新东方
XDF.CN

CW01642579

学习方法：①预习词根
②听一遍英文，跟读着
③再听中文，最后看书对照拼写
④有词根的跳回去看词根表加深印象
⑤会的单词跳
⑥多复习

加强版

雅思词汇

词根+联想记忆法

俞敏洪 编著

浙江教育出版社·杭州

图书在版编目(CIP)数据

雅思词汇词根+联想记忆法：加强版 / 俞敏洪编著
. -- 杭州：浙江教育出版社，2015.1（2018.1重印）
ISBN 978-7-5536-2415-0

Ⅰ. ①雅… Ⅱ. ①俞… Ⅲ. ①IELTS—词汇—记忆术
—自学参考资料 Ⅳ. ①H313

中国版本图书馆CIP数据核字（2014）第252699号

雅思词汇词根 + 联想记忆法：加强版
YASI CIHUI CIGEN + LIANXIANG JIYIFA: JIAQIANGBAN
俞敏洪 **编著**

责任编辑 罗 曼
美术编辑 韩 波
封面设计 大愚设计
责任校对 刘文芳
责任印务 时小娟
出版发行 浙江教育出版社
地址：杭州市天目山路40号
邮编：310013
电话：（0571） 85170300 - 80928
邮箱：dywh@xdf.cn
网址：www.zjeph.com
印 刷 北京海石通印刷有限公司
开 本 720mm×960mm 1/16
成品尺寸 170mm×230mm
印 张 33.5
字 数 570 000
版 次 2015年1月第1版
印 次 2018年1月第8次印刷
标准书号 ISBN 978-7-5536-2415-0
定 价 59.00元

词汇向来都是英语学习的基础。如果把英语学习比作构建大厦，词汇便是深埋于地下的基石，虽不浮于表面，但决定了这座语言大厦的坚固与否。词汇量的匮乏严重影响并制约着一个人听、说、读、写等各方面能力的发展，更会成为各种英语考试的严重障碍。雅思考试在中国开展多年，考生人数逐年增加，但考生的平均分数却始终没有显著的提高，尤其是听说环节。究其根源，与考生对词汇的掌握程度有很大关系。

学习词汇至关重要的一步在于选择一本好的词汇书，那么何谓"好的词汇书"？简而言之，一本好的词汇书应该具备科学的词汇学习理念与方法、合理的编排和设计、全面而实用的内容以及轻松有趣的记忆方法。经广大考生多年实践证明，"词根＋联想"学习法无疑是种科学高效的学习方法。因此本书以词根、词缀记忆法为主体，利用单词的分拆、同反义词、谐音，并配合幽默的插图形成了一套高效实用、生动有趣的记忆方法，帮助考生记忆单词，轻松应对雅思考试。本书特色如下：

一、重点词汇"一网打尽"，全面突破雅思词汇大关

本书以历次雅思考试为依据，精心选取约4500个核心单词及1200多个核心词组，给出重点单词的同、反义词，补充大量的派生词，共收录约8000个常用单词，将雅思考试重点词汇"一网打尽"。

二、"词根＋联想"，记忆障碍一扫而光

如果缺少科学的方法，记忆单词将是个枯燥无味的过程。实践证明，"词根＋联想"记忆法能够帮助考生最大程度地提升单词记忆的趣味性和成就感。词根、词缀记忆法通过归纳常用词根、词缀，使考生可以举一反三，用"四两拨千斤"的"巧力"构建自己的词汇大厦，短时间内记忆海量单词。例如：

词根：vis = to see（看见）

invisible = in-（不）+ vis（看见）+ -ible（可…的）→ 看不见的，无形的

envisage = en-（在…之内）+ vis（看见）+ age → 在内部看见 → 展望，想象；面对

supervise = super-（超过）+ vis（看见）+ e → 在超出别人的高度看 → 监督，管理；指导

visual = vis（看见）+ ual（形容词后缀）→ 视觉的

考生在掌握词根vis的意思后，配合常见的词缀in-, -ible, en-, super-, -ual等就可以轻松记住以上这些单词。而且考试中即使遇到生词，也能够根据其结构推断出词义。

因此，通过词根、词缀的学习，记忆单词将不再单调乏味，而将成为妙趣横生的“拼字游戏”。

联想记忆主要利用单词的拆分、形近词对比、同音词，以及歌曲名、电影名等与英美文化相关的有趣元素，帮助考生强化记忆；发音记忆主要利用英文单词与中文的谐音，帮助考生巧妙记忆单词。

所有这些灵活有趣的记忆方法把考生从记忆单词的枯燥劳役中解放出来，有助于考生克服背诵单词的畏惧心理，提高学习效率。

三、幽默插图，开启轻松记忆之旅

除文字助记方法外，本书为单词配以约350幅生动有趣的插图，为考生营造一个轻松的记忆环境。“千言万语抵不过一张图”，一张幽默的插图，能够有效缓解考生疲劳的神经，从而加深对单词的记忆。例如：

survive* [sə'vaɪv]

v. 活下来；幸免于；比…活得长，比…长命

记 词根记忆：sur(在…之上，越过) + viv(生活，度过) + e → 活得更长久→ 比…活得长

例 For most animal species, individuals are less likely to ***survive*** and reproduce. 对于大多数动物物种来说，个体似乎更难存活以及繁衍后代。

派 survival(*n.* 生存；幸存)

四、原汁原味例句，模拟考试语境

与多数国内英语考试相比，雅思考试中出现的句子(尤其是阅读句子)较长、信息量较大。针对这一特点，本书精选大量雅思真题例句以及与历次雅思考试内容相关、难度相当的例句，力求再现真实考试场景，帮助考生熟悉考试难度，了解考查要点，为备考雅思打下坚实的基础。

五、标记听说词汇，攻克听说难关

对大部分中国考生而言，雅思听力、口语是最大的障碍。因此，本书将雅思听力、口语中常见的词汇、词组用*标出，方便考生在备考听说时更加有的放矢，并牢记这部分词汇的发音。

六、返记菜单，实时反馈

不少考生在记忆单词时一味追求效率，忽视了效果，往往等到一本单词书看完，最先背的单词已经忘得差不多了。本书在页面最下方都设置了"返记菜单"，帮助考生随时检查自己的记忆效果。

"千里之行始于足下"。对大多数考生而言，背单词是一个相当漫长的过程，是对脑力与意志的巨大挑战。但只要目标明确，勇往直前，定能攀上英语学习的顶峰，无限风光尽收眼底。

最后，感谢汇智博纳的金利、关晓蕙、王锋、张森、李素素、张大川等各位编辑，是他们的努力工作使得本书能够与大家见面。

俞敏洪

新东方教育科技集团董事长

使用说明

单元前的词根、词缀预习表帮助考生掌握常用词根、词缀，迅速扩大词汇量。

借助英文单词与中文的谐音，灵活记忆单词。

配有 435 分钟录音，对所有英文单词及中文释义进行朗读，有效提高对单词的理解程度和记忆效果，扫描二维码即可收听。

Word List 21

音频

词根、词缀预习表

fract	碎裂	fraction *n.* 小部分	-ile	易…的	fragile *a.* 脆弱的
-ment	表名词	fragment *n.* 片段	frequ	频繁	frequent *a.* 频繁的
-ent	表形容词	frequent *a.* 频繁的	fund	基础	fundamental *a.* 基础的
germ	芽	germ *n.* 微生物，细菌	fus	流	fusion *n.* 熔化
gen	产生	general *a.* 普遍的	-ous	多…的	generous *a.* 慷慨的

fortnight [ˈfɔːtnaɪt]

n. 两星期，十四天

记 联想记忆：fort(看作 fourteen，十四) + night(夜晚) → 十四个日日夜夜 → 两星期

例 It's a *fortnight* to National Day. 离国庆节还有两星期的时间。

forum [ˈfɔːrəm]

n. 论坛；讨论会

记 联想记忆：for + u(看作 you，你) + m(看作 me，我) → 让你我说话的地方 → 论坛

例 The huge development in rocket technology is a good thing, but at the same time, rockets cause devastating results in the *forum* of war. 火箭研制技术的长足进步是件好事，但同时火箭被用于战争也带来了惨痛的结果。

fossil [ˈfɒsl]

n. 化石；老顽固

记 发音记忆："佛说" → 一开口就是"佛说…"，真是个老顽固 → 老顽固

例 Fuel produced from crop residues is rarely competitive with *fossil* fuels at the present time. 由农作物残渣制成的燃料目前还不具备与矿物燃料竞争的实力。

foster [ˈfɒstə(r)]

v. 培养，培育(某物)；鼓励，促进；领养 *a.* 收养的

记 联想记忆：fost（看作 fast，快速的）+ er → 促进；培养

例 The old couple have *fostered* over 60 children during the past ten years. 这对老夫妇在过去的十年间领养了 60 多名儿童。

派 fosterling(*n.* 养子，养女)；fosterer(*n.* 养育者)

同 nurture(*vt.* 抚育，教养)；cultivate(*vt.* 教养，培养)

□ fortnight　□ forum　□ fossil　□ foster

真题例句以及大量难度适当的例句帮助考生记忆单词，熟悉考试难度。

丰富派生词，横向扩充词汇量。

页面底部设置返记菜单，考生结束每页学习后可以及时进行复习和自测，有助于巩固对单词的掌握。

标注听力、口语常用词汇，便于考生备考听说，有的放矢。

通过单词的分拆、谐音和词与词之间的联系将难词化简、联词成串，轻松高效地记忆单词。

编写大量词根记忆法，考生可举一反三，达到事半功倍的效果。

foul*
[faʊl]

a. 发臭的；肮脏的；邪恶的 *n.* 犯规

记 联想记忆：邪恶的(foul)心灵(soul)

例 The football player was penalized for his *foul*. 那名足球运动员因为犯规而被判罚。

foundation*
[faʊnˈdeɪʃn]

n. 基础；地基；创立

记 联想记忆：found(建立)+ation(表状态，名词后缀)→建立基础→基础；地基

例 Most of the rocks will become the *foundations* for the airport's runways and taxiways. 大多数石块将用作铺设机场跑道和飞机滑行道的地基。

fountain
[ˈfaʊntən]

n. 喷泉

记 联想记忆：大山(mountain)里有喷泉(fountain)

例 There is a beautiful *fountain* in the centre of the square. 广场中心有个漂亮的喷泉。

fraction
[ˈfrækʃn]

n. 小部分，片断

记 词根记忆：fract(打碎)+ion→碎的部分→小部分，片断

搭 a fraction closer 稍微靠近一点；a fraction of 一小部分

例 The little boy has done only a *fraction* of his homework. 那小男孩只做了一小部分家庭作业。

派 fractional(*a.* 很少的，微不足道的)

fracture
[ˈfræktʃə(r)]

n. 断裂，折断；骨折 *v.* (使)断裂

记 词根记忆：fract(打碎)+ure→(使)断裂

搭 a compound fracture 开放性骨折

例 *Fractures* on tools indicate that a majority of ancient people were right-handed. 从工具上的裂痕我们可以看出，大多数古人都是惯用右手的。

同 crack[*v.*(使)破裂，(使)发出爆裂声 *n.* 裂缝，爆裂声]；split[*v.*(使)分裂，分离 *n.* 裂口]

fragile
[ˈfrædʒaɪl]

a. 脆弱的；虚弱的；易碎的；易受伤害的

记 词根记忆：frag(打碎)+ile(易…的)→容易被打碎的→脆弱的；易碎的

例 The *fragile* boxes arrived intact. 这些易碎的箱子被完好无损地运到了目的地。

同 delicate(*a.* 易碎的，脆弱的)；brittle(*a.* 易碎的，易损坏的；脆弱的)；frail(*a.* 体弱的；易破碎的，易损的)

反 unbreakable(*a.* 打不破的，牢不可破的)；sturdy(*a.* 强壮的，强健的)

fragment

[ˈfrægmənt] *n.* 碎片，小部分，片断

[frægˈment] *v.* 分裂；破碎

记 词根记忆：frag(打碎)+ment(名词后缀)→碎片，片断

例 The gigantic explosion from eruption of the volcano tore its summit into *fragments*. 火山喷发引起的强烈爆炸将山顶炸成了碎片。

fragment

□ foul □ foundation □ fountain □ fraction □ fracture □ fragile □ fragment

归纳常考词组和搭配，帮助考生迅速抓住考试重点。

大量同、反义词，帮助考生更好地理解单词，并迅速扩大词汇量。

幽默有趣的插图将单词含义形象化，辅助记忆的同时增加学习的趣味性。

目 录

Word List 1

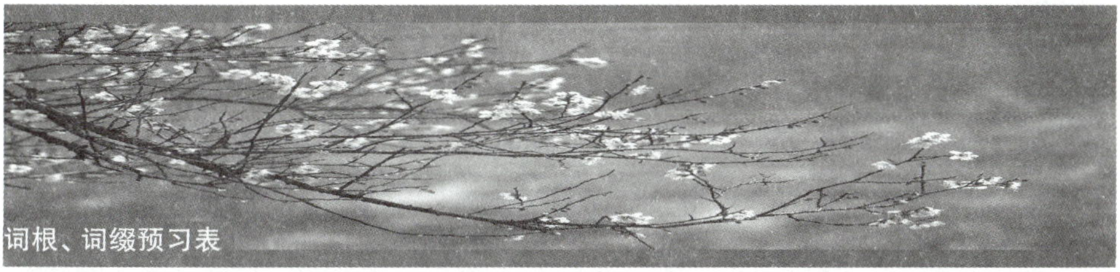

词根、词缀预习表

sorb	吸收	absorb *v.* 吸收；同化	**sent**	送	absent *a.* 不在场的
solut	松开	absolute *a.* 完全的，绝对的	**us**	使用	abuse *v./n.* 滥用
tract	拉，抽	abstract *vt.* 摘要，提炼	**celer**	快速的	accelerate *v.* 加速；促进
cess	走	access *vt.* 进入 *n.* 通道	**cumul**	堆积	accumulate *v.* 累积
bat	走	acrobat *n.* 杂技演员	**apt**	适合的	adapt *v.* 使适合；适应

abandon
[əˈbændən]

vt. 放弃，遗弃

记 联想记忆：a + band（乐队）+ on → 乐队解散，放弃演出 → 放弃

例 She and her tribe had to *abandon* their lands and retreat to Canada. 她和她的部落被迫放弃了土地，退到加拿大。

派 abandonment（*n.* 放弃，遗弃）

abate
[əˈbeɪt]

v. 减轻；降价

记 联想记忆：a（表加强）+ bate（减弱，减少）→ 减轻

例 After the closedown of the airport, noise pollution *abated*. 机场关闭后，噪音污染减轻了。

abhorrent
[əbˈhɒrənt]

a. 可恶的，可恨的

记 词根记忆：ab（表加强）+ horr（发抖）+ ent（形容词后缀）→ 让人发抖的 → 可恶的，可恨的

例 As far as I'm concerned, the practice of killing rare wild animals for food and money is utterly *abhorrent* and should be punished by law. 我认为，为获取食物和金钱而猎杀珍稀野生动物的行径可恶至极，应该受到法律的制裁。

abide
[əˈbaɪd]

v. 停留，逗留；容忍，忍受

记 词根记忆：a + bide（停留）→ 停留，逗留

搭 abide by 遵守，遵循

例 Anyone can *abide* by what he or she said, but it doesn't mean all of them are correct. 任何人都可以坚持自己所说的话，但这并不意味着他们全都是正确的。

□ abandon □ abate □ abhorrent □ abide

ability* [ə'bɪləti]	*n.* 能力；本领；才能 搭 have the ability to do sth. 有做…的能力；to the best of one's ability 尽全力 例 Classes are organised according to ***ability*** level. 根据能力水平进行分班。
abode* [ə'bəʊd]	*n.* 房屋，家，住所 搭 right of abode 居住权；fixed abode 固定住所；permanent abode 永久住所 例 I do not dare to linger in that gloom-hidden ***abode***. 我不敢在那个隐没于黑暗中的房屋里逗留。
abolish [ə'bɒlɪʃ]	*vt.* 废止，废除 例 The ancient Olympics were ***abolished*** by the Roman Emperor Theodosius in 393 AD, after Greece lost its independence. 在希腊丧失主权之后，罗马皇帝狄奥多西于公元 393 年废除了古代奥林匹克运动会。 同 annul(*vt.* 废除，取消)；destroy(*vt.* 破坏，消灭)
abound* [ə'baʊnd]	*vi.* 富于；充满 记 联想记忆：a(一个) + bound(界限，范围) → 所有物品都在一个范围内 → 富于；充满 例 The mountain streams ***abound*** with fish. 山溪里有许多鱼。
absent* ['æbsənt]	*a.* 不在场的；心不在焉的 记 词根记忆：ab(离去) + sent(送) → 送走 → 不在场的 例 Why were you ***absent*** from my birthday party yesterday? 你昨天怎么没来参加我的生日派对呢? 派 absence(*n.* 缺席，不在；缺乏)
absenteeism* [ˌæbsən'tiːɪzəm]	*n.* 旷课；旷工 记 联想记忆：absent(缺席) + ee(表人) + ism → 旷课；旷工 例 In an attempt to reduce the level of ***absenteeism*** amongst employees, the company introduced three different strategies. 该公司采用了三种不同的策略，希望以此降低员工的旷工率。
absolute* ['æbsəluːt]	*a.* 完全的，绝对的，纯粹的 记 词根记忆：ab(表加强) + solut(松开) + e → 完全松开 → 完全的，绝对的，纯粹的 搭 absolute trust 绝对信任；absolute zero 绝对零度 例 There is no ***absolute*** standard for beauty. 美没有绝对的标准。
absorb* [əb'sɔːb]	*v.* 吸收；吸引…的注意，使全神贯注；把…并入，同化 记 词根记忆：ab(离去) + sorb(吸收) → 吸收掉 → 吸收 搭 be absorbed into/in 全神贯注于… 例 Trees can ***absorb*** carbon dioxide. 树木可以吸收二氧化碳。// The writer was so ***absorbed*** in his writing that he forgot to flick the ashes from his cigar. 作家全神贯注地写作，忘了弹去雪茄烟的烟灰。 派 absorption(*n.* 吸收)

□ ability □ abode □ abolish □ abound □ absent □ absenteeism
□ absolute □ absorb

abstract [ˈæbstrækt] *a.* 抽象的；抽象派的 *n.* 摘要，梗概；抽象 [æbˈstrækt] *vt.* 摘要，提炼；抽象化

记 词根记忆：abs + tract(拉，抽) → 抽象化

搭 abstract noun 抽象名词；abstract science 抽象科学

例 Thus, we concluded that the blind interpret *abstract* shapes as sighted people do. 于是，我们得出结论：盲人与视力正常者对抽象形状的理解是一样的。

派 abstracted(*a.* 抽象的)

abstraction [æbˈstrækʃn] *n.* 抽象

例 Logic, rationality and *abstraction* have their origins in the left hemisphere. 逻辑、推理和抽象思维都源自大脑左半球。

absurd [əbˈsɜːd] *a.* 荒谬的，荒唐的

例 Wearing a swimming suit during a snowstorm is *absurd.* 下雪天穿泳装可真荒唐。

派 absurdism(*n.* 荒诞主义)

同 ridiculous(*a.* 荒谬的，可笑的)

abundance* [əˈbʌndəns] *n.* 大量，丰富，充足，充裕

记 来自 abundant(*a.* 丰富的，充裕的)

搭 in abundance 丰富

例 At the party, there was food and drink in *abundance.* 宴会上，食品和饮料供应充足。

同 profusion(*n.* 丰富)；affluence(*n.* 富足)；wealth(*n.* 大量)

反 scarcity(*n.* 缺乏，不足)；deficiency(*n.* 缺少)

abuse* [əˈbjuːs] *n.* 滥用，妄用；虐待，伤害；辱骂，毁谤 [əˈbjuːz] *v.* 滥用，妄用；虐待，伤害；辱骂，毁谤

记 词根记忆：ab(偏离) + us(使用) + e → 使用不当 → 滥用

搭 drug abuse 滥用药物，吸毒；abuse one's authority/office 滥用权威/职权；child abuse 虐待儿童；verbal abuse 口头谩骂

例 Biometrics may raise thorny questions about privacy and the potential for *abuse.* 生物测定学可能会引起棘手的隐私问题，也可能导致对此技术的滥用。

academic [ˌækəˈdemɪk] *a.* 学院的；学术的；不切实际的 *n.* 学者；大学教师

搭 academic achievements 学术成就；academic study 学术研究；academic problems 学术问题；academic teaching staff 师资力量

例 Once in higher education, you can apply for a loan at any time in the *academic* year. 进入高校以后，你就可以在学年内的任何时间申请贷款。

派 academically(*ad.* 学术上)；academia(*n.* 学术界；学术生涯)

accelerate [ək'seləreɪt]

v. 加速；促进

记 词根记忆：ac(=to) + celer(快速的) + ate(使…) → 加速；促进

例 The leader lost ground as the rest of the runners *accelerated*. 领先者在其余赛跑者加速时逐渐失去了优势。

acceptable* [ək'septəbl]

a. 可接受的

例 The salesman's attitude is simply not *acceptable* by the customers. 那个售货员的态度是顾客所不能接受的。

access* ['ækses]

vt. 进入；使用 *n.* 通道，入径；机会；权利

记 词根记忆：ac + cess(走) → 走进去 → 进入

搭 access to 接近/进入…的方法/通路；使用…的权利；have/gain access to 可以获得

例 The students could *access* the Internet in the library. 学生们可以在图书馆上网。

accessible [ək'sesəbl]

a. 能接近的；易达到的

例 He pointed his telescope to every *accessible* part of the sky and recorded what he saw. 他将望远镜指向天空中所有可以达到的地方，并记录下所看到的。

accessory* [ək'sesəri]

n. 附件，零件；[常 *pl.*] (尤指女性的)服装搭配物，装饰品；【律】同谋，帮凶

记 联想记忆：ac(附近) + cess(走) + ory → 接近主体部件 → 附件，零件

搭 accessory to …的附件

例 The uniforms for women in the company were white frocks decorated with purple, white and green *accessories*. 这家公司的女式工作服是配有紫色、白色和绿色装饰物的白色裙装。

acclaim* [ə'kleɪm]

vt. 向…欢呼，为…喝彩 *n.* 称赞；欢迎

记 词根记忆：ac(向) + claim(大声呼喊) → 向某人大声叫喊 → 向…欢呼，为…喝彩

搭 win worldwide acclaim 赢得广泛的赞誉；receive great acclaim 备受赞扬

例 There's lots to see and to do, including the internationally-*acclaimed* climbing wall built on the site of the old aquarium. 这里有很多可看的和可玩的，其中包括那个建在水族馆旧址上享誉世界的攀岩墙。

派 acclaimed(*a.* 受欢呼的，受称赞的)

同 cheer(*v.* 欢呼，喝彩)

acclimatise* [ə'klaɪmətaɪz]

v. (使…)服水土；(使…)适应新环境

例 After a couple of days to *acclimatise* yourself, you'll start the trek on day three walking through the enormous Katiba Forest which will take the whole of the day. 前两天让自己适应环境，第三天要开始徒步穿越巨大的卡蒂巴森林，这需要一整天的时间。

□ accelerate □ acceptable □ access □ accessible □ accessory □ acclaim □ acclimatise

accommodation* [əˌkɒməˈdeɪʃn]

n. 住处，膳宿；适应，调节

accommodation

记 联想记忆：ac + commod（看作 common，普通的）+ ation(名词后缀）→ 再普通的人都需要住处 → 住处，膳宿

搭 student accommodation 学生宿舍；accommodation facilities 住宿设施

例 If you are booking *accommodation* through the school, your course and *accommodation* deposit will be $200. 如果你通过学校预订食宿，你的课程和膳宿押金是 200 美元。

accompany [əˈkʌmpənɪ]

vt. 陪伴；伴随，与…同时发生；伴奏

记 联想记忆：ac(表加强）+ company(同伴；陪伴）→ 陪伴；伴随

搭 accompany training 陪练；accompany a singer 伴唱

例 Your enrolment form must be *accompanied* by the course deposit of $100. 你的登记表和 100 美元的课程押金必须一起上交。

accomplish [əˈkʌmplɪʃ]

vt. 达到(目的)，完成(任务)，实现(计划、诺言等)

记 联想记忆：ac + compl(看作 complete，完成）+ ish(使…）→ 完成

搭 accomplish one's object 达到了某人的目的；accomplish one's mission 完成了某人的任务

例 We must *accomplish* the task before noon. 我们必须在中午之前完成这项任务。

account* [əˈkaʊnt]

v. 说明，解释；(在数量、比例方面)占；导致 *n.* 账，账户；叙述，说明

记 联想记忆：ac(表加强）+ count(数）→ 账目需要一数再数 → 账

搭 take... into account 考虑…；account for 解释，说明(原因等)；(数量等)占；on account of 因为，由于；give sb. an account of 给某人说明或解释(理由)；not on any account 绝对不

例 Coal is expected to *account* for almost 27 percent of the world's energy needs. 预计对煤炭的需求将几乎占世界能源需求的 27%。

accountancy [əˈkaʊntənsi]

n. 会计工作，会计职业

例 He works in *accountancy* since he graduated from university. 他大学毕业后一直从事会计工作。

accountant [əˈkaʊntənt]

n. 会计师

记 联想记忆：account(账目）+ ant(表人）→ 管账的人 → 会计师

accredit [əˈkredɪt]

vt. 信任，相信，委任，授权；把…归于

记 联想记忆：ac + credit(相信）→ 信任，相信

例 Scolded by the boss for many times, the young man was *accredited* as department manager, which is a suddenness for everybody. 这个多次被老板训斥的年轻人却荣升部门经理，这让所有的人都始料不及。

accreditation* [əˌkredɪˈteɪʃn]

n. 证明合格，鉴定合格

记 来自 accredit(*vt.* 委任，授权)

例 Our school has already reached the standards for the *accreditation* of colleges. 我们学校已经达到了学院资格认定的标准。

□ accommodation □ accompany □ accomplish □ account □ accountancy □ accountant
□ accredit □ accreditation

accumulate
[əˈkjuːmjəleɪt]

v. 积累；堆积

记 词根记忆：ac(表加强) + cumul(堆积) + ate → 不断堆积 → 积累

搭 accumulate funds 积累资金

例 The debris that ***accumulated*** at the foot of the volcano reached a depth, in places, of 200 feet. 堆积在火山脚下的岩屑在一些地方有 200 英尺厚。

派 accumulation(*n.* 积累；堆积物)

accuracy
[ˈækjərəsi]

n. 准确(性)，精确(性)

记 词根记忆：ac(表加强) + cur(注意，关心) + acy → 一再关心，使其精确 → 准确(性)，精确(性)

例 The technician placed the machine in the correct spot with complete ***accuracy***. 技术员分毫不差地将机器安放在正确的位置。

accurate
[ˈækjərət]

a. 正确无误的；精确的

例 The forecast was soon proved ***accurate***. 不久，预言就被证明是正确的。

派 inaccurate(*a.* 错误的，不准确的)

accustom
[əˈkʌstəm]

vt. 使习惯于

记 联想记忆：ac(表加强) + custom(风俗，习惯) → 使成为习惯 → 使习惯于

例 If you go abroad for further study, it will take a period of time for you to ***accustom*** yourself to the new environment, the new culture and all the new rules and regulations. 如果你出国留学，那么你需要花上一些时间让自己习惯新的环境、新的文化和所有新的规则与制度。

achievement*
[əˈtʃiːvmənt]

n. 成就，成绩；达到，完成，实现

记 来自 achieve(*v.* 达到，完成)

搭 sense of achievement 成就感

例 His ***achievements*** spread from the sun and moon to remote galaxies. 他的研究成果从太阳、月亮延伸到遥远的星系。

acid*
[ˈæsɪd]

n. 酸 *a.* 酸的；尖刻的

例 DNA is the short form of deoxyribonucleic ***acid***. DNA 是脱氧核糖核酸的缩写形式。

acknowledge
[əkˈnɒlɪdʒ]

v. 承认，确认；致意；感谢

记 联想记忆：ac + know(知道) + ledge → 大家都知道了，所以不得不承认 → 承认

例 Plagiarism is taking other people's work without ***acknowledging*** it, that is, without saying where it comes from. 剽窃就是引用了人家的作品却不承认，即不注明出处。

acoustic
[əˈkuːstɪk]

a. 原声的；声音(学)的；听觉的

例 In the houses near the highway special ***acoustic*** seals should be fitted to the doors to reduce noise. 位于公路旁的住房的房门上应该安装专门的隔音封条，以降低噪音。

□ accumulate □ accuracy □ accurate □ accustom □ achievement □ acid
□ acknowledge □ acoustic

1

acquaint [əˈkweɪnt]

vt. (使)认识；(使)熟悉

例 Film provides an ideal opportunity to ***acquaint*** viewers with something unknown. 电影给观众提供了一个了解未知事物的绝佳机会。

同 inform(*v.* 通知，告知)

acquaintance [əˈkweɪntəns]

n. 熟人；认识，了解

记 联想记忆：acquaint(使熟悉)+ ance(名词后缀)→熟人；认识

搭 a speaking acquaintance 见面聊几句的朋友；nodding acquaintance 点头之交

例 It was in the United States that I made the ***acquaintance*** of Professor Jones. 我是在美国结识琼斯教授的。

acquire* [əˈkwaɪə(r)]

vt. 取得，获得

记 词根记忆：ac(表加强)+ quir(追求)+ e → 不断追求才能够获得 → 获得，取得

例 In the process of evolution, monkeys have not ***acquired*** the art of speech. 在进化的过程中，猴子未能获得语言能力。

acquisition [ˌækwɪˈzɪʃn]

n. 取得；获得物

例 Tom's newest ***acquisition*** is a luxurious sports car. 汤姆新得了一辆豪华跑车。

acrobat* [ˈækrəbæt]

n. 特技演员；杂技演员

记 词根记忆：acro(高)+ bat(走)→ 高空走的人 → 杂技演员

例 They are ***acrobats*** with the Albanian State Circus. 他们是阿尔巴尼亚国家马戏团的杂技演员。

acrobatic* [ˌækrəˈbætɪk]

a. 杂技的；杂技般的；杂技演员的

例 Jane used to be an ***acrobatic*** dancer but three years ago, she started to learn fencing. 简曾经是一名杂技舞蹈演员，但是三年前她开始学习击剑。

activate* [ˈæktɪveɪt]

vt. 激活；使活动，使活化

记 词根记忆：act(做)+ iv + ate(使…)→ 使活跃 → 激活

例 Nicotine in cigarette smoke ***activates*** small blood cells that increase the likelihood of blood clots, thereby affecting blood circulation throughout the body. 香烟中的尼古丁会激活小的血细胞，这些血细胞增加了血栓的可能性，从而影响体内的血液循环。

派 activator(*n.* 催化剂)

actual* [ˈæktʃuəl]

a. 实际的；真实的

搭 in actual fact 实际上

例 Is this vase an ***actual*** antique or a copy? 这个花瓶是真古董还是赝品？

派 actually(*ad.* 实际上；居然)

□ acquaint □ acquaintance □ acquire □ acquisition ■ acrobat □ acrobatic
□ activate □ actual

acumen
[ˈækjəmən]

n. 敏锐；精明

记 词根记忆：acu(尖，锐利，酸) + men → 敏锐；精明

例 Sometimes, organizations with sound financial backing, good product ideas and market ***acumen*** underperform and fail to meet shareholders' expectations. 有时，拥有雄厚的资金保障、良好的产品理念和对市场的精准把握的公司却表现不佳，不能达到股东们的期望。

acupuncture
[ˈækjupʌŋktʃə(r)]

n. 针刺疗法，针灸

例 ***Acupuncture*** is a kind of Chinese method of treating pain and illness using special thin needles. 针灸是一种中医疗法，通过使用特殊的细针来治疗病痛。

acute
[əˈkjuːt]

a. 灵敏的；剧烈的，猛烈的

例 Dogs have very ***acute*** hearing. 狗的听觉很灵敏。

adapt*
[əˈdæpt]

v. 使适合；改编；适应

记 词根记忆：ad + apt(适合的) → 使适合；适应

搭 adapt to 适应…；adapt from 根据…改编

例 All those older buildings in the city have been ***adapted*** for present-day use. 城里的旧建筑已经全部经过改造，以作今日之用。

派 adaptable(*a.* 能适应的；可修改的)

adaptation
[ˌædæpˈteɪʃn]

n. 适应；改编；改制物

记 联想记忆：adapt(改编；适应) + ation(名词后缀) → 适应；改编

例 The simplicity of Indian ways of life has been judged an evolutionary ***adaptation*** to forest ecology. 印第安人的生活方式很简单，这被认为是在进化中适应森林生态环境的结果。

addict
[ˈædɪkt]

n. 吸毒成瘾的人，有瘾的人，对…入迷的人

例 The most tragical sight of all is the very young ***addicts***. 最悲惨的一幕是目睹那些非常年轻的吸毒者。

addiction*
[əˈdɪkʃn]

n. 瘾；沉溺

搭 television addiction 看电视上瘾

例 For his severe illness he had to fight his ***addiction*** to alcohol. 因为病情严重，他不得不克服自己的酒瘾。

addition*
[əˈdɪʃn]

n. 加，增加(物)

记 联想记忆：add(加) + ition → 加，增加(物)

搭 in addition 另外；in addition to... 除…之外

例 This fruit is a welcome ***addition*** to the English diet. 这种添加在英式食谱中的水果很受欢迎。

additional*
[əˈdɪʃənl]

a. 附加的；追加的

搭 additional charges 附加费用；additional outlay 额外开支；additional cost 额外费用，新增成本

例 In recent years a number of ***additional*** countries have subscribed to the Ottawa Charter. 近几年，又有许多国家同意加入《渥太华宪章》。

address* [ə'dres]

vt. 致函，写姓名地址；向…讲话，演说；处理，对付 *n.* 地址；致词

搭 address a letter 给信写上地址；address sb. 向…致词

例 In the marketing course we *address* all these commercial issues. 在营销课上，我们讨论所有这些商业问题。

adequate* ['ædɪkwət]

a. 充足的；合适的，合格的

记 词根记忆：ad(表加强) + equ(平等) + ate → 比平等多的 → 充足的

搭 be adequate for 适合于…

例 Good living habits and *adequate* health care are critical factors of governing health. 良好的生活习惯和适当的卫生保健是保持健康的关键因素。

派 inadequate(*a.* 不充足的；不适当的)

adhere* [əd'hɪə(r)]

vi. 黏附；遵守；坚持

记 词根记忆：ad(表加强) + her(黏附) + e → 黏附；遵守

搭 adhere to 坚持；黏附；遵守

例 Our firm has a set of standards which *adhere* to international requirements. 我们公司拥有一套符合国际要求的标准。

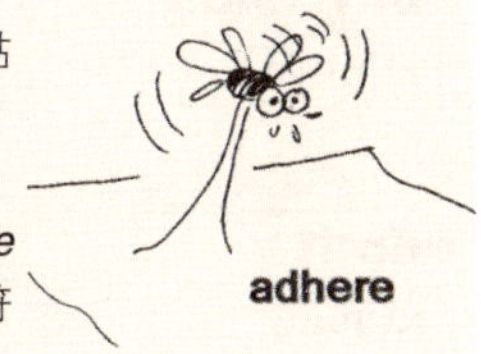

adjacent [ə'dʒeɪsnt]

a. 邻近的，毗连的

例 People living in houses *adjacent* to the airport are tormented by noise for years. 住在机场附近的居民常年受到噪音的折磨。

同 adjoining(*a.* 邻接的)；contiguous(*a.* 接近的)

反 detached(*a.* 分开的)；separate(*a.* 个别的，单独的)

adjunct ['ædʒʌŋkt]

n. 附加物，附件；附加语，修饰语

记 词根记忆：ad + junct(结合，连接) → 连在上面的东西 → 附加物

例 Alternative medicine appears to be an *adjunct*, sought in times of disenchantment when conventional medicine seems not to offer the answer. 替代医学似乎变成了一种附加物。在传统医学因为无法提供答案而令人倍感失望的时候，人们发现了替代医学。

adjust* [ə'dʒʌst]

v. 校准；调节；使…适应

记 词根记忆：ad + just(正确) → 使正确 → 校准；调节；使…适应

搭 adjust a policy 调整政策；adjust expenses to income 量入为出；adjust a watch 调表；adjust to 适应，调节

例 Research shows that older readers are having difficulty in *adjusting* to texts without pictures. 调查显示，年纪较大的读者在阅读那些不带图画的文章时比较费劲。

administer* [əd'mɪnɪstə(r)]

v. 掌管；给予

搭 administer to 有助于；给予

例 The personnel director *administers* the attendance policy. 人事经理负责考勤。// Doctors can *administer* curative drugs to treat lung cancer. 医生可以开一些医疗药物来治疗肺癌。

□ address □ adequate □ adhere □ adjacent □ adjunct □ adjust
□ administer

administration* [ədˌmɪnɪˈstreɪʃn]

n. 管理(部门)；行政(机关)

记 联想记忆：ad + ministr(看作 minister，部长) + ation → 部长的工作 → 管理；行政

例 The *administration* office is opposite the car park on the left. 管理办公室在停车场的对面左边。

administrative* [ədˈmɪnɪstrətɪv]

a. 管理的，行政的

例 Jack used to work in an *administrative* position. 杰克曾担任行政工作。

administrator* [ədˈmɪnɪstreɪtə(r)]

n. 管理者，管理人员；行政人员

例 For sports *administrators* we provide a four-month certificate course. 对于体育管理人员，我们提供为期四个月的证书课程。

admission [ədˈmɪʃn]

n. 允许进入，加入权，进入权；招供，招认；入场券

记 词根记忆：ad(表加强) + miss(送) + ion → 允许送入 → 允许进入

例 If you have any questions, please contact the *Admissions* & Information Office. 如果你有任何问题，请与招生信息办公室联系。

admit* [ədˈmɪt]

v. 承认；准许…进入；准许…加入

记 词根记忆：ad(表加强) + mit(送) → 能送进去 → 准许…进入

例 Bill was forced to *admit* that he had cheated on the test. 比尔被迫承认他在考试中作弊了。

派 admittance(*n.* 进入权；进入)

adobe [əˈdəʊbi]

n. 土坯，泥砖

例 Gharib has already been contacted by a civil engineer in Nicaragua, who wants to put up buildings with *adobe* roofs supported by concrete arches on a site that heavy equipment can't reach. 尼加拉瓜的一名土木工程师联系了加里卜，该工程师想在一个地方建造由混凝土拱支撑的砖顶大楼，但是重型设备到不了该地。

adolescence [ˌædəˈlesns]

n. 青春，青春期

记 联想记忆：ado(看作 adult，成年人) + lescence (看作 licence，许可证) → 青少年即将拿到成年的许可证 → 青春，青春期

例 *Adolescence* brings about major changes in a young person's body and mind. 青春期给年轻人的身心带来巨大改变。

adolescence

adolescent [ˌædəˈlesnt]

n. 青少年 *a.* 青春期的；青少年的

记 联想记忆：adol(看作 adult，成年人) + esc(计算机上退出键) + ent(人) → 好想从成年人退回到青少年 → 青少年

搭 an adolescent girl 一个妙龄少女

例 The *adolescent* always respects parents who admit their mistakes. 青少年往往尊敬能承认错误的父母。

□ administration □ administrative □ administrator □ admission □ admit □ adobe □ adolescence □ adolescent

adopt* [ə'dɒpt]	*v.* 采用，采取，采纳；收养，领养；正式通过，批准 记 联想记忆：这个被收养(adopt)的孩子必须适应(adapt)新的环境 搭 adopt the new policy 通过新政策；adopt a new technique 采用新技术 例 After becoming independent of the local authority and ***adopting*** its new title, our College continued to build on its first class reputation. 自从我们学院脱离当地部门并改了新名之后，就一直致力于打造一所一流院校。
advance [əd'vɑːns]	*a.* 预先的；先行的 *v.* 前进，向前移动；取得进展；预付 *n.* 前进，前移；增长，提高；预付(款等) 搭 in advance 预先，提前；book in advance 提前预订 例 It is essential to reserve a computer three days in ***advance*** if you want to use one. 如果你想使用电脑，最好提前三天预订。
advanced* [əd'vɑːnst]	*a.* 先进的 例 Prehistoric Amazonians developed technology and art that were ***advanced*** for their time. 史前亚马孙人创造了当时先进的技术和艺术。

Today is the first day of the rest of my life, I wake as a child to see the world begin. On monarch wings and birthday wonderings, want to put on faces, walk in the wet and cold. And look forward to my growing old, to grow is to change, to change is to be new, to be new is to be young again, I barely remember when.

——美国乡村歌手 约翰·丹佛(John Denver)

Word List 2

音频

词根、词缀预习表

vent	来	advent *n.* 到来；出现	**vers**	转	adverse *a.* 不利的，有害的
naut	航行	aeronautics *n.* 航空学	**flict**	打击	afflict *vt.* 使苦恼；折磨
flu	流	affluent *a.* 丰富的，富裕的	**ag**	行动	agency *n.* 机构；代理
grav	重的	aggravate *vt.* 加重，恶化	**gress**	走	aggressive *a.* 有进取心的
cult	种植；培养	agriculture *n.* 农业	**ali**	其他的	alienate *vt.* 使疏远

advantage* [əd'vɑːntɪdʒ]

n. 优点，优势

搭 be/work to one's advantage 对…有利；take advantage of 利用；to advantage 有效地，出色地；使优点突出

例 I suppose your survey has the *advantage* of more detailed information. 我认为你调查的优势在于拥有更加详细的资料。

advantageous [ˌædvən'teɪdʒəs]

a. 有利的

记 来自 advantage(*n.* 优势)

例 A free trade agreement would be *advantageous* to both countries. 自由贸易协议对两国都有益处。

advent* ['ædvent]

n. 到来；出现

记 词根记忆：ad + vent(来) → 到来；出现

搭 the advent of sth. …的到来

例 Sea ports have been transformed by the *advent* of powered vessels, whose size and draught have increased. 配有引擎的货船体积更加庞大，可以装载更多货物，它们的出现改变了海港原有的样子。

派 adventitious(*a.* 偶然发生的，非计划中的)

adventure [əd'ventʃə(r)]

n. 冒险，冒险活动；异乎寻常的经历，奇遇

搭 spirit of adventure 冒险精神；adventure playground 儿童游乐园；an adventure film 惊险电影

例 Hypotheses are *adventures* of the mind. 假定是思想的冒险。

adventurous [əd'ventʃərəs]

a. 喜欢冒险的，敢作敢为的；充满危险和刺激的，惊险的

例 The street may be attractive to children as a place to find *adventurous* play and money. 这条街应该对孩子们非常具有吸引力，他们可以在这里找到惊险刺激、乐趣，还有金钱。

2

adverse [ˈædvɜːs]	*a.* 不利的，有害的 记 词根记忆：ad(向) + vers(转) + e → 转向不希望的一方 → 不利的，有害的 搭 adverse circumstances 逆境 例 Smoking can produce substantial ***adverse*** effects on the heart and lungs. 吸烟会对人的心脏和肺造成严重的危害。 同 unfavorable(*a.* 不利的)；harmful(*a.* 有害的)
advertise* [ˈædvətaɪz]	*vt.* 为…做广告；宣传；(在报刊、电视、广播中)公告，公布 搭 advertise for 为…做广告 例 The total number of jobs ***advertised*** in the journal was 120. 这本杂志上共刊登了 120 个职位。 派 advertiser(*n.* 广告客户，登广告者)
advertisement* [ədˈvɜːtɪsmənt]	*n.* 广告，公告；广告活动，宣传 搭 advertisement industry 广告业；advertisement expense 广告费用 例 The newspapers are full of ***advertisements*** for promotion activities of various shops. 报纸上全是各大商店促销活动的广告。
advice* [ədˈvaɪs]	*n.* 劝告，忠告；建议，(医生等的)意见 搭 write to sb. for advice 写信给某人征求建议；expert advice 专家意见 例 I was told to come here for ***advice*** about math courses. 有人告诉我到这里来咨询一些关于数学课程的建议。
advisable* [ədˈvaɪzəbl]	*n.* 可取的，适当的；明智的 记 联想记忆：advis(e)(建议，劝告) + able(能…的) → 能够听取别人的劝告的 → 明智的 例 A: Do I have to book the seat in advance? B: Oh, yes, it's ***advisable***. A: 我必须提前预订座位吗？ B: 哦，是的，这样更好。
advocate	[ˈædvəkeɪt] *vt.* 拥护，支持；提倡 [ˈædvəkət] *n.* 拥护者，支持者；提倡者 记 词根记忆：ad(表加强) + voc(大声呼喊) + ate → 大声喊 → 提倡 例 Some architects ***advocated*** the use of masonry in the construction of skyscrapers. 一些建筑师提倡采用石工技术建造摩天大楼。
aeration* [ˌeəˈreɪʃn]	*n.* 通风 记 词根记忆：aer(空气) + ation → 能通空气 → 通风 例 The tunnels abandoned by the beetles provide excellent ***aeration*** and water channels for root systems of plants. 被甲虫遗弃的地下通道为植物的根系提供了绝佳的通风和汲水管道。
aerobics [eəˈrəʊbɪks]	*n.* 有氧运动 记 词根记忆：aero(空气) + b + ics(…活动) → 有氧运动 例 This room is used mainly for badminton and ***aerobics***. 这间屋子主要用作羽毛球室和有氧运动室。

□ adverse □ advertise □ advertisement □ advice □ advisable □ advocate
□ aeration □ aerobics

aeronautics *

[ˌeərəˈnɔːtɪks]

n. 航空学

记 词根记忆：aero（空气）+ naut（航行）+ ics（…学）→ 航空学

例 The *Aeronautics* Building is on the left side of the university campus. 航空学大楼位于校园的左侧。

---

aeroplane

[ˈeərəpleɪn]

n. 飞机

记 联想记忆：aero（空气）+ plane（飞机）→ 飞机

例 The manager will travel in a private *aeroplane* from Sydney to Queensland. 经理将乘坐私人飞机从悉尼飞往昆士兰。

---

aerospace

[ˈeərəʊspeɪs]

n. 宇宙空间；航空航天技术

记 联想记忆：aero（空气）+ space（太空）→ 宇宙空间

例 This article is mainly about the applications of AI to *aerospace*. 这篇文章主要论述了人工智能在航空航天领域的应用。

---

aesthetic

[iːsˈθetɪk]

a. 美学的；审美的

记 词根记忆：(a)esthet（感觉）+ ic（形容词后缀）→ 美感的 → 美学的

例 What are utilitarian objects to a Westerner may be prized *aesthetic* objects in other cultures. 被西方人视为功利性的东西，在其他文化中可能会因其美学价值而备受推崇。

---

affect *

[əˈfekt]

v. 影响；感染

记 词根记忆：af + fect（做）→ 使人做 → 影响

例 No activity *affects* more of the earth's surface than farming. 耕种是对地表影响最大的人类活动。

---

afflict *

[əˈflɪkt]

vt. 使苦恼；折磨

记 词根记忆：af（向）+ flict（打击）→ 向某人发出攻击 → 使苦恼；折磨

搭 be afflicted with/by 被…折磨

例 Financial difficulties *afflicted* the Smiths. 经济问题困扰着史密斯一家。

同 torment（*vt.* 折磨）；torture（*vt.* 拷问，折磨）

---

afflicting

[əˈflɪktɪŋ]

a. 痛苦的

例 It is said that cancer is increasingly torturing the *afflicting* developing countries due to tobacco and alcohol abuse, unhealthy diets and the lack of exercise. 据称，由于吸烟、酗酒、不健康的饮食以及缺乏锻炼，癌症正日益折磨着痛苦的发展中国家。

---

affluent

[ˈæfluənt]

a. 丰富的，富裕的

记 词根记忆：af（表加强）+ flu（流）+ ent（形容词后缀）→ 不断流出 → 富得流油 → 富裕的

搭 an affluent fountain 丰富的源泉

例 *Affluent* someone may be born, but he is usually uncertain of how to create an admiring life with it or cherish all he has. 有些人可能生于富裕之家，但却往往不知道如何利用其先天优势来创造一个令人称羡的生活或是珍惜所拥有的一切。

□ aeronautics □ aeroplane □ aerospace □ aesthetic □ affect □ afflict
□ afflicting □ affluent

2

afford*
[əˈfɔːd]

v. 负担得起

记 联想记忆：af + ford（看作 Ford，美国大财阀福特家族）→ 财大气粗 → 负担得起

搭 afford to do sth. 负担得起做…；afford to 买得起

例 They would not be able to *afford* cars or homes. 他们买不起汽车和房子。

派 affordable(*a.* 能负担的，承担得起的)

afield
[əˈfiːld]

ad. 在野外，在田中；在战场上；离乡背井地；到远方，在远处

例 The private school enrolls students from Europe, Australia and even further *afield*. 这所私立学校招收来自欧洲、澳大利亚甚至更远地区的学生。

agency*
[ˈeɪdʒənsi]

n. 机构；代理，代办

记 词根记忆：ag（行动）+ ency（表状态，名词后缀）→ 代为行动 → 代理

例 We establish links and access to the organisation's *agencies*. 我们同这一组织的代理机构建立了联系，能直接进入这些机构。

派 agent(*n.* 代理人；代理商)

agenda*
[əˈdʒendə]

n. 议程；议程表

记 词根记忆：ag(做，行动) + enda(表名词复数) → 做的事情 → 议程

例 Blueprinting a meeting involves creating an *agenda* and clarifying rules for the meeting. 起草会议计划包括制定会议议程和明确会议章程。

aggravate*
[ˈæɡrəveɪt]

vt. 恶化，加重，加剧

记 词根记忆：ag + grav(重的) + ate(使…) → 使重 → 加重，恶化

搭 aggravate poverty 加重贫困；aggravate the situation 使环境恶化

例 The pollution problems in the area will be further *aggravated* by the heavy industry. 重工业的发展将使该地区的污染问题进一步恶化。

派 aggravated(*a.* 恶化的，加重的；罪行严重的)

同 burden(*vt.* 使担负)；increase(*v.* 增加)

反 decrease(*v.* 减少)；lessen(*v.* 减少，减轻)

aggravation
[ˌæɡrəˈveɪʃn]

n. 加重；恶化；愤怒，恼怒

搭 leave in aggravation 愤怒地离开；a state of aggravation 愤怒的状态

例 Carrying heavy boxes can cause *aggravation* of prior back injuries. 背部受伤时搬重物，会加重病情。

aggressive*
[əˈɡresɪv]

a. 侵犯的，侵略的，挑衅的；有进取心的，有冲劲的

记 词根记忆：ag + gress(行走) + ive(形容词后缀) → 不断行走，四处闯荡 → 有进取心的

搭 aggressive behavior 挑衅行为

例 The incentive for the more *aggressive* use of rockets came not from within the European continent but from far-away India. 将火箭用作更具攻击性武器的动机并非来自欧洲大陆，而是来自遥远的印度。

派 aggressively(*ad.* 放肆地)

同 militant(*a.* 好战的)；enterprising(*a.* 有进取心的)

□ afford □ afield □ agency □ agenda □ aggravate □ aggravation
□ aggressive

aggressiveness*
[əˈgresɪvnɪs]

n. 侵略；争斗；攻击

例 The message behind a crushing handshake is *aggressiveness* and a desire to compete. 在和他人握手时如果很用力，它传达的信息是争斗或想和对方竞争。

agile
[ˈædʒaɪl]

a. 敏捷的，灵活的，机敏的

记 词根记忆：ag(行动，做) + ile → 敏捷的

例 On the contrary to traditional idea, many interviewers prefer candidates with *agile* mind to those with high marks at universities. 与传统观点相反，许多面试官更喜欢思维敏捷的求职者，而不是那些在大学取得高分的人。

agriculture
[ˈægrɪkʌltʃə(r)]

n. 农业；农学

记 词根记忆：agri(田地；农业) + cult(种植；培养) + ure → 农业；农学

派 agricultural(*a.* 农业的；农学的)

ailment*
[ˈeɪlmənt]

n. (不严重的)疾病

记 联想记忆：a(一个) + il(看作 ill，生病的) + ment(名词后缀) → 疾病

例 New medical technology will cure more *ailments* that afflict humanity. 新的医学技术可以治愈更多困扰人类的疾病。

airtight*
[ˈeətaɪt]

a. 密闭的；无懈可击的

记 组合词：air(空气) + tight(紧密的) → 密不透气的 → 密闭的

例 Bill put the beer in an *airtight* glass container. 比尔把啤酒装进了一个密闭的玻璃容器里。

aisle
[aɪl]

n. 走廊，通道；(教堂的)侧廊

记 联想记忆：ai(看作 air，空气) + sle → 让空气流通的道 → 通道

搭 an aisle seat 靠过道的座位

例 In the supermarket, the end of an *aisle* is usually used for promoting special offers. 超市过道的尽头常用来促销特价商品。

alarm*
[əˈlɑːm]

n. 惊恐，恐慌；报警器；闹钟；警报 *vt.* 使惊恐；使担心

记 联想记忆：al + arm(武器) → 受了惊吓，拿起武器 → 惊恐

搭 a burglar alarm 防盗警报；alarm call 叫醒电话；告警声

alarm

例 Everytime when you leave your house, make sure the windows and doors are shut, and set the burglar *alarm*. 每次出门时都应确定门窗已关好，并打开防盗警铃。

albeit
[ˌɔːlˈbiːɪt]

conj. 虽然，尽管

例 A program for low-carbon energy finally got through this month, *albeit* in substantially scaled-down form. 一项低碳能源的计划本月最终获得通过，尽管其规模大大缩小。

□ aggressiveness □ agile □ agriculture □ ailment □ airtight □ aisle
□ alarm □ albeit

alchemist* [ˈælkəmɪst]

n. 炼金术士

记 联想记忆：al + chemist(化学家)→ 炼金术士

alcohol [ˈælkəhɒl]

n. 含酒精饮料，酒；酒精

例 Passive smoking is the third most preventable cause of death after active smoking and *alcohol*-related diseases. 被动吸烟是除主动吸烟和酗酒引发的疾病外的第三大可预防的致死原因。

alert [əˈlɜːt]

a. 警惕的 *n.* 警戒；警报 *vt.* 警告

记 联想记忆：Red Alert 红色警戒，20 世纪 90 年代风靡全球的电脑游戏

例 We must keep fully *alert*. 我们必须保持高度警惕。

algebra [ˈældʒɪbrə]

n. 代数

例 To Chinese overseas students, *algebra* or any course is not a real challenge, but using English anywhere and anytime. 对中国留学生来说，真正的挑战不是代数或是任何一门课程，而是随时随地都要用英语进行交流。

alienate [ˈeɪliəneɪt]

vt. 使疏远，使不友好；转让，让渡(财产等)

记 词根记忆：ali(其他的)+ en + ate(使…)→ 使具备其他的性质 → 使疏远，使不友好

例 Very talented people may feel *alienated* from the public. 天才出众的人可能觉得与大众格格不入。

派 alienated(*a.* 疏远的，被隔开的)

同 estrange(*vt.* 使疏远)

alienation* [ˌeɪliəˈneɪʃn]

n. 疏远；离间

搭 alienation from 与…疏远；sense of alienation 疏离感

例 The creation of healthy social environment must address issues such as poverty, pollution, natural resource depletion, social *alienation* and poor working conditions. 要营造健康的社会环境，必须解决贫困、污染、自然资源枯竭、社会关系疏离以及工作环境恶劣等问题。

alight* [əˈlaɪt]

a. 点着的 *vi.* 降落，飞落；从(公共汽车等)下来

记 联想记忆：a + light(点着)→ 点着的

搭 set alight 使…燃烧；alight on/upon (偶然)想到，注意到

例 The earliest peoples probably stored fire by keeping slow burning logs *alight* or by carrying charcoal in pots. 最原始人类保存火种的方法可能是让缓慢燃烧的原木保持不灭，或是将木炭装进罐子里。

alignment [əˈlaɪnmənt]

n. 排成直线；联盟

记 联想记忆：a + lign(看作 line，线)+ ment → 排成直线

例 If your bed doesn't give enough support, back muscles and ligaments will work all night trying to correct spinal *alignment*, so you wake up with a tired aching back. 如果你的床不能给你足够的支撑，背部肌肉和韧带便会整晚工作以校直脊椎，因此在第二天醒来时你就会觉得腰酸背痛。

□ alchemist □ alcohol □ alert □ algebra □ alienate □ alienation
□ alight ☒ alignment

allege* [ə'ledʒ]

vt. 断言，宣称

记 词根记忆：al（向）+ leg（送）+ e → 用力向某人寄送 → 断言，宣称

例 The police *alleged* that the man was murdered but they have not given proof yet. 警方宣称这个人被谋杀了，但是他们还没有给出证据。

allergic [ə'lɜːdʒɪk]

n. 过敏的，（对…）变态反应的，变应性的

记 词根记忆：all + erg（起作用）+ ic →（过敏反应）起作用 → 过敏的

搭 an allergic reaction 过敏性反应；allergic to 反感，厌恶

例 If you're not sure what's triggering your *allergic* cough, your doctor can give you a skin test or blood test to pinpoint the allergen. 如果你不能确定是什么引发了过敏性咳嗽，医生可以为你进行皮肤测试或验血来确定过敏源。

alleviate [ə'liːvieɪt]

vt. 减轻，缓解，缓和

记 词根记忆：al + lev（轻）+ iate → 减轻

例 An injection did little to *alleviate* Jane's pain after operation. 注射一针并没有缓解简手术后的疼痛。

alley* ['ælɪ]

n. 小巷；胡同

例 There are many blind *alleys* in this town. 这个镇子里有很多死胡同。

allocate ['æləkeɪt]

vt. 分配；分派

记 词根记忆：al（=ad 向）+ loc（地方）+ ate → 向地方发送 → 分配；分派

例 The world-wide coal industry *allocates* extensive resources to researching and developing new technologies. 全球的煤炭业为新技术的研发提供了广泛的资源。

allocation* [ˌælə'keɪʃn]

n. 配给，分配，安置；配给量

记 来自 allocate（*vt.* 分派）

例 People approved the *allocation* of food to those who need it most. 人们赞成把食物分给那些最需要的人。

allowance [ə'laʊəns]

n. 津贴；允许，容忍

记 联想记忆：allow（允许）+ ance → 允许，容忍

搭 make allowance（s）for 考虑到，顾及；体谅，原谅；为…留余地；at no allowance 无限制，尽情地；financial allowance 财政津贴；daily allowance 日常补贴

例 I have a good retirement *allowance* that will make it easy for me to buy a nice house. 我有一笔丰厚的退休金，买一栋漂亮的房子没什么经济上的困难。

allure [ə'lʊə(r)]

n./v. 诱惑，吸引

例 According to the statistics, the *allure* of the big city has weakened because of high housing prices. 数据显示，高房价降低了大城市的吸引力。

派 alluring（*a.* 有吸引力的，迷人的）

同 charm（*n.* 魅力）；attract（*vt.* 吸引）

□ allege □ allergic □ alleviate □ alley □ allocate □ allocation
□ allowance □ allure

alluvial* [əˈluːviəl]

a.【地】冲积的，淤积的 *n.* 冲积土(或层、矿床)，淤积土

搭 alluvial gold 冲积沙金

例 The seabed here consisted of *alluvial* silt and mud deposits. 此地的海床由冲击到这里的细沙和沉积的淤泥构成。

almond* [ˈɑːmənd]

n. 杏树；杏仁

例 Mary prefers *almonds* to peanuts. 和花生比，玛丽更喜欢杏仁。

alter [ˈɔːltə(r)]

vt. 改变；变动

记 本身为词根，意为“改变状态”

例 We may be able to *alter* our genetic inheritance if we so choose. 如果愿意，我们可以改变自己的基因遗传。

alternate

[ˈɔːltəneɪt] *v.* (使)轮流，(使)交替

[ɔːlˈtɜːnət] *a.* 轮流的；间隔的；交替的

记 词根记忆：altern(其他人或物) + ate → 其他的 → 轮流的；交替的

例 Snow and rain *alternated*, and it was very cold outside. 外面雨雪交加，非常寒冷。

alternative* [ɔːlˈtɜːnətɪv]

a. 可供替代的；非传统的，另类的 *n.* 可供选择的事物

记 词根记忆：altern(其他的) + at + ive(形容词后缀) → 可供替代的

搭 an alternative lifestyle 另一种生活方式

例 The coal industry should be abandoned in favour of *alternative* energy sources. 应该用其他的替代能源来取代煤炭业。

派 alternatively(*ad.* 二选一地)

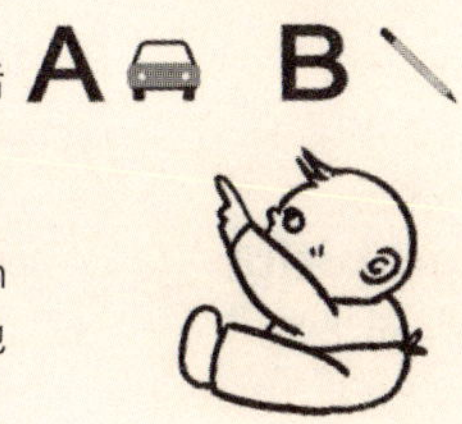

altitude [ˈæltɪtjuːd]

n. 海拔，高度；[*pl.*] 高地，高处

记 词根记忆：alt(高) + i + tude(表状态，名词后缀) → 海拔，高度

搭 high/low altitude 高海拔/低海拔

例 One common type of coffee bean, called Robusta, is grown at *altitudes* below 600 metres. 罗布斯塔咖啡豆是常见的一种咖啡豆，生长在海拔 600 米以下的地方。

altruistic [ˌæltruˈɪstɪk]

a. 无私的，为他人着想的

搭 altruistic act 无私的行为

例 Her motives for donating the money are *altruistic*? She is probably seeking for publicity. 她这次募捐真的是毫无私心吗？恐怕更多的是想为自己做宣传罢了。

aluminium [ˌæljəˈmɪniəm]

n. 铝

例 The US produces 300 million *aluminium* drink cans each day. 美国每天要生产三亿只铝质饮料罐。

amass [əˈmæs]

vt. 积聚

记 联想记忆：a + mass(大量) → 使大量东西汇聚到一起 → 积聚

例 The monopoly capitalists *amassed* fabulous wealth during World War II. 二战期间，垄断资本家大发横财。

☐ alluvial ☐ almond ☐ alter ☐ alternate ☐ alternative ☐ altitude
☐ altruistic ☐ aluminium ☐ amass

amateur [ˈæmətə(r)]	*n.* 外行；业余爱好者 *a.* 业余的 记 词根记忆：amat(爱)+eur(表人)→业余爱好者 搭 radio amateur 业余无线电爱好者 例 Only *amateur* athletes are allowed to compete in this sports games. 这次运动会只允许业余运动员参加。 反 expert(*n.* 专家)；professional(*a.* 职业的，专业的)
amaze [əˈmeɪz]	*vt.* 使惊奇，使惊愕 例 We are *amazed* at the perfect symmetry of the building. 我们惊诧于这座建筑物完美的对称。
ambassador* [æmˈbæsədə(r)]	*n.* 大使，使节 搭 a former ambassador to the UN 前任驻联合国大使
ambiguity [ˌæmbɪˈgjuːəti]	*n.* 模棱两可；不明确 记 词根记忆：amb(周围)+ig(走，驱动)+uity→转圈开→模棱两可 例 There was an element of *ambiguity* in the actor's reply. 演员的回答有些模棱两可。
ambiguous [æmˈbɪgjuəs]	*a.* 含糊其辞的；不明确的，模棱两可的 记 词根记忆：amb(周围)+ig(走，驱动)+uous(形容词后缀)→在周围走动的→模棱两可的 例 Thinking in categories enables us to categorise phenomena that are essentially *ambiguous*. 分类思考能使我们对一些本质上含糊不清的现象进行分类。
ambition* [æmˈbɪʃn]	*n.* 雄心，抱负；野心 记 词根记忆：amb(周围)+it(走)+ion→在周围走动→雄心；野心 搭 fulfill one's ambition 实现抱负 例 Bob's *ambition* was to study medicine. 鲍勃有志于学医。
ambitious* [æmˈbɪʃəs]	*a.* 有抱负的，有雄心的，有野心的 记 词根记忆：amb(周围)+it(走)+ious(多…的)→四处多走动的→有野心的 例 The Human Genome Project is the most *ambitious* scientific project since the Apollo programme, which landed a man on the moon. 人类基因工程是继阿波罗登月计划后最具雄心的科学项目。 
ambulance [ˈæmbjələns]	*n.* 救护车；野战医院 记 词根记忆：ambul(行走)+ance(名词后缀)→到处流动的车→救护车 例 There is a car accident, please send an *ambulance* as soon as possible. 这里发生了一起车祸，请尽快派救护车来。
amorphous* [əˈmɔːfəs]	*a.* 无固定形状的；无组织的 记 词根记忆：a(无)+morph(形状)+ous→无固定形状的 搭 amorphous phosphorus 无定形磷 例 The Swedish chemist called Pasch discovered *amorphous* phosphorus. 瑞典化学家帕施发现了无定形磷。

□ amateur □ amaze □ ambassador □ ambiguity □ ambiguous □ ambition
□ ambitious □ ambulance □ amorphous

amount*

[ə'maʊnt]

n. 总额 *vi.* 合计

搭 amount of 许多；amount to 总计…

例 The chart shows the *amount* spent on six consumer goods in European countries. 这张图表显示了欧洲国家在六种消费品上的总花费。

amphibious*

[æm'fɪbiəs]

a. 两栖的；水陆两用的

例 The newly built Noah's Ark is a kind of *amphibious* vehicle. 新建的诺亚方舟是水陆两用的运载工具。

amplify

['æmplɪfaɪ]

v. 详述；放大(声音等)

记 词根记忆：ampl(大) + ify(使…) → 放大

例 Let me *amplify* so that you will understand the overall problem. 让我来详细解释一下，这样你就会理解整个问题了。

同 expand(*v.* 使膨胀；扩张)；increase(*v.* 增加)

反 deflate(*vt.* 放气；使缩小)；shrink(*v.* 缩小)

analogous*

[ə'næləgəs]

a. 类似的

记 来自 analogy(*n.* 类比；类推)

搭 be analogous to 与…类似

例 The task was strictly *analogous* to the one that we had finished before. 这个任务和我们先前完成的那个极为相似。

analogy

[ə'nælədʒi]

n. 类推；类比

记 词根记忆：ana(类似) + log(说话) + y → 放在一起说 → 类推；类比

搭 draw an analogy between... and... 把…比作

例 Most of the time, it is easier for us to illustrate an abstract concept by *analogy* with something concrete. 大多数情况下，我们更易于通过与具体有形的东西进行类比来理解某个抽象的概念。

派 analogue(*a.* 模拟的)

同 likeness(*n.* 相似)

analyse*

['ænəlaɪz]

vt. 分析；分解

记 词根记忆：ana(贯穿) + lys(分开) + e → 整个分开 → 分析；分解

搭 analyse data 分析数据

例 The objective of the Human Genome Project is to map and *analyse* every single gene within the double helix of humanity's DNA. 人类基因工程的目标就是绘制和分析人类呈双螺旋状的 DNA 中的每一个基因。

派 analyst(*n.* 分析家；化验员)

□ amount □ amphibious □ amplify □ analogous □ analogy □ analyse

Word List 3

音频

lys	分开	analysis *n.* 分析；分解	**tomy**	切	anatomy *n.* 解剖(学)
angl	角	angle *n.* 角；角度	**ann**	年	annual *a.* 每年的，年度的
bio	生命	antibiotic *n.* 抗生素	**cip**	拿，取	anticipate *v.* 先于…行动
dot	给予，捐赠	antidote *n.* 解毒药	**sept**	腐烂的	antiseptic *n.* 防腐剂
para	排列	apparatus *n.* 器械，器具	**plaud**	击，打	applaud *v.* 鼓掌，喝彩

analysis* [ə'næləsɪs]

n. 分析；分解

记 词根记忆：ana(贯穿) + lys(分开) + is → 整个分开 → 分析；分解

搭 self analysis 自我分析；intelligence analysis 情报分析

例 Further ***analysis*** of the experimental result is needed. 试验结果需要进行进一步分析。

anatomy* [ə'nætəmi]

n. 解剖(学)；解剖结构

记 词根记忆：ana(分开) + tomy(切) → 切开机体组织 → 解剖(学)

搭 human anatomy 人体解剖(学)；animal anatomy 动物解剖(学)

例 Leon devoted his life to studying the human ***anatomy***. 利昂毕生致力于研究人体解剖学。

派 anatomical(*a.* 解剖学的)

ancestral [æn'sestrəl]

a. 祖先的；祖传的

例 The family lived at Mary's ***ancestral*** home. 一家人住在玛丽的祖居里。

anchor ['æŋkə(r)]

n. 锚；给人安全感的人(或物)；精神支柱；顶梁柱 *v.* 抛锚；使固定，系牢；使基于；主持(电视节目等)

记 发音记忆："安客" → 船抛锚，客安心 → 抛锚

例 When a ship ***anchors***, it means sailors can stay in the town for a short time to live as locals. 轮船抛锚，意味着船员们可以在小镇稍作停留，过一下当地人的生活。

ancient ['eɪnʃənt]

a. 古老的；年老的

记 发音记忆："安神的" → 那古老的旋律让人心安神宁 → 古老的

例 The ***ancient*** Greeks used lenses to concentrate the sun's rays on dry leaves to light fire. 古希腊人用透镜将太阳光聚集在干树叶上生火。

同 antique(*a.* 古老的)

反 modern(*a.* 现代的)

 □ analysis □ anatomy □ ancestral □ anchor □ ancient

and so forth*

等等

例 In many parts of Australia, standing water — that is dams, puddles *and so forth* — dry up rapidly. 澳大利亚大部分地方的积水，即水库、水坑等地的水，干得很快。

anecdotal* [ˌænɪkˈdəʊtl]

a. 轶话的，轶闻趣事的

例 There is only *anecdotal* evidence of life on Mars. 火星上存在生命仅仅是传言。

anecdote [ˈænɪkdəʊt]

n. 短故事；趣闻，轶事

记 联想记忆：a + nec（看作 neck，脖子）+ dote（溺爱）→ 一个人伸着脖子听喜爱的趣闻、轶事 → 趣闻，轶事

例 In the historical lessons, our teacher quoted many *anecdotes* to attract students' attention. 在历史课上，我们的老师借用大量的趣闻轶事来吸引学生的注意力。

angle [ˈæŋgl]

n. 角；角度；观点，立场 *v.* 移向；使成角度移动；从（某角度）报道

记 词根记忆：angl（角）+ e → 角

例 When you are stuck by a problem, you should change the *angle* to find some valid solutions. 当你被一个难题卡住的时候，应该换一种角度去寻找有效的解决方法。

派 angular（*a.* 有角的；尖角的）

animate

[ˈænɪmət] *a.* 活的，有生命的

[ˈænɪmeɪt] *vt.* 赋予生命；使生机勃勃

记 词根记忆：anim（生命；精神）+ ate → 赋予生命

例 A smile suddenly *animated* her face through hearing the good news. 听到这个好消息，她的脸上立刻浮现出了笑容。

announce* [əˈnaʊns]

vt. 宣布；声称

例 In 1989, a team of American and Canadian archaeologists *announced* that they had found the site of an ancient city. 1989 年，一个由美国和加拿大的考古学家组成的考古小组宣布，他们发现了一处古城遗址。

派 announcement（*n.* 宣告；发布）；announcer（*n.* 广播员，播报员）

annoy [əˈnɔɪ]

vt. 使烦恼；打搅

例 The bathroom light which flickered quite badly *annoyed* me very much. 浴室里的灯闪来闪去，真让我心烦。

annual* [ˈænjuəl]

a. 每年的，年度的 *n.* 年刊，年鉴；一年生植物

记 词根记忆：ann（年）+ ual → 每年的，年度的

搭 an annual report 年度报告；annual rainfall 年降雨量；annual budget 年度预算；annual income 年收入

例 All students at the college are entitled to become members of the Sports Centre for an *annual* fee of $200. 大学里的学生只需交 200 美元的年费，就可以成为运动中心的会员。

派 annually（*ad.* 一年一次，每年）

□ and so forth　□ anecdotal　□ anecdote　□ angle　□ animate　□ announce
□ annoy　□ annual

anthropologist*

[ˌænθrəˈpɒlədʒɪst]

n. 人类学家

記 词根记忆：anthrop(人，人类) + olog(y)(…学) + ist(表人) → 研究人类学的人 → 人类学家

例 The lecturer is an *anthropologist*. 演讲者是位人类学家。

---

antibiotic

[ˌæntibaɪˈɒtɪk]

n. 抗生素，抗菌素 *a.* 抗菌的

記 词根记忆：anti(反) + bio(生命) + tic → 抗生素

搭 antibiotic medicine 抗菌药

例 Although *antibiotic* can be used against infection, doctors won't persuade their patients to take it for a long time. 虽然抗菌素可以用来防止感染，但医生并不建议病人长期服用。

---

anticipate*

[ænˈtɪsɪpeɪt]

v. 预期，预料，期望；先于…行动

記 词根记忆：anti(在…之前) + cip(拿，取) + ate(动词后缀) → 在…之前取得 → 先于…行动

搭 anticipate doing sth. 期待做某事

例 We need someone who can *anticipate* and respond to changes in the fashion industry. 我们需要一个能预见时装业变化并能应对这些变化的人。

---

anticipation

[ænˌtɪsɪˈpeɪʃn]

n. 预料

搭 by anticipation 预先，事先；in anticipation 预先；预料，期待

例 According to the *anticipation* of economists, the global economy will get a burst growth in the second quarter of 2010. 据经济学家预测，全球经济在 2010 年第二季度将会迎来突破性增长。

---

antidote*

[ˈæntidəʊt]

n. 解毒药；矫正方法

記 词根记忆：anti(反) + dot(给予，捐赠) + e → 解毒药

搭 antidote to …的解毒剂

例 Researchers could not say for sure which medicine might be a successful *antidote* to bacterial infection. 研究人员不能确定哪种药可以有效地治疗细菌感染。

---

antiquated

[ˈæntɪkweɪtɪd]

AW

a. 陈旧的，过时的；废弃的

例 In comparison with modern mass media, ordinary radio looks positively *antiquated*. 与现代大众媒体相比，普通收音机肯定显得过时了。

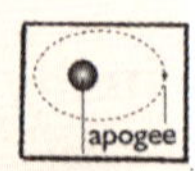

---

antique*

[ænˈtiːk]

a. 古时的，古老的 *n.* 古物，古董

記 词根记忆：anti(在…之前) + que → 以前的 → 古时的，古老的

搭 an antique shop 古玩店

例 There is an *antique* mahogany desk exhibited in the corner. 拐角处展出的是一把古老的红木书桌。

antique

□ anthropologist □ antibiotic □ anticipate □ anticipation □ antidote □ antiquated □ antique

antiquity* [æn'tɪkwəti]	*n.* 古，古老；古代；古人；古迹，古物 记 联想记忆：antiqu(=antique 古代的) + ity → 古代 搭 Roman antiquities 罗马古迹 例 No one knows how much *antiquity* has been stolen or destroyed. 没人知道有多少古迹被偷盗或毁坏了。
antiseptic [ˌænti'septɪk]	*a.* 防腐的，抗菌的 *n.* 防腐剂，抗菌剂 记 词根记忆：anti(反) + sept(腐烂的) + ic → 防腐剂，抗菌剂 例 In old times, the bodies of most of emperors were dealt with *antiseptic* for lasting for ever. 古时，为了死后长存，大多数皇帝的遗体都要做防腐处理。
anxious* ['æŋkʃəs]	*a.* 渴望的；忧虑的 例 He is *anxious* to enter the competition. 他急切希望能加入比赛。
apace* [ə'peɪs]	*ad.* 快速地，急速地 例 The research went on *apace*. 研究进展迅速。
apart [ə'pɑːt]	*ad.* 相间隔；分离；除去 *a.* 分离的 记 联想记忆：a + part(分开) → 分离的 例 *Apart* from the Second World War period, the Winter Olympics were held every four years. 除了二战期间，冬奥会每四年举行一次。
ape* [eɪp]	*n.* 猿 *vt.* 模仿 搭 go ape 发疯；变得狂热 例 It is pretty well agreed that *apes* and men come from a common ancestor. 人们普遍认为类人猿和人类有共同的祖先。
apparatus [ˌæpə'reɪtəs]	*n.* 器械，器具，仪器；机构，组织 记 词根记忆：ap(靠近) + para(排列) + tus → 靠近排列 → 器械，器具 例 This *apparatus* has been thoroughly tested. 这套设备已经过全面测试。
apparent* [ə'pærənt]	*a.* 显然的；表面上的 记 联想记忆：ap + parent(父母) → 父母对儿女的爱是显而易见的 → 显然的 例 This tendency was *apparent* in the late 1980s. 这种趋势在 20 世纪 80 年代末很明显。
apparently* [ə'pærəntli]	*ad.* 显然；看来，似乎 例 *Apparently*, a caretaker government seemed not to be potent. 看来，临时政府似乎无法胜任工作。
appeal* [ə'piːl]	*vi.* 呼吁；起诉，上诉；吸引 *n.* 上诉，申诉；呼吁；感染力，吸引力 搭 appeal for 请求；appeal to 诉诸；吸引 例 You should read things that *appeal* to you. 你应该阅读一些让你感兴趣的东西。 同 accuse(*vt.* 控告)
appear* [ə'pɪə(r)]	*v.* 出现，显露，公开露面；出场，问世；仿佛，似乎 搭 appear to 看上去；appear on behalf of sb.（作为律师）出庭 例 It *appears* that there is a grammar mistake in the composition. 这篇作文好像有处语法错误。

□ antiquity □ antiseptic □ anxious □ apace □ apart □ ape
□ apparatus □ apparent □ apparently □ appeal □ appear

appearance* [əˈpɪərəns]

n. 出现；外观

记 联想记忆：appear(出现) + ance(名词后缀) → 出现

例 His sudden *appearance* surprised me greatly. 他的突然出现让我大吃一惊。

appetite [ˈæpɪtaɪt]

n. 食欲，胃口；欲望

记 词根记忆：ap(向，往) + pet(寻找) + ite → 往到处寻找 → 食欲

搭 appetite for... 对…的食欲；对…的兴趣

例 My supper by this time was cold, and my *appetite* was gone. 我的晚餐这时候已经凉了，我也没胃口了。

applaud [əˈplɔːd]

v. (向…)鼓掌，喝彩；称赞

记 词根记忆：ap(表加强) + plaud(击，打) → 双手击打 → 鼓掌，喝彩

例 They *applaud* their favorite comedienne as she comes on the stage. 当他们最喜欢的女喜剧演员登台时，他们鼓掌欢迎。

appliance [əˈplaɪəns]

n. 用具，器具

记 联想记忆：appli(看作 apply，使用) + ance → 可用的东西 → 用具，器具

搭 household appliances 家用器具

例 On Wednesdays, I repair electrical *appliances* free of charge. 每逢周三，我都给人免费修理电器。

applicant [ˈæplɪkənt]

n. 申请人

例 We have interviewed twenty-six *applicants* and none of them are qualified. 我们已经面试了 26 个申请者，没一人符合条件。

application* [ˌæplɪˈkeɪʃn]

n. 请求，申请(书、表)；应用，运用；施用，敷用

记 词根记忆：ap(=ad 向，靠近) + plic(折叠) + ation(名词后缀) → 折得很近 → 申请；应用

搭 application for 申请…；an application form 申请表；application process 申请过程；job application 应聘

例 I think this invention has many useful *applications*. 我认为这项发明非常有用，会被广泛应用。

apply* [əˈplaɪ]

v. 申请；应用，使用；涉及

记 联想记忆：这家服务站免费提供(supply)打气筒给行人使用(apply)

搭 apply for 申请；apply to 与…有关；适用；应用；apply to the customs 报关；apply oneself to 致力于

例 If you would like more information on how to *apply* for a student loan, then you should contact The Student Loans Company. 如果你想获得更多有关申请学生贷款的信息，那么你应该和学生贷款公司联系。

□ appearance □ appetite □ applaud □ appliance □ applicant □ application □ apply

appoint [ə'pɔɪnt]

vt. 任命，委任；指定(时间、地点等)

记 联想记忆：ap(表加强)＋point(指向，指出)→指定某人做某事→任命，委任

搭 appoint to 任命，委任；an appointed official 受委派的官员；appoint sb. to a post 派某人任某职

例 He is *appointed* to administer funds. 他被指派去管理基金。

appointment* [ə'pɔɪntmənt]

n. 约会

搭 make an appointment 约会

例 If for some reason you cannot keep your *appointment*, please telephone. 如果由于某种原因不能赴约，请您电话告知。

apportion [ə'pɔːʃn]

vt. 分派，(按比例或计划)分配

记 词根记忆：ap＋portion(部分)→分成部分→分派，分配

例 We *apportion* the money before valuing the price of the souvenir. 在对纪念品估价之前，我们先分配一下花销。

appraisal [ə'preɪzəl]

n. 评估，评价

记 词根记忆：ap(给，向)＋prais(价格)＋al→给定价→评价

例 Susan's *appraisal* of the writer's work was favorable. 苏珊对这位作家的作品给予了肯定的评价。

appreciate* [ə'priːʃieɪt]

v. 赏识，鉴赏；感激；涨价，增值

记 词根记忆：ap(向)＋preci(价值)＋ate→对价值予以肯定→赏识

搭 appreciate doing sth. 对…表示感激

例 I deeply *appreciate* your care, but I'm fine now. 我对你的关心深表感激，但是现在我很好。

派 appreciation(*n.* 欣赏；体谅；感激)；appreciative(*a.* 感谢的；赞赏的)；appreciable(*a.* 值得重视的；可感知的)

approach* [ə'prəʊtʃ]

v. 靠近，接近；来临 *n.* 靠近，接近；方法，途径

搭 approach to 接近，近似

例 As autumn *approaches*, the beekeepers pack up their hives and go south. 秋天来临，养蜂人收好蜂房前往南方。

派 approachable(*a.* 易亲近的；友善的)

appropriate*

[ə'prəʊpriət] *a.* 适当的 [ə'prəʊprieɪt] *vt.* 占有，挪用；拨出(款项)

记 词根记忆：ap(=to)＋propr(自身的，固有的)＋iate→变为自己的→占有，挪用

搭 be appropriate to 适于；appropriate sth. for 拨出(款项)供…之用

例 Personality questionnaires are used by companies to put people in *appropriate* areas of work. 很多公司通过性格测试的方式把员工安排到合适的工作岗位。

□ appoint □ appointment □ apportion □ appraisal □ appreciate □ approach
□ appropriate

approval
[ə'pruːvl]

n. 赞成，同意；正式批准

记 词根记忆：ap(向) + prov(试验) + al(名词后缀) → 向某人进行试验 → 赞成，同意；正式批准

例 Mining is subject to stringent controls and *approval* processes. 采矿要接受严格的控制和审批程序。

---

approve*
[ə'pruːv]

v. 赞成；批准，同意

记 联想记忆：ap + prove(证实) → 经过证实才能批准 → 批准，同意

搭 approve of 同意…

例 You can begin making purchases immediately after your application is *approved*. 你的申请得到批准后，马上就可以购买了。

---

approximate

[ə'prɒksɪmət] *a.* 近似的 [ə'prɒksɪmeɪt] *vt.* 近似

记 词根记忆：ap(向) + prox(近) + imate → 接近的 → 近似的

例 I would like to know the *approximate* price of this car. 我想了解一下这辆车的大概价位。

---

approximately*
[ə'prɒksɪmətli]

ad. 近似，大约

例 The next bus will come in *approximately* five minutes. 下一班公交车大约会在五分钟后到达。

---

apt
[æpt]

a. 易于…的；适宜的；敏捷的

记 本身为词根，意为"适应；能力"

搭 a particularly apt comment 特别恰当的评论

例 Artists are *apt* at revealing the inner world of human beings. 艺术家们善于表现人的内心世界。

---

aptitude*
['æptɪtjuːd]

n. 天资，天赋，天生的才能

记 联想记忆：感激(gratitude)上苍让你具备这种才能(aptitude)

搭 aptitude for …的能力

例 Each branch of this company had employees of comparable *aptitudes*. 该公司的所有分公司都雇用能力相当的员工。

---

aquarium*
[ə'kweəriəm]

n. 养鱼池；玻璃缸；水族馆

记 词根记忆：aqu(a)(水) + arium(表场所，名词后缀) → 水族馆

例 We are going to take the kids to the new *aquarium* this weekend. 这周末我们打算带孩子们去新开的水族馆。

---

arable*
['ærəbl]

a. 可耕作的 *n.* 耕地

记 联想记忆：ar(看作 art，技术) + able(能够的) → 通过技术认定可耕 → 可耕作的

搭 arable land 耕地

例 On the top of the hill, the *arable* ground has been seeded. 山顶上那片可耕种的土地已经播种了。

arboreal
[ɑːˈbɔːriəl]
a. 树木的；栖于树木的
记 词根记忆：arbor(树) + eal → 树木的
搭 arboreal insects 栖树的昆虫
例 Koala is an *arboreal* animal. 树袋熊是一种树栖动物。

arcade*
[ɑːˈkeɪd]
n. 拱廊，有拱廊的街道
例 The most exciting place to visit is the new entertainment complex with a seven-screen cinema, bowling alley and video games *arcade*. 最值得参观的地方是新娱乐中心，里面有一家七放映厅的电影院，该娱乐中心还设有保龄球馆和游戏室。

architect
[ˈɑːkɪtekt]
n. 建筑师，设计师；创造者
例 Among mathematicians and *architects*, left-handers tend to be more common. 在数学家和建筑师中，惯用左手者往往更为常见。

architecture*
[ˈɑːkɪtektʃə(r)]
n. 建筑学；建筑设计，建筑风格；【计】体系结构
例 The trend in *architecture* now favours smaller-scale building design. 现在建筑设计的流行趋势是小户型。
派 architectural(*a.* 建筑的)

archive

archive*
[ˈɑːkaɪv]
n. 档案；档案室 *vt.* 存档
例 The museum drew on its *archive* collection for its exhibition. 博物馆为举办展览使用了收藏的档案文件。

argue*
[ˈɑːgjuː]
v. 争论；说服
记 发音记忆："阿Q" → 阿Q喜欢和人争论 → 争论
搭 argue sb. into/out of doing 说服某人做/不做某事；argue for 赞成；要求；argue about 议论…；argue over 辩论/争论…
例 The study *argues* that the type of action needed against passive smoking should be similar to that being taken against AIDS. 该研究认为人们需要采取类似防范艾滋病的方法来防范被动吸烟。
派 arguably(*ad.* 可论证地，可辩解地)

argument*
[ˈɑːgjumənt]
n. 争吵，争论；观点，论据；说理，论证
例 Support your *argument* with examples and relevant evidence, please. 请用实例和相关证据来支持你的论点。

aridity
[əˈrɪdəti]
n. 干旱；乏味
记 联想记忆：arid(干旱的) + ity → 干旱
例 The most challenging natural problem of Australia is *aridity*. 干旱是澳大利亚面临的最具挑战性的自然问题。

arithmetic*
[əˈrɪθmətɪk]
n. 算术
记 词根记忆：arithm(数字) + etic(表学问、学科，名词后缀) → 算术

arousal
[əˈraʊzl]
n. 唤起，激起
例 The physiological *arousal* declined quickly to the same levels as those of the control subjects. 生理激发水平迅速下降到了同受控对象一样的程度。

□ arboreal □ arcade □ architect □ architecture □ archive □ argue
□ argument □ aridity □ arithmetic □ arousal

arrange *
[ə'reɪndʒ]

v. 安排；排列

记 联想记忆：ar(表加强) + range(排列) → 有序地排列 → 安排；排列

搭 arrange for sb./sth. to do sth. 安排…做…；arrange the conference room 布置会议室；arrange the accommodation 安排住宿

例 The Language Institute activities coordinator can assist students to *arrange* any sport and leisure activities. 语言学院的活动负责人可以帮助学生安排任何体育和休闲活动。

arrangement *
[ə'reɪndʒmənt]

n. 安排；[常 *pl.*] 准备工作

搭 course arrangement 课程安排；seat arrangement 座位安排

例 Larger firms appear to be more willing to experiment with flexible working *arrangements*. 较大型的企业似乎更愿意尝试弹性工作制。

array *
[ə'reɪ]

n. 陈列；大批 *vt.* 部署

记 联想记忆：ar + ray(光线) → 像光线一样整齐排列 → 陈列；大批

搭 an array of 一批，一列

例 Corso's drink corner is a shelf with an *array* of bottles and glasses on it. 科尔索的酒水区是一个陈列着许多酒瓶和玻璃杯的架子。

arrogance
['ærəgəns]

n. 傲慢，自大

记 词根记忆：ar(增加) + rog(要求) + ance(名词后缀) → 一再地要求 → 傲慢，自大

例 His *arrogance* impressed us most unfavourably. 他的傲慢态度给我们留下了极坏的印象。

artefact *
['ɑːtɪfækt]

n. 人工制品，手工艺品

记 词根记忆：arte(技巧) + fact(制作) → 用技巧制作的东西 → 人工制品

例 The museum collections included approximately 300,000 *artefacts*. 博物馆里收藏了大约 30 万件手工艺品。

artery
['ɑːtəri]

n. 动脉；干线，要道

记 联想记忆：和 vein(*n.* 静脉)一起记

例 The patient underwent an operation to unblock his coronary *artery*. 这位病人接受了一次冠状动脉疏通手术。

arthritis *
[ɑː'θraɪtɪs]

n. 关节炎

记 词根记忆：arthr(连结；关节) + itis(炎症) → 关节炎

例 Rheumatoid *arthritis* belongs to the family of autoimmune diseases. 类风湿性关节炎属于自体免疫系统类疾病。

artificial *
[ˌɑːtɪ'fɪʃl]

a. 人工的，人造的；假的，矫揉造作的；模拟的

记 词根记忆：arti(技巧) + fic(做) + ial(形容词后缀) → 利用技巧制作的 → 人工的；假的

搭 artificial color 人工色素，合成色素；artificial intelligence 人工智能

例 We use no *artificial* additives of any kind in our products. 我们的产品绝不含任何人工添加剂。

□ arrange □ arrangement □ array □ arrogance □ artefact □ artery
□ arthritis □ artificial

as for/to	至于，关于 例 *As for* the glass changing colours instantly, that may come true. 至于让玻璃瞬间变换色彩，也会成为现实。
as if/though	好像，仿佛 例 The little girl's lips quiver, *as if* she is about to cry. 小女孩的嘴唇颤抖着，好像要哭了。
ascend* [ə'send]	*v.* 攀登；上升，升高 记 词根记忆：a(向) + scend(爬) → 向上爬 → 攀登；上升 搭 ascend to 追溯到 例 The air became colder and more rarefied as we *ascended*. 我们越往上攀登，空气就变得越冷越稀薄。
ascertain [ˌæsə'teɪn]	*vt.* 弄清，查明；确定 记 词根记忆：as + cert(确定) + ain → 弄清，查明；确定 例 It must be *ascertained* whether he is the property owner before you make a down payment. 在交首付之前，你必须查明他是否为该房产的业主。 同 discover(*v.* 发现)；clarify(*v.* 澄清) 反 conceal(*vt.* 隐瞒)；cover(*v.* 掩盖)
ascribe [ə'skraɪb]	*vt.* 把…归因于 记 词根记忆：a + scrib(写) + e → 把…写上去 → 把…归因于 例 The report *ascribes* the rise in asthma to the increase in air pollution. 该报告将哮喘的增加归因于空气污染。

Man errs so long as he strives.
人只要奋斗就会犯错误。

——德国诗人、剧作家 歌德
(Johann Wolfgang Goethe, German poet and dramatist)

Word List 4

音 频

词根、词缀预习表

spir	呼吸	aspiration *n.* 强烈的愿望	**saul**	跳	assault *n./vt.* 攻击，袭击
sembl	一样，相等	assemble *v.* 集合，装配	**sert**	放置	assert *v.* 断言
soci	结交，同伴	associate *v.* 交往	**astro**	星	astrology *n.* 占星学
nomy	法则；学科	astronomy *n.* 天文学	**tach**	接触	attach *v.* 使附属
tempt	诱惑	attempt *n./v.* 尝试，试图	**tent**	伸展	attention *n.* 注意(力)

ash
[æʃ]

n. 灰；灰烬；[*pl.*] 骨灰，遗骸

搭 cigar ash 烟灰

例 The volcanic ***ash*** caused a lot of damage in the village. 火山灰给村庄造成了很大的破坏。

aspect*
[ˈæspekt]

n. 方面；(建筑物的)朝向，方向；外貌，外观样子

记 词根记忆：a + spect(看)→看上去的样子→外貌

搭 in all aspects 全面；aspect of …方面

例 A great deal of empirical evidence shows that pictures in a book interfere in a damaging way with all ***aspects*** of learning to read. 大量经验表明，书中的插图给学习阅读的各方面都造成了不利影响。

aspiration
[ˌæspəˈreɪʃn]

n. 强烈的愿望；志向

记 词根记忆：a(无) + spir(呼吸) + ation→(渴望得快要)窒息了→强烈的愿望

例 A building reflects the ideas and ***aspirations*** of the designer and client. 建筑物反映出设计者和客户的理念与要求。// She has never had any ***aspiration*** to earn a lot of money. 她从未企求赚很多钱。

派 aspirational(*a.* 渴望成功的)

aspire
[əˈspaɪə(r)]

v. 向往，渴望，追求；有志于，有抱负

记 联想记忆：a + spire(塔尖，尖顶)→向塔尖看→向往，渴望，追求

例 The looks on children who ***aspired*** to go to school in some poor areas deeply moved me. 在一些贫困地区，孩子们渴望上学的眼神深深地打动我。

派 aspiring(*a.* 有抱负的，有志向的)

assault
[ə'sɔːlt]

n. (武力或口头上的)攻击，袭击；侵犯人身罪；冲击；抨击 *vt.* 攻击，袭击；使难受

记 词根记忆：as(向) + saul(跳) + t → 跳向某人 → 攻击，袭击

搭 assault carrier 航空母舰；an assault force 突击队

例 With the recent increase in sexual ***assaults***, the police have taken action to curb the crime and protect women. 随着近来性攻击事件的增加，警方已采取措施遏制犯罪，保护女性。

同 attack(*n.*/*v.* 攻击，抨击)

assemble*
[ə'sembl]

v. 集合；装配

记 词根记忆：as(接近) + sembl(一样，相等) + e → 使接近一样 → 集合

例 All components were ***assembled*** in the front workshop. 所有部件都是在前面的车间组装的。

派 assembly(*n.* 集会；组装)

assert*
[ə'sɜːt]

v. 断言，声称；坚持

记 词根记忆：as(表加强) + sert(放置) → 强行放入 → 断言

搭 assert oneself 坚持自己的权利，表现自己的权威；assert one's rights 维护自己的权利；assert national independence 维护国家独立

例 The arrested offender continued to ***assert*** that she was innocent. 被捕的罪犯仍然在强调她是清白的。

派 assertive (*a.* 断言的；武断的)；assertiveness (*n.* 坚定而自信，果断)；assertion(*n.* 断言；主张)

同 declare(*v.* 断言，宣称)；protest(*v.* 断言)；avow(*v.* 承认，宣称)

assess*
[ə'ses]

vt. 评定；估价

例 Core samples are always extracted to ***assess*** the quality and quantity of coal at a site before mining. 在开采前，通常会收集选地的矿样来评估矿质和储量。

assessment*
[ə'sesmənt]

n. 判定，评定；核定的付款额；看法，评价

搭 research assessment 研究评估；assessment methods 评估方法

例 The teacher made a careful ***assessment*** of the exam. 老师对本次考试作了细致的评估。

asset
['æset]

n. 财产；优点

例 Organizations should recognize that their employees are a significant part of their financial ***assets***. 公司应该承认员工是其财产的重要组成部分。

assign*
[ə'saɪn]

vt. 指派，分配；指定

记 联想记忆：as + sign(签名) → 找那个大牌明星签名的任务指派给你了 → 指派，分配

搭 assign sth. to sb. 给某人指派…

例 In the United States, more land is ***assigned*** to car use than to housing. 美国的土地更多地被指定为停车之用，而不是建造住宅。

assignment*
[ə'saɪnmənt]

n. 任务，工作

记 来自 assign(*vt.* 指派，分配)

例 Have you been given any writing ***assignments*** yet? 有人给你布置写作作业了吗？

☐ assault ☐ assemble ☐ assert ☐ assess ☐ assessment ☐ asset
☐ assign ☐ assignment

assimilate [ə'sɪməleɪt]

v. 吸收；使同化

记 词根记忆：as + simil(相同) + ate(使…) → 使相同 → 使同化

例 We *assimilate* some kinds of food more easily than others. 和其他食物相比，有些食物更容易被吸收。

同 absorb(*vt.* 吸收)；digest(*v.* 消化)

assimilation [əˌsɪmə'leɪʃn]

n. 吸收；(被)吸收和同化的过程

搭 cultural assimilation 文化同化

例 Language *assimilation* is the progressive process whereby a speech community of a language shifts to speaking another language. 语言同化是指讲话群体由一种语言转向另一种语言的渐进的过程。

assist* [ə'sɪst]

v. 帮助，援助，协助

记 词根记忆：as(近) + sist(站立) → 站在近旁 → 帮助，协助

搭 assist with/in 帮助

例 The Student Union is intended to *assist* in teachers' work. 学生会旨在协助老师工作。

assistance [ə'sɪstəns]

n. 协助，援助

记 联想记忆：assist(援助，帮助) + ance → 协助，援助

搭 military assistance 军事援助

例 Farmers are to receive financial *assistance* to help see them through the worst drought in over 50 years. 农民们将得到经济援助，以度过这场50多年来最严重的旱灾。

assistant* [ə'sɪstənt]

a. 助理的；副的 *n.* 助理

例 The employees felt that their *assistant* manager was closer to them than the manager. 和经理相比，员工们感觉助理经理与他们更亲近。

assistantship* [ə'sɪstənˌʃɪp]

n. (给研究生的)半工半读助学金，(大学)研究生助教奖学金

例 The organization has contributed a lot to the social welfare activities such as *assistantship* programs. 这个组织为社会福利作了很多贡献，比如给学生提供助教学金。

associate*

[ə'səʊsieɪt] *v.* 使联合；使有联系；交往

[ə'səʊsiət] *n.* 伙伴；同事 *a.* 副的；联合的，合伙的

记 词根记忆：as(表加强) + soci(结交；同伴) + ate(动词后缀) → 交往

搭 associate with 和…相关，联合；business associate 商业伙伴；associate professor 副教授

例 People always *associate* noise with headaches, and for most of us excessive noise creates the conditions for a headache. 人们总是把噪音和头痛联系在一起，对于我们大多数人来说，过多的噪音是引起头痛的原因。

同 combine(*v.* 结合，联合)；join(*v.* 加入，结合)

association* [əˌsəʊsi'eɪʃn]

n. 协会

例 Our long *association* with your company has brought great benefits. 我方和贵公司的长期合作已经带来了巨大的利益。

□ assimilate □ assimilation □ assist □ assistance □ assistant □ assistantship
□ associate □ association

assume* [ə'sjuːm]

vt. 假定，设想；承担(责任)，就(职)

记 词根记忆：as + sum(拿，取) + e → 预先拿取 → 假定，设想

搭 assume an obligation 承担义务；assume responsibility 承担责任

例 Ecologists have ***assumed*** that tropical ecosystems were shaped entirely by natural forces. 生态学家设想热带生态系统完全是由自然的力量形成的。

assumption [ə'sʌmpʃn]

n. 假定，假设；担任，承担

例 The ***assumption*** has been shown to be incorrect by recent research. 最近的研究证明这一假设不正确。

assurance [ə'ʃʊərəns]

n. 信心；保证；保险

记 联想记忆：assur(=assure 保证) + ance → 保证

搭 quality assurance system 质量保证体系

assure* [ə'ʃʊə(r)]

vt. 使确信，使确保；保证，向…保证

记 联想记忆：as + sure(确定的) → 使确信，使确保

例 The young boy ***assured*** us of his ability to solve the problem. 那个小男孩向我们保证他有能力解决这问题。

asthma* ['æsmə]

n. 哮喘症

例 A world-wide rise in ***asthma***, over the past four decades is said to be linked with increased air pollution. 据说，在过去的 40 年里，世界范围内哮喘病发病率升高与越来越严重的空气污染有关。

astonish [ə'stɒnɪʃ]

vt. 使惊讶，使吃惊

记 联想记忆：a(一个) + ston(看作 stone，石头) + ish → 一石激起千层浪，怎不叫人惊讶 → 使惊讶

例 The news ***astonished*** everyone. 这个消息使所有人大吃一惊。

astound [ə'staʊnd]

v. (使)震惊

记 联想记忆：as + tound(看作 sound，声音) → 像被奇怪的声音吓倒 → 震惊

例 The eruption in May 1980 of Mount St. Helens, Washington State, ***astounded*** the world with its violence. 1980 年 5 月，位于华盛顿的圣海伦斯火山喷发所产生的强大破坏力震惊了世界。

astray [ə'streɪ]

ad. 迷路地；误入歧途地

记 联想记忆：as(像) + tray(盘子) → 像在盘子里转圈圈 → 迷路地；误入歧途地

例 Follow the guide or you'll go ***astray*** in the jungle. 跟着导游，否则你们会在丛林里迷路的。

astrology [ə'strɒlədʒi]

n. 占星学；占星术

记 词根记忆：astro(星) + (o)logy(…学) → 占星学

astronaut* ['æstrənɔːt]

n. 宇航员

例 The rocket transported the ***astronauts*** to mysterious realms beyond the Earth. 火箭将宇航员运载到地球以外的神秘领域。

astronomy [ə'strɒnəmi]

n. 天文学

记 词根记忆：astro(星星) + nomy(法则；学科) → 研究星星的学科 → 天文学

例 ***Astronomy*** is an extensive science, which can connect with physics, optics and astrology. 天文学是一门涉及广泛的科学，可以与物理学、光学和占星学相关联。

派 astronomical(*a.* 天文学的；天文的)；astronomer(*n.* 天文学家)

asymmetry* [ˌeɪ'sɪmətri]

n. 不对称

记 联想记忆：a(不) + symmetry(对称，匀称) → 不对称

例 ***Asymmetry*** is a common feature of the human body. 不对称是人体共同的特点。

派 asymmetric(*a.* 不对称的，不均匀的)

at least*

至少

例 Fulltime courses last ***at least*** one academic year in this college. 这所大学的全日制课程至少要上一学年。

at random

随便地，任意地

例 Each programme was assigned ***at random*** a division that had been historically high in productivity and a division that had been below average in productivity. 每个项目被随机分配给一个生产效率历来都很高的部门和一个生产效率低于平均水平的部门。

athlete ['æθliːt]

n. 运动员；体育家

记 发音记忆："爱死你的" → 运动员体格健美让人喜爱 → 运动员

派 athletic(*a.* 运动的，运动员的)

atmosphere* ['ætməsfɪə(r)]

n. 大气；气氛；环境

记 词根记忆：atmo + spher(球体) + e → 围绕地球的空气 → 大气

搭 atmosphere of …的氛围

例 Uranus' ***atmosphere*** consists largely of hydrogen and helium. 天王星的大气主要由氢和氦组成。

atmospheric* [ˌætməs'ferɪk]

a. 大气的，空气的；大气层的；大气所引起的

搭 atmospheric pressure 大气压；atmospheric conditions 大气状况

例 The main reason of ***atmospheric*** pollution is the increase of carbon dioxide emissions. 大气污染的主要原因是二氧化碳排放量的增加。

atomic [ə'tɒmɪk]

a. 原子(能)的

例 ***Atomic*** energy powers the submarine. 原子能给潜艇提供动力。

attach [ə'tætʃ]

v. 系，贴；认为有重要性(或意义、价值等)；使附属，附加

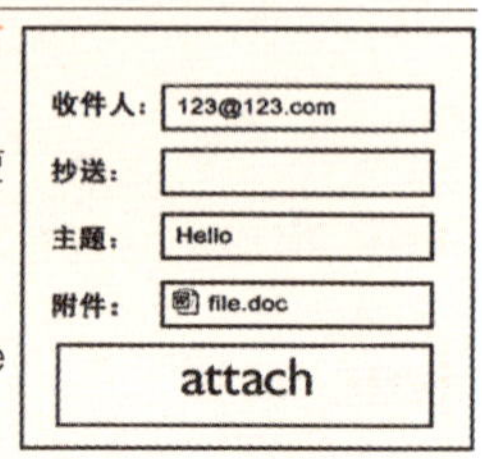

记 词根记忆：at + tach(接触) → 接触上 → 贴；使附属

搭 attach to 使依恋；把…贴在，附加

例 They ***attached*** the coupon to the front of the letter. 他们把优惠券附在信的正面。

派 attachment(*n.* 附件；依恋；忠诚)

□ astronomy □ asymmetry □ at least □ at random □ athlete □ atmosphere
□ atmospheric □ atomic □ attach

attack* [əˈtæk]

n./v. 进攻；抨击；(疾病等)突然发作

记 联想记忆：at(表加强) + tack(看作 tank，坦克) → 用坦克加强进攻 → 进攻；抨击

例 Passive smoking causes between 30,000 and 60,000 deaths from heart *attacks* each year in the United States. 在美国，被动吸烟每年导致三到六万人死于心脏病。

attain [əˈteɪn]

vt. 达到；获得；完成

记 词根记忆：at + tain(拿住) → 稳稳拿住 → 达到；获得；完成

例 Sustainable development is to *attain* a perpetual balance between population, economic growth and the environment. 可持续发展就是要实现人口、经济增长和环境三者之间的永久平衡。

派 attainment(*n.* 成就，造诣；获得，达到)

attainable [əˈteɪnəbl]

a. 可获得的，可达到的，可实现的

例 The newly set standard is easily *attainable* by most students. 大部分学生可以轻松地达到新标准。

attempt* [əˈtempt]

n./v. 尝试，试图；努力

记 词根记忆：at(表加强) + tempt(诱惑) → 试图引诱别人 → 尝试，试图

搭 make attempt 尝试；attempt (doing) sth. 尝试做…；attempt to do sth. 尝试/努力做…

例 A series of lectures organised by the Students' Union is part of the union's *attempt* to help students stay healthy. 学生会举办的一系列讲座是为帮助学生保持健康而努力做的事情之一。

搭 attempted(*a.* 未遂的)

attend* [əˈtend]

v. 出席，参加；随同，陪同；专心，注意

记 词根记忆：at + tend(伸展) → 伸长脖子看 → 专心

例 Students under the age of 16 cannot *attend* any of the courses offered by the college. 未满 16 岁的学生不能学习本学院的任何课程。

attendance* [əˈtendəns]

n. 到场，出席；出勤；伺候，照料

搭 take attendance 点名；attendance record 考勤记录

例 I do not think there is a need to make class *attendance* every day at universities. 我认为在大学里没必要每天点名。

attention* [əˈtenʃn]

n. 注意(力)，留心；立正

记 词根记忆：at + tent(伸展) + ion → (听得)伸长了脖子 → 注意(力)

搭 attract/draw (sb's) attention to 吸引注意力，令(某人)注意某事物；divert attention from 转移注意力；pay attention to 注意；catch the attention of 引起…的注意

例 One problem that deserves *attention* now is the severe climate. 现在，恶劣的气候是需要引起人们关注的一个问题。

attentive* [əˈtentɪv]

a. 注意的，专心的；关心的，体贴的；留意的

例 Kate is *attentive* to her work. 凯特工作很专心。

□ attack ■ attain □ attainable □ attempt □ attend □ attendance
□ attention □ attentive

attitude*
[ˈætɪtjuːd]

n. 态度，看法；姿势

记 发音记忆："爱踢球的"→尽管人们对国足态度不一，但青少年踢球的热情无法阻挡→态度

搭 attitude to/towards 对…的态度

例 We've been looking at the ***attitudes*** of various social and cultural groups towards the management of their personal finances. 我们一直关注不同的社会和文化群体对个人理财的看法。

attract*
[əˈtrækt]

vt. 吸引，招引，引诱，引起(注意等)

记 词根记忆：at + tract(拉)→把注意力拉过来→吸引，招引

搭 attract sb.'s attention 引起人们的注意；attract people's interest 引起人们的兴趣

例 We kept the price low to ***attract*** more visitors here. 我们保持低价以吸引更多的游客前来。

派 attractant(*n.* 引诱物)

attraction
[əˈtrækʃn]

n. 爱慕，吸引；吸引力；具有吸引力的事(或人)

搭 a tourist attraction 旅游胜地

例 The ***attraction*** of single-speed cycles is their simplicity and reliability. 单速自行车吸引人之处在于其简单性和可靠性。

attractive*
[əˈtræktɪv]

a. 吸引的，有吸引力的；引起注意的

搭 an attractive offer 有吸引力的工作；attractive personality 有魅力的个性

例 My landlord is a slender ***attractive*** woman in her mid-thirties. 我的房东35岁，身材苗条，魅力四射。

派 attractively (*ad.* 迷人地，动人地)；attractiveness (*n.* 魅力，吸引力)；unattractive(*a.* 不引人注意的)

attribute

[əˈtrɪbjuːt] *vt.* 把…归于 [ˈætrɪbjuːt] *n.* 属性；品质

记 词根记忆：at + tribut(给予) + e→把…归于

搭 attribute to 归结于，归功于，因为

例 The global increase in greenhouse gases has been ***attributed*** to industrial pollution in developed countries. 全球温室气体的增加归咎于发达国家的工业污染。

同 ascribe(*vt.* 归因于，归咎于)；quality(*n.* 质量，性质)

audacious*
[ɔːˈdeɪʃəs]

a. 大胆的；有冒险精神的；鲁莽的；厚颜无耻的

记 词根记忆：audac(=audax 大胆) + ious→大胆的

搭 audacious spirit 冒险精神

例 The ***audacious*** proposal was quickly denied by the committee. 这个冒险的提议很快就被委员会否决了。

audio
[ˈɔːdiəʊ]

a. 听觉的；声音的

记 词根记忆：aud(听) + io→听觉的

例 Teams of typists transcribed the ***audio*** tapes to produce a computerised database of ten million words. 声音录入组将磁带转录以制成包含一千万单词的电脑数据库。

□ attitude □ attract □ attraction □ attractive ■ attribute ■ audacious □ audio

audit
['ɔːdɪt]

vt. 审计，查账；旁听 *n.* 审计，查账

记 词根记忆：aud(听) + it → 听…报告 → 审计；旁听

例 It is a busy time for him that he has to ***audit*** the accounts of that company. 这段时间他很忙，需要审计那家公司的账目。

audition
[ɔː'dɪʃn]

n. 试演；试听，试音

记 词根记忆：aud(听) + ition → 试听

例 I became a professional singer after I took many ***auditions***. 经过多次试唱，我成了一名职业歌手。

auditorium*
[ˌɔːdɪ'tɔːriəm]

n. 礼堂；观众席

记 词根记忆：aud(听) + it + orium(表场所、地点，名词后缀) → 听(讲座等)的地方 → 礼堂；观众席

搭 the school auditorium 学校礼堂

例 Will audience find any difference in the ***auditorium***? 观众们会发现这个礼堂有什么不同吗?

augment
[ɔːg'ment]

vt. 增加，提高，扩大

记 词根记忆：aug(增加) + ment → 增加，提高，扩大

例 Bush insisted on ***augmenting*** forces in Iraq, when his allies were withdrawing step by step. 当布什政府的盟友都在逐步撤退的时候，他还是坚持对伊拉克增兵。

派 augmentation(*n.* 增加)

authentic
[ɔː'θentɪk]

a. 真品的，真迹的；真正的，真实的，逼真的

例 Scientists have derived ***authentic*** data about the age of the skeleton from carbon dating tests. 科学家利用碳定年法得出了这具骨架的准确年代。

派 authenticity(*n.* 真实性，可靠性)

同 real(*a.* 真的)；genuine(*a.* 真实的)

反 artificial(*a.* 人造的，假的)；fake(*a.* 假的)

authenticate
[ɔː'θentɪkeɪt]

vt. 鉴别，证明

记 联想记忆：authentic(真实的；真正的) + ate → 证明…是真的 → 鉴别，证明

例 There is no way to ***authenticate*** the recording at present, but the voice sounds like Lily's. 目前还不能鉴别这盘录音带的真伪，但是声音听起来像莉莉的。

authorise
['ɔːθəraɪz]

vt. 批准，认可；授权

例 When an ***authorised*** user wishes to enter or use the facility, the system scans the person's corresponding characteristics and attempts to match them against those on record. 被授权的用户如果想进入或使用这一工具，系统会对其相应的特征进行扫描并与记录里的资料进行核对。

派 unauthorised(*a.* 未经授权的，未批准的)；authoritative(*a.* 权威性的；命令式的)

authority*
[ɔː'θɒrəti]

n. 权力，管辖权；[*pl.*] 官方，当局；权威，专家

搭 in authority 持有权力；one leading authority 一个极具有权威的人

例 Dark colours give an aura of ***authority*** while lighter pastel shades suggest approachability. 深色调给人一种权威的感觉，而清淡柔和的色调使人感到亲切。

□ audit □ audition □ auditorium □ augment □ authentic □ authorise
□ authority

autobiography* [ˌɔːtəbaɪˈɒɡrəfi]

n. 自传

记 词根记忆：auto(自己)+bio(生活)+graph(写)+y→写自己的一生→自传

例 The TV series was based on the *autobiography* of the famous writer. 这部电视连续剧是根据那位著名作家的自传改编的。

autocratic [ˌɔːtəˈkrætɪk]

a. 独裁的，专制的

记 词根记忆：auto(自己)+crat(统治)+ic→独自统治的→独裁的，专制的

例 A doctor calls on the full power of *autocratic* suggestion by insisting that the patient take precisely this white capsule precisely three times a day before meals. 医生坚持要求病人一日三餐前按时服用这种白色胶囊，以此呼吁要遵从医嘱的绝对权威。

autoimmune [ˌɔːtəʊɪˈmjuːn]

a. 自身免疫的

记 联想记忆：auto(自身)+immune(免疫的)→自身免疫的

例 Once this immune tolerance break down, the immune system would attack its own tissue, and cause *autoimmune* diseases. 一旦这种免疫耐受受到损害，免疫系统就会攻击自身的组织，引发自身免疫疾病。

automatically* [ɔːtəˈmætɪkli]

ad. 自动地；无意识地

例 Cars will be *automatically* controlled by computer in the future. 未来的汽车将由计算机自动控制。

autonomy [ɔːˈtɒnəmi]

n. 自治，自治权；人身自由，自主权

记 词根记忆：auto(自己)+nom(法律)+y→以法律确定自治权→自治，自治权

例 Hong Kong and Macao maintain their capitalistic mode of production and life style unchanged within 50 years, enjoying extensive *autonomy* on polity and economy. 香港和澳门在享有广泛的政治经济自治的同时，保持其资本主义的生产制度和生活方式50年不变。

派 autonomous(*a.* 自治的；独立自主的)

avail [əˈveɪl]

vt. 有帮助，有益，有用 *n.* 效用；利益

记 词根记忆：a(对，向)+vail(价值)→对…有价值→有帮助，有益

例 *Avail* yourself of every opportunity to enrich your knowledge. 利用每一个机会丰富自己的知识。

availability [əˌveɪləˈbɪləti]

n. 可利用性，可得性；利用的可能性；可利用的人或物

记 来自available(*a.* 可用的)

例 Free Water Served is subject to *availability*. 提供免费茶水。

available* [əˈveɪləbl]

a. 可获得的，可得到的；可用的；有空的

记 联想记忆：avail(有用)+able(能…的)→可用的

搭 be available to 可用于；available facilities 可用的器械

例 We hope that ostrich meat will be *available* soon and before long will be as cheap as beef. 我们希望不久就可以买到鸵鸟肉，而且希望它的价格不久就会变得和牛肉一样便宜。

□ autobiography □ autocratic □ autoimmune □ automatically □ autonomy □ avail □ availability □ available

avalanche
[ˈævəlɑːnʃ]

n./v. 雪崩

例 An earthquake triggered an ***avalanche***. 地震引起一场雪崩。

avenge
[əˈvendʒ]

vt. 报仇，复仇，向(某人)报仇

记 词根记忆：a(对) + veng(惩戒) + e → 对某人进行惩戒 → 报仇，复仇，向(某人)报仇

例 Study shows that some people are likely to ***avenge*** society once they are treated unequally. 研究发现，一些人一旦受到不公平的待遇，就很可能报复社会。

同 revenge(*v.* 复仇)

avenue
[ˈævənjuː]

n. 林阴道，大街；方法，途径

例 They explored every ***avenue*** to cure his cancer. 他们寻找各种方法来治疗他的癌症。

average*
[ˈævərɪdʒ]

n. 平均(数) *a.* 平均的；平常的，普通的 *v.* 平均达到；平均为

搭 average age 平均年龄；average price 平均价格；on average 平均起来

例 How many hours a day on ***average*** do you watch TV? 你平均每天看几个小时电视?

Ordinary people merely think how they shall spend their time; a man of talent tries to use it.
普通人只想到如何度过时间，有才能的人设法利用时间。
——德国哲学家 叔本华(Arthur Schopenhauer, German philosopher)

Word List 5

音 频

词根、词缀预习表

avi	鸟	aviation *n.* 航空，飞行	**barbar**	外来者	barbaric *a.* 野蛮的
barr	条，棒	barrage *n.* 弹幕射击	**fit**	做	benefit *n.* 益处，好处
reav	抢夺	bereave *vt.* 使丧失，剥夺	**bibl**	书	bibliography *n.* 参考书目
lingu	语言	bilingual *a.* (说)两种语言的	**later**	侧面，边	bilateral *a.* 双边的
ocul	眼睛	binoculars *n.* 双筒望远镜	**graphy**	写	biography *n.* 传记

aviation [ˌeɪviˈeɪʃn]

n. 航空，飞行；航空制造业

记 词根记忆：avi(鸟) + at + ion(名词后缀) → 像鸟一样飞 → 航空，飞行

例 It can be seen that Yang Liwei's travel in outer space around the earth's orbit is a milestone of China's ***aviation***. 杨利伟在外太空绕地球轨道航行可以说是中国航天史上的一座里程碑。

avoid* [əˈvɒɪd]

vt. 避免；躲开

记 联想记忆：a(表加强) + void(空旷，空虚) → 越来越空虚，使人想躲开 → 躲开

搭 avoid doing sth. 避免做…；avoid mistakes 避免犯错误

例 Building big commercial buildings underground can be a way to ***avoid*** disfiguring or threatening a beautiful landscape. 在地下建商业大楼可以避免破坏或威胁到美丽的风景。

派 avoidance(*n.* 避免)

award* [əˈwɔːd]

n. 奖；评判；授予 *vt.* 授予；给予

搭 award a prize 颁奖；be awarded for 因…而被授奖；get one's award 得奖；an award ceremony 颁奖仪式；win/receive an award 获奖

例 Our experience would suggest that the long-term effects of incentive ***awards*** on absenteeism are questionable. 我们的经验表明，以激励奖来解决旷课问题的长期效果值得质疑。

aware* [əˈweə(r)]

a. 知道的；意识到的

搭 be aware of 意识到…

例 Most ecologists were ***aware*** that the areas of Amazonia they were working in had been shaped by human settlement. 大多数生态学家意识到他们研究的亚马孙地区已经受到人类居住的影响。

派 unaware(*a.* 不知道的，未意识到的)；awareness(*n.* 知道)

awful* [ˈɔːfl]

a. 糟糕的

例 The food at the hostel was *awful*. 这家饭店的食物很糟糕。

axle [ˈæksl]

n. 车轴，轮轴

例 There is a crack in the front *axle* of the car which was found by the garage mechanic. 汽车修理厂机修工发现汽车的前车轴上有一条裂缝。

bachelor [ˈbætʃələ(r)]

n. 学士；单身汉

搭 bachelor's degree 学士学位；Bachelor of Arts 文学士；Bachelor of Science 理学士

例 Tom is working towards a *Bachelor* of Social Science degree in the university of Cambridge. 汤姆正在剑桥大学攻读社会学的学士学位。

backbone* [ˈbækbəʊn]

n. 脊椎；骨干；支柱

例 The Ottawa Charter for Health Promotion outlined in 1986 remains as the *backbone* of health action today. 1986 年起草的《渥太华健康促进宪章》仍是今天健康活动的支柱。

background* [ˈbækgraʊnd]

n. 背景；经历；后台；不重要或不引人注目的地方

记 组合词：back(背面的) + ground(范围) → 背景

搭 educational/cultural/family background 教育/文化/家庭背景；theoretical background 理论背景；background music 背景音乐

例 The job requires applicants with a business *background*. 这份工作要求求职者有商业背景。

bacterial [bækˈtɪəriəl]

a. 细菌的；由细菌引起的

搭 bacterial infection 细菌感染

例 Leaving any remaining nonviable tissue may create an environment for *bacterial* growth. 留下任何残存的死组织都可能为细菌生长创造环境。

badge [bædʒ]

n. 徽章；标记；象征

例 Are there any marks or *badges* on your briefcase that make it stand out? 你的公文包上是否有什么记号或标记能让它区别于其他公文包?

同 token(*n.* 象征；记号)；mark(*n.* 标志，记号)

badminton [ˈbædmɪntən]

n. 羽毛球

例 There is a sports hall for squash, *badminton*, volleyball and several other indoor sports in my university. 我所在的大学有一个体育馆，可以在里面打壁球、羽毛球、排球，以及进行其他室内运动。

baffle* [ˈbæfl]

vt. 使困惑，难倒 *n.* 挡板，隔板

记 联想记忆：战役(battle)开始，一向忠诚的 tt 反戈，令人费解(baffle) → 使困惑

例 All of us are *baffled* why she didn't give us the notice. 我们都很困惑她为什么没有通知我们。

派 bafflement (*n.* 迷惑不解)

同 disconcert(*vt.* 使为难)

□ awful □ axle □ bachelor □ backbone □ background □ bacterial
□ badge □ badminton ■ baffle

balance*
[ˈbæləns]

n. 平衡；余额 *vt.* 平衡

记 联想记忆：bal（看作 ball，球）+ ance → 球操选手需要很好的平衡能力 → 平衡

搭 lose balance 失去平衡；keep balance 保持平衡；balance of payments 国际收支差额

例 If you have a well-***balanced*** diet, then you should be getting all the vitamins that you need for normal daily activities. 如果你饮食均衡合理，就会获得每天正常活动所需的所有维生素。

balcony
[ˈbælkəni]

n. 阳台；楼座

记 发音记忆："白给你" → 把整个楼座都"白给你" → 楼座

例 From your cabin ***balcony*** you'll find that you cannot see anyone else and the only sound you should hear is the birds' singing. 从你小屋的阳台看不到任何人，听到的只有鸟鸣。

bamboo
[ˌbæmˈbuː]

n. 竹子

记 发音记忆："颁布" → 古时颁布的法令有些是刻在竹简上的 → 竹子

band*
[bænd]

n. 乐队；群，伙；带，箍；条纹；波段，频带
vt. 用带绑扎

记 联想记忆：乐队（band）的成员需要用手（hand）来弹吉他和键盘

例 The drum ***band*** will be appearing on stage in the next show. 下一个节目将是鼓乐队表演。

bankrupt
[ˈbæŋkrʌpt]

a. 破产的

记 联想记忆：bank（银行）+ rupt（词根 rupt 表打破）→ 银行里的账户被打破 → 破产的

例 The theatre went ***bankrupt*** with over ten billion dollars of debt last January. 去年一月份，那家剧院因负债超过一百亿美元而破产。

bankruptcy
[ˈbæŋkrʌptsi]

n. 破产；彻底失败

记 联想记忆：bank（柜台）+ rupt（看作 rupture，破裂）+ cy → 柜台被打破，无法继续经营 → 破产

例 Unwise investment led the firm into ***bankruptcy***. 草率的投资导致了这家公司的破产。

banner*
[ˈbænə(r)]

n. 横幅；旗帜

记 联想记忆：ban（禁止）+ ner → 禁止悬挂横幅 → 横幅

例 On the wall is the ***banner*** welcoming the Friends of Italian Opera. 墙上挂着一条"欢迎意大利歌剧团的朋友们"的横幅。

bar*
[bɑː(r)]

n. 酒吧；栅栏；棒，条状物 *vt.* 闩（门、窗等）；阻拦

记 发音记忆："吧" → 酒吧

例 Architects in the 18th and 19th centuries began to create buildings by using steel, glass and concrete strengthened steel ***bars***. 18、19 世纪的建筑师开始使用钢铁、玻璃和混凝土加固的钢条来建造房屋。

□ balance □ balcony □ bamboo □ band □ bankrupt □ bankruptcy
□ banner □ bar

barbaric
[bɑːˈbærɪk]

a. 野蛮的，粗鲁的；残暴的，残忍的；原始部落的

记 词根记忆：barbar(外来者) + ic(形容词后缀) → 外来者的 → 野蛮的，粗鲁的；残忍的

例 The animal protectors consider the idea of killing wild animals for pleasure extremely ***barbaric***. 动物保护者认为以猎杀野生动物为乐的想法极其野蛮。

---

barbecue*
[ˈbɑːbɪkjuː]

n. 金属烤肉架；烧烤野餐

记 词根记忆：barb(条，棒) + ecue → 用木条支撑着进行烧烤 → 烧烤野餐

例 Membership gives wide access to activities like basketball and football as well as ***barbecues*** and other social functions. 会员可以参加各种活动，诸如打篮球、踢足球、烧烤以及其他社交集会。

---

bare*
[beə(r)]

a. 赤裸的，光秃的

例 Certain plants can cause irritation if you touch them with ***bare*** skin. 某些植物直接接触皮肤时，会引起皮肤过敏。

bare

---

barely*
[ˈbeəli]

ad. 仅仅，几乎不；赤裸裸地，无遮蔽地

例 Rainfall ***barely*** penetrates the soil in this area. 在该地区，降雨很少渗入土壤。

---

bargain
[ˈbɑːgən]

vi. 讨价还价 *n.* 协议；交易；便宜货

例 The employees and the employer reached a ***bargain***. 雇员和老板达成了一项协议。

---

barge*
[bɑːdʒ]

n. 驳船 *v.* 猛撞；闯

记 发音记忆："八只" → 八只驳船 → 驳船

搭 barge in 闯入；barge into 与…相撞

例 Beekeepers moved beehives on ***barges*** along the river to their next destination. 养蜂人用驳船载着蜂箱顺流而下，驶往下一个目的地。

---

bark*
[bɑːk]

vi. 吠叫 *n.* 犬吠声；树皮

记 发音记忆："巴克" → 巴克是《野性的呼唤》中的狗 → 犬吠

例 Our neighbor's dog ***barks*** constantly. 邻居家的狗总是叫个不停。// Almost all the trees of the surrounding forest were flattened, and their branches and ***bark*** ripped off by the shock wave of the explosion from the erupting volcano. 火山喷发引起爆炸，爆炸带来的巨浪将周围的树林夷为平地，树枝和树皮也剥落下来。

---

baron
[ˈbærən]

n. 贵族；男爵

记 发音记忆："白人" → 过去，欧洲的贵族一般都是白人 → 贵族

例 The Frenchman ***Baron*** Pierre de Coubertin, an educator and scholar, founded the modern Olympics. 法国教育家及学者皮埃尔·德·顾拜旦男爵创办了现代奥运会。

---

barrage
[ˈbærɑːʒ]

n. 弹幕射击；火力网

记 词根记忆：barr(条，棒) + age → (火力)像棒子一样长或连续 → 弹幕射击；火力网

例 The army has laid down a ***barrage***. 军队已经布设了火力网。

□ barbaric □ barbecue □ bare □ barely □ bargain □ barge
□ bark □ baron □ barrage

barrel* [ˈbærəl]

n. 桶，圆筒

记 联想记忆：bar(横木) + rel → 横木围成桶，经久又耐用 → 桶

例 The milk is poured into *barrels* for shipment. 牛奶被倒进桶里以便装运。

barren [ˈbærən]

a. (土地等)贫瘠的，荒芜的；不结果实的，不育的；无益的，无效果的

记 联想记忆：bar(=bare 光秃的) + ren → 荒芜的；不结果实的

搭 barren land 不毛之地；a barren effort 无用之功

例 Geographers made great efforts to find that millions of years ago the region was a *barren* desert. 地理学家经过极大的努力发现，数百万年前该地区是一片荒芜的沙漠。

同 fruitless(*a.* 不结果实的；徒劳的)；devoid(*a.* 全无的，缺乏的)；lacking (*a.* 缺乏的)

反 fertile(*a.* 肥沃的，富饶的；多产的)；fecund(*a.* 多产的，丰饶的)

barrier* [ˈbæriə(r)]

n. 栅栏；关卡，检票口；障碍，隔阂；屏障

记 联想记忆：bar(栅栏) + rier → 栅栏

搭 language barrier 语言障碍；trade barrier 贸易壁垒

例 The language *barrier* presents itself in stark form to firms who wish to market their products in other countries. 对于那些希望在其他国家销售自己产品的公司来说，语言成了他们明显的障碍。

basis* [ˈbeɪsɪs]

n. 基础；根据；原则

搭 on the basis of 根据…，在…的基础上

例 Water transport means cheap access, the chief *basis* of all port economies. 水路运输意味着运费低廉，这也是建立所有港口经济的主要基础。

batch [bætʃ]

n. 一批，一组，一群；一批生产量

记 联想记忆：bat(蝙蝠) + ch → 蝙蝠都是群居生活 → 一批，一群

搭 in batch 成批地；a batch of 一批，大量

例 The *batch* number is printed on the bottom of each jar. 每个罐的瓶底都印有生产批号。

battery [ˈbætəri]

n. 电池(组)，蓄电池(组)

记 联想记忆：bat(蝙蝠) + tery → 给蝙蝠玩具提供能量 → 电池(组)

例 When your car's *battery* run low, you can go to the nearest *battery* maintenance point for a replacement. 当你的汽车电池电量不足时，你可以到最近的电池给养站换电池。

bay [beɪ]

n. 海湾

记 联想记忆：baby 中间少了一个 b，宝宝(baby)不愿意去海湾(bay)玩。

例 There were hundreds of boats in the *bay* enjoying the good weather. 海湾里停泊着上百艘船，船上的人们享受着好天气。

bead [biːd]

n. 珠子；(水、血、汗的)小滴

记 联想记忆：做面包(bread)的工人汗滴(bead)如雨下

例 Don't trifle that string of purple *beads* which values more than five million dollars. 别小瞧了那串紫色的珠子，它价值高达 500 多万美元。

□ barrel □ barren □ barrier □ basis □ batch □ battery
□ bay □ bead

beam*
[biːm]

n. (光线等的)束；梁；笑容，喜色 *v.* 面露喜色；发射电波，播送

记 联想记忆：be + am → 做我自己，成为国家的栋梁 → 梁

搭 a beam of light 一束光

例 The little girl *beamed* a warm smile at him. 那个小女孩对他热情地微笑。

beehive*
[ˈbiːhaɪv]

n. 蜂窝；蜂箱

记 组合词：bee(蜜蜂) + hive(蜂房，蜂箱) → 蜂窝；蜂箱

例 A *beehive* is where bees live. 蜂箱是蜜蜂居住的地方。

beforehand
[bɪˈfɔːhænd]

ad. 预先，事先

记 组合词：before(在…以前) + hand(手) → 抢在…之前下手 → 预先，事先

例 The experiment will last for one year. *Beforehand*, several months are devoted to planning. 试验将持续一年的时间。在此之前，要用几个月的时间制订计划。

反 afterward(*ad.* 然后，后来)

begrimed
[bɪˈgraɪmd]

a. 污秽的

例 In recent years, more and more *begrimed* articles and videos have spread by means of Internet and mobile phones. 近年来，越来越多内容污秽的文章和视频通过因特网和手机进行传播。

begrudge
[bɪˈgrʌdʒ]

vt. 对…感到不满；嫉妒；勉强做，不乐意地做

例 The rich, who saw their income slashed, did *begrudge* sharing their gains with the poor. 那些发现自己的收入大幅减少的富人对与穷人分享收益表示不满。

behalf
[bɪˈhɑːf]

n. 利益；代表

记 联想记忆：be + half(半) → 变成两半，一变二，当然生利 → 利益

搭 on one's behalf 代表；on behalf of 代表；为了

例 He made an impassioned speech on *behalf* of his country. 他代表他的国家发表了一个热情洋溢的演说。

behave
[bɪˈheɪv]

v. 表现；(机器等)运转；(事物)起作用；表现得体；使检点

记 联想记忆：be + have(有) → 表现所拥有的 → 表现

搭 behave oneself 注意自己的言行

例 Managers often *behave* very differently outside the office. 通常，经理在办公室内外的举止判若两人。

belief*
[bɪˈliːf]

n. 信仰，信条；相信

例 The *belief* that rain and murky weather make people more unhappy is borne out by a study in Belgium. 人们相信雨天和阴沉的天气会让人更加忧郁，这种想法已被比利时的一项研究所证实。

□ beam　□ beehive　□ beforehand　□ begrimed　□ begrudge　□ behalf
□ behave　□ belief

belt *
[belt]

n. 腰带；地带

例 Molten glass travelled over a moving ***belt*** of perforated steel oozing through the holes into moulds. 融化的玻璃流过一根移动的带孔钢条，通过孔眼滴入模具内。

beneath *
[bɪˈniːθ]

prep./ad. 在下方

记 联想记忆：be + neath(在…之下) → 在下方

例 Shall we have a rest in the shade ***beneath*** these trees? 我们在树阴里休息一下好吗？

beneficial
[ˌbenɪˈfɪʃl]

a. 有利的，有益的

记 词根记忆：bene(善，好) + fic(做) + ial → 做好事 → 有益的

搭 be beneficial to 对…有益、有利；mutually beneficial 互惠的

例 How ***beneficial*** do you think it would be to group students according to their level of ability? 你认为把学生按照能力的高低分组的做法有多大益处？

同 advantageous(*a.* 有利的)

反 harmful(*a.* 有害的)；baleful(*a.* 有害的，恶意的)

benefit *
[ˈbenɪfɪt]

v. 使受益；有益于，得益于 *n.* 益处，好处；恩惠；救济金，保险金，津贴

记 词根记忆：bene(善，好) + fit(做) → 益处，好处

搭 benefit from/by 从…得益，受益于；material benefit 物质利益；for the benefit of 为了…的利益(或好处)；social benefits 社会效益

例 Increased leisure time would ***benefit*** two-career households. 增加休息时间会使双职工家庭受益。

benevolent
[bəˈnevələnt]

a. 善心的，仁心的

记 词根记忆：bene(善，好) + vol(意念) + ent → 好意的 → 善心的，仁心的

例 Some people think that with the belief in the existence of a ***benevolent*** God, many westerners are easier to feel grateful. 一些人认为因为相信仁慈的上帝的存在，西方人更容易懂得感恩。

派 benevolence(*n.* 善心，仁心)

bent *
[bent]

a. 被弄弯的，弯曲的 *n.* 爱好，天赋

搭 a bent nail 弯曲的钉子；be bent on doing sth. 决意做某事

例 If you are buying a cot, do make sure that any metal present is not rusted or ***bent*** in any way. 购买婴儿床的时候，一定要确保床的金属不能生锈或怎么都不会被弄弯。

bereave
[bɪˈriːv]

vt. 使丧失，剥夺

记 词根记忆：be(使…) + reav(抢夺) + e → 使丧失，剥夺

例 Nobody can ***bereave*** wild animals and plants of their survival on the blue planet where we live together. 没人能够剥夺野生动植物在我们共有的蓝色星球上生存的权利。

besides *
[bɪˈsaɪdz]

prep. 除…之外 *ad.* 而且

例 ***Besides*** turning floral nectar into honey, these hardworking insects also pollinate crops for farmers. 除了将花蜜酿成蜂蜜，这些辛勤的昆虫还给农民的庄稼授粉。

□ belt □ beneath □ beneficial □ benefit □ benevolent □ bent
□ bereave □ besides

bet*
[bet]

v. 赌，打赌 *n.* 打赌，赌注
搭 bet on 打赌；赌博；bet with sb. 和…打赌
例 Anyway I *bet* there are some things you didn't know about bananas. 不管怎样，我敢说对于香蕉，你肯定有不知道的地方。

betray*
[bɪˈtreɪ]

vt. 出卖，泄露(秘密等)；辜负；流露情感
记 发音记忆："被踹"→被人暗地里踹了一脚→出卖
搭 betray oneself 原形毕露
例 If you treat him as a friend, he will treat you well and will never *betray* you. 如果你把他当作朋友，他就会对你很好而且绝对不会背叛你。
同 reveal(*vt.* 揭示；暴露)

beverage*
[ˈbevərɪdʒ]

n. 饮料
记 联想记忆：b(看作 be) + ever(曾) + age(年龄)→对我们这个年龄的人来说，饮料在我们孩童时曾是奢侈品→饮料
例 The hotel provided the best available accommodation, food and *beverage*, and meeting facilities in Sydney's southern suburbs. 在悉尼南部市郊，这家旅馆提供的住房、餐饮及会议设施是最棒的。

beware
[bɪˈweə(r)]

v. 谨防，当心
记 联想记忆：be(使) + ware(音似：歪耳)→使歪耳，侧耳偷听→谨防，当心
例 There are some venomous snakes to *beware* of in this area. 该地区有毒蛇，要小心。

bewilder*
[bɪˈwɪldə(r)]

vt. 使迷惑，使昏乱
记 联想记忆：be + wild(荒野的) + er→迷失荒野中→使迷惑
例 His sudden change of mood completely *bewildered* me. 他情绪突然转变使我完全摸不着头脑。
派 bewilderment(*n.* 困惑，迷惑)；bewildering(*a.* 令人困惑的)
同 puzzle(*vt.* 使迷惑，为难)；confuse(*vt.* 使糊涂)

bewilder

beyond*
[bɪˈjɒnd]

prep. 在…较远的一边；超出，除…之外
记 联想记忆：香港红极一时的乐队"Beyond"就是这个词
例 The computer was *beyond* repair. 计算机已损坏得无法修理。

biased
[ˈbaɪəst]

a. 有偏见的；片面的
例 Mothers might be *biased* to always think their children are the best in the world. 妈妈们可能有些偏颇，她们总是认为自己的孩子是世界上最棒的。

bibliography
[ˌbɪbliˈɒɡrəfi]

n. 参考书目；书目；文献学
记 词根记忆：bibl(书) + io + graph(写) + y→写作中用的书→参考书目
搭 universal bibliography 世界文献目录；classified bibliography 分类书目
例 I'm looking for those books which my professor lists in the *bibliography*. 我正在找教授列在参考书目单上的那些书。

□ bet □ betray □ beverage □ beware □ bewilder □ beyond
□ biased □ bibliography

bid
[bɪd]

n./v. 出价；投标

记 发音记忆："必得"→抱着必得的态度出价→出价；投标

例 Those willing to extend the validity of their *bid* shall be neither required nor permitted to modify it. 那些愿意延长其投标有效期的投标人，不需要也不允许修改其投标。

bilateral*
[ˌbaɪˈlætərəl]

a. 双边的；双方的

记 词根记忆：bi(双，两)+later(侧面，边)+al(形容词后缀)→双边的

例 The two countries worked out a *bilateral* agreement. 两国达成了双边协议。

bilingual
[ˌbaɪˈlɪŋgwəl]

a. (说)两种语言的

记 词根记忆：bi（双，两）+ lingu（语言）+ al →（说）两种语言的

搭 bilingual education 双语教育

例 She works as a *bilingual* assistant for an American boss. 她是一位美国老板的双语助理。

bin*
[bɪn]

n. 大箱子；仓

例 After trucks collect garbage, the empty *bins* are put outside of the house. 垃圾车收走垃圾后，空垃圾箱会放在房子外面。

bind
[baɪnd]

v. 捆绑，系；约束；凝结

记 发音记忆："绑的"→捆绑

例 The laws must *bind* everyone, high and low, or they are not laws at all. 法律必须约束所有人，不论贵贱，否则根本就不能算是法律。

binoculars*
[bɪˈnɒkjələz]

n. 双筒望远镜

记 词根记忆：bin(o)(双，两)+ocul(眼睛)+ars→两只眼睛→双筒望远镜

例 The park's viewing shelter is a favourite spot for bird watchers who can use it to spy through *binoculars*. 公园的野鸟观测遮蔽处是鸟类观赏者喜爱的去处，在那儿他们可以使用双筒望远镜来观赏鸟类。

biodiversity*
[ˌbaɪəʊdaɪˈvɜːsəti]

n. 生物多样性

搭 loss of biodiversity 生物多样性的丧失

例 The oilfield engineering threatens one of the world's richest areas of *biodiversity*. 油田工程对世界上一块拥有最丰富物种多样性的地域造成了威胁。

biography
[baɪˈɒgrəfi]

n. 传记

记 词根记忆：bio(生活)+graph(写)+y→记录生活的文字→传记

例 He found a career entirely devoted to *biography*. 他找了一份专门从事传记创作的职业。

□ bid □ bilateral □ bilingual □ bin □ bind □ binoculars
□ biodiversity □ biography

biological [ˌbaɪəˈlɒdʒɪkl]	*a.* 生物的；生物学的，有关生物学的 例 Scientists are doing research to find the *biological* effects of radiation. 科学家正在进行研究，想发现辐射的生物效应。
biometrics* [ˌbaɪəʊˈmetrɪks]	*n.* 生物测定学 例 *Biometrics* is a little-known but fast-growing technology. 生物测定学是一门鲜为人知但发展迅速的技术。
bistro* [ˈbiːstrəʊ]	*n.* 小酒馆；小餐馆 例 The Geneva *Bistro* is always a popular place in this area. 这家杜松子酒馆在这一带很受欢迎。
bit* [bɪt]	*n.* 少许；小片；小块 例 Hot coffee is a *bit* hard to carry. 热咖啡有点不好拿。
bizarre [bɪˈzɑː(r)]	*a.* 奇形怪状的；怪诞的 记 联想记忆：集市(bazaar)上都是奇形怪状的(bizarre)货物 搭 a bizarre story 怪诞的故事 例 The story has a certain *bizarre* interest. 这个故事有一种怪诞的趣味。 同 fantastic(*a.* 奇异的；荒谬的)；outlandish(*a.* 古怪的，奇异的) 

In order that people may be happy in their work, these things are needed: they must be fit for it; they must not do much of it; and they must have a sense of success in it.

为了使人们在工作时感到快乐，必须做到以下三点：他们一定要胜任自己的工作，他们不可做得太多；他们必须对自己的工作有成就感。

——英国作家 罗斯金 .J. (John Ruskin, British writer)

Word List 6

音 频

词根、词缀预习表

bio	生活	biography *n.* 传记	**brilli**	发光	brilliant *a.* 光辉灿烂的
bronch	气管	bronchitis *n.* 支气管炎	**calc**	石灰	calcium *n.* 钙
-let	表小东西	booklet *n.* 小册子	**-ary**	表场所	boundary *n.* 边界
-itis	炎症	bronchitis *n.* 支气管炎	**burg**	花蕾	burgeon *vi.* 迅速成长
bureau	桌子	bureaucracy *n.* 官僚机构	**cracy**	统治	bureaucracy *n.* 官僚机构

blade* [bleɪd]

n. 刀片；桨叶；(草的)叶片

记 联想记忆：热门电影《刀锋战士》英文为 *Blade*

例 The rotating ***blades*** can shave away the wax that covers each cell. 旋转的刀片可以刮掉附在每个蜂房内壁上的蜂蜡。

blame* [bleɪm]

vt. 责怪，责备

搭 blame sth. on sb./sth. 把…归咎于…；only have yourself to blame 只能怪你自己

例 The British diet could be partially to ***blame*** for the increase in back pain. 英式饮食应为背部疼痛的加重承担部分责任。

派 blameless(*a.* 无过错的，无可指摘的)

blank* [blæŋk]

a. 空白的

记 联想记忆：b(看作 be，是) + lank(看作 lack，缺乏) → 缺乏“是什么” → 缺乏内容 → 空白的

搭 blank cheque 空白支票

例 Would you mind my asking about your salary? Or we can leave it ***blank***. 你介意我问一下你的薪水吗？或者我们也可以不填这一项。// He turned to a ***blank*** page in his notebook. 他翻开笔记本的一张空白页。

blanket* [ˈblæŋkɪt]

n. 毯子；厚的覆盖物

记 联想记忆：blank(空的) + et(放在词尾表小玩意) → 毯子铺在一小块空地上 → 毯子

搭 a blanket of cloud 厚厚的一层云

例 It is so strange that this hotel does not provide sheets, ***blankets***, or towels. 这家旅馆不提供被单、毯子和毛巾，真是奇怪。

blast* [blɑːst]

v. 爆破，炸毁 *n.* 一阵(大风)；冲击

记 联想记忆：b + last(最后) → 最后一声 b → 爆炸

搭 have a blast 玩得很开心；a blast of 一阵(风)；at full blast 全力以赴地；最大音量地

例 The granite was *blasted* into boulders no bigger than two metres in diameter. 花岗岩被炸成直径不超过两米的大石头。

blaze [bleɪz]

v. 熊熊燃烧；发(强)光；迸发 *n.* 火焰

记 联想记忆：复仇的火焰(blaze)烧得正旺，人们谴责(blame)不断

例 The fires *blaze* fiercely on the plain. 大火在草原上熊熊燃烧。

bleak [bliːk]

a. 寒冷的，阴沉的；阴郁的，暗淡的；没有希望的，不乐观的；荒凉的；索然无味的

记 联想记忆：寒(bleak)风呼啸而过，打破(break)黑夜的沉寂

搭 a bleak wind 寒风；a bleak prospect 前景暗淡

例 It's reported that many Americans faced a financially *bleak* Christmas last year because of the financial crisis. 据报道，由于金融危机，很多美国人在去年的圣诞节遭遇财政寒冬。

同 cold(*a.* 冷淡的)；raw(*a.* 阴冷的)；dismal(*a.* 阴沉的，凄凉的)

blend* [blend]

v. (使)混合，(使)混杂 *n.* 混合物；混合，交融

搭 blend in 掺入；blend with 与…混合

例 The music gradually *blended* into the city noises. 音乐逐渐和城市的噪音混杂在了一起。

block [blɒk]

n. 一排房屋，街区；阻塞；大块木料(或石料、金属) *vt.* 阻塞，拦阻；封锁

搭 office blocks 办公大楼；block of flats 公寓楼

例 New residential *blocks* are to be completed in three months. 新的住宅区预计三个月后完工。

派 blockage(*n.* 障碍物)

blonde [blɒnd]

a. (人)白肤金发碧眼的 *n.* 白肤金发碧眼的女人

例 He married a *blonde* last year. 他去年娶了个金发碧眼的女人。

bloom* [bluːm]

n. 花；开花(期)；青春焕发(的时期) *v.* (使)开花

记 联想记忆：杜鹃花开(bloom)鲜红如血(blood)

搭 be in full bloom 盛开

例 By the time the flowers *bloom*, the new queens will be laying eggs. 鲜花盛开之时，新的蜂王便会产卵。

blueprint* [ˈbluːprɪnt]

n. 蓝图；方案

记 组合词：blue(蓝) + print(印刷的图) → 蓝图

例 The plans for improving the financial system have only reached the *blueprint* stage so far. 改善金融体系的计划目前尚处于筹划阶段。

blunt [blʌnt]

a. 钝的；率直的 *vt.* 把…弄钝；使减弱

记 发音记忆："不拦的" → 口无遮拦的 → 率直的

例 The bad weather has *blunted* our enthusiasm for camping. 坏天气打击了我们去露营的热情。

□ blast □ blaze □ bleak □ blend □ block □ blonde
□ bloom □ blueprint □ blunt

board* [bɔːd]

n. 板；委员会

搭 board of education 教育委员会

例 All ceilings will require double-thickness plaster ***board*** to be used in the construction. 在建造过程中，所有天花板都需要使用双层厚的灰泥板。

boast* [bəʊst]

n./v. 自夸；夸耀

记 联想记忆：北京的烤鸭（roast duck）值得夸耀（boast）

例 She is always ***boasting*** about how wonderful her children are. 她总是夸耀她的孩子们多么出色。

派 boastful(*a.* 自夸的，自吹自擂的)

bold [bəʊld]

a. 粗(字)体的；大胆的，鲁莽的，勇敢的；醒目的

记 联想记忆：b + old(年长) → 年长的人通常不会太鲁莽 → 鲁莽的

例 The International Style was largely characterised by the ***bold*** use of new materials and simple, geometric forms. "国际风格"的特征主要体现在大胆使用新材料和简单的几何形状上。

bolster* [ˈbəʊlstə(r)]

vt. 支持，支撑；改善 *n.* 垫子

搭 bolster up 改善，激活

例 To protect airports near the sea, the coastline is being ***bolstered*** with twelve kilometres of sea defences. 为了保护近海的机场，海岸线上支起了12公里长的沿海防护栏。

bonus [ˈbəʊnəs]

n. 奖金，红利；好处

记 联想记忆：bon（好的）+ us（我们）→ 一发奖金，我们大家都说好！→ 奖金，红利

例 Scrapping farm-price support and protection for coal-mining offers a two-fold ***bonus***: a cleaner environment and a more efficient economy. 取消农产品价格补贴和煤矿开采保护有双重好处：第一，营造了更干净的环境；第二，发展了更高效的经济。

booklet [ˈbʊklət]

n. 小册子

记 联想记忆：book(书) + let(表小东西) → 小册子

例 If you look on the back of the ***booklet***, you'll see a map of the school. 看一下这本小册子的背面，你就会看到这所学校的地图。

同 pamphlet(*n.* 小册子)

bookrest* [ˈbʊkrest]

n. 阅书架

例 Using a ***bookrest*** which raises the material you are reading 45 degrees to the desk will help reduce your chance of a headache. 阅书架可以将阅读材料呈45度地摆放在桌子上，使用它可以降低因阅读引起头疼的几率。

booming* [ˈbuːmɪŋ]

a. 发展迅速的；激增的

记 来自 boom(*n./vi.* 繁荣)

搭 a booming economy 蓬勃发展的经济

□ board □ boast □ bold □ bolster □ bonus □ booklet
□ bookrest □ booming

boost [buːst]

vt. 使增长，使兴旺；鼓励，促进；为…作宣传，宣扬 *n.* 增加，提高；帮助，激励

记 联想记忆：自吹(boast)自擂，宣扬(boost)自我

搭 boost sb's confidence 增强…的信心

例 Apparently, stock prices were *boosted* by the President's recovery report and supportive policies from the government. 显而易见，股票价格随着总统的经济复苏报告和政府的扶持政策而一路上扬。

派 booster(*n.* 升降压器；支持者)

boot* [buːt]

n. (长筒)靴子；(汽车后部的)行李箱；[the ~] 解雇

记 联想记忆：足(foot)蹬长靴(boot)

例 You'd better take along a good pair of hiking *boots* if you want to take advantage of the wonderful trails in the mountains. 如果想要领略在山中徒步旅行的惊险刺激，你最好带上一双好点儿的户外长靴。

booth [buːð]

n. (隔开的)小房间；公用电话亭；售货棚

记 联想记忆：他在公用电话亭(booth)里打电话说他牙(tooth)不好

例 In our company, we work in separate *booths*. 在公司里，我们在隔间里工作。

border* [ˈbɔːdə(r)]

n. 边缘；边界 *v.* 与…接壤；接近，毗邻

记 联想记忆：b + order(命令) → 听从命令不许出边界 → 边缘；边界

搭 border controls 边境管制

例 We passed the *border* into Mexico. 我们穿越边境进入了墨西哥。

bore* [bɔː(r)]

v. 使厌烦；钻孔 *n.* 令人讨厌的人(或事)

例 There is such a wide variety of cultures in this program that it is difficult to get *bored*. 这次的节目中有很多关于不同文化的知识，因此不太容易使人感到厌倦。

bother* [ˈbɒðə(r)]

v. 打扰，烦扰；烦恼，操心 *n.* 麻烦，烦扰

搭 bother sb. about/with sth. 用…打扰…；bother to do sth. 操心做…

例 I'm sorry to *bother* you so early, Mrs Smith. 史密斯女士，很抱歉这么早就来打扰您。

boulder* [ˈbəʊldə(r)]

n. 大石头；鹅卵石

例 The *boulder* is too big to put into the cave. 石头太大了，塞不进洞里。

bounce [baʊns]

v. 弹起，反弹；(使)上下晃动 *n.* 弹跳；反弹力；活力，精力

记 联想记忆：弹跳 (bounce) 起来掀翻了一盎司(ounce)酒

搭 bounce back 卷土重来，恢复过来

例 Don't *bounce* on the bed, you'll break the springs! 别在床上乱蹦，你会把弹簧弄断的。

bouncing [ˈbaʊnsɪŋ]

a. 健壮的，茁壮的

例 The new invention can put the ***bouncing*** person into a trance-like state and provide wonderful relaxation. 这项新发明能将精力充沛的人引入一种恍惚状态，给人带来愉悦的放松。

bound* [baʊnd]

a. 负有义务的；一定的，必然的

例 Because these courses start every Monday, there's ***bound*** to be one that fits in with your academic, personal or professional commitments. 因为这些课程每周一都开，所以一定有适合你学习、针对你个人或工作内容的课程。

boundary [ˈbaʊndəri]

n. 分界线；边界

记 联想记忆：bound(bind 过去分词，束缚)＋ary(表场所，名词后缀)→ 分界线；边界

搭 push back the boundary of 扩大…的范围

例 Mount St. Helens is located along the ***boundary*** of two of the moving plates that make up the Earth' s crust. 圣海伦斯火山位于组成地壳的两大移动板块的边界线上。

bow*

[baʊ] *v.* 低下(头)；弯腰，鞠躬 [bəʊ] *n.* 弓

记 联想记忆：彩虹(rainbow)没有了雨(rain)就变成了弓(bow)

例 When you're introduced to a stranger, you may simply ***bow*** to each other. 当你被介绍给一个陌生人的时候，你们可能只是彼此点一下头。

branch* [brɑːntʃ]

n. 树枝；分部，分科

搭 main branch 主枝；主要的支行；local branch 本地分店

例 You may pay your account at ***branches*** of the Federal Bank. 你可以在联邦银行的分行支付款项。

brand [brænd]

n. 商标；品牌 *vt.* 铭刻，打烙印于；丑化

搭 name brand 名牌；leading brand 驰名品牌；brand image 品牌形象；co-branded card 联名卡

例 What ***brand*** of cola do you like? 你喜欢喝什么牌子的可乐？

派 branded(*a.* 名牌的)

brass* [brɑːs]

n. 黄铜；黄铜器；铜管乐器

记 联想记忆：敲击黄铜器(brass)，声音低沉(bass)

搭 brass band 军乐队；as bold as brass 大模大样地，粗鲁无礼地；the brass ring 成功机遇，(来之不易的)成功

例 A ***brass*** knocker was fixed on the door. 门上装了一个黄铜门环。

brazen [ˈbreɪzn]

a. 黄铜制的，黄铜色的；厚颜无耻的

例 How can you believe such a ***brazen*** lie? 你怎能相信如此厚颜无耻的谎言？

breakdown [ˈbreɪkdaʊn]

n. 垮台，倒塌，破裂；(健康、精神等)衰竭，衰弱；(机器等的)损坏，故障；分类

记 来自词组 break down(打破，破坏)

例 Gloomy people are likely to suffer from a nervous ***breakdown***. 忧郁的人容易精神崩溃。

同 disintegration(*n.* 瓦解)；classification(*n.* 分类)

breakthrough [ˈbreɪkθruː]

n. 突破；重大进展

记 组合词：break(打破) + through(通过) → 打破通道 → 突破

例 A brilliant intellectual ***breakthrough*** does not ensure that the transition is made from theory to practice. 重大的学术突破并不能保证从理论到实践的成功转变。

breakwater* [ˈbreɪkwɔːtə(r)]

n. 防浪堤

记 组合词：break(超过) + water(水) → 超过水位 → 防浪堤

例 A harbour can be consolidated by building ***breakwaters***. 可以通过修建防浪堤来加固海港。

breed [briːd]

v. 饲养，养殖，繁殖；养育，培育；酿成，招致 *n.* 种，品种

搭 breed fish 养鱼

例 Rabbits ***breed*** very quickly. 兔子繁殖得非常快。

breeze [briːz]

n. 微风，和风

记 联想记忆：和风(breeze)吹化了冰冻的(freeze)河流

例 The systems mix light, sounds, ***breezes*** and scents to stimulate people who spend long periods below ground. 该系统综合了光线、声音、微风和香味来刺激长期待在地下的人。

brew* [bruː]

v. 酿造；冲泡；酝酿

记 联想记忆：自酿(brew)苦酒，紧皱起眉头(brow)

例 When there is a thunderstorm ***brewing***, some people complain of the air being "heavy" and of feeling irritable. 当暴风雨即将来临，人们抱怨空气沉闷而且感觉烦躁。

派 brewery(*n.* 啤酒厂)

brief [briːf]

a. 短时间的，短暂的；简短的，简洁的 *n.* 概要，摘要 *vt.* 向…介绍基本情况，为…提供资讯

搭 in brief 简单地说，简言之；a brief of …的摘要；brief introduction 简短的介绍

例 The lecture is a ***brief*** history of civil engineering development. 这次的讲座内容是土木工程发展的简史。

briefcase [ˈbriːfkeɪs]

n. 公文包

记 组合词：brief(简捷的) + case(手提箱) → 简捷的手提箱 → 公文包

例 She had papers, pens and a novel inside her ***briefcase***. 她的公文包里有论文、钢笔和小说。

briefly* [ˈbriːfli]

ad. 暂时地；简要地

例 He paused ***briefly*** before continuing. 他停了片刻又继续进行。

□ breakdown □ breakthrough □ breakwater □ breed □ breeze □ brew
□ brief □ briefcase □ briefly

brilliant
[ˈbrɪliənt]

a. 光辉灿烂的；卓越的，有才华的

记 词根记忆：brilli(发光) + ant(形容词后缀) → 发光的 → 光辉灿烂的

搭 brilliant sunshine 灿烂的阳光；brilliant idea 极好的想法

例 That's a ***brilliant*** solution to the problem. 那可真是一个解决问题的好办法。

bring around/round

说服；使恢复知觉(或健康)

例 Tom fainted! Send him to the hospital at once to ***bring*** him ***round***. 汤姆昏过去了，赶紧送他去医院，让他苏醒过来！

bring out

出版；激起；鼓励

例 Mary is very shy; try to ***bring*** her ***out***. 玛丽很怕羞，要设法鼓励她说话。

brittle
[ˈbrɪtl]

a. 易碎的，易损坏的；靠不住的；冷淡的，不友好的；(声音)尖利的

记 联想记忆：br(看作 break，打破) + ittle(看作 little，小的) → 打破成小块 → 易碎的

搭 a brittle temper 易发怒的脾气，急脾气

例 The heritage antiques are ***brittle*** with age. 这些古董年代久远，极其易碎。

派 brittleness(*n.* 脆弱)

brochure*
[ˈbrəʊʃə(r)]

n. 小册子；说明书

记 发音记忆："不用求" → 有了说明书，就不用求别人了 → 说明书

例 Please inform us of your trade terms and forward samples and a product ***brochure***. 请告知贵方的交易条款，并寄来货样及产品小册子。

bronchitis*
[brɒŋˈkaɪtɪs]

n.【医】支气管炎

记 词根记忆：bronch(气管) + itis(炎症) → 支气管炎

例 Smoking can cause problems such as pneumonia, ***bronchitis*** and influenza. 吸烟能引起肺炎、支气管炎和流行性感冒等疾病。

brood
[bruːd]

v. 沉思；孵蛋 *n.* (雏鸡等)一窝

记 联想记忆：这一窝（brood）小鸡是同一个品种（breed）

例 In the ***brood*** chamber, the bees will stash honey to eat later. 蜜蜂在巢箱中贮藏蜂蜜，以供日后食用。

同 meditate(*v.* 想，考虑)；hatch(*v.* 孵化)

broom
[bruːm]

n. 扫帚

broom

例 He picks up the ***broom*** and bangs on the ceiling. 他拿起扫把，猛击天花板。

browse*
[braʊz]

v. 吃嫩叶或草；浏览 *n.* 嫩叶，嫩芽；吃草；浏览

记 联想记忆：brow(眉毛) + se → 像眉毛一样纤细的嫩叶 → 嫩叶

例 Vera ***browsed*** the shelves for something interesting to read. 薇拉浏览了一下书架，希望找到一些有意思的读物。

派 browser(*n.* 浏览器；吃嫩叶的动物；浏览图书报刊者)

同 skim(*v.* 浏览，略读)；graze(*v.* 放牧，吃草)

□ brilliant □ bring around/round □ bring out □ brittle □ brochure □ bronchitis
□ brood □ broom □ browse

brunt *

[brʌnt]

n. 冲击；冲力

记 联想记忆：b + run(跑) + t → 飞奔着冲过去 → 冲击；冲力

例 The *brunt* of a typhoon can be abated by the breakwaters. 防浪堤可以缓解台风的冲击力。

brutal

[ˈbruːtl]

a. 野兽般的，残忍的；无情的，冷酷的

记 来自 brute(*a.* 残忍的 *n.* 残忍的人)

搭 a brutal attack 残忍的攻击

例 It was not the first time to report the *brutal* treatment towards prisoners by American army. 这已经不是第一次报道美军虐待战俘的情况了。

派 brutality(*n.* 残酷，兽行)

同 cruel (*a.* 残忍的，残暴的，兽性的)；bestial (*a.* 野兽的，兽性的，残忍的)；feral(*a.* 野蛮的，凶猛的)

bubble

[ˈbʌbl]

vi. 冒泡，起泡；发出冒泡的声音 *n.* 泡，泡沫；气泡；幻想的计划

记 发音记忆：拟声词，指水冒泡的声音

搭 bubble economy 泡沫经济

例 The water in the pan was beginning to *bubble*. 锅里的水开始冒泡。

bucket

[ˈbʌkɪt]

n. 水桶

例 I knocked over the *bucket* and the water poured out all over the floor. 我把水桶弄翻了，水洒了一地。

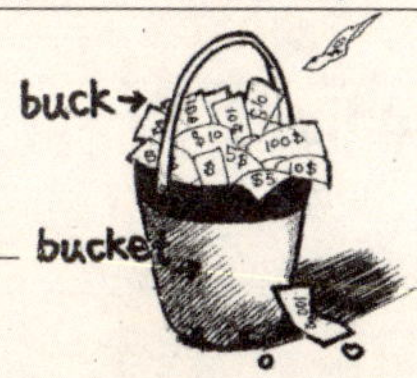

buckle

[ˈbʌkl]

n. 皮带扣环 *v.* 扣紧；(使)变形；弯曲

记 联想记忆：扣紧(buckle)雄鹿(buck)，拿来煮肉

例 Buildings, pipes and roads tend to *buckle* and crack because of the movement of the earth. 由于地壳的运动，建筑物、地下管道以及道路等往往会变形甚至破裂。

bud *

[bʌd]

n. 花蕾；叶芽 *v.* 发芽，萌芽

记 联想记忆：泥土(mud)中发出的芽(bud)

搭 taste bud 味蕾

例 Jasminum mesnyi has the first *buds* in spring. 野迎春在春天里长出第一批花蕾。

budget *

[ˈbʌdʒɪt]

n. 预算，预算经费 *v.* 做预算

搭 budget deficit 预算赤字；cut down the budget 减少预算；plan a budget 做预算；on a budget 节省费用

例 I'm going to talk about ways of making sure that you eat well while at the same time staying within your *budget*. 我将会谈到一些方法，让你在不超过预算的前提下吃好。

buffalo *

[ˈbʌfələʊ]

n. 水牛；(北美)野牛

例 The Native Americans followed the wounded *buffalo* until it fell dead. 这些印第安人紧追这头受伤的水牛不放，直到它倒地死去。

bulb *

[bʌlb]

n. 灯泡

例 Light *bulbs* are made by a machine at the rate of 66,000 an hour. 电灯泡是由一台机器以每小时 66000 只的速度生产的。

□ brunt □ brutal □ bubble □ bucket □ buckle □ bud
□ budget □ buffalo □ bulb

bulge [bʌldʒ]	*n./v.* 膨胀；凸出；塞满 例 In early May, the northern flank of the mountain ***bulged***, and the summit rose by 500 feet, which indicated that the volcano would erupt. 五月初，火山的北部山脊隆起，最高峰升高了 500 英尺，这预示着它即将喷发。
bulk * [bʌlk]	*n.* 大量；大批 记 联想记忆：公牛(bull)总是大批(bulk)地行动 例 Ports take advantage of the need for breaking up ***bulk*** material. 港口充分利用了分解大宗原料的需求。
bullet * [ˈbʊlɪt]	*n.* 枪弹，子弹 记 联想记忆：bull(芝加哥公牛队) + et → 芝加哥公牛队队员如子弹般在球场中穿梭 → 枪弹，子弹 例 In reaction to the forward discharge of ***bullets***, the gun moves backward. 发射子弹所产生的后坐力，会使枪向后动一下。
bulletin * [ˈbʊlətɪn]	*n.* (报纸、电台等的)新闻简报；公告；学报；期刊(尤指机关刊物) 记 联想记忆：芝加哥公牛队(Bull)又上新闻(bulletin)了 搭 bulletin board (电子)公告牌；news bulletin 新闻简报 例 Tom is going for some news ***bulletins***. 汤姆正在寻找一些新闻简报。
bully [ˈbʊli]	*n.* 恃强凌弱者 *vt.* 恐吓；胁迫，欺负 记 联想记忆：他仗着自己力大如公牛(bull)欺负(bully)别人 例 When confronted with ***bullying*** and threats, most of the people will choose to give in or keep silent. 当面对恐吓和威胁时，大多数人选择屈服或沉默。 同 intimidate(*vt.* 恐吓，威胁)；bluster(*n./v.* 威吓，吓唬)
bump * [bʌmp]	*v.* 碰，撞；颠簸着前进 *n.* 碰撞；隆起物 记 发音记忆：物体碰撞的声音 搭 bump against 碰到；bump along/down 颠簸着前进 例 The policeman ran after the thief, ***bumping*** against people in his hurry. 那个警察追赶小偷，匆忙中撞到了人。 派 bumper[*n.* (汽车上的)保险杠，缓冲器 *a.* 特大的；丰盛的]；bumpy[*a.* (路等)崎岖不平的；(车等)颠簸的]
bump into	不期而遇，邂逅 例 I was glad I ***bumped into*** you. 很高兴碰到你。
bunch [bʌntʃ]	*n.* 群，伙；束，串，捆 *v.* 集中，挤在一起；使成一束(或一群等) 搭 a bunch of 一些 例 He picked me a ***bunch*** of flowers. 他给我采了一束花。
bungalow * [ˈbʌŋɡələʊ]	*n.* (带走廊的)平房 例 Developers do not build the tiny ***bungalows*** that served the first postwar generation of home buyers. 开发商不建造供应给战后第一代买房人的小平房。
bureau [ˈbjʊərəʊ]	*n.* 办公室；机构；局；处；所 记 本身为词根，意为"桌子"，引申为"政府的局" 搭 an employment bureau 职业介绍所

□ bulge □ bulk □ bullet □ bulletin □ bully □ bump
□ bump into □ bunch □ bungalow □ bureau

bureaucracy [bjʊəˈrɒkrəsi]	*n.* 官僚主义；官僚机构 记 词根记忆：bureau（桌子，引申为“政府的局”）+ cracy（统治）→ 官僚机构 例 Since you hate *bureaucracy*, you must learn to work with *bureaucracy* to save it from itself. 既然你们痛恨官僚主义，那你们就必须学会与官僚主义共事，只有这样才能将其克服。
burgeon* [ˈbɜːdʒən]	*vi.* 迅速成长；发展 记 词根记忆：burg（=bud 花蕾）+ eon → 像花蕾一样成长 → 迅速成长 例 To serve the *burgeoning* tourist industry, an array of professionals has emerged. 为了满足日益繁荣的旅游业的发展需求，已经出现了一大批专业人员。

Every day I remind myself that my inner and outer life are based on the labors of other men, living and dead, and that I must exert myself in order to give in the same measure as I have received and am still receiving.

每天我都提醒着自己：我的精神生活和物质生活都是以别人的劳动为基础的，我必须尽力以同样的分量来报偿我所获得的和至今仍在接受着的东西。

———美国科学家 爱因斯坦（Albert Einstein, American scientist）

Word List 7

音频

词根、词缀预习表

calcul	计算	calculate *v.* 计算；推测	**cap**	抓住	capable *a.* 有能力的
-ity	表状态、情况	capacity *n.* 能力	**capt**	抓住	captivity *n.* 囚禁，拘留
cas	落下	cascade *n.* 小瀑布	**cau**	小心	cautious *a.* 谨慎的
cel	天空	celestial *a.* 天体的	**cens**	审查，评估	censor *vt.* 审查，检查
enn	年	centennial *n.* 百年纪念	**cert**	确认	certify *vt.* 证明，保证

burglar
[ˈbɜːglə(r)]

n. 窃贼

记 联想记忆：burg(看作 bag，包) + lar → 背着大包潜入室内 → 窃贼

例 When you leave the house, make sure the windows and doors are shut, and set the *burglar* alarm. 当你离开房子时，务必关好门窗，并打开防盗报警器。

派 burglary(*n.* 夜盗行为；夜盗罪)

burrow*
[ˈbʌrəʊ]

v. 挖掘，钻进；翻寻 *n.* 地洞

记 联想记忆：用犁(furrow)来挖(burrow)地

搭 burrow into 探查

例 Most dung beetles *burrow* into the soil and bury dung in tunnels. 大多数蜣螂在地下挖洞，并将粪球埋在地下。

burst
[bɜːst]

v. (使)爆炸；突然发作；破裂 *n.* 爆炸

搭 burst into 突然爆发；burst out 突然激动地喊叫；突然开始做；a sudden burst of anger 怒火的迸发

例 Water pipes often *burst* in cold weather. 水管在寒冷的天气里经常冻裂。

bury*
[ˈberi]

vt. 埋葬；埋藏，掩藏

例 Some birds *bury* their eggs under the ground. 有些鸟将自己的蛋埋在地下。

派 burial(*n.* 埋葬，埋藏；葬礼)

bypass
[ˈbaɪpɑːs]

n. (绕过市镇的)旁道 *vt.* 绕过

记 来自词组 pass by(经过)

例 If we take the *bypass*, we'll avoid the town centre. 我们走小路的话，就能绕开镇中心。

同 circumvent(*vt.* 绕行，避开)

cable* [ˈkeɪbl]

n. 缆绳；电缆；电报 *v.* (给…)发电报

记 联想记忆：他在工作台(table)上夜以继日地研究电缆(cable)

搭 underground cables 地下电缆

例 The street is blocked off because workers are laying telephone *cables*. 因为工作人员正在铺设电话线，所以这条街被封锁了。

cafeteria [ˌkæfəˈtɪəriə]

n. 自助餐馆；自助食堂

记 联想记忆：cafe(咖啡馆) + teria → 自助餐馆

例 Bill had lunch in the school *cafeteria*. 比尔在学校食堂吃的午饭。

calcium [ˈkælsiəm]

n. 钙

记 词根记忆：calc（石灰）+ ium → 石灰中含碳酸钙 → 钙

例 *Calcium* is essential for developing healthy bones. 钙对骨骼的健康生长至关重要。

calculate [ˈkælkjuleɪt]

v. 计算，推算；估计，推测；计划，打算

记 词根记忆：calcul(计算) + ate → 计算；推测

搭 be calculated to do sth. 旨在，打算；故意做

a calculated crime 有预谋的犯罪

例 It has been *calculated* that 17 percent of lung cancer cases can be attributed to high levels of exposure to second-hand tobacco smoke. 据统计，有17%的肺癌是由于长期处于二手烟环境而引起的。

calendar* [ˈkælɪndə(r)]

n. 日历；月历；日程表

搭 calendar year 日历年

例 Their five-year-old son is able to use the *calendar* to count how many days until his birthday. 他们五岁的儿子能用日历数出离他的生日还有多少天。

calf [kɑːf]

n. 牛犊；崽，幼兽

记 联想记忆：小牛(calf)是半(half)大的牛

例 A cow produces only one *calf* a year. 牛一年只生一胎。

calibrate [ˈkælɪbreɪt]

vt. 标定，划分；校准刻度

例 People can establish their genetic "distance", which itself can be *calibrated* to give an indication of the length of time since these populations last interbred. 人们能够确定遗传距离，这一距离的划定将表明族群自上一次杂交迄今的时间长度。

calibre* [ˈkælɪbə(r)]

n. 质量，才干，能力；口径

例 They suggest that the *calibre* of these institutions be carefully examined. 他们建议要仔细调查这些机构的资质。

calm [kɑːm]

a. 镇静的；平静的 *v.*（使）平静；（使）镇静

记 联想记忆：她手掌(palm)心出汗，内心很不平静(calm)

例 The pilot managed to bring the aircraft and its 50 passengers down safely in the *calm* waters of the bay. 飞行员成功地将飞机降落在风平浪静的海湾中，确保了 50 名乘客的安全。

calorie [ˈkæləri]

n. 卡(路里)，大卡(食物的热量)

记 发音记忆："卡路里"

例 The energy content of food is measured in *calories*. 食物中所含热量通过卡路里进行衡量。

camel* [ˈkæml]

n. 骆驼

记 联想记忆：came(来) + l → 把骆驼牵过来 → 骆驼

例 A characteristic of the *camel* is its ability to live for a long time without water. 骆驼的一大特点是不喝水也能活很长时间。

cameral [ˈkæmərl]

a.（立法机关）院的

camouflage [ˈkæməflɑːʒ]

v./n. 掩饰，伪装

记 联想记忆：cam(看作 came，来) + ou(看作 out) + flag(旗帜) + e → 扛着旗帜出来 → 伪装成革命战士 → 掩饰，伪装

例 Her size was properly *camouflaged* by the long loose dress she wore in the evening party. 晚宴上，她一席宽松的长裙恰到好处地掩饰了自己的体形。

campaign* [kæmˈpeɪn]

vi. 参加活动；作战 *n.* 战役；活动

搭 launch a campaign 发起活动；campaign funds 竞选经费

例 Local authorities in London *campaigned* to be allowed to enforce anti-pollution laws themselves. 伦敦当地政权发起一场要求赋予他们执行反污染法案权力的运动。

camper* [ˈkæmpə(r)]

n. 露营者，宿营者

记 联想记忆：camp(露营，宿营) + er → 露营者，宿营者

例 I'm afraid I'm not a very good *camper*, I feel a bit frightened sleeping outdoors. 恐怕我不是个很好的露营者，因为我有点害怕睡在户外。

campfire [ˈkæmpfaɪə(r)]

n. 营火

记 组合词：camp(露营，宿营) + fire(火) → 营火

例 The *campfire* smoldered for hours after the blaze died out. 营火在火焰熄灭后闷烧了好几个小时。

campus* [ˈkæmpəs]

n. 校园

记 联想记忆：camp(营地) + us(我们) → 校园是学生们学习的营地 → 校园

例 There isn't enough room on *campus* for everyone to park. 学校里没有足够的空间为每个人提供车位。

□ calm □ calorie □ camel □ cameral □ camouflage □ campaign
□ camper □ campfire □ campus

cancel*
[ˈkænsl]

v. 取消，废除；抵消，对消；删去，划掉

搭 cancel out 抵偿

例 Could you please call the dentist at 816-25285 and *cancel* the appointment for me? 你能拨打 816-25285 帮我取消和牙医的预约吗？

candidate*
[ˈkændɪdət]

n. 候选人，候补者；申请求职者；报考者

记 联想记忆：can(能) + did(做) + ate → 踏实能干才能当候选人 → 候选人

搭 a candidate for …的候选人

例 These forms have to be filled out by the *candidates*. 这些表格需要由申请者来填写。

cannon*
[ˈkænən]

n. 加农炮，大炮

记 发音记忆："加农"

例 They relied on grenades and *cannons* to repel their enemies. 他们用手榴弹和大炮击退了敌人。

canoe*
[kəˈnuː]

n. 独木舟

例 The waves spun the *canoe* a hundred and eighty degrees. 急流使独木舟旋转了 180 度。

canteen
[kænˈtiːn]

n. 餐厅，食堂

记 发音记忆："看停" → 小孩一看到餐厅就停下不走了 → 餐厅

例 Why don't I go to the *canteen* and buy something while you stay here and wait? 要不我去食堂买吃的，你在这等我？

Cantonese*
[ˌkæntəˈniːz]

n./a. 广东人(的)；广东话(的)

例 She wrote a book of *Cantonese* recipes. 她写了本粤菜菜谱。

cap*
[kæp]

vt. 盖在…上面 *n.* 帽子

例 The sand dredged from the waters will be used to provide a two-metre *capping* layer over the granite platform. 从水里挖出的沙子将被用来覆盖在大理石平台上，该覆盖层厚达两米。

capable
[ˈkeɪpəbl]

a. 有能力的；能够的

记 词根记忆：cap(抓住) + able(能…的) → 能抓得住的 → 有能力的

例 The bridge is *capable* of carrying 150-tonne trucks. 这座桥能够承受载重 150 公吨的卡车。

capacity*
[kəˈpæsəti]

n. 容量，容积；能量，能力

记 词根记忆：cap(拿住) + ac + ity(表状态、情况，名词后缀) → 能拿住 → 能力

搭 the capacity of …的容量；the capacity to do/for doing sth. 做…的能力；have the capacity to do sth. 有能力做

例 Without genetic variability a species lacks the *capacity* to evolve and cannot adapt to changes in its environment. 如果没有遗传的多样性，物种就会缺乏进化的能力，也就不能适应其环境的变化。

□ cancel □ candidate □ cannon □ canoe □ canteen □ Cantonese
□ cap □ capable □ capacity

capsize [kæp'saɪz]

v. (使船)翻，倾覆

记 联想记忆：cap(帽子) + size(大小) → 像帽子一样小的船容易翻 → 翻，倾覆

例 Things are always contradictory and interdependent to each other, as water can carry the boat, but it can also *capsize* it. 事物总是相互对立又相互依存的，正如"水能载舟，亦能覆舟"。

capsule ['kæpsjuːl]

n. 胶囊；航天舱，太空舱

记 联想记忆：cap（帽子）+ sule（音似：seal，"密封"）→ 帽状物 → 胶囊；密封舱

例 A *capsule* is long and thin, and you can open it up and take out what's in it. 胶囊通常长而薄，你可以把它打开，把里面的东西倒出来。

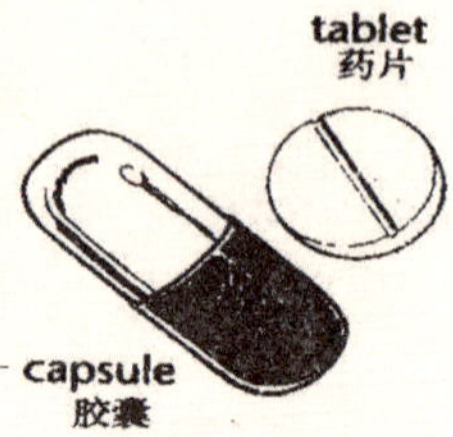

captive* ['kæptɪv]

a. 被抓住的，被捕获的；受控制的；受垄断的

n. 被抓住的人或动物

记 词根记忆：capt(抓住) + ive → 被抓住的，被捕获的

搭 captive audience 受制而走不开的听众；captive market 垄断市场

例 Today approximately 10 species might be said to have been "saved" by *captive* breeding programmes. 据说现在约有 10 个物种在抓捕繁殖计划中获得"拯救"。

captivity [kæp'tɪvəti]

n. 囚禁，拘留

记 词根记忆：capt(抓住) + ivity → 被抓住 → 被俘 → 囚禁，拘留

例 Animals bred in *captivity* would probably not survive if they were released into the wild. 圈养的动物如果被放生野外，它们将很难生存下来。

capture* ['kæptʃə(r)]

vt. 捕获，俘获；夺取或赢得 *n.* 捕获；战利品

记 词根记忆：capt(抓住) + ure(表行为) → 抓住 → 捕获，俘获

搭 capture sb's attention 引起某人的注意

例 Her beautiful smile was *captured* through a camera by her husband. 她的动人笑容被她丈夫用照相机捕捉了下来。

cardiovascular* [ˌkɑːdiəʊ'væskjələ(r)]

a. 心血管的

搭 cardiovascular disease 心血管疾病

例 People who smoke cigarettes are continually damaging their *cardiovascular* system. 吸烟者在不断地损害自身的心血管系统。

career* [kə'rɪə(r)]

n. 生涯；经历；职业

记 发音记忆：和同音词 Korea(*n.* 韩国)一起记

搭 career break 离职期；a careers adviser 职业顾问

例 The idea of having a single *career* is becoming old fashioned. 只从事一种职业的想法现在已经开始变得落伍了。

carousel* [ˌkærə'sel]

n. 行李式传送带

例 I put my baggage on the airport *carousel*. 我把行李放到机场的行李传送带上。

□ capsize □ capsule □ captive □ captivity □ capture □ cardiovascular
□ career □ carousel

carry* [ˈkæri]

v. 运送，搬运；传送，传播 *n.* 运载；射程

搭 carry off 夺去；carry on 继续下去，坚持下去；carry out 贯彻，实现；carry... through 成功完成，顺利实现

例 We advised the students to *carry* either euros or dollars. 我们建议学生带欧元或美元。

carve [kɑːv]

v. 切；雕刻

搭 carve in stone（决定、计划）等不能改变的

cascade* [kæˈskeɪd]

n. 小瀑布

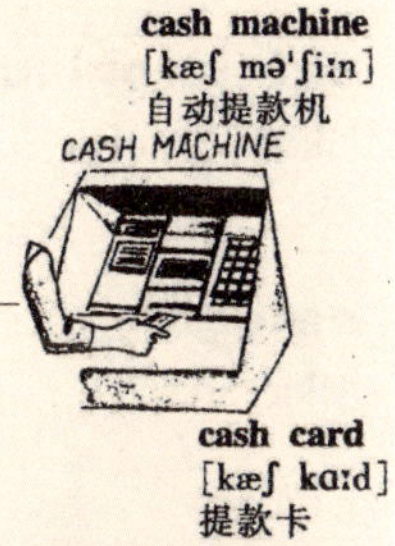

记 词根记忆：cas（落下）+ cad（落下）+ e → 疑是银河落九天 → 小瀑布

例 The *cascade* falls over a tall cliff. 瀑布从万丈悬崖上倾泻而下。

cash [kæʃ]

n. 现金，现款 *vt.* 把…兑现

例 You can withdraw *cash* from a cashpoint machine with a cashcard. 你可以用提款卡在取款机上提取现金。

cassette [kəˈset]

n. 盒式录音（或录像）带

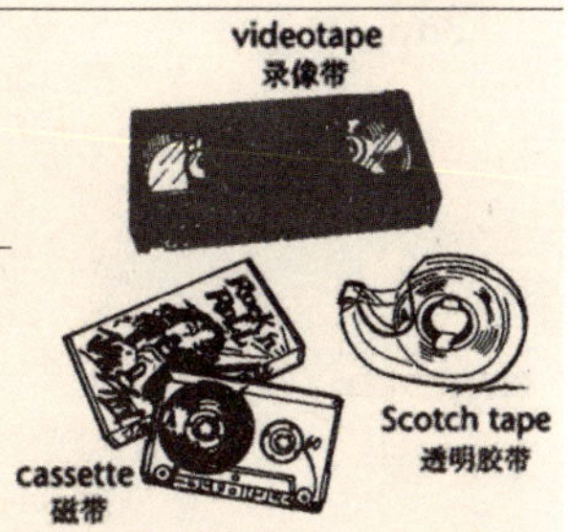

例 There are *cassettes* for students to borrow to practise their English. 这里的磁带可供学生借用练习英语。

cast [kɑːst]

v. 投射（光、视线等）；把…加于；投，扔；丢弃，剔除；脱落，蜕（皮）；浇铸，铸造

n. 演员表，全体演员；石膏绷带；铸模，铸件；外貌，特征

搭 cast iron 铸铁

例 When we finally stop at the centre of an aisle, we pause and take stock, *casting* our eyes along the length of it. 我们最后到了过道的中间，停下来评估过道的状况，目测其长度。

casual* [ˈkæʒuəl]

a. 偶然的，碰巧的，不经意的；临时的，非正式的

记 联想记忆：平常（usual）时候可以穿非正式的（casual）服装

搭 casual meeting 邂逅；a casual worker 临时工；casual clothes 便装

例 Helen occasionally wears *casual* clothes during classes. 海伦有时候在课上穿便装。

派 casualness（*n.* 偶然性）

casualty [ˈkæʒuəlti]

n. 伤亡（人员），伤亡者；损失的东西；伤亡事故

记 词根记忆：cas（掉落）+ ual + ty（表物）→ 掉落下来，造成事故 → 伤亡（人员）；伤亡事故

例 The major *casualty* of cutting down forests on a large scale has been the environment. 受大规模森林砍伐影响最多的是环境。

同 victim（*n.* 受害人）

catalogue* [ˈkætəlɒg]

n. 目录；系列 *vt.* 编目录；记载

例 It is a new *catalogue* of the language books in the library. 这是图书馆语言类图书的新目录。

catastrophe [kəˈtæstrəfi]

n. 大灾难

记 词根记忆：cat(a)(落下) + astro(星星) + phe → 星星坠落，古人认为星星坠落预示大难临头 → 大灾难

例 The flood was a major *catastrophe*, reducing population sizes in areas involved. 洪水是一场大灾难，使受灾地区的人口减少。

同 disaster(*n.* 灾难)

catastrophic [ˌkætəˈstrɒfɪk]

a. 悲惨的；灾难性的

例 The scientists have confirmed that the earth will face a *catastrophic* explosion in 2012 is only a rumor. 科学家已经证实地球将在 2012 年遭遇毁灭性爆炸的说法只是谣言。

category [ˈkætəgəri]

n. 种类；类别；范畴

例 After the final interview, potential recruits were divided into three *categories*. 经过最后的面试，可能入选的新学员被分成三类。

cater [ˈkeɪtə(r)]

v. 提供饮食；迎合；满足需要(或欲望)

记 联想记忆：cat(小猫) + er → 小猫饿了，喂点猫粮 → 提供饮食

搭 cater for sb./sth. 迎合…；为…提供饮食及服务；cater to sth. 迎合…，满足…的需求

例 The role of tourism is to *cater* to the needs of the tourists in accordance with their class. 旅游业就是一个满足各阶层人士旅游需求的行业。

派 catering(*n.* 餐饮业)

caustic [ˈkɔːstɪk]

n. 腐蚀剂 *a.* 腐蚀性的；(指评论)讽刺的，挖苦的

记 联想记忆：caus(看作 cause，造成) + tic → 造成腐蚀的 → 腐蚀性的

搭 caustic remarks 讽刺性的言论

例 This paper mainly introduce the test status of filtrating equipment in medicine industry used for diaphragm *caustic* soda cooling process. 这篇文章主要论述了医药行业用于隔膜烧碱冷却工序的过滤装置的试验情况。

caution [ˈkɔːʃn]

n. 谨慎，小心 *v.* 提醒，警告

记 发音记忆："考生" → 考生要谨慎答题 → 谨慎，小心

例 You should exercise extreme *caution* when driving in fog. 在雾中开车要格外小心。

cautious [ˈkɔːʃəs]

a. 十分小心的，谨慎的

记 词根记忆：cau(小心) + ti + ous(多…的) → 谨慎的

例 We should be more *cautious* not to make any mistakes in our papers. 我们要更加小心以避免在试卷上出现任何错误。

cavort [kəˈvɔːt]

vi. 欢跃，跳跃；嬉戏

记 发音记忆："渴望他" → 看到他便兴奋得跳跃 → 跳跃

例 Playful young animals use around two or three percent of their energy *cavorting*, and in children that figure can be close to fifteen percent. 动物幼崽会花去 2%~3%的精力去玩，而小孩子会花去近 15%。

□ catalogue □ catastrophe □ catastrophic □ category □ cater □ caustic
□ caution □ cautious □ cavort

cease* [siːs]	*v.* 停止，终止 记 联想记忆：c + ease（安逸，安心）→ 生于忧患，死于安乐 → 停止，终止 例 The music *ceased*, and the audience broke into applause. 音乐停了，观众爆发出热烈的掌声。
celebrate* [ˈselɪbreɪt]	*v.* 赞扬，歌颂；庆祝 例 The architectural style *celebrated* scientific and engineering achievements by openly parading the sophisticated techniques used in construction. 该建筑风格通过公开展示建筑中的先进技术来称颂科学和工程方面的成就。 派 celebration（*n.* 庆祝，庆典）
celebrity* [səˈlebrəti]	*n.* 名声；知名人士 例 The lecture will be given by a sports *celebrity*. 这场讲座将由一位体育名人主讲。
celestial* [səˈlestiəl]	*a.* 天体的，天上的 记 词根记忆：cel（天空）+ est + ial → 天体的 例 The moon and the galaxy are all *celestial* bodies. 月亮和银河都是天体。
cell* [sel]	*n.* 细胞；小房间；电池 搭 blood cells 血细胞 例 Scientists are doing cellular research, looking at changes in *cells* when the body is under stress. 科学家正在进行细胞研究，观察身体在压力下细胞内部发生的变化。 派 cellular（*a.* 细胞的）
censor* [ˈsensə(r)]	*vt.* 审查，检查（书报）*n.* 检查员 记 词根记忆：cens（审查，评估）+ or → 审查，检查（书报） 例 Should films and television be *censored* or should we be free to choose what we see? 电影和电视应该接受审查还是由我们自由选择？ 派 censorship（*n.* 审查制度）
censure* [ˈsenʃə(r)]	*vt./n.* 指责，谴责，责难 记 词根记忆：cens（审查，评估）+ ure → 可以评估的 → 指责，谴责 例 The warden *censured* the guard for letting the prisoner escape. 监狱长责骂狱警让罪犯逃走了。
centennial [senˈteniəl]	*n.* 百年纪念 *a.* 一百年的 记 词根记忆：cent（百）+ enn（年）+ ial → 百年纪念；一百年的 例 Many statesmen attended the *centennial* celebration of the founding of the republic. 许多政治家出席了该共和国成立百年的纪念庆典。
centigrade [ˈsentɪɡreɪd]	*a.* 百分度的；摄氏度的 记 联想记忆：centi（百）+ grade（等级）→ 百分度的 例 This substance has a relatively high ignition temperature of 182 degrees *centigrade*. 这种物质的燃点相对较高，达到 182 摄氏度。
centrifugal force*	离心力 例 *Centrifugal force* throws the honey out of the combs. 离心力使蜂蜜从蜂巢里掉了出来。

7

□ cease □ celebrate □ celebrity □ celestial □ cell ☒ censor
□ censure □ centennial □ centigrade □ centrifugal force

ceramic
[sə'ræmɪk]

a. 陶器的 *n.* [*pl.*] 陶瓷器

记 联想记忆：c + era(时代，时期) + mic → 古时中国以陶器而闻名 → 陶瓷器

例 Glass ***ceramics*** can serve as nose cones of missiles. 玻璃瓷可用来制造导弹的头锥体。

cereal
['sɪəriəl]

n. 谷类植物；谷物；谷类食物

记 联想记忆：ce + real(真正的) → 真正的健康食品 → 谷类食物

例 The east of the UK is its great ***cereal***-producing region. 英国东部地区是英国最大的产谷区。

同 grain(*n.* 谷物；谷粒)

ceremony
['serəmənɪ]

n. 典礼；仪式

记 联想记忆：cere(蜡) + mony(看作 money，钱) → 为办典礼花钱去买蜡 → 典礼

例 The graduation ***ceremony*** in many universities is an important occasion. 在很多大学，毕业典礼非常重要。

certificate*
[sə'tɪfɪkət]

n. 证书，执照

记 词根记忆：cert(确认) + ific(做) + ate → 确认某人有做某事的资格 → 证书，执照

搭 a teaching certificate 执教证书；a birth certificate 出生证明；a marriage certificate 结婚证；a certificate of childcare 儿童保育证书

例 We provide a four-month ***certificate*** course, but you should be aware that this is designed for those who are employed. 我们提供为期四个月的资格认证课程，但是你要明白这一课程是专为在职人员开设的。

certify
['sɜːtɪfaɪ]

vt. 证明，保证

记 词根记忆：cert(确认) + ify → 使得到确认 → 证明，保证

例 The council, which was founded in 1996, ***certifies*** fisheries that meet high environmental standards, enabling them to use a label that recognizes their environmental responsibility. 成立于 1996 年的委员会为达到高环境标准的渔场提供证明，准许他们使用一种认可他们所承担的环境责任的标签。

cervical*
['sɜːvɪkl]

a. 子宫颈的；颈部的

例 Smoking is thought to cause about 14 percent of leukemia and ***cervical*** cancers. 约 14%的白血病和宫颈癌被认为是由吸烟引发的。

chain
[tʃeɪn]

n. 链，链条；一连串，一系列；[*pl.*] 枷锁，镣铐；联号，连锁店 *vt.* 用链条拴住

搭 food chain 食物链

例 During the show he will be ***chained*** and thrown into a sealed aquarium from which he will try to escape. 在表演中他会被用链条捆起来，然后被扔到一个密封的养鱼缸里，他要设法从那里逃出来。

□ ceramic □ cereal □ ceremony □ certificate □ certify □ cervical □ chain

challenge* [ˈtʃælɪndʒ]	*n.* 挑战；质疑；艰巨任务，难题 *vt.* 挑战；质疑 搭 face a challenge 面对挑战；take up challenges 接受挑战 例 The greatest *challenge* in this respect is time. 这一方面面临的最大挑战是时间问题。
chamber* [ˈtʃeɪmbə(r)]	*n.* 室；洞穴；(枪)膛 例 In the brood *chamber* below, the bees will stash honey to eat later. 在蜂巢的下部，蜜蜂会贮藏蜂蜜，以供日后食用。

7

A man is not old as long as he is seeking something. A man is not old until regrets take the place of dreams.

只要一个人还有所追求，他就没有老。直到后悔取代了梦想，一个人才算老。

——美国演员 巴里穆尔(J. Barrymore, American actor)

□challenge □chamber

Word List 8

音 频

词根、词缀预习表

chron	时间	chronic *a.*（疾病）慢性的	scrib	画	circumscribe *vt.* 限制
civ	市民，公民	civilization *n.* 文明	clar	清楚	clarity *n.* 清楚
-ify	使	classify *vt.* 把…归类	gn	知道	cognition *n.* 认知
her	黏附	cohesion *n.* 结合，团结	labor	工作	collaboration *n.* 合作
cid	切	coincide *vi.* 一致	lat	搬运	collate *vt.* 对照；核对

champion* [ˈtʃæmpiən]

n. 冠军

记 发音记忆："产品"→冠军是付出无数汗水后的"产品"→冠军

chancellor* [ˈtʃɑːnsələ(r)]

n. 大臣；总理；首席法官；大学校长

记 联想记忆：chance（运气）+ llor → 运气好，当了总理 → 总理

例 Harold was the first *chancellor* of our university. 哈罗德是我们大学的第一任校长。

channel* [ˈtʃænl]

n. 频道；[常 *pl.*] 渠道，途径；沟渠；海峡，水道；航道

记 联想记忆：卫视音乐台就是 Channel V

搭 the English channel 英吉利海峡

例 We're doing some market research for a new television *channel* starting in two years' time. 我们正在为日后两年内开通一个新的电视频道做市场调查。

chaos* [ˈkeɪɒs]

n. 混乱

记 发音记忆：chao（拼音"吵"）+ s（音似：死）→ 吵死啦！ → 混乱

搭 molecular chaos 分子混沌，分子混沌态

例 The house was in *chaos* after Christmas party. 圣诞晚会过后，房间一片狼藉。

派 chaotic（*a.* 混乱的，无秩序的）

chapel [ˈtʃæpl]

n. 小教堂；祈祷室

记 联想记忆：chap（看作 chamber，房间）+ el（小）→ 小房间 → 小教堂

例 Jack was the organist in the Octagon *Chapel* in the city of Bath. 杰克是巴斯市八角教堂的风琴师。

character* [ˈkærəktə(r)]

n. 性格，品质；性质，特性；人物，角色；(书写或印刷)符号，(汉)字

记 联想记忆：char + acter(看作 actor，演员) → 演员刻画人物性格，惟妙惟肖 → 性格

搭 character traits 性格特征；character flaws 性格缺陷；cartoon characters 卡通人物；in character 适合；相称；out of character 不适合；不相称

例 The interview does give you a bit of information about an applicant's *character.* 面试确实能给你提供一些和应聘者性格有关的信息。

characteristic* [ˌkærəktəˈrɪstɪk]

n. 特性；特征 *a.* 特有的；典型的

例 Many *characteristics*, such as height and intelligence, result not from the action of genes alone. 诸如身高、智力等这些特征并不完全是基因作用的结果。

charcoal* [ˈtʃɑːkəʊl]

n. 炭，木炭

记 组合词：char(烧焦) + coal(煤) → 将煤烧焦 → 炭

搭 charcoal grey 深灰色

例 Unable to make flame for themselves, the earliest peoples probably stored fire by carrying *charcoal* in pots. 由于自己不能生火，最早的人类可能是将木炭装在罐中来保存火种。

charge* [tʃɑːdʒ]

n. 价钱，费用；管理；照管；掌管；控告，指控；电荷，电量 *v.* 索取(金额)，要价；控告，指控；委以；指示；(使)充电

搭 take charge of 担任，负责；in charge (of) 负责，主管；no charge / free of charge 免费；extra charge 额外费用

例 Drivers will be *charged* according to the roads they use. 根据司机行驶的公路对其收费。

charity [ˈtʃærəti]

n. 慈善；施舍；慈善机构

搭 charity donation 慈善捐款；charity hospital 慈善医院

例 I have some things to give to the local *charity* in a box in the front room. 前厅有个盒子，里面装了些东西，我准备捐给当地的慈善机构。

chart* [tʃɑːt]

n. 图，图表；海图 *vt.* 记录；用图表表示；制图

搭 bar chart 条形图；flow chart 流程图

例 The first *chart* shows the reasons why adults decide to study. 第一张图表显示成年人决定进行学习的原因。

charter [ˈtʃɑːtə(r)]

n. 纲领，宣言；宪章；包租 *vt.* 包租(飞机、船等)；特许设立，给…发许可证，给予特权

例 There's the Ticket Shop, where you can get inexpensive *charter* flights. 那是票务窗口，在那里你可以买到便宜的包机航班票。

chase* [tʃeɪs]

v. 追捕；追求；雕镂

记 联想记忆：谁动了我的奶酪(cheese)，我就去追(chase)谁

搭 chase after 追赶，追逐；追求

例 The babysitter *chased* the kids around the yard. 照看孩子的人跟着孩子满院子地跑。

□ character □ characteristic □ charcoal □ charge □ charity ■ chart
■ charter □ chase

cheat* [tʃiːt]

v. 欺骗；作弊 *n.* 欺骗；骗子

例 Tour operators try to ***cheat*** tourists. 旅行社的工作人员试图欺骗游客。

check* [tʃek]

v. 检查，核对；阻止，制止 *n.* 检查，核对；制止，抑制；支票，账单

例 The teacher has ***checked*** Kate's answers. 老师检查了凯特的答案。

派 checker(*n.* 检验员，审查员)；check-in(*n.* 登记；登记处)；check-out(*n.* 办理退房)；checklist(*n.* 清单)；checked(*a.* 有格子图案的)

check-up* [ˈtʃekʌp]

n. 检查

例 I go to my dentist for a ***check-up*** every two months. 我每两个月去牙医那里检查一次。

chef* [ʃef]

n. 厨师长，厨师

记 联想记忆：厨师长(chef)是厨房的长官(chief)

例 ***Chefs*** wore white because they worked with flour, but the main ***chef*** wore a black hat to show he supervised. 厨师穿戴白色衣物是因为他们整天和面粉打交道，但主厨会戴黑色的帽子以示其管理者的身份。

chemical* [ˈkemɪkl]

a. 化学的 *n.* 化学制品

搭 toxic chemicals 有毒的化学物品；chemical reaction 化学反应；chemical engineering 化学工程

例 The ***chemicals*** will contaminate water resources when drained into the river. 这些化学物质如果被排放到河里会污染水源。

cherry* [ˈtʃeri]

n. 樱桃(树)

记 联想记忆：要会分清浆果(berry)和樱桃(cherry)

例 Farmers will rent the bees to pollinate almond and ***cherry*** trees. 农民会租蜜蜂来给杏树和樱桃树授粉。

chest* [tʃest]

n. 胸；金库，资金

例 Numerous fund-raising activities are combined to fill the coffers of the "war ***chest***". 很多集资活动一起为筹集"战争专款"添砖加瓦。

chew* [tʃuː]

v. 咀嚼；回味；熟思

搭 chew sth. over 深思熟虑；详细讨论；chew up 咀嚼

例 Rats like to ***chew*** on something hard. 老鼠喜欢咀嚼硬物。

chief* [tʃiːf]

a. 主要的；为首的

例 Paula is the ***chief*** counsellor at Liverpool's famous pain clinic. 波拉是利物浦著名的疼痛治疗诊所的首席顾问。

chill* [tʃɪl]

v. (使)变冷，冷藏 *n.* 寒意；寒战；寒心 *a.* 寒冷的；扫兴的

记 联想记忆：c + hill(小山) → 山上 → 高处不胜寒 → 寒冷

例 The group asks for a specially designed camping cool box, which will keep food and drinks ***chilled***. 这个团体在寻求一种设计独特的野营冷藏箱，用以冷藏食物和饮料。

□ cheat □ check □ check-up □ chef □ chemical □ cherry
□ chest □ chew □ chief □ chill

chink* [tʃɪŋk]

n. 裂缝，裂口；一缕光；叮当声 *v.* (使)发出叮当声

记 联想记忆：chin(看作 china，瓷器) + k(口) → 瓷器有缺口 → 裂口

例 Closer inspection revealed a *chink* of sky-light through window. 走近点儿看就会发现有一缕自然光透过窗户射入。

chip* [tʃɪp]

n. 碎片；芯片；瑕疵 *v.* 削(或凿)下(屑片或碎片)

记 联想记忆：大家对 KFC 的炸薯条(fried chips)一定不陌生

搭 chip away at sth. 不停地削(或凿)；chip off 损坏，剥落

例 Electronic *chips* recorded the presence of a vehicle in a given high traffic area at a given time. 电子芯片记录了特定时间内，车辆在某一繁忙路段的通行情况。

8

cholesterol [kəˈlestərɒl]

n. 胆固醇

记 组合词：chole(胆，胆汁) + sterol(固醇) → 胆固醇

例 Ostrich meat is much lower in fat and *cholesterol* than beef. 鸵鸟肉中的脂肪和胆固醇含量比牛肉中的低很多。

chorus [ˈkɔːrəs]

n. 合唱，合唱曲；合唱队；副歌，叠句；齐声，齐声说的话(或发出的喊声) *v.* 齐声说

搭 in chorus 异口同声；female/male chorus 女/男声合唱；a mixed chorus 混声；chorus master 合唱队指挥

例 The *chorus* usually plays a large part in the music festival. 合唱在音乐节上通常扮演着重要的角色。

chronic [ˈkrɒnɪk]

a. (疾病)慢性的；积习难改的

记 词根记忆：chron(时间) + ic(形容词后缀) → 长时间的 → (疾病)慢性的

搭 a chronic problem 长期的问题；a chronic smoker 积习难改的烟民；a chronic disease 慢性疾病；a chronic war 持久战

例 Jim suffers from *chronic* back pain after the car-wreck. 车祸后吉姆一直受背痛的折磨。

同 inveterate(*a.* 根深蒂固的，成癖的)

chunk [tʃʌŋk]

n. 大块；相当大的部分(或数量)

记 发音记忆："常客" → 饭馆的常客占客人总数的很大一部分 → 相当大的部分

例 Research and development now takes up a sizeable *chunk* of the military budget. 现在研发经费占军事预算相当大的一部分。

churn [tʃɜːn]

n. (制作黄油用的)搅乳器 *v.* 用搅乳器搅拌；剧烈搅动；猛烈翻滚；反胃，恶心

例 The butter *churn* have two paddles to whip the cream. 黄油搅乳器有两根搅棍用来搅打奶油。

cinematography [ˌsɪnəməˈtɒgrəfi]

n. 电影摄影术

例 The new film provided the raw material for the introduction of *cinematography* a few years later. 新的电影胶片为几年后电影摄影术的诞生提供了原材料。

□ chink □ chip □ cholesterol □ chorus □ chronic □ chunk
□ churn □ cinematography

circle* [ˈsɜːkl]

n. 圆；圈，环状物；圈子，阶层；周期，循环 *v.* 圈出；盘旋，环绕…移动

例 What you are doing will start up a vicious *circle*. 你的所作所为会引起恶性循环。

派 circular(*a.* 圆形的；循环的 *n.* 通知)

circulation [ˌsɜːkjəˈleɪʃn]

n. (体液的)循环，(水、空气等的)流通；流传，传播；发行，发行量

记 来自 circulate(*v.* 循环，流通)

例 Nicotine and other toxins in cigarette smoke will affect blood *circulation* throughout the body. 香烟中的尼古丁和其他毒素会影响人体内的血液循环。

同 flow(*n.* 流动)

circumscribe [ˈsɜːkəmskraɪb]

vt. 在…周围画线；限制

记 词根记忆：circum(周围) + scrib(画)+ e → 画地为牢 → 限制

例 The power of the monarchy was severely *circumscribed* by the newly promulgated laws. 新颁布的法律严格限制了君主的权力。

circumstance* [ˈsɜːkəmstəns]

n. 环境；[*pl.*] 境况，情况

记 词根记忆：circum(周围) + st(站) + ance → 站在周围的事物 → 环境

搭 in/under...circumstances 在…情况下；in/under no circumstances 在任何情况下都不

例 In social *circumstances*, dress has often been used as a sign of professional role. 在社交圈内，服装通常被看作是某种职业角色的标志。

circus* [ˈsɜːkəs]

n. 马戏团；环形广场

记 词根记忆：circ(圆，环形) + us → 环形广场

例 The *circus* trainer snapped his whip. 马戏团驯兽师把鞭子抽得啪啪响。

cite* [saɪt]

vt. 引用；引证

例 Studies of the sources *cited* in publications lead to a conclusion: the use of foreign-language sources is often found to be as low as 10 percent. 对于出版物中引用的原始资料的研究得出了一个结论：外语资料的使用仅占 10%。

civil [ˈsɪvl]

a. 国民的；民用的；政府的

例 Personality questionnaires were used by the ancient Chinese for picking out *civil* servants. 古代中国人用性格问卷来挑选政府文职人员。

civilization [ˌsɪvəlaɪˈzeɪʃn]

n. 文明(社会)，文化

记 词根记忆：civ(=citizen 市民，公民) + iliza + tion(名词后缀) → 文明

例 Many important *civilizations* developed from Asia. 许多重要的文明发源于亚洲。

claim* [kleɪm]

v. 要求；声称，主张；索赔 *n.* 要求；主张，断言；索赔

记 本身为词根，意为"大声呼喊" → 要求；声称

搭 lay claim to 对…提出所有权要求；make/put forward a claim to sth. 提出要得到某物；claim to do sth. 声称要做某事

例 Many people *claim* they feel better in negatively charged air. 很多人称处在富含负离子的空气中让他们感觉更舒服。

□ circle □ circulation □ circumscribe □ circumstance □ circus □ cite
□ civil □ civilization □ claim

clamp [klæmp]	*v.* (用夹具等)夹紧 *n.* 夹钳 例 If you do not have a parking sticker, the workers will *clamp* your car wheel and give you a fine. 如果你没有停车许可证，工作人员会夹住你的车轮并对你进行罚款。
clarify [ˈklærəfaɪ]	*vt.* 澄清；阐明 记 词根记忆：clar(清楚) + ify(使…) → 使清楚 → 澄清 例 Talking to students about the requirements of a course helps to *clarify* what needs to be done. 告诉学生课程要求有助于他们了解自己所需要完成的工作。 派 clarification(*n.* 澄清；阐明)
clarity [ˈklærəti]	*n.* 清楚 记 词根记忆：clar(清楚) + ity → 清楚 例 This article was written with *clarity*. 这篇文章思路清晰。
clash* [klæʃ]	*v.* 发生冲突；不协调；砰地相撞，发出刺耳的撞击声 *n.* 冲突；不协调；(金属等的)刺耳的撞击声 记 发音记忆：物体撞碎的声音 搭 personality clashes 性格冲突 例 In the *clash* between environmentalists and developers, the Native Americans have suffered the most. 在环境保护主义者和开发者之间的冲突中，印第安人受到的伤害最大。
classical* [ˈklæsɪkl]	*a.* 古典的；传统的；经典的 搭 classical music 古典音乐 例 Some architects look back to the *classical* tradition. 一些建筑师追忆起古典的建筑风格。
classification [ˌklæsɪfɪˈkeɪʃn]	*n.* 分类；级别 记 联想记忆：classifi(=classify 把…归类) + cation → 分类 例 The *classification* and analysis of this species occupied scientists for years. 科学家们花费了数年的时间对该物种进行分类和分析。
classify [ˈklæsɪfaɪ]	*vt.* 把…归类，把…分级 记 联想记忆：class(类别) + ify(使…) → 把…归类 例 The researcher has *classified* environmental tobacco smoke in the highest risk category for causing cancer. 研究人员将环境烟害归类于最容易致癌的因素。
clay* [kleɪ]	*n.* 泥土，黏土 记 联想记忆：c + lay(层) → 泥土一层一层分布 → 泥土 搭 clay pigeon 泥制飞靶；容易被捉弄的人 例 The ancient Egyptians moved *clay* hives, probably on rafts, down the Nile to follow the bloom. 古埃及人带着泥制的蜂箱，可能是乘着筏子，沿尼罗河而下去寻找花源。
clench* [klentʃ]	*v.* 握紧；咬紧(牙关等)；牢牢抓住 例 The doctor told him to relax and not to *clench* his hands like that. 医生告诉他放松，别像那样紧握拳头。

□ clamp □ clarify □ clarity □ clash □ classical □ classification
□ classify □ clay □ clench

clerk
[klɑːk]

n. 办事员；职员

例 The *clerks* aren't allowed to accept any collect long-distance calls. 职员不允许接听由接听方付费的长途电话。

派 clerical(*a.* 书记的；职员的)

client*
[ˈklaɪənt]

n. 委托人；顾客，客户

例 Physical fitness instructors prepare exercise routines to suit the individual *client's* age and level of fitness. 健身教练会根据每一位学员的年龄和健康层次安排他(或她)的常规训练。

clientele
[ˌkliːənˈtel]

n. (医生、律师等的)顾客，主顾，客户

例 If they see potential *clientele* going elsewhere, they might want to be able to offer a similar service. 如果他们看到一位潜在客户去了别处，他们应该希望能提供一种相似的服务。

climate*
[ˈklaɪmət]

n. 气候；风气，思潮

例 Farmed ostriches don't need African *climates*. 养殖鸵鸟并不要求一定有非洲的气候条件。

climatic
[klaɪˈmætɪk]

a. 气候(上)的

搭 climatic phenomenon 气候现象

例 The proposal of preventing global *climatic* changes was fiercely discussed in the meeting held in Copenhagen. 预防全球气候变化的提议在哥本哈根会议上引发激烈讨论。

clinic
[ˈklɪnɪk]

n. 门诊部，诊所

例 The majority of our patients at the *clinic* tend to be women. 来我们诊所的病人大多数为女性。

clinical
[ˈklɪnɪkl]

a. 临床的；冷静客观的；简朴的，不装饰的

记 联想记忆：clinic(诊所)+al→临床的

例 The experiment results show that the proposed evaluation method has good *clinical* value, which will be further accepted by more medical workers. 实验结果表明，提出的评价方法具有良好的临床价值，而且将进一步被更多的医学工作者所接受。

clip
[klɪp]

n. (弹簧)夹子，回形针，别针；弹夹；修剪；剪报，电影(或电视)片断

v. (用夹子、回形针等)夹住，扣住；剪，修剪

搭 clip on 用夹子夹上去，可夹住

例 It is said that the US produces 300 million aluminium paper *clips* each day. 据说美国每天生产三亿个铝制纸夹。

同 clutch(*v.* 抓住)

cloakroom
[ˈkləʊkruːm]

n. 衣帽间；〈英〉洗手间

记 组合词：cloak(披风)+room(房间)→衣帽间

例 The *cloakroom* where you can hang your coat or leave your bags is just behind us here. 衣帽间就在我们后面，你可以在那儿挂大衣或放包。

clockwise
[ˈklɒkwaɪz]

a./ad. 顺时针方向的/地

记 组合词：clock(时钟)+wise(方向)→指针转动的方向→顺时针方向的(地)

例 You should turn the key *clockwise* to open the door. 你应该按顺时针方向转动钥匙来开门。

□ clerk □ client □ clientele □ climate □ climatic □ clinic
□ clinical □ clip □ cloakroom □ clockwise

clot*
[klɒt]

n. (血液)凝块 *v.* 凝结成块
搭 blood clot 血液凝块

clue
[kluː]

n. 线索；提示
记 发音记忆："刻录" → 警方凭一张刻录光盘找到了犯罪分子 → 线索
例 If you do not know a word, you can look to the picture in this book for a *clue* to its meaning. 如果你碰到不认识的单词，可以通过书中的插图来推测它的意思。

clumsy
[ˈklʌmzi]

a. 笨拙的；不得体的
例 These oversized *clumsy* cars would slow down traffic. 这些体形硕大而笨拙的汽车会减缓交通的速度。

cluster*
[ˈklʌstə(r)]

n. 串，束，群 *v.* 成群；群集
记 联想记忆：clu(看作 clue，线索) + ster → 由一条线索贯穿的 → 串，群
搭 a cluster of 一束…
例 Their villages were little more than *clusters* of thatched huts. 他们的村子比茅草屋群强不了多少。

clutch
[klʌtʃ]

n. 离合器；[常 *pl.*] 控制 *v.* 企图抓；抓紧
记 联想记忆：和 catch(*v.* 抓住)一起记
例 The driver released the *clutch* to engage the gears and make his car go. 司机松开离合器，挂上挡，这样汽车就开动起来了。

coach*
[kəʊtʃ]

n. 教练；指导；长途汽车 *vt.* 训练；辅导
例 They play just as important a role as the *coach* in our team. 在我们队里，他们扮演着和教练同等重要的角色。

coarse*
[kɔːs]

a. 粗的；粗糙的；粗劣的
记 联想记忆：coar(看作 coal，煤炭) + se → 煤炭是很粗糙的 → 粗糙的
例 It's good for you to walk on the *coarse* sand with bare feet. 光脚在粗沙上走动对你有好处。

code
[kəʊd]

n. 密码；代码 *vt.* 把…编码
搭 an error code 错误代码；break a code 破译密码
例 What is the postal *code* for Black Street? 布莱克街的邮编是多少？

coexist
[ˌkəʊɪɡˈzɪst]

vi. 共存
记 联想记忆：co(共同) + exist(存在) → 共存
例 Many foreigners believe that traditional Chinese medicine cannot *coexist* with western medicine in the west. 许多外国人认为，在西方传统的中医很难与西医共存。

coffer
[ˈkɒfə(r)]

n. 保险箱
记 联想记忆：把昂贵的咖啡(coffee)装进保险箱(coffer)
例 The thief managed to open the *coffer*, but it turned out to be empty. 小偷费尽心思打开了保险箱，却发现里面空空如也。

□ clot □ clue □ clumsy □ cluster □ clutch □ coach
□ coarse □ code □ coexist □ coffer

cognition [kɒɡˈnɪʃn]	*n.* 感知，认知；认识力 记 词根记忆：co(共同) + gn(知道) + ition → 共同知道 → 认知 例 Child studies center on theories of ***cognition*** of two-year-old children. 儿童研究集中研究两岁孩子的认知理论。
coherent [kəʊˈhɪərənt]	*a.* 条理清楚的，连贯的；一致的，协调的 记 词根记忆：co(共同) + her(黏附) + ent → 黏附在一起 → 连贯的 例 The archaeologist has to develop a picture of the past, just as the scientist has to develop a ***coherent*** view of the natural world. 考古学家需要提供一张过去的图片，就如同科学家需要描绘出自然世界的连贯图景。 派 coherently(*ad.* 条理清楚地；一致地)；coherence(*n.* 一致；连贯性) 同 cohesive(*a.* 黏着的)；coordinated(*a.* 同等的，并列的)；consistent(*a.* 一致的)
cohesion* [kəʊˈhiːʒn]	*n.* 结合，团结；凝聚力 记 词根记忆：co(共同) + hes(黏附) + ion(名词后缀)→ 黏附在一起 → 结合，团结；凝聚力 例 The Women's Social and Political Union (WSPU) brought the suffragette movement the ***cohesion*** and focus it had previously lacked. 妇女社会政治同盟为妇女参政运动带来了前所未有的凝聚力。
coincide [ˌkəʊɪnˈsaɪd]	*vi.* 同时发生；一致 记 词根记忆：co(共同) + in + cid(切) + e → 切成一样的 → 一致 例 My religious beliefs don't ***coincide*** with yours. 我的宗教信仰与你的不同。 派 coincidence(*n.* 同时发生的事情；一致) 同 concur(*vi.* 一致)；agree(*v.* 与…一致)
collaboration [kəˌlæbəˈreɪʃn]	*n.* 合作，协作；勾结，通敌 记 词根记忆：col(共同) + labor(工作) + ation → 合作，协作 搭 in collaboration with 与…合作；与…勾结 例 Museum staff carried out the anthropological projects in ***collaboration*** with a wide variety of national governments. 博物馆工作人员与多国政府合作完成这些人类学工程。
collapse* [kəˈlæps]	*v./n.* 坍塌，崩溃；晕倒 记 联想记忆：col + lapse(滑倒) → 一出门就滑倒，真让人崩溃 → 崩溃 例 The whole market ***collapsed***, as a matter of fact, and coffee became cheaper than it had been for the previous 25 years. 事实上，(咖啡)市场全盘崩溃，咖啡的售价跌到 25 年来的最低。
collate* [kəˈleɪt]	*vt.* 对照；核对；整理(文件、书页等) 记 词根记忆：col(共同) + lat(搬运) + e → 一起搬运 → 对照；核对 例 Customers' comments are ***collated*** regularly to identify opportunities for improvement. 顾客的意见会定期核对，以确保公司能在适当的时机进行改进。

□ cognition □ coherent □ cohesion □ coincide □ collaboration □ collapse
□ collate

Word List 9

音频

词根、词缀预习表

later	侧面，边	collateral *a.* 并行的	**lect**	收集	collect *v.* 收集，搜集
col	耕种	colony *n.* 殖民地	**bat**	打	combat *n.* 战斗，搏斗
com-	共同	combine *v.* 联合，结合	**men**	引导	commence *v.* 开始，着手
merc	交易	commerce *n.* 贸易，商业	**miser**	同情	commiserate *vi.* 同情，怜悯
mit	送	commit *v.* 提交	**mod**	样式	commodity *n.* 商品，货物

collateral
[kɒˈlætərəl]

a. 并行的；间接的，附带的

记 词根记忆：col(共同) + later(侧面，边) + al(形容词后缀)→ 两个相同的侧面相对 → 并行的

例 The cost is in the *collateral* damage of the very methods of food production that has made the food cheaper. 某些食品生产方法降低了食物的价格，但代价是带来附带性的危害。

collect*
[kəˈlekt]

v. 收集，搜集；领取，接走；收(税等)；聚集；积累

记 词根记忆：col(一起) + lect(收集) → 收集，搜集

例 I've *collected* maps and other data to prepare a guidebook. 我已收集了地图和其他信息准备写本指南。

派 collective(*a.* 共同的；集体的)

collection*
[kəˈlekʃn]

n. 收集，积聚；收藏(品)

例 The textile *collection* of the museum is the largest in the world. 这家博物馆收藏的纺织品是全世界最多的。

collision
[kəˈlɪʒn]

n. 碰撞；冲突，抵触

记 来自 collide(*vi.* 冲撞)

例 These fracture zones, where the *collisions* occur, are where earthquakes happen. 这些断裂带是碰撞发生的地方，也是地震发生区。

colony*
[ˈkɒləni]

n. 殖民地；(动植物的)群体

记 词根记忆：col(耕种) + on + y(表场所，名词后缀) → 在某处耕种 → 将那里变为自己的殖民地 → 殖民地

例 The Olympics brought together states in Greece and their *colonies*. 奥运会让希腊的各城邦和其殖民地的人齐聚一堂。

colossal [kə'lɒsl]	*a.* 巨大的，庞大的 例 The damage that the earthquake has caused has been *colossal*. 地震带来极大的破坏。
colour-blind* ['kʌləblaɪnd]	*a.* 色盲的 例 People who are *colour-blind* may be not able to see the difference between particular colours. 色盲患者无法辨认某些特定的颜色。
column ['kɒləm]	*n.* 柱；柱形物；专栏(文章)，栏目 搭 the financial column 财经专栏 例 My friend has his own *column* in the magazine. 我朋友在该杂志上有自己的专栏。
comb* [kəʊm]	*n.* 梳子；蜂巢；(鸡等的)肉冠，冠状物 *v.* 梳理；搜寻，彻底搜查 搭 comb through sth. for sth. 搜寻 例 These temporary hive extensions contain frames of empty *comb* for the bees to fill with honey. 这些临时扩充的蜂箱里有用来让蜜蜂贮存蜂蜜的空蜂巢。
combat ['kɒmbæt]	*n.* 战斗，搏斗 *vt.* 战斗，与…搏斗；防止 记 词根记忆：com(共同) + bat(打) → 战斗，搏斗 例 The state government is spending millions of dollars in its attempt to *combat* gun abuse. 州政府花费数百万美元试图防止滥用枪支。 派 combatant(*n.* 参战者，战士)；combative(*a.* 好斗的)
combination* [ˌkɒmbɪ'neɪʃn]	*n.* 结合(体)，联合(体)；化合 记 来自 combine(*v.* 结合) 例 The old man's treatment was a *combination* of surgery, radiation and drugs. 对那位老人的治疗集外科手术、放射治疗以及药物治疗于一体。
combine* [kəm'baɪn]	*v.* 联合，结合 记 词根记忆：com(共同) + bi(两个) + ne → 使两个在一起 → 联合，结合 搭 combine...with... 联合…和… 例 The next step was to *combine* the holder with a small camera. 下一步是将支架和一台小型相机连接起来。
combustion* [kəm'bʌstʃən]	*n.* 燃烧；燃烧过程 记 联想记忆：combust(消耗；燃烧) + ion → 燃烧；燃烧过程 搭 combustion chamber 燃烧室 例 *Combustion* and gasification techniques are now at pilot and demonstration stages. 燃烧技术和气化技术现在处于试用和验证阶段。 派 combustibility(*n.* 燃烧性，可燃性)
comedy* ['kɒmədi]	*n.* 喜剧；喜剧性(事件) 记 联想记忆：大家一起来(come)看喜剧(comedy) 例 I really like to watch some of the old *comedy* shows. 我真想看一些以前的喜剧表演。 派 comedian(*n.* 喜剧演员)

□ colossal □ colour-blind □ column □ comb □ combat □ combination
□ combine ■ combustion □ comedy

comet
[ˈkɒmɪt]

n. 彗星

记 联想记忆：come(来)+t → 偶尔来一次的星体 → 彗星

例 The newly-discovered object was considered a *comet*. 人们认为这一新发现的物体是彗星。

comic*
[ˈkɒmɪk]

a. 可笑的，滑稽的；喜剧的 *n.* 喜剧演员

搭 comic strip（常登载于报纸的）连环漫画

例 Henry's accident of slipping on the banana skin brought some *comic* relief to this boring performance. 亨利意外踩到香蕉皮滑倒给这场沉闷的表演带来了些许喜剧色彩，缓和了氛围。

9

commence*
[kəˈmens]

v. 开始，着手

记 词根记忆：com(共同)+men(引导)+ce → 共同引导 → 开始，着手

搭 commence with 由…开始；commence doing sth. 开始做某事

例 Most courses *commence* at 9 a.m. and run until 3 p.m. 大部分课程上午 9 点开始，下午 3 点结束。

同 begin(*v.* 开始)；start(*v.* 开始)

反 end(*v.* 结束)；finish(*v.* 结束，终止)

commencement
[kəˈmensmənt]

n. 开始，开端；毕业典礼

例 The high school seniors engaged in high jinks after *commencement*. 毕业典礼后，中学毕业生狂欢了一场。

comment*
[ˈkɒment]

n. 注释，评论，意见 *v.* 注释，评论

记 词根记忆：com(共同)+ment(想法) → 共同进行思考 → 评论

搭 comment on/about... 评论…

例 Customer's *comments*, both positive and negative, are recorded by staff and are collated regularly to identify opportunities for improvement of products. 员工记录来自顾客的正反两方面意见，(公司)定期整理核查这些意见，以确定是否能根据意见来提高产品的质量。

派 commentator(*n.* 评论员；讲解员)

commentary*
[ˈkɒməntri]

n.（尤指电台或电视台所作的）实况报道，现场解说；注释，解释；批评；评价

记 来自 comment(*v.* 评论)

例 The bus company runs all its tours with a live *commentary* in English. 这家公交公司给其各条运营线路都配有生动的英文解说。

commerce
[ˈkɒmɜːs]

n. 贸易，商业；交往，交流

记 词根记忆：com(共同)+merc(交易)+e → 贸易，商业

例 In the US, Washington is the seat of government and New York is the chief seat of *commerce*. 在美国，华盛顿是政府所在地，纽约是主要的商业中心。

□ comet □ comic □ commence □ commencement □ comment □ commentary □ commerce

commercial*
[kəˈmɜːʃl]

a. 商业的，商品化的，贸易的 *n.* 商业广告

记 联想记忆：commerc(e)(商业) + ial(形容词后缀) → 商业的

搭 commercial intercourse 通商，贸易往来；commercial venture 商业投资；commercial television 商业电视台；commercial centre 商业中心

例 The research findings report *commercial* rather than political trends. 这些研究结果反映了商业趋势而非政治趋势。

commiserate
[kəˈmɪzəreɪt]

vi. 同情，怜悯

记 词根记忆：com(带有) + miser(同情) + ate → 带有同情之心 → 同情，怜悯

例 We deeply *commiserated* with job hunters who were on the loss of their jobs. 我们对那些失去工作的求职者深表同情。

commission
[kəˈmɪʃn]

n. 委托；佣金 *vt.* 授权，委托

记 词根记忆：com(共同) + miss(送) + ion → 送交给某人 → 委托

搭 in/out of commission 可/不可使用

例 He now has a new *commission* to design a glass sculpture for the headquarters of a pizza company. 他现在有新的委托事务，为一家比萨公司的总部大楼设计一件玻璃雕塑。

commit*
[kəˈmɪt]

v. 把…交托给，提交；犯(错误)，干(坏事)

记 词根记忆：com(共同) + mit(送) → 送交 → 把…交托给，提交

搭 commit crimes 犯罪；commit suicide 自杀；commit oneself to 使自己承担

例 The drivers refused to *commit* themselves to the traffic accident. 司机们拒绝承担这起交通事故的责任。

派 committed(*a.* 尽心尽力的；坚信的)

commitment
[kəˈmɪtmənt]

n. 委托；许诺；承担义务

记 词根记忆：com(共同) + mit(送出) + ment → 一起送出 → 委托

例 This *commitment* has been clearly defined in the act. 这项法案中明确定义了这一义务的内容。

committee*
[kəˈmɪti]

n. 委员会，全体委员

记 词根记忆：com(共同) + mitt(=mit 发送) + ee(表人) → 共同发送指令的人 → 委员会，全体委员

例 The *committee's* decisions are often determined by the members' vote. 委员会的决议常常由委员投票决定。

commodity*
[kəˈmɒdəti]

n. 商品，货物；日用品

记 词根记忆：com(共同) + mod(样式) + ity → 市场上的商品种类繁多 → 商品，货物

搭 commodity economy 商品经济；a commodities fair 商品交易会；commodity price 商品价格；agricultural commodities 农业产品；commodity inspection 商品检查

例 Nowadays, the airlines are treating their seats like a *commodity*. 现在，航空公司把客机的席位看作是一种商品(进行出售)。

同 goods(*n.* 货物)

□ commercial □ commiserate □ commission □ commit □ commitment □ committee □ commodity

commonwealth [ˈkɒmənwelθ]

n. [the C-] 英联邦；联合体

记 组合词：common(共同的) + wealth(财富) → 共创财富 → 联合体

例 George was a scientist at the *Commonwealth* Scientific and Industrial Research Organisation at that time. 那时乔治是(澳大利亚)联邦科学与工业研究组织的一名科学家。

community [kəˈmjuːnəti]

n. 社会；社区；团体；(动植物的)群落；共同体

记 词根记忆：com(共同) + mun(服务) + ity → 为大家服务 → 社区；团体

搭 the Asian community 亚洲人聚居的社区；sense of community 社区意识；community spirit 团体精神

例 Detailed surveys of social and economic trends in the European *Community* show that Europe's population is falling and getting older. 欧共体开展的关于社会经济趋势的详细调查显示，欧洲人口在减少且开始呈现老龄化趋势。

commute [kəˈmjuːt]

v. (乘公共汽车等)上下班往返，经常往返；交换，抵偿；减刑 *n.* 上下班路程

记 词根记忆：com(=with 以) + mut(改变) + e → 以一物改变另一物 → 交换，抵偿

例 Eventually, it is predicted that many people may be able to work at home instead of *commuting* at office in the future. 据预测，在未来许多人最终可以在家办公，而不用乘公交往返上下班。

派 commuter(*n.* 上下班往返的人；通勤者)

同 compensate(*v.* 赔偿，补偿)

compact* [kəmˈpækt]

a. 紧密的，结实的；简明的；紧凑的 *vt.* 使紧凑，压缩

记 词根记忆：com(表加强) + pact(系紧) → 紧密的

搭 a compact car 小型客车；a compact narration 简明的叙述

例 The bag must be *compact* and light for easy transport. 这个包必须轻便结实以便于运输。

派 compaction(*n.* 压紧，紧束的状态)；compactness(*n.* 紧密)

companion [kəmˈpænɪən]

n. 共事者；同伴

记 词根记忆：com(共同) + pan(面包) + ion → 共享面包的人 → 共事者；同伴

例 Tom was my only Chinese *companion* during my stay in Switzerland. 汤姆是我在瑞士期间唯一的一位中国伙伴。

comparable [ˈkɒmpərəbl]

a. 可比较的，类似的；比得上的

记 词根记忆：com(共同) + par(相等) + able(能…的) → 能等同的 → 可比较的

例 A *comparable* apartment in the east of this city would cost twice as much. 一套类似的房子在城东部就要贵一倍。

同 similar(*a.* 相似的，类似的)；like(*a.* 相似的，同样的)

comparative* [kəmˈpærətɪv]

a. 比较的；相当的

记 词根记忆：com(共同) + par(相等) + ative → 差不多的 → 相当的

搭 comparative advantage 相对优势；comparative validity 相对合法性

例 Tom is living in *comparative* comfort. 汤姆现在过得比较舒服。

□ commonwealth □ community □ commute □ compact □ companion □ comparable □ comparative

comparatively* [kəmˈpærətɪvli]

ad. 相对地；比较地

例 The standard of living in this city is *comparatively* high. 这个城市的生活水平相对比较高。

compare* [kəmˈpeə(r)]

v. 比较；对比

记 词根记忆：com(共同) + par(相等) + e → 放在一起看看是否相等 → 对比

搭 compare to 比喻成…；compare with 与…比较

例 How are the expectations of today's school leavers different *compared* with those of the previous generation? 与上一届相比，现在毕业生的期望有何不同？

comparison* [kəmˈpærɪsn]

n. 比较，对比，对照；比喻，比拟

记 词根记忆：com(共同) + par(相等) + ison → 放在一起看看是否相等 → 比较，对比

搭 by comparison 比较起来；make a comparison 进行对比；fair comparison 公平比较；in comparison 比较起来

例 We generally think of Africa as being a very hot and dry place, but it is not in *comparison* with Australia. 通常我们认为非洲炎热干燥，但是它与澳洲无法比。

compass [ˈkʌmpəs]

n. 罗盘，罗盘仪；界限，范围；[*pl.*] 圆规

记 联想记忆：com(共同) + pass(通过) → 双边共同通过的地方 → 界限，范围

例 Nearly two thousand years have passed since the invention of *compass*, which is the pride of Chinese people. 指南针的发明是中国人的骄傲，距今已有差不多 2000 年的历史了。

compassionate* [kəmˈpæʃənət]

a. 有同情心的，表示怜悯的

搭 compassionate attitude 热诚的态度；compassionate leave 照顾性准假(一般指丧假)

例 We should try our best to create a more *compassionate* society. 我们应该竭尽全力营造一个更人性化的社会。

compatible [kəmˈpætəbl]

a. 兼容的；合得来的

记 词根记忆：com(共同) + pat(=path 感觉) + ible → 有共同感觉的 → 兼容的；合得来的

搭 be compatible with 与…相适应/不矛盾；compatible software 可兼容的软件；compatible blood groups 相容的血型

例 Accuracy is not always *compatible* with haste. 忙中难免出错。

compatriot* [kəmˈpætriət]

n. 同胞；同国人

记 联想记忆：他的同伴(companion)跟他是同一个国家的人(compatriot)

例 In France, Bob bumped into a *compatriot* from Denver. 鲍勃在法国偶遇了来自丹佛的同胞。

□ comparatively □ compare □ comparison □ compass □ compassionate □ compatible □ compatriot

compel *

[kəm'pel]

vt. 强迫

记 词根记忆：com(共同)+pel(推)→强迫

搭 compel sb. to do sth. 强迫某人做某事

例 The boss *compels* workers to spend more time on the job. 老板强迫工人花更多的时间在工作上。

compendium *

[kəm'pendiəm]

n. 简要，概略

记 词根记忆：com(共同)+pend(悬挂)+ium→把重要的部分抽出来挂在一起→简要，概略

例 The human genome is the *compendium* of all these inherited genetic instructions. 人类基因组是所有这些遗传基因说明的一个缩影。

compensate

['kɒmpenseɪt]

v. 补偿，赔偿；弥补

记 词根记忆：com(以)+pens(偿还)+ate→以某物来偿还→补偿，赔偿；弥补

搭 compensate (sb.) for sth. 弥补，补偿；赔偿

例 Nothing can *compensate* for the loss of one's health. 失去的健康是无法弥补的。

同 indemnify(*vt.* 赔偿，补偿)

compensation

[ˌkɒmpen'seɪʃn]

n. 补偿，赔偿；赔偿物，赔偿金

搭 make compensation for sb.'s losses 补偿某人的损失

例 The company was paid a sum of money by an insurance agent as *compensation* for its loss in a fire. 那家公司从保险公司那里得到一笔火灾损失赔偿。

compete *

[kəm'piːt]

vi. 竞争；比赛

记 词根记忆：com(共同)+pet(追求，寻求)+e→共同追求(一个目标)→竞争

搭 compete against/with 与…竞争；compete for 为…比赛

例 A series of tests and interviews eventually left 280 applicants *competing* for the 120 advertised positions. 经过一系列的测试和面试之后，最终留下280名申请者来竞争招聘广告上的120个职位。

派 competitive(*a.* 竞争的)；competitor(*n.* 竞争者，对手)

competent

['kɒmpɪtnt]

a. 有能力的；能胜任的

记 联想记忆：compet(e)(竞争)+ent(形容词后缀)→能在竞争中取胜的→有能力的

例 This new manager was really *competent*. 新任经理的确很能干。

同 sufficient(*a.* 充分的，足够的；能胜任的)

反 inefficient[*a.* (指人)不能胜任的]

competition *

[ˌkɒmpə'tɪʃn]

n. 竞争；比赛

例 The workers opened small businesses in direct *competition* with their former employer. 工人们开办了小型公司，直接和他们以前的雇主竞争。

compile

[kəm'paɪl]

vt. 汇编；编纂

记 联想记忆：com(共同)+pile(堆)→堆在一起→汇编；编纂

例 The daily paper is *compiled* at the editorial headquarters in the heart of the city. 日报是在位于市中心的编辑总部完成的。

□ compel □ compendium □ compensate □ compensation □ compete □ competent
□ competition □ compile

complain *

[kəmˈpleɪn]

v. 抱怨；投诉

记 联想记忆：com + plain(平淡的) → 不要抱怨生活的平淡 → 抱怨

搭 complain about 抱怨

例 John *complains* that the resource centre has limited opening hours. 约翰抱怨说信息中心的开放时间有限。

---

complaint *

[kəmˈpleɪnt]

n. 抱怨；投诉；控告；(尤指不严重、常影响身体某部位的)疾病

例 My friend told me that he had gotten a kidney *complaint*. 我朋友对我说他肾不舒服。

---

complementary

[ˌkɒmplɪˈmentri]

a. 互补的；补充的，补足的

记 联想记忆：complement(补充物) + ary → 互补的；补充的，补足的

例 The survey suggested that *complementary* medicine is probably a better term than alternative medicine. 调查显示，比起替代医学，辅助性医学这一术语可能更加恰当。

---

complete *

[kəmˈpliːt]

a. 彻底的；完成的；绝对的 *vt.* 完成；结束

记 词根记忆：com(表加强) + plet(满，填满) + e → 完成；结束

例 Some people believe that children's leisure activities must be educational, otherwise they are a *complete* waste of time. 有些人认为孩子们的休闲活动必须具有教育意义，否则那完全就是浪费时间。

派 completion(*n.* 完成；实现)；completely(*ad.* 十分；完全)

---

complex *

[ˈkɒmpleks]

n. 综合体，集合体；建筑群；情结 *a.* 合成的，综合的；复杂的，难懂的

记 词根记忆：com(共同) + plex(重叠) → 重叠交叉的 → 复杂的

搭 inferiority complex 自卑感，自卑情结

例 The new sports *complex* has everything needed for many different activities. 新建的综合体育馆能为多种活动提供所需的一切设施。

同 complicated (*a.* 复杂的，难解的)；intricate (*a.* 复杂的，错综的)；involved(*a.* 棘手的)；knotty(*a.* 棘手的，困难多的)

反 simple(*a.* 简单的，简易的)

---

complexity

[kəmˈpleksəti]

n. 复杂，复杂性；复杂的事物

例 Students in our class are all astonished by the great *complexity* of this event. 我们班里的所有同学都被这次事件的复杂性震惊了。

---

complicate *

[ˈkɒmplɪkeɪt]

vt. 使变复杂

记 词根记忆：com(共同) + plic(重叠) + ate(使…) → 使重叠在一起 → 使变复杂

搭 complicate matters 使事情复杂化；complicate the business 使生意难做

例 This problem was *complicated* beyond all reason. 这个问题被毫无道理地复杂化了。

---

complicated *

[ˈkɒmplɪkeɪtɪd]

a. 复杂的；难懂的

记 词根记忆：com(共同) + plic(重叠) + ated → 重叠在一起的 → 复杂的

例 The other hat we made was more *complicated*. 我们制作的另外一项帽子更加复杂。

□ complain □ complaint ■ complementary □ complete □ complex □ complexity
□ complicate □ complicated

compliment*
[ˈkɒmplɪment]

n. 赞美；[*pl.*] 问候，祝贺

记 词根记忆：com（共同）+ pli（满，填满）+ ment（名词后缀）→ 一起满足某人的愿望 → 赞美

例 Thank you for your *compliments*. 谢谢你的称赞。

comply
[kəmˈplaɪ]

vi. 遵从；服从

记 词根记忆：com（表加强）+ ply（装满）→ 完全装满 → 完全满足 → 遵从；服从

搭 comply with the law 守法

例 The patient was unwilling to *comply* with the physician's orders. 这位病人不愿意遵从医生的嘱咐。

component*
[kəmˈpəʊnənt]

n. 成分；零部件 *a.* 构成的，组成的

记 词根记忆：com（共同）+ pon（放）+ ent → 放到一起（的东西）→ 成分

搭 key component 主要成分；component parts 部件

例 It is often easier to check individual *components* before assembly takes place in many manufacturing processes. 在许多生产工序中，在组装之前先检查单个零部件通常更容易。

同 ingredient（*n.* 成分）；element（*n.* 要素，元件）；constituent（*a.* 组成的）

compose
[kəmˈpəʊz]

v. 组成，构成；写，创作（乐曲等）；使安定

记 词根记忆：com（共同）+ pos（放）+ e → 放到一起 → 组成，构成

搭 be composed of 由…组成

例 All of the subjects which you undertake in the first year are *composed* of lectures and tutorials. 你第一年所要学习的所有科目都由讲座和辅导课构成。

composition*
[ˌkɒmpəˈzɪʃn]

n. 作品；写作，作曲；结构，组成，成分

搭 composition of …的组成

例 There are many grammar errors in your *composition*. 你的作文中有很多语法错误。

compound*

[kəmˈpaʊnd] *vt.* 使恶化，加重；使化合，使合成 [ˈkɒmpaʊnd] *n.* 化合物，复合物；（有围墙或篱笆等的）楼群，大院 *a.* 复合的，化合的；综合的

记 词根记忆：com（一起）+ pound（放置）→ 放到一起使合成 → 化合物

例 Government policies have frequently *compounded* the environmental damage that farming can cause. 政府推行的政策往往会加重农业对环境的破坏。

comprehension*
[ˌkɒmprɪˈhenʃn]

n. 理解；理解力

记 词根记忆：com（共同）+ prehens（抓住）+ ion → 共同抓住要领 → 理解

例 The teacher's task of improving *comprehension* is made harder by influences outside the classroom. 老师提高学生理解力的工作因为课堂外的影响而变得更加困难。

□ compliment □ comply □ component □ compose □ composition □ compound
□ comprehension

comprehensive * [ˌkɒmprɪˈhensɪv]

a. 全面的，广泛的；综合的；包容的

记 词根记忆：com（共同）+ prehens（抓住）+ ive → 全部抓住 → 全面的；综合的

搭 comprehensive school 综合中学

例 His account of the meeting was most *comprehensive*. 他对会议的叙述面面俱到。

compress

[kəmˈpres] *v.* 压紧；压缩 [ˈkɒmpres] *n.* 敷布，压布

记 联想记忆：com(表加强) + press(压) → 使劲压 → 压紧；压缩

搭 compress sth. into sth. 把…压缩成…

例 Puffs of *compressed* air shape the glass. 吹出的压缩空气使玻璃成型。

comprise [kəmˈpraɪz]

vt. 包含；由…组成

记 词根记忆：com(共同) + pris(抓住) + e → 共同抓住 → 包含

搭 be comprised in 归入…

例 The hotel *comprises* 82 one-bedroom apartments and 12 suites. 这家酒店有82间单人床位的公寓和12间套房。

compromise [ˈkɒmprəmaɪz]

n. 妥协，折中办法 *v.* 妥协，放弃(原则、理想等)；危及

记 联想记忆：com + promise(保证) → 相互保证 → 妥协

搭 reach a compromise over sth. 就某事达成妥协；compromise with sb. on sth. 与某人就某事妥协

例 This means that the choice you make will probably be determined by the amount of money you want to pay, your own personal needs, what is actually available or a *compromise* of all three things. 这意味着你所作的选择可能会取决于你想花多少钱、你的个人需要和你实际能买到的(商品)，或者你也可以将三者折中一下。

compulsively * [kəmˈpʌlsɪvli]

ad. 强制地；禁不住地

例 If you do *compulsively* grind your teeth in your sleep, ask your dentist for a soft mouthguard. 如果你睡觉时禁不住要磨牙，可以向牙医要一个质地柔软的护牙套。

compulsory [kəmˈpʌlsəri]

a. 义务的；必须做的；强制性的；(课程)必修的

记 词根记忆：com(共同) + puls(推) + ory → 共同推进的 → 义务的；必修的

派 compulsory education 义务教育；compulsory subjects 必修课

例 These counselling sessions are *compulsory* for all students. 所有学生都必须参加这些咨询课。

同 mandatory(*a.* 命令的，强制的)；enforced(*a.* 强迫的)

computerize [kəmˈpjuːtəraɪz]

vt. 使计算机化；用计算机做；用计算机储存(信息)

记 来自 computer(*n.* 计算机)

例 It's reported that 80% of sections in the company have been completely *computerized*. 据报道，该公司80%的部门已经完全计算机化了。

派 computerization(*n.* 计算机化)

□ comprehensive □ compress □ comprise □ compromise □ compulsively □ compulsory □ computerize

conceal [kən'siːl]	*vt.* 隐藏；隐瞒；掩盖 记 联想记忆：con + ceal(看作 seal，密封) → 密封起来 → 隐藏；隐瞒；掩盖 例 Men were very aware that thieves might be *concealed* behind the car. 人对窃贼可能藏在车后很警觉。
concede [kən'siːd]	*v.* (不情愿地)承认；让步 记 词根记忆：con(带着) + ced(走) + e → 带着某物走 → 让步 例 The defeated side had to *concede* some of their territory to the enemy. 战败的一方不得不把部分领土割让给敌人。
conceive [kən'siːv]	*v.* (构)想出，构想，设想；怀孕 记 词根记忆：con(共同) + ceiv(抓住) → 怀有一种想法 → 想出 搭 conceive of 设想；conceive a child 怀孕 例 These scientific advances can offer a new way to test whether a *conceived* baby is healthy or not. 这些科学上的进步为检测孕育中的婴儿是否健康提供了一种新方法。 同 think(*v.* 想，认为)；imagine(*v.* 想象，设想)

9

You have to believe in yourself. That's the secret of success.
人必须相信自己，这是成功的秘诀。
——美国演员 卓别林(Charles Chaplin, American actor)

□ conceal □ concede □ conceive

Word List 10

音频

词根、词缀预习表

centr	中心	concentrate *v.* 集中，聚焦	**cern**	观察	concern *vt.* 关心；关注
clud	关闭	conclude v. 推断出；作结论	**cur**	跑	concur *v.* 一致
dem	伤害；诅咒	condemn *vt.* 极力谴责	**duct**	引导	conduct *n./v.* 指导
fin	界限	confine *vt.* 限制；管制	**firm**	坚固的	confirm *vt.* 证实；肯定
front	额头，脸	confront *vt.* 遭遇；面对	**gest**	搬运	congested *a.* 拥挤不堪的

concentrate* [ˈkɒnsntreɪt]

v. 全神贯注，全力以赴；集中，聚集；浓缩 *n.* 浓缩物，浓缩液

记 词根记忆：con(共同)+centr(中心)+ate → 置于同一个中心 → 集中，聚集

搭 concentrate on 集中，专心，倾全力于，全神贯注于

例 The Ancient Greeks used lenses or concave mirrors to *concentrate* the sun's rays. 古希腊人利用透镜或凹面镜来聚集太阳光。

concentration [ˌkɒnsnˈtreɪʃn]

n. 集中；专心，专注；浓缩，浓度

例 This *concentration* of vehicles makes air quality in urban areas unpleasant and sometimes dangerous to breathe. 交通工具如此集中造成城市地区空气质量的恶劣，有时甚至不宜呼吸。

concept* [ˈkɒnsept]

n. 概念，观念；设想

记 词根记忆：con(共同)+cept(拿，取) → 共同拿取 → 概念

例 The *concept* of health holds different meanings for different people and groups. 健康观念因人和群体的不同而不同。

conception [kənˈsepʃn]

n. 观念，概念

例 This book is designed to help Ph.D. students by explaining different *conceptions* of the research process. 本书旨在通过解释研究过程中出现的不同概念来帮助博士生进行学习。

派 misconception(*n.* 误解)

conceptual [kənˈseptʃuəl]

a. 观念的，概念的

记 来自 concept(*n.* 观念，概念)

例 There is only *conceptual* framework of the play which needs the actor to develop themselves. 这部戏到现在为止只有一个概念框架，需要演员们自行发挥。

 □ concentrate □ concentration □ concept □ conception □ conceptual

concern* [kən'sɜːn]	*vt.* 涉及；使关心；让(人)担忧 *n.* 关心；关注 记 词根记忆：con(表加强)＋cern(观察)→关心；关注 搭 as/so far as...be concerned 就…来说；concern oneself with/about 关心；be concerned with 涉及，有关；concern with/about 关心… 例 What most *concerns* me is I'm still not doing very well on my homework. 最让我担心的是我现在还不能很好地完成家庭作业。 派 concerned(*a.* 担心的，忧虑的；关注的，感兴趣的)；concerning(*prep.* 关于，涉及)
concert ['kɒnsət]	*n.* 音乐会，演奏会 记 联想记忆：那个得了癌症(cancer)的音乐家举行了最后一次个人音乐会(concert) 例 All their musical instruments were lost and they couldn't play at their *concert*. 他们所有的乐器都不见了，所以无法在演奏会上表演。
concession [kən'seʃn]	*n.* 让步，迁就；特许权；承认，认可 记 词根记忆：con(共同)＋cess(行走，前进)＋ion→要想大家共同进步，必须都做出让步→让步 例 You will get what is called a "student account", which is a current account with special *concessions* for students. 你将获得一个称为"学生账户"的活期账户，这是专为学生开设的，有特殊优惠措施。
conclude* [kən'kluːd]	*v.* 推断出；作结论 记 词根记忆：con(共同)＋clud(关闭)＋e→共同关闭→推断出；作结论 搭 conclude with 以…作结论；to conclude 最后 例 They *concluded* that the children were incapable of deductive reasoning. 他们得出结论：儿童没有推理能力。
conclusion* [kən'kluːʒn]	*n.* 结论，推论；结束，结尾；【法】缔结，议定 搭 in conclusion 最后，总之；draw a conclusion 得出结论；at the conclusion of 当…结束时 例 At the clinic we have come to the *conclusion* that the major cause of back pain is not with the design of chairs, but in the way we sit in them. 临床试验得出的结论是，背痛不是由椅子的设计引起的，而是我们的坐姿造成的。
concrete* ['kɒŋkriːt]	*a.* 混凝土制的；确实的，具体的；有形的，实在的 *n.* 混凝土 记 词根记忆：con＋cre(产生)＋te→产生(事物)→具体存在的事物→实在的；具体的 搭 reinforced concrete 钢筋混凝土
concur [kən'kɜː(r)]	*v.* 同时发生；意见相同，一致 记 词根记忆：con(共同)＋cur(跑)→一起跑→一致 例 He *concurs* that orthodox doctors could learn a lot about bedside manner and advising patients on preventative health from alternative therapists. 他认同这种观点：传统医生在对待病人的态度、举止上以及如何给予病人预防保健的建议上可以从替代疗法专家那里学到很多。

□ concern □ concert □ concession □ conclude □ conclusion □ concrete
□ concur

condemn [kən'dem]	*vt.* 声讨，极力谴责；给…判刑 记 词根记忆：con（共同）+ dem（伤害；诅咒）+ n → 极力谴责 搭 condemn sb. to death 判某人死刑；be condemned to 被宣告… 例 The police offer those *condemned* to spend five days a week in an urban environment with an unrivalled area of freedom to unwind and take part in a range of leisure activities, such as hunting, riding and hiking. 警察让那些死刑犯每周有五天时间在无比自由的城市环境中度过，在那里放松放松，参加诸如打猎、骑马、徒步旅行等一系列休闲活动。 派 condemnation（*n.* 谴责；定罪）
condensation [ˌkɒnden'seɪʃn]	*n.* 浓缩，凝结 记 来自 condense（*v.* 凝结；精简，压缩） 例 The essay was publicly recognized as a readable *condensation* of the recent scientific literature. 这篇散文被公认为是近期科普读物的浓缩通俗版。
condense* [kən'dens]	*v.* (使)压缩，精简；(使)凝结 记 联想记忆：con + dense（密集的）→ 变得密集的 →（使）压缩 例 This article has been adapted and *condensed* from the article by William and Slater. 这篇文章改编自威廉姆和斯莱特的文章，并进行了精简。
condition* [kən'dɪʃn]	*n.* 状况，状态；[*pl.*] 环境，形势；条件，前提 *vt.* 训练；使适应，使习惯于；对…有重要影响 搭 indoor conditions 室内环境；out of condition 情况不好；on (the) condition that 以…为条件 例 The research ignored the social and environmental *conditions* affecting health. 这一研究忽略了影响人类健康的社会环境和自然环境。
conditioner* [kən'dɪʃənə(r)]	*n.* 护发素，护发剂；调节物；调节器，调节装置 搭 soil conditioner 土壤调节剂；air conditioner 空调 例 If your hair is dry in winter, you can use some hair *conditioner* every day. 如果头发在冬天时干燥，可以每天用一些护发素。
condone [kən'dəʊn]	*v.* 宽恕，赦免；纵容，容忍 记 词根记忆：con（完全）+ don（给予）+ e → 完全给予 → 宽恕，赦免 例 If the government *condones* violent conflict between the two parties, the bloodshed will never stop. 如果政府无视两党之间的暴力冲突，流血事件将永远不会停止。
conduce* [kən'djuːs]	*v.* 有益于，有助于；导致 搭 conduce to 导致；有助于 例 Money, fame and wealth do not always *conduce* to happiness. 金钱与名利并不一定就能给人们带来幸福。
conduct*	['kɒndʌkt] *n.* 举止；指导；管理 [kən'dʌkt] *v.* 指导；管理，实施；指挥 记 词根记忆：con（表加强）+ duct（引导）→ 指导 搭 conduct oneself（行为）表现 例 Some experiments are *conducted* by this professor and others are not. 有些实验是这位教授指导的，有些不是。

□ condemn □ condensation □ condense □ condition □ conditioner □ condone
□ conduce □ conduct

conductive [kən'dʌktɪv]	*a.* 能传导电(或热)的，导电(或热)的 例 Scientists found that this kind of new material was more *conductive* at extremely low temperature than at the ordinary temperature. 科学家发现，这种新材料在极端的低温条件下比在常温下导电性更好。
conference ['kɒnfərəns]	*n.* (正式)会议 例 I'm going to a *conference* in London. 我要去伦敦参加一个会议。
confidence ['kɒnfɪdəns]	*n.* 信任；信心 搭 be in sb's confidence 受某人信任 例 The message is that you have little *confidence*. (反馈出的)信息就是你没什么自信。
configuration [kənˌfɪgə'reɪʃn]	*n.* 结构，配置；轮廓，外形 记 联想记忆：con + figur(e)(形状) + ation → 轮廓，外形 搭 aircraft configuration 飞机结构 例 This seminar aims to introduce the *configuration* and composing of the papain and the use in foodstuff, medicine and industry. 本次研讨会旨在介绍木瓜蛋白酶的结构、组成，及其在食品、医药和工业中的用途。 派 configure(*vt.* 配置，使成型)
confine [kən'faɪn]	*vt.* 限制，仅限于；管制，禁闭 *n.* [*pl.*] 界限，范围 记 词根记忆：con(表加强) + fin(界限) + e → 限制；管制 搭 be confined to (局)限于…，(被)限制/封闭在…；between the confines of 在…界线之间；beyond the confine of 超出…的范围；confine oneself to 只涉及…，只限于… 例 It's important not to *confine* yourself to reading on your subject. 不要仅限于阅读本专业的书籍，这一点很重要。
confirm* [kən'fɜːm]	*vt.* 证实，确定；肯定；批准，使有效 记 词根记忆：con(表加强) + firm(坚固的) → 使更加坚固 → 证实；肯定 例 If a prediction based on a hypothesis is fulfilled, then the hypothesis is *confirmed*. 如果基于某一假设的预测得到实现，那么该假设就被证实是正确的。
confirmation* [ˌkɒnfə'meɪʃn]	*n.* 证实，确认；批准 例 Hundreds of students are waiting for *confirmation* of the test results. 数百名学生都在等待着确认考试成绩。
conflict*	['kɒnflɪkt] *n.* 冲突 [kən'flɪkt] *vi.* 冲突，抵触 记 词根记忆：con(共同) + flict(击，打) → 互相打 → 冲突，抵触 搭 come into conflict with sb. 与…起冲突 例 Friction management means handling *conflicts* in a positive and constructive manner. 摩擦管理就是指用一种积极的有建设性的方式来处理冲突。

10

□ conductive □ conference □ confidence □ configuration □ confine □ confirm
□ confirmation □ conflict

conform
[kənˈfɔːm]

vi. 遵守，服从；适应，顺应；相一致，相符合

记 词根记忆：con(共同)+form(形状)→形状相同→相一致

搭 conform to the custom of society 遵从社会习俗；conform with the regulations 遵守规章制度

例 All students must *conform* to the school rules. 所有的学生都必须遵守校规。

同 adapt(*v.* 适应，顺应)

conformity*
[kənˈfɔːməti]

n. 符合，一致

例 One of the most important tasks of managers is to consider the needs of the individual on one hand and group cooperation and *conformity* on the other. 管理者最重要的任务之一是在考虑个人需求的同时还要兼顾团队的合作和一致性。

confront*
[kənˈfrʌnt]

vt. 遭遇；面对，正视

记 词根记忆：con(一起)+front(额头，脸)→一起对顶额头→遭遇；面对

搭 confront with 遭遇；面对；be confronted with 面临

例 Growth and environmentalism can actually go hand in hand, if politicians have the courage to *confront* the vested interest that subsidies create. 如果政客们有勇气面对财政补助所产生的既得利益，那么经济增长和环境保护实际上可以共同发展。

confuse*
[kənˈfjuːz]

vt. 使混乱，混淆；使迷惑，使糊涂

记 词根记忆：con(共同)+fus(流)+e→流到一起，混合→混淆；使迷惑

搭 confuse...with 把…和…混淆，把…和…混为一谈

例 I'm afraid I'm a bit *confused* by what you said just now. 恐怕我被你刚才说的话弄得有点糊涂。

派 confused(*a.* 困惑的)

confusion
[kənˈfjuːʒn]

n. 困惑，糊涂；混淆；混乱，杂乱，无秩序状态，骚乱

记 联想记忆：confus(=confuse 使混乱)+ion→困惑，糊涂

例 This medicine may cause hair loss, depression or *confusion*, and yellowing of skin or eyes. 服用该药可能导致脱发、精神抑郁或神志不清，还可能致使肤色或眼睛发黄。

congested*
[kənˈdʒestɪd]

a. 拥挤不堪的；充塞的

记 词根记忆：con(一起，共同)+gest(搬运)+ed→都搬运到一起→拥挤不堪的；充塞的

例 Can the world avoid being locked into *congested* and polluting means of transport? 世界能否避免受拥挤而污染的交通方式的困扰？

congestion
[kən'dʒestʃən]

n. 拥挤，充塞；充血

记 词根记忆：con + gest(搬运) + ion → 运了一大堆 → 拥挤，充塞

搭 traffic congestion 交通阻塞；congestion surcharge (港口)拥挤附加费

例 Alleviation of mass illiteracy on a global scale is essential to that of health, hunger and other major world problems such as traffic *congestion*, environment pollution, etc. 在全球范围内大规模扫盲是缓解卫生、饥饿及其他重大世界性问题，如交通堵塞、环境污染等所不可或缺的条件。

congratulate
[kən'grætʃuleɪt]

vt. 祝贺

记 词根记忆：con(共同) + grat(喜好) + ulate → 同喜同贺 → 祝贺

例 I wanted to *congratulate* you all on having passed the exam. 大家都通过了考试，我向你们表示祝贺。

congress*
['kɒŋgres]

n. (代表)大会；(美国等国的)国会，议会

记 词根记忆：con(共同) + gress(行走) → 走到一起去开会 → 大会

搭 the support of Congress 国会的支持；the People's Congress 人民代表大会

例 The *congress* called on the local governments to reopen schools after the war. 战后，国会号召地方政府重开学校。

派 congressional(*a.* 大会的；国会的)

conjunction
[kən'dʒʌŋkʃn]

n. 连接；连词

记 词根记忆：con(表加强) + junct(连接，联合) + ion → 连接

例 Seat belts are more effective when used in *conjunction* with air bags. 安全带和安全气囊一起使用，效果更好。

connect*
[kə'nekt]

v. 连接，衔接；联合，关联；由…联想到；给…接通电话

记 词根记忆：con(共同) + nect(绑) → 与…绑在一起 → 连接

搭 connect with/to 与…连接

例 What special food and activities are *connected* with this festival? 有什么特别的食物和活动与这个节日相关？

connection
[kə'nekʃn]

n. 连接；关系

搭 in connection with 与…有关，与…相关

例 A link between weather and mood is made believable by the evidence for a *connection* between behaviour and the length of the daylight hours. 证据显示人的行为与昼长有关系，据此我们可以相信气候和情绪之间是有联系的。

conquer*
['kɒŋkə(r)]

vt. 征服，战胜，占领；克服，破除(坏习惯等)

记 词根记忆：con(全部) + quer(寻求；询问) → 全部寻求到 → 征服

搭 conquer your fear 战胜恐惧

例 Many people have made attempts to *conquer* the peaks of Everest. 许多人都试图征服珠穆朗玛峰。

派 conqueror(*n.* 征服者)

□ congestion □ congratulate □ congress □ conjunction □ connect □ connection
□ conquer

conquest* [ˈkɒŋkwest]

n. 征服；战利品

搭 military conquest 军事征服

例 The king completed the *conquest* of the country. 国王彻底征服了那个国家。

conscious [ˈkɒnʃəs]

a. 自觉的；意识到的；神志清醒的

记 词根记忆：con(共同) + sci(知道) + ous → 共同知道的 → 自觉的；意识到的

搭 conscious of 意识到；注意到

例 Deep inside he was *conscious* that music was not his destiny. 在内心深处，他知道音乐并不是自己的归宿。

consecutive* [kənˈsekjətɪv]

a. 连续不断的，连贯的

记 词根记忆：con + secut(跟随) + ive → 一个接一个的 → 连续不断的，连贯的

搭 consecutive days 连续几天；consecutive years 连年

例 You should give a clear and *consecutive* narrative for your report. 你应该就你的报告给出一个清晰、连贯的陈述。

同 successive(*a.* 继承的；连续的)

consensus* [kənˈsensəs]

n. 共识；(意见)一致

记 词根记忆：con(共同) + sens(感觉) + us → 感觉相同 → 共识

搭 value consensus 价值共识

例 The general *consensus* is that the reform is a good thing. 改革是件好事，这是共识。

同 unanimity(*n.* 全体一致)

consequence* [ˈkɒnsɪkwəns]

n. [常*pl.*] 结果，影响；重要意义

记 词根记忆：con + sequ(跟随) + ence(名词后缀) → 跟随其后 → 结果，影响

搭 as a consequence 因而，结果

例 The *consequence* of the Human Genome Project goes far beyond a narrow focus on disease. 人类基因工程的重要意义远远不止于治愈疾病。

consequent [ˈkɒnsɪkwənt]

a. 作为结果的；随之发生的

记 词根记忆：con + sequ(跟随) + ent(形容词后缀) → 随之发生的

例 There is always confusion *consequent* to an earthquake. 地震过后总是会发生混乱。

consequential [ˌkɒnsɪˈkwenʃl]

a. 结果的，随之发生的

例 The teacher discusses with his students about the *consequential* matters after the financial crisis. 老师在跟同学们一起讨论金融危机后可能产生的一些问题。

consequently* [ˈkɒnsɪkwəntli]

ad. 因此，因而

例 Mr. Foster has never been to China. *Consequently* he knows very little about it. 福斯特先生从未到过中国，所以对中国知之甚少。

□ conquest □ conscious □ consecutive □ consensus □ consequence □ consequent
□ consequential □ consequently

conservation* [ˌkɒnsəˈveɪʃn]

n. 保存；保护

记 联想记忆：con(表加强) + serv(e)(服务) + ation → 一再为其服务 → 保存；保护

例 We just set up a new wildlife *conservation* programme here. 我们刚刚在这里启动了一个新的野生动物保护项目。

派 conservationist(*n.* 自然环境保护主义者)

conservative [kənˈsɜːvətɪv]

a. 保守的；传统的；守旧的 *n.* 保守的人

搭 Conservative Party (英国的)保守党

例 The obstacle to our development has been *conservative* local authorities. 保守的地方当局一直是我们发展的障碍。

conserve [kənˈsɜːv]

vt. 保护；保存，储存；节约

记 词根记忆：con + serv(保持) + e → 保持住 → 保存，储存；节约

例 People living in the desert have a special way to *conserve* water. 生活在沙漠里的人有一种特别的储水方法。

considerable [kənˈsɪdərəbl]

a. 相当大(或多)的，可观的；值得考虑的，重要的

记 联想记忆：consider(考虑) + able(能…的) → 能纳入考虑范围的 → 值得考虑的

例 The heavy snow blocks the highway, so we have to take *considerable* detours. 大雪使得公路封锁，我们不得不绕道而行，为此多走了很多路。

consideration* [kənˌsɪdəˈreɪʃn]

n. 考虑；思考；体谅

搭 in consideration of 考虑到…；由于…

例 After a few moments' *consideration*, they refused the invitation. 他们考虑片刻后，拒绝了邀请。

consignment* [kənˈsaɪnmənt]

n. 交付，委托；投递，发送；所托运的货物

搭 on consignment 以寄售方式；a large consignment of grain 托运大批粮食；consignment store 寄售店

例 We are glad to hear of the post office's making a *consignment* of bikes. 听说邮局可以托运自行车，我们很高兴。

consist* [kənˈsɪst]

vi. 由…组成，由…构成；在于，存在于

记 词根记忆：con(共同) + sist(站) → 站在一起 → 由…构成

搭 consist of 由…组成，由…构成；consist in 在于，存在于

例 Each hour *consists* of 50-minute tuition and a 10-minute break. 每小时的内容安排是 50 分钟的讲解和 10 分钟的休息。

同 comprise(*vt.* 组成，构成)

consistent [kənˈsɪstənt]

a. 一致的，协调的；相符的，相容的

记 词根记忆：con(共同) + sist(站立) + ent → 站在一起的 → 一致的

例 The survey results are entirely *consistent* with our earlier research. 调查的结果与我们早期的研究结果完全一致。

派 consistently(*ad.* 始终如一地)；consistency(*n.* 一致性，连贯性)

□ conservation □ conservative □ conserve □ considerable □ consideration □ consignment
□ consist □ consistent

consolation * [ˌkɒnsəˈleɪʃn]	*n.* 安慰；慰问 记 词根记忆：con(=with 以) + sol(安慰) + ation → 可用来给人安慰的东西 → 安慰；慰问 搭 consolation prize 安慰奖 例 The results of this research may be a great *consolation* to left-handers. 这项研究的结果对惯用左手者来说可能是个极大的安慰。
consolidation * [kənˌsɒlɪˈdeɪʃn]	*n.* 合并；巩固 记 词根记忆：con(共同) + solid(结实的) + ation → 联合在一起使更加结实 → 合并；巩固 例 The global airline industry was heading towards more *consolidation*. 全球航空业的合并之风日益盛行。
consortium * [kənˈsɔːtɪəm]	*n.* 集团；财团；社团，协会 记 联想记忆：consort(陪伴，结交) + ium → 结交组成团体 → 社团，协会 例 The *consortium* that won the contract for the island opted for an aggressive approach. 赢得这座岛屿(开发)合同的财团采取了一种野蛮的开发方式。
constant * [ˈkɒnstənt]	*a.* 经常的，不断的；坚定的，永恒的，忠实的；持续的，不变的 *n.* 常数，恒量 记 词根记忆：con(共同) + stant(站立) → 永远站在一起 → 坚定的，永恒的，忠实的 搭 constant temperature 恒温；constant speed 恒定速度；constant value 不变价值 例 We need to have a *constant* supply of bikes to tourists. 我们需要不断地向游客提供自行车。 派 constancy(*n.* 恒定不变)
constantly [ˈkɒnstəntli]	*ad.* 经常；不断地 例 Atlas's teaching methodology is *constantly* revised as more is discovered about the process of learning a new language. 随着新语言学习过程中有了更多的发现，阿特拉斯的教学法不断得以改进。
constituent [kənˈstɪtjuənt]	*n.* 成分，要素；选区内的选民 *a.* 组成的；有宪法制定或修改权的 记 词根记忆：con(共同) + stit(=stat 站立) + uent → 站在一起 → 成分 搭 a constituent assembly 立宪会议 例 The language which develops along with nationality's development is a national culture *constituent*. 随着民族的发展而发展的语言，是民族文化的组成部分。 派 constituency(*n.* 选区；选区的选民) 同 component(*a.* 组成的，构成的)
constitute [ˈkɒnstɪtjuːt]	*v.* 组成；构成；设立，成立 记 词根记忆：con(共同) + stit(站立) + ute → 设立 例 The lid *constitutes* twenty-five percent of the can's total weight. 盖子占罐子总重的 25%。

□ consolation □ consolidation □ consortium □ constant □ constantly □ constituent □ constitute

constitution* [ˌkɒnstɪˈtjuːʃn]

n. 宪法，章程；体质，体格；组成，形成

例 Many people are concerned that such an emphasis on humanity's genetic *constitution* may distort our sense of values. 许多人担心，对人类基因组成如此重视可能会歪曲我们的价值观。

constrain [kənˈstreɪn]

vt. 迫使；约束

记 词根记忆：con（表加强）+ strain（拉紧）→ 约束

例 The evidence was so compelling that he felt *constrained* to accept it. 证据是那样的令人折服，他觉得不得不接受。

派 constraint（n. 限制，约束）

construct*

[kənˈstrʌkt] vt. 建造；构思，构筑；创立 [ˈkɒnstrʌkt] n. 构想，观念

记 词根记忆：con（表加强）+ struct（建立）→ 建造；构筑

搭 construct a model 制作模型；construct an argument 建立论点

例 This anticipation is *constructed* through films, TV and literature. 这一预想通过电影、电视和文学得以构思成形。

construction [kənˈstrʌkʃn]

n. 建造；建筑物；构造

例 They spent years completing the *construction* of the new airport. 他们花了数年的时间才建成新机场。

consulate* [ˈkɒnsjələt]

n. 领事馆；领事职位，领事任期

例 Peter's father used to be a consul worked in the American *consulate* in China. 彼得的父亲曾经是一名领事，在美国驻中国领事馆工作。

consult [kənˈsʌlt]

v. 请教；查阅；商议

记 联想记忆：不顾侮辱（insult），不耻请教（consult）

例 You do not need to *consult* your doctor immediately if the tablets give you a side-effect. 如果药片对你产生副作用，你不必立即请医生诊治。

派 consultation（n. 请教；咨询）

consultant* [kənˈsʌltənt]

n. 顾问；专科医生

记 联想记忆：consult（请教；查阅）+ ant（表人）→ 供咨询的人 → 顾问

搭 school consultant 校方顾问；legal consultant 司法顾问；study abroad consultant 留学顾问

例 Marketing *consultants* have been gathering information about customers' shopping habits. 市场顾问一直在收集有关消费者购物习惯的资料。

consumer [kənˈsjuːmə(r)]

n. 消费者；用户

例 Many *consumers* feel that government and business have taken on the environmental agenda. 许多消费者认为政府和商家已经将环保提上了日程。

派 consumerism（n. 消费主义）

consumption [kənˈsʌmpʃn]

n. 消耗（量）；消费（量）

记 词根记忆：con（共同；完全）+ sumpt（使用）+ ion → 消耗；消费

搭 consumption pattern 消费模式；consumption of electricity 耗电量

例 Fuel *consumption* and exhaust emissions depend on which cars are preferred and how they are driven. 耗油量和排气量取决于用户偏爱的车型及其驾驶方式。

☐ constitution ☑ constrain ☐ construct ☐ construction ☐ consulate ☐ consult
☐ consultant ☐ consumer ☐ consumption

contact* [ˈkɒntækt]	*n.* 接触；联系 *vt.* 与…取得联系，联络 记 词根记忆：con(共同) + tact(接触) → 接触 搭 contact list 联系人清单；eye contact 目光交流；in contact with sb. 与某人保持联系；come into contact with sb. 接触某人；contact lens 隐形眼镜 例 For further details, ***contact*** Mr. Smith, please. 欲知详情，请与史密斯先生联系。
contain* [kənˈteɪn]	*vt.* 包含，容纳，装有；控制，阻止，遏制 记 词根记忆：con(共同) + tain(拿住) → 全部拿住 → 包含 搭 contain oneself 自制 例 It is traditionally accepted that children's books should ***contain*** a few pictures. 从传统意义上来说，人们普遍认为儿童读物中应该配有一些插图。 派 container(*n.* 容器)

Trouble is only opportunity in work clothes.
困难只是穿上工作服的机遇。
——美国实业家 凯泽(H. J. Kaiser, American businessman)

Word List 11

音 频

词根、词缀预习表

tempor	时间	contemporary *a.* 同时间的	**text**	编织	context *n.* 上下文
ting	触摸	contingency *n.* 可能性	**tract**	拉，拽	contract *n.* 契约，合同
dict	说话；断言	contradict *v.* 反驳	**st**	站	contrast *n./v.* 对比；对照
tribut	给予	contribute *v.* 捐赠，捐助	**ve**	走	contrived *a.* 不自然的
contro-	反	controversy *n.* 争论，辩论	**ven**	来	convenience *n.* 便利设施

contaminant *
[kən'tæmɪnənt]

n. 致污物，污染物
搭 biological contaminant 生物污染物
例 Before shipment we have to make sure that all equipment is clean and free of *contaminants*. 装船之前我们需要确定所有的设备都是整洁的、未受到污染的。

contaminate
[kən'tæmɪneɪt]

vt. 污染
搭 a contaminated river 被污染的河流
例 Chemical fertilisers and pesticides may *contaminate* water supplies. 化肥和杀虫剂可能会污染水源。
同 taint(*vt.* 污染，玷污)；pollute(*vt.* 弄脏，污染)；defile(*vt.* 弄脏，污损)

contemplate
['kɒntəmpleɪt]

v. 思量，沉思；注视，凝视；打算，预期
记 联想记忆：con + templ(看作 temple，庙) + ate → 庙里的和尚常常打坐→ 思量，沉思
例 In order to compete in the world market, we *contemplate* improving our present product. 为了参与国际市场的竞争，我们打算改进现有产品。
派 contemplative(*a.* 沉思的，深思熟虑的)
同 consider(*v.* 考虑；认为)；ponder(*v.* 沉思，考虑)

contemporary
[kən'tempərəri]

a. 当代的；同时代的 *n.* 同代人
记 词根记忆：con(共同) + tempor(时间) + ary → 同时代的
例 Some *contemporary* tribes still live among the earthworks of earlier cultures. 当代一些部落仍生活于早期文明的建筑之中。
同 modern(*a.* 近代的，现代的)；current(*a.* 当前的；现在的)

□ contaminant □ contaminate □ contemplate □ contemporary

contempt [kən'tempt]	*n.* 轻视，鄙视，不尊重；蔑视 记 词根记忆：con(共同)+tempt(尝试)→小意思！大家都能试→轻视 例 The officer's tone of voice towards the stowaway was loaded with *contempt*. 警官对偷渡者说话的语气充满了轻蔑。 同 disdain(*n.* 轻蔑)
content*	['kɒntent] *n.* 内容；满意 [kən'tent] *vt.* 使满意 *a.* 满意的 记 词根记忆：con(全部)+tent(拥有)→全部都拥有→满意的 搭 be content with 对…感到满足、满意；table of contents 目录 例 The meeting leader concerns himself with the *content* of the meeting. 会议的主办者本人很关心会议的内容。
context ['kɒntekst]	*n.* 上下文；背景；环境 记 词根记忆：con(共同)+text(编织)→共同编织在一起→上下文 例 You can guess the meaning of the word from the *context*. 你可以根据上下文猜出这个词的意思。 派 contextual(*a.* 根据上下文的)
continent ['kɒntɪnənt]	*n.* 大陆，陆地；洲 例 Australia is a dry *continent*, second only to Antarctic in its lack of rainfall. 澳洲大陆很干燥，降水量之少仅次于南极洲，位居世界第二。
continental* [ˌkɒntɪ'nentl]	*a.* 欧洲大陆的；大陆性的 *n.* 欧洲大陆人 例 The company grew rapidly and has been providing holidays in *continental* Europe for the last fifteen years. 公司发展迅速，在过去 15 年里一直为员工提供去欧洲大陆度假的机会。
contingency* [kən'tɪndʒənsi]	*n.* 偶然性，可能性；意外事件；附带事件 记 词根记忆：con+ting(触摸)+ency→触摸引起的→可能性 例 The extra people can cover *contingencies*, such as when crises take people away from the workplace. 编外人员可以弥补紧急事件所造成的职位空缺，比如当危急事件使得人们离开工作岗位的时候。
continually [kən'tɪnjuəli]	*ad.* 连续地，持续地 例 The diver was *continually* fascinated by the beauty of the sea. 潜水者一直陶醉于大海的美丽。
continuity [ˌkɒntɪ'njuːəti]	*n.* 连续(性)；持续(性) 记 联想记忆：continu(=continue 连续)+ity→连续(性) 例 This country took steps to enhance its *continuity* of government operation. 该国采取了措施来加强政府运作的连续性。
continuous [kən'tɪnjuəs]	*a.* 连续的，不断的 记 来自 continue(*v.* 连续) 搭 continuous flow 持续气流；continuous performance cinema 循环场电影院 例 There's a *continuous* video showing today about the voyages of Captain Cook. 今日将连续放映有关库克船长航海的录像。 派 continuously(*ad.* 不断地，连续地)

□ contempt □ content □ context □ continent □ continental □ contingency
□ continually □ continuity □ continuous

contract* ['kɒntrækt] *n.* 契约，合同 [kən'trækt] *v.* 缩小；签约

记 词根记忆：con(共同) + tract(拉，拽) → 将双方拉到一起 → 契约，合同

例 Both sides should abide by the *contract*. 双方都应该遵守合同。

contradict [ˌkɒntrə'dɪkt]

v. 反驳，驳斥；与…发生矛盾；相抵触

记 词根记忆：contra(反) + dict(说话；断言) → 说反话 → 反驳

例 The statement *contradicts* the writer's views. 这一陈述与作者的观点不符。

同 deny(*vt.* 驳斥，反对)

11

contradiction [ˌkɒntrə'dɪkʃn]

n. 矛盾，不一致；否认，反驳

记 词根记忆：contra(反) + dict(说话；断言) + ion → 反着说 → 否认，反驳

例 It is a *contradiction* that what you said just now is not consistent with what you said one year before. 你刚说的话与一年前说的话不符，真是自相矛盾。

contrary ['kɒntrəri]

a. 相反的 *n.* 相反

记 词根记忆：contra(反) + ry → 相反的；相反

搭 to the contrary 反之，正相反；on the contrary 反之，正相反；contrary to 与…相反；quite the contrary 恰恰相反；contrary opinions 相反的观点

例 *Contrary* to what you might imagine, the size of the cycle is not determined by the size of the wheels, but by the size of the frame. 与你可能想象的相反，自行车的大小不是由车轮的尺寸决定的，而是由车架的大小决定的。

contrast ['kɒntrɑːst] *n.* 对比；对照 [kən'trɑːst] *v.* 对比；对照；形成对比

记 词根记忆：contra(反) + st(=stand 站立) → 反着站 → 对比；对照

搭 by contrast 对比之下；(与…)相对照；in contrast with/to 与…形成对比；contrast A with B 把 A 与 B 进行对比

例 This white peak *contrasts* finely with the blue sky. 这座雪白的山峰同蔚蓝的天空交相辉映。

contribute [kən'trɪbjuːt; 'kɒntrɪbjuːt]

v. 捐赠，捐助；起作用，影响

记 词根记忆：con(全部) + tribut(给予) + e → 无偿给予 → 捐赠，捐助

搭 contribute to 有助于；捐助，贡献；a contributing factor 起作用的因素

例 Industrial emissions and automobile exhausts *contribute* to high pollution. 工业排放物和汽车尾气共同造成了重污染。

派 contribution(*n.* 作用，影响)；contributor(*n.* 促成因素)

contrive [kən'traɪv]

v. 计划，图谋；设计；发明

记 联想记忆：contri(看作contra，反) + ve(=vene走) → (和普通人不同)反着走 → 设计，发明

例 She finds it more difficult to *contrive* to live as prices are rising every month. 物价每月都在上涨，她觉得越来越难维持生计了。

同 devise(*vt.* 设计，发明)；plan(*v.* 计划，设计)；manage(*v.* 管理；设法做到)

contrived* [kən'traɪvd]

a. 不自然的；人为的

记 词根记忆：contri(看作contra，反) + ve(=vene走) + d → 故意反着走 → 不自然的；人为的

例 The story is really touching, but the ending is rather *contrived*. 这个故事确实感人，但结尾颇有斧凿之嫌。

controversial* [ˌkɒntrə'vɜːʃl]

a. 争论的

记 词根记忆：contro(反) + vers(转) + ial → 反着转 → 争论的

例 The appearance of individual buildings is often *controversial*. 私人建筑的外观常常会引起争议。

controversy* ['kɒntrəvɜːsi; kən'trɒvəsi]

n. 争论，辩论，论战

记 词根记忆：contro(反) + vers(转) + y → 因反对而转向另一方 → 争论，辩论

例 There exists a *controversy* over a plan for new teaching building. 建造新教学楼的计划存在争议。

controversy

convection [kən'vekʃn]

n. 传送；对流

例 The flow, thought to be in the form of *convection* currents, is powerful enough to fracture the "eggshell" of the crust into plates. 这股水流，人们认为其呈对流的形式，其能量足以将地壳表面如"蛋壳"的坚硬物质冲破成板块。

convenience [kən'viːniəns]

n. 方便；便利设施

记 词根记忆：con(共同) + ven(来) + ience → 共同行动来维护便民设施 → 便利设施

搭 convenience food/store 便利食品/商店；at sb.'s convenience 在方便时；在适宜的地点

例 The newly-built apartment building provides gas, electricity and other modern *conveniences*. 这幢新盖的公寓大楼提供煤气、电以及其他一些现代化便利设施。

派 inconvenience(*n.* 麻烦，不方便)

convenient* [kən'viːniənt]

a. 方便的，便利的；适宜的

记 发音记忆："肯为你的" → 肯为你提供方便的 → 方便的

搭 be convenient for... 对…来说方便；be convenient to do 方便做…

例 Cars easily surpass trains or buses as a flexible and *convenient* mode of personal transport. 小汽车轻而易举地就超过火车及公共汽车，成为一种灵活便捷的个人交通工具。

□ contrive □ contrived □ controversial □ controversy □ convection □ convenience □ convenient

convention* [kən'venʃn]

n. 大会，会议；惯例，常规，习俗；公约，协定

记 词根记忆：con(共同) + vent(来) + ion → 大家共同来到 → 大会，会议

搭 social conventions 社会习俗

例 The city's *convention* center is also a famous landmark in the country. 该市的会议中心也是这个国家的一个著名地标。

conventional* [kən'venʃənl]

a. 普通的，习惯的；常规的，因循守旧的，传统的

搭 conventional food 普通食物；conventional crime 传统性犯罪；conventional value 传统价值

例 Most people prefer *conventional* housing now. 现在很多人偏爱传统式的住宅。

派 conventionally(*ad.* 按照惯例地)；unconventional(*a.* 非传统的)

conversation* [ˌkɒnvə'seɪʃn]

n. 会话，谈话

记 来自 converse(*vi.* 交谈，谈话)

例 The *conversation* between the new students touched on many new subjects. 新同学之间的对话涉及很多新话题。

派 conversational(*a.* 适于交谈的)

converse

[kən'vɜːs] *vi.* 谈话，会谈 ['kɒnvɜːs] *a.* 逆向的 *n.* 相反的事物；反面

记 词根记忆：con + vers(转) + e → 一起转向→ 交谈，会谈

例 The *converse* was also found to be true. 反之同样成立。

conversely ['kɒnvɜːsli]

ad. 相反地，颠倒地

记 词根记忆：con + vers(转) + e + ly → 转过去 → 相反地，颠倒地

例 *Conversely*, achievements in applied science and technology often play a direct stimulus to the development of pure science. 相反，应用科学技术的成果通常可以直接促进纯科学的发展。

conversion [kən'vɜːʃn]

n. 转化；转变，变换；兑换；改变信仰，皈依

记 词根记忆：con + vers(转) + ion → 转化；转变

例 Clean coal is another avenue for improving fuel *conversion* efficiency. 洁净煤是提高燃烧效率的另一种途径。

convert [kən'vɜːt]

v. (使)改变信仰，皈依；(使)转变，(使)转化；改装

记 词根记忆：con(完全地) + vert(转) → 完全转变 → (使)转变，(使)转化

搭 convert to/into 把…转化为…

例 The original house was *converted* into a residential college. 原来的房子被改建成一所寄宿学院。

convey* [kən'veɪ]

vt. 传送，运送；表达，传递

记 词根记忆：con + vey(搬运) → 传送，运送

搭 convey a message 传递信息

例 His poem *conveyed* a sense of sorrow. 他的诗表达了一种悲伤的情感。

派 conveyance(*n.* 传送，运送；运载工具)

conviction* [kən'vɪkʃn]

n. 定罪；坚信，确信

例 The information led to the *conviction* of those who were found guilty of treason. 这些资料足以给那些叛国者定罪。

□ convention □ conventional □ conversation □ converse □ conversely □ conversion
□ convert □ convey □ conviction

convince* [kən'vɪns]	*vt.* (使)确信；说服 记 词根记忆：con(完全)+vinc(征服，克服)+e → 彻底征服对方 → 说服 搭 convince sb. to do sth. 说服某人做某事；be convinced of 确信，承认；be convinced that 确信，承认；convince sb. of 使某人承认，使某人信服 例 Men try to *convince* employers that any shortcomings they have will not prevent them from doing a good job. 男人们努力让雇主相信，他们身上的任何缺点都不会妨碍他们做好工作。 派 convincing(*a.* 有说服力的，令人信服的)
cookery* ['kʊkəri]	*n.* 烹调法 记 联想记忆：cook(烹调)+ery → 烹调法 搭 cookery book 烹调书，食谱 例 I took a month' s *cookery* course at a local college last year. 去年，我在当地的一所学院学习了一个月的烹调课程。
cooperate [kəʊ'ɒpəreɪt]	*vi.* 合作，协作 记 词根记忆：co(共同)+oper(工作)+ate → 一起工作 → 合作，协作 搭 cooperate with (sb.) in (sth.) 和(某人)合作(某事) 例 It is meaningful for world nations to *cooperate* with each other. 对世界各国来说，相互合作的意义重大。
cooperation* [kəʊˌɒpə'reɪʃn]	*n.* 合作，协作；配合 例 The President's visit promoted the *cooperation* between the two countries. 总统的访问促进了两国间的合作。
cooperative* [kəʊ'ɒpərətɪv]	*a.* 合作的，协作的 *n.* 合作社 搭 cooperative enterprises 合作企业；make a cooperative effort 共同努力 例 The members in the club are very *cooperative*. 这个俱乐部的成员都非常合作。 派 uncooperative(*a.* 不合作的，不配合的)
coordinate	[kəʊ'ɔːdɪneɪt] *v.* 调整，协调 [kəʊ'ɔːdɪnət] *n.* 同等者，同等物 *a.* 同等的，并列的 记 词根记忆：co(共同)+ordin(顺序)+ate(使…) → 使…顺序一致 → 协调 例 The Makete Integrated Rural Transport Project started in 1985 with financial support from the Swiss Development Corporation and was *coordinated* with the help of the Tanzanian government. 玛科特农村综合交通项目自1985年启动，由瑞士发展公司提供资金支持，在坦桑尼亚政府的协调下进行。// There are around 1,000 zoos capable of participating in *coordinated* conservation programmes. 约有1000家动物园有能力加入这些协作保护计划。
coordinator* [kəʊ'ɔːdɪneɪtə(r)]	*n.* 协调者 记 来自 coordinate(*v.* 调整，协调) 例 He worked in the government as an Economic Development *Coordinator*. 他在政府工作，是一名经济发展协调员。

□ convince □ cookery □ cooperate □ cooperation □ cooperative □ coordinate □ coordinator

cope* [kəʊp]

vi. (成功地)应付；(妥善地)处理

搭 cope with 处理；应付

例 Books are available to help employees *cope* with stress. 书籍有助于员工应对压力。

coral [ˈkɒrəl]

n. 珊瑚；珊瑚虫 *a.* 珊瑚色的，红色的

搭 coral reefs 珊瑚礁

例 According to the research, with a big requirement of decoration, there is a falling number of *coral* in deep ocean in recent years. 据调查，由于装饰品的大量需求，近几年深海珊瑚数量锐减。

cord* [kɔːd]

n. 线；带

记 本身为词根，意为"心"→ 线；带

例 This process could be speeded up by wrapping a *cord* around the drill and pulling on each end. 这个过程可以通过拉缠绕在钻头两端的线来加快速度。

core [kɔː(r)]

n. 果心，果核；(物体的)中心部分；核心，要点，精髓 *vt.* 去掉核

记 词根记忆：cor(心) + e → 果心，果核；核心

搭 to the core 十足，彻底地

例 Any profit company's *core* is trying to transform its product into capital. 任何营利性公司的核心都是要将其产品转化为资本。

cork [kɔːk]

n. 软木塞 *vt.* 用软木塞塞住

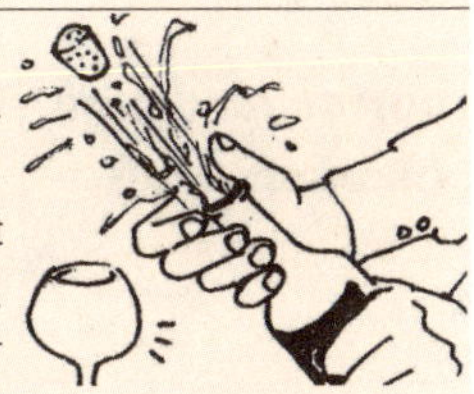

记 发音记忆："犒客"→ 犒劳客人 → 打开酒(瓶上的软木塞)犒劳客人 → 软木塞

例 When a volcano erupts, the shattered summit is ejected like a *cork* from a shaken soda bottle. 火山喷发时，被炸碎的山峰喷射而出，就像是装有汽水的瓶子经过摇晃，上面的软木塞被顶飞出去一样。

派 corkage(*n.* 开瓶费)

corporal [ˈkɔːpərəl]

a. 肉体的，身体的 *n.* (陆军或空军)下士

记 词根记忆：corp(身体) + or + al → 身体的

例 Some claim that teachers have no rights to treat naughty students with *corporal* punishment, while others hold an opposite opinion. 一些人声称教师无权体罚顽皮的学生，而另一些人持相反观点。

corporate* [ˈkɔːpərət]

a. 团体的，共同的；法人的，公司的

记 词根记忆：corp(身体) + or + ate → 团体的

搭 corporate crime 法人犯罪；corporate loan 公司贷款；corporate body 法人团体

例 From uniforms and workwear emerged *corporate* clothing. 在制服和劳动服的基础上出现了工作装。

派 corporation(*n.* 公司；法人)

□ cope □ coral □ cord □ core □ cork □ corporal
□ corporate

corps *
[kɔː(r)]

n. 部队；军团

记 联想记忆：和 cops(警察)一起记，两者都是国家的防卫力量

例 The leaders had built up a *corps* of rocketers and used rockets successfully against the British in the late eighteenth century. 这些领导人组建了火箭部队，并在 18 世纪末成功地用火箭打败了英国人。

corpus *
[ˈkɔːpəs]

n. 文集，文献，汇编；语料库

记 词根记忆：corp(身体) + us → 知识体 → 文集，汇编；语料库

例 We have an existing written *corpus* of language learning materials in the library. 图书馆里有关于语言学习的现成的书面资料。

correlation
[ˌkɒrəˈleɪʃn]

n. 相互关系，相关(性)

记 联想记忆：cor(共同) + relation(关系) → 相互关系

例 There's a high *correlation* between trace element selenium insufficient and functional disease. 微量元素硒不足和官能性疾病有着紧密的联系。

correspond *
[ˌkɒrəˈspɒnd]

vi. 相一致，符合；通信；相当于，相应

记 词根记忆：cor(共同) + re(又，再) + spond(回答，约定) → 又作出相同的反应 → 相一致，符合

搭 correspond to 符合；相当于；correspond with 相一致；与…通信

例 This person's characteristics *correspond* with the witness' description. 这个人的特征与证人的描述相符。

派 corresponding(*a.* 相应的)

correspondence *
[ˌkɒrəˈspɒndəns]

n. 通信，信件；符合，一致；对应

搭 keep correspondence with sb. 与某人保持通信；commercial correspondence 商业信函

例 I have kept *correspondence* with my former classmates. 我一直和以前的同学保持通信。

corridor
[ˈkɒrɪdɔː(r)]

n. 过道，走廊

搭 in the corridor 在走廊里

例 You will notice that at the end of each *corridor* there is another door, but these are fire doors. 你会注意到在每一条走廊的尽头都有另一扇门，但这些是防火门。

corrode *
[kəˈrəʊd]

v. 腐蚀；侵蚀

记 词根记忆：cor(表加强) + rod(咬) + e → 用力咬掉 → 腐蚀；侵蚀

例 Acid rain can *corrode* metal and stone work. 酸雨能腐蚀金属制品和石头制品。

corrupt
[kəˈrʌpt]

v. 腐化，腐蚀；使堕落；破坏，损坏；(计算机文件等)出错 *a.* 堕落的，腐化的；腐败的，贪污的

记 词根记忆：cor(表加强) + rupt(断裂) → 完全断裂 → 腐化，腐蚀

例 People are usually annoyed by the sudden incident that the data on the hard drive of their computers is *corrupted* by the power cut. 电脑硬盘驱动器上的数据因断电而损坏，这类突发事件常常让人很恼怒。

□ corps □ corpus □ correlation □ correspond □ correspondence □ corridor
□ corrode □ corrupt

cosmic* [ˈkɒzmɪk]	*a.* 宇宙的 记 词根记忆：cosm(宇宙)+ic(形容词后缀)→宇宙的 搭 cosmic dust 宇宙尘埃 例 The surface of Earth contains tons of *cosmic* dust. 地球表面存有大量的宇宙尘埃。
cosmopolitan* [ˌkɒzməˈpɒlɪtən]	*a.* 世界性的，全球的 *n.* 世界主义者；四海为家者 记 词根记忆：cosmo(世界，宇宙)+polit(城市)+an→世界城→世界性的；世界主义者 例 A port will make a city *cosmopolitan*. 港口会让一座城市走向世界。
cosset* [ˈkɒsɪt]	*vt.* 宠爱，溺爱 *n.* 宠儿 记 联想记忆：cos(看作 cost，花费)+set(固定)→每天固定花一大笔钱为某人买礼物→宠爱，溺爱 例 Tom is one who *cossets* his health. 汤姆是个悉心保养身体的人。
costume [ˈkɒstjuːm]	*n.* 戏装；(特定场合穿的)成套服装 记 联想记忆：cost(花费)+u(你)+me(我)→你我都免不了花钱买服装→成套服装 例 Mom told me that she had a ballet *costume*. 妈妈告诉我她有一套芭蕾舞服。
cosy [ˈkəʊzi]	*a.* 舒适的，安逸的 例 Learning in a warm and *cosy* classroom is the best dream these children in impoverished mountainous district have wished. 能够在温暖舒适的教室里学习是贫困山区孩子们最大的愿望。
council* [ˈkaʊnsl]	*n.* 理事会，委员会 记 Security Council 联合国安理会 例 The *Council* may convoke a formal conference. 理事会可能会召开一次正式会议。
counsel [ˈkaʊnsl]	*n.* 律师，法律顾问；建议，忠告 *v.* 商议，劝告 记 联想记忆：coun(看作 court，法庭)+sel(看作 sell，卖)→在法庭上卖弄技巧的人→律师 例 Today's Health *Counsel* is presented by Paula Clayburg. 今天的健康忠告由波拉·克莱伯格讲解。
counsellor* [ˈkaʊnsələ(r)]	*n.* 顾问，辅导顾问 例 Paula Clayburg is the chief *counsellor* at Liverpool's famous pain clinic. 保拉·克莱伯格是利物浦一家著名止痛诊所的首席顾问。
counter* [ˈkaʊntə(r)]	*n.* 柜台 *ad.* 相反地 记 联想记忆：与 count(*v.* 计算)一起记 搭 under the counter (商品销售)秘密地，暗地里，非法地 例 The government's plans run *counter* to agreed European policy on this issue. 政府的计划与欧洲在该问题上的既定政策相悖。

□ cosmic □ cosmopolitan □ cosset □ costume □ cosy □ council
□ counsel □ counsellor □ counter

counterpart * [ˈkaʊntəpɑːt]	*n.* 与对方地位相当的人；配对物；副本 记 组合词：counter(相反) + part(部分) → 配对物 例 Researchers say that when women apply for positions they tend to be better qualified than their male *counterparts*. 研究人员声称，女性在申请职位时往往比男性竞争者更具实力。
counterproductive [ˌkaʊntəprəˈdʌktɪv]	*a.* 产生相反效果的，适得其反的 记 联想记忆：counter(相反) + productive(有成效的) → 产生相反效果的 例 This phenomenon can be partly attributed to the common *counterproductive* approach to study, but it also simply reflects the way the brain functions. 这种现象可以部分归因于普通反作用的研究方法，但它也简单地反映出大脑的活动方式。
county * [ˈkaʊnti]	*n.* 郡，县 记 联想记忆：一个国家(country)里有很多县(county) 例 Research being conducted in two *counties* of Southern California is reaching similar conclusions. 在南加州两个县开展的研究得出了相似的结论。
couple * [ˈkʌpl]	*n.* (一)对，(一)双；夫妇 *v.* 连接，联合，结合；结婚 搭 a couple of 两个；几个 例 There are a *couple* of books I'd like you to look at. 有几本书我想让你读一读。
coupon [ˈkuːpɒn]	*n.* 优惠券；票证；配给券；参赛表，订货单 记 联想记忆：co(共同) + upon(在…上) → 商家联合在节假日打折的基础上还发放优惠券 → 优惠券 例 Please fill out the attached *coupon*. 请把附上的参赛表填写好。
courageous * [kəˈreɪdʒəs]	*a.* 勇敢的，有胆量的 记 联想记忆：courage(勇气) + ous(形容词后缀) → 有勇气的 → 勇敢的，有胆量的 例 The message behind a half handshake is that "I'm not a strong or *courageous* person." 握手时只握住手指，其暗含的信息是："我不是强者或有胆量的人。"
course * [kɔːs]	*n.* 过程，进程；路线，方针；跑道；课程 *v.* 追猎；运行；流动 搭 in the course of 在…过程中，在…期间；of course 当然，自然，无疑；beginning courses 初级课程；a basic course 基础课；course code 课程编号 例 You can sign up for this training *course* in advance. 你可以提前报名参加这门培训课程。
courtship [ˈkɔːtʃɪp]	*n.* 求爱或追求；求爱期，追求期 例 This contact may help to maintain order within a group, and stroking or touching are part of the *courtship* ritual in most species. 这种接触也许有助于维持一个群体里的秩序，而在大多数物种中，抚摸或接触是求爱仪式中的一部分。

□ counterpart □ counterproductive □ county □ couple □ coupon □ courageous
□ course □ courtship

cover
[ˈkʌvə(r)]

vt. 盖，覆盖；包含，包括；走过(一段路)；适用于；报道，采访；给…上保险，足够支付；用枪掩护 *n.* 盖子，套子；封面；掩蔽(物)，掩护(物)

搭 cover all the bases 考虑周全，面面俱到；cover over/up （完全）遮住，盖住；the front/back cover 封面/封底；under (the) cover of 在…的掩护下

例 The study *covered* 500 employees in four large companies. 这次研究的对象涉及四家大公司的500名雇员。

If you would go up high, then use your own legs! Do not let yourselves carried aloft; do not seat yourselves on other people's backs and heads.

如果你想要走到高处，就要使用自己的两条腿！不要让别人把你抬到高处；不要坐在别人的背上和头上。

——德国哲学家 尼采(F. W. Nietzsche, German philosopher)

Word List 12

音频

词根、词缀预习表

cred	相信	credential *n.* 证明书	**crim**	罪行	crime *n.* 罪行；犯罪
cri	判断	critic *n.* 批评家	**cruc**	十字形，交叉	crucial *a.* 决定性的
crus	十字	crusade *n.* 十字军	**rud**	天然的	crude *a.* 天然的
culmin	顶	culminate *vi.* 告终；结束	**cult**	种植；培养	cultivate *vt.* 种植；培养
cur	治疗	curative *a.* 有疗效的	**tail**	切割	curtail *vt.* 缩短，削减

coverage [ˈkʌvərɪdʒ]

n. 新闻报道；覆盖范围

记 联想记忆：cover（覆盖）+ age（集体名词后缀）→ 覆盖范围

搭 tonight's live coverage of the basketball game 今晚篮球比赛的现场直播

例 We all watch for live *coverage* of the results of the bombing trial. 我们都等着看这起爆炸审判结果的现场报道。

同 scope（*n.* 范围）

crack [kræk]

n. 裂缝，缝隙；爆裂声 *v.* （使）破裂；（使）发出爆裂声；重击；崩溃，瓦解

搭 at the crack of dawn 黎明，破晓；crack up（身体或精神等）崩溃；crack down on 镇压

例 Viscous lava, accompanied by burning clouds of ash and gas, welled out of the volcano from *cracks* in its flanks. 黏稠的岩浆夹杂着燃烧的火山灰和气团，从火山侧面的裂缝中喷涌而出。

craft* [krɑːft]

n. 工艺，手艺；船；航空器

记 联想记忆：c + raft（筏）→ 筏也就是船 → 船

例 This region is a diverse agricultural area, rich in historic sites, arts and *crafts*. 该地区为多种农作物种植带，且具有众多的历史遗址，艺术形式丰富，手工艺发达。

派 craftsman（*n.* 工匠，手艺人）

crank* [kræŋk]

n. 曲柄，曲轴 *vt.* 用曲柄转动某物

例 That gear is connected to a *crank* which changes the motion. 那个传动装置与一个能改变运动方式的曲柄连接在一起。

crash [kræʃ]	*v.* 碰撞；冲，闯；倒下，坠落；发出撞击(或爆裂)声；垮台，破产 *n.* 碰撞；坠落，坠毁；破裂声，撞击声 *a.* 速成的 记 联想记忆：卡车撞上（crash）路边的一堆垃圾（trash） 搭 crash into 闯入；碰撞；crash out (of sth.) 被淘汰；a crash course 速成课程 例 The two cars *crashed* into each other. 两辆汽车猛烈相撞。 
crater [ˈkreɪtə(r)]	*n.* 火山口；坑 例 After the volcano erupted, lava domes formed inside the new *crater*, and have periodically burst. 火山喷发后，新形成的火山口内部会形成熔岩穹丘，这些熔岩穹丘会周期性地爆发。 
crawl* [krɔːl]	*vi.* 爬，爬行；缓慢行进 *n.* 缓慢(或费力)的行进；自由泳 记 联想记忆：c + raw(生疏的) + l → 对地形生疏，车要开得慢一点 → 缓慢行进 搭 be crawling with sth. 挤满，爬满 例 To prevent the queen from *crawling* up to the top and laying eggs, a screen can be inserted between the brood chamber and the supers. 为了防止蜂王爬到顶部产卵，可在蜂箱育卵室和蜂房上层之间插入一块隔板。
create* [kriˈeɪt]	*vt.* 创造，创作；产生 例 The economic recovery *created* more jobs. 经济复苏带来了更多的工作机会。
creation* [kriˈeɪʃn]	*n.* 创造；作品 记 联想记忆：creat(e)(创造) + ion → 创造 例 The very first fire-*creation* methods involved the use of friction. 最早的取火方法都离不开摩擦。 派 recreation(*n.* 消遣)
creative* [kriˈeɪtɪv]	*a.* 创造性的；创作的 搭 creative thinking 创造性思维 例 We give this system to save children the trouble of developing these *creative* skills. 我们提供这套系统，为孩子们省去了发展这些创造性技巧的麻烦。
credential [krəˈdenʃl]	*n.* 证明书；(学历、资历)资格证书；证件 记 词根记忆：cred(相信) + ential → 让人相信的东西 → 证明书 例 Refused by the enterprise again, she was so upset that she tore up these *credential* documents by hand. 再次被企业拒之门外，她极其沮丧，随手将这些资格证书撕个粉碎。

12

□ crash □ crater □ crawl □ create □ creation □ creative
□ credential

credibility [ˌkredəˈbɪləti]

n. 可信性，可靠性

记 词根记忆：cred(相信) + ibility(可…性) → 可信性，可靠性

例 *Credibility* is an essential characteristic that is built on the elements of integrity, reliability, veracity, competence and commitment. 诚信是一个重要的特征，是建立在正直、可靠、诚实、能力和承诺的基础之上的。

credible [ˈkredəbl]

a. 可信的，可靠的

记 词根记忆：cred(相信) + ible(可…的) → 可信的

例 This witness presented *credible* information to convict the defendant. 这个证人提供了可靠的证据，证明被告有罪。

反 incredible(*a.* 难以置信的)

credit* [ˈkredɪt]

vt. 记入贷方；把…归于 *n.* 信用贷款，赊欠；信任，相信；贷方；荣誉，名望；光荣，功劳；学分

记 词根记忆：cred(相信) + it → 信任，相信

搭 payment by credit card 信用卡支付；give...credit for 因…而称赞…credit limit 信贷限额；on credit 赊账

例 Most historians *credit* the Chinese with the discovery of gun powder. 大多数历史学家认为是中国人发明了火药。

派 discredit(*vt.* 使丧失信誉，使怀疑)

creep* [kriːp]

vi. 悄悄移动；缓慢行进；爬行

记 联想记忆：兔子偷懒睡觉(sleep)时乌龟继续缓慢行进(creep)

搭 creep in/into 开始发生；creep out of... 从某地悄悄出来

例 I *crept* upstairs so as not to wake up other tenants. 我悄悄地爬上楼，以免吵醒其他房客。

派 creeping(*a.* 逐渐发生的)

crescent* [ˈkresnt]

n. 新月，月牙；新月形(物) *a.* 新月形的

记 联想记忆：cre + scent(香味) → 新月长到满月，月饼飘香 → 新月

例 The *crescent* of a new moon hung over the mulberry in the yard. 一弯新月高悬于院子里的桑树之上。

crew [kruː]

n. 全体船员；工作人员；队，组

记 联想记忆：和 crow(*n.* 乌鸦)一起记

例 The rescue *crew* is still looking for survivors. 救援队仍然在寻找生还者。

cricket* [ˈkrɪkɪt]

n. 板球；蟋蟀

记 联想记忆：花钱买票(ticket)去看板球(cricket)比赛

例 Baseball and *cricket* differ. 棒球和板球不同。

□ credibility □ credible □ credit □ creep □ crescent □ crew
□ cricket

crime* [kraɪm]

n. 罪行；犯罪

记 词根记忆：crim(罪行) + e → 罪行；犯罪

搭 campus crime 校园犯罪；hotel crime 旅馆犯罪；crime rate 犯罪率；commit a crime 犯罪

例 Without the death penalty our lives are less secure and violent *crime* will increase. 如果没有死刑，我们的生命会更不安全，暴力犯罪活动也将增加。

criminal [ˈkrɪmɪnl]

a. 犯罪的；刑事的 *n.* 罪犯

搭 criminal acts 犯罪行为

例 The discontent may lead more youths into *criminal* behavior. 这种不满情绪可能会导致更多的年轻人走上犯罪之路。

crisis* [ˈkraɪsɪs]

n. 危机；紧要关头，关键阶段

记 联想记忆：cri(看作 cry，哭) + sis(看作 sos，求救信号) → 哭喊着求救 → 危机

例 In the US, energy-efficient homes became popular after the oil *crisis* of 1973. 美国在经历了 1973 年的石油危机之后，节能型房屋就变得深受欢迎。

crisp [krɪsp]

a. 脆的；利落的 *n.* [*pl.*] 油炸土豆片

记 发音记忆：该词的发音就像咬薯片的声音

例 The answers from the soldiers are *crisp* and assured. 士兵们的回答干脆而肯定。

△ **criterion** [kraɪˈtɪəriən]

n. 标准，准则

记 词根记忆：cri(判断) + ter + ion → 判断的手段 → 标准，准则

例 Success in studying at school is not an appropriate *criterion* of achievement in life. 在学校里学习好并不是衡量人生成就的一个恰当的标准。

critic [ˈkrɪtɪk]

n. 批评家；爱挑剔的人

记 词根记忆：crit(判断) + ic → 判断是非 → 批评家

搭 a music critic 乐评人

例 The coal industry has been targeted by *critics* as a significant contributor to the greenhouse effect. 煤炭业被评论家指责为造成温室效应的主要原因。

critical* [ˈkrɪtɪkl]

a. 批评的，评论的；危急的，紧要的；临界的；挑剔的

记 词根记忆：crit(判断) + ic + al(形容词后缀) → 作出判断的 → 评论的

搭 be critical of 对…吹毛求疵；critical thoughts 批判性思维；be of critical importance 至关重要；critical point 临界点；a critical period 危险期

例 The strike has been stopped, but the situation is still *critical* at the moment. 罢工虽然停止了，但是当前形势仍很危急。

派 uncritical(*a.* 不加批判的)；critically(*ad.* 危急地；批判地)

criticise [ˈkrɪtɪsaɪz]

v. 批评，非难，责备；评论

例 Citizens have the right to *criticise* the government. 公民有权利批评政府。

12

□ crime □ criminal □ crisis □ crisp □ criterion □ critic
□ critical □ criticise

crockery [ˈkrɒkəri]

n. 陶器；瓦器

记 联想记忆：crock（坛子，瓦罐）+ ery → 陶器；瓦器

例 You'll find all sorts of things in the museums: old suitcases, ***crockery***, first-class cabins decorated in the fashion of the day. 在博物馆里你会看到各式各样的东西：旧衣箱、陶罐以及按当时流行风格装修的头等舱。

crocodile [ˈkrɒkədaɪl]

n. 鳄鱼；鳄鱼皮

例 ***Crocodiles*** are being farmed for their meat. 人们饲养鳄鱼以供食用。

crossword* [ˈkrɒswɜːd]

n. 纵横填字游戏

例 They were good at ***crosswords*** and knew a lot of words. 他们擅长做纵横填字游戏，并熟知大量词汇。

crowded* [ˈkraʊdɪd]

a. 拥挤的；塞满的

记 联想记忆：crowd（人群）+ ed → 拥挤的人群 → 拥挤的

例 We live in an increasingly ***crowded*** and complicated world. 我们生活在一个日益拥挤和复杂的世界里。

crown* [kraʊn]

n. 王冠；花冠；齿冠

记 联想记忆：crow（乌鸦）+ n → 给乌鸦戴王冠 → 王冠

例 Here's a hat that looks like a ***crown***. 这里有顶看起来像王冠的帽子。

crucial [ˈkruːʃl]

a. 决定性的；至关重要的

记 词根记忆：cruc（十字形，交叉）+ ial（形容词后缀）→ 十字路口 → 决定性的，至关重要的

搭 crucial to/for 对…至关重要的；at a crucial time 在关键时刻；a crucial question 关键问题

例 The presence of human beings is ***crucial*** to the survival of the forest. 人类的存在对森林的存活至关重要。

crude [kruːd]

a. 天然的；粗糙的；粗俗的

记 词根记忆：c + rud（天然的）+ e → 天然的

例 The tribesmen still use bows, arrows and ***crude*** digging sticks. 该部落成员依然使用弓箭和粗糙的挖掘棍。

cruel* [ˈkruːəl]

a. 残忍的，残暴的

记 发音记忆："刻肉" → 残忍的，残暴的

搭 be cruel to 对…残忍

例 The anthropologist concluded that the tribesmen were unusually aggressive and ***cruel***. 人类学家得出结论，这个部落的人无比凶残，侵略成性。

cruise [kruːz]

v. 航游，巡航；（出租车、船等）缓慢巡行 *n.* 航游，游弋

记 联想记忆：汤姆·克鲁斯（Tom Cruise）在巡游（cruise）

例 The famous Crocodile ***Cruise*** leaves at 11 a.m. each day. 著名的"鳄鱼"号巡游艇每天上午 11 点出航。

□ crockery □ crocodile □ crossword □ crowded □ crown □ crucial
□ crude □ cruel □ cruise

crusade [kruːˈseɪd]

n. 十字军(远征)；斗争，运动 *v.* 加入十字军，投身正义运动

记 词根记忆：crus(十字形) + ade → 十字军

例 With an attempt to recapture Jerusalem, the First *Crusade* played a very important part in Medieval England. 第一次十字军东征企图再次夺回耶路撒冷，这在中世纪的英国起着重要的作用。

crush* [krʌʃ]

vt. 碾碎；压服，压垮；镇压，制服；压碎，压坏

记 联想记忆：碰撞(crash)后被碾碎(crush)

搭 crush a rebellion 压制反抗；crush sb's hopes 打破某人的愿望；crush up 粉碎

例 Be careful not to *crush* my glasses in the bag. 小心别把我包里的眼镜给压碎了。

crushing [ˈkrʌʃɪŋ]

a. 惨重的，毁灭性的；压倒的，决定性的

例 The atomic bomb attack in Hiroshima during World War II was a *crushing* calamity to Japanese people. 二战期间，在广岛投射的原子弹对日本人民来说是一次毁灭性的灾难。

crust [krʌst]

n. 硬层，硬表面，地壳；(一片)面包皮

记 联想记忆：可与 crush(*v.* 压碎)一起记

例 Tectonic plates are the plates which make up the earth's *crust* and mantle. 构造板块是指构成地球地壳及地幔的板块。

派 crusty(*a.* 有脆皮的；脾气暴躁的)

crystallize [ˈkrɪstəlaɪz]

v. (使)结晶；(使)变明确

例 Sometimes, what we suffered in life is not a totally mess, which might help us to *crystallize* pieces of thoughts. 我们生活中所遭遇的并不一定完全是坏事，有时也可以帮我们总结出一些想法。

cube [kjuːb]

n. 立方形；立方

例 The *cube* of 4 is 64. 4 的立方是 64。

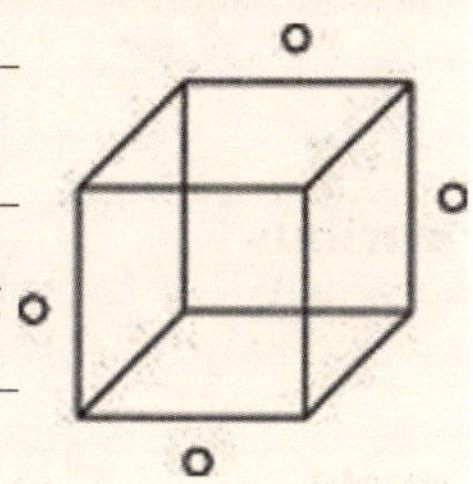

cucumber [ˈkjuːkʌmbə(r)]

n. 黄瓜

例 Eating *cucumber* is good for your health. 吃黄瓜有益健康。

cue [kjuː]

n. 暗示，提示

记 词根记忆：线索(clue)有提示(cue)作用

例 The actor got his *cue* from the director. 那位男演员从导演那里得到了一些提示。

cuisine [kwɪˈziːn]

n. 烹饪；烹调法，烹调风格；菜肴

记 发音记忆："口味新" → 烹饪出新口味 → 烹饪

例 I would choose Chinese *cuisine* compared with French *cuisine*. 比起法国餐，我更喜欢中餐。

culminate* [ˈkʌlmɪneɪt]

vi. (以某种结果)告终；(在某一点)结束

记 词根记忆：culmin(顶) + ate → 达到顶点 → (以某种结果)告终；(在某一点)结束

例 My arguments with my mum got worse and worse, and it all *culminated* in my deciding to give up school. 我和妈妈的争吵越来越严重，最后以我决定辍学而告终。

同 end(*v.* 结束，终结)；terminate(*v.* 停止，结束)；top(*vt.* 达到顶端；结束)

□ crusade □ crush □ crushing □ crust □ crystallize □ cube
□ cucumber □ cue □ cuisine □ culminate

cultivate
[ˈkʌltɪveɪt]

vt. 种植；培养

记 词根记忆：cult（种植；培养）+ ivate → 种植；培养

例 This banana is the first type to be *cultivated* here. 这种香蕉是这里最早种植的品种。

cultivation *
[ˌkʌltɪˈveɪʃn]

n. 耕种，耕作；培养，教育

例 Now, the *cultivation* of crops and the husbandry of livestock can bring great profit. 如今，种植农作物和饲养牲畜能获得丰厚的利润。

cultural *
[ˈkʌltʃərəl]

a. 文化的，人文的

例 The exhibition showed some *cultural* relics of the primeval times. 该展览展出了很多原始时期的文化遗产。

cumulative
[ˈkjuːmjələtɪv]

a. 积累的，渐增的

记 词根记忆：cumul（堆积）+ ative → 积累的，渐增的

搭 a cumulative process 积累的过程

例 The condition appears to result from the *cumulative* effect of a number of factors, with atmospheric pollutants the principal culprits. 这种情况看上去是由大量因素日积月累所导致的，其中大气污染物是罪魁祸首。

curative *
[ˈkjʊərətɪv]

a. 有疗效的；医疗的

记 词根记忆：cur（治疗；关心）+ ative → 有疗效的

curb
[kɜːb]

vt. 控制，抑制，约束 *n.* 路缘，（街道的）镶边石；马勒；起限制作用的事物

例 The effective measure to *curb* the spread of the virus is keeping the computer off. 控制病毒传播最有效的方法就是不开电脑。

curiosity
[ˌkjʊəriˈɒsəti]

n. 好奇，好奇心；稀奇或罕见的事物或人，古玩

记 词根记忆：cur（关心）+ iosity →"家事、国事、天下事，事事关心"→ 好奇心

例 The relentless *curiosity* of scientific researchers brought the forces of nature to light. 科研人员无尽的好奇心是自然力量发现的源泉。

curious *
[ˈkjʊəriəs]

a. 好奇的；奇怪的

搭 be curious about 对…好奇

例 Further observation by astronomers revealed two *curious* facts. 宇航员经过进一步观察发现了两个奇怪的现象。

curly
[ˈkɜːli]

a. 卷曲的，波浪式的

记 联想记忆：curl（使卷曲）+ y → 卷曲的

例 The package was decorated with *curly* ribbon. 包裹用卷丝带装饰了起来。

currency
[ˈkʌrənsi]

n. 货币；通用，流行

搭 paper currency 纸币

例 The paper *currency* of the United States is green and white. 美国的纸币由绿色和白色组成。// Many good words just have no *currency* these days and are useless in conversation. 许多很好的词现在都不太流行，而且交谈中也用不到。

□ cultivate □ cultivation □ cultural □ cumulative □ curative □ curb
□ curiosity □ curious □ curly □ currency

current* [ˈkʌrənt]	*a.* 流通的；流动的；现行的，当前的 *n.* (水、气等的)流动；电流；潮流 搭 the current situation 当前形势；current affairs 时事；air currents 气流；ocean current 洋流；alternating current 交流电 例 I would like to open a *current* account. 我想开一个活期存款账户。
currently [ˈkʌrəntli]	*ad.* 当前，现时，目前 记 联想记忆：current(当前的) + ly(副词后缀) → 当前，现时，目前 例 Fingerprint scanners are *currently* the most widely deployed type of biometric application. 指纹扫描是目前生物测定技术中发展最为迅速的应用项目。
curriculum [kəˈrɪkjələm]	*n.* 课程，(学校等的)全部课程 例 The teacher expects that the *curriculum* will successfully attract students. 老师希望这种课程安排能成功地吸引学生。
curry [ˈkʌri]	*n.* 咖喱，咖喱饭菜 *vt.* 把(肉、蔬菜等)做成咖喱食品；梳刷(马毛等) 搭 curry powder 咖喱粉 例 Which kind of *curry* do you like, mild or peppery? 你喜欢哪种咖喱，微辣的还是辛辣的?
curtail [kɜːˈteɪl]	*vt.* 缩短，削减；剥夺 记 词根记忆：cur(关注) + tail(切割) → 专注地切短 → 缩短，削减 例 The new constitution imposed a dogmatic property rules which had severely *curtailed* the people's interest. 新宪法强制推行专断财产法，严重损害了民众的利益。 同 abridge(*vt.* 缩减，减短)；shorten(*v.* 缩短)
curtain* [ˈkɜːtn]	*n.* 窗帘，门帘 例 The last thing on the list you should buy is the kitchen *curtains*. 清单上你要买的最后一件东西是厨房的窗帘。
cylinder [ˈsɪlɪndə(r)]	*n.* 圆柱体；圆筒；汽缸 搭 brake cylinders 制动圆筒 例 The earliest British rocket was encased in a stout, iron *cylinder*, terminating in a conical head. 英国最老式的火箭装在一个坚固的铁筒内，顶部成圆锥形。
dairy [ˈdeəri]	*n.* 奶制品；乳品店 *a.* 乳制品的 记 联想记忆：每天(daily)吃乳制品(dairy)强壮骨骼 搭 dairy cattle 乳牛；dairy farm 乳牛场 例 Try using low-lactose *dairy* foods, such as yogurt, instead of milk. 尝试用一些低乳的奶制品，如奶酪，来代替牛奶。
damage* [ˈdæmɪdʒ]	*n.* 损害；[*pl.*] 损害赔偿(金) *vt.* 损害 例 Smoking may be doing you quite serious long-term *damage*. 吸烟会给你带来长期、严重的伤害。

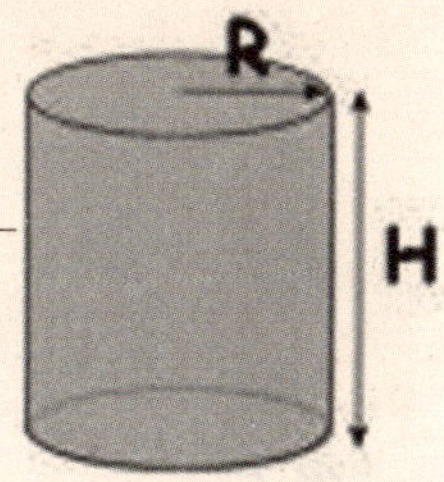

12

□ current □ currently □ curriculum □ curry □ curtail □ curtain
□ cylinder □ dairy □ damage

damp [dæmp]

a. 潮湿的 *n.* 潮湿，湿气 *vt.* 使潮湿；减弱，抑制；(使)沮丧

记 联想记忆：dam(水坝) + p → 水坝上很潮湿 → 潮湿的

搭 damp course 防潮层

例 The ground is very *damp* in the rainforest. 热带雨林的地面非常潮湿。

darkroom [ˈdɑːkrʊm]

n. 暗室

例 Plate cameras were heavy, and required access to a *darkroom* for loading and processing the plates. 感光相机很重，而且还需要一间暗室来装载和处理使用过的底片。

dash [dæʃ]

v. 飞奔，猛冲；猛掷；使破灭，使沮丧 *n.* 飞奔，猛冲；破折号；精力，干劲

记 联想记忆：d + ash(灰尘) → 群马飞奔而过，扬起漫天灰尘 → 飞奔

例 I *dashed* off the letter. 我急急忙忙地把信写完了。

data* [ˈdeɪtə]

n. 数据；资料

记 联想记忆：数据(data)与日(date)更新

例 You have to spend a bit of time making the *data* a lot clearer. 你要花一点时间把这些数据整理得更清晰些。

database [ˈdeɪtəbeɪs]

n. 数据库

记 组合词：data(数据) + base(基础) → 数据库

例 The *database* can help lexicographers to search for a word and find out how frequently it is used. 该数据库能够帮助词典编纂人员搜索单词，了解其使用频率。

daunt* [dɔːnt]

vt. 使气馁，使胆怯

记 联想记忆：d(看作 devil，魔鬼) + aunt(姨妈) → 姨妈被鬼故事吓倒了 → 使胆怯

例 Now, the Semira Mountains are among the highest in the world but you mustn't be too *daunted*, we will mainly be trekking in the foothills only, although there will be spectacular views even in the foothills. 如今，赛米拉山位于世界最高山脉之列，但你们不必太胆怯，我们基本上只在山麓徒步行走，但也能领略壮观的景色。

dazzle [ˈdæzl]

v. 使目眩；使倾倒 *n.* 耀眼眩目；令人眼花缭乱的东西

记 联想记忆：爵士乐(jazz)使人头晕目眩(dazzle)

例 Despite a lot of razzle-*dazzle*, the home basketball team has been beaten by 20 points. 主场篮球队尽管有许多迷惑人的假动作，但仍以 20 分之差落败。

deadline* [ˈdedlaɪn]

n. 最后期限

记 组合词：dead(死) + line(线) → 死期 → 最后期限

例 If you can't meet a *deadline* for an essay, you should go and see your lecturers. 如果你不能按时交论文，就应该去找你的导师(说明情况)。

dealer [ˈdiːlə(r)]

n. 商人，经销商

记 联想记忆：deal(交易) + er(表人) → 进行交易的人 → 商人

例 The collector bought antiques from a local *dealer*. 收藏家从一个当地商人那里买了些古董。

□ damp □ darkroom □ dash □ data □ database □ daunt
□ dazzle □ deadline □ dealer

12

dean [diːn]	*n.* (基督教的)教长；(大学的)院长，系主任 记 发音记忆："盯" → 院长狠狠地盯着作弊的学生 → 院长 例 At the top of the faculty is a *dean*. 院长是学院里的一把手。
dearth [dɜːθ]	*n.* 缺乏，短缺 记 联想记忆：dear(珍贵的) + th → 物以稀为贵 → 缺乏，短缺 搭 a dearth of water 缺水 例 There is a *dearth* of good young players at the moment. 目前优秀的年轻选手太少了。

When an end is lawful and obligatory, the indispensable means to it are also lawful and obligatory.

如果一个目的是正当而必须做的，则达到这个目的的必要手段也是正当而必须采取的。

——美国政治家 林肯(Abraham Lincoln, American statesman)

□ dean □ dearth

Word List 13

音 频

词根、词缀预习表

de-	表加强	debate *n./v.* 争论，辩论	**deca**	十	decade *n.* 十年，十年期
capit	头	decapitate *vt.* 斩首	**ceiv**	抓住	deceive *v.* 欺骗，蒙骗
clar	清楚	declare *v.* 正式宣布；声明	**clin**	弯曲	decline *n./v.* 下降；衰退
decor	装饰	decorate *v.* 装饰，装潢	**cre**	生长	decrease *v./n.* 减少
dic	分配，分派	dedicate *vt.* 献(身)	**fect**	做	defect *n.* 缺点，不足之处

debate [dɪˈbeɪt]

n./v. 争论，辩论

记 词根记忆：de(表加强) + bat(打) + e → 竞选双方在打口水战 → 争论，辩论

搭 beyond debate 无异议，无可争辩；open the debate 在辩论时首先发言；debate upon/on 讨论(问题)

例 There's a *debate* in the meeting room about next year's budget. 会议室里(大家)就来年的预算产生了争论。

同 dispute (*v./n.*争论，辩论)

debris [ˈdebriː]

n. 碎屑，残骸；【地质】岩屑

记 发音记忆："堆玻璃" → 一堆碎玻璃 → 碎屑，残骸

搭 clear the debris from... 清理残骸(或废弃物)

例 As the sliding ice and snow melted, it touched off devastating torrents of mud and *debris*, which destroyed all life in their path. 下滑中的冰雪融化后会引发泥石流，破坏力极大，毁灭途经的一切生物。

debt* [det]

n. 债，债务

记 发音记忆："贷的" → 贷款 → 债务

搭 be in debt 欠债，欠情；in debt to sb./ in one's debt 欠某人的债

例 The freshman misconducted his expenditure so he's deep in *debt*. 这名大一新生没有合理地规划开销，所以债台高筑。

派 debtor(*n.* 债务人)

decade* [ˈdekeɪd]

n. 十年，十年期

记 词根记忆：deca(十) + de → 十年，十年期

例 In Tokyo builders are planning a massive underground city to be begun in the next *decade*. 在东京，建筑师们正计划在今后的十年里大规模兴建地下城。

decapitate* [dɪˈkæpɪteɪt]
vt. 斩首
记 词根记忆：de(去掉)+capit(头)+ate → 把头去掉 → 斩首
例 The fisherman *decapitated* the fish. 渔民把鱼头给剁了。

decay* [dɪˈkeɪ]
n. 腐烂，腐朽；衰败(或衰退)状态 *v.* 腐烂，腐朽；衰败，衰退
记 联想记忆：骗(decoy)人变坏(decay)
搭 dental decay 龋齿
例 The wooden bridge was unsafe due to *decay*. 木桥腐烂了，不安全。

deceive [dɪˈsiːv]
v. 欺骗，蒙骗
记 词根记忆：de(分离)+ceiv(拿，抓)+e → 欺骗，蒙骗

例 deceive oneself 欺骗自己；deceive sb. into doing sth. 骗某人做某事
例 Mary *deceived* the interviewer about her past experience. 玛丽在自己的过去经历上对面试官撒了谎。
派 deceptive(*a.* 迷惑的；虚伪的)

decent [ˈdiːsnt]
a. 大方的，体面的，像样的；正派的，合乎礼仪的
例 You can't get anything *decent* under $15. 花不到 15 美金不可能买到像样的东西。

deception* [dɪˈsepʃn]
n. 欺骗；诡计
记 词根记忆：de(分离)+cept(拿，抓)+ion → 拿开 → 欺骗
搭 intentional deception 故意的欺骗行为
例 The young boy didn't have the courage to admit his *deception*. 那个男孩没有勇气承认他的欺骗行为。

decibel* [ˈdesɪbel]
n. 分贝
记 词根记忆：deci(十分之一)+bel(贝尔，为十个分贝) → 分贝
例 The normal noise threshold for private housing is 55 *decibels*. 正常情况下私人住宅区的最高噪音是 55 分贝。

decipher [dɪˈsaɪfə(r)]
vt. 破译；解释
记 联想记忆：de(去掉)+cipher(密码) → 解开密码 → 破译
例 The scientists use the techniques to *decipher* disorder-related genes. 科学家使用这些技术，成功破解了与(遗传)紊乱有关的基因。

decisive [dɪˈsaɪsɪv]
a. 决定性的；果断的
记 来自 decide(*v.* 决定)
例 Automobiles and televisions have the most *decisive* influences on American habits. 汽车和电视对美国人的生活习惯最具决定性的影响。

declaration [ˌdekləˈreɪʃn]
n. 宣布；宣言，声明(书)
记 来自 declare(*v.* 正式宣布)
例 This *declaration* seemed to calm the discontented party members somewhat. 这项声明似乎让那些心存不满的党派成员稍微平静了点。

declare
[dɪˈkleə(r)]

v. 正式宣布；声明；断言

记 词根记忆：de(表加强) + clar(清楚) + e → 说清楚 → 正式宣布；声明

例 The government ***declared*** that the ballots cast were inconclusive. 政府宣布这次投票不具有决定性。// The area has been ***declared*** a national park. 该地区已宣布为国家公园。

派 declarative(*a.* 陈述的)

decline*
[dɪˈklaɪn]

n./v. 下降，减少；衰退，衰落

记 词根记忆：de(向下) + clin(弯曲) + e → 向下弯曲 → 下降；衰退

搭 on the decline 在衰退中；in decline 下降；rapid decline 飞速减少；phase of decline 衰退期

例 Technological advances helped bring about the ***decline*** of rural industries and an increase in urban populations. 技术进步加速了乡镇企业的衰落和城市人口的增长。

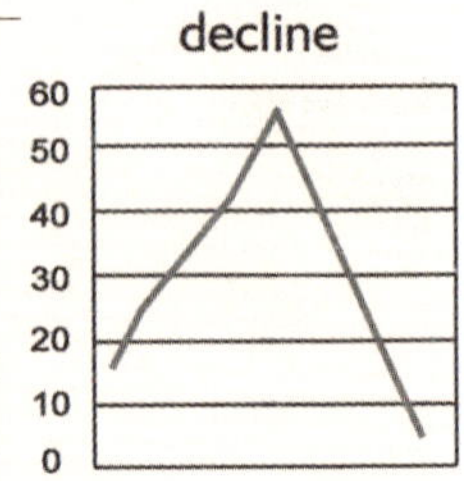

decompose*
[ˌdiːkəmˈpəʊz]

v. (使)分解，(使)腐烂

记 联想记忆：de(分离) + compose(组成) → 把组合在一起的东西分开 → 分解

例 Earthworms ***decompose*** the dung further to provide essential soil nutrients. 蚯蚓将粪进一步分解，给土壤提供了重要的养分。

decompression
[ˌdiːkəmˈpreʃn]

n. 减压；减压室

记 联想记忆：de(减) + compress(压缩) + ion → 减压

搭 a decompression chamber 减压舱

例 A manifestation of ***decompression*** sickness that is caused by the formation of nitrogen bubbles in the blood and tissues after a rapid reduction in the surrounding pressure and is characterized by pain in the joints and abdomen. 减压病是因周围压力急剧减少，在血液和组织中形成氮气泡而引发的一种疾病，其症状表现为关节和腹部疼痛。

decorate*
[ˈdekəreɪt]

v. 装饰，装潢，布置；授勋

记 词根记忆：decor(装饰) + ate(动词后缀) → 装饰，装潢

搭 decorate sb. for 因…授予某人奖章等；decorate sth. with sth. 用某物装饰…

例 We moved in our new apartment before it was ***decorated***. 新公寓还没有装修，我们就搬进去了。

派 decorative(*a.* 装饰性的，作装饰用的)；decoration(*n.* 装饰，装潢；装饰品)

decouple*
[diːˈkʌpl]

v. 减弱，减少

例 Increased production has been almost entirely ***decoupled*** from employment. 增加的产量几乎完全被就业问题抵消了。

decrease*

[dɪˈkriːs] *v.* 减少，减小 [ˈdiːkriːs] *n.* 减少；减少量

记 词根记忆：de(相反) + cre(生长) + ase → 减少

搭 decrease to 减少到

例 Do you think the cinema has increased or *decreased* in popularity in recent years? 你认为近年来电影受欢迎的程度是提高了还是降低了？

decrepit*

[dɪˈkrepɪt]

a. 破旧的；衰老的

记 词根记忆：de + crep(发出破裂声) + it → 破旧的

例 Our aim is to remove the heaviest-polluting, most-*decrepit* vehicles from the roads. 我们的目标是清除公路上造成最严重污染、最破旧的车辆。

派 decrepitude(*n.* 衰老，老朽；破旧)

dedicate

[ˈdedɪkeɪt]

vt. 献(身)；(在著作等上)题献词

记 词根记忆：de(表加强) + dic(分配，分派) + ate(动词后缀) → 为…献出 → 献(身)

搭 dedicate oneself to 献身于

例 We have come to *dedicate* a portion of that field as a final resting place for those who gave their lives here. 我们已经贡献出那片土地的一部分，作为那些在此献出了生命的人们的安息之地。

同 devote(*vt.* 投入于，献身于)

13

deduce

[dɪˈdjuːs]

v. 演绎，推断

记 词根记忆：de(向下) + duc(拉) + e→ 向下拉 → 演绎，推断

例 They cannot *deduce* very much from these simple figures. 他们无法从这些简单的数据中推断出很多东西。

deem

[diːm]

vt. 认为

记 联想记忆：和 seem(*v.* 似乎)一起记

例 The WHO *deems* that a city with more than ten million inhabitants has exceeded the healthy level. 世界卫生组织认为，人口在一千万以上的城市已经超过了健康标准的要求。

同 assume(*vt.* 假定，设想)；consider(*v.* 认为)；believe(*v.* 认为，想)

defeat*

[dɪˈfiːt]

n./vt. 击败；挫败；战败

记 联想记忆：击败(defeat)敌人，战绩(feat)累累

例 Now both coaches know semifinal *defeat* could cost them their jobs. 现在双方的教练都很清楚，半决赛失败可能会让他们丢掉工作。

defect

[ˈdiːfekt] *n.* 缺点，不足之处 [dɪˈfekt] *vi.* 叛变

记 词根记忆：de(离开) + fect(做) → 没做好 → 缺点，不足之处

例 Foetuses can be tested for genetic *defects* while in the womb. 胎儿还在子宫里时就可以通过检查看其是否存在基因缺陷。

派 defective(*a.* 有缺点的；不完全的)

□ decrease □ decrepit □ dedicate □ deduce □ deem □ defeat
□ defect

defence* [dɪ'fens]

n. 防御，保护；辩护；答辩；[*pl.*] 防务工事

记 来自 defend(*v.* 防护；辩护)

搭 natural defence mechanisms 先天性防御机制；defence against 防御…

例 The *defence* of the country must be reinforced. 该国的防务工事必须加强。

派 defenceless(*a.* 不能自卫的，无防御能力的)

defendant [dɪ'fendənt]

n. 被告 *a.* 处于被告地位的；为自己辩护的

记 联想记忆：defend(辩护) + ant → 需要为自己辩护的一方 → 被告

例 The judge told the *defendant* to stand when the verdict was read. 法官要求被告在宣读判决结果的时候起立。

deficiency [dɪ'fɪʃnsi]

n. 缺乏，不足

记 词根记忆：de(离开) + fic(做) + iency → 做事不力，缺乏能力 → 缺乏

例 The short child of tall parents very likely had a hormone *deficiency* early in life. 父母个子高而孩子个子矮，极有可能是由幼年分泌的荷尔蒙不足造成的。

同 inadequacy(*n.* 不充分，不足)

deficit ['defɪsɪt]

n. 不足额，赤字

记 词根记忆：de(向下) + fic(做) + it → 经济走下坡路 → 赤字

搭 a trade deficit 贸易逆差

例 The weak dollar plays an significant role in helping U.S. government to reduce trade *deficit.* 疲软的美元在帮助美国政府降低贸易赤字上起着重要的作用。

define [dɪ'faɪn]

vt. 下定义；限定

记 词根记忆：de + fin(界限，范围) + e → 划定界限 → 下定义；限定

例 Health in the physical sense has been *defined* as the absence of disease or illness. 就身体而言，健康的意思是不受疾病的困扰。

definite* ['defɪnət]

a. 明确的，肯定的；清楚的

记 词根记忆：de + fin(界限，范围) + ite → 划定界限的 → 明确的，肯定的

例 I have no *definite* plans for my future. 我对未来并没有明确的规划。

派 definitive(*a.* 决定性的，不可更改的)

definition [ˌdefɪ'nɪʃn]

n. 定义，释义；清晰(度)

例 The *definition* of any individual's role in any situation will be a combination of the role expectations. 任何情况下任何个人角色的定义都会是对角色期待的综合。

deflect [dɪ'flekt]

v. (使)偏斜，(使)转向

记 词根记忆：de(离开) + flect(弯曲) → 弯到旁边 → (使)偏斜

例 The bullet hit a wall and then *deflected* from its course. 子弹击中墙壁后改变了方向。

□ defence □ defendant □ deficiency □ deficit □ define □ definite
□ definition □ deflect

degenerate	[dɪˈdʒenəreɪt] *vi.* 退化 [dɪˈdʒenərət] *a.* 退化的 记 词根记忆：de(向下)+ gen(产生) + erate → 毁掉产生的东西 → 退化；退化的 例 Similarly, although at least some cetaceans have taste buds, the nerves serving these have ***degenerated*** or are rudimentary. 同样，尽管至少一些鲸鱼是有味蕾的，但是控制味蕾的神经已经退化了或者根本就没有充分发展。 派 degeneration(*n.* 恶化，退化的过程) 同 vicious(*a.* 堕落的，有错误的) 反 develop(*v.* 发展，生长)；evolve〔*v.*(使)发展，(使)进化〕
degrade [dɪˈgreɪd]	*v.* (使)降级；(使)堕落；(使)降解；(使)退化 记 联想记忆：de(向下) + grade(级别) → 降低级别 → 降级 例 You should not ***degrade*** yourself by telling such a lie. 你不该说这样的谎话来降低自己的人格。 同 demote(*vt.* 使降级，使降职)；decompose(*v.* 分解)；abase(*vt.* 降低)
delay* [dɪˈleɪ]	*n./v.* 耽搁，延迟，延期，迟滞 记 联想记忆：de + lay(放下) → 放下不管 → 耽搁 搭 without delay 立即，刻不容缓 例 After a ***delay*** of two days, the whole team continued the journey. 耽搁了两天后，整个小组继续行进。
delegate	[ˈdelɪgət] *n.* 代表，代表团成员 [ˈdelɪgeɪt] *vt.* 委派…为代表；授(权)给…，把…委托给… 搭 delegate sb. to do sth. 委派某人做某事 例 Negotiation progressed fairly with confidence felt among ***delegates***. 谈判进行得很顺利，代表们也都充满信心。
deliberate	[dɪˈlɪbərət] *a.* 故意的；深思熟虑的；从容不迫的 [dɪˈlɪbəreɪt] *v.* 深思熟虑；审议 记 词根记忆：de(表加强) + liber(权衡) + ate → 反复权衡 → 深思熟虑的 例 Wilson has a slow, ***deliberate*** way of acting. 威尔逊动作缓慢而谨慎。 同 ponder(*v.* 沉思，考虑) 反 hasty(*a.* 匆忙的，草率的)
delicate [ˈdelɪkət]	*a.* 纤细的；精巧的；微妙的 例 Cowhide can be treated to produce about half a square metre of very ***delicate*** leather. 牛皮可以被加工成面积约为 0.5 平方米且极其精致的皮革。
delinquency* [dɪˈlɪŋkwənsi]	*n.* 失职；行为不良 记 来自 delinquent(*a.* 有违法倾向的) 搭 juvenile delinquency 青少年犯罪 例 Young people now experience many problems, such as juvenile ***delinquency***. 现在的年轻人面临很多问题，比如青少年犯罪。

□ degenerate □ degrade □ delay □ delegate □ deliberate □ delicate
□ delinquency

delinquent [dɪˈlɪŋkwənt]

a. 失职的；违法的；拖欠的 *n.* 违法者，罪犯（尤指少年犯）

记 词根记忆：de(分离) + linqu(离开) + ent(形容词后缀) → 离开自己的岗位的 → 失职的；违法的

例 A recent research shows that there has been a sharp increase in the rate of juvenile ***delinquent*** related to domestic violence. 最近的一项调查显示，与家庭暴力相关的青少年犯罪率剧增。

deliver* [dɪˈlɪvə(r)]

v. 交付，递送；发表，表达；释放；接生

记 词根记忆：de(使…) + liver(=liber 自由) → 使自由 → 递送；释放

搭 deliver a speech 发表演讲；deliver a judgement 作出判决

例 The President ***delivered*** a televised speech to the whole nation on October 1st. 总统在 10 月 1 日向全国发表了电视讲话。

delivery [dɪˈlɪvəri]

n. 投递，交付；分娩

例 The invention of the motor vehicle brought personal mobility to the masses and made rapid freight ***delivery*** possible over a much wider area. 机动车的发明带来了人员的大规模流动，同时使得相当大区域内的快速货运成为可能。

delta [ˈdeltə]

n. 三角洲；希腊字母表的第四个字母

搭 the Nile Delta 尼罗河三角洲

例 River ***deltas*** are difficult places for map makers. 河流三角洲地带是让地图绘制者感到头疼的地方。

demand* [dɪˈmɑːnd]

n. 要求；需求(量) *v.* 要求；需要；询问

记 词根记忆：de(向下) + mand(命令) → 向下命令 → 要求；需要

搭 in great demand 需求量大；demand for 对…(的)需求

例 Tall buildings were constructed to help meet the ***demand*** for more economical use of land. 高层建筑的建造是为了满足节约用地的需求。

demerit* [diːˈmerɪt]

n. 过失；缺点，短处

例 I was asked to discuss my best friend's merits and ***demerits*** objectively. 我需要客观地讨论我最好朋友的优缺点。

democratic* [ˌdeməˈkrætɪk]

a. 民主的，有民主精神的

搭 Democratic Party 民主党；democratic reform 民主改革

例 The school held a ***democratic*** election for student-council officers. 学校进行了一次民主选举来挑选学生会成员。

demographic [ˌdeməˈgræfɪk]

a. 人口统计学的；人口的

记 来自 demography(*n.* 人口统计；人口学)

例 Early attempts to predict population viability were based on ***demographic*** uncertainty. 早期对人口生存能力预测的尝试是以人口的不确定性为基础的。

demolish* [dɪˈmɒlɪʃ]

vt. 破坏；拆除；驳倒(论点等)，推翻

记 词根记忆：de(表加强) + mol(磨) + ish → 完全磨成粉 → 破坏；拆除

例 Many of the buildings which were poorly designed and constructed have been ***demolished***. 许多设计和建造粗糙的建筑物都被拆除了。

□ delinquent □ deliver □ delivery □ delta □ demand □ demerit
□ democratic □ demographic □ demolish

demolition* [ˌdeməˈlɪʃn]

n. 拆除；破坏，毁坏

例 Creating the park required the ***demolition*** of lots of derelict buildings on the site. 建造公园需要摧毁旧址上大量的废弃建筑物。

demonstrate* [ˈdemənstreɪt]

v. 论证，证实；演示，说明；举行示威游行(或集会)

记 词根记忆：de(完全) + monstr(展示) + ate → 完全展示 → 论证；说明

搭 demonstrate one's ability 显示自己的能力

例 Crick and Watson ***demonstrated*** the structure of the DNA molecule in their academic papers. 克里克和沃森在他们的学术论文中论证了 DNA 的分子结构。

demonstrate

派 demonstrative(*a.* 感情外露的；指示的)

同 display(*v.* 展览；显示)；show(*v.* 说明，显示)；illustrate(*vt.* 举例说明，阐明)

demonstration* [ˌdemənˈstreɪʃn]

n. 论证，证明；示范；显示，表露；示威游行

记 词根记忆：de(完全) + monstr(展示) + ation → 论证；示范

例 Thousands of people took part in the ***demonstration***. 数千人参加了示威游行。

denomination* [dɪˌnɒmɪˈneɪʃn]

n. 命名；(货币等的)单位；宗教派别

记 来自 denominate(*vt.* 命名，取名)

例 Christians of all ***denominations*** attended the conference. 各教派的基督徒都参加了会议。

denote* [dɪˈnəʊt]

v. 表示，指示；意味着

记 词根记忆：de(向下) + not(知道) + e → 深究 → 表示，指示；意味着

例 The uniforms ***denoted*** a hierarchy. 制服体现了一种等级关系。

同 signify(*v.* 表示，意味)；indicate(*v.* 指出，显示)；mean(*v.* 意味，用意)

dense [dens]

a. 密集的；浓厚的

记 联想记忆：在雨中，感觉(sense)雨丝很密集(dense)

例 The airport was closed because of the ***dense*** fog. 机场因为大雾而关闭了。

density [ˈdensəti]

n. 密集；浓度，密度

搭 population density 人口密度；the density of settlement 居住密度

例 The house has some high-***density*** insulation materials in the roof. 房子的屋顶采用了一些高密度的绝缘材料。

deny* [dɪˈnaɪ]

v. 否认，否定；拒绝

记 发音记忆："抵赖" → 否认

搭 deny oneself 节制，戒绝，摒弃；deny doing sth. 否认做过某事；deny a charge 否认控告

例 If you don't acknowledge the source of your information, you might be ***denied*** entry into the university. 如果你不供认信息的来源，你可能会被这所大学拒收。

13

□ demolition ■ demonstrate □ demonstration □ denomination ■ denote □ dense
□ density □ deny

depart* [dɪˈpɑːt]	*vi.* 离开，起程 记 词根记忆：de（去掉，离开）+ part（离开）→ 离开，起程 例 Tom *departs* at sundown to fishing. 汤姆黄昏时分出发捕鱼。
departmental* [ˌdiːpɑːtˈmentl]	*a.* 部门的 例 I saw a book in the *departmental* library that would be helpful. 我在系图书馆看到一本书，可能有用。
departure [dɪˈpɑːtʃə(r)]	*n.* 离开，出发；背离，违反 搭 the departure time 离站时间 例 The local people had received no news of him since his *departure* from hometown. 自从他离开家乡之后，乡亲们就没有听到过他的消息。
depend* [dɪˈpend]	*vi.* 依靠，依赖；信赖，相信；决定于，视…而定 记 词根记忆：de（在…之下）+ pend（悬挂）→ 悬挂于之下 → 依靠，依赖 搭 depend on/upon 取决于 例 A: How much do the trips cost? B: Between five and fifteen pounds a head, *depending* on distance. A: 旅行费是多少？ B: 每个人 5 到 15 磅不等，取决于距离。 派 dependable（*a.* 可信赖的）；dependence（*n.* 依赖）；dependent（*a.* 依赖的；取决于…的）
depict [dɪˈpɪkt]	*vt.* 描绘，描述 记 词根记忆：de（表加强）+ pict（描写，画）→ 描绘，描述 例 The photographs *depicted* vivid scenes of a young girl's life. 这些照片栩栩如生地描绘出一个年轻女孩的生活。 同 describe（*v.* 描写，描述）；represent（*vt.* 表现，描绘）；picture（*vt.* 画，描绘）
deplete* [dɪˈpliːt]	*vt.* 倒空；（使）枯竭；消耗 记 词根记忆：de + plet（满，填满）+ e → 不满 → 倒空；（使）枯竭 例 When local resources became *depleted*, the tribe moved on. 当地资源濒临枯竭时，部落会迁往他处。
depletion [dɪˈpliːʃn]	*n.* 削减；消耗 记 词根记忆：de（去掉）+ plet（满，填满）+ ion → 使不满 → 削减；消耗 例 Many western countries have taken measures to prevent the *depletion* of their precious dollar reserves. 许多西方国家已经采取措施，防止损耗其宝贵的美元储备。
deploy* [dɪˈplɔɪ]	*vt.* 部署；使用，运用 记 联想记忆：de（表加强）+ ploy（策略）→ 运用策略 → 使用，运用 搭 deploy resources 利用资源 例 Resources must be *deployed* to bring about vigorous development in agriculture. 必须充分利用资源，以大力发展农业。 派 deployment（*n.* 部署，运用）

□ depart ☑ departmental □ departure □ depend □ depict □ deplete
□ depletion □ deploy

deposit [dɪˈpɒzɪt]	*v.* 存放；储蓄；使沉淀；付(保证金) *n.* 存款；保证金，押金；沉积物  记 联想记忆：de + posit（看作 position，位置）→ 将钱放在安全的位置，存入银行 → 储蓄 搭 savings deposit 储蓄存款；a fixed deposit 定期存款；20% deposit 20%押金；bank deposit 银行存款 例 Overseas students must pay a ***deposit*** when they apply for a course at the college. 外国学生如果申请这所大学的课程，需要付一定的押金。
depress* [dɪˈpres]	*vt.* 使沮丧；使不景气；降低，减少 记 联想记忆：de(向下) + press(挤压) → 情绪向下挤压 → 使沮丧 例 The recession has ***depressed*** the housing market. 经济衰退导致住房市场不景气。
depression* [dɪˈpreʃn]	*n.* 忧愁，消沉；低气压，低压；不景气，萧条(期) 记 来自 depress(*vt.* 使沮丧；使不景气) 搭 the Great Depression 大萧条；economic depression 经济萧条 例 The economic ***depression*** of the 1930s and the Second World War prevented the advanced ideas from being widely realized. 20 世纪 30 年代的经济萧条和第二次世界大战阻碍了先进思想的传播，使其不能得到广泛认识。
deprive [dɪˈpraɪv]	*vt.* 剥夺；使丧失 记 词根记忆：de(离开) + priv(私有的) + e → 使某物离开某人 → 使丧失 搭 deprive sb. of sth. 剥夺某人某物 例 The accident ***deprived*** him of his feet. 这场意外事故使他失去了双脚。 同 remove(*vt.* 去除；解除)
deputy [ˈdepjuti]	*n.* 代理人；代表 记 联想记忆：de + puty(看作 duty，责任) → 应负责任的人 → 代理人 例 If you have any question, you may ask my ***deputy***. 如果有任何问题，可以咨询我的代理人。
derelict* [ˈderəlɪkt]	*a.* 被抛弃的；衰退的，破败的 *n.* 遗弃物；无家可归者，社会弃儿 记 词根记忆：de(表加强) + re(后) + lict(分离) → 完全置后 → 被抛弃的 搭 derelict land 荒废的土地 例 The building has been ***derelict*** for many years. 该建筑物已经废弃多年。
derive* [dɪˈraɪv]	*v.* 取得；起源 记 联想记忆：de + rive(r) → 黄河是中华文明的发源地 → 起源 搭 derive from 源自 例 France ***derives*** three quarters of its electricity from nuclear power. 法国四分之三的电力来自核能。 派 derivative(*n.* 派生词；衍生物)

13

□ deposit □ depress □ depression □ deprive □ deputy □ derelict
□ derive □ decend

descend [dɪˈsend]	*v.* 下来，下降；遗传 记 词根记忆：de(向下) + scend(爬) → 往下爬 → 下降；遗传 搭 descend on/upon (结伙)袭击；突然来访；be descended from sb. 是…的后裔；descend into 逐渐陷入 例 As would have been predicted by Robert Williams's work, all three groups appear to be ***descended*** from the same ancestral population. 正如罗伯特•威廉斯的文章所预测的，三组人都是同一祖先的后裔。 派 descendant(*n.* 后代，子孙；派生物)

If you put out your hands, you are a laborer; if you put out your hands and mind, you are a craftsperson; if you put out your hands, mind, heart and soul, you are an artist.

如果你用双手工作，你是一个劳力；如果你用双手和头脑工作，你是一个工匠；如果你用双手和头脑工作，并且全身心投入，你就是一个艺术家。

——美国电影 *American Heart and Soul*

Word List 14

音频

词根、词缀预习表

scrib	写	describe *vt.* 描述	**serv**	服务	deserve *v.* 应得；值得
sper	希望	desperate *a.* 绝望的	**struct**	建立	destruction *n.* 破坏
tach	接触	detach *v.* 分离	**ter**	吓唬	deter *v.* 威慑，吓住
termin	结束	determine *v.* 决定	**val**	价值	devalue *v.* 使贬值；贬低
vic	看	device *n.* 装置，装备	**lect**	讲	dialect *n.* 方言，土语

describe* [dɪˈskraɪb]

vt. 描述，描写，形容

记 词根记忆：de(表加强) + scrib(写) + e → 描述

例 The lecturer *describes* four processes which may contribute to the extinction of a species. 演讲者描述了可能导致一个物种灭绝的四个过程。

派 description(*n.* 描述；类型)

desert*

[ˈdezət] *n.* 沙漠；荒地 *a.* 沙漠的；荒凉的 [dɪˈzɜːt] *v.* 舍弃

记 词根记忆：de(分开) + sert(放置) → 不放进去 → 舍弃

例 The new estates around the city often proved to be windswept *deserts* because they lacked essential social facilities and services. 城市周边新建的住宅区因缺少基本的社区服务和设施，常常沦落为只有冷风飕飕吹过的荒凉之地。

deserve* [dɪˈzɜːv]

v. 应得；值得

记 词根记忆：de + serv(服务) + e → 花钱享受应得的服务 → 应得；值得

例 These poor people *deserve* our help. 这些可怜的人值得我们帮助。

design [dɪˈzaɪn]

n. 设计，构想；图样，图案；企图，图谋 *v.* 设计；谋划，构思

记 联想记忆：de + sign(标记) → 做标记 → 设计

例 Architecture is the art and science of *designing* buildings and structures. 建筑学是一门设计建筑物及其结构的艺术科学。

派 designer(*n.* 设计师)

desirable [dɪˈzaɪərəbl]

a. 值得拥有的；合意的；可取的，有利的

记 来自 desire(*v.* 渴望)

例 Selecting the right person for the job involves more than identifying the essential or *desirable* range of skills. 为一份工作选择合适的人选，不能只看他是否拥有胜任这份工作的基本技能和相应专长。

□ describe　□ desert　□ deserve　□ design　□ desirabe

desire*

[dɪˈzaɪə(r)]

v./n. 想望，期望；要求

记 联想记忆：*A Street Car Named Desire*《欲望号街车》

搭 a strong desire to do sth. 做…的强烈愿望

例 Many old folks ***desire*** to learn English in China. 在中国，很多老年人都想学英语。

desperate*

[ˈdespərət]

a. 绝望的；拼命的，不顾一切的；极度渴望的；危急的

记 词根记忆：de(去掉) + sper(希望) + ate → 去掉希望 → 绝望的

例 Tom was ***desperate*** to find friends with common interests. 汤姆渴望结交一些志趣相投的朋友。

despite*

[dɪˈspaɪt]

prep. 不管，尽管

搭 despite oneself 尽管(自己)不愿意

例 Los Angeles suffers from chronic highway blockages, ***despite*** efforts to encourage people to use public transport. 尽管当局积极鼓励人们使用公共交通工具，洛杉矶仍然长期存在公路拥堵现象。

despoil

[dɪˈspɔɪl]

vt. 抢夺，掠夺；蹂躏，破坏

例 If human beings continue to ***despoil*** the natural resources crazily, they will be doomed to be punished by nature. 如果人类继续疯狂地掠夺自然资源，他们必将遭到自然的惩罚。

destination

[ˌdestɪˈneɪʃn]

n. 目的地，终点；目标

记 联想记忆：destin(看作 destine，预定) + ation → 预定的地方 → 目的地

搭 holiday destination 度假胜地；final destination 最终目的地；arrive at/reach one's destination 到达目的地

例 The tourists rest there and then go to various ***destinations***. 游客们在那里稍事休息，然后去往不同的目的地。

destiny

[ˈdestəni]

n. 命运，定数

记 联想记忆：音乐组合 Destiny's Child(真命天子)

例 Mark was conscious that music was not his ***destiny***. 马克意识到音乐并不是他的最终归宿。

派 destined(*a.* 命中注定的)

destruction*

[dɪˈstrʌkʃn]

n. 破坏，毁灭，摧毁

记 词根记忆：de(去掉) + struct(建立) + ion → 毁坏建好的东西 → 破坏

搭 environmental destruction 环境破坏

例 The importation of cheap goods has often contributed to the ***destruction*** of local skills and indigenous markets. 进口廉价商品常常会给当地的手工业和本土市场带来毁灭性的打击。

同 ruin(*n.* 毁灭；崩溃)

反 establishment(*n.* 确立，制定)；construction(*n.* 构筑)

□ desire □ desperate □ despite □ despoil □ destination □ destiny
□ destruction

destructive* [dɪˈstrʌktɪv]

a. 破坏(性)的

记 词根记忆：de(去掉) + struct(建立) + ive(形容词后缀) → 毁坏建好的东西 → 破坏(性)的

例 The lungs of children who grow up in polluted air offer further evidence of its *destructive* power. 那些呼吸着污浊空气长大的孩子们的肺部状况进一步证明，污浊空气是有害的。

detach [dɪˈtætʃ]

v. 分开，分离；分遣

记 词根记忆：de(去掉) + tach(接触) → 去掉接触 → 分离

搭 detach from... 从…分离；拆下；使分开；semi-detached house 半独立式住宅

例 The mechanic *detached* the oil filter. 机工拆开了滤油器。

同 disconnect(*vt.* 切断，使分离)；separate(*v.* 分开，分离)

反 attach(*v.* 系；附加)

detail [ˈdiːteɪl]

n. 细节，详情；枝节，琐事 *vt.* 详述，详细说明

记 联想记忆：de(向下) + tail(切) → 向下切，使变成小份，露出细节 → 细节

搭 in detail 详细地；with details of 关于…的细节

例 I'll put up a notice with *details* of the restaurant and the menu. 我会张贴一份有关饭店和菜单内容的详细通知。

detect* [dɪˈtekt]

vt. 发现，察觉；侦查，探测

记 词根记忆：de(去掉) + tect(遮盖) → 去掉遮盖 → 发现，察觉

例 The robots can *detect* unauthorised personnel and alert security staff immediately. 机器人能够发现未经允许擅自闯入的人员，并马上向保安人员发出警报。

派 undetected(*a.* 未被发现的)

detective [dɪˈtektɪv]

n. 侦探 *a.* 侦探的

例 The *detective* tailed the man. 侦探盯上了那名男子。

deter* [dɪˈtɜː(r)]

v. 威慑，吓住，(使)断念

记 词根记忆：de + ter(=terr 吓唬) → 威慑，吓住

例 They would be *deterred* from buying a product if it had been tested on animals. 他们不会买在动物身上做过试验的产品。

detergent [dɪˈtɜːdʒənt]

a. 净化的，清洁的 *n.* 清洁剂

记 词根记忆：de(去掉) + terg(擦) + ent → 擦掉(脏)东西 → 清洁的

例 The auto beauty company often use the professional cleaning *detergent* foam, and then wipe the car slightly with a clean soft cloth. 汽车美容公司通常会使用专业泡沫清洁剂进行清洁，然后用干净的软布轻轻擦拭。

□ destructive □ detach □ detail □ detect □ detective □ deter
□ detergent

deterioratе* [dɪˈtɪəriəreɪt]

v. 变坏，恶化；退化

记 词根记忆：de(向下) + ter(地) + ior + ate → 向地面下降 → 变糟糕 → 变坏

例 Air quality in many of the world's major cities has ***deteriorated***. 世界上很多大城市的空气质量越来越糟糕。

反 improve(*v.* 改善，改进)；ameliorate(*v.* 改善，改进)

deterioration [dɪˌtɪərəˈreɪʃn]

n. 恶化；堕落

例 There is a serious ***deterioration*** in relations between the two countries. 两国的关系严重恶化。

determine* [dɪˈtɜːmɪn]

v. 确定；决定；(使)下决心

记 词根记忆：de + termin(结束) + e → 已经结束 → 决定

例 Before enrollment, students must take a test to ***determine*** the level of class they enter. 入学前，学生必须参加入学考试来确定他们进入何种等级的班级。

detour [ˈdiːtʊə(r)]

n. 弯路，便道 *v.* 迂回，绕道

记 联想记忆：de(离开) + tour(走) → 绕着走 → 迂回，绕道

例 You can take a ***detour*** to get there and avoid Black Street. 你可以绕道去那，不走布莱克大街。

detract* [dɪˈtrækt]

v. 去掉，减损

记 词根记忆：de(向下) + tract(拉) → 向下拉 → 去掉，减损

例 These buildings were stripped of unnecessary decoration that would ***detract*** from their primary purpose. 这些大楼已经去掉了会削弱它们主要功能的多余装饰。

detrimental* [ˌdetrɪˈmentl]

a. 不利的，有害的

记 联想记忆：detriment(损害，伤害) + al(形容词后缀) → 不利的，有害的

搭 be detrimental to 对…有害；detrimental effect 不良影响

例 Smoking cigarettes is ***detrimental*** to your health. 吸烟有害健康。

devalue [ˌdiːˈvæljuː]

v. 使(货币)贬值；贬低

记 词根记忆：de(去掉) + val(价值) + ue → 去掉价值 → 使贬值；贬低

例 Let's not ***devalue*** his work unjustly. 我们不要不公正地贬低他的工作。

派 devaluation(*n.* 贬值)

devastate* [ˈdevəsteɪt]

vt. 破坏，毁坏；使震惊，使极为悲痛

记 词根记忆：de(表加强) + vast(空) + ate(使…) → 使完全变空 → 破坏，毁坏

搭 be devastated by 被…破坏

例 The writer had been ***devastated*** by the death of his seven-year-old elder daughter. 作者因七岁的大女儿夭折而崩溃了。

devastating* [ˈdevəsteɪtɪŋ]

a. 毁灭性的；强有力的

搭 devastating effect 毁灭性的影响

例 The ***devastating*** earthquake caused great damage to the city. 那场毁灭性的地震给这个城市造成了巨大的损失。

□ deteriorate □ deterioration □ determine □ detour □ detract □ detrimental
□ devalue □ devastate □ devastating

develop* [dɪˈveləp]

v. 发展；生长，形成；开发

例 When a country *develops* its technology, the traditional skills and ways of life die out. 一个国家在发展技术的同时，会造成传统手工艺和原有生活方式的消亡。

派 development(*n.* 发展)；undeveloped(*a.* 欠发达的)；developing(*a.* 发展中的)

deviance* [ˈdiːviəns]

n. 异常；偏常行为

记 词根记忆：de(偏离) + vi(路) + ance → 偏离正路 → 偏常行为

例 The investigation of *deviance* can reveal interesting and significant aspects of "normal" societies. 对偏常行为的研究会揭露出"正常"社会中一些有趣且重要的情况。

派 deviant(*a.* 不正常的；偏离常规的)

device* [dɪˈvaɪs]

n. 装置，设备，仪表；方法；设计；手段，策略

记 词根记忆：de(向下) + vic(看) + e → 用于向下观看的(东西) → 装置

搭 a marketing device 营销手段；leave sb. to their own devices 听任其人自行其是，对某人不加干涉

例 A wide range of pollution control *devices* is in place at most modern mines. 大多数现代矿井都配备了大量的污染控制设备。

devise* [dɪˈvaɪz]

vt. 设计，发明

记 联想记忆：科学家发明(devise)出许多现代化的机械设备(device)

例 Ford *devised* the first moving auto assembly line. 福特发明了第一条移动的汽车装配线。

devote* [dɪˈvəʊt]

vt. 将…奉献给；致力(于)

记 联想记忆：de + vote(投票) → 把票全投给那个候选者 → 将…奉献给

搭 devote oneself to 专注于…；devote sth. to sth. 把…用于…

例 The local newspapers were mainly *devoted* to regional news and gossip. 当地报纸主要报道地方新闻和小道消息。

派 devotion(*n.* 奉献；忠诚)

diagnose [ˈdaɪəgnəʊz]

v. 诊断；判断

记 词根记忆：dia + gno(知道) + se → 专家会诊，知道病情 → 诊断；判断

例 Lupus can be difficult to *diagnose* because symptoms vary from person to person. 狼疮很难诊断，因为其症状因人而异。

派 diagnosis(*n.* 诊断；判断)

diagram [ˈdaɪəgræm]

n. 图解，图表

记 词根记忆：dia(穿过) + gram(写，图) → 画带有交叉点的图 → 图解，图表

例 He tossed the *diagram* of the bridge to Brian. 他把桥的结构图扔给了布赖恩。

□ develop □ deviance □ device □ devise □ devote □ diagnose □ diagram

dialect [ˈdaɪəlekt]	*n.* 方言，土语 记 词根记忆：dia(相对) + lect(讲) → 相对于普通话方言更亲切 → 方言 例 The tourists were confused by the unfamiliar ***dialects*** in this area. 游客被该地奇特的方言弄得满头雾水。
diameter [daɪˈæmɪtə(r)]	*n.* 直径 记 词根记忆：dia(穿过) + meter(测量) → 穿过圆的中心进行测量 → 直径 例 The ***diameter*** of the pipe is three inches. 这根管子的直径为三英寸。
dictation [dɪkˈteɪʃn]	*n.* 听写 例 If you plan to take examinations, there are ***dictation*** and listening comprehension cassettes for you to practise with. 如果你打算参加考试，这里有听写和听力理解的录音带可供你练习。
diesel [ˈdiːzl]	*n.* 柴油；柴油机；柴油车 搭 a diesel engine 柴油机 例 Because of the development of new energies, less and less ***diesel*** engines are used in daily life. 由于新能源的开发，柴油机在日常生活中的使用日益减少。
dietary [ˈdaɪətəri]	*a.* 饮食的 搭 a dietary expert 饮食专家；dietary habits 饮食习惯 例 For tourists with special ***dietary*** requirements, we will offer a variety of delicious food for them to choose. 对于有特殊饮食要求的游客，我们会提供各种美食供其选择。
differ [ˈdɪfə(r)]	*vi.* 不同，相异；(在意见方面)发生分歧 例 French ***differs*** from English in this respect. 法语在这方面不同于英语。
differentiate [ˌdɪfəˈrenʃieɪt]	*v.* 区分，区别；差别对待，区别对待 记 词根记忆：dif(分开) + fer(搬运) + ent + iate → 分开搬运 → 区分，区别；差别对待 例 The main aim of the management course is to teach us how to ***differentiate*** primary work from secondary work in the office. 该管理课程的主要目的是教我们如何区分首要工作和次要工作。 派 differentiation(*n.* 区别，差别) 同 discriminate(*v.* 区别；歧视)
diffuse	[dɪˈfjuːz] *v.* 散布，传播；(光等)漫射；(使气体或液体)扩散，弥漫 [dɪˈfjuːs] *a.* 扩散的，漫射的；(文章等)冗长的，难解的 记 词根记忆：dif(分开) + fus(倾泻) + e → 分开倾泻 → 散布；漫射；扩散 例 Nowadays, Internet has become a powerful means of ***diffusing*** knowledge and information instead of television. 如今，因特网已取代电视成为传播知识和信息的有力媒介。 派 diffusion(*n.* 扩散；传播；普及)；diffused(*a.* 普及的；漫射的)；diffuser(*n.* 扩散器，柔光镜) 同 wordy(*a.* 冗长的)

□ dialect □ diameter □ dictation □ diesel □ dietary □ differ
□ differentiate □ diffuse

digest	[daɪˈdʒest] *v.* 消化；领会 [ˈdaɪdʒest] *n.* 文摘 记 词根记忆：di(分开) + gest(搬运) → 运来食物，接着分解 → 消化 例 Chemists were searching for a fat that could be ***digested*** more easily by infants. 药剂师们正在寻找一种婴儿能更容易消化的脂肪。 同 absorb(*vt.* 吸收，吸引)；comprehend(*v.* 领会，理解)
digestive* [daɪˈdʒestɪv; dɪˈdʒestɪv]	*a.* 消化的；和消化有关的 记 词根记忆：di(分开) + gest(搬运) + ive → 消化的 搭 digestive tract 消化道 例 Professor introduced the feeding habits and ***digestive*** systems of starfish. 教授介绍了海星摄取食物的习惯以及它们的消化系统。
digital [ˈdɪdʒɪtl]	*a.* 数码的，数字的 记 词根记忆：digit(手指，脚趾) + al → 用手指数的 → 数字的 例 In some respects, ***digital*** automation tends to diminish the quality of our lives. 从某些方面来看，数字自动化会降低我们的生活质量。
dimension [daɪˈmenʃn; dɪˈmenʃn]	*n.* 尺寸，(长、宽、厚、深)度；方面，特点；维，元；[*pl.*] 面积 记 词根记忆：di + mens(测量) + ion → 测量 → 尺寸；面积 例 Good health is a major resource for social, economic and personal development and an important ***dimension*** of quality of life. 健康是社会、经济和个人发展的重要源泉，同时也是体现生活质量的一个重要方面。
dimensional [daɪˈmenʃnl]	*a.* …度空间的，…维的 搭 three-dimensional image 三维图像 例 In a similar way, a three-***dimensional*** truss can be built up of tetrahedra. 采用类似的方法，三维托架可以由四面体构成。
diminish* [dɪˈmɪnɪʃ]	*v.* 减少；降低；贬低，轻视 记 词根记忆：di + min(小) + ish → 减少；降低 例 Our farmland was losing topsoil at a rate likely to ***diminish*** the soil's productivity. 我们农田的地表土正在流失，照这样下去，很可能会降低土壤的生产力。 同 curtail(*vt.* 缩减，减少(经费等))；decrease(*v.* 减少) 反 increase(*v.* 增加，加大)
dioxide* [daɪˈɒksaɪd]	*n.* 二氧化物 记 联想记忆：di(二) + oxide(氧化物) → 二氧化物 例 At present, the U.K. produces as much sulphur ***dioxide*** as France, Germany and Sweden. 目前，英国所产生的二氧化硫与法国、德国和瑞典三个国家产生的一样多。
diploma [dɪˈpləʊmə]	*n.* 毕业文凭(或证书)；资格证书 记 联想记忆：做外交官(diplomat)需要资格证书(diploma) 例 Tim got a ***diploma*** at a private college. 蒂姆拿到了一所私立学院的毕业证书。
direction [daɪˈrekʃn; dɪˈrekʃn]	*n.* 方向；趋势，动向；[*pl.*] 用法说明；指导 例 Shall we ask somebody for ***directions*** again? 我们还要找人问一下路吗？

14

□ digest □ digestive □ digital □ dimension □ dimensional □ diminish
□ dioxide □ diploma □ direction

directory [də'rektəri]

n. 人名地址录；(电话)号码簿

记 联想记忆：direct(指引) + ory(表物) → 指引人们查询的东西 → 人名地址录

例 For our addresses, just check in your local telephone ***directory***. 你可以在当地的电话簿中找到我们的地址。

disable* [dɪs'eɪbl]

vt. 使丧失能力，使伤残；使不能正常运转，使无效

记 联想记忆：dis(不) + able(有能力的) → 使丧失能力，使伤残

例 There were so many people ***disabled*** and killed in the war. 这场战争造成了太多人的伤残和死亡。

disadvantage [ˌdɪsəd'vɑːntɪdʒ]

n. 缺点，不利

记 联想记忆：dis(不) + advantage(优点) → 不是优点 → 缺点

例 What are the advantages and ***disadvantages*** of making films of real-life events? 根据真实事件拍摄的电影，其优势和劣势分别是什么呢？

disagree* [ˌdɪsə'griː]

v. 不同意；不一致

记 联想记忆：dis(不) + agree(同意；一致) → 不同意；不一致

搭 disagree with 不同意；不一致

例 They ***disagreed*** about love. 他们对爱情持有不同的看法。

派 disagreement(*n.* 争执，不和)

disappointing* [ˌdɪsə'pɔɪntɪŋ]

a. 令人失望的

记 来自 disappoint(*v.* 失望)

例 The students find the exhibition ***disappointing***. 学生们觉得这个展览令人失望。

派 disappointment(*n.* 失望)

disapprove* [ˌdɪsə'pruːv]

v. 不赞成，反对

记 联想记忆：dis(不) + approve(赞成) → 不赞成

例 They ***disapprove*** of paying farmers for not cultivating the land. 他们不赞成付钱给未耕种土地的农民。

disastrous [dɪ'zɑːstrəs]

a. 损失惨重的，灾难性的；极坏的

记 词根记忆：dis(分离) + astr(o)(星星) + ous(形容词后缀) → 古人认为星位发生偏离就预示有灾难发生 → 灾难性的

例 The ***disastrous*** Hanshin earthquake in 1995 killed 6,400 people, toppled elevated highways, flattened office blocks and devastated the port area of Kobe. 1995 年的阪神大地震极具灾难性，使 6400 人丧生，高架公路倒塌，办公大楼夷为平地，神户港口地区变成废墟。

discard* [dɪs'kɑːd]

vt. 丢弃，遗弃

记 联想记忆：dis(分离) + card(纸牌) → 出牌，把牌扔出去 → 丢弃，遗弃

例 10% of the data was ***discarded*** as unreliable. 10%的数据因不可靠而被废弃。

discerning* [dɪ'sɜːnɪŋ]

a. 有识别力的，眼光敏锐的

记 词根记忆：dis(分离) + cern(分开) + ing → 能分清楚的 → 有识别力的

例 Only the ***discerning*** customers can recognize this jade decoration as a high quality product. 只有眼光敏锐的顾客才能识别出这件玉饰是高品质产品。

□ directory □ disable □ disadvantage □ disagree □ disappointing □ disapprove
□ disastrous □ discard □ discerning

discharge

[ˈdɪstʃɑːdʒ] *n.* 排出(物)；获准离开，免职；履行，执行；(债务的)清偿

[dɪsˈtʃɑːdʒ] *v.* 解雇；释放；排出，放出；放(电)；完成，履行

记 联想记忆：dis(分离) + charge(职责；电荷) → 解雇；放(电)

搭 discharge one's responsibilities/obligations 履行责任/义务

例 Thousands of marine organisms were murdered as a result of a *discharge* of toxic wastes from a nearby chemical factory. 附近一个化工厂排出的有毒废料造成数以千计海洋生物的死亡。

discipline*

[ˈdɪsəplɪn]

vt. 训练，训导 *n.* 学科；纪律；处分

记 联想记忆：dis(不) + cip + line(线) → 不站成一条线就要受惩罚 → 必须遵守纪律 → 纪律

例 Sports Studies as a *discipline* is still comparatively new. 体育研究仍是一个相对较新的学科。

disclose

[dɪsˈkləʊz]

vt. 揭露；透露；公开

记 词根记忆：dis(不) + clos(关闭) + e → 不关闭 → 揭露；透露；公开

例 She didn't *disclose* those details on tax bills. 她没有透露那些税收法案的相关细节。

同 reveal(*vt.* 展现，揭示)；uncover(*vt.* 揭开，揭露)

反 conceal(*vt.* 隐藏，隐瞒)；hide(*v.* 隐藏，掩藏)

discontinue

[ˌdɪskənˈtɪnjuː]

v. 停止；中断；不连续

例 Without first consulting their health care provider, patients shall not *discontinue* the use of these medication. 在没有咨询过医护人员前，患者不应该中断使用这些药物。

discount*

[ˈdɪskaʊnt] *n.* (价格、债款等)折扣

[dɪsˈkaʊnt] *vt.* 给…打折；漠视，低估

记 联想记忆：dis(分离) + count(计算) → 不计算在内的部分 → 折扣

搭 make a discount 打折；a discount store 廉价商店；at a discount 打折；不值钱，不受重视；discount rates 贴现率

例 For those of you who are up and about early in the morning, we are introducing a 50 percent "morning *discount*" this year. 今年，我们将为你们这些早起的人推出五折的"早间折扣"。

discourage

[dɪsˈkʌrɪdʒ]

vt. 使泄气，使灰心；阻止，劝阻

记 词根记忆：dis(消失) + cour(精神) + age → 使精神消失掉 → 使泄气

例 Tom was *discouraged* from using the new car because of its bad assembly. 汤姆不愿意驾驶这辆新车，因为它的配置很差，这让汤姆很泄气。

discourteous

[dɪsˈkɜːtiəs]

a. 无礼的，粗鲁的

记 词根记忆：dis(离开) + court(花园，引申为"宫廷") + eous → 离开宫廷的 → 无礼的，粗鲁的

例 It would be *discourteous* for young people to ignore their parents' basic request for living together. 年轻人无视父母要求住在一起的基本请求是无礼的。

discover* [dɪˈskʌvə(r)]

vt. 发现，找到；发觉

例 Scientists are working to ***discover*** the links between the weather and people's moods and performance. 科学家正致力于通过研究来发现天气和人的情绪、行为之间的联系。

discovery [dɪˈskʌvəri]

n. 发现

例 Herschel's ***discovery*** was the most important find of the last three hundred years. 赫舍尔的发现是过去三百年中最重要的发现。

discredit* [dɪsˈkredɪt]

vt. 使怀疑；使丧失信誉，使丢脸

记 联想记忆：dis（不）+ credit（信任）→ 不信任 → 使怀疑

例 The ugly gossip would ***discredit*** us all. 恶毒的流言飞语会使我们所有人丧失信誉。

discrepancy [dɪsˈkrepənsi]

n. 不同；矛盾

记 词根记忆：dis（分开）+ crep（发出破裂声）+ ancy → 裂开 → 矛盾

例 We noticed the obvious ***discrepancy*** between these two agreements signed by the two parties. 我们注意到双方签订的这两份合同有着明显的不同之处。

同 difference（*n.* 差别，分歧）

反 accord（*n.* 一致，符合）

discretion [dɪˈskreʃn]

n. 判断力；谨慎，审慎；明智

记 来自 discreet（*a.* 小心的，谨慎的）

搭 act at one's discretion 自行决断；with discretion 慎重地，审慎地

例 The services that the bank will offer you will depend on your individual circumstances and on the ***discretion*** of the bank manager involved. 银行提供给你的服务将取决于你的个人情况和相关银行经理的判断力。

discriminate [dɪsˈkrɪmɪneɪt]

v. 区别；歧视

记 词根记忆：dis（分开）+ crimin（分开）+ ate → 分开对待 → 区别；歧视

例 We must learn to ***discriminate*** right from wrong. 我们必须学会明辨是非。

同 distinguish（*v.* 区别，辨别）

disdain [dɪsˈdeɪn]

v./n. 鄙视，蔑视

记 词根记忆：dis（不）+ dain（=dign 高贵）→ 把人弄得不高贵 → 鄙视，蔑视

例 Paul ***disdains*** to join in this leader election with such ignorant persons. 保罗不屑于和这些无知的人一同参加领导人的竞选。

Word List 15

音频

词根、词缀预习表

miss	送，放出	dismiss *v.* 解散，解雇	**par**	平等	disparage *vt.* 贬低
pen	重量	dispense *vt.* 分配	**pos**	放置	disposable *a.* 一次性的
dis-	不	disregard *vt.* 不理会，模式	**rupt**	打破，断裂	disrupt *vt.* 使中断
semin	种子	disseminate *v.* 散布，传播	**stinct**	刺	distinct *a.* 明显的
sting	刺	distinguish *v.* 区别，辨别	**tort**	卷缠	distort *vt.* 扭曲

disempower [ˌdɪsɪmˈpaʊə(r)]

vt. 使失去权力或影响

例 You *disempower* yourself to do anything about it, because you always think it beyond your ability. 你总是觉得这件事超出了你的能力，所以根本没有给自己力量去做些什么。

disenchantment [ˌdɪsɪnˈtʃɑːntmənt]

n. 失望，不抱幻想

例 *Disenchantment* with orthodox medicine has seen the popularity of alternative therapies in Australia climb steadily during the past 20 years. 过去的 20 年中，在澳大利亚，人们对传统医学的失望促进了替代医学的日益流行。

disfigure* [dɪsˈfɪɡə(r)]

vt. 使毁容，使变丑

记 联想记忆：dis(消失) + figure(形体) → 正常的形体消失了 → 使毁容

例 Buildings here *disfigured* such a beautiful landscape. 这里的建筑破坏了如此美丽的风景。

disharmony [ˌdɪsˈhɑːməni]

n. 不一致；不和谐

记 联想记忆：dis(不) + harmony(一致，协调) → 不一致；不和谐

搭 social disharmony 社会不协调

例 The *disharmony* of a person-environment mismatch is likely to result in low job satisfaction. 工作环境的不和谐很可能会导致工作满意度不高。

disillusion [ˌdɪsɪˈluːʒn]

vt. 使醒悟

记 联想记忆：dis(不) + illusion(幻想) → 不要再幻想了，快醒醒吧 → 使醒悟

例 A better educated and less accepting public has become *disillusioned* with the experts in general. 受教育水平更高而更为挑剔的公众一般来说对专家已不再抱有幻想。

□ disempower □ disenchantment □ disfigure □ disharmony □ disillusion

disillusionment* [ˌdɪsɪˈluːʒnmənt]

n. 幻灭；觉醒，醒悟

记 联想记忆：dis(不) + illusion(幻想) + ment → 不再幻想 → 觉醒，醒悟

例 *Disillusionment* at the failure of many poor imitations of Modernist architecture led to interest in various styles and ideas from the past and present. 这种对现代主义建筑风格模仿的失败引起了建筑师们的觉醒，继而激发了他们对过去和现在多重风格和理念的兴趣。

disintegrate [dɪsˈɪntɪgreɪt]

v. (使)碎裂，瓦解，解体

记 联想记忆：dis(不) + integrate(一体化，使完整) → 使不完整 → (使)碎裂，瓦解

例 The plane flew into a mountain and *disintegrated* on impact. 飞机冲向一座山，撞得粉碎。

dismantle* [dɪsˈmæntl]

vt. 拆除；废除，取消

记 联想记忆：dis(去掉) + mantle(覆盖) → 拆除；废除

例 Most have been forced to *dismantle* their individualistic homes and return to more conventional lifestyles. 大多数人被迫拆除了他们极具个性的房子，回归更加传统的生活方式。

dismiss* [dɪsˈmɪs]

v. 解雇，解散；驳回，不受理

记 词根记忆：dis(分开) + miss(送，放出) → 解散，解雇

搭 dismiss sb. (from sth.) 解雇

例 As sales declined, the manager had to *dismiss* several workers. 由于销售额下跌，经理不得不解雇一些员工。

disobey [ˌdɪsəˈbeɪ]

v. 不服从，违抗

记 联想记忆：dis(不) + obey(服从) → 不服从，违抗

例 In China, children usually cannot *disobey* the orders of their parents, but it is not the same situation in America. 在中国，孩子通常不能违抗父母之命，但在美国却不然。

disorder* [dɪsˈɔːdə(r)]

n. 混乱；失调，紊乱，疾病

记 联想记忆：dis(不) + order(顺序) → 无序 → 混乱

例 The couple knew through the examination that they would have a baby free from the *disorder*. 通过检查，这对夫妇知道自己会生一个健康的宝宝。

派 disorderly(*a.* 混乱的，无秩序的)

disorientate [dɪsˈɔːriənteɪt]

vt. 使失去方向感；使迷茫，使不知所措(=disorient)

例 The woman felt shocked and totally *disorientated* by her mother's crazy behaviour. 这个女人因其母亲的疯狂举动而感到震惊不已，不知所措。// You wake up in the middle of the night in a strange hotel miles away from home, *disoriented* most probably from jet lag. 午夜时分，在一个离家很远的陌生旅馆醒来，你极可能会因为时差而晕头转向。

disparage [dɪˈspærɪdʒ]

vt. 贬抑，贬低；轻蔑，轻视

记 词根记忆：dis(去掉) + par(平等) + age → 剥夺平等 → 贬抑，贬低

例 The charitable work, which public figures, especially actors and singers have done, has been *disparaged* by the press as an attempt to get publicity. 公众人物，尤其是演员和歌手，所做的慈善工作被媒体贬抑为自我宣传。

□ disillusionment □ disintegrate □ dismantle □ dismiss □ disobey □ disorder
□ disorientate □ disparage

dispense* [dɪˈspens]

vt. 分发，分配；提供

记 词根记忆：dis(分开) + pens(重量) + e → 把重量分开 → 分配

搭 dispense with sb./sth 摒弃，不再使用；dispense advice 给予忠告；a dispensing chemist 药剂师

例 Those in the business travel industry maintain that these serviced apartments *dispense* with all the unwanted and expensive hotel services that business travellers don't want. 那些商务旅行行业的人士认为这些服务式公寓省去了商务旅行者不需要的昂贵的酒店服务。

dispenser* [dɪsˈpensə(r)]

n. 药剂师，配药师；分配者，施予者；自动售货机

记 词根记忆：dis(分开) + pens(付钱) + er(表人) → 分开付钱的人 → 分配者

例 Japan's largest maker of cash *dispensers* is developing new machines that incorporate iris scanners. 日本最大的提款机制造商正在开发配有虹膜扫描仪的新机器。

dispersal [dɪˈspɜːsl]

n. 散布，分散；消散，疏散

例 After receiving the fire alarm, the firefighters rushed to the scene and quickly finished the *dispersal* of the crowd that had gathered. 接到火警后，消防人员迅速赶到现场，紧急疏散聚集的人群。

dispiriting* [dɪˈspɪrɪtɪŋ]

a. 令人沮丧的，使人气馁的

记 联想记忆：dis(没有) + spirit(精神) + ing → 使人没精神的 → 令人沮丧的

例 Sometimes even the most expensive hotel can seem empty and *dispiriting*. 有时甚至最昂贵的酒店也会让人感觉空虚和沮丧。

displace [dɪsˈpleɪs]

vt. 取代；迫使(人们)离开家园；撤职，使失业

记 联想记忆：dis(分离) + place(位置) → 使从位置上离开 → 取代

例 Each year rain and flooding *displace* millions of people and result in thousands of deaths. 每年，暴雨和洪水不仅使数百万人背井离乡，还会导致数千人丧生。

display* [dɪsˈpleɪ]

vt./n. 陈列，展览；显示，表现

记 联想记忆：dis(分开) + play(播放，表演) → 分开播放 → 陈列，展览

搭 on display 展示，陈列

例 The windows *display* postcards and greeting cards designed by women artists for Christmas. 橱窗陈列着女艺术家为圣诞节设计的明信片和贺卡。

disposable [dɪˈspəʊzəbl]

a. 一次性的；可动用的

记 词根记忆：dis + pos(放置) + able → 不能长久放置的 → 一次性的

搭 disposable income 可支配收入

例 In domestic market, people are increasing their *disposable* income, which provides China a huge potential market. 在国内市场，民众的可支配收入不断增加，为中国提供了一个巨大的潜在市场。

□ dispense □ dispenser □ dispersal □ dispiriting □ displace □ display
□ disposable

disposal *
[dɪ'spəuzl]

n. 处理，处置；布置，安排

记 来自 dispose(*v.* 处理，处置)

搭 waste disposal 废物处理；at one's disposal 任某人处理，供某人支配

例 The main use of water in most families is washing and waste *disposal*. 在大多数家庭中，水的主要用途是洗漱和废物处理。

dispute *
[dɪ'spjuːt]

n. 争论，争端，争吵 *v.* 对…表示异议；争论，争吵

记 词根记忆：dis(分开) + put(思考) + e → 分开思考 → 争论，争吵

搭 in dispute 在争论中，未决的；beyond dispute 毫无争议，不容争辩；dispute over 就…争论；dispute with 与…争论/争执

例 When participants get into *disputes* with each other, it's time for the facilitator to take on the role of "friction manager". 当与会者发生争执时，会议干事就要担起"摩擦消除者"的角色。

disqualify *
[dɪs'kwɒlɪfaɪ]

vt. 使丧失资格

记 联想记忆：dis(不) + qualify(具有资格) → 使不具有资格 → 使丧失资格

搭 disqualify sb. from (doing) sth. 使某人丧失(做)某事的资格

例 Will this *disqualify* me from getting a student loan? 这会不会让我失去获得学生贷款的资格？

disregard
[ˌdɪsrɪ'gɑːd]

vt. 不理会，漠视 *n.* 忽视，漠视

记 联想记忆：dis(不) + regard(关心) → 不关心 → 不理会，漠视

例 In his dissertations on tourism, Boorstin said that the mass tourists found pleasure in inauthentic contrived attractions, *disregarding* the real world outside. 布尔斯廷在关于旅游业的论文中写道，众多游客都在人造景观中找寻乐趣，而对外面的真实世界无动于衷。

disrespectful *
[ˌdɪsrɪ'spektfl]

a. 失礼的，无礼的

例 Camping there on one's own may be *disrespectful* to the people of that culture, and certainly don't make fires, however romantic it may seem. 在那里单独露营可能会冒犯当地人，而且不管看起来多浪漫，一定不能生火。

disrupt
[dɪs'rʌpt]

vt. 使中断；扰乱

记 词根记忆：dis(分开) + rupt(打破，断裂) → 切断 → 使中断

例 Work of any company may be *disrupted* by absence of its employees. 任何一家公司的工作都可能因员工的旷工而中断。

disruption
[dɪs'rʌpʃn]

n. 动乱；打乱；破坏

例 The accident on the main road through the high way caused widespread *disruption* for car drivers. 公路主干道上的事故给汽车司机带来很大不便。

disruptive
[dɪs'rʌptɪv]

a. 制造混乱的；分裂性的；破坏性的

例 The school accident happening in Hunan preliminarily resulted from some *disruptive* students in the crowd. 湖南省发生校园事故的初步原因是一些学生在人群中制造混乱。

□ disposal □ dispute □ disqualify □ disregard □ disrespectful □ disrupt
□ disruption □ disruptive

dissatisfied* [dɪsˈsætɪsfaɪd]

a. 不满意的，不满足的

例 They were ***dissatisfied*** with the treatment of animals at the London Zoo. 他们对伦敦动物园对待动物的方式表示不满。

disseminate [dɪˈsemɪneɪt]

v. 散布，传播

记 词根记忆：dis(分开) + semin(种子) + ate(动词后缀) → 散布，传播

例 University libraries should aim at ***disseminating*** popular culture as well as leading the dissemination of the mainstream culture. 大学图书馆应传播大众文化，还要引导主流文化的传播。

dissemination* [dɪˌsemɪˈneɪʃn]

n. 散布，传播

记 来自 disseminate(*v.* 散布)

例 Whether the activity is tourism research, business, or data ***dissemination***, the lack of a common language can severely impede progress. 不管是旅游研究、贸易还是资料的传播，缺少一种共同的语言都会严重阻碍这些活动的发展。

dissertation [ˌdɪsəˈteɪʃn]

n. 专题论文

记 来自 dissert(*vi.* 论述，写论文)

例 What I'd like to do in this session is to give you the opportunity to ask questions on writing the ***dissertation***. 在这节课，我想做的就是给你们机会就写专题论文进行提问。

dissolve [dɪˈzɒlv]

v. 溶解；解散；结束

记 联想记忆：dis(分开) + solve(解决) → 分开解决 → 溶解；解散

dissolve

搭 dissolve in 溶解

例 None of the forms of carbon ***dissolves*** in ordinary solvents, although melted iron does ***dissolve*** carbon to a certain extent. 任何状态的碳都不溶于普通溶剂，但能在一定程度上溶于铁水。

distance [ˈdɪstəns]

n. 距离；远方；一长段时间

记 来自 distant(*a.* 遥远的)

例 Underground water can flow very large ***distances*** and can be kept in underground reservoirs for a very long time. 地下水可以流经很长的距离，并能在地下含水层中储藏相当长时间。

distill [dɪˈstɪl]

vt. (使)蒸馏，提取

例 The vacuum distillation unit ***distills*** heavy and light gas oils. 真空蒸馏装置精炼出重柴油和轻柴油。

distinct [dɪsˈtɪŋkt]

a. 清楚的，明显的；有区别的，不同的

记 词根记忆：di + stinct(刺) → 刺眼的 → 明显的

搭 be distinct from 与…截然不同；a distinct minority 明显的少数

例 Why do humans, alone among all animal species, display a ***distinct*** left- or right-handedness? 为什么唯独人类和其他动物不一样，会出现独特的惯用左手或右手现象呢？

派 distinction(*n.* 差别，不同)

□ dissatisfied □ disseminate □ dissemination □ dissertation □ dissolve □ distance
□ distill □ distinct

distinctive* [dɪˈstɪŋktɪv]

a. 出众的；有特色的

记 来自 distinct(*a.* 明显的)

例 If you require any further information regarding the convention, you can talk to one of the many convention helpers wearing a ***distinctive*** blue and gold jackets. 如果你想获得更多关于本次会议的信息，可以询问大会工作人员，他们穿着显眼的金蓝相间的夹克。

同 characteristic(*a.* 特别的，特殊的)

distinguish [dɪˈstɪŋgwɪʃ]

v. 区别，辨别；辨认出；使杰出

记 词根记忆：di(分开) + sting(刺) + uish → 将刺挑出来 → 区别，辨别

搭 distinguish between 辨别，弄清；distinguish...from 把…与…区别开；distinguish oneself 使自己脱颖而出

例 A port must be ***distinguished*** from a harbour. Harbour is a physical concept, port is an economic concept. 必须分清港口和海港的区别，海港是一个物理概念，港口是一个经济概念。

同 discern(*v.* 洞悉，辨别)；dignify(*vt.* 使尊荣，使高贵)

distort [dɪsˈtɔːt]

vt. 扭曲；曲解；变形

记 词根记忆：dis(分开) + tort(卷缠) → 扭曲

例 Many people are concerned that an excessive emphasis on humanity's genetic constitution may ***distort*** our sense of values. 许多人担心过分强调人类基因构成可能会扭曲人类的价值观。

distortion [dɪˈstɔːʃn]

n. 扭曲，变形；曲解，歪曲

例 This novel reflects the struggle and bitterness of people in such a society which is full of ***distortion***. 这篇小说反映出人们在一个扭曲的社会里的挣扎和痛苦。

distract [dɪˈstrækt]

vt. 转移(注意力)；使分心

记 词根记忆：dis(分开) + tract(拉) → (注意力)被拉开 → 使分心

搭 distract attention from 转移注意力

例 Researchers claim that when children come to a word they already know, the pictures are unnecessary and ***distracting***. 研究人员称，当孩子们碰到认识的单词时，配有的相关图画是多余的，还会使他们分心。

同 divert(*v.* 转移)

反 attract(*v.* 吸引，引起注意)

distraction* [dɪˈstrækʃn]

n. 分散注意力的事；使人分心的事；娱乐，消遣

例 There are a lot of ***distractions*** at home. 家里有很多叫人分心的事。

distribute [dɪˈstrɪbjuːt; ˈdɪstrɪbjuːt]

vt. 分发，分配，分送；散布，分布；分类，分区

记 词根记忆：dis(分开) + tribut(给予) + e → 分开给予 → 分发，分送

搭 distribute sth. equally 平均分配；distribute expenses 分配经费

例 The port of the city draws to it raw materials and ***distributes*** them in many other forms. 城市港口的功能主要在于集中原材料，然后通过其他形式把它们分送出去。

□ distinctive □ distinguish □ distort □ distortion □ distract □ distraction □ distribute

distribution* [ˌdɪstrɪˈbjuːʃn]	*n.* 分发，分配；配给物；散布，分布 搭 distribution channel 分配渠道 例 A society can achieve a fair ***distribution*** of resources only under conditions of economic growth. 只有在经济增长的前提下，社会才可能对资源进行公平分配。
district [ˈdɪstrɪkt]	*n.* 区，地区 例 If you go up to the banana-growing ***districts***, you'll see all these banana trees with plastic bags on them. 如果你去香蕉种植区，就会看见所有的香蕉树上都罩着塑料袋。
disturb* [dɪˈstɜːb]	*v.* 扰乱；弄乱，打乱；打扰，使烦恼 记 词根记忆：dis(分开)＋turb(晃动，搅动)→扰乱；打乱 搭 disturb the peace 扰乱和平；disturb the balance of the environment 破坏环境平衡 例 One of the most concerning elements of acid rain is that it ***disturbs*** the natural balance of lakes and rivers. 在酸雨带来的破坏中，最令人担心的是它破坏了河流和湖泊的自然生态平衡。
disturbance* [dɪˈstɜːbəns]	*n.* 扰乱，打扰；骚乱，混乱；心神不安，烦恼 记 词根记忆：dis(分开)＋turb(晃动，搅动)＋ance→扰乱，打扰 例 The construction work is creating constant noise, dust and ***disturbance***. 建筑工程带来持续不断的噪音、灰尘以及骚乱。
diverge [daɪˈvɜːdʒ]	*vi.* (道路，线条等)分开，岔开；(意见、观点等)分歧，相异；偏离，违背 记 词根记忆：di(分离)＋verg(转)＋e→分别转换方向→分开，岔开；分歧 搭 diverge from the norm 与常态不符 例 They had been living together for ten years, but then their paths ***diverged***. 尽管他们在一起生活了十年，最后还是分道扬镳。 派 divergence (*n.* 分歧；偏离)；divergent(*a.* 分叉的；分歧的)
diverse [daɪˈvɜːs]	*a.* 不同的，多样的 记 词根记忆：di(分离)＋vers(转)＋e→转开→不同的，多样的 搭 diverse cultures 不同的文化 例 Millions of years ago, changes in the Earth's climate gave rise to ***diverse*** species in the tropical rain forest. 数百万年前，地球气候的变化导致了这片热带雨林物种的多样性。 
diversify* [daɪˈvɜːsɪfaɪ]	*v.* (使)多样化 例 Farms have ***diversified*** in recent years. 近年来，农业种植开始多样化。 派 diversification(*n.* 变化，多样化)
diversion* [daɪˈvɜːʃn]	*n.* 转向，转移，转换；转移视线的事物；娱乐 记 词根记忆：di(分离)＋vers(转)＋ion→转向，转移，转换 搭 create a diversion 转移注意力 例 Most water ***diversion*** projects are harmful to the fish population. 大多数的水系改道工程都会危及鱼群。

15

□ distribution □ district □ disturb □ disturbance □ diverge □ diverse
□ diversify □ diversion

diversity* [daɪˈvɜːsəti]

n. 多样性；差异

记 词根记忆：di(分离)+vers(转)+ity(名词后缀)→转开→多样性；差异

搭 cultural diversity 文化的多样性；diversity of 各种各样的

例 The study of primitive peoples has discovered a great *diversity* of customs, values, feelings, and thoughts. 对原始人类的研究发现其在风俗习惯、价值观、情感以及思想上具有丰富的多样性。

divert [daɪˈvɜːt]

vt. 使绕道，转移；娱乐，供消遣

记 词根记忆：di(分离)+vert(转)→转移

例 Out of a country's health budget, a large proportion should be *diverted* from treatment to health education. 在一个国家的医疗预算中，大部分费用应从治疗转移到健康教育上。

派 diverting(*a.* 娱乐的，消遣性的)

divide* [dɪˈvaɪd]

v. 分开，分隔；分配，分享；除(以) *n.* 分歧，差异；分界线，分水岭

搭 divide into 分成；divide sth. from sth. 把某物和某物分开

例 All the students will be *divided* into groups of 12 to 15 students. 所有的学生将被分组，每组12到15人。// I *divided* the candies in even proportions among the children. 我把糖果平均分给了孩子们。

dividend [ˈdɪvɪdend]

n. 红利，股息；回报，效益；被除数

例 We pay a *dividend* of 15 percent. 我们所付的股息为15%。

divine* [dɪˈvaɪn]

a. 神的；神授的，天赐的

例 To early man, fire was a *divine* gift delivered in the form of lightning, forest fire or burning lava. 对早期的人类来说，火是伴随着闪电、森林大火或是燃烧的岩浆而来的神赐之物。

division [dɪˈvɪʒn]

n. 分开，分隔；分配；分歧；除(法)；部门，科，司

记 词根记忆：di+vis(看)+ion→看出不同→分歧

搭 division of labor 分工

例 The study covered 500 clerical employees in four parallel *divisions*. 这一研究涉及四个平行部门的500名文员。// I wanted to heal the *division* between Tom and his wife, but I didn't know how. 我想要调和汤姆夫妇之间的分歧，但不知该怎样去做。

divisional* [dɪˈvɪʒənl]

a. 部门的

例 Each branch has a *divisional* head. 每个分部都有部门领导。

dizziness [ˈdɪzinəs]

n. 头昏眼花，眩晕

例 With a sudden *dizziness*, he fell down the floor, which frightened his family. 突然一阵眩晕，他跌倒在地上，把家人都吓坏了。

□ diversity □ divert □ divide □ dividend □ divine □ division
□ divisional □ dizziness

dizzy [ˈdɪzi]

a. 头晕目眩的，眩晕的；(使)人头晕的

记 联想记忆：di(二) + zz(打鼾声) + y → 室友打鼾，吵得睡不着 → 眩晕的

例 He is *dizzy* and confused and does not want to be here. 他感到眩晕迷惑，不想待在这儿。

同 giddy(*a.* 眼花缭乱的；头晕的)

dock [dɒk]

v. (使)靠码头 *n.* 码头

例 There are a number of historic ships *docked* in the harbour. 港口停泊着很多具有历史价值的船只。

doctoral [ˈdɒktərəl]

a. 博士的

例 This is Changhong Liu, a *doctoral* student from China. 这位是刘长红，来自中国的博士生。

doctorate* [ˈdɒktərət]

n. 博士学位

例 After getting his *doctorate* last year, he decided to continue that research. 去年取得博士学位后，他决定继续那项研究。

document* [ˈdɒkjumənt]

n. 公文，文件，证件 *vt.* 用文件(或文献等)证明；记载

例 In the English-speaking scientific world, surveys of books and *documents* consulted in libraries and other information agencies have shown that very little foreign-language material is ever consulted. 在以讲英语为主的科学界里，调查显示，科学家们几乎不参考图书馆及其他信息机构中非英语书籍和文献。

派 documentary(*n.* 纪录片 *a.* 文献的，纪实的)

documentation* [ˌdɒkjumenˈteɪʃn]

n. 文件证据，文献资料，文件

例 When you open a bank account, you should take some *documentation* with you. 当你去银行开户时，要随身携带一些文件资料。

dolphin [ˈdɒlfɪn]

n. 海豚

例 Driftnets are killing tens of thousands of *dolphins* in the Mediterranean. 地中海里数以万计的海豚因漂网而死。

dome [dəʊm]

n. 圆屋顶；穹顶

记 联想记忆：和 home(*n.* 家)一起记

例 The bottom of the can is shaped like a *dome* to resist the internal pressure. 罐子的底部呈内凹的圆顶形，这是为了承受来自罐内的压力。

domestic [dəˈmestɪk]

a. 本国的；家庭的；驯养的

记 词根记忆：dom(家) + estic → 家庭的

搭 domestic appliances 家用器具；gross domestic product (GDP) 国内生产总值；domestic market 国内市场；domestic violence 家庭暴力；domestic animals 家畜

例 The evidence we have suggests that *domestic* trade was greater than external trade at all periods. 我们掌握的证据表明，无论在哪个时期，国内贸易都要比对外贸易发达。

□ dizzy □ dock □ doctoral □ doctorate □ document □ documentation
□ dolphin □ dome □ domestic

domesticate [dəˈmestɪkeɪt]

vt. 驯养，教化；使喜爱家居生活

记 联想记忆：domestic(家庭的) + ate(使…) → 使成为家养的 → 驯养

例 It seems that ants are continually ***domesticating*** new species. 蚂蚁似乎也在不断地驯化新品种。

dominant [ˈdɒmɪnənt]

a. 占优势的；统治的；居高临下的

记 词根记忆：domin(统治) + ant → 统治的

搭 a dominant power in the world 世界头号强国；a dominant position 统治地位

例 Of all the media, television is clearly ***dominant***, with newspapers a close second. 在所有的媒体中，电视显然占统治地位，报纸紧随其后，位居第二。

dominate [ˈdɒmɪneɪt]

v. 支配，统治；耸立于

记 词根记忆：domin(统治) + ate → 支配，统治

例 Cities cease to be port cities when other functions ***dominate***. 当城市的其他功能占统治地位时，它就不再是港口城市了。

domination [ˌdɒmɪˈneɪʃn]

n. 控制，统治，支配

记 词根记忆：domin(统治) + ation → 控制，统治，支配

例 The two companies are fighting for the ***domination*** of the market. 这两家公司在争夺对市场的控制权。

donate* [dəʊˈneɪt]

vt. 捐赠，赠送

记 词根记忆：don(给予) + ate → 给出去 → 捐赠，赠送

搭 donate money and materials 捐赠钱和物资

例 I should also like to say if you do have a bike to ***donate***, it doesn't matter what condition it is in. 我还想说如果你有自行车可以捐赠，那么不管它是什么状况都没关系。

派 donator(*n.* 捐赠者)

同 contribute(*v.* 捐助，捐献)；present(*vt.* 赠送)

donation [dəʊˈneɪʃn]

n. 捐款；捐赠

记 词根记忆：don(给予) + ation → 免费给予 → 捐赠

例 The work of the charity is funded by voluntary ***donations***. 这家慈善机构工作所需资金是人们自愿捐赠的。

doom [duːm]

vt. 注定…失败(或遭殃、死亡等)，使…在劫难逃 *n.* 毁灭；厄运，劫数

例 Some people hold that if this kind of rare animal is not well protected, it will be ***doomed*** to extinction. 一些人认为，如果这种珍稀动物得不到很好的保护，它注定会灭绝。

□ domesticate □ dominant □ dominate □ domination □ donate □ donation □ doom

Word List 16

音频

词根、词缀预习表

dorm	睡眠	dormancy *n.* 休眠；冬眠	**dub**	不确定	dubious *a.* 靠不住的，不确定的
plic	重叠	duplicate *n.* 复制品	**dur**	持续	duration *n.* 持续的时间
dynam	力量	dynamic *a.* 动力的；活跃的	**centr**	中心	eccentric *a.* 古怪的，反常的
lip	离开	ecliptic *a.* 日(或月)食的	**eco**	家庭	ecology *n.* 生态学
ed	吃	edible *a.* 可食用的	**ject**	扔	eject *v.* 驱逐，逐出

dorm
[dɔːm]

n. 宿舍

例 There are eight students in each *dorm*. 每个宿舍住八个学生。

dormancy *
[ˈdɔːmənsi]

n. 休眠；催眠状态；冬眠；隐匿

记 词根记忆：dorm(睡眠) + ancy → 休眠；催眠状态；冬眠

例 That huge volcano erupted after one hundred years of *dormancy*. 在长达一百年的休眠之后，那座火山又喷发了。

dormant
[ˈdɔːmənt]

a. 休眠的；静止的；隐匿的

搭 a dormant volcano 休眠火山；lie dormant 潜伏着

例 Mount St. Helens lay *dormant* for more than a century. 圣海伦斯火山休眠了一个多世纪。

dormitory *
[ˈdɔːmətri]

n. (集体)宿舍

记 词根记忆：dorm(睡眠) + it + ory(表地点，名词后缀) → 睡觉的地方 → 宿舍

例 The club has long-term *dormitory* accommodation. 俱乐部提供长期的宿舍住宿服务。

dose *
[dəʊs]

n. 剂量，一剂

记 联想记忆：玫瑰(rose)对生气中的女孩是一剂(dose)良药

例 Nick injected the dog with a strong *dose* of morphine. 尼克给狗注射了一剂强效吗啡。

dot *
[dɒt]

n. 点，小圆点 *v.* 打点于；散布于，点缀

记 联想记忆：和 pot(*n.* 壶)一起记；pot(壶)上有许多可爱的 dot(小圆点)

例 The full stop at the end of this sentence is a *dot*. 这句话结尾的地方是一个句点。

□ dorm □ dormancy □ dormant □ dormitory □ dose □ dot

download* [ˌdaʊnˈləʊd]

v. 下载

例 Do they *download* the song from the Internet? 他们从网上下载这首歌了吗?

downpour* [ˈdaʊnpɔː(r)]

n. 暴雨

记 组合词：down(往下) + pour(倒) → 倾盆而下的雨 → 暴雨

例 We were at home during the *downpour*. 下大雨时我们正待在家里。

downsize* [ˈdaʊnsaɪz]

v. 缩小，紧缩

记 组合词：down(往下) + size(大小，尺寸) → 尺寸减小 → 缩小，紧缩

例 Some firms are even *downsizing* as their profits climb. 一些公司甚至在利润增长的同时也在裁员。

draft* [drɑːft]

n. 草稿，草案；汇票；征兵，服役；通风，气流 *vt.* 起草，草拟；选派，抽调；征募，征召…入伍

搭 bank draft 银行汇票；first draft 草案，初稿

例 You must think a great deal before you start writing your *draft*. 你在开始打草稿之前一定要考虑周全。

drainage [ˈdreɪnɪdʒ]

n. 排水(系统)

记 联想记忆：drain(排水) + age(集体名词后缀) → 排水(系统)

例 *Drainage* within and off the mining site is carefully designed. 矿井内部及周围的排水系统都是经过精心设计的。

dramatic* [drəˈmætɪk]

a. 引人注目的；戏剧性的；激动人心的；戏剧的

记 词根记忆：dra(推动) + ma + tic → 巨大的推动(产生戏剧性变化) → 戏剧性的

搭 dramatic irony 戏剧性的讽刺；dramatic effect 戏剧性的效果

例 The changes in China's Pearl River Delta are more *dramatic* than these natural fluctuations. 中国珠江三角洲的变化比这些自然界的变化更大。

派 dramatically(*ad.* 引人注目地；戏剧性地)

drawback [ˈdrɔːbæk]

n. 缺点；不利条件

记 联想记忆：draw(拉) + back(向后) → 拖后腿 → 缺点；不利条件

例 The only *drawback* to your plan is the expense. 你计划的唯一缺点就是费用问题。

dreadful [ˈdredfl]

a. 可怕的；令人不快的

例 He became an orphan after the *dreadful* disaster. 那场可怕的灾难后他就成了孤儿。

dredge* [dredʒ]

v. 挖掘；疏浚；挖出，吸出；重提(不愉快或令人难堪的)旧事

记 发音记忆："掘机" → 挖掘

搭 dredge up 挖掘；疏浚

例 Those harbours were expensively improved by enlarging, *dredging* and building breakwaters. 这些港口的情况通过扩建、疏浚及建造防浪堤得以改善，但是花销巨大。

派 dredger(*n.* 挖泥船，挖泥机)

□ download □ downpour □ downsize □ draft □ drainage □ dramatic
□ drawback □ dreadful □ dredge

drill
[drɪl]

v./n. 钻；训练

记 联想记忆：dr + ill(生病的) → 生病了还坚持训练 → 训练

例 This small hole was ***drilled*** with an auger. 这个小洞是用钻孔机钻出来的。

droplet
[ˈdrɒplət]

n. 小滴

记 词根记忆：drop(=drip 水滴) + let(表小东西) → 小水滴 → 小滴

例 Study of atmospheric particles formed from the explosion showed that ***droplets*** of sulphuric acid, acting as a screen between the Sun and the Earth's surface, caused a distinct drop in temperature. 对爆炸后形成的大气颗粒的研究显示，硫酸微粒在太阳与地球表面之间形成了一层屏障，使气温明显降低。

drought*
[draʊt]

n. 干旱，旱灾

记 联想记忆：dr(看作 dry，干燥的) + ought(应该) → 干旱时到处都应该很干燥 → 干旱

例 The government has pledged two hundred and fifty million dollars to help the ***drought***-stricken farmers. 政府承诺发放 2.5 亿美元的救济金，以帮助遭受旱灾侵袭的农民。

drum*
[drʌm]

n. 鼓，鼓状物

记 发音记忆："壮" → 他很壮，腰像鼓似的 → 鼓

例 There is a golden tiger sitting on the top of a large bronze ***drum***. 在一个大青铜鼓上卧着一只金虎。

dubious
[ˈdjuːbiəs]

a. 怀疑的；靠不住的，不确定的

记 词根记忆：dub(不确定，不明确) + ious → 靠不住的，不确定的

例 The greatly respected American Association of Zoological Parks and Aquariums (AAZPA) has had extremely ***dubious*** members, too. 在备受人们尊敬的美国动物园水族馆协会中，也有一些身份极其可疑的成员。

同 doubtful(*a.* 可疑的，不确定的)；questionable(*a.* 可疑的)

due*
[djuː]

a. 到期的，预期的；应有的，应得的；正当的

记 发音记忆："丢" → 应有的东西丢了 → 应有的，应得的

搭 due to 由于；in due course 及时地，在适当的时候

例 The greenhouse effect is a natural phenomenon involving the increase in global surface temperature ***due*** to the presence of greenhouse gases. 温室效应是一种自然现象，指由于温室气体的出现而导致地球表面温度升高。

dull*
[dʌl]

a. 乏味的；阴沉的

记 联想记忆：和充实的(full)相反的是乏味的(dull)

例 We all think his tutorial topic is ***dull***. 我们都认为他的辅导主题令人乏味。

□ drill □ droplet □ drought □ drum □ dubious □ due
□ dull

dump*
[dʌmp]

vt. 倾卸，倾倒 *n.* 垃圾场

记 发音记忆："当铺"→到当铺去倾销→倾卸，倾倒

搭 dump on 把…倾倒在…上

例 Dredgers suck up clay and mud and *dump* them in deeper waters. 挖泥船挖出黏土和泥，然后将其倒入更深的水域。

dupe
[djuːp]

n. 上当者，受骗者 *vt.* 欺骗，愚弄

例 Most historians reached the conclusion that the Indian were innocent *dupes*, blameless in the battle. 许多历史学家都得出这样的结论：印第安人是无辜的受骗者，他们无需担负这场战争的责任。

duplicate

[ˈdjuːplɪkeɪt] *vt.* 复制，复写；重复 [ˈdjuːplɪkət] *a.* 完全相同的；副本的 *n.* 复制品

记 词根记忆：du(两，双) + plic(重叠) + ate → 两种重叠状态 → 完全相同的；复制品

搭 duplicate copy 副本

例 These methods include strength training that *duplicates* what they are doing in their running events as well as plyometrics. 这些方法包含力量训练，这与他们在跑步中以及肌肉增强训练中所做的完全一致。

派 duplication(*n.* 副本；复制)

同 copy(*n.* 副本 *v.* 复印，复制)

durable
[ˈdjʊərəbl]

n. 耐用品 *a.* 耐久的；耐用的

记 词根记忆：dur(持续) + able(可…的) → 耐久的；耐用的

搭 a durable peace 持久的和平

例 The table shows the consumer *durables* (telephone, refrigerator, etc.) owned in Britain from 1972 to 1983. 该表格显示了从1972年到1983年英国耐用消费品(如电话、电冰箱等)的拥有情况。

派 durability(*n.* 耐久性；耐用性)

duration
[djuˈreɪʃn]

n. 持续，持续的时间，期间

记 词根记忆：dur(持续) + ation → 持续的时间

例 The school was used as a hospital for the *duration* of the war. 整个战争期间这所学校都被用作医院。

dusk
[dʌsk]

n. 薄暮，黄昏

记 联想记忆：她趴在书桌(desk)上看着窗外的黄昏(dusk)

例 You can catch a glimpse of some more of the rainforest's wildlife as it comes out at *dusk* to feed. 黄昏时分，当雨林中的野生动物出来觅食时，你能看见更多的野生动物。

dwell
[ˈdwel]

vi. 居住，栖身

例 This kind of ground-*dwelling* herbivore may go extinct within a decade. 这种穴居食草动物也许在十年内就会灭绝。

派 dwelling (*n.* 住宅，寓所)

□ dump □ dupe □ duplicate □ durable □ duration □ dusk □ dwell

dweller* [ˈdwelə(r)]	*n.* 居住者，居民 例 An underground *dweller* himself, Carpenter has never paid a heating bill, thanks to solar panels and natural insulation. 作为地下居住者，得益于太阳能板和天然的保温条件，卡彭特从未交过取暖费。
dwindle [ˈdwɪndl]	*v.* (使)变小，(使)缩小 记 联想记忆：d + wind(风) + le → 随风而去，越来越小 → (使)缩小 搭 dwindle down to 缩减到…；dwindle out 逐渐消失 例 The lake has *dwindled* to a third of its former size in the last decade because of global warming. 由于全球气候变暖，十年间，这个湖泊已经缩减到了原来的三分之一。
dynamic* [daɪˈnæmɪk]	*a.* 动力的；活跃的，充满活力的，精力充沛的 记 词根记忆：dynam(力量) + ic → 力量的 → 动力的；活跃的 搭 a dynamic personality 充满活力的个性 例 The market is so *dynamic* that the figures change almost every two weeks. 这个市场很活跃，数据几乎每两周就会发生改变。 派 dynamism(*n.* 精力，活力) 同 active(*a.* 积极的，活动的，活跃的) 反 static(*a.* 静态的，静力的)
dystrophy* [ˈdɪstrəfi]	*n.* 营养障碍；营养不良 记 词根记忆：dys(坏) + troph(营养) + y → 营养不良 搭 muscular dystrophy 肌肉萎缩症 例 In 1986, American researchers identified the genetic defect underlying one type of muscular *dystrophy*. 1986 年，美国研究人员确认了导致一种肌肉萎缩症的遗传缺陷。
earthquake [ˈɜːθkweɪk]	*n.* 地震 记 组合词：earth(地球) + quake(震动) → 地震 例 At the same moment in which the volcano erupted, an *earthquake* with an intensity of 5 on the Richter scale was recorded. 火山喷发的同时，据记载还发生了里氏五级的地震。
earthwork* [ˈɜːθwɜːk]	*n.* 土方(工程) 例 Some contemporary tribes still live among the *earthworks* of earlier cultures. 一些同时代的部落依然生活在早期文化风格的建筑里。
earthworm* [ˈɜːθwɜːm]	*n.* 蚯蚓；小人 记 组合词：earth(地上) + worm(蚯蚓；小人物) → 蚯蚓；小人 例 The digested dung in these burrows is an excellent food supply for the *earthworms*. 这些洞里(蜣螂)消化过的粪球给蚯蚓提供了极好的食物来源。
easy-going* [ˈiːziˌɡəʊɪŋ]	*a.* 脾气随和的，心平气和的；随便的 例 The interview don't tell you if applicants are *easy-going* or hate smoking or whatever. 从面试中你看不出求职者是否随和或者讨厌吸烟什么的。

16

□ dweller □ dwindle □ dynamic □ dystrophy □ earthquake □ earthwork
□ earthworm □ easy-going

eccentric
[ɪk'sentrɪk]

a. 古怪的，反常的 *n.* 古怪的人

记 词根记忆：ec(=e 出) + centr(中心) + ic → 偏离中心的 → 古怪的，反常的

例 Psychologists are trying to find the reason why some children cultivate *eccentric* behavior to separate themselves from their peers. 心理学家正致力于为一些孩子远离同伴孤立自己的古怪行为找出原因。

派 eccentrically(*ad.* 古怪地)；eccentricity(*n.* 古怪；古怪行为)

同 abnormal(*a.* 反常的，变态的)；peculiar(*a.* 奇特的)

反 ordinary(*a.* 平常的，普通的)；normal(*a.* 正常的)

ecliptic
[ɪ'klɪptɪk]

n.【天】黄道 *a.* 黄道的，日(或月)食的

记 词根记忆：ec(没有) + lip(离开) + tic → 因离开而没有了 → 日(或月)食的

例 There is an angle between the *ecliptic* plane and the equatorial plane which is called the obliquity of the ecliptic. 黄道面与赤道面之间有一个夹角被称为黄赤交角。

eco-friendly
[ˌiːkəʊ'frendli]

a. 环保的

例 Reusable bag is an *eco-friendly* product which was famous for its slogan "I am not a plastic bag!" 可再利用袋是一种环保产品，它曾以"我不是塑料袋"的标语而闻名。

ecological
[ˌiːkə'lɒdʒɪkl]

a. 生态学的，生态的

例 Some scientists claim that the destruction of the rainforests is an *ecological* disaster that is threatening the survival of life on earth. 一些科学家声称，雨林的破坏是一场生态灾难，正威胁着地球上生命的生存。

ecology
[iː'kɒlədʒi]

n. 生态，生态学；生态环境

记 词根记忆：eco(家庭) + logy(…学) → 研究(地球这个大)家庭事务的学科 → 生态学

例 If the beetles successfully adapt to their new environment, they'll soon become a part of the local *ecology*. 如果甲虫完全适应了新的环境，它们很快就会成为当地生态环境的一部分。

economic*
[ˌiːkə'nɒmɪk]

a. 经济的；经济上的，经济学的

搭 economic climate 经济形势，经济气候

例 They encouraged farmers to use greater quantities of fertilizers than are needed to get the highest *economic* crop yield. 他们鼓励农民使用远远超过作物实际所需量的化肥，以获得最高的经济作物产量。

economical
[ˌiːkə'nɒmɪkl]

a. 节约的；经济的

例 The government set some policies to help meet the demand for more *economical* use of land. 政府制定了一些政策，以满足更为经济地利用土地的需要。

派 economically(*ad.* 节约地；经济上)

ecosystem*
['iːkəʊsɪstəm]

n. 生态系统

记 词根记忆：eco(家庭的) + system(系统) → 有关家庭的系统 → 生态系统

搭 balanced ecosystem 平衡的生态系统

例 One tool for assessing the impact of forestry on the *ecosystem* is population viability analysis (PVA). 种群生存力分析是评定林业对生态系统影响的一种方法。

□ eccentric □ ecliptic □ eco-friendly □ ecological □ ecology □ economic
□ economical □ ecosystem

edible [ˈedəbl]	*a.* 可食用的 记 词根记忆：ed(吃) + ible(可…的) → 可食用的 例 The seeds of these plants are *edible*. 这些植物的种子是可食用的。 派 inedible(*a.* 不可食用的) 同 eatable(*a.* 可以吃的)
edify [ˈedɪfaɪ]	*v.* 陶冶，教化；启发，启迪 记 词根记忆：ed(吃) + ify(使…) → 使吃下去 → 陶冶，教化 例 Good books not only *edify* but also entertain their readers. 好书不仅可以陶冶读者的情操，还可以娱乐读者。
effect* [ɪˈfekt]	*n.* 作用，影响；结果；效果 *vt.* 使产生，招致；实现 记 词根记忆：ef(出) + fect(做) → 做出来的 → 效果 搭 carry/bring into effect 使生效，实施；in effect 有效；实际上；take effect 生效，起作用；side effects 副作用；a positive effect 积极影响；cause and effect 原因和结果 例 The report suggests that the smoke experienced by many people in their daily lives is enough to produce substantial adverse *effects* on a person's heart and lungs. 报告指出，许多人在日常生活中吸入的(香烟)烟雾足以给他们的心脏和肺造成严重的负面影响。
effective* [ɪˈfektɪv]	*a.* 有效的，生效的；给人深刻印象的，显著的 记 来自 effect(*n.* 影响；效果) 搭 effective measures 有效措施；an effective remedy 有效药物 例 Which advertisement is the most *effective*? 哪一种广告最有效？ 派 ineffective(*a.* 无效的)；effectiveness(*n.* 效力)；effectively(*ad.* 有效地)
efficiency [ɪˈfɪʃnsi]	*n.* 效率；功效，效能 记 词根记忆：ef(出) + fic(做) + iency → 做出东西又快又好 → 效率；功效 例 Clean coal is an avenue for improving fuel conversion *efficiency*. 提高煤的纯度是提高燃料转换效率的一个途径。
efficient* [ɪˈfɪʃnt]	*a.* 有效的，效率高的；有能力的，能胜任的 记 词根记忆：ef(出) + fic(做) + ient → 能做出来的 → 有能力的；有效的 搭 energy efficient 节能的；efficient methods 有效的方法；the efficient use of energy 能源的有效利用 例 The financial analyst found *efficient* ways for the company to save money. 财务分析师找到了能够有效地替公司省钱的方法。 派 efficiently(*ad.* 有效率地；有效地)
effort* [ˈefət]	*n.* 努力，艰难的尝试；成就 搭 make an/every effort 努力，出力，费力 例 Henry has put a lot of *effort* into communicating with new friends. 亨利非常努力地与新朋友进行交流。 派 effortless(*a.* 容易的，轻松自如的)

□ edible □ edify □ effect □ effective □ efficiency □ efficient
□ effort

eject [iˈdʒekt]

v. 弹出；喷出；驱逐，逐出

记 词根记忆：e(出) + ject(扔) → 扔出来 → 驱逐，逐出

搭 eject from 从…逐出

例 The quantity of dust *ejected* by Mount St. Helens amounted to a quarter of a cubic mile. 圣海伦斯火山喷出的粉尘多达四分之一立方英里。

同 expel(*vt.* 驱逐；开除)；remove(*vt.* 开除；移交)；evict(*vt.* 驱逐，逐出)

ejection [iˈdʒekʃn]

n. 喷出；排出物

例 The reaction to the *ejection* of these small particles inside the rocket causes the rocket to move forwards. 喷出这些火箭内部颗粒的反作用力使得火箭向前运动。

elaborate

[ɪˈlæbərət] *a.* 详尽的；复杂的；精心制作的 [ɪˈlæbəreɪt] *v.* 详述；详细制定

记 联想记忆：e(出) + labor(劳动) + ate → 辛苦劳动做出来的 → 精心制作的

搭 elaborate designs 精心的设计

例 Archaeological traces of far more *elaborate* cultures have been dismissed in this region. 排除了该地区有更为复杂和高级文明存在的考古遗迹的可能。

elaboration [ɪˌlæbəˈreɪʃn]

n. 精心之作；详尽阐述

记 联想记忆：e(出) + labor(劳动) + ation → 辛苦劳动做出来的东西 → 精心之作；详尽阐述

例 Whether homosexuals could get married legally or not needs further *elaboration*. 对于同性恋结婚是否合法的问题，还需进一步探讨。

elastic [ɪˈlæstɪk]

a. 有弹性的；灵活的 *n.* 松紧带

记 联想记忆：e(出) + last(延长) + ic(形容词后缀) → 可延长的 → 有弹性的；灵活的

例 The ropes are made of *elastic* fabrics. 这些绳子是由弹性纤维制成的。// Their plans are fairly *elastic*. 他们的计划具有相当大的灵活性。

elbow [ˈelbəʊ]

n. 肘；(衣服的)肘部

记 联想记忆：力在肘(elbow)，弓(bow)在手

例 His forearms were black and blue from wrist to *elbow*. 他的小臂从手腕到肘部又青又紫。

electrical* [ɪˈlektrɪkl]

a. 电的，电学的，有关电的

搭 an electrical fault 电故障

例 The small battery-powered gadget can deliver subliminal *electrical* pulses to the skin. 这种小的电池驱动装置可以向皮肤传达微小的电脉冲。

派 electrically(*ad.* 电力地)

electronic* [ɪˌlekˈtrɒnɪk]

a. 电子的

记 来自 electric(*a.* 电的)

例 Computers make up of the so-called *electronic* media. 所谓的电子媒介是由计算机构成的。

□ eject □ ejection □ elaborate □ elaboration □ elastic □ elbow
□ electrical □ electronic

element* [ˈelɪmənt]

n. 要素；元素；[the -s] 基本原理

记 联想记忆：e + lemen（看作 lemon，柠檬）+ t → 柠檬是水果的一种 → 要素；元素

例 Impressed by the ***element's*** combustibility, several 17th century chemists used phosphorus to manufacture fire-lighting devices. 磷的燃烧性给 17 世纪的几位化学家留下了深刻印象，他们开始用这种元素制造点火装置。

派 elementary（*a.* 初步的；基本的）

elevate [ˈelɪveɪt]

vt. 提升…的职位；举起；使更有修养

记 词根记忆：e（向外）+ lev（升）+ ate（使…）→ 使…升起来 → 举起

例 John has been ***elevated*** to manager. 约翰已被提升为经理。

派 elevating（*a.* 发人深思的，有启发性的）

elicitation [ɪˌlɪsɪˈteɪʃn]

n. 引出，诱出

记 词根记忆：e（出）+ lic（诱骗）+ itation → 诱骗到外边来 → 引出，诱出

例 There are also several direct methods of ***elicitation***, such as asking information to fill in the blanks. 这里也有一些直接的引导办法，例如在空格处填上所问的信息。

eligible [ˈelɪdʒəbl]

a. 符合条件的；合适的

记 词根记忆：e + lig（=lect 选择）+ ible → 能被选择出来的 → 符合条件的

搭 be eligible to 有资格做…

例 You are ***eligible*** for a student loan if you are a UK resident. 如果你是英国居民，就可以申请学生贷款。

同 desirable（*a.* 值得要的，合意的）；qualified（*a.* 有资格的）；suitable（*a.* 适当的，相配的）

eliminate [ɪˈlɪmɪneɪt]

vt. 消灭，消除；淘汰

记 词根记忆：e（出）+ limin（界限）+ ate → 划在界限之外 → 消灭，消除

搭 eliminate poverty 消除贫困；eliminate crime 消除犯罪

例 Job descriptions ***eliminate*** role ambiguity for managers. 职位描述消除了经理们对角色认识的模糊不清。

elite* [eɪˈliːt]

n. 精英，中坚 *a.* 卓越的，精锐的

记 联想记忆：e + lite（看作词根 lig，选择）→ 选出来的都是精英 → 精英

搭 social elite 社会精英

例 This country's Internet ***elite*** have begun to emerge in recent years. 近年来，该国涌现出一批网络精英。

派 elitism（*n.* 精英统治；精英主义）

elucidate [iˈluːsɪdeɪt]

vt. 阐明，使…清楚

记 联想记忆：e + lucid（清晰的）+ ate → 弄清晰 → 阐明，使…清楚

例 The notes in this book could help you ***elucidate*** the confusing and difficult parts. 书中的注释可以帮你弄清楚难懂的部分。

□ element □ elevate □ elicitation □ eligible □ eliminate □ elite □ elucidate

elusive [iˈluːsɪv]

a. 难懂的，难捉摸的；易忘的

记 联想记忆：e(出) + lus(看作词根 lust，光) + ive → 没有灵光出来的 → 难懂的，难捉摸的

例 Even if these peripheral details are a bit *elusive*, they come back readily in hypnosis or when we relive the event imaginatively, as in psychodrama. 即使这些细枝末节有点容易忘却，但它们也会在我们处于催眠状态下或者重温往事时在脑海里生动地浮现出来，就像在心理剧里那样。

embankment* [ɪmˈbæŋkmənt]

n. 筑堤；堤岸，路基

记 联想记忆：em(使…) + bank(岸) + ment → 使有堤岸 → 筑堤

例 It was the Tilburg architect Jo Hurkmans who hit on the idea of making use of noise *embankments* on main roads. 蒂尔堡的建筑师约·胡尔克曼斯灵机一动，想到在主干道上使用防噪音路基的办法。

embark [ɪmˈbɑːk]

v. (使)上船或飞机；(使)从事

搭 embark on/upon 从事，着手，开始工作

例 Without hesitation Alexander *embarked* on his new career as a musician. 亚历山大毫不犹豫地开始他的新职业，当一名音乐家。

同 board〔*v.* 上(船、飞机等)〕

反 disembark〔*v.* 下车(或船、飞机等)〕

embassy* [ˈembəsi]

n. 大使馆；大使馆全体官员

搭 the American Embassy in Paris 美国驻巴黎大使馆

例 Your visa application is being processed at the UK *Embassy*. 你的签证正由英国大使馆办理。

embed* [ɪmˈbed]

vt. 把…嵌入(或埋入、插入)，扎牢；使深留脑中

记 联想记忆：em(进入…中) + bed(床) → 把…放入床中 → 把…嵌入

搭 be embedded in 植根于

例 The traditional idea is deeply *embedded* in our university. 这个传统的想法在我们大学根深蒂固。

派 embedment(*n.* 嵌入)

同 wedge(*vt.* 楔入，楔进)；fix(*v.* 使固定)

embezzlement* [ɪmˈbezlmənt]

n. 贪污，盗用

记 联想记忆：em + bezzle(看作 bezzant，金银币) + ment → 将金银币据为己有 → 贪污，盗用

例 The three criminals are arrested for *embezzlement* of company funds. 这三名罪犯因为盗用公司资金而被逮捕。

embody [ɪmˈbɒdi]

vt. (作品等)表达，体现；具体表现，使具体化；包括，包含

记 词根记忆：em(给予) + body(身体) → 给予身体 → 使具体化

例 As a rule, if you want to write a good essay, you'd better list some relevant examples *embodying* the gist. 通常，如果你想写出好文章，你最好列举一些体现文章主旨的相关例子。

同 contain(*vt.* 包含，容纳)；incarnate(*vt.* 使具体化)

□ elusive □ embankment □ embark □ embassy □ embed □ embezzlement □ embody

emboss [ɪm'bɒs]	*vt.* 使…凸出；压花(纹) 记 联想记忆：em(出)+boss(老板)→老板通常都有凸出来的啤酒肚→使…凸出；压花(纹) 例 The hotel's name was ***embossed*** on all the towels. 所有毛巾上都压印有旅馆的名字。
embrace [ɪm'breɪs]	*v./n.* 拥抱；包括；欣然接受 记 词根记忆：em(使…)+brac(胳膊)+e→使在胳膊里→拥抱 例 The students tearfully ***embraced*** each other on their last day of school. 在校的最后一天，学生们流着泪相互拥抱。 

Jovons saw the kettle boil and cried out with the delighted voice of a child; Marshal too had seen the kettle boil and sat down silently to build an engine.

杰文斯看见壶开了，高兴得像孩子似地叫了起来；马歇尔也看见壶开了，却悄悄地坐下来造了一部蒸汽机。

——英国经济学家 凯恩斯(John Maynard Keynes, British economist)

16

Word List 17

音频

词根、词缀预习表

bryo	变大	embryo *n.* 胚胎	**merg**	浸没	emerge *vi.* 显露
min	突出	eminent *a.* 杰出的，显赫的	**mit**	送	emit *vt.* 发出，散发
phas	说	emphasize *vt.* 强调，着重	**emul**	竞争	emulate *vt.* 赶上
code	电码，密码	encode *vt.* 把…译成电码	**croach**	钩子	encroach *vi.* 侵入，侵占
dur	持续	endure *v.* 忍受；持久	**enigm**	谜	enigma *n.* 谜

embryo*
[ˈembriəʊ]

n. 胚，胚胎；事物的萌芽期

记 词根记忆：em + bryo（变大）→ 种子等变大 → 胚胎

搭 in embryo 在胚胎阶段，在萌芽时期

例 Two American researchers studied the brains of human ***embryos*** and discovered that the left-right asymmetry exists before birth. 两位美国研究人员在对人类胚胎的大脑进行研究后发现，左右脑不对称的现象在出生前就存在。

派 embryonic（*a.* 胚胎期的，萌芽期的）

emerge*
[iˈmɜːdʒ]

vi. 出现；显露，（事实等）暴露

记 词根记忆：e（出）+ merg（浸没）+ e → 从浸没物之中出来 → 显露

例 A new style of architecture ***emerged*** to reflect more idealistic notions for the future. 一种新的建筑风格出现了，它反映了未来更为理想的建筑理念。

emergency*
[iˈmɜːdʒənsi]

n. 紧急情况，突发事件

记 联想记忆：emerge（出现）+（e）ncy → 突然出现 → 紧急情况，突发事件

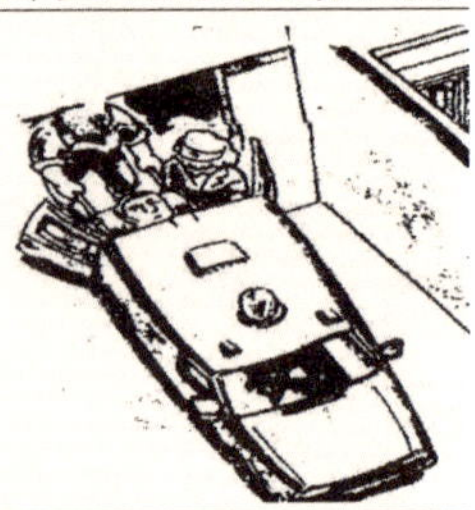

搭 emergency funding 应急基金；emergency contact person 紧急联系人；emergency shelter 应急避难所

例 If it's an ***emergency***, you can phone at any time. 如果发生紧急情况，你可以随时来电。

emeritus
[iˈmerɪtəs]

a. 保留头衔而退休的，荣誉退休的

例 Michael Yessis, an ***emeritus*** professor of Sports Science at California State University at Fullerton, maintains that genetics only determined about one third of what an athlete can do. 位于富勒顿的加州大学体育科学系名誉教授迈克尔·耶西认为基因对一名运动员的能力来说只起 1/3 的作用。

eminent*
['emɪnənt]

a. 杰出的，显赫的

记 词根记忆：e(出) + min(突出) + ent → 杰出的，显赫的

例 He was then the most ***eminent*** architect in England. 他是当时英格兰最著名的建筑师。

emission*
[i'mɪʃn]

n. (光、热等的)散发；散发物

记 词根记忆：e(出) + miss(送) + ion → 送出 → (光、热等的)散发

搭 greenhouse gas emissions 温室气体排放；zero-emission cars 零排放车辆

例 The new fuel can save energy and cut carbon dioxide ***emissions***. 新型燃料可以节约能源，降低二氧化碳的排放量。

emit*
[i'mɪt]

vt. 发出(光、热、声音等)，射出，散发，排放

记 词根记忆：e(出) + mit(送) → 发出，散发

搭 emit light 发光

例 Older trucks, buses and taxis ***emit*** excessive levels of smoke and fumes. 老式卡车、公交车和出租车排放出过量的烟和废气。

17

emotion*
[ɪ'məʊʃn]

n. 感情；情绪

记 词根记忆：e(出) + mot(动) + ion(名词后缀) → 心里释放出的东西 → 感情；情绪

例 Doing sports can be a good way to release suppressed ***emotion***. 运动是一个释放压抑情绪的好方法。

emotional*
[ɪ'məʊʃənl]

a. 感情(上)的，情绪(上)的；引起情感的，表示情感的；情绪激动的，易动感情的

记 词根记忆：e(出) + mot(动) + ion + al → 动出(感情) → 感情(上)的

例 Mother is the most essential part in a family for which she often provides ***emotional*** support. 母亲是一个家庭中最重要的成员，她常常要为整个家庭提供情感支持。

派 emotionally(*ad.* 在情绪上)

emperor
['empərə(r)]

n. 皇帝；君主

例 The executive of a republic cannot do what a king or an ***emperor*** does. 共和国的领导者不能像国王或君主那样行事。

emphasis
['emfəsɪs]

n. 强调；重要性

记 词根记忆：em(表加强) + phas(说) + is → 强调；重要性

搭 place emphasis on 把重点放在…上面，强调…

例 The President's statement gave ***emphasis*** to the crisis. 总统在声明中强调了这次危机。

emphasize
['emfəsaɪz]

vt. 强调，着重

例 This report ***emphasizes*** that cancer is not caused by a single element in cigarette smoke. 这一报告强调，癌症并不是由香烟烟雾中的某单一成分导致的。

□ eminent □ emission □ emit □ emotion □ emotional □ emperor
□ emphasis □ emphasize

empire* [ˈempaɪə(r)]

n. 帝国

记 联想记忆：一个大帝国(empire)肯定需要一个贤明的君主(emperor)

例 Isaac's epic stories charted the future of the galactic ***empire***. 伊萨克的史诗故事描绘出了那个超级帝国的未来。

empirical* [ɪmˈpɪrɪkl]

a. 经验主义的，以经验为依据的

例 Amazingly, there is virtually no ***empirical*** evidence to support the use of illustrations in teaching reading. 令人惊讶的是，事实上并没有实践经验性的证据可以证明图表在阅读教学中的作用。

反 theoretical(*a.* 理论的)

employ* [ɪmˈplɔɪ]

n./vt. 雇用；用，使用

例 Actually, the person did not do the work himself but rather asked a young Scotsman in his ***employ*** to design the system. 实际上那个人没有亲自做这项工作，而是雇了一个苏格兰年轻人来设计该系统。

派 employee(*n.* 职员，雇员)；employer(*n.* 雇主)；employment(*n.* 雇用)；employable(*a.* 可利用的)

emulate [ˈemjuleɪt]

vt. 与…竞争，赶上；仿真，模仿

记 词根记忆：emul(竞争) + ate → 与…竞争，赶上

例 While suggestopedia has gained some reputation through success in the teaching of modern languages, few teachers are able to ***emulate*** the spectacular results of Lozanov and his associates. 在现代语言教学所取得的成功中，暗示教学法已经享有一定的声誉，几乎没有教师可以取得像洛扎诺夫及其同僚们那样引人注目的成果。

派 emulation(*n.* 竞争；仿效)

enable* [ɪˈneɪbl]

vt. 使能够，使成为可能

记 联想记忆：en(使…) + able(能够的) → 使能够，使成为可能

搭 enable sb. to do sth. 使…能够做…

例 The bank service ***enables*** you to withdraw cash from your account at any time. 这种银行服务使你能随时从账户中取钱。

enact [ɪˈnækt]

v. 通过(法律)；扮演(角色)

记 联想记忆：en(使) + act(法令) → 使成为法令 → 通过(法律)

例 Under the new law, Internet bars must ***enact*** relevant policies to prevent young people's admission. 新的法律规定，网吧必须制定相关政策制止未成年人进入。

encapsulate [ɪnˈkæpsjuleɪt]

vt. 装入胶囊；压缩；总结，概述

记 来自 capsule(*n.* 胶囊)；en(进入) + capsul(e) + ate (使…)→ 装入胶囊

例 The movie ***encapsulated*** tens of romantic stories and recomposed them, which grasped many youth' s eyes. 这部电影收纳了数十个浪漫故事，并将其改编，引起大量年轻人的关注。

encase* [ɪnˈkeɪs]

vt. 装入，包住

记 联想记忆：en(进入) + case(容器) → 被装入容器中 → 装入，包住

搭 encase sth. in sth. 将…装入…

例 The resin oozed out of the tree and the spider or leaf became ***encased*** in it. 树脂从树里渗出来，把蜘蛛或树叶包在了里面。

□ empire □ empirical □ employ □ emulate □ enable □ enact □ encapsulate □ encase

enclose
[ɪn'kləʊz]

vt. 围住；附上；把…装入信封

记 联想记忆：en(进入) + close(关闭) → 关闭在里面 → 围住

例 The farmer *enclosed* his land and kept cattle away from his crops. 农民在田地四周筑起围栏，以使牛群远离庄稼。

---

enclosure
[ɪn'kləʊʒə(r)]

n. 四周有篱笆(或围墙等)的场地，围场；(信中的)附件

记 联想记忆：en(进入…之中) + clos(看作 close) + ure → 被围在当中 → 围场

例 Overseas trade, colonial plunder and the *enclosure* movement had accumulated abundant capital for greedy capitalists in Western countries. 海外贸易、殖民掠夺和圈地运动为西方贪婪的资本家积累了雄厚的资本。

enclosure

17

---

encode
[ɪn'kəʊd]

vt. 把(电文等)译成电码(或密码)，把…编码

记 词根记忆：en + code(电码，密码) → 把…译成电码

例 Engineers need to *encode* the message into computer language. 工程师需要将信息转化为计算机语言。

---

encompass
[ɪn'kʌmpəs]

vt. 包含；包围；环绕

记 联想记忆：en(进入) + compass(范围) → 收入所属范围之内 → 包含；包围

例 It would not worry trustbusters, because it seems unlikely to *encompass* advertising area in any deal between the *New York Post* and the *Daily News*. 《纽约邮报》和《每日新闻》之间的任何合作似乎都不可能包含广告领域，因此反垄断人士不会担心。

encompass

---

encounter*
[ɪn'kaʊntə(r)]

vt./n. 遭遇，遇到

记 联想记忆：en(使…) + counter(相反的) → 使从两个相反的方面来 → 遇到，遭遇

搭 encounter problems 遇到问题

例 I *encountered* a lot of difficulty when I tried to take a rest. 当我打算休息一下时遇到了很多麻烦。// Our *encounter* at the train station caught me by surprise. 我们在车站的相遇让我大吃一惊。

---

encourage*
[ɪn'kʌrɪdʒ]

v. 鼓励；促进，激发

记 联想记忆：en(使…) + courage(精神) → 使有精神 → 鼓励

搭 encourage sb. to do sth. 鼓励某人做某事

例 To *encourage* the bees to produce as much honey as possible, the beekeepers open the hives and stack extra boxes on top. 为了让蜜蜂尽可能多地产蜜，养蜂人打开蜂箱，在上面加放了一些盒子。

encroach [ɪnˈkrəʊtʃ]

vi. 侵入，侵占，侵犯；侵蚀，蚕食(土地)

记 词根记忆：en(进入) + croach(=croch 钩子) → 使进入钩子 → 侵入，侵占

例 It has been proved that human activities have *encroached* upon the survival of the creatures in nature. 经证实，人类的活动已经侵害了自然界中生物的生存。

endanger [ɪnˈdeɪndʒə(r)]

vt. 危及，危害

记 联想记忆：en(使…) + danger(危险) → 危及

例 Navajo is considered *endangered* despite having 150,000 speakers. 尽管有 15 万人使用纳瓦霍语，它还是濒临(灭绝的)危险。

同 imperil(*vt.* 使陷于危险，危及)

endeavour* [ɪnˈdevə(r)]

n./vi. 努力，尽力；尝试

记 联想记忆：end(尽头) + eav(看作 eager，热情) + our(我们的) → 用尽了我们的热情 → 努力，尽力

搭 endeavour to do sth. 努力做某事

例 I wished the result of my *endeavours* to be respectable. 我希望我努力的结果能得到尊重。// On the basis of tradition, the calligraphists in China and South Korea *endeavour* to explore modern styles, making the ever-lasting literal handwriting art go forward in new era. 中韩两国书法家立足传统，努力探索现代书写风格，使这门经久不衰的文字书写艺术在新时期继续发展。

endorse* [ɪnˈdɔːs]

vt. 支持，赞同

搭 endorse a candidate 支持候选人

例 The socio-ecological view of health was *endorsed* at the first International Conference of Health Promotion. 关于健康的社会生态学观点在第一届世界健康促进会上得到了认可。

endure [ɪnˈdjʊə(r)]

v. 忍受；持久，持续

记 词根记忆：en(使) + dur(持续) + e → 忍受；持久，持续

例 The pain was almost too great to *endure*. 这种疼痛几乎难以忍受。

energetic* [ˌenəˈdʒetɪk]

a. 有力的，精力旺盛的；积极的

记 来自 energy(*n.* 精神，活力)

搭 an energetic person 精力旺盛的人

例 I don't like doing *energetic* exercises in the evening. 我不喜欢在晚上做剧烈运动。

enforce [ɪnˈfɔːs]

vt. 实施，执行；强制，迫使

记 联想记忆：en(使…) + force(强迫) → 强制，迫使

搭 enforce laws 执法；enforce a demand 竭力要求

例 Do they *enforce* that rule? 他们执行那条规则了吗？// The teacher did not like to *enforce* rigid rules on the children. 那个老师不喜欢将陈规旧条强加到孩子们身上。

派 enforcement(*n.* 实施，执行)

□ encroach □ endanger □ endeavour □ endorse □ endure □ energetic
□ enforce

enfranchise* [ɪnˈfræntʃaɪz]

vt. 给予…政治权利(尤指选举权); 解放(奴隶)

记 联想记忆: en(使…) + franchise(选举权) → 使…有选举权 → 给予…权利

例 The third Reform Act *enfranchised* the agricultural labourer. 第三版《改革法案》赋予了农业劳动者选举权。

派 enfranchisement(*n.* 给予权利; 解放)

engage* [ɪnˈgeɪdʒ]

v. 吸引(某人的注意力等); 占用(某人的时间); 使从事于, 使忙于; 雇用, 聘用; 与(某人)交战; (指机器零件等)啮合, 衔接

搭 engage in doing sth. 从事于…

例 In many countries, children *engage* in some kind of paid work. 在很多国家, 儿童会做某些付费工作。

engrave* [ɪnˈgreɪv]

vt. (在…上)雕刻; (使)铭记

记 联想记忆: en(进入) + grave(坟墓) → 进入坟墓也要记着, 真是刻骨铭心 → (使)铭记

搭 be engraved with one's name 刻着某人的名字

例 Many researchers now think that these were pictures the wise men *engraved* for themselves. 现在许多研究者认为这些图是智者为他们自己雕刻的。

engross [ɪnˈgrəʊs]

vt. 使全神贯注, 占去(某人的)全部注意力和时间

记 联想记忆: en(进入) + gross(总的) → 全身心进入一种状态 → 使全神贯注

例 As the number of students grew, it totally *engrossed* him. 随着学生人数的增多, 他全身心投入了这项工作。

enhance [ɪnˈhɑːns]

vt. 提高, 增强, 增进

搭 enhance one's reputation 提高声誉; enhance one's confidence 增强信心; enhance the ability 提高能力

例 Organisations provide a range of opportunities for women to *enhance* their skills. 一些组织为妇女提供大量提高她们技能的机会。

enhancer [ɪnˈhɑːnsə(r)]

n. 增强剂; 放大器

搭 flavour enhancers 增味剂

例 Although not all people like the flavor of onion, ginger or garlic, they are good immune system *enhancer*. 尽管不是所有人都喜欢洋葱、姜、蒜的味道, 但它们都具有极佳的增强免疫的功能。

enigma [ɪˈnɪgmə]

n. 谜, 谜一样的人或事

记 词根记忆: enigm(谜) + a → 谜

例 Up to now, researchers and scientists cannot explain the whole *enigma* of Mayan civilization's disappearance. 研究者和科学家至今都无法解释玛雅文明消失这个谜团。

enjoyable* [ɪnˈdʒɔɪəbl]

a. 令人愉快的, 使人快乐的

例 There is going to be a very *enjoyable* TV programme this evening. 今天晚上将有一期非常有意思的电视节目。

□ enfranchise □ engage □ engrave □ engross □ enhance □ enhancer
□ enigma □ enjoyable

enlarge [ɪnˈlɑːdʒ]

v. 扩大，放大，扩充

记 联想记忆：en(使…) + large(大的) → 使…变大 → 扩大，放大

例 The new headmaster *enlarged* his office and installed expensive carpet. 新校长扩充了他的办公室，并铺上了昂贵的地毯。

派 enlarger(*n.* 放大机，缩放机)；enlargement(*n.* 扩大，扩充；扩大物，放大物)

enlighten [ɪnˈlaɪtn]

vt. 启发；开导；阐明

记 词根记忆：en(使…) + light(点亮) + en → 使心灵点亮 → 启发；开导

例 Would you *enlighten* me on your plans for the future? 能否给我讲讲你未来的计划?

enlist [ɪnˈlɪst]

v. 征募；从军，参军；谋取(帮助、支持等)

记 联想记忆：en(进入) + list(名单) → 进入名单 → 征募；从军，参军

例 At present, tens of thousands of volunteers are being *enlisted* all over the country to serve the approaching World Expo. 目前，正在全国范围内招募成千上万的志愿者，为即将到来的世博会服务。

enormous* [ɪˈnɔːməs]

a. 巨大的，庞大的，极大的

记 联想记忆：e(出) + norm(规范) + ous(形容词后缀) → 超出规范的 → 巨大的

搭 enormous expenditure 巨额开支；an enormous amount of 大量的

例 We grow an *enormous* number of bananas each year. 我们每年都大量种植香蕉。

派 enormously(*ad.* 巨大地，庞大地)

enquire* [ɪnˈkwaɪə(r)]

v. 打听，询问；查问，调查

记 词根记忆：en(向内) + quir(追问) + e → 追问到里面 → 询问；查问

搭 enquire into 调查，查究，查问

例 If you have any question, welcome to call the Students' Union to *enquire*. 有任何问题，欢迎致电学生会询问。

enquiry [ɪnˈkwaɪəri]

n. 询问；调查；探索

记 联想记忆：enquir(=enquire 询问) + y → 询问

例 Before I continue, is there any *enquiry* into what I've said? 在我继续讲之前，对我刚才所说的，还有什么想问的吗?

enrich [ɪnˈrɪtʃ]

vt. 充实，使丰富；使富裕

记 联想记忆：en(使…) + rich(富有的) → 使富裕

搭 enrich one's experience 丰富…的经历

例 Ports can *enrich* the life of a city. 港口可以丰富一座城市的生活。

enroll* [ɪnˈrəʊl]

v. 入学；登记；加入；招收

记 联想记忆：en(进入) + roll(名单) → 上了名单 → 登记

搭 enroll on 加入，参加；注册；入学

例 Places are available here even for students *enrolled* in the minimum length course. 这里甚至为那些报名参加最短课时的学生提供上课场所。

□ enlarge □ enlighten □ enlist □ enormous □ enquire □ enquiry
□ enrich □ enroll

enrolment
[ɪnˈrəʊlmənt]

n. 登记(人数)，注册(人数)；入学，入伍；登记簿，名册

记 联想记忆：enrol(登记；入学) + ment → 登记；入学

搭 enrolment form 登记表

例 When you apply for a student loan, most banks ask you to bring your passport and your letter or certificate of *enrolment*. 申请学生贷款的时候，很多银行会要求你随身携带护照、入学介绍信或入学证明。

enslave
[ɪnˈsleɪv]

vt. 奴役，征服，使受控制

记 联想记忆：en(使…) + slave(奴隶) → 使成为奴隶 → 奴役，征服，使受控制

例 Nowadays, more and more Americans have realized that they are being *enslaved* by the credit-card debt. 如今，越来越多的美国人意识到了自己正沦为信用卡债务的奴隶。

派 enslavement(*n.* 奴役，征服)

ensue
[ɪnˈsjuː]

vi. 继而发生；接着发生

记 联想记忆：确定(ensure)的事情就会继而发生(ensue)

例 If a forest fire cannot be extinguished, devastation is sure to *ensue*. 如果不能扑灭森林火灾，毁坏一定会随之发生。

ensure
[ɪnˈʃʊə(r)]

vt. 确保，保证；担保；赋予

记 联想记忆：en(使…) + sure(确定的) → 使确定 → 确保，保证

例 How can you *ensure* that your diet contains enough of the vitamins you need? 你怎样才能确保你的饮食中包含了自己所需的足量的维生素呢？

entail *
[ɪnˈteɪl]

vt. 牵涉；需要

记 联想记忆：en + tail(尾巴) → 被人抓住尾巴 → 牵涉

例 The work *entailed* the processing of accounts and generating of invoices. 这份工作需要处理账目和开具发票。

enterprise *
[ˈentəpraɪz]

n. 企业，公司；事业

记 词根记忆：enter(进入) + pris(握住) + e → 进入市场，把握先机 → 企业，公司

搭 a backbone enterprise 骨干企业；joint enterprise 合资企业；state enterprise 国有企业

例 The land can be considered part of the *enterprise's* assets. 这块土地可以归入该公司的资产。

entertain *
[ˌentəˈteɪn]

v. (使)欢乐，(使)娱乐；招待

记 词根记忆：enter(进入) + tain(拿住) → 拿着东西进入 → 招待

搭 entertain sb. with sth. 以…娱乐某人；以…招待某人

例 The spectators go to be *entertained* rather than out of loyalty to a team. 观众去观看体育比赛与其说是忠于某支球队，还不如说是为了娱乐。

□ enrolment □ enslave □ ensue □ ensure □ entail □ enterprise
□ entertain

entertainment* [ˌentəˈteɪnmənt]

n. 招待，款待；娱乐(业)；供消遣的事物

记 来自 entertain(*v.* 娱乐；招待)

搭 the entertainment industry 娱乐产业

例 The use of some ***entertainment*** can be addicted. 参与一些娱乐项目是会上瘾的。

enthusiasm [ɪnˈθjuːziæzəm]

n. 热情，热心，积极性；热衷的事物

例 She shows great ***enthusiasm*** for the movie. 她对这部电影表现出了极大的热情。

enthusiastic [ɪnˌθjuːziˈæstɪk]

a. 热情的；热心的

记 联想记忆：enthusias(=enthusiasm 热情，热心)+tic → 热情的

搭 enthusiastic applause 热烈的掌声；enthusiastic reception 热诚的接待

例 With lights flashing and horns honking, the newly-manufactured vehicles poured into the world like ***enthusiastic*** machines from a science-fiction movie. 车灯闪烁，喇叭轰鸣，新生产出来的汽车就像是科幻电影中充满动力的机器一样涌入大千世界。

同 eager(*a.* 渴望的)；anxious(*a.* 渴望的，盼望的)；passionate(*a.* 充满热情的)

entice [ɪnˈtaɪs]

v. 怂恿，引诱

记 联想记忆：全部(entire)被引诱(entice)了

例 With the festivals coming, supermarkets begin to push out all sorts of tricks to ***entice*** customers to consumption. 随着节日的来临，超市使出各种各样的手段吸引顾客消费。

entire* [ɪnˈtaɪə(r)]

a. 全部的，整个的

记 词根记忆：en(进去)+tir(拉)+e → 拉进去，不留在外的 → 全部的，整个的

例 Hughes claims that in the twenty-first century, consumers will be encouraged to think more about the ***entire*** history of the products and services they buy. 休斯声称，21 世纪消费者将受到鼓励多考虑他们所购买的产品和服务的整个历史。

派 entirely(*ad.* 完全地，一概地)

entitle [ɪnˈtaɪtl]

vt. 给…权利(或资格)；给(书、文章等)题名；给…以称号

记 联想记忆：en(使…)+title(题目，标题) → 使有题目或标题 → 给(书、文章等)题名

搭 be entitled to 有权…，有资格…

例 As a member of the museum you would be ***entitled*** to use the members' lounge for refreshments. 作为博物馆的会员，你有权在会员休息室内享用茶点。

entrepreneur [ˌɒntrəprəˈnɜː(r)]

n. 企业家；承包人

记 词根记忆：entr(=inter 在…之间)+pren(=prehend 拿)+eur(表人) →在多人之间拿取的人 → 承包人

例 The owner of the company is an American ***entrepreneur***. 这家公司的老板是一位美国企业家。

entrepreneurial [ˌɒntrəprəˈnɜːriəl]

a. 创业的

例 The provision of small loans to support the ***entrepreneurial*** dreams and ambitions of youth can be an effective means to help them change their lives. 小额贷款为年轻人的创业梦想与雄心提供支持，可以成为帮助他们改变人生的有效方式。

entrust* [ɪnˈtrʌst]

vt. 委托，交付，托付

记 联想记忆：en + trust(信任) → 十分信任才会委托 → 委托

例 As a hotelier, how do you go about attracting people to give up the security of their own home and ***entrust*** themselves to staying in a completely strange place and sleeping in an unfamiliar bed? 作为旅馆经营者，你是如何吸引人们使他们放弃自己家里的安全感，却把自己托付给你，让自己待在一个完全陌生的地方并睡在一张不熟悉的床上呢?

entwine [ɪnˈtwaɪn]

vt. 使缠住，使盘绕

记 联想记忆：en(使…) + twine(缠绕) → 使缠住，使盘绕

例 The history of human civilization is ***entwined*** with the history of the ways we have learned to manipulate water resources. 人类文明的历史与人类学习利用水资源的历程是相互交织在一起的。

environment* [ɪnˈvaɪərənmənt]

n. 周围状况；环境

搭 working/learning environment 工作/学习环境；the political environment 政治环境

例 The one kind of subsidy whose removal appeared to have been bad for the ***environment*** was the subsidy to manage soil erosion. 取消对土地流失管理部门的补助金给环境带来了不利影响。

派 environmental(*a.* 环境的)

envisage [ɪnˈvɪzɪdʒ]

vt. 展望，想象；面对

记 词根记忆：en(在…之内) + vis(看见) + age → 在内部看见 → 展望

搭 It is envisaged that... 预计…；envisage an bright future 展望美好的未来

例 It's just a chance for you to say anything about the equipment and problems you ***envisage***. 这对你来说是个机会，你可以就设备和想到的问题谈一谈自己的看法。

同 imagine(*vt.* 想象，设想)；fancy(*vt.* 想象，设想)

epidemic* [ˌepɪˈdemɪk]

a. 流行性的 *n.* 流行病

记 词根记忆：epi + dem(=demo 人民) + ic → 在人民之中的 → 流行性的

搭 an epidemic of measles 麻疹的流行

例 The government declared that no major ***epidemic*** diseases prevailed in this area. 政府宣布该地区没有流行重大的传染性疾病。

同 contagious(*a.* 传染性的，会感染的)；prevalent(*a.* 流行的)

17

episodic
[ˌepɪˈsɒdɪk]

a. 偶然发生的，不定期的；由许多片段组成的，松散的

记 来自 episode(*n.* 片段；插曲)

例 An *episodic* format is the writer's favorite, when he tries to relax by writing. 当这个作家想要用写作来放松自己时，他最爱用一种松散的形式来创作。

epitomise*
[ɪˈpɪtəmaɪz]

vt. 集中体现；概括

记 词根记忆：epi(在…上) + tom(切) + ise → 剪切下来放在上面 → 概括

例 Indeed, in many respects the Siriono *epitomise* the popular conception of life in Amazonia. 的确，西里奥诺人的生活在很多方面集中体现了亚马孙河流域普遍的生活理念。

equal
[ˈiːkwəl]

a. 相等的 *vt.* 比得上

搭 equal pay 同酬；on equal terms 处于平等的地位

例 These four firms had *equal* levels of productivity. 这四家公司的生产力水平不相上下。

派 equality(*n.* 同等，平等)；equally(*ad.* 平等地，相等地)

equation
[ɪˈkweɪʒn]

n. 方程式，等式；平衡；等同，相等

搭 identical equation 恒等式

例 The researchers thought that human beings should not be left out of the *equation* in the rainforest. 研究人员认为，不应该忽略人类在雨林的生态平衡中的作用。

equator
[ɪˈkweɪtə(r)]

n. (地球)赤道

记 联想记忆：equat(看作 equal，相等的) + or → 把地球等分的线 → 赤道

例 The *equator* divides the earth into two hemispheres. 赤道把地球划分为两个半球。

派 equatorial(*a.* 赤道的；赤道地区特有的)

equip*
[ɪˈkwɪp]

vt. 装备，配备；使有能力，使有准备

搭 be equipped with 配备有，装备有

例 Underground offices in Japan are *equipped* with "virtual" windows and mirrors. 日本的地下办公室装有虚拟的窗户和镜子。

派 equipment(*n.* 装备)

Word List 18

音频

词根、词缀预习表

val	力量	equivalent *a.* 相等的，等量的	**rod**	咬	erode *v.* 侵蚀，腐蚀
ess	存在	essential *a.* 本质的，基本的	**err**	徘徊	erroneous *a.* 错误的
st	站立	establish *vt.* 建立；确立	**val**	价值	evaluate *vt.* 评价，估价
vacu	空	evacuate *v.* 疏散；撤离	**act**	做	exact *a.* 精确的；准确的
volv	卷	evolve *v.* 演变，进化	**vid**	看见	evidence *n.* 根据，证据

equipment [ɪˈkwɪpmənt]
n. 设备，装备
例 Last week we talked about buying camping ***equipment***. 上周我们讨论了有关购买露营装备的事情。

equity* [ˈekwəti]
n. 公平，公正
记 词根记忆：equ(相等) + ity → 等价交换→ 公平，公正
例 The ***equity*** of the committee's decision was accepted by everyone. 委员会所做决定的公正性得到了大家的一致认可。

equivalent [ɪˈkwɪvələnt]
a. 相等的，等量的 *n.* 相等物，等价物
记 词根记忆：equi(相等) + val(力量) + ent → 力量相等的 → 相等的，等量的
搭 equivalent to 相当于
例 At that time, the cost of a bulb was ***equivalent*** to half a day's pay for the average worker. 那时，每个灯泡的成本相当于普通工人半天的工资。

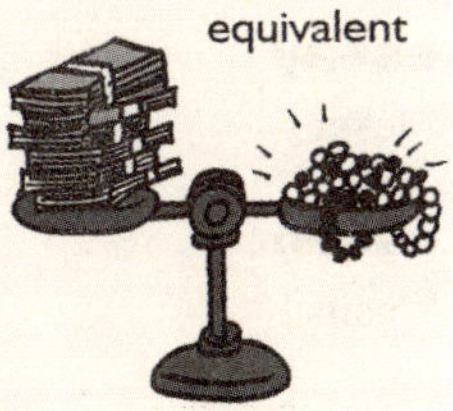

era* [ˈɪərə]
n. 纪元；时代
记 联想记忆：反过来拼写 are(是)
例 Dallas is a very wealthy city in Texas which has grown up in an ***era*** when cars were considered essential to move about. 达拉斯是德克萨斯州一个非常富裕的城市，兴起于汽车成为人们基本交通工具的时代。

erode [ɪˈrəʊd]
v. 侵蚀，腐蚀；削弱，损害
记 词根记忆：e(去掉) + rod(咬) + e → 咬掉 → 侵蚀，腐蚀
例 The sharp increase in food price over the last few months has ***eroded*** the public's confidence in the government's policy. 过去几个月食品价格大幅上涨，削弱了公众对政府政策的信心。
同 corrode(*v.* 腐蚀，侵蚀)

通常用于被动语态、强调物理侵蚀

↳ 主动、被动皆可，强调化学变化.

□ equipment □ equity □ equivalent □ era □ erode

erosion
[ɪˈrəʊʒn]

n. 腐蚀；磨损

搭 soil erosion 土壤侵蚀；coastal erosion 海岸侵蚀

例 Often dams are built to protect the area from soil ***erosion*** and to serve as permanent sources of water. 人们建造水坝常常是用为了防止水土流失，并将水坝(所在地)作为永久的水源。

同 corrosion(*n.* 侵蚀)；deterioration(*n.* 退化，堕落)

erroneous
[ɪˈrəʊnəs]

a. 错误的，不正确的

记 词根记忆：err(徘徊)+oneous→在正确事物旁边徘徊→错误的，不正确的

例 It seems that the boy is under the ***erroneous*** impression that the pretty girl is in love with him. 看起来这个男孩子是误以为那个漂亮女孩喜欢他了。

eruption
[ɪˈrʌpʃn]

n. (火山、战争等)爆发；(疾病)发作

记 来自 erupt(*v.* 爆发；喷出)

例 Geologists forecasted that an ***eruption*** of the volcano would take place before the end of the century. 地质学者预测，在本世纪结束之前该火山可能会喷发一次。

escalate
[ˈeskəleɪt]

v. (使)逐步增长或发展，(使)逐步升级

记 来自 Escalator，原来是自动电梯的商标，后来才出现了动词 escalate

例 Instigated by a small number of people with ulterior motives, the demonstration quickly ***escalated*** into a riot. 在少数别有用心的人的煽动教唆下，游行示威很快升级演变成一场暴动。

escalator*
[ˈeskəleɪtə(r)]

n. 〈美〉自动扶梯

例 The new store has an ***escalator*** to carry customers from one floor to another. 这家新商店有自动扶梯，将顾客从一个楼层运送到另一个楼层。

essay
[ˈeseɪ]

n. (作为课程作业的)短文，文章；评论文

例 You have to complete a 3000-word ***essay*** on the topic. 你需要就该主题写一篇 3000 字的文章。

essence
[ˈesns]

n. 本质；精髓

记 词根记忆：ess(存在)+ence→存在即是本质→本质

例 Psychologists claimed that the ***essence*** of reasoning lies in the putting together of two “behaviour segments” in some novel way to reach the goal. 心理学家声称，推理的本质就在于将两个行为片断用某种全新的方式结合起来，以达到预期的目的。

essential
[ɪˈsenʃl]

a. 本质的，基本的；必要的，必不可少的；极其重要的 *n.* 要素；实质，本质；要点

记 词根记忆：ess(存在)+ential→存在的东西→要素；实质，本质

搭 be essential to/for 对…必不可少

例 It is ***essential*** that the glass be thicker on the outside than on the inside. 外层的玻璃应该比内层的玻璃厚，这一点很重要。

派 essentially(*ad.* 本质上，基本上)

□ erosion □ erroneous □ eruption □ escalate □ escalator □ essay
□ essence □ essential

establish* [ɪ'stæblɪʃ]

vt. 建立；确立；安置，使定居

记 词根记忆：e(出) + st(站立) + abl(能…的) + ish(使…) → 使能够站立出来 → 建立；确立

搭 establish goals 树立目标；establish relations 建立联系

例 You may have to ***establish*** new eating habits in order to keep healthy. 为了保持健康，你需要养成一些新的饮食习惯。

派 establishment（*n.* 建立；确立；机构，组织）；established（*a.* 已获确认的；著名的，公认的）

---

estate [ɪ'steɪt]

n. 个人财产，(尤指)遗产；土地，地产，(尤指)庄园

搭 estate agent 房地产经纪人；real estate 房地产；房地产所有权

例 My accountant estimated the value of my ***estate***. 我的会计师评估了我的个人财产值。

---

esteem [ɪ'stiːm]

n./vt. 尊重；尊敬

记 联想记忆：e(音似：一) + stee(看作 steel，钢铁) + m(看作 man，人) → 一个有钢铁般意志的人值得尊敬 → 尊重；尊敬

搭 have great esteem for 对…大为敬佩；be held in high esteem by sb. 深受某人敬佩

例 We had great ***esteem*** for this dedicated and imaginative scientist. 对这位乐于奉献、富于想象力的科学家，我们深表敬佩。

同 regard(*vt./n.* 尊敬；尊重)

反 disesteem(*n./vt.* 轻视)

---

estimate*

['estɪmeɪt] *v.* 估计，估量；估价；评价 ['estɪmət] *n.* 估计，估量；估价；评价

记 联想记忆：评估(estimate)地产(estate)

搭 estimated time of arrival (ETA) 预测到达时间；estimated time of departure (ETD) 预计出发时间；estimated number of people 预计人数；conservative estimate 保守估计

例 The deal is ***estimated*** to be worth around £1.5 million. 这笔交易估计价值 150 万英镑左右。// I can give you a rough ***estimate*** of the amount of wood you will need. 我可以粗略估计一下你所需的木材量。

---

estrange [ɪ'streɪndʒ]

vt. 使疏远，使分离

例 If the government continues to increase the tax, it will ***estrange*** itself from the public in the end. 如果政府继续增加税收，终将脱离民众。

---

estuary* ['estʃuəri]

n. (江河入海的)河口，河口湾

记 联想记忆：est(看作 east，东) + uary(看作 February，二月) → 二月春水向东流，流到河口不回头 → 河口，河口湾

搭 estuary deposits 河口沉积，港湾沉积

例 This area is in a sheltered part of the ***estuary***. 这一区域处于河口的隐蔽处。

eternal [ɪˈtɜːnl]	*a.* 永恒的 记 联想记忆：外部(external)世界是永恒的(eternal)诱惑 例 Muslims believe the soul of anyone who commits suicide will suffer ***eternal*** damnation. 穆斯林信徒相信自杀者的灵魂将受到永无休止的诅咒。 同 endless（*a.* 无止境的）；everlasting（*a.* 永恒的，持久的）；permanent（*a.* 永久的，持久的） 反 momentary(*a.* 瞬间的，刹那的)；temporary(*a.* 暂时的)
ethereal [iˈθɪəriəl]	*a.* 太空的；轻巧的 记 来自 ether(*n.* 太空；苍天) 搭 ethereal beauty 娇柔、飘逸之美 例 Entering the resort and breathing the clear and ***ethereal*** air, you will find yourself strolling in a haven of peace. 进入度假胜地，呼吸着清新飘渺的空气，你就发现自己仿佛进入了世外桃源。
ethical* [ˈeθɪkl]	*a.* (有关)道德的；伦理的 搭 ethical standards 道德标准；ethical problems 道德问题 例 The behavior is not strictly ***ethical***. 严格来讲，这种行为是不道德的。
evacuate [ɪˈvækjueɪt]	*v.* 疏散；撤离 记 词根记忆：e(出) + vacu(空) + ate(动词后缀) → 空出去 → 疏散；撤离 例 The hotel's fire officer will instruct you in how to ***evacuate*** the building if a fire breaks out. 饭店消防人员会告诉你们万一着火该如何撤离。 派 evacuation(*n.* 撤退，撤离) 同 remove(*vt.* 移动；开除)；depart(*v.* 离开)
evaluate [ɪˈvæljueɪt]	*vt.* 评价，估价 记 词根记忆：e(出) + val(价值) + uate → 使给出价值 → 评价，估价 例 We ***evaluated*** the students' skills on the basis of test results. 我们在考试成绩的基础上对学生的技能进行评估。
evaluation [ɪˌvæljuˈeɪʃn]	*n.* 估价，评价 记 来自 evaluate(*v.* 评价，估价) 例 Employees should make a copy of their completed Self ***Evaluation*** Form for their supervisor in advance of the review meeting. 开评审会之前，雇员应该复印一份填好的自我评估表交给主管。
evaporate* [ɪˈvæpəreɪt]	*v.* (使)蒸发；消失；不复存在 记 词根记忆：e(出) + vapor(水汽) + ate(使…) → 使水汽出去 → 蒸发 例 He thought water could ***evaporate*** quickly in sandy soils. 他认为水在砂土中会很快蒸发。 派 evaporation(*n.* 蒸发；消失) 同 vanish(*vi.* 消失)；vaporize〔*vt.* (使)蒸发〕
event* [ɪˈvent]	*n.* 事件；比赛项目 例 Your graduation from college is an important ***event***. 你大学毕业了，这是件大事。

□ eternal □ ethereal □ ethical □ evacuate □ evaluate □ evaluation
□ evaporate □ event

evidence* [ˈevɪdəns]

n. 根据，证据；形迹，迹象

记 词根记忆：e + vid(看见) + ence → 所看见的人或物 → 形迹，迹象

搭 a piece of evidence 一项证据；in evidence 明显地

例 As an international student you will need to provide ***evidence*** that you can fund yourself for however long your course lasts. 作为国际学生，你需要提供证据，证明无论课程持续多长时间你都有足够的资金维持学业。

evoke [ɪˈvəʊk]

vt. 唤起

记 词根记忆：e(出) + vok(喊) + e → 喊出声来 → 唤起

例 This fragrance ***evokes*** the memory of a cool, summer evening. 这种香味唤起了我对一个清凉夏夜的回忆。

派 evocation(*n.* 唤起；重现)

evolution [ˌiːvəˈluːʃn]

n. 进展；进化

记 词根记忆：e(出) + volu(滚，转) + tion → 滚出外边 → 人类的进化就是不停向前滚的过程 → 进化

搭 the evolution of man 人类的进化；Darwin's theory of evolution 达尔文的进化论

例 The scientist has suggested that ***evolution*** of speech went with right-handed preference. 科学家认为，语言的进化伴随着使用右手的倾向而产生。

evolve* [iˈvɒlv]

v. (使)逐渐形成；(使)演变，(使)进化

记 词根记忆：e(出) + volv(滚，转) + e → 转出来 → (使)进化

搭 evolve from 由…进化而来；evolve into 进化成为…

例 According to brain researchers, as the brain ***evolved***, one side became specialised for fine control of movement. 根据大脑研究人员的说法，随着大脑的进化，一边的脑半球专门用来精确控制动作。

exacerbate* [ɪgˈzæsəbeɪt]

vt. 恶化，加剧

记 词根记忆：ex(表加强) + acerb(苦涩的，痛苦的) + ate(动词后缀) → 使非常痛苦 → 恶化

例 More intensive farming and the abandonment of fallow periods tend to ***exacerbate*** soil erosion. 更密集的耕种和取消休耕期会加剧土壤的侵蚀。

exact* [ɪgˈzækt]

a. 精确的；准确的

记 词根记忆：ex(出) + act(做) → 做出精确的结果 → 精确的；准确的

例 What is the ***exact*** amount left in your savings account? 你储蓄账户上的准确余额是多少?

派 exactly(*ad.* 正确地；完全地)

exaggerate *

[ɪɡˈzædʒəreɪt]

v. 夸大，夸张

记 词根记忆：ex(出) + ag(表加强) + ger(搬运) + ate → 过多搬运 → 夸大，夸张

例 The witness ***exaggerated*** the seriousness of the accident. 目击者夸大了事故的严重性。

派 exaggeration (*n.* 夸张)；exaggerated (*a.* 夸张的；故作姿态的)

---

examine *

[ɪɡˈzæmɪn]

vt. 检查；调查，研究；测验

例 He ***examined*** the work of other researchers. 他检查了其他研究人员的工作。// The medical students ***examined*** patients under the supervision of a doctor. 医科学生在一名医生的监督下对患者进行了检查。

派 examiner(*n.* 主考者)；examination(*n.* 考试；检查)

---

excavate *

[ˈekskəveɪt]

vt. 挖掘，开凿

记 词根记忆：ex(出) + cav(洞) + ate (动词后缀) → 挖出洞 → 挖掘，开凿

例 Some large species of dung beetles originating from France ***excavate*** tunnels to a depth of approximately 30cm below the dung pat. 一些法国的大型蜣螂品种会在粪堆下挖一条大约 30 厘米深的隧道。

---

excavation *

[ˌekskəˈveɪʃn]

n. 挖掘，发掘；出土文物

例 The new ***excavations*** are open to the public this weekend in Shanxi Museum. 新出土的文物将于本周末在山西博物馆对公众开放展览。

---

exceed

[ɪkˈsiːd]

v. 超过，胜过

记 词根记忆：ex(出) + ceed(走) → 走出 → 超过，胜过

搭 exceed speed limit 超速

例 World population in the twenty-first century will probably ***exceed*** 8 billion. 世界人口总数在 21 世纪有可能超过 80 亿。

派 exceedingly(*ad.* 极其，非常，特别)

---

excellent *

[ˈeksələnt]

a. 极好的；杰出的

记 联想记忆：excel(优于，超过) + lent → 杰出的

例 Under several metres of earth, noise is minimal and insulation is ***excellent***. 在地下几米的地方，噪音很小，隔热效果也很好。

派 excellence(*n.* 优秀，杰出，卓越)

---

except *

[ɪkˈsept]

vt. 将…除外 *prep.* 除…外

记 词根记忆：ex(出) + cept(拿，抓) → 不拿 → 将…除外

例 The hotel was built into a hill and little could be seen from outside ***except*** a glass facade. 这家旅馆建在山体内，从外面看，除了旅馆正面的玻璃墙什么也看不到。

□ exaggerate □ examine □ excavate □ excavation □ exceed □ excellent □ except

exceptional [ɪk'sepʃənl]

a. 例外的；异常的
记 来自 except(*prep.* 除…之外)
例 Kate has quite an *exceptional* music ability. 凯特具有非凡的音乐才能。
同 extraordinary(*a.* 非常的，特别的)；outstanding(*a.* 突出的)；unusual(*a.* 不平常的)
反 ordinary(*a.* 平常的，普通的)；common(*a.* 普通的)

excess*

[ɪk'ses] *n.* 超越；过量 ['ekses] *a.* 过量的，额外的
记 词根记忆：ex(出)＋cess(行走)→走出界限→超越；过量
搭 excess baggage 超重行李
例 I am burdened with an *excess* of public attention. 公众的过度关注使我感到不堪重负。

excessive [ɪk'sesɪv]

a. 过多的，极度的，过分的
例 Each month, managers would analyse the pattern of absence of staff with *excessive* sick leave. 每个月，经理们都会分析请过多病假的员工的缺勤模式。

exchange [ɪks'tʃeɪndʒ]

v. 交换，调换；交易；兑换；交流；谈话，争论 *n.* 交换，调换；交易(所)；兑换(率)；交流
搭 in exchange for 交换；stock exchange 证券交易(所)；part exchange 部分抵价交易；exchange rate 汇率
例 Are you one of the *exchange* students? 你是交换生之一吗？// I shook hands and *exchanged* a few words with the manager. 我与经理握手并交谈了几句。

18

excitement* [ɪk'saɪtmənt]

n. 激动；兴奋；令人兴奋的事
记 词根记忆：ex(出)＋cit(激起，召唤)＋e＋ment(名词后缀)→激动，兴奋
例 The *excitement* died down. 激动的情绪已经平息了。

exclude [ɪk'skluːd]

vt. 把…排斥在外；将(某物)排除，不包括
记 词根记忆：ex(出)＋clud(关闭)＋e→关出去→把…排斥在外
搭 exclude sth. from sth. 把…排除在…之外
例 Thick curtains help to *exclude* street noises. 厚窗帘有助于阻挡街上的噪音。

exclusive [ɪk'skluːsɪv]

a. 奢华的；独有的；排他的 *n.* 独家新闻
例 He is part of an *exclusive* social circle. 他所属的社交圈子很排外。

exclusively [ɪk'skluːsɪvlɪ]

ad. 专有地，专门地
例 In open-cut operations, the land is used *exclusively* for mining, but land rehabilitation measures generally progress with the mine's development. 在露天开采时，土地仅限采矿使用，但土地复原措施的实行通常与采矿的进度保持一致。

excreta* [ɪk'skriːtə]

n. 排泄物
例 Dung is the droppings or *excreta* of animals. "Dung"就是兽粪或动物的排泄物。

excursion [ɪk'skɜːʃn]

n. 远足，短途旅游；【物】偏移，漂移
搭 Saturday excursion 周六短途旅行
例 Our family took a two-week *excursion* to France. 我们一家人去法国旅行了两周。

□ exceptional □ excess □ excessive □ exchange □ excitement □ exclude
□ exclusive □ exclusively □ excreta □ excursion

excusable* [ɪkˈskjuːzəbl]

a. 可原谅的；可谅解的；可容许的

记 来自 excuse(*n./vt.* 原谅)

搭 an excusable mistake 可原谅的错误

例 Absent-mindedness is an ***excusable*** human weakness. 心不在焉是人的一种可以原谅的缺点。

同 forgivable(*a.* 可原谅的；可谅解的)

execute [ˈeksɪkjuːt]

vt. 将…处死；实施，执行

记 联想记忆：ex(表加强)+ecut(追踪)+e→加强追踪→实施，执行

例 We ***execute*** company policy for homeowners. 我们执行公司针对业主的政策。

派 executive(*a.* 执行的；行政的 *n.* 执行者，主管领导)

execution [ˌeksɪˈkjuːʃn]

n. 执行，实施；处决

记 词根记忆：ex(表加强)+ecut(追踪)+ion→加强追踪→执行，实施

例 The manager had failed in the ***execution*** of her duty. 经理未能履行职责。

派 executioner(*n.* 行刑者)

exemplify [ɪgˈzemplɪfaɪ]

vt. 作为…的典型；例证，举例说明

记 来自 example(*n.* 实例)，注意区分 a 和 e

例 Robin Hill Park ***exemplifies*** the standards in natural zoos. 罗宾山郊野公园是自然动物园的典范。

同 demonstrate(*v.* 证明，论证)；illustrate(*v.* 举例说明，阐明)

exhale* [eksˈheɪl]

v. 呼出(气)；散发(气味、蒸汽等)

记 词根记忆：ex(出)+hale(气)→呼出(气)；散发

例 Passive smoking, the breathing in of the side-stream smoke from the burning of tobacco or of the smoke ***exhaled*** by a smoker, also causes a serious health risk. 被动吸烟，从燃烧的烟草中吸入侧流烟或吸烟者呼出的烟，都会使健康受到严重威胁。

exhaust* [ɪgˈzɔːst]

v. 使非常疲倦，使疲惫不堪；用尽，耗尽

n. (机器排出的)废气，蒸汽

搭 be exhausted from 因…而十分疲乏；exhaust pipe 排气管；exhaust emission 尾气排放；intake and exhaust system 进气和排气系统

例 She was ***exhausted*** by her four kids. 四个孩子让她精疲力尽。

exhaustible [ɪgˈzɔːstəbl]

a. 可耗尽的，会枯竭的

例 Stone, brick, metal and plastic are all derived from ***exhaustible*** mineral sources. 石料、砖、金属和塑料都是从可耗尽矿产资源中提取的。

exhaustion [ɪgˈzɔːstʃən]

n. 精疲力竭；耗尽

例 The runner collapsed from ***exhaustion***. 那个奔跑的人因为极度疲劳而昏倒了。

□ excusable □ execute □ execution □ exemplify □ exhale □ exhaust
□ exhaustible □ exhaustion

exhaustive [ɪɡˈzɔːstɪv]

a. 包揽无遗的，彻底的，详尽的

例 During the course of this ***exhaustive*** study, Reznikova has grown so attached to her laboratory ants that she feels she knows them as individuals even without the paint spots used to mark them. 经过详尽的学习，热兹尼科娃深深爱上了她实验室里的蚂蚁，她觉得自己甚至不用通过油漆点标记也可以辨认出每一只蚂蚁。

exhibit* [ɪɡˈzɪbɪt]

n. 展览品 *v.* 陈列，展览；显示

记 词根记忆：ex(出) + hib(拥有；拿住) + it → 把自己拥有的拿出来 → 显示；展览

例 Some of the ***exhibits*** at the Museum are very precious. 这个博物馆的一些展品非常珍贵。// The artist ***exhibited*** his paintings in a local gallery. 画家在当地的美术馆展出了自己的画作。

exhibition [ˌeksɪˈbɪʃn]

n. 展览(会)；陈列

搭 an education exhibition 教育展

例 The woman's ***exhibition*** met with great opposition from Parliament. 女性(作品)展览会遭遇了国会的强烈反对。

18

exhilaration [ɪɡˌzɪləˈreɪʃn]

n. 高兴；兴奋

例 Many astronauts have testified that they experienced the ***exhilaration*** of weightlessness. 许多宇航员都证实他们体验到了失重的兴奋感。

exile* [ˈeksaɪl; ˈeɡzaɪl]

vt. 放逐，流放，使流亡 *n.* 流放，流亡；被流放者，背井离乡者，流犯

记 联想记忆：ex(出) + il(=sil 跳跃) + e → 跳出去 → 放逐，流放

搭 in exile 流放中；drive sb. into exile 流放某人

例 The former President was ***exiled*** for more than twenty years. 前总统被流放了二十多年。

同 expel(*vt.* 驱逐，开除)；banish(*vt.* 流放，驱逐)

exist* [ɪɡˈzɪst]

vi. 存在；生存

例 Two American brain researchers studied the brains of human embryos and discovered that the left-right asymmetry ***exists*** before birth. 两名美国大脑研究人员研究了人类胚胎的大脑后发现，大脑的左右半球不对称在婴儿出生前就已存在。

派 existent(*a.* 存在的；实有的)

existence* [ɪɡˈzɪstəns]

n. 存在；生活(方式)

记 联想记忆：exist(存在) + ence → 存在；生活(方式)

搭 come into existence 产生

例 There are no scientists in ***existence*** who really wait until they have all the evidence in front of them before they try to work out what it might possibly mean. 从来没有哪个科学家真的要等到所有的证据都摆在他面前才试图研究可能的规律。

派 coexistence(*n.* 共存，共处)

□ exhaustive □ exhibit □ exhibition □ exhilaration □ exile □ exist
□ existence

exodus
[ˈeksədəs]

n. 大批离去，成群外出

记 词根记忆：ex(出)+od(路)+us→走上外出的道路→大批离去

例 There are a mass *exodus* of workers from the villages to the towns in this country. 该国有大批工人从乡村涌向城市。

exorbitant
[ɪɡˈzɔːbɪtənt]

a. 过分的，不合理的

记 联想记忆：ex(出)+orbit(轨道，常规)+ant→走出常规→过分的，不合理的

例 Glass as instant curtains is available now, but the cost is *exorbitant*. 现在玻璃可作为即时窗帘用，但成本过于昂贵。

exotic
[ɪɡˈzɒtɪk]

a. 外来的；奇异的；醒目的，吸引人的

搭 exotic experience 异国体验

例 Their *exotic* apparel stands them out from the locals. 奇装异服将他们与当地人区分开来。

同 foreign(*a.* 外国的，外来的)

反 native(*a.* 本国的，本地的)；indigenous(*a.* 本土的)

expand*
[ɪkˈspænd]

v. (使)膨胀，(使)扩张；张开，展开；详述

记 词根记忆：ex(向外)+pand(张开)→向外张开→(使)膨胀，(使)扩张

搭 expand one's knowledge 扩大知识面；expand our horizon 拓宽视野

例 The goal of university should be to *expand* the minds of students. 大学的目标应该是开阔学生的视野。

派 expanding(*a.* 扩大的)；expanse(*n.* 宽广空间)

expansion
[ɪkˈspænʃn]

n. 扩大，扩张

记 来自 expand(*v.* 膨胀，扩张)

例 Even without further *expansion* the school could recruit around 2,000 students every year. 即使没有进一步的扩建，学校每年仍可招收 2000 名学生。

expectancy*
[ɪkˈspektənsi]

n. 期待，期望；预期数额(如寿命等)

搭 life expectancy 平均寿命

例 Smoking will cause a shortened life *expectancy*. 吸烟会导致寿命缩短。

expectation
[ˌekspekˈteɪʃn]

n. 期待，预期；[*pl.*]前程，成功的前景

记 联想记忆：expect(期待)+a+tion(名词后缀)→期待，预期

搭 role expectations 角色期待

例 The company failed to meet shareholders' *expectations*. 公司没有满足股东的期望。

expedition
[ˌekspəˈdɪʃn]

n. 远征，探险，考察；(短途的)旅行，出行；远征队，探险队，考察队

记 词根记忆：ex(出)+ped(脚)+ition→出行

搭 on an expedition to 去…探险；go/start on an expedition 去远征(探险、考察)；a shopping expedition 外出购物

例 I talked to Charles Owen, the leader of the *expedition* group, about the trip. 我和探险队队长查尔斯·欧文谈了关于出行的事。

□ exodus □ exorbitant □ exotic □ expand □ expansion □ expectancy
□ expectation □ expedition

expel
[ɪk'spel]

vt. 把…开除；驱逐

[记] 词根记忆：ex(出) + pel(驱动，推) → 把…开除；驱逐

[例] John has been ***expelled*** from the firm and is operating on his own. 约翰被那家公司开除了，现在自己单干。// Conrad ***expelled*** the enemy from his dominions. 康拉德将敌人驱逐出自己的领地。

expense*
[ɪk'spens]

n. 花费，开支；消费，消耗；代价，损失

[记] 词根记忆：ex(出) + pens(支付) + e → 花费；消费

[搭] at the expense of 以…为代价；at sb's expense 由…付费，由…负担费用；public expenses 公共开支；fixed expenses 固定支出；optional expense 选择性支出；miscellaneous expenses 杂费

[例] I am sure you are concerned about ***expenses*** such as books and uniforms when your child starts studying. 我敢肯定，当你的孩子开始上学时，你会关心书本、制服等花费。

[派] expensive(*a.* 昂贵的，费钱的)

The supreme happiness of life is the conviction that we are loved.
生活中最大的幸福是坚信有人爱我们。
——法国小说家 雨果(Victor Hugo, French novelist)

Word List 19

音频

词根、词缀预习表

plo	折叠	exploit *vt.* 剥削；开发	**plod**	击掌	explode *v.* 爆炸；爆发
pir	呼吸	expire *v.* 期满；终止	**port**	运	export *v.* 出口；输出
plor	哭泣，流泪	explore *v.* 探险	**tend**	伸展	extend *v.* 延长；扩大
pos	放	exposure *n.* 暴露；显露	**tol**	举起	extol *vt.* 赞颂，赞美
vag	走	extravagance *n.* 奢侈；挥霍	**tract**	拉	extract *n.* 摘录，选段

expire* [ɪkˈspaɪə(r)]

v. 期满；终止

记 词根记忆：ex(出) + pir(呼吸) + e → 呼出气 → 期满

例 The lease on this house *expires* at the end of the year. 这房子租约年底到期。

同 run out(到期，失效)

expiry* [ɪkˈspaɪəri]

n. 满期，终结

搭 date of expiry 有效期限

例 The *expiry* date of my credit card is November 12th 2012. 我的信用卡有效期限是到 2012 年 11 月 12 日。

explode [ɪkˈspləʊd]

v. (使)爆炸；爆发；激增

记 词根记忆：ex(出) + plod(击掌) + e → 众人齐声鼓掌声响如爆炸 → 爆炸；爆发

例 The experts have thought of a way to *explode* the dynamite below this building. 专家们已经想出了一种方法来引爆埋在这幢楼下面的炸药。

派 explosion(*n.* 爆炸)

同 blow up(爆炸，爆裂)

exploit*

[ɪkˈsplɔɪt] *vt.* 剥削；开发，开拓；利用

[ˈeksplɔɪt] *n.* 英勇行为；业绩，功绩

记 词根记忆：ex(出) + plo(折叠) + it → 向外折 → 开拓；利用

例 Our company was quick to *exploit* a money-making opportunity provided by the government. 我们公司很快就抓住了政府提供的赚钱机会。

exploitation
[ˌeksplɔɪˈteɪʃn]

n. 开采，开发；剥削，榨取；自私的利用

例 There is a report on the *exploitation* of child workers which attracts broad attention. 有一篇关于剥削童工的报道引起广泛的关注。

exploitative
[ɪkˈsplɔɪtətɪv]

a. 开发的，利用的；剥削的

例 It is also a place where some children are exposed, with little or no protection, to *exploitative* employment. 在这里有的孩子只能得到些许保护或根本没有保护，被雇主无情压榨。

exploratory
[ɪkˈsplɒrətri]

a. 探测的；勘探的；探索的

例 The patient is having some *exploratory* tests done to find out what's causing the illness. 病人正在接受检查，以找到致病原因。

explore
[ɪkˈsplɔː(r)]

v. 探险，探索；仔细检查，探究

记 词根记忆：ex(出) + plor(哭泣，流泪) + e → 流出眼泪 → 探索，探究

例 Architects began to *explore* ways of creating buildings using the latest technology. 建筑师开始探索利用最新技术来建造房屋的方法。

派 exploration(*n.* 探险；探究)

explorer*
[ɪkˈsplɔːrə(r)]

n. 勘探者，探险者

记 来自 explore(*v.* 探险，探索)

例 Underground reservoirs were rare sources of permanent water and were vital to early *explorers* of inland Australia. 地下含水层是罕见的长期水源，对早期进入澳大利亚腹地的探险者至关重要。

explosive*
[ɪkˈspləʊsɪv]

n. 爆炸物，炸药 *a.* 爆炸的，爆发的；使人冲动的

搭 explosive device 引爆装置

例 The bomb was packed with several pounds of *explosive*. 这枚炸弹装有几磅炸药。

export*

[ɪkˈspɔːt] *v.* 出口；输出，传播 [ˈekspɔːt] *n.* 出口；输出；出口商品

记 词根记忆：ex(出) + port(运) → 把东西运出去 → 出口

搭 export rebates 出口退税；export finance 出口信贷；export restriction 出口限制

例 In Africa, the feathers of ostriches were used for tribal ceremonial dress and they were also *exported* to Europe and America. 在非洲鸵鸟毛经常用在部落的典礼服饰上，同时也出口到欧洲和美洲。

expose*
[ɪkˈspəʊz]

vt. 使暴露，揭露

记 词根记忆：ex(出) + pos(放) + e → 放出来 → 使暴露，揭露

搭 expose oneself (to sth.) 使自己面临、遭受(危险或不快)

例 He has been widely *exposed* on television to the public. 他经常在电视上向公众露面。

派 exposed(*a.* 无遮蔽的；易受攻击的，无保护的)

19

□ exploitation □ exploitative □ exploratory □ explore □ explorer □ explosive
□ export □ expose

exposure* [ɪk'spəʊʒə(r)]	*n.* 暴露；显露；接触；曝光 记 词根记忆：ex(出)+pos(放)+ure → 放出来 → 暴露；显露 例 On the positive side, ***exposure*** to such diversity helps encourage creativity which is generally an asset to a company. 从积极的一面来看，处于这样的多样性下有助于激发创造性，这对公司来说通常都是一笔财富。
express* [ɪk'spres]	*vt.* 表达，表示 *a.* 特快的，快速的；明确的 *n.* 快车，快运，快递 记 联想记忆：ex(出)+press(挤压) → 挤出心里话 → 表达，表示 例 The chart on the wall ***expresses*** the economic movements differently from the last year. 墙上的这张图表反映了经济趋势与去年的不同。 派 expression(*n.* 表达，表述)；expressive(*a.* 表现的，有表现力的)
extend* [ɪk'stend]	*v.* 延长；扩大 记 词根记忆：ex(出)+tend(伸展) → 伸展出去 → 延长 例 I ***extended*** my tour for another week here. 我把在这里的旅行时间延长了一周。
extendable* [ɪk'stendəbl]	*a.* 可延伸的，可展开的，可扩张的 搭 extendable rod 拉杆；extendable bond 可延长债券 例 The visa is for 15 days, ***extendable*** to one month. 此签证有效期为15天，可延期到一个月。
extension* [ɪk'stenʃn]	*n.* 伸展；延长部分；电话分机 搭 one month extension 延期一个月；the extension of vocabulary 词汇的扩展；extension to …的延伸部分 例 These temporary hive ***extensions*** contained frames of empty comb for the bees to fill with honey. 这些临时加上去的蜂箱中放有空的蜂巢结构的架子，用于让蜜蜂存放蜂蜜。
extensive [ɪk'stensɪv]	*a.* 广大的，广阔的；广泛的 搭 make extensive use of 广泛应用；extensive reading 泛读；extensive knowledge 广博的知识；extensive efforts 巨大的努力 例 ***Extensive*** underground water resources are available over more than half of Australia's land area. 在澳大利亚，超过一半的土地上广泛分布着可利用的地下水资源。
extent* [ɪk'stent]	*n.* 范围；面积；广度，长度；程度 记 词根记忆：ex(出)+tent(伸展) → 伸展出的距离 → 范围；广度 搭 to some extent 在某种程度上 例 That old race track in the sport center is nearly six miles in ***extent***. 体育中心的旧跑道将近六英里长。
exterior [ɪk'stɪərɪə(r)]	*a.* 外部的，外表的 *n.* 外部，外表 记 联想记忆：金玉其外(exterior)，败絮其中(interior) 搭 an exterior policy 对外政策 例 All ***exterior*** doors in this especially noisy pocket will have to be solid wood core doors with hinges. 在这个特别吵闹的地区，所有通向外面的门都必须是带铰链的坚固木芯门。

□ exposure □ express □ extend □ extendable □ extension □ extensive
□ extent □ exterior

external* [ɪkˈstɜːnl]	*a.* 外面的，表面的 记 词根记忆：ex(外)+ternal → 外面的 搭 an external wound 外伤；external pressure 外界压力；external affairs 外交事务；an external member 外部构件，套件；external auditor 外部审计师 例 The evidence we have suggests that domestic trade was greater than *external* trade at all periods. 我们掌握的证据表明，无论在哪个时期，国内贸易都要比对外贸易发达。
externally [ɪkˈstɜːnəli]	*ad.* 外表上，外形上 记 联想记忆：external(表面的)+ly → 外表上，外形上 例 The medicine is used *externally* only. 这种药只能外用。
extinct* [ɪkˈstɪŋkt]	*a.* 灭绝的；废弃的 记 词根记忆：ex(没有)+tinct(刺) → 用针刺使没有的 → 灭绝的 搭 extinct volcano 死火山 例 A species becomes *extinct* when the last individual dies. 当最后一个个体死亡后，该物种便灭绝了。 同 vanished(*a.* 消失的，不见的) 反 thriving(*a.* 兴旺的，兴盛的)
extinction [ɪkˈstɪŋkʃn]	*n.* 灭绝，绝种；熄灭 记 来自 extinct(*a.* 灭绝的) 搭 on the verge of extinction 濒临灭绝 例 It's a mass *extinction*, and whether we will ever rebound from the loss is difficult to know. 这是大规模的物种灭绝，我们是否能从中恢复还是个未知数。
extinguish* [ɪkˈstɪŋgwɪʃ]	*vt.* 熄灭，扑灭；消灭，使破灭 记 词根记忆：ex(没有)+ting(刺)+uish → 用针刺使没有 → 熄灭，扑灭；消灭 例 This is non-smoking section. Please *extinguish* all cigarettes. 这里是非吸烟区，请将所有香烟熄灭。
extinguisher [ɪkˈstɪŋgwɪʃə(r)]	*n.* 灭火器；灭火者 记 来自 extinguish(*vt.* 熄灭；消灭) 例 If you discover a fire, shout "FIRE" and activate the nearest fire alarm. Attack the fire with an *extinguisher* but do not take any risks. 如果发现火情，应大喊"着火了"，并按响离你最近的火警铃。使用灭火器去灭火，但不要冒险。
extol* [ɪkˈstəʊl]	*vt.* 赞颂，赞美，颂扬 记 词根记忆：ex(外，上)+tol(举起) → 举起双手，赞美上帝 → 赞美 例 Weld *extolled* Kerry's debate skills, saying he has "the speed of a welterweight." 韦尔德称赞克里的辩论技巧，说他有"次中量级拳击手的速度"。

19

□ external □ externally □ extinct □ extinction □ extinguish □ extinguisher
□ extol

extra *

[ˈekstrə]

a. 额外的；特别的 *ad.* 额外地，另外；特别地

记 本身为词根，意为“额外的；特别的”

例 Today, almost all companies have employees work overtime rather than hire ***extra*** personnel. 如今，几乎所有的公司宁愿让员工加班也不愿意雇用额外的职员。

---

extract *

[ˈekstrækt] *n.* 摘录，选段；提出物，精，汁 [ɪkˈstrækt] *vt.* 取出；提取

记 词根记忆：ex(出) + tract(拉) → 拉出 → 取出；提取

搭 extract from 从…中提取

例 You will hear an ***extract*** from a BBC television program on acid rain. 你将会听到一段来自 BBC 电视节目的有关酸雨的摘录。

同 remove(*vt.* 移开，挪走)；cull(*vt.* 挑选，精选)；abstract(*n.* 摘要，梗概)

---

extracurricular *

[ˌekstrəkəˈrɪkjələ(r)]

a. 课外的

记 组合词：extra(额外的) + curricular(课程的) → 课外的

例 What role do you think ***extracurricular*** activities play in education? 你认为课外活动在教育中起着怎样的作用?

---

extraordinary *

[ɪkˈstrɔːdnri]

a. 不同寻常的，非常的

记 组合词：extra(以外的) + ordinary(平常的) → 平常之外的 → 不同寻常的，非常的

例 It's ***extraordinary*** that he managed to sleep through the party. 真想不到他竟然从聚会一开始一直睡到结束。

---

extravagance

[ɪkˈstrævəgəns]

n. 奢侈，挥霍；放肆的言行

记 词根记忆：extra(超过的) + vag(走) + ance → 超出正常尺度的走的行为 → 放肆的言行

例 He lived in ***extravagance*** far beyond his means, which brought his career to a premature end and led to bankruptcy. 他过着超出他收入能力的奢侈生活，从而过早结束了自己的职业生涯，走向破产。

---

extravagant

[ɪkˈstrævəgənt]

a. 奢侈的，铺张的；(言行等)无节制的，过分的，放肆的

搭 an extravagant price 过高的价格；extravagant act 行为放肆

例 The majority of people maintain that mass media has no rights to report the ***extravagant*** lifestyle and privacy of a star. 绝大多数人认为大众媒体无权报道明星奢侈的生活方式以及隐私。

派 extravagantly(*ad.* 挥霍无度地)

同 excessive(*a.* 过分的，过多的)；lavish(*a.* 过分慷慨的，奢侈的)

---

extreme

[ɪkˈstriːm]

a. 极度的；最后的 *n.* 极端，过分

记 联想记忆：extre(看作 extra，以外的) + me(我) → 在我能忍受的极限以外 → 极端，过分

搭 in the extreme 极其

例 One mistake we often make when stricken with ***extreme*** back pain is to go to bed and stay there. 当背部出现剧痛时我们经常犯的一个错误就是上床躺着。

派 extremely(*ad.* 极端地，非常地)

extrovert* [ˈekstrəvɜːt]

n. 性格外向的人；爱交际的人

记 词根记忆：extro(外) + vert(转) → 向外转的人 → 性格外向的人

例 Most sales people are *extroverts* that they like communicating with others. 大多数的销售人员都很外向，喜欢与人交流。

extrusion [ɪkˈstruːʒn]

n. 挤出，推出，挤压

记 词根记忆：ex(出) + trus(刺) + ion → 挤出

例 Vast bubbles of magma—molten rock from the mantle inch towards the surface, cooling slowly, to show through as granite *extrusion*. 岩浆，也就是熔岩，鼓着巨大的泡泡从地幔中涌向表面，慢慢冷却，看上去就像经过挤压后的花岗岩。

exuberant [ɪɡˈzjuːbərənt]

a. 繁茂的，丰富的；非凡的；华而不实的

搭 an exuberant imagination 丰富的想象力

eyesight [ˈaɪsaɪt]

n. 视力

记 组合词：eye(眼睛) + sight(看见) → 视力

例 You must stop taking the medicine if your *eyesight* is affected. 如果药物影响了你的视力，必须停止服用。

fabrication* [ˌfæbrɪˈkeɪʃn]

n. 捏造，伪造；制作；构成

搭 metal fabrication 金属预制件

例 The paper is a pure *fabrication*. 这篇论文纯粹是瞎编的。

fabulous [ˈfæbjələs]

a. 寓言式的；极为巨大的；极好的

记 联想记忆：fab(看作 fable，寓言) + ulous → 寓言式的

搭 fabulous heroes 神话中有名的英雄

例 There is a *fabulous* performance this weekend in accordance with the poster. 海报上说，这周末有一场很棒的演出。

façade* [fəˈsɑːd]

n. 正面；(虚伪的)外表

记 联想记忆：faç(看作 face，正面) + ade → 正面

例 Preserving historic buildings or keeping only their *façades* grew common. 对历史建筑或对它们的正面外观的保护变得越来越普遍。

facial [ˈfeɪʃl]

a. 面部的；面部用的

记 词根记忆：fac(面) + ial → 面部的

搭 facial expressions 面部表情

例 I can not guess what he means from his *facial* expressions. 从他的面部表情我猜不出他是什么意思。

facilitate [fəˈsɪlɪteɪt]

vt. 使便利，使容易；推动，帮助

记 词根记忆：fac(做) + ilit + ate(使…) → 使便利，使容易

例 The new strategies have *facilitated* and improved cooperation and communication between management and staff. 新策略有助于员工和管理层之间进行更为有效的沟通与合作。

facility [fəˈsɪləti]

n. [*pl.*] 设备，设施；便利条件

记 词根记忆：fac(做) + ility → 辅助人们做事的东西 → 设备，设施

搭 communication facilities 通信设施

例 There are *facilities* for high-energy particle experiments in our research centre. 我们研究中心有高能粒子实验设备。

19

□ extrovert　□ extrusion　□ exuberant　□ eyesight　□ fabrication　□ fabulous
□ façade　□ facial　□ facilitate　□ facility

facsimile [fæk'sɪməli]

n. 复制品；副本

记 词根记忆：fac(做) + simil(相同) + e → 做出相同的东西 → 复制品；副本

例 The painting is a *facsimile* edition that is not so valuable. 这幅画是复制品，不是很值钱。

---

fact sheet*

(尤指英国广播或电视节目中有关讨论题目的)资料页

例 The *fact sheets* have a summary of all the information contained in the programme. 这些资料页包含该节目的所有信息摘要。

---

factual* ['fæktʃuəl]

a. 事实的；真实的，确凿的

记 联想记忆：fact(事实) + ual → 事实的；真实的

例 The task is intended to test your skills of skimming for *factual* information. 该任务旨在测试你略读事实信息的能力。

---

faculty ['fæklti]

n. 才能；学院，系；(学院或系的)全体教学人员

搭 mental/intellectual faculty 智力；the faculty of law 法学院

例 Here on this campus we have the *faculties* of Architecture and Law. 这所大学里设有建筑学院和法学院。

---

fade [feɪd]

v. (使)变淡，变暗；褪色；凋谢；逐渐消失

记 联想记忆：褪色(fade)的记忆何以面对(face)

例 His smile *faded* as he heard the answer. 听到这个答案，他脸上的笑容渐渐消失了。

---

fair* [feə(r)]

a./ad. 公平的/地

例 This part of the island is warmer than the southern half, but it wouldn't be *fair* to say that the southern half is cold. 小岛的这部分区域比南部区域暖和，但是因此说南部冷是不公平的。

派 unfair(*a.* 不公平的)

---

fairly* ['feəli]

ad. 相当地；公平地；简直，完全地

例 I felt she hadn't treated me *fairly*. 我觉得她没有公平地对待我。

---

faith [feɪθ]

n. 信任，信用；信仰，信条

记 联想记忆：屡败(fail)屡战，信心(faith)不倦

搭 have faith in 信任…，相信…；lose faith in 不信任…，不相信…；religious faith 宗教信仰

例 People have to have *faith* in their ability to carry out the task their boss has set them. 大家必须相信自己有能力完成老板布置的任务。

---

fake [feɪk]

a. 假的 *n.* 假货；骗子 *v.* 伪装

记 联想记忆：打击造(make)假(fake)

例 He's holding the *fake* credit card, but dares not use it. 他手里攥着伪造的信用卡，却不敢用。

---

fallow* ['fæləʊ]

a. (土地)休耕的；休闲的

记 联想记忆：几个伙伴(fellow)一起在休耕的(fallow)田地上玩耍

例 Overuse of fertilisers may cause farmers to stop rotating crops or leave their land *fallow*. 过度使用肥料可能会导致农民停止农作物的轮作或让土地休耕。

□ facsimile □ fact sheet ☑ factual □ faculty □ fade □ fair
□ fairly □ faith □ fake ☑ fallow

familiarise* [fə'mɪliəraɪz]

vt. 使熟悉，使通晓；使家喻户晓

记 来自 familiar(*a.* 熟悉的)

搭 familiarise yourself with sth. 使自己熟悉某事物

例 Read the flow chart to ***familiarise*** yourself with the task. 阅读流程图以使你熟悉自己的任务。

fancy ['fænsi]

a. 别致的 *vt.* 想象 *n.* 想象力

记 联想记忆：fan(迷，狂热者) + cy → 着迷(的事) → 爱好

例 Maureen tiptoed around the room in her ***fancy*** shoes. 莫林穿上她那双精致的鞋，踮着脚尖在房间里走来走去。// She tries to ***fancy*** what the flame of a candle looks like after the candle is blown out. 在蜡烛被吹灭后，她努力想象烛焰的样子。

fantastic [fæn'tæstɪk]

a. 极好的；荒诞的，奇异的；不切实际的

例 Kids like spending a great deal of pocket money on ***fantastic*** toys instead of useful books. 孩子们喜欢花大量的零花钱购买奇特的玩具，而不是有用的书籍。

派 fantastically(*ad.* 极其)

同 marvelous(*a.* 惊人的，奇迹般的)；super(*a.* 极好的，上等的)

反 awful(*a.* 极坏的，可怕的)；ordinary(*a.* 普通的，平常的)

19

fantasy ['fæntəsi]

n. 想象

例 Those pleasures were produced through daydreaming and ***fantasy***. 那些快乐是通过白日梦和想象产生的。

fare* [feə(r)]

n. 费，票价 *vi.* 进展

记 联想记忆：若愿与我同行，我不在乎(care)船费(fare)

例 According to Susan, air ***fares*** are the lowest. 据苏珊说，机票价格是最便宜的。// How did you ***fare*** while you were abroad? 你在国外时过得好吗?

farewell [ˌfeə'wel]

n. 告别；欢送会

记 联想记忆：fare(看作 far，远) + well(好) → 朋友去远方，说些告别话 → 告别

搭 a farewell party 欢送会

例 We bid our old friends ***farewell***. 我们向老友们告别。

fascinate ['fæsɪneɪt]

v. 强烈地吸引，使着迷

记 联想记忆：fasc(看作 fast，牢固的) + in(里面的) + ate → 牢牢地陷在里边 → 使着迷

搭 be fascinated by 被…迷住

例 The very style of the old house ***fascinates***. 这个老房子的风格本身就令人着迷。

□ familiarise □ fancy □ fantastic □ fantasy □ fare □ farewell
□ fascinate

fascinating [ˈfæsɪneɪtɪŋ]

a. 迷人的

搭 find sth. fascinating 发现…吸引人

例 The museum has a *fascinating* collection of Celtic artifacts. 该博物馆藏有极其吸引人的凯尔特手工艺品。

fashion* [ˈfæʃn]

n. 方式；流行款式；时装

记 联想记忆：f + ash(灰) + ion → 我灰头土脸的，和商场里的时装格格不入 → 时装；流行款式

例 You'll find all sorts of things in the museum: old suitcases, ships' crockery, and classical cabins decorated in the *fashion* of the day. 在博物馆里你会找到各类东西：陈旧的手提箱、陶制船模型，还有以当时风格装饰的古典小屋。

派 fashionable(*a.* 时髦的)

fasten* [ˈfɑːsn]

v. 扎牢，扣住

记 联想记忆：fast(牢固的) + en(使…) → 扎牢

例 The driver must *fasten* his seat belt before driving. 司机在开车前必须系好安全带。

fatal* [ˈfeɪtl]

a. 致命的；重大的；命中注定的；灾难性的

记 来自 fate(*n.* 命运)

搭 a fatal accident 一场严重的事故

例 The majority of single-gene defects are *fatal*. 大部分的单基因缺陷都是致命的。

fate* [feɪt]

n. 命运，天数

例 The airport was built in a different way, to avoid the same sinking *fate*. 该机场用一种不同的方法建造而成，希望能够避免沉没的命运。

fatigue [fəˈtiːg]

n. 疲劳，劳累 *v.* (使)疲劳

记 联想记忆：fat(胖) + igue → 胖的人容易累 → 疲劳

例 Part-time workers are less likely to succumb to *fatigue* in stressful jobs. 兼职工人在有压力的工作中不太可能被疲劳压垮。

fault [fɔːlt]

n. 缺点，瑕疵，毛病

例 Any *fault* should be reported to the local *fault* repair service. 出现任何问题都应报知当地的维修中心。

faulty [ˈfɔːlti]

a. 有错误的，有缺点的；不完美的

记 来自 fault(*n.* 缺点)

例 In addition to *faulty* brake, this terrible accident which has caused 3 dead and 1 injured, was attributed to drunk driving. 除了刹车有问题之外，酒后驾车也是导致这起三死一伤严重事故的原因。

fauna* [ˈfɔːnə]

n. (某地区或某时期的)所有动物

记 来自 Fannus(潘纳斯，罗马神话中的动物之神)

搭 land and marine faunas 陆地和海洋动物区系

例 They tried their best to protect native flora and *fauna*. 他们竭尽全力来保护当地的动植物。

favour [ˈfeɪvə(r)]	*n.* 帮忙；偏爱；赞同；恩惠 *vt.* 赞同；较喜欢，偏袒；有利于  记 发音记忆：“飞吻”→ 姑娘比较喜欢那个小伙子，于是给了他一个飞吻 → 较喜欢 例 Darkness *favoured* their escape. 黑暗有利于他们逃跑。// I *favour* a state income tax over a raise in the sales tax. 我赞成用收取所得税来代替提高营业税。
favourite* [ˈfeɪvərɪt]	*a.* 特别喜欢的，宠爱的 *n.* 特别喜欢的人或物；亲信 例 Lucy's *favourite* colour is pink which her twin sister doesn't like at all. 露西最喜欢粉色，而她的双胞胎妹妹却一点儿也不喜欢。
feasible [ˈfiːzəbl]	*a.* 可行的，可能的；可做的，可实行的 记 联想记忆：f + easi(看作 easy，容易的) + ble → 容易做到的 → 可能的 搭 a feasible plan 可行的计划；feasible suggestions 可行的建议 例 Better integration of transport systems is made more *feasible* by modern computers. 现代计算机的应用使得交通系统得到更好的统筹。
feather [ˈfeðə(r)]	*n.* 羽毛，翎毛 记 联想记忆：父亲(father)爱戴插有羽毛(feather)的帽子 例 *Feather* fans and decorated hats went out of fashion. 羽毛扇和配有装饰的帽子已经过时了。

19

And gladly would learn, and gladly teach.

勤于学习的人才能乐于施教。

——英国诗人 乔叟(Chaucer, British poet)

□favour □favourite □feasible □feather

Word List 20

音 频

词根、词缀预习表

femin	女	feminism *n.* 女权主义	**-ism**	…主义	feminism *n.* 女权主义
fer	带来	fertile *n.* 肥沃的，多产的	**fin**	最后	finance *vt.* 为…提供资金
fin	界限	finite *a.* 有限的	**flam**	燃烧	flame *n.* 火焰 *v.* 燃烧
flex	弯曲	flexible *a.* 易弯曲的	**flour**	花	flourish *v.* 繁荣；茂盛
flu	流动	fluctuate *v.* (使) 起伏	**form**	形状	formality *n.* 认真遵守规范

feature* [ˈfiːtʃə(r)]

n. 特征，特色；[*pl.*]面貌，相貌；特写，专题节目；故事片 *v.* 以…为特色；由…主演；占重要地位

记 联想记忆：我的未来(future)由我主演(feature)

搭 a distinguishing feature 显著特色

例 Asymmetry is a common *feature* of the human body. 不对称是人体的一个普遍特征。

federal [ˈfedərəl]

a. 联邦的，联盟的

记 联想记忆：FBI(联邦调查局)的 F 就是 federal 的缩写

例 I opened a current account at the *Federal* Bank. 我在联邦银行开了一个活期账户。

federation [ˌfedəˈreɪʃn]

n. 联邦；同盟

记 来自 federal(*a.* 联邦的)

例 A study by the European *Federation* for Transport found that car transport is seven times as costly as rail travel. 欧洲运输联盟的一项研究发现，汽车运输所需的费用是铁路运输费用的七倍。

feeble [ˈfiːbl]

a. 虚弱的；无效的

记 联想记忆：fee(费用) + ble → 需要花钱看病 → 虚弱的

例 I felt *feeble* when I was ill. 我生病的时候感到很虚弱。

feed [fiːd]

v. 喂养，为…提供食物；吃，以…为食 *n.* 饲料

搭 feed into 向…提供；feed on 以…为食

例 To *feed* an increasingly hungry world, farmers need every incentive to use their soil and water effectively and efficiently. 为了养活世界上日益增加的人口，农民需要利用每一个激励措施来有效并且高效地使用他们的土地和水资源。

feedback* [ˈfiːdbæk]

n. 反馈；反馈信息

记 组合词：feed（喂养；提供）+ back（反）→ 反馈

搭 provide feedback 提供反馈信息；feedback on 关于…的反馈信息

例 Employee *feedback* is reviewed daily and some suggestion will be implemented within 48 hours. 员工反馈信息每天都会被查看，一些建议也会在 48 小时之内被采纳实施。

female [ˈfiːmeɪl]

a. 女(性)的；雌的 *n.* 女子

记 联想记忆：fe（音似：非）+ male（男子）→ 非男子 → 女子

例 A cow produces only one calf a year whereas a *female* ostrich can lay an egg every other day. 一头奶牛一年只能生一头小牛，而一只雌鸵鸟每隔一天就下一个蛋。

feminism* [ˈfemənɪzəm]

n. 男女平等主义；女权主义；女权运动

记 词根记忆：femin（女）+ ism（…主义）→ 女权主义

例 We discuss everything from personal experience to future society and *feminism*. 我们从个人阅历、未来社会或男女平等主义的角度来讨论每件事。

ferry [ˈferi]

n. 渡船；摆渡 *v.* 渡运

记 词根记忆：fer（带来）+ ry → 渡运

例 In Venice, which is famous as the city of water, the children there need to be *ferried* between school and home every day. 在著名的水城威尼斯，孩子们每天都要乘船来往于学校和家之间。

fertile [ˈfɜːtail]

a. 肥沃的，多产的，富饶的；能繁殖的

记 词根记忆：fer（带来）+ tile → 可带来果实的 → 多产的

搭 fertile land/field/soil 肥沃的土地；fertile eggs 受精卵

例 The east of this region is flatter and more low-lying, with *fertile* soils. 这一地区的东部土壤肥沃，地势较为平坦，海拔也比较低。

fertilise* [ˈfɜːtəlaɪz]

vt. 使肥沃，使多产；施肥于；使受精

记 词根记忆：fert（=fer 带来）+ ilise → 带来果实 → 使肥沃，使多产

搭 fertilised eggs 受精卵；cross-fertilise 异花受精

例 Mature breeding birds are very expensive—even a *fertilised* ostrich egg isn't cheap. 这种鸟的成鸟很贵，甚至一个受精的鸵鸟蛋都不便宜。

fibre [ˈfaɪbə(r)]

n. 纤维

记 联想记忆：多食富含纤维（fibre）的水果，有助消化降火（fire）

例 Today *fibre* optics are used to obtain a clearer image of smaller objects than ever before—even viruses. 现在人们利用纤维光学来获取更小物体的画面，其清晰程度前所未有，甚至病毒的图像都很清楚。

fickle* [ˈfɪkl]

a. 易变的，无常的

例 I knew that he was a *fickle* man, and one you could never rely on. 我知道他是个反复无常的人，你绝不能依赖他。

□ feedback □ female □ feminism □ ferry □ fertile □ fertilise
□ fibre □ fickle

fiction* [ˈfɪkʃn]

n. 小说

记 发音记忆："费口舌"→费口舌瞎编→小说

搭 science fiction 科幻小说

例 Suddenly, the stuff of science *fiction* doesn't seem so fanciful anymore. 这些科幻小说似乎突然就不再那么让人充满幻想了。

fieldwork* [ˈfiːldwɜːk]

n. 实地调查，野外考察

记 组合词：field(场地)+work(工作)→实地调查

例 A series of acquisitions might represent a decade's *fieldwork*. 一系列的发现可能代表着十年的实地调查。

fierce* [fɪəs]

a. 凶猛的；强烈的

记 发音记忆："飞蛾死"→凶猛的飞蛾扑火而死→凶猛的

搭 fierce loyalty 极度的忠诚

例 There is *fierce* competition in the examination. 考试竞争非常激烈。

figure* [ˈfɪɡə(r)]

n. 数字；人物；体态，体形；轮廓；(插)图，图表；雕像，塑像 *v.* 是重要部分；认为；计算，估计

搭 leading figures 主要人物，领导人物

例 The most recent available *figures* show that about a quarter of a million people are incapacitated with back pain every day. 最新数字显示，每天大约有25万人因受背部疼痛的折磨而无法正常工作与生活。

filter* [ˈfɪltə(r)]

n. 过滤器 *v.* 过滤；(消息等)走漏

记 发音记忆："非要它"→香烟的过滤嘴是非要不可的→过滤器

搭 filter tip (香烟的)过滤嘴；filter sth. out 把…滤出

例 Workers find that machines work much better if they change the *filters* regularly. 工人们发现如果他们能定期更换机器里的过滤器，机器就会运转得更好。

finale* [fɪˈnɑːli]

n. (音乐的)终曲；终场

记 联想记忆：final(最后的)+e→终场

例 No other performer has managed to equal their grand *finale*. 他们的压轴大戏令其他表演者望尘莫及。

finance* [ˈfaɪnæns; faɪˈnæns]

vt. 为…提供资金 *n.* 财政，金融；[常 *pl.*] 财务情况

记 词根记忆：fin(最后)+ance→最后起作用的东西→财政，金融

搭 college of finance and economics 财经学院；raise finance for 为…提供更多资金；to finance education 支付教育费用

例 Opponents of smoking *financed* this study. 反对吸烟的人为这一研究提供了资金。

派 financial(*a.* 财政的，金融的)；financially(*ad.* 财政上，金融上)

fingerprint* [ˈfɪŋɡəprɪnt]

n. 指纹，手印

记 组合词：finger(手指)+print(印迹)→指纹，手印

例 Systems using *fingerprints*, hands, voices and faces are already on the market. 市场上已出现了利用指纹、手印、声音和面部进行识别的系统。

□ fiction □ fieldwork □ fierce □ figure ■ filter □ finale
□ finance □ fingerprint

finite [ˈfaɪnaɪt]	*a.* 有限的；限定的 记 词根记忆：fin(界限，范围) + ite → 限定范围的 → 限定的 例 The *finite* fossil fuel reserves will hinder the development of a country. 有限的矿物燃料储备将阻碍一个国家的发展。
finitude [ˈfɪnɪtjuːd]	*n.* 有限；限定，界限 例 It is far beyond human *finitude* to climb this mountain. 爬越这座山远远超出人类的极限。
firm* [fɜːm]	*n.* 公司 *a.* 坚实的，稳固的，坚定的 例 Some *firms* are even downsizing as their profits climb. 一些公司即使在利润上升的情况下也会裁员。
fitness [ˈfɪtnəs]	*n.* 健康；适合(某事物) 记 联想记忆：fit(健康的) + ness(名词后缀) → 健康 例 Specific behaviours which were seen to increase risk of disease, such as smoking, lack of *fitness* and unhealthy eating habits, were targeted. 一些被认为会加大疾病威胁的特定行为成为攻击的目标，如吸烟、缺少锻炼和不健康的饮食习惯。
fitting [ˈfɪtɪŋ]	*n.* 试穿；装置 *a.* 适合的 例 If you want to buy a pair of trousers, a *fitting* is very necessary. 如果你想买裤子，试穿非常必要。
flame* [fleɪm]	*n.* 火焰；强烈的感情 *v.* 发火焰，燃烧 记 词根记忆：flam(燃烧) + e → 燃烧 例 The house was in *flames*. 房子失火了。// After hearing the news, her cheeks *flamed* with rage. 听到消息后，她愤怒得两颊通红。 
flap [flæp]	*v.* 拍打；(翅膀)拍动 *n.* 薄片；封盖；振动；激动 记 联想记忆：f(看作 fly，飞) + lap(拍打) → 拍动 搭 flap wings 振动翅膀；get in a flap over sth. 因某事而激动/不安 例 Mike bended the *flap* of an envelope over and stuck it with glue. 迈克把信封的封口折过来用胶水黏好。  同 agitation(*n.* 骚动，不安)；commotion(*n.* 骚动，动乱)；flutter(*v.* 振翼；飘动)
flash [flæʃ]	*v.* 闪光，闪耀 *n.* 闪烁；闪光灯 搭 a flash of lightning 一道闪电；a flash in the pan 昙花一现的人物，一时的成功 例 The air can become slightly positively charged when large thunderclouds are generating the intense electrical fields that cause lightning *flashes*. 当大团的雷雨云产生了引发闪电的强烈电场时，空气会略带正电。 派 flashlight(*n.* 闪光信号灯；手电筒)

20

□ finite □ finitude □ firm □ fitness □ fitting □ flame
□ flap □ flash

flask [flɑːsk]	*n.* 长颈瓶；烧瓶 记 联想记忆：和 flash(*v.* 闪光)一起记 例 After the science experiment, students washed the ***flasks***. 科学实验后，同学们将烧瓶清洗干净。
flat* [flæt]	*a.* 平的；(价格)固定的 *n.* 单元住宅 记 联想记忆：菜不放盐(salt)味道平平(flat) 例 ***Flat*** shoes may cure your back pain. 穿平底鞋能治疗背部疼痛。
flavour [ˈfleɪvə(r)]	*n.* 风味，滋味 *vt.* 给…调味 记 联想记忆：喜欢(favour)加上 l(看作 love，爱)，生活更有味道(flavour) 搭 a flavour of …的味道 例 Each country's coffee has a different ***flavour***. 各国的咖啡都别具风味。
flaw [flɔː]	*n.* 缺点；瑕疵 例 The worst ***flaw*** in this document was the naive faith it embodied. 这份文件最大的缺点就是它所表达的思想太天真了。
flee [fliː]	*v.* 逃走；逃避 例 Citizens were forced to ***flee*** the besieged city. 居民们被迫逃离这座被围困的城市。
fleet* [fliːt]	*n.* 舰队，船队 *a.* 快速的，敏捷的 *v.* 疾驰，飞逝，掠过 记 联想记忆：舰队(fleet)遇到问题赶紧逃跑(flee) 例 Governments assembled the world's largest ***fleet*** of dredgers to suck up mud in the ocean. 各国政府共同组建了世界上最大的挖泥船队，去挖掘大洋海底沉积的淤泥。
flexibility [ˌfleksəˈbɪləti]	*n.* 柔韧，有弹性；柔顺，温顺；灵活性；适应性 记 来自 flexible(*a.* 易弯曲的；柔韧的) 搭 flexibility of mind 头脑的灵活性 例 PE teachers help the development of coordination, balance, posture, and ***flexibility*** with activities like simple catching and throwing. 体育老师利用简单抓取和投掷等活动帮助学生提高身体的协调性、平衡度以及改善他们的体态和柔韧性。
flexible [ˈfleksəbl]	*a.* 易弯曲的；柔韧的；灵活的 记 词根记忆：flex(弯曲) + ible → 易弯曲的；柔韧的 搭 a flexible schedule 可变通的日程表；flexible working hours 弹性工作时间 例 Cars easily surpass trains or buses as a ***flexible*** and convenient mode of personal transport. 小汽车轻易地超越火车和公共汽车，成为一种灵活、便利的个人交通工具。
flexitime* [ˈfleksitaɪm]	*n.* 弹性工作制 例 ***Flexitime*** is one good method to reduce the number of vehicles traveling together at rush hour. 采用弹性工作制是降低交通高峰期时车流量的好方法。
flicker [ˈflɪkə(r)]	*n./vi.* 闪烁；一闪而过 记 联想记忆：flick(弹) + er → 弹指一挥间星光闪烁 → 闪烁 例 The light ***flickers*** quite badly and it's giving me headaches. 灯光闪得厉害，弄得我头疼。

□ flask □ flat □ flavour □ flaw □ flee □ fleet
□ flexibility □ flexible □ flexitime □ flicker

flight
[flaɪt]

n. 航班

搭 flight attendant (客机的)乘务员；flight crew 机组人员；flight path (飞机的)飞行路线

例 She's already booked a *flight* to Queensland. 她已经预订了去昆士兰的航班。

flint*
[flɪnt]

n. 火石，打火石

记 联想记忆：f + lint(看作 line，线) → 火石产生的火光如同一条线 → 火石

例 In Europe, the combination of steel, *flint* and tinder remained the main method of firelighting until the mid 19th century. 在欧洲，19 世纪中期以前，钢铁、火石和火绒的混合物一直都是点火的主要工具。

flip
[flɪp]

v. 轻抛；轻弹

例 A switch was *flipped* and the machine began to operate. 轻弹开关，机器便开始运作。

flora*
[ˈflɔːrə]

n. (某地区或时期的)一切植物，植物群

记 联想记忆：希腊神话里，花神名叫弗洛拉(Flora)

搭 flora and fauna 动植物

例 The theme of the meeting is the protection of native *flora* and fauna. 本次会议以保护当地动植物为主题。

floral
[ˈflɔːrəl]

a. 花的，像花的；绘有花的，饰以花的；植物群的

例 He devoted much time to *floral* design in his study room, with the inspiration from a cartoon. 他花费了很多时间对书房进行花饰设计，创作灵感来源于一幅漫画。

flourish*
[ˈflʌrɪʃ]

v. 繁荣；茂盛；兴旺；健康幸福 n. (为引起注意的)夸张动作；修饰

记 词根记忆：flour(=flor 花) + ish → 像花一样绽放 → 繁荣；茂盛

搭 with a flourish 兴旺；in full flourish 盛极一时

例 Research in Britain has shown the "green consumers" continue to *flourish* as a significant group amongst shoppers. 英国的调查表明，作为购物人群重要组成部分的"绿色消费者"仍然很活跃。

fluctuate
[ˈflʌktjueɪt]

v. (使)涨落，(使)起伏；(使)变化

记 词根记忆：flu(流动) + ctu + ate → (水)流动 → 起伏，涨落

例 Australia's environment *fluctuates* enormously from year to year. 澳大利亚的环境每年变化都很大。

同 waver(vi. 摇摆，摆动)；vary(v. 变化)

fluctuation*
[ˌflʌktjuˈeɪʃn]

n. 波动，起伏；动摇

记 来自 fluctuate(v. 起伏)

搭 display a fluctuation 显示波动

例 The decision was affected by his *fluctuation* of mood. 这个决定受他情绪波动的影响。

fluency
[ˈfluːənsi]

n. 流利，流畅；通顺

记 词根记忆：flu(流动) + ency → 话从口中流出 → 流利

例 *Fluency* in French is required for this job. 这项工作要求能讲一口流利的法语。

□ flight □ flint □ flip □ flora □ floral □ flourish
□ fluctuate □ fluctuation □ fluency

flush
[flʌʃ]

v. 冲洗，清除；(使)发红；(使)脸红；奔流 *n.* 脸红，红光 *a.* 齐平的，同高的

记 联想记忆：在闪烁(flash)的镁光灯下，她的脸通红(flush)

搭 flush away 冲洗掉，冲洗去

例 You can *flush* a wound with iodine to prevent the infection. 可以用碘酒冲洗伤口，以防止感染。

同 redden[*v.*（使某物）变红；（脸因羞涩、愤怒等）发红]；douche(*vt.* 冲洗，灌洗)

flutter
[ˈflʌtə(r)]

v. 振(翅)，拍打(翅膀)；飘动，晃动；(快速而不规则地)跳动

记 联想记忆：fl（看作 fly）+ utter（看作 butter）→ 蝴蝶(butterfly)振翅而飞 → 振(翅)

例 Her heart began to *flutter* with fear. 她害怕得心怦怦乱跳。

foam
[fəʊm]

n. 泡沫；泡沫材料 *vi.* 起泡沫

记 联想记忆：肥皂(soap)变成了很多泡沫(foam)

例 The orange juice in its *foam* overflew. 橙汁冒着泡，溢了出来。

focus*
[ˈfəʊkəs]

v. (使)聚焦，(使)集中 *n.* 焦点，焦距；(注意力、活动等的)中心

记 联想记忆：foc(看作 for，为了) + us → 焦点访谈的口号是为人民大众服务 → 焦点

搭 focus (sth.) on 使聚集，集中；(使)聚焦

例 The primary *focus* of attention in the twentieth century has been on small-scale societies. 在 20 世纪，小型社会成了人们首要关注的焦点。

foetus*
[ˈfiːtəs]

n. 胎儿；胚胎

记 联想记忆：foe(敌人) + t(看作 to) + us(我们) → 对我们来说，胎儿是自由的敌人 → 胎儿；胚胎

例 Every brain is initially female in its organisation and it only becomes a male brain when the male *foetus* begins to secrete hormones. 每一个大脑在结构上最初都是雌性的，只有当雄性胚胎开始分泌荷尔蒙时才变成雄性。

foil
[fɔɪl]

n. 箔；箔纸

例 The freezer is filled with *foil*-wrapped packages. 冷藏室里塞满了用箔纸包裹着的东西。

fold
[fəʊld]

v. 折叠 *n.* 皱；折

例 He decided to *fold* up Phoebe's massage table. 他决定把菲比的按摩桌折叠起来。

for instance*

例如

例 Fish can be flavored with tomato, cheese or chocolate *for instance*. 可以在鱼里加些东西来调味，例如：西红柿、奶酪或巧克力。

for the sake of

为了

例 *For the sake of* future generations, please save water. 为了子孙后代，请节约用水。

□ flush □ flutter □ foam □ focus □ foetus □ foil
□ fold □ for instance □ for the sake of

force* [fɔːs]

vt. 强迫 *n.* [*pl.*] 军队；力气；影响力

搭 bring into force 开始生效，开始实施；the forces of nature 自然力量

例 She'd like to finish the studies she was ***forced*** to give up earlier in life. 她想完成自己早年被迫放弃的研究。

forecast* [ˈfɔːkɑːst]

n./vt. 预报；预测；预想

记 联想记忆：fore(前面) + cast(扔) → 预先扔下 → 预报；预测；预想

搭 weather forecast 天气预报

例 The economic report ***forecast*** a sharp drop in unemployment for the next year. 据经济报告预测，来年的失业人数将明显减少。

foreland* [ˈfɔːlənd]

n. 前沿地；岬角

记 组合词：fore(前面) + land(土地) → 前面的土地 → 前沿地

例 The south ***foreland*** is also open to visitors. 南部前沿地也向游客开放。

foremost [ˈfɔːməʊst]

a. 最好的；最重要的

记 组合词：fore(前面) + most(最) → 放在最前面的 → 最重要的

例 The ***foremost*** research center of the day is in the USA. 当今最先进的研究中心在美国。

foresee [fɔːˈsiː]

vt. 预见，预知

记 联想记忆：fore(预先) + see(看) → 预先看到 → 预见，预知

例 What changes do you ***foresee*** in the educational field in the next 50 years? 在未来的50年里，你认为教育界会发生什么变化？

同 predict(*v.* 预言，预测)；foretell(*vt.* 预言，预示)

foreseeable [fɔːˈsiːəbl]

a. 可预知的，能预测的

例 For the ***foreseeable*** future, records will be made to be broken. 在不久的将来，记录将被打破。

forfeit* [ˈfɔːfɪt]

v. (因犯规等而)丧失，失去 *n.* 罚款；代价

记 联想记忆：for(因为) + feit(看作词根 fect，做) → 因为做错事，所以被处罚 → 罚款

例 He ***forfeited*** his driving licence because he drove after drinking. 他因酒后驾车被没收了驾照。

forgo* [fɔːˈɡəʊ]

vt. 放弃，抛弃；作罢

记 联想记忆：for(往，向) + go(走) → 走向他处，放弃了目前所在地 → 放弃

例 Jack has to ***forgo*** his vacation so as to take a summer English course. 杰克为了参加暑期英语班只好放弃他的假期。

form* [fɔːm]

n. 形式；外形；表格 *v.* (使)形成，(使)出现

例 You have to fill in a ***form***, but it doesn't take long. 你得填写一张表格，但不会耽误太久。// The council ***formed*** new policies at the meeting last night. 昨晚的会议上，委员会产生了一些新政策。

派 formability(*n.* 可成形性)

□ force □ forecast □ foreland □ foremost □ foresee □ foreseeable
□ forfeit □ forgo □ form

formal
[ˈfɔːml]

a. 正式的；正规的

例 They held the first *formal* international meeting on the subject. 他们就这一主题举行了第一届正式的国际会议。

派 informal(*a.* 非正式的)

formality
[fɔːˈmæləti]

n. 认真遵循规范、礼节等；例行公事；正式手续

记 词根记忆：form(形状) + al + ity(表性质，名词后缀) → 认真维持形状 → 认真遵守规范、礼节等

例 Juventus are not underestimating anyone and if there is someone who considers this match a pure *formality,* then they do not belong to this team. 尤文图斯队不会低估任何一个对手，如果哪个队员认为这场比赛只是个形式，他就不属于这支球队。

format*
[ˈfɔːmæt]

vt. 使格式化 *n.* 安排，计划；版式；格式

记 联想记忆：form(形式) + at → 固定的形式 → 版式；格式

例 You can use a computer to *format* your disc. 你可以用计算机将磁盘格式化。

派 formation(*n.* 构成)；formative(*a.* 形成的)

former*
[ˈfɔːmə(r)]

a. 以前的 *n.* 前者

记 联想记忆：form(形成) + er(表人或物) → 已形成的东西 → 前者

例 The world's food production will move from Western Europe to the *former* communist countries and parts of the developing world. 世界粮食生产将从西欧转移到前社会主义国家和一些发展中国家。

派 formerly(*ad.* 从前，以前)

formidable*
[ˈfɔːmɪdəbl]

一般

a. 可怕的；难以应付的，难以克服的

例 The new coastline is being bolstered with a *formidable* twelve kilometres of sea defences. 新的海岸线被一条 12 公里长的坚固海防线保护起来。

同 dreadful(*a.* 可怕的，令人畏惧的)；awesome(*a.* 使人敬畏的，使人惊惧的)；insurmountable(*a.* 不能克服的，不能超越的)

反 manageable(*a.* 能处理的)

formula*
[ˈfɔːmjələ]

n. 公式；配方；准则

记 联想记忆：form (形式，形态) + ula → 使具备形式、形态的方式、过程 → 公式；配方

搭 mathematical formula 数学公式

例 John Walker, an English pharmacist, borrowed the *formula* from a military rocket-maker called Congreve. 一名叫做约翰•沃克的英国药剂师从一位名叫康格里夫的军用火箭制造商那里借用了配方。

formulate
[ˈfɔːmjuleɪt]

vt. 系统阐述，明确表达；构想出(计划、方法等)，规划(制度等)

记 词根记忆：form(形式，形态) + ul + ate(使…) → 使具备形式 → 系统阐述

例 She cannot *formulate* her idea in a few words. 她无法用几句话阐明自己的思想。

□ formal □ formality □ format □ former □ formidable □ formula
□ formulate □ formulation □ forth □ forthcoming

formulation [ˌfɔːmjuˈleɪʃn]	*n.* 公式化，格式化；确切的表达 例 Could you choose another ***formulation***? 你能选择另一种表达方式吗?
forth* [fɔːθ]	*ad.* 离去，外出；向前；向某处 搭 call forth 使产生，引起；bring forth 提出；set forth 阐明，陈述；and so forth 等等；back and forth 来回地，往返，来来往往地 例 From this day ***forth*** I will study much harder. 从今以后我将更加努力学习。
forthcoming [ˌfɔːθˈkʌmɪŋ]	*a.* 即将到来的 记 组合词：forth(往前)+coming(就要来的)→即将到来的 例 This is the list of ***forthcoming*** books. 这是即将出版的书籍目录。

The man who has made up his mind to win will never say "impossible".

凡是决心取得胜利的人是从来不说"不可能的"。

——法国皇帝 拿破仑(Bonaparte Napoleon, French emperor)

Word List 21

音频

词根、词缀预习表

fract	碎裂	fraction *n.* 小部分	**-ile**	易…的	fragile *a.* 脆弱的
-ment	表名词	fragment *n.* 片段	**frequ**	频繁	frequent *a.* 频繁的
-ent	表形容词	frequent *a.* 频繁的	**fund**	基础	fundamental *a.* 基础的
germ	芽	germ *n.* 微生物，细菌	**fus**	流	fusion *n.* 熔化
gen	产生	general *a.* 普遍的	**-ous**	多…的	generous *a.* 慷慨的

fortnight
[ˈfɔːtnaɪt]

n. 两星期，十四天

记 联想记忆：fort（看作 fourteen，十四）+ night（夜晚）→ 十四个日日夜夜 → 两星期

例 It's a *fortnight* to National Day. 离国庆节还有两星期的时间。

forum
[ˈfɔːrəm]

n. 论坛；讨论会

记 联想记忆：for + u（看作 you，你）+ m（看作 me，我）→ 让你我说话的地方 → 论坛

例 The huge development in rocket technology is a good thing, but at the same time, rockets cause devastating results in the *forum* of war. 火箭研制技术的长足进步是件好事，但同时火箭被用于战争也带来了惨痛的结果。

fossil
[ˈfɒsl]

n. 化石；老顽固

记 发音记忆："佛说" → 一开口就是"佛说…"，真是个老顽固 → 老顽固

例 Fuel produced from crop residues is rarely competitive with *fossil* fuels at the present time. 由农作物残渣制成的燃料目前还不具备与矿物燃料竞争的实力。

foster
[ˈfɒstə(r)]

v. 培养，培育(某物)；鼓励，促进；领养 *a.* 收养的

记 联想记忆：fost（看作 fast，快速的）+ er → 促进；培养

例 The old couple have *fostered* over 60 children during the past ten years. 这对老夫妇在过去的十年间领养了 60 多名儿童。

派 fosterling（*n.* 养子，养女）；fosterer（*n.* 养育者）

同 nurture（*vt.* 抚育，教养）；cultivate（*vt.* 教养，培养）

foul *
[faʊl]

a. 发臭的；肮脏的；邪恶的 *n.* 犯规

记 联想记忆：邪恶的(foul)心灵(soul)

例 The football player was penalized for his *foul*. 那名足球运动员因为犯规而被判罚。

foundation *
[faʊnˈdeɪʃn]

n. 基础；地基；创立

记 联想记忆：found(建立) + ation(表状态，名词后缀) → 建立基础 → 基础；地基

例 Most of the rocks will become the *foundations* for the airport's runways and taxiways. 大多数石块将用作铺设机场跑道和飞机滑行道的地基。

fountain
[ˈfaʊntən]

n. 喷泉

记 联想记忆：大山(mountain)里有喷泉(fountain)

例 There is a beautiful *fountain* in the centre of the square. 广场中心有个漂亮的喷泉。

fraction
[ˈfrækʃn]

n. 小部分，片断

记 词根记忆：fract(打碎) + ion → 碎的部分 → 小部分，片断

搭 a fraction closer 稍微靠近一点；a fraction of 一小部分

例 The little boy has done only a *fraction* of his homework. 那小男孩只做了一小部分家庭作业。

派 fractional (*a.* 很少的，微不足道的)

fracture
[ˈfræktʃə(r)]

n. 断裂，折断；骨折 *v.* (使)断裂

记 词根记忆：fract(打碎) + ure → (使)断裂

搭 a compound fracture 开放性骨折

例 *Fractures* on tools indicate that a majority of ancient people were right-handed. 从工具上的裂痕我们可以看出，大多数古人都是惯用右手的。

同 crack〔*v.*(使)破裂，(使)发出爆裂声 *n.* 裂缝，爆裂声〕；split〔*v.*(使)分裂，分离 *n.* 裂口〕

fragile
[ˈfrædʒaɪl]

a. 脆弱的；虚弱的；易碎的；易受伤害的

记 词根记忆：frag(打碎) + ile(易…的) → 容易被打碎的 → 脆弱的；易碎的

例 The *fragile* boxes arrived intact. 这些易碎的箱子被完好无损地运到了目的地。

同 delicate(*a.* 易碎的，脆弱的)；brittle(*a.* 易碎的，易损坏的；脆弱的)；frail(a. 体弱的；易破碎的，易损的)

反 unbreakable(*a.* 打不破的，牢不可破的)；sturdy(*a.* 强壮的，强健的)

fragment

[ˈfrægmənt] *n.* 碎片，小部分，片断

[frægˈment] *v.* 分裂；破碎

记 词根记忆：frag(打碎) + ment(名词后缀) → 碎片，片断

例 The gigantic explosion from eruption of the volcano tore its summit into *fragments*. 火山喷发引起的强烈爆炸将山顶炸成了碎片。

fragment

□ foul　□ foundation　□ fountain　□ fraction　□ fracture　□ fragile
□ fragment

fragrance
[ˈfreɪɡrəns]

n. 芳香，香味；香水

记 联想记忆：frag(打碎) + rance(看作 France，法国) → 从法国买回来的香水瓶被打碎，芳香四溢 → 芳香；香水

例 The rose sends out strong *fragrance*. 玫瑰散发出浓郁的香味。

同 scent(*n.* 香味，香气)；perfume(*n.* 香味；香水)

反 stink(*n.* 臭味，恶臭)；stench(*n.* 臭气，恶臭)

frame
[freɪm]

n. 框架 *vt.* 给…镶框

搭 a picture frame 画框；frame of mind 心态，心绪

例 The tall buildings have been made possible by the development of light steel *frames* and safe passenger lifts. 轻型钢框架和安全客梯的改良使得高层建筑的建造成为可能。

派 framework(*n.* 结构，机制)

frank*
[fræŋk]

a. 坦白的，直率的

搭 to be frank 坦白说

例 Will you be *frank* with me about this matter? 在这件事上你能不能坦白地跟我说？

fraud*
[frɔːd]

n. 诈骗罪；骗子；伪劣品，冒牌货

记 发音记忆：“富饶的” → 骗子愿意去富饶的地区骗人 → 骗子

例 The votes are invalidated because of voter *fraud*. 选民的欺骗行为使得这些选票都作废了。

fraught
[frɔːt]

a. 充满…的；担心的，烦恼的

记 可能来自 freight(*n.* 货物)

例 During a period *fraught* with difficulties and marked by very extraordinary events, the United States has flourished beyond example. 在一段困难重重、风云跌宕的岁月里，美国拥有史无前例的繁荣。

freefone
[ˈfriːfəʊn]

n. 免费电话

例 The special call services of this telephone company include alarm calls, credit card calls, fixed time calls and *freefone* calls. 这家电话公司的特殊电话业务包括紧急号码呼叫、信用卡付费呼叫、定时呼叫和免费电话呼叫。

freight
[freɪt]

n. 货物 *vt.* 运送(货物)；货运

例 Heavy *freight* could only be carried by water or rail. 大型货物只能通过水路或铁路来运输。

frequency*
[ˈfriːkwənsi]

n. 频繁；频率

记 词根记忆：frequ(频繁；频率) + ency(名词后缀) → 频繁；频率

例 There is an increasing *frequency* of terrorist attacks in this primitive tribe. 这个原始部落受到越来越频繁的恐怖袭击。

frequent*
[ˈfriːkwənt]

a. 频繁的，常见的，常用的

记 词根记忆：frequ(频繁；频率) + ent(形容词后缀) → 频繁的，常见的

例 *Frequent* failures did not affect his morale. 屡屡失败并未让他泄气。

派 frequently(*ad.* 常常，频繁地)

□ fragrance　□ frame　□ frank　□ fraud　□ fraught　□ freefone
□ freight　□ frequency　□ frequent

friction [ˈfrɪkʃn]

n. 摩擦(力)；矛盾，冲突

记 联想记忆：润滑油的功能(function)是减小摩擦力(friction)

例 Studies of primitive societies suggest that the earliest method of making fire was through *friction*. 有关史前社会的研究表明，摩擦取火是最早的取火方式。

同 discord(*n.* 不和，纷争)；conflict(*n.* 冲突，争论)；attrition(*n.* 磨损；摩擦)

反 accord(*n.* 一致，符合)；harmony(*n.* 相符，一致；和谐)

frightened* [ˈfraɪtnd]

a. 受惊的；受恐吓的

例 The *frightened* child spoke in a halting voice. 这个受了惊吓的孩子说话结结巴巴。

frock* [frɒk]

n. 上衣；连衣裙

例 WSPU members wear their official uniforms of a white *frock* decorated with purple, yellow and green accessories. 妇女社会与政治同盟的成员穿着白色的制服裙，上面配有紫、黄、绿三色配饰。

frontier [ˈfrʌntɪə(r)]

n. 边境，边界；开发地区的边缘地带；[常 *pl.*] 前沿，新领域

记 联想记忆：front(前方) + ier → 一国最前方的地域 → 边境，边界

例 The police are closely spread over the *frontier* between the land of China and that of Nepal. 警力密布于中国与尼泊尔的边境上。

front-line* [frʌnt ˈlaɪn]

a. 前线的；第一线的

例 Decision-making has been forced down in many cases to *front-line* employees. 很多时候，决策权被迫下放到第一线的雇员手中。

frown* [fraʊn]

vi. (表示愤怒或烦心而)皱眉

记 联想记忆：f(音似：翻) + row(看作 brow，眉毛) + n → 翻眉毛 → 皱眉

搭 frown on/upon 反对；厌恶

例 Colleges always *frown* on late nights out. 大学向来不赞成深夜外出。

fruitful [ˈfruːtfl]

a. 多产的，富饶的；富有成效的

记 联想记忆：fruit(果实) + ful(=full 满满的) → 硕果累累的 → 多产的

例 The researchers' hard working has led to some *fruitful* discoveries. 研究人员经过努力工作，终于有了一些卓有成效的发现。

frustrate [frʌˈstreɪt]

vt. 使沮丧；挫败

例 This is the place where we *frustrated* the enemy. 我们就是在此处挫败了敌人。

frustrating* [frʌˈstreɪtɪŋ]

a. 令人泄气的，使人沮丧的

例 I find it *frustrating* to have so few teaching resources. 我发现教学资源太少，这真令人沮丧。

□ friction □ frightened □ frock □ frontier □ front-line □ frown
□ fruitful □ frustrate □ frustrating

frustration [frʌˈstreɪʃn]

n. 沮丧，不满

例 However, you have to admit that you need him so much when the moment of sadness, fear or an acute sense of *frustration* descends. 但你不得不承认的是，当悲伤、痛苦或是极度沮丧的时候，你如此需要他。

fuel [ˈfjuːəl]

n. 燃料 *v.* 给…加燃料

搭 solid fuel 固体燃料；nuclear fuels 核燃料；add fuel to the fire/flames 火上浇油

例 Such *fuels* produce far less carbon dioxide than coal or oil. 这些燃料所产生的二氧化碳要比煤和石油产生的少得多。

fulfil* [fʊlˈfɪl]

vt. 实现，完成；满足

记 联想记忆：ful(看作 full，充满的) + fil(l)(装满) → 做得圆满，把梦想实现 → 实现

搭 fulfil oneself 实现某人自己的抱负

例 The prophecy was *fulfilled*. 预言应验了。

fulfillment [fʊlˈfɪlmənt]

n. 履行；实现

例 The company gains its reputation from delivering fast and accurate order *fulfillment* services. 该公司因其快速而准确地完成订单而声名远播。

fumes* [fjuːmz]

n. 烟，气，汽

例 Moscow has joined the list of capitals afflicted by congestion and traffic *fumes*. 莫斯科已成为受交通堵塞和尾气排放之苦的首都之一。

function [ˈfʌŋkʃn]

vi. 运行，起作用 *n.* 功能；职责，作用；函数

搭 vital functions 生命机能；public function 正式社交集会

例 The dams store water for a variety of *functions*. 大坝贮存的水用途广泛。

fund [fʌnd]

n. 基金，专款；储备，蕴藏；[*pl.*] 存款，资金 *vt.* 为…提供资金，给…拨款

搭 raise funds 筹集资金；additional/extra fund 额外款项；mutual fund 互助基金

例 They provide *funds* for zoos in underdeveloped countries. 他们为不发达国家的动物园提供资金。

fundamental [ˌfʌndəˈmentl]

a. 基础的，基本的 *n.* [*pl.*] 基本原理

记 词根记忆：fund(基础) + ament + al → 基础的

搭 fundamental innovation 基础性的创新；fundamental process 基本过程；fundamental elements 基本元素；fundamental differences 根本差异

例 The *fundamental* conditions and resources for health are peace, education, food, a viable income, and a stable eco-system. 和平、教育、食物、足以维持生计的收入和稳定的生态系统是健康的基本条件和源泉。

furious [ˈfjʊəriəs]

a. 狂怒的；激烈的

例 The *furious* workers agitated for a strike. 愤怒的工人们鼓动罢工。

同 irate(*a.* 暴怒的，极其愤怒的)；fierce(*a.* 强烈的，狂热的)；turbulent(*a.* 汹涌的，狂暴的)

反 meek(*a.* 温顺的，驯服的)；calm(*a.* 镇静的，平静的)；unperturbed(*a.* 宁静的；泰然自若的)

□ frustration □ fuel □ fulfil □ fulfillment □ fumes □ function
□ fund □ fundamental □ furious

furnace [ˈfɜːnɪs]

n. 熔炉

例 This meeting room is like a *furnace*. 这个会议室热得像火炉。

furnish* [ˈfɜːnɪʃ]

vt. 布置，为…配备家具；供应，提供；装备

记 联想记忆：fur(皮毛) + nish → 供应皮毛 → 提供

搭 furnish sth. with sth. 用…布置…

例 You can get free advice on *furnishing* your home from the interior designer. 你可以从室内设计师那儿免费获得关于家居装潢的建议。

派 unfurnished(*a.* 无家具的)

furniture [ˈfɜːnɪtʃə(r)]

n. 家具

搭 office furniture 办公室家具

fuse [fjuːz]

n. 保险丝 v. 因保险丝烧断而断电；熔合；熔化

例 We have to insert a new *fuse* because the former one has malfunctioned. 保险丝烧断了，我们必须换一根新的。

同 merge(*v.* 合并，并入)；meld〔*v.*(使)混合，(使)合并〕；smelt(*v.* 熔解，熔炼)

反 divide(*v.* 分，分开，分隔)；separate(*v.* 使分离，使分开)；split〔*v.*(使)分裂，分离〕

fusion* [ˈfjuːʒn]

n. 熔化，熔合；聚变

记 词根记忆：fus(流) + ion → 流到一起 → 熔合

例 Singapore culture is a successful *fusion* of Eastern and Western features. 新加坡文化成功融合了东西方文化的特点。

futile [ˈfjuːtaɪl]

a. 无效的，无用的，无意义的；(人)没出息的；琐细的

记 词根记忆：fut(=fus 流) + ile → 流走的 → 无用的

例 Our attempts to improve performance are *futile*. 我们努力提高业绩，却付诸了东流。

gadget* [ˈgædʒɪt]

n. 小巧的器械，精巧的装置；小玩意

记 联想记忆：gad(尖头棒) + get(得到) → 好不容易得到的尖头棒是他钟爱的小玩意 → 小玩意

搭 kitchen gadgets 厨房小用具

例 We have tried out some of the latest *gadgets* on show. 我们试用了展出的一些最新小玩意。

派 gadgetry(*n.* 小器具，小装置)

galaxy [ˈgæləksi]

n. [the G-] 银河；星系；群英

例 Scientists intend to discover a sun-like fixed star in remote *galaxies*. 科学家们试图在遥远的星系中找到一颗类似太阳的恒星。

gallery [ˈgæləri]

n. 美术馆

例 We'll go to the Picture *Gallery* with a marvellous collection of paintings all by Australian artists. 我们将前往美术馆，那里收藏了一些优秀的画作，它们全部出自澳大利亚画家之手。

■ furnace □ furnish □ furniture □ fuse ■ fusion ■ futile
□ gadget □ galaxy □ gallery

gallop* ['gæləp]

v./n. 奔驰，飞跑，飞驰

记 联想记忆：汽车加了一加仑(gallon)油，于是飞驰(gallop)而去

搭 at a gallop 以最快速度，急速地

例 My sister set off at a *gallop* this morning. 今天早上我姐姐匆忙出发。

gamble ['gæmbl]

v. 赌博，打赌；投机；冒险

记 联想记忆：gamb(看作 game，游戏) + le → 赌博可不仅仅是小小的游戏 → 赌博

搭 gamble on 把…押在…上；投机；碰运气 gamble away 赌博输掉；a gambling house 赌场；gamble in stocks 做股票投机

例 For vacation, I went to Las Vegas to *gamble*. 假期我去拉斯维加斯赌博了。// Bob might show up on time, but I wouldn't *gamble* on it. 鲍勃也许会准时露面，但我不想冒这个险。

同 bet(v. 打赌，赌博)；wager(v. 打赌；赌博)；stake(vt. 以…打赌，拿…冒险)

gang [gæŋ]

n. 一帮 v. 结成一伙

例 A *gang* of young men attacked the police station with machine guns. 一群手持机关枪的年轻人袭击了警察局。

gather* ['gæðə(r)]

v. 聚集，集合，聚拢；收集，采集；逐渐增加；猜想，推测

搭 gather in 收割

例 In the beginning of a new semester, all the new students will *gather* in the playground to meet the Principal and the rest of the faculty. 新学期伊始，所有的新生在操场上集合与校长和其他老师见面。

gauge [geɪdʒ]

n. 测量仪表；规格，标准；计量器 vt. 测量，度量

记 发音记忆："规矩" → 规格

例 These new monitors can *gauge* the exhaust from a passing vehicle. 这些新的监视器可以测量驶过车辆的尾气排放量。

同 measure(n. 量具，计量单位 v. 测量，度量)；criterion(n. 评判的标准，尺度)；estimate (v. 估计，估量)；evaluate(vt. 评价，估计)

gear [gɪə(r)]

n. 齿轮，传动装置，(排)挡；(从事某项活动所需的)用具、设备、衣服等 vt. 调节，调整，使适应

搭 bottom gear 最低挡；gear to/towards 调整，使合适；gear the plan 调整计划

例 Single-speed cycles are bikes with no *gears*. 单速自行车就是没有变速齿轮的自行车。

gelatin ['dʒelətɪn]

n. 明胶

例 *Gelatin* dry plates are used in the film-making industry. 明胶干燥后制成的底版被用于电影制造业。

gender* ['dʒendə(r)]

n. 性别；(语法中的)性

记 联想记忆：女性大体上属于温柔的(tender)性别(gender)

搭 gender equality 男女平等

例 The *gender* gap is being attenuated in modern society. 在现代社会里，性别差距正在弱化。

□ gallop □ gamble □ gang □ gather □ gauge □ gear
□ gelatin □ gender

gene
[dʒiːn]

n. 基因

记 发音记忆："基因"

搭 a dominant/recessive gene 显性/隐形基因；gene pool 基因库

例 *Gene* is only an inborn factor in deciding one's intelligence, while a healthy diet and a good education are the extrinsic ones. 基因只是决定智力高低的一个先天因素，健康的饮食习惯和良好的教育是其后天因素。

---

general *
[ˈdʒenrəl]

a. 一般的，普通的；全体的，普遍的；大体的，概括的；首席的 *n.* 将军

记 词根记忆：gen(产生) + er + al → 产生一切的 → 普遍的

搭 in general 通常，大体上；general science 大众科学

例 The book on the desk is a *general* one. 课桌上的那本书很普通。

---

generalise
[ˈdʒenrəlaɪz]

v. 概括；推广

记 联想记忆：general(概括的) + ise → 概括

例 It's impossible to *generalise* about children's books, as they are all different. 儿童读物差别很大，很难概括。

派 generalisation (*n.* 概括，归纳；泛论)

---

generate
[ˈdʒenəreɪt]

vt. 发生，产生(光、热、电等)；引起，导致

记 词根记忆：gen(产生) + er + ate(使…) → 产生；引起

搭 generate electricity 发电

例 Compared with ordinary coal, "new clean coals" may *generate* power more efficiently. 和普通煤相比，新型的"高纯度"煤可以提高发电效率。

派 generation(*n.* 产生；一代)

---

generative
[ˈdʒenərətɪv]

a. 生殖的，生产的；有生产能力的

例 The convenience of this approach makes it widely used, and it is considered the norm in the *generative* approach to linguistics. 这种方法的便捷性使其被广泛应用，并且被视为语言学生成研究的规范。

---

generic
[dʒəˈnerɪk]

a. 一般的，普通的，通用的；种的，属的

记 词根记忆：gen(产生) + er + ic → 产生不同种属的 → 种的，属的；注意不要和 genetic(*a.* 遗传的；起源的)相混

搭 generic name 属名

例 The *generic* term for that plant is difficult to remember. 那种植物的种类名称很难记。

---

generous
[ˈdʒenərəs]

a. 慷慨的；大量的

记 词根记忆：gen(产生) + er + ous(多…的) → 产生很多的 → 慷慨的；大量的

搭 a generous gift 一份慷慨的礼物

例 People in disaster-affected areas received *generous* aid from the government. 受灾地区的人民从政府那里得到了大量的救济物资。

genetic* [dʒəˈnetɪk]	*a.* 遗传的 *n.* [-s] 遗传学 记 联想记忆：gene(基因) + tic → 基因的 → 遗传的 搭 genetic code 遗传密码；genetic engineering 基因工程；one's genetic makeup 一个人的基因结构 例 *Genetic* inheritance determines a baby's characteristics. 遗传基因决定了婴儿的特征。 派 genetical(*a.* 遗传的；起源的) 同 hereditary(*a.* 遗传的，遗传性的)；inherited(*a.* 遗传的)；congenital(*a.* 先天的，天生的)
genuine* [ˈdʒenjuɪn]	*a.* 真正的；真实的 记 词根记忆：gen(出生，产生) + uine → 生来就有的 → 真正的 例 Sixteen American states now use biometric fingerprint verification systems to check that people claiming welfare payments are *genuine*. 现在美国的 16 个州利用生物指纹识别系统来确保要求领取福利金的人们的信息真实无误。
geographical [ˌdʒiːəˈgræfɪkl]	*a.* 地理学的；地理的 例 The new *geographical* report covers a wide range of *geographical* area. 新的地理学报告涵盖了大范围的地理区域。
geological [ˌdʒiːəˈlɒdʒɪkl]	*a.* 地质的，地质学的 记 词根记忆：ge(o)(地球，地) + olog(y)(…学) + ical → 关于地球的学科 → 地质学的 搭 a geological textbook 地质学教科书 例 There is a *geological* survey that there will be an earthquake in the south part of the country. 地质学调查显示该国南部地区将有一次地震发生。
geology [dʒiˈɒlədʒi]	*n.* 地质学；地质概况 记 词根记忆：geo(地球，地) + logy(…学) → 地质学 例 The *geology* varies a good deal from region to region even in one country. 即使是在同一个国家，不同地区的地况也极为不同。
geometric [ˌdʒiːəˈmetrɪk]	*a.* 几何的，几何学的 记 来自 geometry(*n.* 几何学) 搭 geometric configuration 几何构型 例 He indulged in the study on *geometric* configuration even though he felt tired of math. 尽管不喜欢数学，他却对研究几何构型充满兴趣。
geometry [dʒiˈɒmətri]	*n.* 几何；几何学 例 Reading novels during *geometry* class is a misuse of your time. 在几何课上看小说是滥用你自己的时间。
germ [dʒɜːm]	*n.* 微生物，细菌；起源，萌芽 记 本身是词根，意为"芽" → 微生物，细菌 例 The patient had not the strength to throw off the *germs* that had invaded his immune system. 病人已无力摆脱已经侵入他免疫系统的病菌。

□ genetic　■ genuine　□ geographical　□ geological　□ geology　□ geometric
□ geometry　□ germ

germinate
[ˈdʒɜːmɪneɪt]

v. (使)发芽，(使)生长；发展

记 词根记忆：germ(芽) + in + ate(使…)→（使)发芽

例 The cat puts many fishes, which she has caught, in the soil in order to *germinate* them and pray for a good harvest in next year. 小猫把它捉来的鱼种到地里，希望它们发芽生长，并祈祷来年获得大丰收。

gesture*
[ˈdʒestʃə(r)]

n. 姿势，姿态；手势 *v.* 做手势

例 Sometimes you may simply bow, or make no *gesture* at all, when you're introduced to a stranger. 在介绍你和陌生人认识时，你可以只鞠躬，也可以不做任何动作。

get off track*

离题，偏离目标

例 It's all too easy for discussion in a meeting to *get off track*. 会议上的讨论极容易离题。

gigantic
[dʒaɪˈgæntɪk]

a. 巨大的，庞大的

记 词根记忆：gigant(=giant 巨人) + ic → 巨大的

搭 a gigantic sculpture 一座巨大的雕像

例 A *gigantic* explosion tore buildings around the bomb to fragments. 巨大的爆炸将炸弹周围的建筑物炸得粉碎。

同 colossal(*a.* 巨大的，庞大的)；enormous(*a.* 巨大的，极大的)

反 tiny(*a.* 极小的，微小的)；microscopic(*a.* 极小的)

gill
[gɪl]

n. 鳃

例 Unlike human beings, most fish are breathing with *gills*. 与人类不同，大多数鱼类都靠鳃呼吸。

21

We often hear of people breaking down from overwork, but in nine cases out of ten they are really suffering from worry or anxiety.

我们常常听人说，人们因工作过度而垮下来，但是实际上十有八九是因为饱受担忧或焦虑的折磨。

—— 英国银行家 卢伯克 .J.（John Lubbock, British banker）

□germinate □gigantic □gill

Word List 22

音频

词根、词缀预习表

germ	芽	germinate *v.*(使)发芽	**glac**	冰	glacial *a.* 冰期的
glob	球体	global *a.* 全球的	**gran**	颗粒	granite *n.* 花岗岩
graph	书写	graphic *a.* 文字的	**-ology**	…学	graphology *n.* 笔迹学
grav	重的	gravel *n.* 沙砾	**greg**	群体	gregarious *a.* 群居的
hab	生活	habitat *n.* 栖息地	**-ual**	表形容词	habitual *a.* 惯常的

given* [ˈɡɪvn]

a. 规定的，特定的；假设的

例 It is often important that you make it clear what your particular role is at a ***given*** time. 明确自己在特定时间内的特定角色通常很重要。

glacial* [ˈɡleɪʃl]

a. 冰期的；冰川的；寒冷的，冰冷的；冷若冰霜的

记 词根记忆：glac(冰) + ial → 冰期的

搭 the glacial period 冰期

例 These giant stones are part of an ancient ***glacial*** deposit. 这些巨石是古冰川沉积物的一部分。

glacier [ˈɡlæsiə(r)]

n. 冰川，冰河

记 词根记忆：glac(冰) + ier → 冰川，冰河

例 ***Glacier*** Bay, located in southeast Alaska, United States, is a narrow inlet of the Pacific Ocean which runs from northwest to southeast for about 105 kilometers. 冰川湾，位于美国阿拉斯加东南部，是太平洋的一个狭窄入海口，它自西北流向东南，全长约 105 公里。

glamor [ˈɡlæmə(r)]

n. 魅力；诱惑力

记 联想记忆：g + lamor(看作 labor，劳动) → 劳动人民最有魅力 → 魅力

例 Traveling abroad can offer you an opportunity to enjoy the ***glamor*** of other countries. 出国旅游能为你提供一个领略异国风情的机会。

gland [ɡlænd]

n. 腺

例 This type of hormone is only produced in the pineal ***gland*** in the brain. 只有脑部的松果腺才分泌这类荷尔蒙。

gleam [ɡliːm]

vi. 闪烁；流露 *n.* 闪光

例 The church steeple ***gleamed*** in the sunlight. 教堂的尖塔在阳光下闪闪发光。

 □ given □ glacial □ glacier □ glamor □ gland □ gleam

glide
[glaɪd]

vi./n. 滑行，滑翔

记 联想记忆：和 slide(*n./v.* 滑动)一起记

例 The pilot managed to ***glide*** down to a safe landing. 飞行员成功地使飞机向下滑行并安全着陆。

同 slide(*n./v.* 滑动，下滑)；slip(*v.* 滑倒；溜)

glimpse
[glɪmps]

vt. 瞥见 *n.* 一瞥，一看

记 联想记忆：glim（灯光）+ pse → 像灯光一闪 → 一瞥

例 We ***glimpsed*** the profile of the church steeple against the last glow of the sunset. 我们瞥见了在最后一抹晚霞映衬下的教堂尖顶的轮廓。

glitter
[ˈglɪtə(r)]

n./vi. 闪光

记 联想记忆：g + litter(看作 little，小) → 一闪一闪小星星 → 闪光

例 Wealth's ***glitter*** never washed a foul life clean. 财富的光辉永远洗不净肮脏的生涯。

同 gleam(*vi.* 闪亮，闪烁 *n.* 闪光，闪亮)；radiate[*v.* 发出(光或热)]；sheen(*n.* 光辉，光泽)

22

global*
[ˈgləʊbl]

a. 全球的，全世界的；整体的，全面的

记 词根记忆：glob(球体) + al → 全球的，全世界的

搭 global warming 全球变暖；global village 地球村，世界村

例 Does the media in your country pay more attention to ***global*** or national events? 你们国家的媒体更关注全球事件还是国内事件？

glorious
[ˈglɔːriəs]

a. 光荣的；壮丽的

记 发音记忆："哥劳累死" → 劳累致死，荣誉来之不易 → 光荣的

例 Our country has a ***glorious*** past. 我们的祖国有着辉煌的历史。

gloss*
[glɒs]

n. 光泽，色泽；虚假的外表，假象；注解，解释 *v.* 使具有光泽；掩饰；曲解；作注释；发光，发亮

记 可能来自 glow(*v.* 闪光)；注意不要和 gross(*a.* 总的，粗略的)相混

例 The kitchen ware can be polished to a ***gloss***. 那些厨房用具能被擦得闪闪发亮。

glossary*
[ˈglɒsəri]

n. 词汇表；术语表

例 You'll find the meaning of the difficult words used on this website in the ***glossary***. 你能在词汇表中查到此网页上难词的意思。

glossy
[ˈglɒsi]

a. 有光泽的，光滑的

记 来自 gloss(*n.* 光泽，色泽)

例 Out of sudden, the sun broke through from the heavy clouds, shining on her ***glossy*** hair, giving it a metallic luster. 突然间，太阳冲破阴云，照在她光滑的头发上，给头发镀上了一层金属的光泽。

□ glide □ glimpse □ glitter □ global □ glorious □ gloss
□ glossary □ glossy

glove* [glʌv]

n. 手套

记 联想记忆：g + love(喜欢) → GG 喜欢 MM 给他织的手套 → 手套

例 It is not necessary to wear *gloves* or a beekeeper's veil because the hives are not being opened and the bees should remain relatively quiet. 蜂箱尚未打开，蜜蜂应该还相对安静，没有必要戴手套或蒙上养蜂人专用面罩。

glue [gluː]

n. 胶水 *vt.* 胶合，张贴

记 联想记忆：用胶水(glue)把那幅蓝色的(blue)画贴上

例 I've prepared this so that I don't get *glue* everywhere. 我已经有所准备，这样就不会把胶水弄得到处都是。

glutamate* [ˈgluːtəmeɪt]

n. 谷氨酸；谷酸盐

例 But it wasn't until 1908 that the ingredient in kombu which was responsible for the improvement in flavour was actually discovered to be *glutamate* by scientists working there. 直到 1908 年，在那里工作的科学家才发现，改善了海藻味道的成分实际上是谷氨酸。

goal* [gəʊl]

n. 球门；射门，进球得分；目标

例 Once you have achieved the first *goals*, you will move up to a higher level of study. 一旦你达到了最初的目标，就可以进行更深层次的研究了。

goggles* [ˈgɒglz]

n. 护目镜；风镜；游泳镜

例 Racecar drivers all wear *goggles* when they are in a race. 赛车选手比赛时都佩戴护目镜。

goodwill* [ˌgʊdˈwɪl]

n. 友好，善意；信誉

记 组合词：good(好的) + will(意愿) → 善意

例 The manufacturer will lose customers and *goodwill* if word gets around that the product is unreliable. 一旦产品不可靠的消息传了出去，生产商便会失去顾客及信誉。

gorge* [gɔːdʒ]

v. 狼吞虎咽，塞饱 *n.* 山峡，峡谷

例 After a long journey, he started to *gorge* himself on cream cakes. 走了很长一段路后，他开始拼命吃奶油蛋糕。

gorgeous [ˈgɔːdʒəs]

a. 华丽的；极好的

记 联想记忆：gorge(峡谷) + ous → 峡谷很美丽 → 华丽的

例 The garden with azaleas is *gorgeous*. 花园里杜鹃花盛开，绚丽多彩。

gorilla [gəˈrɪlə]

n. 大猩猩

例 You cannot believe that most *gorillas* with scary faces and huge bulk like in *King Kong* are vegetarian. 你不会相信大多数像《金刚》里那样长相可怕身躯庞大的大猩猩居然都是素食动物。

govern [ˈgʌvn]

v. 统治，管理；控制，支配

例 The discovery that language can be a barrier to communication is quickly made by all who travel, study, *govern* or sell. 旅行者、学习者、管理人员或销售人员很快就会发现语言可能会成为他们交流的障碍。

派 government(*n.* 政府)

□ glove □ glue □ glutamate □ goal □ goggles □ goodwill
□ gorge □ gorgeous □ gorilla □ govern

grab [græb]

v./n. 抓，夺

记 联想记忆：螃蟹(crab)用钳子抓(grab)人

搭 grab at/for sth. 抓住/夺得某物；up for grabs 可供争夺的

例 Promotions in the store stand out and *grab* our attention. 商店里的促销广告非常显眼，吸引了我们的视线。

graduate*

[ˈgrædʒuət] *n.* (尤指大学)毕业生；研究生 [ˈgrædʒueɪt] *v.* (使)毕业；获得学位

搭 graduate school 研究生院；college graduates 大学毕业生；graduate from 从…毕业

例 Nowadays, there are not many job opportunities which *graduates* can look forward to. 现在，本科毕业生所能期望的就业机会并不多。

grand* [grænd]

a. 宏伟的；大的

例 Some 60 biometric companies around the world pulled in at least $22 million last year and that *grand* total is expected to mushroom to at least $50 million by 1999. 去年，全球大约 60 家生物测定公司的收入至少是 2200 万美元，到 1999 年总收入预计至少会猛增到 5000 万美元。

granite* [ˈgrænɪt]

n. 花岗岩，花岗石 22

记 词根记忆：gran(=grain 颗粒) + ite → 颗粒状石头 → 花岗岩，花岗石

例 This provided 7,000 cubic metres of *granite* to add to the island's foundations. 这为小岛地基的建设提供了 7000 立方米的花岗石。

grant* [grɑːnt]

n. 授予物；补助金，助学金，津贴；授权 *v.* 同意，承认；给予，授予

记 联想记忆：授予(grant)显赫的(grand)贵族爵位

搭 take...for granted 想当然，认为…理所当然；grant a request 答应请求；award a research grant 得到一笔研究经费

例 The loan is intended to supplement the *grant* for living costs. 这笔贷款是打算用来补贴生活费的。

graph* [grɑːf;græf]

n. 图，图表，曲线图

记 本身为词根，意为“书写；图” → 图表

搭 bar graph 条形图

例 The *graph* below shows the population growth over the past several years. 下图显示了过去几年的人口增长情况。

graphic [ˈgræfɪk]

a. 文字的；生动的，形象的；绘画的，图表的

记 词根记忆：graph(书写) + ic(形容词后缀) → 文字的；生动的

例 The *graphic* record shows three waves are arriving. 图表记录显示有三股浪潮正在靠近。

同 lifelike(*a.* 逼真的，栩栩如生的)；vivid(*a.* 逼真的)；pictorial(*a.* 绘画的；用图片表示的)

反 vague(*a.* 含糊的，模糊的)；obscure(*a.* 模糊的；费解的)

□ grab □ graduate □ grand □ granite □ grant □ graph
□ graphic

graphology [græˈfɒlədʒi]

n. 笔迹学，笔相学

记 词根记忆：graph（书写）+ ology（…学）→ 笔迹学

例 *Graphology* is not a good predictor of future job performance. 笔相学并不是预测未来工作成就的好方法。

grasp [grɑːsp]

vt. 抓紧；掌握，全面理解 *n.* 抓住；支配；理解

记 联想记忆：他见到她宛如抓住（grasp）一根救命稻草（grass）

例 Mary finally *grasped* the material after reading the textbook very carefully. 在非常仔细地阅读了课本后，玛丽最终领会了这段材料的意思。// Success is within our *grasp*. 成功尽在我们掌握之中。

grassy* [ˈgrɑːsi]

a. 草绿色的；似草的

例 To the east of us, you'll see no building at all—just trees and flowers and a huge *grassy* area. 在我们东面，你根本看不到建筑物，唯有树木、花卉和大片的绿地。

grateful [ˈgreɪtfl]

a. 感激的，感谢的

例 I'd be *grateful* if you could tell me a little about your time since you've been here in Cambridge. 如果你能够说说来剑桥以后的一些情况，我将不胜感激。

gravel [ˈgrævl]

n. 沙砾，砾石

记 词根记忆：grav（重的）+ el（表小玩意、小东西）→ 重的小东西 → 沙砾

例 There is a *gravel* path from my home to school. 从我家去学校有一条沙砾小路。

gravity [ˈgrævəti]

n. 重力

例 This increased the arrow's stability by moving the centre of *gravity* to a position below the rocket. 通过将重心移到火箭下方来增加整支箭的稳定性。

greasy* [ˈgriːsi; ˈgriːzi]

a. 多脂的；油滑的

记 联想记忆：greas(e)（油脂）+ y → 多脂的

例 Fish contains a lot of protein, and is not *greasy*. 鱼肉富含蛋白质且脂肪含量低。

greatly* [ˈgreɪtli]

ad. 非常；很；极大地

例 The process of growing bananas was *greatly* reduced with modern growing methods. 现代种植技术大大缩短了香蕉的种植过程。

gregarious [grɪˈgeəriəs]

a. 群居的；合群的；爱交际的

记 词根记忆：greg（群体）+ ari + ous（形容词后缀）→ 群体的 → 群居的；合群的；爱交际的

例 Dr. Green, a famous zoologist at the Harvard University, claimed that wild goose remains *gregarious* during the migration. 哈佛大学著名的动物学家格林博士称，大雁在迁徙中保持群居。

grid* [grɪd]

n. 格子，栅格；地图上的坐标方格；输电网，煤气输送网

搭 power grid 电力网

例 New York is laid out on a *grid*, which makes it easier to find your way around. 纽约市的布局十分整齐，因此你不容易迷路。

□ graphology □ grasp □ grassy □ grateful □ gravel □ gravity
□ greasy □ greatly □ gregarious □ grid

grieve
[griːv]

v. (使)伤心

例 I ***grieved*** very much for what I have done. 我为自己的行为感到非常痛心。

同 lament(*v.* 哀悼；悲痛)；bemoan(*vt.* 哀怨；悲叹)；sadden(*vt.* 使伤心，使悲哀)

反 cheer(*v.* 欢呼)；rejoice(*v.* 感到高兴，充满喜悦)

grill *
[grɪl]

vt. 烧烤；拷问，盘问 *n.* 烤架

例 Our leader ***grilled*** us about why we were absent from evening party after meeting. 我们领导盘问我们为什么缺席会议之后的晚会。

grim
[grɪm]

a. 严厉的；可怕的；讨厌的

记 联想记忆：g + rim(边框) → 给出条条框框来约束 → 严厉的；可怕的

例 We gradually found his laugh ***grim***. 我们渐渐觉得他的笑声让人讨厌。

grimy
['graɪmi]

a. 积满污垢的，肮脏的

例 The increasingly serious air pollution is threatening the health of people living in the ***grimy*** industrial cities. 日益严重的空气污染正威胁着生活于肮脏的工业城市中的人们的健康。

grin
[grɪn]

v./n. 咧嘴笑

记 联想记忆：gr(看作 girl，女孩) + in → 女孩叫，咧嘴笑 → 咧嘴笑

搭 grin from ear to ear 笑得合不拢嘴

例 The suicide-bomb attacker made a wolfish ***grin*** and exploded the car he was driving. 自杀式爆炸的制造者露出狰狞的一笑，随后引爆了他驾驶的汽车。

grind
[graɪnd]

n. 〈口〉苦差事 *v.* 磨(碎)，碾；折磨

记 联想记忆：将一块大(grand)石头磨碎(grind)

搭 the daily grind 繁重的日常工作

例 Tension may cause you to chew too forcefully or ***grind*** your teeth when you are sleeping. 紧张可能导致你在睡觉时用力咀嚼或是磨牙。

grip
[grɪp]

v. 握紧，抓牢；吸引住…的注意力(或想象力等) *n.* 紧握，抓牢；掌握，控制

搭 be in the grip of 在…的掌控下

例 She ***gripped*** on to the railing with both hands. 她双手紧紧抓住栏杆。

groan
[grəʊn]

vi. 呻吟；叹息 *n.* 呻吟声，叹息声

记 联想记忆：受到折磨(groan)，发出呻吟(moan)

例 The roof creaked and ***groaned*** under the weight of the snow. 屋顶在雪的重压下发出嘎吱嘎吱的声响。

grocery *
['grəʊsəri]

n. 杂货店；食品，杂货

例 I assisted in a ***grocery*** store last semester. 上学期，我在一家杂货店帮忙。

grope
[grəʊp]

v. (暗中)摸索

记 联想记忆：g + rope(绳子) → 抓住绳子向前走 → (暗中)摸索

例 The man ***groped*** for the light switch in the dark room. 男子在黑洞洞的屋里摸索着寻找电灯开关。

□ grieve □ grill □ grim □ grimy □ grin □ grind
□ grip □ groan □ grocery □ grope

gross
[grəʊs]

a. 总的，毛的

搭 Gross Domestic Product(GDP) 国内生产总值；Gross National Product (GNP) 国民生产总值

例 Agriculture and its supporting industries account for around 20% of our *Gross* National Product. 农业及其辅助产业占我国国民生产总值的20%左右。

grove*
[grəʊv]

n. 树丛，小树林

记 联想记忆：g(音似：哥) + rove(看作 love，爱) → 哥哥在小树林里谈恋爱 → 小树林

例 At this time, beehives are in particular demand by farmers who have almond *groves*. 这时，拥有杏树林的农民就尤其需要蜂箱。

grudge
[grʌdʒ]

n. 不满，积怨，怀恨 *v.* 勉强做；不情愿地给，吝惜

搭 hold grudges 心存怨恨；a grudge match 势不两立的比赛

例 Owing a *grudge* against somebody or something consumes one's energies and finally accomplishes nothing at all. 对某个人或某件事记仇会耗费一个人的精力，到最后一无所获。

grudge

guarantee*
[ˌgærən'tiː]

v. 保证；允诺 *n.* 保证；担保物

记 联想记忆：guar(看作 guard，保卫) + ant(蚂蚁) + ee → 蚁后允诺要开展一场保卫战 → 允诺；保证

搭 guarantee to 保证…；guarantee sb. sth. 保证某人某事

例 The box is made of stainless steel which is *guaranteed* for 20 years. 这个盒子是不锈钢的，品质保证为20年。

guidance*
['gaɪdns]

n. 指引，指导

记 联想记忆：guid(e)(指引，指导) + ance(名词后缀) → 指引，指导

搭 guidance system 向导系统；moral guidance 精神指导

例 We will solicit *guidance* and aid from legal experts. 我们将向法律专家寻求指导和帮助。

guideline*
['gaɪdlaɪn]

n. [常 *pl.*] 指导方针；准则，行动纲领

记 组合词：guide(指导) + line(路线) → 指导方针

例 These standards are based on *guidelines* set out by the major control boards. 这些标准是基于主管委员会拟定的指导方针制定的。

guilty*
['gɪlti]

a. 内疚的；有罪的

搭 be guilty of doing sth. 因做某事而内疚；因做某事而获罪

例 The information can lead to the conviction of any person *guilty* of placing metal pieces in its products. 这些信息可以将那些把金属片非法放入他们产品中的人绳之以法。

guinea
['gɪni]

n. 几尼(英国的旧货币单位，现值1.05镑)

记 发音记忆："几尼"

例 A *guinea* equals 5 dollars. 一几尼相当于五美元。

□ gross □ grove □ grudge □ guarantee □ guidance □ guideline
□ guilty □ guinea

gullibly *
[ˈɡʌləbli]

ad. 轻信地，易受欺骗地

记 来自 gullible(*a.* 易受骗的)

例 The tourist finds pleasure in landscapes and ***gullibly*** enjoys pseudo-events. 游客从欣赏风景中得到快乐，并且可以轻易享受模拟活动所带来的乐趣。

guzzle
[ˈɡʌzl]

v. 狂饮，暴饮；大量消耗

例 As its cars ***guzzle*** fuel, this car company has decreasing sales figures in recent years. 由于其生产的汽车耗油量太大，该汽车公司近几年的销售量一直在下滑。

派 guzzler(*n.* 耗油量大的汽车；暴饮暴食者)

habitable
[ˈhæbɪtəbl]

a. 适于居住的，可居住的

记 词根记忆：hab(生活，居住) + it + able(能…的) → 能让人生活的 → 适于居住的

例 Some areas of the earth are not ***habitable*** because of extreme climate conditions, such as low temperature. 地球上的一些区域由于低温之类的极端气候条件而不适合人类居住。

habitat *
[ˈhæbɪtæt]

n. 栖息地，住处

记 词根记忆：hab(生活，居住) + it + at → 住的地方 → 栖息地，住处

搭 natural habitat 自然保护区

例 They have focused their research on ***habitats*** they believe have escaped human influence. 他们已将研究重心放在他们认为不受人类影响的物种栖息地上。

habitual
[həˈbɪtʃuəl]

a. 惯常(性)的，通常的

记 联想记忆：habit(习惯) + ual(形容词后缀) → 惯常的，通常的

搭 a habitual criminal 惯犯

例 New curricula requires teachers to alter not just their teaching concepts but also their ***habitual*** teaching methods and behaviors. 新课程要求教师不仅要改变教育理念，还要调整他们习以为常的教学方式和教学行为。

hall *
[hɔːl]

n. 门厅；礼堂

例 There is a pay phone in the entrance ***hall***. 门廊里有一个投币式公用电话。

hallowed
[ˈhæləʊd]

a. 受崇敬的；神圣(化)的

记 联想记忆：hall(大厅) + ow + ed → 放在大厅里供奉起来 → 神圣(化) 的

例 In ancient Greece, sports games were held on ***hallowed*** ground near Mount Olympus every four years. 古希腊人每四年就要在奥林匹斯山附近的圣地举行运动会。

halt *
[hɔːlt]

v. 暂停；踌躇；停住 *n.* 暂停

记 联想记忆：h + alt(高音) → 高处不胜寒，该停下来了 → 停住

例 Iraq ***halted*** most oil exports. 伊拉克暂停了大部分的石油出口。

□ gullibly □ guzzle □ habitable □ habitat □ habitual □ hall
□ hallowed □ halt

halve* [hɑːv]

v. 二等分，减半

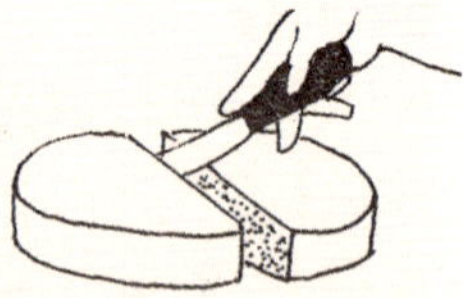

例 A development of 194 houses would take up 14 hectares of land above ground and occupy 2.7 hectares below it, while the number of roads would be *halved*. 建造 194 栋房子要占用 14 公顷的地上面积和 2.7 公顷的地下面积，而道路的数量则会减半。

---

hamlet* [ˈhæmlət]

n. 小村庄

例 I was born in a *hamlet* in the most south part of the city. 我出生于这个城市最南端的一个小村庄。

---

hamper [ˈhæmpə(r)]

vt. 妨碍，阻挠 *n.* 有盖的大篮子；盒装食物

记 联想记忆：篮子(hamper)在左手，锤子(hammer)在右手

例 Fierce storms have been *hampering* rescue work and there is now little chance of finding more survivors. 猛烈的暴风雨阻碍了救援工作，现在找到更多幸存者的机会已经很小。

---

hamster* [ˈhæmstə(r)]

n. 仓鼠

例 In the laboratory, *hamsters* put on more weight when the nights get shorter. 在实验室里，仓鼠的体重会随着夜晚的缩短而增加。

---

handicapped [ˈhændikæpt]

a. 残废的，有生理缺陷的

记 联想记忆：hand(手) + i + cap(帽子) + ped → 没法用手来戴帽子 → 残废的，有生理缺陷的

搭 mentally handicapped 心理缺陷

例 Toilets for *handicapped* people are located on this floor, with a sign of wheelchair on the door. 残疾人厕所就在本楼层，门上有一个轮椅的标志。

---

handle [ˈhændl]

v. 处理；操作，操纵；触，抚摸 *n.* 手柄，把手

记 联想记忆：hand(手) + le → 用手操作的东西 → 手柄，把手

搭 door handle 门把手

例 Friction management means *handling* conflicts in a positive and constructive manner. 摩擦管理是指以积极的、建设性的态度来处理各种冲突。

同 manage(*v.* 操纵，控制；管理)；regulate(*v.* 管制，控制)

派 mishandle(*vt.* 错误地处理)

---

handout [ˈhændaʊt]

n. 传单，分发的印刷品；救济品

记 组合词：hand(手) + out(向外) → 从手里发出去 → 传单；救济品

例 You should each have a *handout* with names and addresses. 你们每个人手头都应该有一张写有名字和地址的单子。

---

handy* [ˈhændi]

a. 方便的；手边的；手巧的

搭 come in handy 有用处，派上用场

例 To do this work needs *handy* men. 做这项工作需要些手巧的人。// Scissors are a *handy* tool to have in the kitchen. 剪刀是厨房里的一种便利工具。

Word List 23

音频

词根、词缀预习表

en-	使…	heighten *v.*（使）增强	**helic**	螺旋	helicopter *n.* 直升飞机
hemi	半	hemisphere *n.* 半球	**herb**	草	herbivore *n.* 食草动物
her	继承人	hereditary *a.* 遗传性的	**-age**	表集体名词	heritage *n.* 遗产；传统
hes	黏附	hesitate *vi.* 犹豫	**hier**	神圣	hierarchy *n.* 等级，层次
horr	害怕	horrify *vt.* 使恐惧	**hosp**	主人	hospitality *n.* 好客；热情

hang* [hæŋ]	*v.* 悬挂，吊，垂下；吊死，绞死 搭 hang out with 与…闲逛 例 The waiter did me a favor to *hang* my coat up on the hook. 服务员帮我将外衣挂在了衣钩上面。
hang on*	抓住；坚持下去；别挂断 例 "*Hang on*. I'll just get a pen." Tom said. "别挂断，我去拿一支笔过来。"汤姆说道。
haphazard* [hæpˈhæzəd]	*a.* 无秩序的，无计划的，组织混乱的 记 联想记忆：hap(机会，运气) + hazard(冒险) → 运气加冒险，就能成功 → 偶然情况 → 无计划的 例 There are books piled on shelves in a *haphazard* fashion. 书架上无序地堆放着一些书。
harbour [ˈhɑːbə(r)]	*n.* 港湾 *v.* 停泊；隐匿 记 发音记忆："哈勃" → 哈勃望远镜停泊在太空中 → 停泊 例 A port must be distinguished from a *harbour*. 港口和港湾在概念上必须区分开来。// *Harbouring* criminals is an offense in law. 窝藏罪犯是犯法的。
harmony* [ˈhɑːməni]	*n.* 相符，一致；和谐，融洽；【音】和声 搭 live in harmony 生活和谐；in harmony (with) (与…)和睦相处，(与…)协调一致 例 All his brothers and sisters are living together in perfect *harmony*. 他的兄弟姐妹们生活在一起并相处得非常融洽。 派 harmonize (*v.* 协调；配和声)；harmonious (*a.* 和睦的；协调的；悦耳的)；harmoniously(*ad.* 和谐地，和睦地)

□ hang □ hang on □ haphazard □ harbour □ harmony

harness* [ˈhɑːnɪs]

vt. 控制，利用；上马具 *n.* 马具

记 联想记忆：har（看作 hard，结实的）+ ness → 马具通常都很结实 → 马具

搭 harness a river 治理河流；harness nuclear energy 利用核能

例 The dam stores water for such functions as the irrigation of crops and the ***harnessing*** of the force of gravity for the generation of electricity. 大坝的存水可以用来灌溉农作物或利用重力来发电等。

harridan* [ˈhærɪdən]

n. 凶恶的老妇；老巫婆

例 Those people depicted a suffragette as a fierce ***harridan*** bullying her poor, abused husband. 那些人把妇女参政论者刻画成虐待她们可怜丈夫的悍妇。

harsh [hɑːʃ]

a. 严厉的，严酷的；粗糙的，毛糙的；刻薄的；（天气或生活环境）恶劣的；刺耳的，刺目的

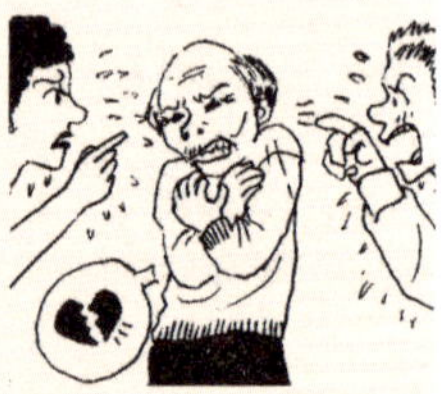

记 联想记忆：har（看作 hard，坚硬的）+ sh → 态度强硬的 → 严厉的

搭 harsh measures 严厉的措施；a harsh climate 恶劣的气候

例 The report has ***harsh*** words for the countries that sold these weapons. 这篇报道严厉谴责了出售这些武器的国家。

hassle* [ˈhæsl]

n. 困难，麻烦；分歧，争论

记 联想记忆：可能是 haste（急忙）+ tussle（争执；扭打）的缩合词 → 分歧，争论

例 Bob didn't want the ***hassle*** of commuting to work, so he took a job close to his home. 鲍勃不想每天很麻烦地乘车往返于家和公司之间，于是就在离家不远的地方找了份工作。

hasty [ˈheɪsti]

a. 草率的，匆忙的

记 联想记忆：hast（看作 fast，快的）+ y → 快速完成的 → 匆忙的

例 It is unwise to make a ***hasty*** conclusion. 草率地得出结论是不明智的。

同 impetuous（*a.* 草率的，匆忙的）

hatch [hætʃ]

v. 孵出，孵化；策划 *n.*（门、地板或天花板上的）开口；（飞机等的）舱门

记 联想记忆：要想赢得比赛（match）得有准备和策划（hatch）

例 Almost all the eggs in the farm will ***hatch*** into chicks. 农场里几乎所有的鸡蛋都会孵化成小鸡。

同 design（*vt.* 筹划，构思）；devise（*vt.* 策划，图谋）；scheme（*v.* 计划，策划）

haul [hɔːl]

vt. 用力拖；搬运

记 联想记忆：他们忙着往礼堂（hall）里搬（haul）东西

例 Every spring a beekeeper may move up to flowering fields and ***haul*** the hives back to where he starts out in winter. 每年春天，养蜂人都会迁往花地，冬天再将蜂箱搬运回来。

□ harness □ harridan □ harsh □ hassle □ hasty □ hatch
□ haul

hawk
[hɔːk]

n. 鹰，隼

记 发音记忆："好客"→好客的主人硬要送给客人一只鹰→鹰

例 The *hawk* swooped on its prey. 老鹰向猎物猛扑过去。

hazard
[ˈhæzəd]

n. 危险，冒险 *v.* 尝试着做(或提出)；冒…风险

记 发音记忆："骇死人的"→危险

搭 a safety/health hazard 安全/健康隐患

例 Traffic pollution is a major health *hazard*. 交通污染是主要的健康公害。

hazardous
[ˈhæzədəs]

a. 危险的，冒险的；有害的

记 联想记忆：hazard(危险，冒险)+ous(形容词后缀)→危险的，冒险的；有害的

搭 hazardous waste 有害废物

例 The acid rain in big cities can be *hazardous* to the environment where people live and their health. 大城市中的酸雨会危害人们生活的环境以及他们的健康。

headline
[ˈhedlaɪn]

n. 大字标题；[常 *pl.*] 头版头条新闻

记 联想记忆：head(头部)+line(行列)→写在文章顶头的内容→大字标题

例 What sort of national events make *headlines* in your country? 在贵国，哪种类型的国内事件会成为头条新闻呢？

headmaster*
[ˌhedˈmɑːstə(r)]

n. (中小学)校长

例 The new *headmaster* boosted his school with rallies and fund drives. 新校长通过集会和募捐来宣传学校。

headquarters*
[ˌhedˈkwɔːtəz]

n. 总部，总公司；大本营；司令部

记 组合词：head(头)+quarters(部分)→总部，总公司

例 The daily paper is compiled at the editorial *headquarters*. 日报由编辑部总部编纂。

heal
[hiːl]

v. 治愈，康复；调停

例 The wound took months to *heal*. 这个伤口花了几个月才治愈。

healing
[ˈhiːlɪŋ]

n. 康复，复原 *a.* 有治疗作用的

记 来自 heal(*v.* 治愈，康复)

例 Hypnosis, yoga, Silva mind-control, religious ceremonies and faith *healing* are all associated with successful suggestion. 催眠、瑜伽、席尔瓦心灵术、宗教仪式和信仰疗法都与成功的暗示相关。

heap*
[hiːp]

n. (一)堆；大量 *vt.* (使)成堆

记 联想记忆：通过大量(heap)量变一跃(leap)发生质变

搭 heaps of 许多，大量；heap sth. on sth. 在…上放很多…

例 The *heap* of boulders does not fill the space perfectly. 成堆的大块鹅卵石不能严丝合缝地填充这个空间。

23

□ hawk □ hazard □ hazardous □ headline □ headmaster □ headquarters
□ heal □ healing □ heap

heartless [ˈhɑːtləs]	*a.* 无情的，狠心的；无生气的，没精打采的 例 In employees' mind, employers are cold and ***heartless***, showing no concern for their welfare. 在员工的心目中，雇主冷酷无情，不关心他们的福利。
hectare* [ˈhekteə(r)]	*n.* 公顷 记 联想记忆：hect(=hecto 一百) + are(公亩) → 一百公亩 → 公顷 例 The farms there are quite large，typically around 800 ***hectares***. 那里的农场都很大，一般都在 800 公顷左右。
height* [haɪt]	*n.* 海拔；身高 例 Many characteristics, such as ***height*** and intelligence, result from subtle interactions between genes and the environment. 许多特征，如身高和智力，都是基因和环境间相互微妙作用的结果。
heighten [ˈhaɪtn]	*v.* (使)增强，(使)加剧 记 联想记忆：height(高度，海拔) + en(使…) → 提高 → (使)增强，(使)加剧 例 Competition is a kind of friendship. You can ***heighten*** the degree of your wisdom with the help of your rivals. 竞争就是一种友谊。在对手的帮助下，你能够变得更聪明。 同 intensify〔*v.* (使)增强，(使)加剧〕 反 lessen〔*v.* (使)变少，(使)减轻，(使)减少〕
heir [eə(r)]	*n.* 继承人 记 发音记忆："儿啊" → 儿子当然是继承人了 → 继承人 例 The man murdered the legal ***heir*** and disguised himself his victim. 该男子谋杀了合法继承人并冒名顶替。
helicopter* [ˈhelɪkɒptə(r)]	*n.* 直升飞机 记 词根记忆：helic(螺旋) + opter → 带螺旋翼的飞机 → 直升飞机 例 Here used to be a big factory manufacturing ***helicopter*** engines. 这里曾经有家生产直升飞机引擎的大工厂。
helix* [ˈhiːlɪks]	*n.* 螺旋(形)，螺旋结构 记 联想记忆：heli(看作 helic，螺旋) + x → 螺旋(形)，螺旋结构 例 The DNA molecule is a double ***helix***, resembling a ladder that's been twisted along its height. DNA 分子是双螺旋结构，就像是顺其长度螺旋扭转的梯子。
hemisphere [ˈhemɪˌsfɪə(r)]	*n.* (地球的)半球；大脑半球 记 词根记忆：hemi(半) + spher(球) + e → 半球 例 The left ***hemisphere*** of the brain controls the right half of the body. 左脑控制身体的右半部分。
hence* [hens]	*ad.* 因此，所以；今后，从此 记 发音记忆："恨死" → 恨死你，从此不相往来 → 从此 例 People all believe firmly that the true consequences will be known several days ***hence***. 人们都坚信几天后真实的结果将公之于众。

□ heartless □ hectare □ height □ heighten □ heir □ helicopter
□ helix □ hemisphere □ hence

herbal
[ˈhɜːbəl]

a. 草本植物的；药草(制)的 *n.* 草本植物志；药草书

搭 herbal medicine 草药；herbal practitioner 草药医生

例 *Herbal* medicine is well recognized as a non-toxic treatment. 草药被公认为一种无毒害的治疗方法。

herbivore*
[ˈhɜːbɪvɔː(r)]

n. 食草动物

记 词根记忆：herb(草) + i + vor(吃) + e → 食草动物

例 Ground-dwelling *herbivores* may return within a decade to this area. 地栖食草动物可能会在十年内返回这一地区。

herdsman*
[ˈhɜːdzmən]

n. 牧人

记 组合词：herds(畜群) + man(人) → 牧人

例 The *herdsman* talked to the cattle as if they were children. 牧人对着牛说话，好像它们是自己的孩子一样。

hereditary
[həˈredɪtri]

a. (尤指疾病)遗传的，遗传性的；可继承的，世袭的

记 词根记忆：her(=heir 继承人) + edit + ary → 遗传的，遗传性的；世袭的

搭 a hereditary title 世袭的头衔；hereditary rulers 世袭统治者

例 Albinism is a *hereditary* disease, which can be visual when the recessive gene does work. 白化病是一种遗传性疾病，当隐性基因表现出来时就会发病，显示性状。

heritage
[ˈherɪtɪdʒ]

n. 遗产；传统

记 词根记忆：her(遗传) + it + age(集体名词后缀) → 遗传下来的东西 → 遗产；传统

搭 cultural heritage 文化遗产

例 The highland games are part of Scotland's cultural *heritage*. 高地竞技是苏格兰文化遗产的一部分。

同 legacy(*n.* 遗产，遗留之物，遗赠物)；inheritance(*n.* 遗产，继承物；遗赠)

23

hesitate
[ˈhezɪteɪt]

vi. 犹豫；不情愿

记 词根记忆：hes(黏附) + it + ate → 脚像被黏住了一样 → 犹豫；不情愿

例 Mary *hesitated* before she answered this question because she didn't know what to say. 玛丽在回答这个问题前犹豫了一下，因为她不知道要说什么。

hesitation*
[ˌhezɪˈteɪʃn]

n. 犹豫，踌躇

搭 without hesitation 毫不犹豫；have no hesitation in doing sth. 做某事时没有犹豫

例 Tom bought the house immediately without *hesitation*. 汤姆毫不犹豫，当即买下了这幢房子。

hiccup
[ˈhɪkʌp]

n. 嗝，呃逆；暂时(或小的)困难(或挫折) *vi.* 打嗝

例 We've had a few slight *hiccups*, but progress has generally been quite steady. 我们遇到过一些小挫折，但是总的来说还在稳步前进。

□ herbal □ herbivore □ herdsman □ hereditary □ heritage □ hesitate
□ hesitation □ hiccup

hide
[haɪd]

v. (躲)藏 *n.* 皮革，兽皮

例 It is improbable that there is a planet ***hidden*** behind the sun. 在太阳的背后不可能藏着一颗行星。

hierarchy
[ˈhaɪərɑːki]

n. 领导层；层次，等级

记 词根记忆：hier(神圣) + arch(统治) + y(名词后缀) → 统治 → 领导层

例 It is likely that all uniforms make symbolic sense, namely, denoting a ***hierarchy***. 很可能所有的制服都具有象征意义，即体现了穿衣人的等级。

highland
[ˈhaɪlənd]

n. 高地，高原

记 组合词：high(高处) + land(陆地) → 高地，高原

例 Angela planned to take leave to see the southern ***highlands***. 安格拉计划休假去参观南部高原。

highlight
[ˈhaɪlaɪt]

vt. 强调，突出；以强烈光线照射；集中注意力于 *n.* 最精彩的部分，最重要的事件

记 组合词：high(高的) + light(发光) → 高调地发光 → 强调，突出

例 You'd better underline or ***highlight*** new words in this paragraph. 你最好把这个段落的生词画线或高亮标出。

high-tech*
[ˈhaɪˈtek]

n. 高科技

记 组合词：high(高的) + tech(科技) → 高科技

例 The architectural style usually referred to as ***high-tech*** was emerging. 经常被称为高科技的建筑风格涌现了出来。

highway
[ˈhaɪweɪ]

n. 公路

记 联想记忆：high(高的) + way(路) → 高速的路 → 公路

例 Los Angeles suffers from chronic ***highway*** blockages, despite efforts to encourage people to use public transport. 尽管(政府)竭力鼓励人们使用公共交通工具，但长期以来洛杉矶仍饱受公路交通拥堵的困扰。

hike
[haɪk]

v. 徒步旅行；提高(价格等) *n.* 远足，徒步旅行；猛增

记 联想记忆：穿着 Nike 鞋徒步旅行(hike)

例 My classmates want to ***hike*** through the forest in summer. 我的同学们想在夏天做一次穿越森林的徒步旅行。

hinder
[ˈhɪndə(r)]

vt. 阻碍，妨碍

记 联想记忆：阻碍(hinder)发展，落在后面(behind)

搭 hinder from 阻碍，妨碍

例 The survey reveals that most of the candidates' job applications have been ***hindered*** by their lack of relevant working experience. 调查显示，大部分求职者因缺乏相关的工作经验而导致其工作申请受阻。

派 unhindered(*a.* 不受妨碍的，不受阻碍的)；hindrance(*n.* 阻碍)

反 impede(*vt.* 阻碍，妨碍，阻止)；encumber(*vt.* 阻碍，妨碍)；hamper(*vt.* 妨碍，阻碍)

hinge*
[hɪndʒ]

n. 合叶；铰链 *v.* 依…而定

记 发音记忆："很紧" → 铰链很紧，转不动 → 铰链

例 The two metal tubes joined at a ***hinge*** at one end. 这两根铁管的末端连接在一个铰链上。

□ hide □ hierarchy □ highland □ highlight □ high-tech □ highway
□ hike □ hinder □ hinge

hinterland* [ˈhɪntəlænd]

n. 内地，腹地，内陆

记 组合词：hinter(=hinder 后面的) + land(土地) → 内地，腹地，内陆

例 A port is a centre of land-sea exchange which requires good access to a *hinterland*. 港口是海陆交易的中心，它需要与内陆有着便利的通道。

hire [ˈhaɪə(r)]

v./n. 租用；雇用

例 She was *hired* three years ago. 她是三年前录用的。

historian [hɪˈstɔːriən]

n. 历史学家，历史工作者

例 Most *historians* of technology credit the Chinese with the discovery of gunpowder. 大多数技术历史学家认为是中国人发明了火药。

historic* [hɪˈstɒrɪk]

a. 有历史意义的；历史的，历史性的

搭 historic moment 历史性的时刻

例 There are a number of *historic* ships docked in the habour. 这个港湾停泊了很多具有历史意义的船舶。

hitherto [ˌhɪðəˈtuː]

ad. 到目前为止，迄今

记 联想记忆：hit(打) + her + to → 迄今为止，他的爱还没有打动她 → 到目前为止，迄今

例 *Hitherto*, virtually all photographers developed and printed their own pictures. 事实上，到目前为止，所有的摄影师都亲自冲印自己拍摄的照片。

hive* [haɪv]

n. 蜂房，蜂箱；蜂房内的蜂群；闹市，忙碌之地 *v.* (使)入蜂箱；群居

记 联想记忆：生活(live)忙，建蜂房(hive)

例 For the three-week long bloom, beekeepers can hire out their *hives* for $32 each. 在长达三周的花期里，养蜂人可以将他们的蜂箱以每个 32 美元的价格租出去。

23

hockey [ˈhɒki]

n. 曲棍球；冰球

记 联想记忆：一只猴子(monkey)在玩曲棍球(hockey)

例 Both skating and ice *hockey* were included in the Antwerp Olympic Games in 1920. 1920 年在安特卫普举办的奥运会包括滑冰和冰球两个项目。

holistic [həʊˈlɪstɪk]

a. 整体的，全面的；功能整体性的

搭 holistic medicine 整体医学

例 Usually, the *holistic* solutions are required for the environment problems. 通常来说，环境问题需要整体性的解决方案。

holistically [həʊˈlɪstɪkli]

ad. 整体地，全盘地

例 In the innovation time, the firm must design its innovation process *holistically*. 在这个创新的时代，企业必须全面设计自己的创新流程。

hollow [ˈhɒləʊ]

a. 空的，空洞的；(声音)沉闷的；虚伪的，空虚的 *v.* 挖空，凿空

例 Dung beetles' homes are *hollowed* out from within. 蜣螂的家是从里面往外挖空的。

homesick* [ˈhəʊmsɪk]

a. 想家的，思乡的

记 组合词：home(家) + sick(病的) → 想家想到生病 → 思乡的

例 I was *homesick* at first and missed my family. 起初，我思乡心切，想念我的家人。

homesick

□ hinterland □ hire □ historian □ historic □ hitherto □ hive
□ hockey □ holistic □ holistically □ hollow □ homesick

homestay* [ˈhəʊmsteɪ]	*n.* 在当地居民家居住的时期 搭 homestay family 寄宿家庭 例 A: I've heard that you want to move into a ***homestay*** family. Is that correct? B: Yes, that's right. A: 我听说你想搬入一个寄宿家庭，是吗? B: 是的。
homogeneous [ˌhɒməˈdʒiːniəs]	*a.* 同种类的，由相同(或同类型)事物(或人)组成的 记 联想记忆：homo(同类的) + gene(基因) + ous → 相同基因的 → 同种类的 搭 homogeneous light 单色光，均匀光；a homogeneous mixture 相同成分组成的混合物 例 Uniforms can project the image of a company and unite the workforce into a ***homogeneous*** unit. 工装能展示一个公司的形象，并使公司内部的员工凝聚为一个整体。 同 identical(*a.* 相同的，相等的)；kindred(*a.* 同类的，类似的)；uniform(*a.* 相同的，一致的) 反 heterogeneous(*a.* 异类的，不同的)；dissimilar(*a.* 不同的，相异的)
honour [ˈɒnə(r)]	*n.* 光荣；尊敬 *vt.* 向…示敬意；信守，执行(承诺) 例 The planet was for a time called Herschel in ***honour*** of its discoverer. 为了纪念这颗行星的发现者，它一度被称为赫舍尔星。
hook* [hʊk]	*n.* 钩，吊钩，钩状物 *v.* (使)钩住，挂住；钓(鱼) 记 联想记忆：书(book)在手，月如钩(hook) 搭 hook up with sb. 与某人来往 例 It is common in the Internet cafes that computers from different manufacturers can be ***hooked*** together. 在网吧里不同厂家的电脑可以联网是很普通的。
horizon* [həˈraɪzn]	*n.* 地平线；范围；眼界 记 联想记忆：ho + riz(音似：rise"升起") + on → 太阳从地平线上升起 → 地平线 搭 expand one's horizons 开阔眼界 例 It is in technology and commerce that glass has widened its ***horizons***. 玻璃在技术和商业领域扩大了应用范围。
horizontal [ˌhɒrɪˈzɒntl]	*a.* 地平线的，水平的 记 来自 horizon(*n.* 地平线) 例 Gharib and Graff set themselves the task of raising a 4.5-metre stone column from ***horizontal*** to vertical, using no source of energy except the wind. 加里卜和格拉夫为自己制定了这样一项任务，除了风以外，不借助其他任何能源，把 4.5 米高的石柱由水平抬高成垂直状态。 派 horizontally(*ad.* 水平地)
horrify* [ˈhɒrɪfaɪ]	*vt.* 使恐惧，使惊骇；使震惊；使感到厌恶 记 词根记忆：horr(害怕) + ify(使…) → 使恐惧，使惊骇 例 I had been ***horrified*** by several newspaper reports. 我对几篇新闻报道的内容感到震惊。

□ homestay □ homogeneous □ honour □ hook □ horizon □ horizontal
□ horrify

horror [ˈhɒrə(r)]

n. 害怕，恐怖

例 He was filled with ***horror*** at the sight of the dog. 他看见狗就害怕。

hose* [həʊz]

n. 软管 *vt.* 用软管淋

记 联想记忆：要想玫瑰花(rose)开，需把软管(hose)拿来浇水

例 The water entered through a ***hose*** to the machine. 水通过软管流入机器。

hospitable* [hɒˈspɪtəbl]

a. 好客的，殷勤的，热情友好的；(气候、环境)宜人的；(对新思想等)易接受的，开通的

记 词根记忆：hosp（=host 主人）+ it + able → 主人的盛情款待让人难忘 → 好客的，热情友好的

例 The villagers were very ***hospitable*** towards anyone who passed through. 村民们对所有经过村子的路人都十分热情友好。

hospitality [hɒspɪˈtæləti]

n. (对客人的)友好款待，好客；盛情；招待礼节

搭 corporate hospitality 企业联谊

例 The ***hospitality*** of the host greatly impressed every guest. 主人的殷勤好客给每一位客人留下了深刻印象。

host* [həʊst]

n. 主人；东道主；主办方；大量，许多 *v.* 主办；招待

搭 a host of 大量的；host country 东道国，主办国

例 We will be ***hosting*** more than 250 participants for the lectures and workshops. 我们将接待 250 多位参加讲座和讨论会的人员。

hostel* [ˈhɒstl]

n. (青年)招待所；学生宿舍

记 联想记忆：host(主人) + el → 房间临时的主人 → 招待所；学生宿舍

搭 student hostel 学生宿舍；youth hostel 青年旅舍

例 Claudia doesn't like youth ***hostels*** because there' s no privacy. 克劳迪娅不喜欢住青年旅舍，因为那里毫无隐私可言。

hostile* [ˈhɒstaɪl]

a. 敌方的；不友善的；不利的

记 联想记忆：host(主人) + ile → 鸿门宴的主人 → 不友善的

例 The luxuriant forests of Amazonia seem ageless, unconquerable, a habitat totally ***hostile*** to human civilization. 茂密的亚马孙丛林似乎是永恒的，无法征服的，是一个完全不利于人类文明存在的地方。

hostility* [hɒˈstɪləti]

n. 敌意，敌对，对抗；抵制，反对，否决；[*pl.*] 交战，战争

例 The ***hostility*** of the indigenous population to North American influences is still very strong. 当地人对来自北美的影响仍怀有很深的敌意。

household [ˈhaʊshəʊld]

n. 家庭；户，全家人 *a.* 家庭的，家用的，普通的；家喻户晓的

记 组合词：house(房屋) + hold(拥有) → 有房屋才像个家 → 家庭

搭 single-parent households 单亲家庭；household appliances 家用电器

例 I've been investigating four new ***household*** gadgets and sorting out their advantages and disadvantages. 我已就四种家居新产品做了调查，并将它们的优缺点分门别类。

□ horror □ hose □ hospitable □ hospitality □ host □ hostel
□ hostile □ hostility □ household

hover
[ˈhɒvə(r)]

v. （鸟等）翱翔，盘旋；逗留在近旁，徘徊；彷徨，犹豫

记 联想记忆：爱人(lover)在自己身边徘徊(hover)

例 It is August 15th in the Chinese lunar calendar and there is a full moon *hovering* in the sky. 今天是农历八月十五，一轮满月挂在夜空中。

同 linger〔*vi.*（因不愿离开而）继续逗留，徘徊〕；flutter〔*v.*（鸟等）振翼，翩然而飞〕

Victory won't come to me unless I go to it.
胜利是不会向我走来的，我必须自己走向胜利。

——美国女诗人 穆尔（M. Moore, American poetess）

Word List 24

音频

词根、词缀预习表

hum	地	humble *a.* 谦卑的	**humid**	潮湿的	humidity *n.* 湿度
id	看	ideal *a.* 理想的	**-ity**	表性质	identity *n.* 身份
gno	知道	ignorance *n.* 无知	**lumin**	光	illuminate *vt.* 照亮
lus	光	illustrate *v.* 阐明	**imit**	模仿	imitate *vt.* 模仿
mens	测量	immense *a.* 巨大的	**mun**	作用	immune *a.* 免疫的

however* [haʊˈevə(r)]

conj. 不管用什么方法，然而 *ad.* 无论如何，不管怎样；可是；仍然

例 I feel a bit sleepy, *however*, I keep studying. 我觉得有点困了，但我还是坚持学习。

huddle [ˈhʌdl]

vi. 聚集在一起 *n.* 杂乱的一堆；拥挤

记 联想记忆：大家聚集在一起（huddle）处理（handle）问题

例 There is a *huddle* of people around the injured man. 一群人聚在伤者周围。

hug [hʌg]

n./v. (热烈的 / 地)拥抱

例 She gave her mother an affectionate *hug* after winning the prize. 获奖后，她紧紧地拥抱了母亲。

hum [hʌm]

n. 嗡嗡声，嘈杂声 *vi.* 哼曲子；发嗡嗡声

记 发音记忆："哼"→ 蚊子、苍蝇的哼哼声

例 The *hum* of conversation died away as the curtain rose. 幕布升起时，嗡嗡的谈话声渐渐消失。

humane [hjuːˈmeɪn]

a. 善良的，人道的，仁慈的，慈悲的；(指学科)促进文明或教化的，人文的

记 词根记忆：hum(人) + ane → 有人性的 → 善良的，人道的，仁慈的

例 A series of campaign for the *humane* treatment of wildlife has been launched throughout the world in recent years. 近年来，全世界发起了一连串的善待野生生物的活动。

humanistic [ˌhjuːməˈnɪstɪk]

a. 人文主义的，人性的

例 It is a *humanistic* study. 这是人文主义方面的研究。

humanity [hjuːˈmænəti]

n. 人类，人；人性；人道，仁慈；[*pl.*] 人文学科

例 The control of fire was the first and perhaps greatest of *humanity's* steps towards a life-enhancing technology. 人类在迈向提高生活质量的技术旅途中，对火的支配是迈出的第一步，可能也是最重要的一步。

同 humankind(*n.*〈总称〉人类)

□ however □ huddle □ hug □ hum □ humane □ humanistic
□ humanity

humble* [ˈhʌmbl]

a. 谦逊的，谦虚的；地位(或身份)低下的，卑贱的；简陋的，低劣的 *vt.* 使谦恭；使卑下；贬低

记 词根记忆：hum(地) + ble → 接近地面的 → 谦逊的；卑贱的

搭 a man of humble origin 出身寒微的人

例 They do not wish to return to the *humble* post-war era. 他们不希望回到那可怜的战后年代。// I was *humbled* by her generosity. 她的大度让我觉得自己渺小。

humid* [ˈhjuːmɪd]

a. 湿的，潮湿的，湿润的，多潮气的

记 词根记忆：hum(地) + id → 接近地的 → 潮湿的，湿润的

搭 humid air 潮湿的空气；humid atmosphere 潮湿的大气；humid climate 湿润的气候

例 Summers in that city are extremely hot and *humid*. 那个城市的夏天非常湿热。

humidity [hjuːˈmɪdəti]

n. 湿度；潮湿

记 联想记忆：humid(潮湿的) + ity → 湿度；潮湿

搭 relative humidity 相对湿度

例 The wooden frame warped in the *humidity*. 木框因受潮而弯曲了。

humour [ˈhjuːmə(r)]

n. 幽默，幽默感

记 发音记忆："幽默"

例 I think our professor must have some sense of *humour*. 我认为我们的教授得有点儿幽默感。

hurdle* [ˈhɜːdl]

n. 障碍；跳栏 *v.* 越过障碍

例 It's still so hard for women to even get on to short lists—there are so many *hurdles* and barriers. 对于女性来说，想要进入最后的候选名单仍然很难，可谓是障碍重重。

hurl [hɜːl]

vt. 猛投，猛摔；大声叫骂

例 Mr. Lee *hurled* the book across the room while he was in a fury. 李先生暴怒之下将书本从房间一头扔向另一头。

hurricane [ˈhʌrɪkən]

n. 飓风

记 联想记忆：hurri(看作 hurry，匆忙) + cane → 来得很匆忙的风 → 飓风

例 The *hurricane* flung their boat upon the rocks. 飓风将他们的船摔到了岩石上。

hybrid* [ˈhaɪbrɪd]

n. 杂交生成的生物体，杂交植物(或动物)；杂种，混血儿；混合物，合成物 *a.* 杂交产生的；混合的，合成的

例 They suggest small low-emission cars for urban use and larger *hybrid* or lean-burn cars for use elsewhere. 他们建议在城市中使用低排量的小型车，而将那些较大的双动力汽车和稀燃车应用在其他地方。

hypnotic [hɪpˈnɒtɪk]

a. 催眠的 *n.* 催眠药

例 Western people believed that being *hypnotic* could help people remember something happening in life. 西方人相信，催眠可以帮助人们记起生活中发生的一些事。

□ humble □ humid □ humidity □ humour □ hurdle □ hurl
□ hurricane □ hybrid □ hypnotic

hypothesis
[haɪˈpɒθəsɪs]

n. 假设，假定；假说；猜想

记 联想记忆：hypo(在…下面) + thesis(论点) → 在论点之下，非真正论点 → 假设，假定；假说

搭 Continental Drift Hypothesis 大陆漂移说；raise a hypothesis 提出一个假设

例 You have to discard or modify your *hypothesis* if shown not to be correct. 如果被证实不正确，你就必须放弃或修改你的假设。

同 supposition(*n.* 假定；猜想)；assumption(*n.* 假定)

---

hypothetical
[ˌhaɪpəˈθetɪkl]

a. 假设的，假定的；爱猜想的

例 Many great discoveries are based on putting a *hypothetical* theory in the laboratory. 许多重大发现都是将假设的理论拿到实验室验证后得出的。

ID card*

身份证(= identity card)

例 Students must have their student *ID cards* with them if they want to attend the conference. 学生必须携带学生证才能参加本次大会。

---

ideal
[aɪˈdiːəl]

a. 理想的，完美的；理想主义的；空想的；唯心的 *n.* 理想；理想的东西(或人)

记 词根记忆：id(看) + eal → 心里想看到的 → 理想的

搭 an ideal companion 理想伙伴

例 She is the *ideal* person for the job. 她是这项工作的最佳人选。

派 idealistic(*a.* 唯心论的，空想主义的)；ideally(*ad.* 理想地，完美地)

---

identical*
[aɪˈdentɪkl]

a. 完全相同的，同一的

例 Even among *identical* twins, one in six pairs will differ in their handedness. 即使是同卵双胞胎，平均六对中也会出现一对在使用左右手习惯上不同的双胞胎。

同 alike(*a.* 同样的，相同的)；duplicate(*a.* 完全相同的)

反 dissimilar(*a.* 不同的，相异的)；distinct(*a.* 有区别的，不同的)

---

identifiable*
[aɪˈdentɪˈfaɪəbl]

a. 可辨认的，可识别的；可确定的，可证明是同一的

记 来自 identify(*v.* 认出，识别)

搭 identifiable characteristics 可识别的特征

---

identification
[aɪˌdentɪfɪˈkeɪʃn]

n. 身份证明；识别，鉴定

记 词根记忆：ident(一样的，相同的) + ific(使…) + tion(名词后缀) → 查看是否相同 → 鉴定；证明

搭 identification card 身份证

例 Give us the ship's name, its *identification* number and ocean region. 告诉我们这艘船的名字、它的登记号以及所处海域。

---

identify*
[aɪˈdentɪfaɪ]

v. 认出，识别；辨别；查明；确定；视…(与…)为同一事物

搭 identify... with... 把…与…视为同一事物

例 In 1986, American researchers *identified* the genetic defect underlying one type of muscular dystrophy. 1986 年，一些美国研究人员发现了可导致某种肌肉萎缩症的遗传缺陷。

同 recognize(*vt.* 认出，识别)；determine(*v.* 确定)；distinguish(*v.* 区别，辨别)

□ hypothesis　□ hypothetical　□ ID card　□ ideal　□ identical　□ identifiable
□ identification　□ identify

identity*
[aɪˈdentəti]

n. 身份；特性；同一性

记 联想记忆：i + dent（牙齿）+ ity（表性质）→ 通过牙齿来确定身份 → 身份

搭 cultural identity 文化特性

例 If people want to enter this building, their *identities* must be authenticated by an electronic scanner. 如果人们想进入这座大楼，需经电子扫描仪进行身份验证。

ignorance
[ˈɪɡnərəns]

n. 无知，愚昧；不知道

记 词根记忆：i（不）+ gno(r)（知道）+ ance → 什么都不知道 → 无知

搭 ignorance about 不知…

例 Not *ignorance*, but the *ignorance* of *ignorance*, is the death of knowledge. 知识的死亡不是无知本身，而是对无知的无知。

ignorant
[ˈɪɡnərənt]

a. 无知的；愚昧的

例 She is very *ignorant* about her own job. 她非常不了解自己的工作。

同 stupid（*a.* 愚蠢的，迟钝的）；retarded（*a.* 弱智的，迟钝的）

ignore*
[ɪɡˈnɔː(r)]

vt. 不顾，不理，忽视

记 联想记忆：ig + nore（看作 nose，鼻子）→ 翘起鼻子不理人 → 不顾，不理，忽视

搭 ignore the fact 忽视事实

例 If you *ignore* these instructions, this medicine could affect your heart rhythm. 如果你没有按说明服药，这种药可能会影响你的心率。

illegal*
[ɪˈliːɡl]

a. 不合法的，违法的

记 联想记忆：il（不，非）+ legal（合法的）→ 不合法的

搭 illegal profit 非法利润；illegal drugs 毒品；illegal activities 非法活动

例 The police arrested the old lady for *illegal* possession of drugs. 警方以非法持有毒品为由逮捕了这位老妇人。

派 illegality（*n.* 非法，违法）；illegally（*ad.* 不合法地，违法地）

illuminate
[ɪˈluːmɪneɪt]

vt. 照亮；阐明，解释；启发

记 词根记忆：il（向内）+ lumin（光）+ ate → 向内投入光 → 照亮；启发

例 The street was *illuminated* by fireworks. 这条街被焰火照得通明。

同 illustrate（*v.* 举例说明，阐明）；demonstrate（*v.* 说明；证实）

illusion
[ɪˈluːʒn]

n. 幻想中的事物，错误的观念；错觉，幻觉，假象

记 联想记忆：il（不，无）+ lus（看作 lust，光）+ ion（名词后缀）→ 看到根本没有的光 → 幻觉，假象

例 He will be presenting his show of magic *illusion* and mystery at 9:30. 他将在 9 点 30 分表演神秘魔幻节目。

同 mirage（*n.* 幻景，幻想）

□ identity □ ignorance □ ignorant □ ignore □ illegal □ illuminate □ illusion

illustrate [ˈɪləstreɪt]

v. (用图等)说明，举例说明，阐明；给…作插图说明

记 词根记忆：il(向内) + lus(光) + tr + ate → 向内投入光 → 阐明

搭 illustrate the point 举例说明要点

例 The diagram *illustrates* the information provided in paragraphs B–F of the reading. 该图说明了阅读材料中 B–F 段出现的信息。

派 illustrator(*n.* 插图画家)

illustration [ˌɪləˈstreɪʃn]

n. 说明；实例；图解，插图

记 联想记忆：illustrat(=illustrate 举例说明，阐明) + ion(名词后缀) → 实例；图解

例 There is virtually no empirical evidence to support the use of *illustrations* in teaching reading. 事实上没有任何实证的经验能够支持在教阅读的时候使用插图。

image [ˈɪmɪdʒ]

n. 形象；印象；图像

例 Their *images* were always dry and dusty. 他们总是一副不修边幅、蓬头垢面的形象。

imagination [ɪˌmædʒɪˈneɪʃn]

n. 想象(力)；想象出来的事物

例 They need to train their powers of *imagination*. 他们需要训练自己的想象力。

imaginative [ɪˈmædʒɪnətɪv]

a. 富有想象力的；创新的

记 来自 imagine(*v.* 想象)

例 Hypotheses are *imaginative* and inspirational in character, and are adventures of the mind. 臆测让人充满想象与灵感，它是思想的冒险。

imagine* [ɪˈmædʒɪn]

v. 想象；猜想

例 The children have no need to *imagine* anything when they read such books. 孩子们阅读这种书时根本不用发挥想象力。

派 imaginable(*a.* 可想象的，可能的)

imitate [ˈɪmɪteɪt]

vt. 模仿，模拟；仿效

记 词根记忆：imit(模仿) + ate(动词后缀) → 模仿

例 Children like to *imitate* adults. 儿童喜欢模仿大人。

imitation [ˌɪmɪˈteɪʃn]

n. 模仿；仿造；仿制品，假货，赝品

搭 in imitation of 模仿，仿效

例 A child learns to talk by *imitation*. 小孩子通过模仿学会说话。

同 fake(*n.* 假货，赝品)；counterfeit(*n.* 赝品)

immediately* [ɪˈmiːdiətli]

ad. 立即，马上；紧接地；直接地

例 You go down to the end of this corridor and turn right. The computer lab is *immediately* on your right. 走到走廊尽头向右拐，右手边就是机房。

immense* [ɪˈmens]

a. 巨大的，广大的

记 词根记忆：im(不) + mens(测量) + e → 不能测量的 → 巨大的，广大的

搭 an immense improvement 巨大的进步

例 The scope of the problem facing the world's cities is *immense*. 全世界的城市面临很多方面的问题。

□ illustrate □ illustration □ image □ imagination □ imaginative □ imagine
□ imitate □ imitation □ immediately □ immense

immigrant
[ˈɪmɪɡrənt]

n. 移民；侨民

记 词根记忆：im（向内）+ migr（迁移）+ ant（表人）→ 向内迁移的人 → 移民；侨民

例 This *immigrant's* citizenship was revoked because he had concealed his criminal record. 这位移民因为隐瞒了犯罪记录而被取消了国籍。

immigration*
[ˌɪmɪˈɡreɪʃn]

n. 外来的移民；移居

记 词根记忆：im（向内）+ migr（迁移）+ ation → 向内迁移 → 移居

搭 immigration law 移民法；immigration controls 移民管制；immigration application 移民申请

例 There will be stricter controls on *immigration* into the country. 以后要移民到这个国家会有更严格的管制。

immune
[ɪˈmjuːn]

a. 免疫的，有免疫力的；有抵抗力的；不受影响的；免除的，免除惩罚的，豁免的

记 词根记忆：im（没有）+ mun（作用）+ e → 没有作用 → 免疫的；免除的

搭 immune system 免疫系统

例 The viruses stimulated the *immune* system. 病毒刺激了免疫系统。

派 autoimmune（*a.* 自体免疫的）

同 resistant（*a.* 有抵抗力的）；invulnerable（*a.* 无法伤害的）

反 susceptible（*a.* 易受…影响或损害）；liable（*a.* 易于…的）

impact*
[ˈɪmpækt]

n. 影响，作用；冲击

例 Cigarette smoke has the same *impact* on smokers as it does on non-smokers. 香烟烟雾对吸烟者和不吸烟者的影响是一样的。

impair
[ɪmˈpeə(r)]

vt. 损害；削弱

记 词根记忆：im（不）+ pair（相等）→ 使…不一样 → 损害

搭 impair one's health 损害健康

例 The performance of divers will be *impaired* if they work in cold water. 如果在冷水中工作，潜水员的工作效率会降低。

同 injure（*vt.* 伤害，损害，损伤）；undermine（*vt.* 削弱，破坏）

反 strengthen（*v.* 加强，巩固）；improve（*v.* 改进，改善）

impart
[ɪmˈpɑːt]

vt. 给予，赋予；传授；告知，透露

搭 impart knowledge 传授知识

例 He told me not to *impart* it to anyone without his own permission. 他告诉我，未经他允许不可以把此事透露给任何人。

impede*
[ɪmˈpiːd]

vt. 阻碍，妨碍

记 词根记忆：im + ped（脚）+ e → 用脚绊倒 → 阻碍，妨碍

例 The lack of a common language can severely *impede* progress. 缺乏一种通用语言会严重阻碍进程。

imperil
[ɪmˈperəl]

vt. 使陷于危险，危及

记 词根记忆：im（进入）+ per（冒险）+ il → 使陷于危险，危及

例 Some people think that the government's housing policy now might *imperil* the whole real estate market. 一些人认为政府的住房政策可能危及当下的整个房地产市场。

□ immigrant □ immigration □ immune □ impact □ impair □ impart
□ impede □ imperil

impetus
[ˈɪmpɪtəs]

n. 推动，促进，刺激；推动力

记 词根记忆：im + pet(追求) + us → 有追求才有动力 → 推动，促进

例 According to the insiders, real estate market's ***impetus*** first came from the effective demand for the release of China's huge population. 据业内人士分析，房地产市场的推动力首先来源于中国巨大人口的有效购房需求。

同 stimulus〔*n.* 促进(因素)，刺激(物)〕；spur〔*n.* 刺激(物)，激励〕

implement

[ˈɪmplɪment] *vt.* 使生效，实施；贯彻，执行 [ˈɪmplɪmənt] *n.* 工具

记 词根记忆：im(里面) + ple(填满) + ment → 把…里面填满 → 实施；执行

例 Policy makers struggle to define and ***implement*** appropriate legislation. 政策制定者们致力于阐释和执行适当的法规。

派 implementation(*n.* 实施；执行)

同 perform(*v.* 做，履行)；execute(*vt.* 执行，履行，实行)；utensil(*n.* 用具)；instrument(*n.* 仪器，器械，工具)

implication
[ˌɪmplɪˈkeɪʃn]

n. 含意；暗示，暗指；卷入，牵连

记 词根记忆：im(里面)+ plic(重叠，折叠) + ation → 有双重意思 → 含意；暗示，暗指

搭 political implication 政治含意

例 What would be the ***implications*** if humanity were to understand, with precision, the genetic constitution? 如果人类准确地破译了基因的构成，那将意味着什么呢?

同 connection(*n.* 联系，关联)；involvement(*n.* 包含；连累)

impose
[ɪmˈpəʊz]

v. 把…强加于；征(税等)；处以(罚款、监禁等)

记 词根记忆：im(使…) + pos(放置) + e → 强行放置 → 征(税)

例 I ***imposed*** certain constraints on them to make things simple. 为了让事情变得简单，我给它们加了一些限制。

impossible*
[ɪmˈpɒsəbl]

a. 不可能的，办不到的

记 联想记忆：汤姆·克鲁斯主演的电影《碟中谍》就是 *Mission Impossible*

例 This kind of research would be ***impossible*** without computers. 没有计算机就无法进行这种研究。

impoverish
[ɪmˈpɒvərɪʃ]

vt. 使贫困；使枯竭，使贫瘠

记 词根记忆：im(进入) + pover(贫困) + ish(使…) → 使进入贫困 → 使贫困

例 Excessive farming had ***impoverished*** the soil here. 过度耕种使得这里的土地变得贫瘠了。

impoverished
[ɪmˈpɒvərɪʃt]

a. 穷困的，赤贫的；贫乏的，贫瘠的；枯竭的

记 词根记忆：im(进入) + pover(贫困) + ish(使…) + ed → 使处于贫困中的 → 穷困的，赤贫的；贫乏的

例 It is necessary to carry out the project of returning farmland to forests since overfarming has created much ***impoverished*** soil. 过度耕作已经造成了大量土地的贫瘠，所以必须实行退耕还林。

□ impetus □ implement □ implication □ impose □ impossible □ impoverish
□ impoverished

imprecise [ˌɪmprɪˈsaɪs]	*a.* 不精确的，不严密的 记 联想记忆：im(不) + precise(精确的，严密的) → 不精确的，不严密的 例 The witness's descriptions were too *imprecise* to be of any real value. 目击者的描述太不精确了，没有任何实际价值。
impress* [ɪmˈpres]	*vt.* 给…留下深刻印象，使铭记；印，压印 *n.* 印记 记 联想记忆：im(=on 在…上) + press(压) → 在上面压 → 压印 例 Those uniforms for the military were originally intended to *impress* and even terrify the enemy. 最初设计军装是为了给敌人留下深刻的印象，甚至威慑敌人。
impression* [ɪmˈpreʃn]	*n.* 印象，感想；印记，压痕 记 联想记忆：impress(印，盖印) + ion → 印象；印记 搭 first impression 第一印象 例 Could you tell us something about your first *impression* of the town when you arrived? 你能不能告诉我当你初到这个小镇时，你的第一印象是什么？
impressive* [ɪmˈpresɪv]	*a.* 给人深刻印象的，令人敬佩的 记 来自 impress(*vt.* 给…以深刻印象) 搭 the most impressive place 给人印象最深的地方 例 I think this figure is especially *impressive*. 我认为这个数字尤其令人印象深刻。 派 impressively(*ad.* 令人难忘地)
improve* [ɪmˈpruːv]	*v.* 改善，改进 搭 improve on/upon sth. 改进，做出更好的业绩 例 In an English course with Atlas English Language College, you *improve* your language skills and make friends from all over the world! 在阿特拉斯英语学院的英语课堂，你可以提高自己的英语水平，同时结识来自世界各地的朋友！
improvement* [ɪmˈpruːvmənt]	*n.* 改进，进步；改进措施；改进处 搭 improvement in 在…有改进/好转 例 His oral English is well, but there's still room for some *improvement*. 他的英语口语不错，但是还有提升的空间。
impulse [ˈɪmpʌls]	*n.* 冲动，突如其来的念头；刺激，驱使；脉冲 记 词根记忆：im(使…) + puls(推) + e → 冲动 搭 on (the) impulse (of...) 凭(…的)冲动；impulse buying 即兴购买 例 Mary bought the dress on *impulse*. 玛丽一时冲动买了这件衣服。 同 desire(*n.* 愿望，欲望)；urge(*n.* 强烈的欲望，迫切的要求)
in accordance with*	按照，依据 例 The rights of children are protected *in accordance with* the law. 儿童的权利依法受到保护。
in addition*	另外；加之 例 *In addition*, this drug may cause problems with vision and hair loss. 此外，这种药可能会导致视力问题和脱发。

□ imprecise □ impress □ impression □ impressive □ improve □ improvement
□ impulse □ in accordance with □ in addition

in addition to*	除…之外 例 *In addition to* its rings, Uranus has 15 satellites. 除了有自己的光环外，天王星还有 15 颗卫星。
in comparison with	与…比较起来 例 Fewer women apply for senior positions *in comparison with* men. 申请高级职位的女性数量比男性少。
in favour of	赞同，支持 例 It is unrealistic to expect people to give up private cars *in favour of* mass transit. 期望人们放弃私家车而选择公共交通工具是不现实的。
in vain*	徒然，无效 例 All our work was *in vain*. 我们的工作全都白干了。
inactive [ɪnˈæktɪv]	*a.* 不活动的；懒散的 例 The volcano has been *inactive* for 50 years. 这座火山已经有 50 年没有喷发了。
inadequate* [ɪnˈædɪkwət]	*a.* 不充分的；不适当的 记 联想记忆：in(不) + adequate(适当的，足够的) → 不充分的；不适当的 搭 inadequate supplies 供应短缺 例 Mary rejected the $3 million compensation as totally *inadequate*. 玛丽拒绝了 300 万美元的赔偿金，她认为那是完全不够的。 派 inadequacy(*n.* 不充分，不足；不胜任)
inalienable [ɪnˈeɪliənəbl]	*a.* 不可剥夺的，不可分割的 记 词根记忆：in(不) + ali(其他的) + en + able(能…的) → 不能让与他人的 → 不可剥夺的，不可分割的 例 From my point of view, childbirth is the *inalienable* right of female employees who work in private companies. 在我看来，生孩子是在私企工作的女性员工不可剥夺的权利。
inaugurate [ɪˈnɔːgjəreɪt]	*vt.* 开始，开创；为…举行就职典礼；为…举行开幕式；为…举行落成仪式 记 词根记忆：in(进入) + augur(占卜，预测) + ate → 进入预测好的未来 → 开始，开创 例 The officials said more subway lines would be *inaugurated* in Beijing to facilitate the public in the recent two years. 政府官员称，在未来两年中，北京将建成更多地铁线路以方便大众出行。 派 inauguration(*n.* 就职，就职典礼)；inaugural(*a.* 就职的；开幕的) 同 commence(*v.* 开始)；initiate(*vt.* 开始，发起)
inborn [ˌɪnˈbɔːn]	*a.* 天生的，先天的，天赋的 记 联想记忆：in + born(出生) → 天生的，先天的，天赋的 例 Many sociologists claim good living habits are not *inborn* but can be learned by hard-working. 许多社会学家声称，好的生活习惯不是天生的，而是可以通过努力习得的。

24

□ in addition to □ in comparison with □ in favour of □ in vain □ inactive □ inadequate
□ inalienable □ inaugurate □ inborn

incapacitate* [ˌɪnkəˈpæsɪteɪt]	*vt.* 使无能力；使伤残；使不适合；使无资格 记 词根记忆：in(无) + capac(=cap 握住) + it + ate(使…) → 使无力握住 → 使无能力；使伤残 例 The figures show that about a quarter of a million people are *incapacitated* with back pain every day. 数据显示，每天约有 25 万人因背痛而无法正常生活。
incendiary* [ɪnˈsendiəri]	*a.* 放火的，能引起燃烧的；煽动性的 记 词根记忆：in + cend(=cand 发白光) + iary → 发出白光的 → 能引起燃烧的；煽动性的 搭 an incendiary bomb 燃烧弹 例 In the early nineteenth century the British began to experiment with *incendiary* barrage rockets. 19 世纪初，英国就开始试验燃烧式扫射火箭。

Few things are impossible in themselves; and it is often for want of will, rather than of means, that man fails to succeed.

事情很少有根本做不成的；其所以做不成，与其说是条件不够，不如说是由于决心不够。

——法国作家 罗切福考尔德(La Rochefoucauld, French writer)

Word List 25

音频

词根、词缀预习表

cent	唱歌	incentive *n.* 激励	**ciner**	灰	incinerate *vt.* 焚化
clin	倾斜	inclination *n.* 倾向	**clud**	关闭	include *v.* 包括
corp	身体	incorporate *vt.* 吸收	**cred**	相信	incredible *a.* 不可信的
lev	轻	alleviate *vt.* 减轻	**cur**	跑	incur *vt.* 招致
gen	产生	indigenous *a.* 本土的	**dol**	悲痛	indolent *a.* 懒惰的

incentive
[ɪnˈsentɪv]

n. 刺激；激励

记 词根记忆：in(在里面) + cent(唱歌) + ive → 在里面唱歌 → 刺激

例 Hypotheses provide the initiative and *incentive* for the inquiry. 假设促使人们主动去调查。

同 motivation (*n.* 刺激，动机)；impetus (*n.* 推动，促进，刺激)

incident
[ˈɪnsɪdənt]

n. 发生的事；事件，事变

例 The most common type of road rage *incident* involves personal violence. 公路上因暴怒而发生的事故中，最常见的都与个人暴力有关。

incinerate
[ɪnˈsɪnəreɪt]

vt. 焚化，焚毁，把…烧成灰烬

记 词根记忆：in(进入) + ciner(灰) + ate(使…) → 使成灰 → 焚化，焚毁

例 Hundreds of residents in the village near the volcano were *incinerated* by the high temperatures generated by the eruption of magma. 火山附近村子里的数百名居民在岩浆喷发产生的高温中化为灰烬。

inclination
[ˌɪnklɪˈneɪʃn]

n. 爱好；趋势；倾斜

记 词根记忆：in(内向) + clin(倾斜) + ation → 倾斜

例 Developing photos require a darkroom and the time and *inclination* to handle the necessary chemicals. 冲洗照片需要一间暗室、一些时间并且愿意接触冲印过程中所必需的一些化学药剂。

include*
[ɪnˈkluːd]

v. 包括，包含；计入

记 词根记忆：in(进入) + clud(关闭) + e → 关进里面 → 包括，包含

搭 be included in 被包括在…

例 Sports administrators' duties *include* booking playing fields with local councils. 体育管理员的职责包括向地方委员会预订比赛场馆。

反 exclude(*v.* 把…排除在外)

□ incentive □ incident □ incinerate □ inclination □ include

inclusive*
[ɪnˈkluːsɪv]

a. 包括一切费用在内的；所有数目(或首尾日期)包括在内的；包容广阔的

记 词根记忆：in(进入) + clus(关闭) + ive(形容词后缀) → 关进里面 → 包括一切费用在内的；包容广阔的

搭 fully inclusive 完全包括在内的

例 The fully *inclusive* fee for the trip to the country will be higher in summer vacation. 暑假去那个国家旅行的全部费用会高一些。

派 inclusively(*ad.* 全部)

incoming*
[ˈɪnkʌmɪŋ]

a. 进来的 *n.* [*pl.*] 收入

例 Telephones in this hall can only be used to call out; they will not receive *incoming* calls. 大厅里的电话只能打出，而不能接听外面打进来的电话。

incompatible
[ˌɪnkəmˈpætəbl]

a. 不兼容的，不能和谐共存的，不协调的，合不来的

记 联想记忆：in(不) + compatible(兼容的，协调的) → 不兼容的，不协调的

例 Any new operating system that is *incompatible* with existing ones has little chance of being used. 任何与现有的操作系统不兼容的新操作系统都几乎得不到使用。

incongruity
[ˌɪnkɒŋˈgruːəti]

n. 不和谐，不相称；不协调或不一致的事物

记 联想记忆：in(不) + congruity(一致，和谐) → 不和谐，不相称

例 It was such a night that sorrow may come to laugh without causing any great sense of *incongruity*. 这个夜晚，哀愁毫不突兀地转变为狂喜。

incongruous
[ɪnˈkɒŋgruəs]

a. 不协调的，不一致的；不适宜的

例 As *incongruous* as it may sound, the little frog with big eyes has no lungs and gets all the oxygen it needs through its skin. 听起来可能不可思议的是，这种身材小巧、眼睛大大的青蛙居然没有肺，所需氧气均要靠皮肤来获得。

incorporate
[ɪnˈkɔːpəreɪt]

vt. 把…合并，纳入；包含，吸收

记 词根记忆：in(进入) + corp(身体) + orate → 进入身体成为一部分 → 把…合并

例 Cash dispensers in the future will *incorporate* face scanners. 未来的取款机将包含面部扫描仪。

派 comprehend(*v.* 包括，由…组成)；embody(*vt.* 包括，包含)

incredible
[ɪnˈkredəbl]

a. 不可信的；难以置信的

记 词根记忆：in(不) + cred(相信) + ible(能…的) → 不可信的

例 The facts have been distorted to an *incredible* degree. 事实已被歪曲到不可信的地步了。

inculcate
[ˈɪnkʌlkeɪt]

vt. 谆谆教诲，反复灌输

记 词根记忆：in(进入) + culc(踩踏) + ate → 为进入某人内心而踩踏 → 谆谆教诲，反复灌输

搭 inculcate sb. with a sense of responsibility 谆谆教导某人要有责任感

例 Chinese parents try to *inculcate* a sense of social responsibility in their children when they are still young. 中国的父母在孩子很小的时候就试图向他们灌输一种社会责任感。

□ inclusive □ incoming □ incompatible □ incongruity □ incongruous □ incorporate
□ incredible □ inculcate

incur* [ɪnˈkɜː(r)]

vt. 招致，遭受

记 词根记忆：in(进入) + cur(跑；发生) → 使发生 → 招致，遭受

搭 incur debt 负债；incur losses 遭受损失

例 Overdrafts usually *incur* charges, though some banks offer interest-free overdrafts to students. 尽管一些银行给学生们提供了免息透支的服务，但一般透支都是要付费的。

independence* [ˌɪndɪˈpendəns]

n. 独立，自主

记 联想记忆：in(不) + depend(依靠) + ence(名词后缀) → 不依靠别人 → 独立，自主

例 With the *independence* of much of Asia and Africa after 1945, it was assumed that economic progress would rapidly lead to the disappearance or assimilation of many small-scale societies. 1945年后，随着亚洲和非洲很多国家的独立，人们推断经济进步将会很快导致小型社会的消失或者被同化。

independent* [ˌɪndɪˈpendənt]

a. 独立的，自主的，不受约束的 *n.* 中立派，无党派议员

搭 be independent of 独立于，不受约束

例 Mary was an *independent*-minded student. 玛丽是个有独立见解的学生。

派 independently(*ad.* 独立地)

indicate* [ˈɪndɪkeɪt]

v. 标示，表示，表明；象征；暗示，示意

记 词根记忆：in + dic(说) + ate → 说出 → 表示，表明

例 Evidence gathered in recent years *indicates* that the region has supported a series of indigenous cultures for eleven thousand years. 近年来收集到的证据表明，这一地区有过持续一万一千多年的土著文明。

派 indicator(*n.* 指示器；指示信号)

indication [ˌɪndɪˈkeɪʃn]

n. 指示，象征

例 Their failure to act is the *indication* of their lack of interest. 他们不行动表示他们没兴趣。

indifferent* [ɪnˈdɪfrənt]

a. 冷漠的，不关心的

搭 be indifferent to 对…漠不关心

例 Tina seems to be totally *indifferent* to the exam result of the higher language course. 蒂娜似乎对高级语言课程的考试结果毫不关心。

indigenous [ɪnˈdɪdʒənəs]

a. 土产的，本地的，本土的

记 词根记忆：indi(内部) + gen(产生) + ous → 内部产生的 → 本地的

搭 the indigenous language 本土语言

例 The emu is *indigenous* to Australia. 鸸鹋是澳大利亚土生土长的鸟类。

25

□ incur □ independence □ independent □ indicate □ indication □ indifferent
□ indigenous

indispensable [ˌɪndɪˈspensəbl]

a. 必不可少的，必需的

记 联想记忆：in(不) + dispensable(可有可无的) → 不是可有可无的 → 必不可少的，必需的

例 A good reference book is *indispensable* for learning a classwork. 一本好的参考书对于学习一门功课是必需的。

同 essential(*a.* 非常重要的，必要的)；vital(*a.* 极其重要的，必不可少的)；requisite〔*a.* (成功所)必要的〕

individual [ˌɪndɪˈvɪdʒuəl]

a. 个别的，单独的；独特的 *n.* 个人，个体

记 联想记忆：in + divid(e)(分割) + ual → 分割开的 → 个别的，单独的

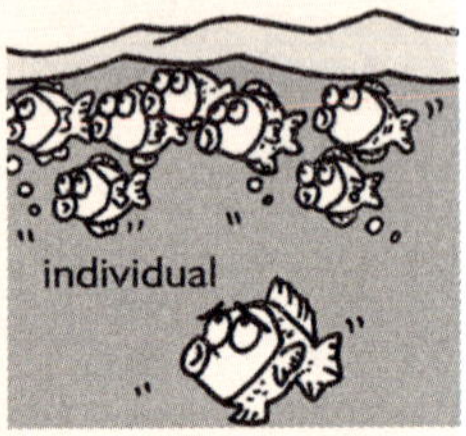

搭 individual effort 个人的努力；individual interest 个人利益

例 The food is served in *individual* portions. 食物是按一人一份供给的。

派 individually(*ad.* 各自地；独特地)；individualistic(*a.* 个人主义的)

indolent [ˈɪndələnt]

a. 懒惰的，倦怠的；不活跃的，无行动的

记 词根记忆：in(不) + dol(悲痛) + ent → 连悲痛也感受不到的 → 懒惰的，倦怠的

例 As a rule, superior living conditions encourage children in rich family to lead an *indolent* life. 通常，优越的生活条件促使富家子弟过着懒散的生活。

induce* [ɪnˈdjuːs]

vt. 引诱，劝使；引起，导致；感应

记 词根记忆：in(内) + duc(拉) + e → 向内拉 → 引诱；引起

搭 induce sb. to do sth. 引诱某人做某事；a drug-induced coma 药物引起的昏迷

例 Nothing would *induce* me to change my idea. 任何事都不能使我改变主意。

派 inducement(*n.* 引诱；劝诱)；inducible(*a.* 可诱导的，可诱发的)

induction* [ɪnˈdʌkʃn]

n. 就职；归纳；感应

记 联想记忆：induct(就任；归纳；感应) + ion → 就职；归纳；感应

例 This mathematician got the result by means of *induction*. 这位数学家通过归纳得出了结果。

inductive* [ɪnˈdʌktɪv]

a. 诱导的，归纳的

搭 inductive reasoning 归纳推理

例 The myth of scientific method is that it is *inductive*. 科学方法的神秘就在于它的归纳性。

inductive reasoning

归纳；推理

例 Michael Cole and his colleagues demonstrated that adult performance on *inductive reasoning* tasks depends on features of the apparatus and procedure. 迈克尔·科尔和他的同事们证明，成人在归纳推理任务上的表现取决于器官和程序的特征。

□ indispensable □ individual □ indolent □ induce □ induction □ inductive
□ inductive reasoning

indulge [ɪnˈdʌldʒ]	*v.* 沉溺于，纵情于；满足(欲望、兴趣等)；放纵，听任 记 词根记忆：in + dulg(屈服，让步) + e → 屈服于欲望 → 满足(欲望等)；放纵 例 Overseas visitors like to come to New Albion to ***indulge*** in one of Astoria's more famous agricultural products—wine. 外国游客喜欢到新英格兰尽情品尝这里的美酒，这是阿斯托里亚较出名的农产品之一。 同 gratify(*vt.* 使满意，纵容)；satisfy(*v.* 满足，(使)满意)；spoil(*v.* 宠坏，溺爱)；pamper(*vt.* 纵容，娇惯)
industrialise* [ɪnˈdʌstriəlaɪz]	*v.* (使)工业化 例 The projects are part of a larger plan to ***industrialise*** northeastern Iceland. 这些项目只是冰岛东北部工业化更大计划中的一部分。 派 industrialisation(*n.* 工业化，产业化)
industrious [ɪnˈdʌstriəs]	*a.* 勤奋的，勤勉的，勤劳的 例 Li Ming used to be such an ***industrious*** student that he usually got the first grade. 李明过去学习非常勤奋，总是排名年级第一。
inescapable [ˌɪnɪˈskeɪpəbl]	*a.* 不可逃避的；难免的 例 The role of governments in environmental management is difficult but ***inescapable***. 政府在环境管理方面担负的任务很艰巨，但这是它们无法推卸的。
inevitable [ɪnˈevɪtəbl]	*a.* 不可避免的，必然(发生)的 记 联想记忆：in(不) + evitable(可避免的) → 不可避免的 例 A further escalation of the economic crisis now seems ***inevitable***. 如今，经济危机的进一步扩大化在所难免。 派 inevitably(*ad.* 不可避免地，必然地)
infection [ɪnˈfekʃn]	*n.* 传染，感染，侵染，传播；传染病 搭 a severe infection 严重的传染病；respiratory infection 呼吸道感染 例 Are you taking oral medicines for fungal ***infections***? 你在吃口服药预防真菌感染吗?
infer [ɪnˈfɜː(r)]	*v.* 推断，猜想 记 词根记忆：in(进入) + fer(带来) → 带进(意义) → 推断，猜想 例 I ***infer*** from your letter that you have not made up your mind yet. 我从你的信中推断出你还没下定决心。
inference [ˈɪnfərəns]	*n.* 推论；推断 记 联想记忆：从这些参考书(reference)里，你能推断(inference)出什么? 例 If the evidence is true then by ***inference*** he is guilty. 如果证据确凿，就可以推断出他有罪。
inferential* [ˌɪnfəˈrenʃl]	*a.* 可推断的，推理的 记 联想记忆：infer(推断) + enti + al → 可推断的 例 For young children, the difficulty lies not in the ***inferential*** processes which the task demands, but in certain perplexing features of the apparatus and the procedure. 对于小孩子们来说，难点不在于任务所需的可推断的方法，而在于某些设备和过程的复杂性。

25

□ indulge □ industrialise □ industrious □ inescapable □ inevitable □ infection
□ infer □ inference □ inferential

inferior
[ɪnˈfɪəriə(r)]

a. 较差的，次的，低劣的；级别低的，较低的

n. 下级；下属，晚辈

搭 inferior goods 劣质商品；an inferior officer 下级军官

例 In general, schooling in suburbs is *inferior* to that in downtown, interior regions to coastal ones, developing countries to developed ones. 一般而言，城郊的学校教育不如市中心的，内陆的不如沿海的，发展中国家的不如发达国家的。

派 inferiority(*n.* 低等，劣等)

infiltrate
[ˈɪnfɪltreɪt]

v. (使)悄悄进入，潜入；渗入，渗透

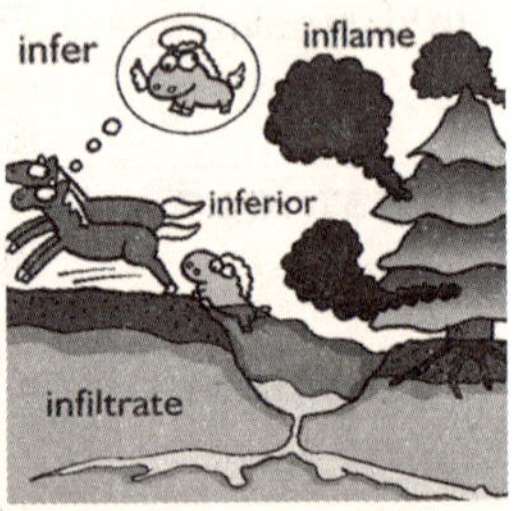

记 联想记忆：in(进入) + filtrate(滤液) → 使进入滤液 → (使)悄悄进入，潜入；渗透

例 Many companies want their new employees to quickly adapt themselves to working environment and *infiltrate* corporate culture. 许多公司希望新员工很快适应工作环境并融入企业文化。

派 infiltration(*n.* 潜入；渗透)；infiltrator(*n.* 潜入者；渗入者)

infirmity
[ɪnˈfɜːməti]

n. 虚弱，衰弱

记 联想记忆：in(不) + firm(坚定) + ity → 不坚强 → 虚弱，衰弱

例 Pathogen infections are among the leading causes of *infirmity* and mortality among humans and animals in the world. 病原体感染是世界上导致人和动物衰弱和死亡的主要原因之一。

inflammable*
[ɪnˈflæməbl]

a. 易燃的；易怒的

记 词根记忆：in + flamm(燃烧) + able(能…的) → 容易着火的 → 易燃的

搭 an inflammable temper 易怒的脾气

例 Impressed by the element's combustibility, several 17th century chemists used it to manufacture fire-lighting devices, but the results were dangerously *inflammable*. 受这种元素可燃性的启发，17 世纪的一些化学家用它来制造点火装置，但这些装置却容易发生危险性的燃烧。

inflate*
[ɪnˈfleɪt]

v. 使充气，使膨胀；使得意，使骄傲；抬高(物价)，使(通货)膨胀

记 词根记忆：in(进入) + flat(吹) + e → 往里面吹气 → 使充气

例 This kind of fish *inflates* itself to twice its size when being attacked. 这种鱼在受到袭击时会膨胀到原来的两倍。

inflation
[ɪnˈfleɪʃn]

n. 通货膨胀

记 词根记忆：in(进入) + flat(吹) + ion(名词后缀) → 往里面吹 → 通货膨胀

例 *Inflation* reduced the purchasing power of the families. 通货膨胀降低了家庭的购买力。

inflict [ɪn'flɪkt]	*vt.* 把…强加给，使遭受，使承受 记 词根记忆：in(对着) + flict(打) → 对着…打 → 把…强加给，使遭受，使承受 搭 inflict oneself on sb. 打搅，搅扰 例 Doctors warned parents that children aged two or three years could *inflict* various injuries in daily life. 医生警告父母：两三岁的儿童在日常生活中可能遭受各种伤害。 派 infliction [*n.*(强加于人身的)痛苦，刑罚] 同 impose(*v.* 把…强加于)
influence* ['ɪnfluəns]	*vt.* 影响 *n.* 影响力；产生影响力的人 例 What factors do you think *influence* these decisions? 你认为影响这些决定的因素有哪些？
influential* [ˌɪnflu'enʃl]	*a.* 有影响力的；有权势的 记 来自 influence(*n./vt.* 影响) 例 The female President is one of the most *influential* figures in local politics. 这位女总统是当地政坛上最有影响力的人物之一。
influenza* [ˌɪnflu'enzə]	*n.* 流行性感冒 记 联想记忆：流行性感冒(influenza)会影响(influence)很多人 例 In 1990, smoking caused more than 84,000 deaths, mainly resulting from such problems as pneumonia, bronchitis and *influenza*. 在 1990 年，吸烟导致了 84000 多人死亡，其中主要是由肺炎、支气管炎及流行性感冒等疾病引发。
inform* [ɪn'fɔːm]	*v.* 通知；向…报告 记 联想记忆：in(进入) + form(形式) → 进入形式，公告于众 → 通知 例 Fancy Foods wishes to *inform* the public that pieces of metal have been found in some jars of Fancy Foods Chicken Curry (Spicy). 美食公司希望告知大众，在他们生产的一些咖喱(辣)鸡块罐头中发现有金属碎片。
informant [ɪn'fɔːmənt]	*n.* 提供消息或情报的人，线人；提供资料的人 例 The journalist refused to reveal the identity of his *informant*. 记者拒绝披露消息提供者的身份。
infrastructure* ['ɪnfrəstrʌktʃə(r)]	*n.* 基础结构，基础设施 记 词根记忆：infra (在…下面) + struct (结构，建造) + ure → 下面的结构 → 基础结构 例 How does the port change a city's *infrastructure*? 港口如何改变一个城市的基础结构？
infringe [ɪn'frɪndʒ]	*v.* 侵犯，侵害；违背，触犯(法规)；干涉，干扰 搭 infringe a rule 违反规章；infringe a law 违法 例 Some students argued that the new school rule would *infringe* on their right to read in the morning. 一些学生争论说，这条新校规将侵犯他们晨读的权利。

□ inflict □ influence □ influential □ influenza □ inform □ informant
□ infrastructure □ infringe

ingenuity
[ˌɪndʒəˈnjuːəti]

n. 心灵手巧，足智多谋；巧妙，精巧

记 词根记忆：in + gen(产生) + uity → 能产生很多点子 → 足智多谋

例 The little girl showed her *ingenuity* in making handicrafts out of scraps of paper. 小女孩将纸片做成工艺品，展示出她的心灵手巧。

ingredient
[ɪnˈɡriːdiənt]

n. (混合物的)组成部分，成分；(烹调的)原料；(构成)要素，因素

记 词根记忆：in(内部) + gred(=grad 进入) + ient → 放入内部的东西 → 组成部分，成分；原料

例 Some time in tenth century, black powder was first compounded from its basic *ingredients* of saltpeter, charcoal and sulphur. 10 世纪的某个时候，黑火药第一次由硝石、木炭和硫磺这些基本成分混制而成。

inhabitant
[ɪnˈhæbɪtənt]

n. 居民，住户，居住者；栖息的动物

记 词根记忆：in(在里面) + hab(居住) + it + ant → 住在里面的人 → 居民，居住者

例 The natural history of the Amazon is to a surprising extent tied to the activities of its prehistoric *inhabitants*. 亚马孙河的自然历史与其史前居民的活动有着极为密切的关系。

inhale*
[ɪnˈheɪl]

v. 吸(烟)，吸气

记 词根记忆：in(进) + hale(气) → 吸气

搭 inhale the cigarette 吸烟

例 Sometimes people have to *inhale* secondhand smoke. 有时候，人们不得不吸入二手烟。

派 inhalation(*n.* 吸入；吸入物)

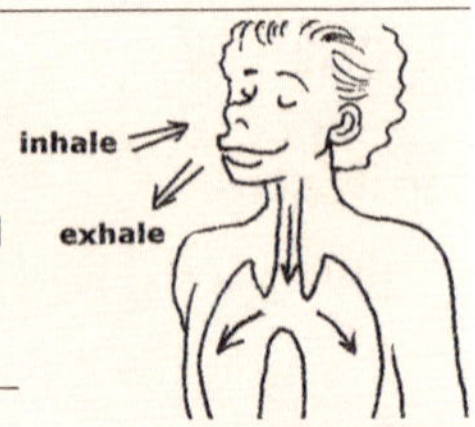

inherent
[ɪnˈhɪərənt]

a. 内在的；生来就有的

记 词根记忆：in(向内) + her(黏附) + ent(形容词后缀) → 黏附在内的 → 内在的；生来就有的

例 Women have an *inherent* love of beauty. 女人天生爱美。

同 natural(*a.* 出于本性的，天赋的)；inborn(*a.* 天生的，天赋的)；innate(*a.* 天生的，天赋的)

inheritance
[ɪnˈherɪtəns]

n. 遗传；继承，继承物；遗产，遗赠

搭 historic inheritance 历史遗产

例 To get rid of being called “NEET Group”, he is too stubborn to accept the *inheritance* from his father. 为了摆脱“啃老族”的称号，他固执地拒绝接受父亲的遗产。

inhibit
[ɪnˈhɪbɪt]

v. 抑制，约束；起抑制作用

记 词根记忆：in(不) + hib(拥有) + it → 使不能拥有 → 抑制，约束

例 Studies show that intake of carbon monoxide *inhibits* the flow of oxygen to the heart. 研究显示，吸入一氧化碳会抑制氧气对心脏的供给。

同 hinder(*v.* 阻碍，妨碍)；obstruct(*vt.* 妨碍，阻止)；impede(*vt.* 阻碍，妨碍，阻止)

反 encourage(*vt.* 激励，促进)

inhumane
[ˌɪnhjuːˈmeɪn]

a. 不近人情的，残忍的，不人道的

例 In sweatshops, skinny men, starved women and small minors are in the same *inhumane* conditions. 血汗工厂里，骨瘦如柴的男人、食不果腹的女人和瘦小的孩子都在同样的惨无人道的环境中工作。

派 inhumanity(*n.* 残酷的行为，无人性，不人道)

---

initial
[ɪˈnɪʃl]

a. 最初的，开始的；词首的 *n.* 词首大写字母

记 词根记忆：in(向里) + it(走) + ial → 开始的

搭 the initial stage 初级阶段；initial offerings 原始股；initial payment 首付

例 Interest will be charged after the *initial* 60-day interest-free period. 过了最初 60 天的免息期后，就要开始收取利息了。

派 initially(*ad.* 最初，开始)

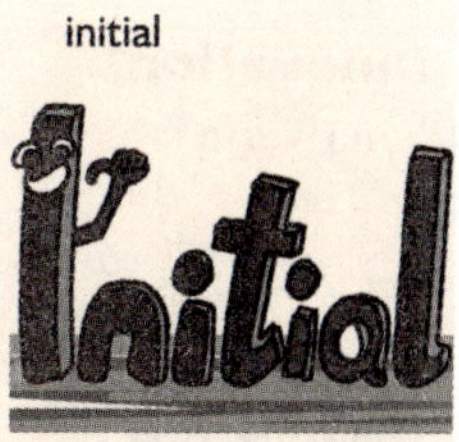

---

initiate

[ɪˈnɪʃieɪt] *vt.* 开始，创造，发起；接纳(新成员)，让…加入

[ɪˈnɪʃiət] *n.* (新)加入组织者

记 词根记忆：in(向内) + it(走) + iate → 向里走 → 开始；让…加入

例 The government has *initiated* a programme of social welfare policy. 政府已经在社会福利政策上发起一项新的计划。

---

initiative
[ɪˈnɪʃətɪv]

n. 倡议，新方案；主动性，积极性；主动权

搭 take the initiative 带头，倡导，发起；seize the initiative 掌握先机；lose the initiative 丧失先机

例 The major *initiative* by this car-manufacturing company was to adopt a totally multi-skilled workforce. 这家汽车制造厂采取的主要措施是雇用掌握多种技能的工人。

25

---

inject
[ɪnˈdʒekt]

vt. 注射；注入，灌输

记 词根记忆：in(进入) + ject(投，掷) → 投进去 → 注入，灌输

例 By *injecting* lime into the land around the water and neutralizing the effects of acid, scientists have created conditions in which fish can survive. 通过对水域周围的土地注入石灰，中和当地的酸性效应，科学家已经创造出能让鱼存活的环境。

派 injection(*n.* 注射)

同 implant(*vt.* 注入，灌输)；infuse(*vt.* 注入，灌输)

---

inland

[ˈɪnlænd] *a.* 内陆的 [ˌɪnˈlænd] *ad.* 向内地(或内陆)

例 Today about 90 per cent of *inland* freight in the United Kingdom is carried by road. 现在，公路承担了英国约 90%的内陆运输。

---

inlet
[ˈɪnlet]

n. 入口；进(水)口，水湾

记 联想记忆：in(进入) + let(让) → 让…进入的地方 → 入口

例 There are a thousand little *inlets* and backwaters all through here. 这里共有上千个小水湾和死水潭。

□ inhumane □ initial □ initiate □ initiative □ inject □ inland
□ inlet

innocent [ˈɪnəsnt]

a. 清白的；无害的；天真的

记 词根记忆：in(不) + noc(伤害) + ent(形容词后缀) → 没受过伤害的 → 天真的

搭 an innocent child 天真无邪的孩子

例 Seeing these *innocent* children, I can't help recalling my own childhood. 看到这些天真无邪的孩子，我不禁想起了自己的童年。

innovation [ˌɪnəˈveɪʃn]

n. 革新，创新

记 词根记忆：in(进入) + nov(新的) + ation → 革新，创新

搭 technological innovation 技术革新

例 The *innovation* of match-making technology made the waterproof possible. 火柴制造技术的革新使人们生产出防水火柴。

同 novelty(*n.* 新奇，新奇的事物)；reformation(*n.* 改革，革新)

innovative [ˈɪnəveɪtɪv]

a. 革新的，创新的，新颖的；富有革新精神的

记 来自 innovation(*n.* 改革，创新)

搭 innovative spirit 创新精神

例 Target pricing is an *innovative* approach used in the initial stages of the new-product development cycle to establish a contract price between a buyer and a seller. 目标定价法是在新产品开发环节的最初阶段，用来在买家和卖家之间建立合同价格的新方法。

input* [ˈɪnpʊt]

n. 投入，输入；输入的数据 *vt.* 把…输入计算机

记 来自词组 put in(投入；输入)

例 The intensity of farming in the rich world should decline, and the use of chemical *inputs* will diminish. 富裕国家应该降低农业生产的密度，这样化学药品的使用将会减少。

insane* [ɪnˈseɪn]

a. 蠢极的，荒唐的；(患)精神病的，精神失常的，疯狂的

记 词根记忆：in(不) + san(健全的) + e → 精神不健全的 → 精神病的

例 The prisoner has been slowly going *insane* and he can not recognize his parents now. 这名犯人在监狱里慢慢变得有些精神失常了，现在已经无法认出自己的父母。

inscribe* [ɪnˈskraɪb]

v. (在某物上)写、题、铭刻；牢记，铭记

记 词根记忆：in(进入) + scrib(写) + e → 刻写进去 → (在某物上)写、题、铭刻

例 Each of the prize winners will receive a golden medal with their names *inscribed* on it. 这个奖项的得主每人将获得一枚金牌，上面刻着他们各自的名字。

insecure* [ˌɪnsɪˈkjʊə(r)]

a. 不安全的，不可靠的

记 联想记忆：in(不) + secure(安全的) → 不安全的

搭 an insecure investment 一笔不可靠的投资

例 The trend towards blurring these roles in dress is probably democratic, but it also makes some people very *insecure*. 淡化服饰角色的趋势或许比较民主，但同时也让一些人觉得很不安全。

派 insecurity(*n.* 不安全，不安全感)

□ innocent □ innovation □ innovative □ input □ insane □ inscribe □ insecure

insert [in'sɜːt]	*v.* 插入，嵌入 记 词根记忆：in(进入) + sert(放置) → 放进去 → 插入，嵌入  例 To prevent the queen from crawling up to the top and laying eggs, a screen can be *inserted* between the brood chamber and the supers. 为了防止蜂王爬到蜂房顶端产卵，可以在育卵室和蜂房上层活动架中间插入一块隔板。
insidious [ɪn'sɪdiəs]	*a.* 潜伏的，隐伏的 记 词根记忆：in(进入) + sid(坐) + ious → 坐在里面的 → 潜伏的 例 Hypertension is usually an *insidious* disease which has few symptoms in the early stage. 高血压通常是一种潜伏性疾病，早期几乎没有症状。
insight ['ɪnsaɪt]	*n.* 洞察力，深刻的了解；顿悟 记 联想记忆：in(内) + sight(眼光) → 眼光深入 → 洞察力 例 The application of our new *insights* into the Amazonian past would change present policies on development in the region. 我们对亚马孙地区的过去有了新的了解，这会改变目前我们针对这一地区的开发政策。 派 insightful(*a.* 富有洞察力的)
insignificant* [ˌɪnsɪg'nɪfɪkənt]	*a.* 无关紧要的，无意义的 记 联想记忆：in(不) + significant(有意义的，重要的) → 无关紧要的，无意义的 例 The consequences are *insignificant* compared to this great idea. 同这种伟大的思想相比，结果并不重要。

My fellow Americans, ask not what your country can do for you, ask what you can do for your country. My fellow citizens of the world: ask not what American will do for you, but what together we can do for the freedom of man.

美国同胞们，不要问国家能为你们做些什么，而要问你们能为国家做些什么。全世界的公民们，不要问美国将为你们做些什么，而要问我们共同能为人类的自由做些什么。

——美国总统 肯尼迪(John Kennedy, American President)

Word List 26

音 频

词根、词缀预习表

sist	站	insist *v.* 坚持	**spect**	看	inspect *vt.* 检查
spir	呼吸	inspiration *n.* 启示	**stil**	掉	instil *vt.* 灌输
stinct	刺激	instinct *n.* 本能	**stit**	站立	institute *vt.* 建立
struct	建筑	instruct *vt.* 教导	**tact**	接触	intact *a.* 完整无缺的
tegr	触摸	integral *a.* 完整的	**lig**	选择	intelligent *a.* 聪明的

insist* [ɪnˈsɪst]

v. 坚持，坚决认为；一定要

记 词根记忆：in(里面) + sist(站) → 一直站在里面 → 坚持

搭 insist on 坚持要求，坚决主张

例 We do not *insist* on any prerequisites for this course. 对于这一课程，我们不一定需要什么先决条件。

inspect [ɪnˈspekt]

vt. 检查，检阅

记 词根记忆：in(向内) + spect(看) → 向内看 → 检查，检阅

例 The general *inspected* the troops. 将军检阅了军队。

派 inspector(*n.* 检查员)；inspection(*n.* 检查，视察)

inspiration [ˌɪnspəˈreɪʃn]

n. 启示，灵感；鼓舞人心的人(或事)，激励

记 词根记忆：in(进入) + spir(呼吸) + ation → 吸入灵气 → 灵感

例 Hypotheses arise from guesswork, or from *inspiration*. 假说由人们的猜测或灵感引起。

派 inspirational(*a.* 鼓舞人心的；启发灵感的)

inspire* [ɪnˈspaɪə(r)]

vt. 鼓舞，激起；给…以灵感

记 词根记忆：in (向内) + spir (呼吸) + e → 吸气 → 鼓气 → 鼓舞

例 Leader in a group is very important and his confident attitude will *inspire* his followers greatly. 一个团队里的领导者是非常重要的，他自信的态度会极大地鼓舞团队成员。

inspiring* [ɪnˈspaɪərɪŋ]

a. 鼓舞(或激励)人心的；启发灵感的

记 词根记忆：in(使…) + spir(呼吸) + ing → 使呼吸的 → 鼓舞人心的

搭 an inspiring successful story 激励人心的成功故事

例 King was an *inspiring* tutor. 金是一位激励人心的老师。

install*
[ɪnˈstɔːl]

vt. 安顿，安置；安装，设置；正式任命，使正式就职

记 词根记忆：in（进入）+ stall（放）→ 放进 → 安置；安装

搭 install drinking machine 安装饮水机；install wood strip flooring 安装木地板条

例 In the noisiest areas, mechanical ventilation will have to be *installed* in the exterior walls. 在最喧闹的地区，其外墙上必须安装机械通风装置。

installment
[ɪnˈstɔːlmənt]

n. 分期付款；（连载或连播的）一集

搭 in installment 以分期付款的形式；monthly installments 按月还款

例 Each *installment* costs $1, and site visitors are given three options. 每一集需付费一美元，网上游览者可以通过三种方式支付。

instil
[ɪnˈstɪl]

vt. 滴注；逐渐灌输；逐步培养（感受、思想等）

记 词根记忆：in（进入）+ stil（掉）→ 掉到里面 → 滴注；逐渐灌输

例 Trust and encouragement can *instil* confidence into a person, which can serve him or her well for life. 信任和鼓励能使人逐步树立起信心，让他们终生受益。

instinct
[ˈɪnstɪŋkt]

n. 本能，直觉；天性

记 词根记忆：in（在…之内）+ stinct（刺激）→ 内在的刺激 → 本能，直觉

例 It is *instinct* that makes salmon swim upstream to lay eggs. 大马哈鱼洄游产卵是出于本能。

instinctual
[ɪnˈstɪŋktʃuəl]

a. 本能的

例 No one will deny that wink is an *instinctual* reaction when something appears before your eyes suddenly. 没人会否认，当有东西突然出现在眼前时，眨眼是一种本能的反应。

institute
[ˈɪnstɪtjuːt]

n. 研究所，学院 *vt.* 建立，设立

记 词根记忆：in + stit（站立）+ ute → 建立，设立

搭 financial institute 金融研究所

例 The language *Institute* provides student support, welfare and activities services. 语言学院为学生提供资助、福利和活动服务。

institution
[ˌɪnstɪˈtjuːʃn]

n. （行业）协会；机构；制度；习俗；团体；设立，制定

搭 institution of higher learning 高等院校；an educational institution 教育机构；a supervisory institution 监督机构

例 Such a record will allow you to present your linguistic credentials to academic *institutions*. 这份记录将允许你将自己的语言证书呈递给学术机构。

instruct
[ɪnˈstrʌkt]

vt. 教导；指示，命令

记 词根记忆：in + struct（建筑）→ 教人如何建筑 → 教导；指示

例 PE teachers *instruct* students how to exercise, play sports, and do other recreational activities correctly and safely. 体育老师指导学生们如何安全正确地锻炼、做运动以及进行其他娱乐活动。

instrument
[ˈɪnstrəmənt]

n. 仪器；手段；工具；乐器

搭 strategic instruments 战略工具；measuring instruments 测量工具；musical instruments 乐器

例 We use questionnaires as our main research *instrument*. 我们将问卷调查作为主要的研究手段。

□ install □ installment □ instil □ instinct □ instinctual □ institute
□ institution □ instruct □ instrument

instrumental [ˌɪnstrəˈmentl]

a. 有帮助的，起作用的；用乐器演奏的

记 来自 instrument(n. 手段；工具)

例 Doctors have been *instrumental* in improving living standards in Western society. 在西方社会，医生在提高人们生活质量方面一直发挥着重要作用。

insufficient* [ˌɪnsəˈfɪʃnt]

a. 不足的，不够的

记 联想记忆：in(不，没有) + sufficient(充分的) → 不足的，不够的

搭 insufficient for 不够做…；不能胜任…

例 The company's funds for research were *insufficient*. 那家公司没有足够的研究资金。

insularity [ˌɪnsjuˈlærəti]

n. 岛国(状态)；与外界隔绝的生活状况；(思想、观点等的)褊狭

例 Japan is an *insularity* and such geographical feature forms its distinctive natural landscape. 日本是一个岛国，这一地理特征形成了它独特的自然景观。

insulate [ˈɪnsjuleɪt]

vt. 使绝缘，使隔热，使隔音；隔离；使隔绝(以免受到影响)

记 词根记忆：insul(岛) + ate(使…) → 使成为孤岛 → 隔离；使隔绝

搭 insulate sb. from/against sth. 使某人与(不良影响)隔绝；insulating tape 绝缘胶带；insulated cable 绝缘电线

例 The familiar native-style hotels could *insulate* the tourist from the strangeness of the host environment. 这种似曾相识的本土风格的旅馆能够避免让游客在异乡产生陌生感。

同 isolate(vt. 使孤立，使隔离)

insulation* [ˌɪnsjuˈleɪʃn]

n. 隔绝，隔绝状态；绝缘(材料)，隔热，隔音

搭 insulation layer 绝缘层；acoustic insulation 隔音；thermal insulation 隔热

例 The good *insulation* will reduce heating loss. 良好的隔热会减少热损失。

insurance [ɪnˈʃʊərəns]

n. 保险；保险费；保险业

记 联想记忆：insur(e)(给…保险) + ance → 保险；保险费；保险业

搭 unemployment insurance 失业保险；accident insurance 意外险；life insurance 人寿险

例 I'd like to get *insurance* for the contents of my home. 我想给我家的财物上保险。

intact [ɪnˈtækt]

a. 完整无缺的；完好无损的

记 词根记忆：in(不) + tact(接触) → 未经触动的 → 完整无缺的

例 She hopes that her honor could remain *intact*. 她希望自己的名誉依旧能完好无损。

同 undamaged(a. 未损坏的，未毁坏的)；sound(a. 健全的，完好的)

反 broken(a. 破碎的)；shattered(a. 粉碎的，破坏的)

intake [ˈɪnteɪk]

n. 吸入，纳入；进气口，入口

记 联想记忆：in(进入) + take(带来) → 被带入里面 → 吸入，纳入

搭 intake of …的摄入

例 It is important not to decrease salt *intake* too much, as sodium is an essential mineral for the body to function. 钠是维持机体运转的重要矿物元素，因此避免过度减少食盐的摄取量非常重要。

□ instrumental □ insufficient □ insularity □ insulate □ insulation □ insurance □ intact □ intake

integral
[ˈɪntɪɡrəl]

a. 不可或缺的，构成整体所必需的；完整的，完备的

记 词根记忆：in(不) + tegr(触摸) + al → 未被触摸的 → 完整的，完备的

搭 an integral number 整数

例 This kind of beetle has become an *integral* part of the successful management of dairy farms in Australia over the past few decades. 在过去的几十年里，这种甲虫已成为澳大利亚乳牛场成功管理所必不可少的一部分。

同 essential(*a.* 非常重要的)；basic(*a.* 基本的，根本的)；fundamental(*a.* 根本的，基础的)

integrate*
[ˈɪntɪɡreɪt]

v. (使)合并，(使)成为一体

记 词根记忆：in(不) + tegr(触摸，接触) + ate → 未被触摸 → (使)成为一体

搭 integrate theory with practice 使理论与实践相结合

例 The researchers don't know how to *integrate* the two actions. 研究者不知该如何将这两种行为融为一体。

派 integration(*n.* 结合，综合)；disintegrate(*vt.* 使分解，使碎裂)

intellectual
[ˌɪntəˈlektʃuəl]

n. 知识分子 *a.* 智力的；理智的

记 词根记忆：intel(在…之间) + lect(选择) + ual → 能从中选择的 → 有辨别力的 → 智力的

搭 intellectual tests 智力测试

例 The development of literacy has far-reaching effects on general *intellectual* development. 文化素质的提高对于人类整体智力的发展有着深远的影响。

intelligence*
[ɪnˈtelɪdʒəns]

n. 智力，理解力；情报

记 词根记忆：intel(在…之间) + lig(选择) + ence → 作出明智的选择 → 智力；理解力

搭 the US Central Intelligence Agency 美国中央情报局

例 The scientists are using genetics to improve the *intelligence* of mice. 科学家们正在利用基因技术提高老鼠的智力。

intelligent*
[ɪnˈtelɪdʒənt]

a. 聪明的，理智的

记 词根记忆：intel(在…之间) + lig(选择) + ent(形容词后缀) → 选择好坏，智愚区别 → 聪明的，理智的

搭 an intelligent reader 聪明的读者

例 The most *intelligent* students do additional reading to supplement the material in the textbook. 最聪明的学生通过课外阅读来补充课本的内容。

intelligible
[ɪnˈtelɪdʒəbl]

a. 可理解的，明白易懂的，清楚的

记 词根记忆：intel(在…之间) + lig(选择) + ible(能…的) → 能在众多选择中作出选择的 → 可理解的

搭 an intelligible speech 清楚的讲话

例 I have failed to make the sentence *intelligible*. 我没能把这个句子弄清楚。

同 clear(*a.* 清楚的，明白的)；distinct(*a.* 清楚的，明显的)

反 unintelligible(*a.* 难解的，无法了解的)；incomprehensible(*a.* 不能理解的，难于领悟的)

26

intend [ɪn'tend]

v. 想要，打算

记 词根记忆：in(向内)＋tend(伸展)→向内伸展→想要，打算

例 I *intend* to prove to you why those people were mistaken. 我要证明给你看为什么那些人错了。

intense [ɪn'tens]

a. 强烈的，剧烈的；紧张的；热情的，热切的

记 联想记忆：in(在…之中)＋tense(紧张)→处于紧张之中→紧张的

搭 intense heat 酷热

例 Large thunderclouds generate the *intense* electrical fields that cause lightning flashes. 巨大的雷雨云产生极强的电磁场，从而形成闪电。

intensify [ɪn'tensɪfaɪ]

vt. 使增强；使加剧

记 词根记忆：in(向内)＋tens(伸展)＋ify(使…)→使向内伸展→使增强

例 The strong wind seemed to *intensify* the cold. 狂风似乎使天气更加寒冷了。

intensity [ɪn'tensəti]

n. 强烈，剧烈；强度

例 The pulse laser is increasing its *intensity*. 脉冲激光的强度在不断增加。

intensive [ɪn'tensɪv]

a. 加强的；密集的

记 来自 intense(*a.* 强烈的)

搭 intensive training 强化训练；intensive readings 精读材料

例 *Intensive* English classes are taught in four-week blocks throughout the year. 强化英语班全年授课，四周为一期。

intent [ɪn'tent]

n. 意图，意向，目的 *a.* 专心的，专注的；急切的

记 词根记忆：in(向内)＋tent(伸展)→向内伸展→意图

例 He came with *intent* to defraud. 他怀着欺骗的意图而来。

intention [ɪn'tenʃn]

n. 意图，目的

记 词根记忆：in(向内)＋tent(伸展)＋ion→向内伸展→意图，目的

例 We all listened carefully as the director outlined his *intentions*. 我们都认真聆听了导演对他的意图的概述。

interact [ˌɪntər'ækt]

vi. 相互作用；相互影响

记 词根记忆：inter(在…之间)＋act(行动)→相互之间有行动→相互作用

搭 interact with 和…相互作用

例 Group work can give employees a chance to *interact* and to share ideas. 分组工作可以给员工一个相互协作和交流的机会。

派 interaction(*n.* 相互作用)

interdependent* [ˌɪntədɪ'pendənt]

a. 互相依赖的，互助的

记 联想记忆：inter(相互)＋dependent(依赖的)→互相依赖的

例 The society, economy and environment are interacting and *interdependent*. 社会、经济和环境相互作用，彼此依赖。

interest* ['ɪntrəst]

n. 兴趣；利息；利益 *vt.* 使感兴趣

例 Many young people are showing less *interest* in higher education. 很多年轻人对高等教育不太感兴趣。

□ intend □ intense □ intensify □ intensity □ intensive □ intent
□ intention □ interact □ interdependent □ interest

interface [ˈɪntəfeɪs]

n. 界面；接口；接合点

记 联想记忆：inter(相互) + face(面) → 界面

例 The new version of the program has a much better user *interface* than the original. 新版程序比旧版的用户界面要好得多。

interfere* [ˌɪntəˈfɪə(r)]

vi. 干涉，干扰，妨碍

记 词根记忆：inter(在…之间) + fer(搬运) + e → 在中间搬弄是非→ 干涉，干扰，妨碍

搭 interfere with 干涉…

例 Carbon monoxide may *interfere* with the blood's ability to deliver oxygen to the heart. 一氧化碳会妨碍血液向心脏供氧。

interior* [ɪnˈtɪəriə(r)]

a. 内部的，里面的 *n.* 内部；内地

搭 interior decoration 室内装潢；interior design 室内设计；interior structure attic 阁楼；in the interior of... 在…内部

例 The secret of the versatility of glass lies in its *interior* structure. 这种多功能玻璃的奥秘就在于它的内部结构。

intermediate* [ˌɪntəˈmiːdiət]

a. 中间的，中级的

记 词根记忆：inter(在…之间，相互) + medi(中间) + ate(形容词后缀) → 中间的

例 Students who have reached an *intermediate* level benefit from learning general English skills. 那些英语水平达到中级的学生从英语综合技能学习中受益匪浅。

intermix [ˌɪntəˈmɪks]

v. 混入，混杂

例 In an insignificant basis of reality, the imagination spins, weaving new patterns and *intermixing* with memories, experience, free fancies, incongruities and improvisations. 在微不足道的现实中，想象力织就着新的世界，混合着记忆、经历、自由幻想、怪异及随想。

intern*

[ɪnˈtɜːn] *vt.* 拘禁，软禁 [ˈɪntɜːn] *n.* 实习生

记 联想记忆：与 internal(*a.* 内部的)一起记

例 Helen worked as an *intern* in that hospital last year. 海伦去年在那家医院实习。

internal [ɪnˈtɜːnl]

a. 内部的；国内的

搭 internal organs 内脏；internal clock 生物钟；internal trade 国内贸易

例 The theory lacks *internal* consistency. 这种理论缺乏内在统一性。

internationalist* [ˌɪntəˈnæʃnəlɪst]

n. 国际主义者 *a.* 国际主义者的

记 联想记忆：international(国际的，世界的) + ist(表人)→ 国际主义者

例 We established links and access to the *internationalist* organisations and their resources. 我们与国际主义者组织建立了联系，并有权使用他们的资源。

internist* [ɪnˈtɜːnɪst]

n. 内科医师

例 The professor who teaches us is a respected *internist*. 教我们的那个教授是一位受人尊敬的内科医师。

□ interface □ interfere □ interior □ intermediate □ intermix □ intern
□ internal □ internationalist □ internist

internship *

[ˈɪntɜːnʃɪp]

n. 实习生身份；实习医师

例 During *internship*, John came into contact with society. 实习期间，约翰开始接触社会。

interplay *

[ˈɪntəpleɪ]

vi./n. 相互作用，相互影响

记 联想记忆：inter（在…之间）+ play（担任角色）→ 相互作用

例 Social factors have *interplayed* with one another over the past hundred years and made the Middle East what it is today. 在过去的一百年间，诸多社会因素相互影响，造成了今天的中东局势。

interpret

[ɪnˈtɜːprɪt]

v. 解释，说明；口译，翻译

记 词根记忆：inter(在…之间) + pret → 在两种语言之间沟通 → 口译，翻译

例 I wanted to discover whether there were differences in how the blind and the sighted *interpreted* colours. 我希望可以发现失明者与有视力者对颜色的描述是否有所不同。

interpretation *

[ɪnˌtɜːprɪˈteɪʃn]

n. 口译；解释，诠释；（表演、演奏的）艺术处理

例 My *interpretation* of the drama was rather superficial. 我对戏剧的理解相当肤浅。

interrelationship *

[ˌɪntərɪˈleɪʃnʃɪp]

n. 相互关联，相互影响

例 This study examined the *interrelationship* between environment and human behaviour. 这项研究考察了环境和人类行为的相互影响。

interrupt *

[ˌɪntəˈrʌpt]

v. 中断，中止；阻碍；打断，打扰

记 词根记忆：inter(在…之间) + rupt(打破，断裂) → 在中间断裂 → 中断，中止；打断，打扰

搭 interrupt the work 打扰工作

例 A: How does your headache affect your daily life?

B: It has *interrupted* my work.

A: 头痛对你的日常生活有什么影响?

B: 它妨碍到了我工作。

派 interruption(*n.* 打扰，打断)

intersection

[ˌɪntəˈsekʃn]

n. 道路交叉口，十字路口

记 词根记忆：inter(在…中间) + sect(切割) + ion(名词后缀)→ 在路面中间切割 → 道路交叉口，十字路口

例 The *intersections* of these streets with Main Street will not be affected. 这些道路与主干道的交叉口将不会受到影响。

同 crossroad(*n.* 十字路口)

interval

[ˈɪntəvl]

n. 间隔，幕间休息；间距

记 词根记忆：inter(在…之间) + val → 处在两者之间的 → 间距；间隔

例 The discussion was so prolonged and exhausting that at *intervals* the speakers stopped for refreshment. 讨论冗长又使人疲倦，以至于发言人不时要停下来休息。

intervene
[ˌɪntəˈviːn]

vi. 干涉，干扰；介于其间

记 词根记忆：inter(在…之间) + ven(来) + e → 来到中间 → 干涉，干扰

例 The bank *intervened* with a large dollar purchase. 那家银行以大量购进美元来进行干预。

同 interfere(*vi.* 介入，干涉，干扰)；interpose(*v.* 置于…之间，介入)

---

intervention
[ˌɪntəˈvenʃn]

n. 干涉，干预，介入

记 来自 intervene(*vi.* 干涉；干扰，介于其间)

例 In decade, more and more governments strengthened health *intervention*, and introduced a series of new health-care system. 十年间，越来越多的政府加强对保健的干预，引入一些新的医疗体系。

---

interview *
[ˈɪntəvjuː]

v./n. 接见，会见；采访；面试

记 联想记忆：inter(相互) + view(看) → 相互观察 → 接见；面试

搭 personal interview 私人会晤；have an interview with sb. 会见某人；job interview 求职面试；group interview 小组访谈

例 We will talk about how applicants put through a short *interview*. 我们将讨论求职者如何成功进行短时间面试。

interview

---

intestine
[ɪnˈtestɪn]

n.【解】肠

记 联想记忆：in(里面) + test(检查) + ine → 对身体内部进行检查 → 肠

例 Food passes from the stomach to the small *intestine* and from there to the large *intestine*. 食物从胃里先到小肠，然后经过小肠到大肠。

---

intimate

[ˈɪntɪmət] *a.* 亲密的，密切的；私人的，个人的；小圈子内的 *n.* 至交，密友 [ˈɪntɪmeɪt] *vt.* 暗示，提示，透露

记 词根记忆：in(不) + tim(害怕) + ate → 关系密切，无须害怕 → 密切的

搭 be intimate with sb. 与某人关系亲密；intimate details 隐私；intimate knowledge of sth. 对…非常了解，熟悉；on intimate terms with sb. 与某人保持亲密关系

例 The dance studio provides a smaller, more *intimate* space, which we use for ballet, modern dance and martial arts. 舞蹈室为我们练习芭蕾、现代舞和武术提供了一个更小更私密的空间。

---

intrigue

[ɪnˈtriːɡ] *v.* 密谋，施诡计；引起极大兴趣，迷住 [ˈɪntriːɡ] *n.* 阴谋，诡计；密谋

记 词根记忆：in(里面) + trig(=tric 小障碍物) + ue → 在里面放入小障碍物使复杂 → 密谋，施诡计

搭 political intrigues 政治阴谋

例 A good teacher knows how to *intrigue* his students to learn. 好老师懂得如何激发学生的学习兴趣。

派 intriguing(*a.* 迷人的，吸引人的)

同 attract(*vt.* 吸引)；captivate(*vt.* 迷住，迷惑，吸引)；appeal(*vi.* 有吸引力)；plot(*v./n.* 密谋，阴谋)

intrinsic*

[ɪnˈtrɪnsɪk]

a. 固有的，内在的；本质的

搭 intrinsic nature 本质

例 Students should realize the ***intrinsic*** value of education. 学生应该认识到教育的内在价值。

派 intrinsically(*ad.* 内在地)

同 inherent(*a.* 内在的，固有的)；essential(*a.* 本质的)；innate(*a.* 天生的，固有的)

反 extrinsic(*a.* 外来的，外在的)；external(*a.* 外面的，表面的)

introduce*

[ˌɪntrəˈdjuːs]

vt. 介绍；传入，引进；提出；采用，推行

搭 introduce a course 介绍一门课程

例 We've ***introduced*** a simpler price structure. 我们引进了一套更为简易的价格结构体系。

introduction*

[ˌɪntrəˈdʌkʃn]

n. 介绍；传入，引进；导言，绪论

记 词根记忆：intro(向内) + duct(拉) + ion → 向内拉 → 介绍；传入，引进

例 By way of ***introduction***, I shall give you the background of the subject. 通过介绍，我将向你讲述该学科的相关背景。

introspection

[ˌɪntrəˈspekʃn]

n. 内省，反省

记 词根记忆：intro(向内) + spect(看) + ion → 看自己的内心 → 内省

例 These situations are best resolved with the minimum of ***introspection*** or self-analysis. 通过最低程度的自我反省或自我分析，圆满地解决了这些问题。

introvert*

[ˈɪntrəvɜːt]

n. 性格内向的人

例 Mr. King was described as an reserved, ***introvert*** man who spoke little. 金先生被描述成一位保守、内向的人，话说得非常少。

intrusion*

[ɪnˈtruːʒn]

n. 闯入；打搅；侵扰

记 词根记忆：in(向内) + trus(刺) + ion → 向内刺 → 闯入

例 In fact, there are people who dislike any kind of perfume and think it's an ***intrusion***. 实际上，有些人讨厌所有香水的气味，并认为别人使用香水是对自己的侵犯。

inundate

[ˈɪnʌndeɪt]

vt. 淹没，泛滥；使不胜负荷，使应接不暇

记 词根记忆：in(进入) + und(波浪) + ate → 卷入波浪 → 淹没，泛滥

例 Due to the successive heavy rain, the dam of the Nile breaks, which ***inundates*** large parts of the town and farmlands. 由于连降大雨，尼罗河大坝溃堤，淹没了该镇的大部分地区和农田。

invade*

[ɪnˈveɪd]

v. 侵犯，侵入，侵略，侵袭

记 词根记忆：in(进入) + vad(走) + e → 未经允许走进来 → 侵犯，侵入

例 Portugal was ***invaded*** by the French in 1807. 法国人在 1807 年入侵葡萄牙。

invader*

[ɪnˈveɪdə(r)]

n. 入侵者

记 来自 invade(*v.* 侵犯，侵入)

例 Their way of life was destroyed by ***invaders***. 他们的生活方式遭到了入侵者的破坏。

□ intrinsic □ introduce □ introduction □ introspection □ introvert □ intrusion
□ inundate □ invade □ invader

invalid

[ɪnˈvælɪd] *a.* (指法律上)无效的，作废的；无可靠根据的，站不住脚的；有病的，伤残的 [ˈɪnvælɪd] *n.* (需要有人照顾的)病弱者，残疾者

记 词根记忆：in(无) + val(价值) + id → 无价值的 → 无效的，作废的

搭 invalid characters 无效字符

例 The judge declared Tom's marriage *invalid*. 法官宣布汤姆的婚姻无效。

同 impotent(*a.* 无效的，不起作用的)；unfounded(*a.* 无事实根据的)

invaluable

[ɪnˈvæljuəbl]

a. 无价的

记 联想记忆：in(无) + valuable(有价值的) → 无价的

反 valueless(*a.* 没有价值的)

invasion*

[ɪnˈveɪʒn]

n. 入侵，侵略

记 词根记忆：in(进入) + vas(走) + ion(名词后缀) → 走进来 → 入侵，侵略

例 The freedom from foreign *invasion* enables a country to develop its natural resources steadily. 不受外来侵略可以使一国的自然资源得到稳定的开发。

invasive

[ɪnˈveɪsɪv]

a. 侵略的，入侵的；(疾病等)侵袭的，扩散的；切入的，开刀的

记 词根记忆：in(进入) + vas(走) + ive(形容词后缀) → 未经许可就进入的 → 入侵的，侵袭的

搭 invasive cancer 扩散性肿瘤；invasive surgery 开刀手术

inventive

[ɪnˈventɪv]

a. 发明的，创造的；善于发明创造的

记 联想记忆：invent(创造，发明) + ive → 发明的，创造的

例 This experiment aims to explore children's imagination and *inventive* learning skill. 该实验的目的在于开发孩子们的想象力和创造性学习技巧。

In our efforts to adjust differences of opinion we should be free from intolerance of passion, and our judgements should be unmoved by alluring phrases and unvexed by selfish interests.

在我们努力协调意见的分歧时，应当抛弃偏执与意气用事；我们的判断不应当被花言巧语蒙骗，也不应被个人私利扰乱。

——美国总统 克利夫兰 .G.（Grover Cleveland, American President）

Word List 27

音频

词根、词缀预习表

vent	来	inventory *n.* 存货	**vers**	转	inversion *n.* 颠倒
viol	违反	inviolable *a.* 不可侵犯的	**vis**	看见	invisible *a.* 无形的
vok	叫喊	invoke *vt.* 恳求	**volv**	卷	involve *vt.* 卷入
rit	擦	irritable *a.* 急躁的	**isol**	岛屿	isolate *vt.* 使隔离
it	走	itinerary *n.* 旅行路线	**journ**	日	journal *n.* 日志

inventory [ˈɪnvəntri]

n. 目录；存货

记 词根记忆：in + vent(来) + ory(表物) → 有关所有进来的货物的 → 目录；存货

例 Managing agents can offer a total service from reliable sourcing, managing *inventory* to budget control and distribution. 运营代理商可以提供从可靠资源获取、库房存货管理以及从预算控制到商品分销的全套服务。

同 checklist(*n.* 清单)

inversion* [ɪnˈvɜːʃn]

n. 倒置，颠倒

记 词根记忆：in(反的) + vers(转) + ion(名词后缀) → 倒转 → 倒置，颠倒

搭 an inversion of word order 词序颠倒

invert* [ɪnˈvɜːt]

vt. (使)倒转，(使)颠倒

记 词根记忆：in(进入) + vert(转) → (使)倒转，(使)颠倒

例 Should the image formed on the retina be *inverted*? 在视网膜上形成的图像应该是颠倒的吗？

invest* [ɪnˈvest]

v. 投资；投入(时间、精力等)；授予，赋予

搭 invest in the stock market 投资股票市场；invest in sth. 购买昂贵有用的东西

例 Supermarkets are able to *invest* millions of pounds in powerful computers which tell them what sells best. 超市可投资数百万英镑用于购买功能强大的计算机，这些计算机能告诉他们什么最畅销。

派 investment(*n.* 投资，投入)；investor(*n.* 投资者)

investigate [ɪnˈvestɪɡeɪt]

v. 调查

记 联想记忆：invest(投资) + i + gate(大门) → 先进行市场调查是通往投资的大门 → 调查

例 We must *investigate* and understand the link between environment and health. 我们必须研究并了解环境与健康之间的联系。

inviolable
[ɪnˈvaɪələbl]

a. 不可侵犯的，不容亵渎的，不容破坏的

记 词根记忆：in（不）+ viol（违反，冒犯）+ able（能…的）→ 不可侵犯的

例 What a man has experienced in the privacy must necessarily remain *inviolable* at any time. 一个人的隐私在任何时候都一定是不可侵犯的。

派 inviolability（*n.* 不可侵犯，神圣）

invisible
[ɪnˈvɪzəbl]

a. 看不见的，无形的

记 词根记忆：in（不）+ vis（看见）+ ible（可…的）→ 看不见的，无形的

搭 invisible earnings 无形收益

例 Could there be another planet there, essentially similar to our own, but always *invisible*? 那里会不会有另一颗星球和我们的星球很相似，但我们却一直看不见呢？

反 visible（*a.* 可见的，有形的）

invoice*
[ˈɪnvɔɪs]

n. 发票 *vt.* 给…开发票

记 联想记忆：in + voice（声音）→ 大声把人叫进来开发票 → 发票；给…开发票

例 The manufacturer *invoiced* me for two computers. 厂商给我开了一张两台电脑的发票。

invoke
[ɪnˈvəʊk]

vt. 恳求，祈求；援用，援引；使用，应用

记 词根记忆：in（使）+ vok（叫喊）+ e → 恳求

例 Police can *invoke* the law of human rights to regulate the perpetrators. 警察可以通过人权法来管理闹事者。

involve*
[ɪnˈvɒlv]

vt. 使卷入，使参与；牵涉，陷入，连累；包含，含有

记 词根记忆：in（进入）+ volv（卷）+ e → 使卷入，牵涉

搭 involve in 卷入，参加；involve sb. in 使某人卷入，使某人陷入

例 No city can be simply a port but must be *involved* in a variety of other activities. 没有哪个城市能够单纯作为港口，它必然还含有其他多种功能。

派 involvement（*n.* 包含；连累）

ion*
[ˈaɪən]

n. 离子

例 The *ion* propulsion system was first activated. 首先激活离子推进系统。

派 ionizer（*n.* 负离子发生器）

iris*
[ˈaɪərɪs]

n.（*pl.* irises 或 irides）虹；（眼球的）虹膜

记 本身为词根，意为“彩虹；虹膜”

例 Systems using fingerprints, hands, voices, *irises*, retinas and faces are already on the market. 使用指纹、手掌、声音、虹膜、视网膜以及面部进行识别的系统都已上市。

iron*
[ˈaiən]

n. 铁；烙铁，熨斗 *v.*（用熨斗）熨，烫平

搭 iron sth. out 熨平（衣服等的皱褶）

例 It will take me about half an hour to *iron* that dress. 烫平那条连衣裙，我大概要花上半个小时的时间。

□ inviolable □ invisible □ invoice □ invoke □ involve □ ion
□ iris □ iron

irony *

[ˈaɪərəni]

n. 反话，讽刺；出人意料的事情

记 联想记忆：iron（铁）+ y → 像铁一样冷冰冰的话 → 反话，讽刺

例 It reveals the power of the pauses and noises we use to play for time, convey emotion, doubt and *irony*. 这表现出停顿和噪音的力量，我们用它们来拖延时间，表达情感、疑惑和讽刺。

派 ironically（*ad.* 讽刺地；嘲讽地）

irony

irrational

[ɪˈræʃənl]

a. 不合理的，不合逻辑的，荒谬的 *n.* 无理数

记 联想记忆：ir（不）+ rational（合理的）→ 不合理的

搭 an irrational fear 无端的恐惧

例 The theory that the earth revolves around the sun, put forward by Polish astronomer Copernicus, seemed to be somewhat *irrational* in 15th century. 15 世纪时波兰天文学家哥白尼提出的地球绕着太阳运转的理论在当时似乎有点荒谬。

irregularity *

[ɪˌregjəˈlærəti]

n. 不规则，无规律

例 To date, the most widely used commercial biometric system is the handkey, a type of hand scanner which reads the unique shape, size and *irregularities* of people's hands. 迄今为止，在商业生物测定系统中应用最广泛的是掌形识别仪，这是一种读取人们手掌独有的形状、大小和不规则性的手掌扫描仪。

irrelevant *

[ɪˈreləvənt]

a. 不相关的；离题的

记 联想记忆：ir（不）+ relevant（有关的）→ 不相关的

例 What you wrote is almost *irrelevant* to the topic. 你写的文章和主题几乎是不相关的。

irresistible

[ˌɪrɪˈzɪstəbl]

a. 无法抵抗的，不能压制的；不能自已的

记 联想记忆：ir（不）+ resistible（可抵抗的）→ 不可抵抗的 → 无法抵抗的

例 Later the lava cools slowly into a huge, hard, stable plug which blocks any further eruption until the pressure below becomes *irresistible*. 随后岩浆慢慢冷却，变成巨大、坚硬而稳固的岩颈，堵塞着火山进一步喷发，直到喷发的压力变得势不可挡。

irrevocable *

[ɪˈrevəkəbl]

a. 无法取消的，不能改变的

记 联想记忆：ir（不）+ revocable（可取消的）→ 无法取消的

例 The powers given to these agents are *irrevocable*. 下放给这些代理商的权力是不可改变的。

irrigation

[ˌɪrɪˈgeɪʃn]

n. 灌溉；冲洗

记 词根记忆：ir（进入）+ rig（水）+ ation → 把水引入 → 灌溉

例 The sea water is too salty to be used for the *irrigation* of crops. 海水太咸了，不能用于农作物灌溉。

irritable

[ˈɪrɪtəbl]

a. 急躁的，易怒的，易受刺激的；过敏的

记 词根记忆：ir（使…成为，进入）+ rit（擦）+ able → 进入摩擦 → 急躁的

例 The old man was so *irritable* that he often jabbed his stick in his servant's face. 那个老人脾气太暴躁，经常用手杖戳佣人的脸。

□ irony □ irrational □ irregularity □ irrelevant □ irresistible □ irrevocable
□ irrigation □ irritable

irritate [ˈɪrɪteɪt]	*vt.* 使烦躁；使疼痛；刺激 例 Foul smelling chemicals are often used to *irritate* the bees and drive them down into the hive's bottom boxes. 气味难闻的化学物质常常被用来刺激蜜蜂并把它们赶到蜂箱底部的箱子。 派 irritant(*n.* 刺激物 *a.* 刺激性的)；irritating(*a.* 恼人的，令人痛苦的)
irritation* [ˌɪrɪˈteɪʃn]	*n.* 激怒，恼怒；刺激物，恼人的事 记 来自 irritate(*vt.* 使烦躁；刺激) 例 Tom couldn't hide his *irritation* that he failed the exam. 汤姆无法掩饰自己因考试不及格而产生的恼怒情绪。
isle [aɪl]	*n.* 小岛，岛 例 The newly established Dinosaur Museum is located on the *Isle* of Wight. 新建的恐龙博物馆位于怀特岛。
isolate* [ˈaɪsəleɪt]	*vt.* 使隔离，使孤立 记 词根记忆：isol(=insul 岛屿) + ate(使…) → 使隔离，使孤立 例 Reasons for higher success rates among women are difficult to *isolate.* 我们很难把造成女性(求职)成功率较高的原因孤立出来看。
isolated [ˈaɪsəleɪtɪd]	*a.* 隔离的，分离的；与世隔绝的，偏僻的；孤立的，孤独的；个别的 记 来自 isolate(*vt.* 使隔离) 例 Old people could easily become a socially *isolated* group, so they should keep moving and maintain interaction with the outside world. 老年人很容易变成与社会脱节的一个群体，所以他们应该不断前进并保持与外界的互动。 同 remote(*a.* 偏远的)
issue* [ˈɪʃuː]	*n.* 问题，争论点；发行；(报刊的)一期；分发，流出 *vt.* 颁布；发行；流出；分发，发给 搭 environmental issues 环境问题；issue a statement 发表声明；issue shares 发行股票；be at issue 是讨论或争议的焦点 例 They care about environmental *issues* but their concern does not affect their spending habits. 他们关心环境问题，但这种关心并没有影响他们的消费习惯。
item* [ˈaɪtəm]	*n.* 条款，项目；(新闻等)一则 搭 single item 单件物品 例 You should pay for each *item* the doctor has prescribed. 你需要为医生列出的各项处方付款。
itinerary* [aɪˈtɪnərəri]	*n.* 行程表；旅行路线，旅行计划 记 词根记忆：it(走) + iner + ary → 行走 → 旅行路线 例 I will be distributing leaflets at the end where you can find out more information, but just for the moment I'll outline the *itinerary*, the main high points of the holiday. 最后，我会分发传单，你们可以从中了解更多的信息，但目前我要概述一下旅行路线，都是假期的热门景点。

□ irritate □ irritation □ isle □ isolate □ isolated □ issue
□ item □ itinerary

jargon
[ˈdʒɑːɡən]

n. 行话，行业术语；黑话

搭 legal jargon 法律术语

例 If you take a presentation on some specific fields, to avoid confusing the audience, you should try to decrease ***jargon*** in your speech. 在做有关某一特定领域的报告时，为避免听众产生疑惑和不解，你应该尽量少用术语。

jaw*
[dʒɔː]

n. 颌

记 发音记忆："嚼"→ 他下颌脱臼了，没法嚼东西 → 颌

例 Necrosis of the mouth is a disease that eats away the ***jaw***. 口腔坏死性疾病是一种腐蚀颌部的疾病。

jealous
[ˈdʒeləs]

a. 嫉妒的；猜疑的

例 Tom is ***jealous*** of anyone who talks to his girlfriend. 汤姆对每个和她女友说话的人都心存猜疑。

jeopardise
[ˈdʒepədaɪz]

vt. 危害，使受危困

例 He has never done anything to ***jeopardise*** his family. 他从来没有做过任何伤害其家庭的事情。

jerk
[dʒɜːk]

v. 使猝然一动；猛拉 *n.* 急推，急扭；抽搐

例 The fierce man grabbed a handful of hair of his wife and ***jerked*** at it. 那个凶狠的男人抓住他妻子的一把头发用力猛拽。

joint
[dʒɔɪnt]

n. 接头；关节 *a.* 连接的；联合的

记 联想记忆：join(结合，连接) + t → 接头；关节

搭 call for joint effort from 需要…的共同努力；joint venture 合资企业

例 The Universities of Oxford and Cambridge recently held ***joint*** conferences to discuss the rapid decline in literacy among their undergraduates. 牛津大学和剑桥大学近日召开联合会议，讨论两校大学生文化素养迅速下降的问题。

jostle*
[ˈdʒɒsl]

v. 推挤；挤开通路

例 In a port city, races, cultures, and ideas, as well as goods from a variety of places, ***jostle***, mix and enrich each other. 在港口城市，种族、文化和理念还有那些来自四面八方的货物，互相推挤、混合又互为补充。

journal*
[ˈdʒɜːnl]

n. 杂志；日报；日志

记 词根记忆：journ(日) + al → 每日都有的 → 日报；日志

例 We are grateful to the author and the *Asia Pacific **Journal** of Human Resources* for allowing us to use the material. 我们感激作者及《亚太人力资源》杂志允许我们使用这些材料。

派 journalese(*n.* 新闻文体；新闻笔调)

journalist
[ˈdʒɜːnəlɪst]

n. 新闻工作者，新闻记者

例 I'm a ***journalist*** who specializes in travel. 我是旅游记者。

□ jargon □ jaw □ jealous □ jeopardise □ jerk □ joint
□ jostle □ journal □ journalist

judgment
[ˈdʒʌdʒmənt]

n. 意见；审判；判断(力)

搭 make a judgment 作出评价

例 The lawyer is a man of good *judgment*. 那位律师具有出色的判断力。

judicious *
[dʒuˈdɪʃəs]

a. 明智的；有见识的

记 词根记忆：jud(判断) + icious → 具有判断力的 → 明智的；有见识的

例 Archaeology makes clear that with *judicious* management selected parts of the region could support more people than anyone thought before. 考古学解释说，利用明智的管理方法，所选地区能够养活的人数能比以往任何人所能想象的都多。

jumble *
[ˈdʒʌmbl]

n. 混杂，掺杂；供义卖的旧杂货 *vt.* 混杂，掺杂

记 联想记忆：jum(看作 jump，跳) + ble → 上蹿下跳，群魔乱舞 → 混杂

搭 a jumble of 杂乱的一堆；jumble sale 废旧杂货廉价义卖；jumble sth. together/up 使乱堆，使杂乱

例 Here is a *jumble* of books and newspaper. 这有一堆杂乱的书和报纸。

junction
[ˈdʒʌŋkʃn]

n. 连接；联结点；交叉路口

记 词根记忆：junct(连接) + ion → 连接

例 The power station was built at the *junction* of two rivers. 那座发电站建于两河的交汇处。

jungle
[ˈdʒʌŋgl]

n. 丛林

例 They ventured deep into the *jungle* and sought out an isolated tribe. 他们冒险进入丛林深处，找到了一个与世隔绝的部落。

27

justice
[ˈdʒʌstɪs]

n. 正义，公正；司法

记 词根记忆：just(正确的) + ice → 正义，公正

例 Where might is master, *justice* is servant. 有强权，就没有正义。

justify
[ˈdʒʌstɪfaɪ]

v. 证明…为正当的；为…辩护

记 词根记忆：just(正确的) + ify(使…) → 证明…为正当的；为…辩护

例 To *justify* this claim, the arguer provided a lot of evidence. 为了证明这个主张是正当的，争辩者提供了许多证据。

juvenile
[ˈdʒuːvənaɪl]

a. 少年的，少年特有的；幼稚的，不成熟的 *n.* 未成年人，少年

记 词根记忆：juven(年轻) + ile → 少年的；幼稚的

例 *Juvenile* delinquency has increased remarkably in the last decade. 在过去的十年里，未成年人犯罪有明显的增加。

同 childish (*a.* 幼稚的)；immature (*a.* 不成熟的)；youngster(*n.* 少年，年轻人)；teenager(*n.* 青少年)

□ judgment □ judicious □ jumble □ junction □ jungle □ justice
□ justify □ juvenile

keen [kiːn]

a. 热衷的，热心的，渴望的；敏锐的，敏捷的；激烈的，紧张的；锋利的

搭 be keen on 渴望，对…喜爱，热衷于；a man of keen perception 知觉敏锐的人

例 I'm not very *keen* on Westerners, although my father likes them. 我不是很喜欢西部人，尽管父亲很喜欢他们。// The dog had a *keen* sense of smell. 狗的嗅觉很灵敏。

keystone* [ˈkiːstəʊn]

n. 拱顶石；(计划、论据等的)基础，主旨

例 Changes to the social welfare system are the *keystone* of the government's reforms. 政府对社会福利系统的改革是政府改革的基础。

kidney [ˈkɪdni]

n. 肾，肾脏

例 The doctor asked Mark whether he had ever suffered from any liver, *kidney* or heart disease. 医生问马克以前是否得过肝、肾或是心脏方面的疾病。

kindergarten [ˈkɪndəgɑːtn]

n. 幼儿园

例 *Kindergarten* is the starting place for children to learn basic morals and how to get along with people. 幼儿园是孩子们学习基本的道德规范和与人相处之道的第一站。

kit [kɪt]

n. 成套工具 *vt.* 装备

搭 a first-aid kit 一套急救用品

例 The plumber reached into his tool *kit* for a wrench. 水管工人伸手从他的成套工具中拿出一个扳手。// They all were *kitted* out for skiing. 他们全都配齐了滑雪的必需品。

kneel [niːl]

vi. 跪

例 Mary *knelt* down to examine the damage to her car. 玛丽跪下来仔细查看她汽车的受损情况。

knob [nɒb]

n. 球形把手；(机器等)旋钮

记 联想记忆：没有门把手（knob），只能敲门（knock）

例 This machine has lots of *knobs* on it. 这台机器上有许多旋钮。

Kung Fu* [ˌkʌŋ ˈfuː]

n. 功夫

例 A lot of people in the U.S. complained that Chinese *Kung Fu* films were particularly violent. 很多美国人抱怨说中国功夫片太暴力了。

label* [ˈleɪbl]

vt. 贴标签于 *n.* 标签，标记；称号；绰号，外号

记 联想记忆：lab（实验室）+ el → 实验室里的试剂瓶上贴有标签 → 标签

搭 label as 把…称为

例 I think we should *label* the lid itself and say that it constitutes twenty-five percent of the total weight. 我认为我们应该在盖子上贴上标签，注明盖子本身占总重的 25%。

laboratory [ləˈbɒrətri]

n. 实验室，研究室

记 联想记忆：labor（工作）+ at（在）+ ory（表地点，名词后缀）→ 工作的地方 → 实验室，研究室

例 Do you have a Computer *Laboratory*? 你们有计算机室吗？

□ keen □ keystone □ kidney □ kindergarten □ kit □ kneel
□ knob □ Kung Fu □ label □ laboratory

labour* [ˈleɪbə(r)]

n. 劳动；劳动力，工人 *v.* 劳动；努力

搭 labour costs 劳动成本；labour away（努力做困难的事）

记 发音记忆："累伯"→农民伯伯劳动很辛苦，很累→劳动

例 As a result, 51% of all women aged 14 to 64 are now economically active in the *labour* market. 结果表明，劳务市场上年龄在14到64岁之间的所有女性中，51%的人在经济方面很活跃。

派 laboured（*a.* 费力的）

lack* [læk]

n./vt. 缺乏，不足，没有

搭 lack of 缺乏，没有；lack (for) nothing 什么都不缺

例 Martin can't afford the book due to *lack* of money. 由于缺钱，马丁买不起这本书。

lag* [læg]

v. 走得慢；落后 *n.*（时间上的）间隔；滞后

记 联想记忆：leg（腿）中间的零件e换成a了→腿坏了→走得慢

搭 time lag 时滞，时间间隔；jet lag 时差，时差反应

例 America *lagged* behind Europe in match technology and safety standards. 美国在火柴技术和安全标准上落后于欧洲。

landfill* [ˈlændfɪl]

n. 垃圾堆；垃圾填筑地，废渣埋填地

记 组合词：land（地）+ fill（充满）→堆满垃圾的地方→垃圾堆

搭 landfill site 垃圾掩埋地点

例 Sand was driven into the seabed to strengthen it before the *landfill* was piled on top. 沙子被运到海床，在垃圾被堆在海床上之前对其进行加固。

landmark* [ˈlændmɑːk]

n. 路标，地标；里程碑

记 组合词：land（土地）+ mark（标志）→路标，地标

搭 landmark decision 里程碑式的决定

例 In fact, I'd just like to spend a few minutes pointing out some of the *landmarks* that can be seen from here. 事实上，我只是想花几分钟时间指出从这里能看到的一些地标。

landscape [ˈlændskeɪp]

n. 风景 *vt.* 对…作景观美化，美化（自然环境等）

例 The *landscape* on the altiplano is the most beautiful I've ever seen. 高原上的风景是我所见过的最美的景色。

landward* [ˈlændwəd]

a./ad. 向陆的/地，近陆的/地

例 It is *landward* access, which is productive of goods for export and which demands imports, that is critical. 近陆的入口非常重要，它既能够生产出口货物，对进口也有需求。

lane* [leɪn]

n. 小巷；行车道

记 联想记忆：小巷（lane）可作行车路线（line）

例 Vehicles carrying more than one person can use special priority *lanes*, which means they can travel more quickly. 载有一位以上乘客的车辆可以使用特殊的优先级车道，这就意味着它们能行驶得更快。

27

□ labour □ lack □ lag □ landfill □ landmark □ landscape
□ landward □ lane

large-scale* [ˈlɑːdʒˈskeɪl]

a. 大规模的，大范围的

例 They invested much money into *large-scale* industrial development. 他们投入大量金钱发展大规模的工业。

larva* [ˈlɑːvə]

n. [*pl.* larvae] 幼虫，幼体

例 Once the beetle *larvae* have finished pupation, the residue is a first-rate source of fertiliser. 一旦甲虫的幼虫完成了化蛹过程，其残留物就是最好的肥料来源。

laser [ˈleɪzə(r)]

n. 激光

记 发音记忆："镭射" → 激光

例 The bar codes on the products are read by *lasers*. 这些产品上的条形码是用激光读取的。

latent* [ˈleɪtnt]

a. 潜在的，潜伏的，不易察觉的

记 联想记忆：lat(看作 late，后面的) + ent(形容词后缀) → 后面的 → 潜在的，潜伏的

搭 latent capital 潜在资本；latent infection 潜伏性传染病；latent period 潜伏期

例 He still has *latent* force to develop in study and research. 在学习和研究方面，他仍有潜力可挖。

lateral* [ˈlætərəl]

a. 侧面的，旁边的

记 词根记忆：later(侧面，边) + al → 侧面的

例 Not even our closest relatives among the apes possess such decided *lateral* asymmetry, as zoologists call it. 正如动物学家所认为的那样，即便是和我们有着最近的血缘关系的猿类也不具备这样明显的侧向不对称性。

派 lateralize(*vt.* 把…移到一侧)

laterality* [ˌlætəˈrælɪti]

n. 对一侧面的偏重，偏向一侧状态

例 His team measured the hand, feet and eyes of 2,611 players and found that there were really three main types of *laterality*. 他的团队对2611名演奏者的手脚和眼睛进行了测量，发现真的有三种主要的侧重类型。

latitude [ˈlætɪtjuːd]

n. 纬度；[*pl.*] 纬度地区；(言行等的)自由

记 联想记忆：和 attitude(*n.* 态度)一起记

例 Our position is *latitude* 40 degrees south. 我们的位置是南纬 40 度。

同 freedom(*n.* 自由，自主)；liberty(*n.* 自由，自由权)

launch [lɔːntʃ]

vt. 将…投放市场；开始从事，发动，发起；发射 *n.* 发射；(产品)上市

记 联想记忆：在午餐(lunch)会上推出(launch)新产品，真是不错的主意。

搭 launch into sth. 开始…；积极投入…；launch an attack 发动攻击；launch pad 发射台；launch the product 将新产品投放市场

例 They set about developing a new camera model, which was *launched* in June 1888. 他们着手研发新的相机款式，并于 1888 年 6 月推出。

派 launcher(*n.* 发射器，发射装置)

□ large-scale □ larva □ laser □ latent □ lateral □ laterality
□ latitude □ launch

laundry * [ˈlɔːndri]	*n.* 洗衣房；待洗衣服 记 词根记忆：lau(洗) + nd + (o)ry(表地点) → 洗衣房 例 You should pay a ***laundry*** fee which covers the cleaning of bed linens and towels. 你必须支付包括清洗床上用品和毛巾在内的所有洗衣费用。
lava * [ˈlɑːvə]	*n.* 岩浆，熔岩 记 联想记忆：幼虫(larva)在岩浆(lava)中熔化 例 ***Lava*** domes have formed inside the new crater and have periodically burst. 熔岩穹丘已在新的火山口形成并周期性地爆发。
lavatory [ˈlævətrɪ]	*n.* 盥洗室，厕所 记 词根记忆：lav(洗) + at + ory(表地点，名词后缀) → 盥洗室 例 Could you tell me the way to the ***lavatory***, please? 请问去盥洗室怎么走?

Every man's work, whether it be literature of music of pictures or architecture of anything else, is always a portrait of himself.

每个人的工作，不管是文学、音乐、美术、建筑还是其他工作，都是自己的一幅画像。

——美国教育家 勃特勒 .S.（Samuel Brtler, American educator）

Word List 28

音 频

词根、词缀预习表

lect	讲	lecture *n.* 演讲	**leg**	送	legacy *n.* 遗赠
len	软	lenient *a.* 宽容的	**lev**	举起	lever *n.* 杠杆
lexico	词	lexicographer *n.* 词典编纂者	**lib**	文字	libel *vt.* 诽谤
lingu	语言	linguistic *a.* 语言学的	**liter**	文字	literacy *n.* 有文化
loc	地点	locate *vt.* 位于	**log**	语言	logic *n.* 逻辑

lawsuit [ˈlɔːsuːt]

n. 诉讼，起诉

记 组合词：law(法律) + suit(起诉，诉讼) → 诉讼

例 The ***lawsuit*** is very much on the lawyer's mind. 律师的脑子里一直浮想着这起诉讼。

lax [læks]

a. 懒散的；松弛的，不严格的，马虎的

例 Much to our surprise, some companies have been ***lax*** in carrying out their social responsibilities. 令我们大为吃惊的是，一些公司在履行其社会职责方面表现得很懈怠。

layer [ˈleɪə(r)]

n. 层，层次

记 联想记忆：lay(层面) + er → 层，层次

例 Between the islands there was a ***layer*** of soft mud. 在小岛之间有一层软泥。

layout [ˈleɪaʊt]

n. 布局，安排，设计

记 来自词组 lay out(布置，安排)

搭 layout of an office 办公室布局；layout of a CV 简历的版面设计；product layout of a supermarket 超市的货品摆放

例 The noise factor will have to be taken into consideration with the ***layout*** of the houses. 噪音因素必须被纳入房屋设计的考虑范围之内。

lead* [liːd] *v.* 指引；领导；致使 [led] *n.* 铅

搭 lead to 导致；通向

例 The road will ***lead*** you into the college grounds. 这条路通向学院校区。// It was assumed that economic progress would rapidly ***lead*** to the disappearance or assimilation of many small-scale societies. 有人认为，经济发展会很快导致小规模社会的消失或被同化。

 □ lawsuit □ lax □ layer □ layout □ lead

leadership* [ˈliːdəʃɪp] *n.* 领导，领导层；领导能力

记 联想记忆：leader（领导者）+ ship（表身份）→ 领导，领导层

例 Last week we talked about the most effective ways of leading meetings, and the advantages and disadvantages of different *leadership* styles. 上周，我们讨论了主持会议最有效的方法以及不同主持风格的利弊。

leaflet [ˈliːflət] *n.* 传单，散页印刷品；小册子 *v.* 散发传单（或小册子）

记 联想记忆：leaf（树叶）+ let（表小东西）→ 大街上的传单如落叶般铺天盖地 → 传单

例 You can find exact information about a patient on the patient information *leaflet*. 你可以在病人信息单中找到有关病人的详细信息。

leak* [liːk] *n.* 漏洞；泄露 *v.*（使）漏，（使）渗出

记 联想记忆：湖（lake）面上的船漏出（leak）很多油

例 If there were a gas *leak* in this room, the average person would notice fairly quickly. 如果这个房间发生煤气泄漏，一般人很快就会察觉到。

leap* [liːp] *n.* 跳跃；激增 *v.* 跳；冲

例 The athlete tensed his muscles for the *leap*. 运动员绷紧肌肉准备跳跃。

lease [liːs] *n.* 租约 *vt.* 出租，租用

记 联想记忆：l + ease（安心）→ 有了租约，可以安心了 → 租约

例 Could I ask how long is the *lease*? 我能问一下租期是多久吗？

leather [ˈleðə(r)] *n.* 皮革，皮革制品

记 联想记忆：天气（weather）对皮革（leather）的保存有影响

例 Michel lounged in the capacious *leather* chair, watching TV. 米歇尔懒洋洋地躺在宽大的皮椅上看电视。

派 leathery（*a.* 似皮革的；粗糙的）

lecture* [ˈlektʃə(r)] *n.* 演讲，讲课

记 词根记忆：lect（讲）+ ure → 演讲，讲课

例 I am giving you the *lectures* on environmental noise this term. 这个学期由我来给你们上环境噪声课。

派 lecturer（*n.* 讲师）

legacy* [ˈlegəsi] *n.* 遗产；遗赠

记 词根记忆：leg（送）+ acy → 去世前送出的东西 → 遗产；遗赠

例 Mary received this house as a *legacy* from her uncle. 玛丽从她叔叔那继承了这所房子。

legal* [ˈliːgl] *a.* 法律的；合法的

记 词根记忆：leg（法律）+ al（形容词后缀）→ 法律的；合法的

例 The Union has its own officers who can give advice on *legal* problems. 该协会拥有自己的人员，负责给法律事务提供建议。

legislation [ˌledʒɪsˈleɪʃn]

n. 法律，法规；立法

记 词根记忆：leg(法律) + islat + ion → 法律，法规；立法

例 The man called for ***legislation*** to adopt a unified response to the challenges posed by climate change and for the issue to receive more political support of the government. 此人呼吁通过立法，采取一致行动来应对气候变化带来的挑战，还呼吁政府给予该问题更多行政支持。

派 legislator(*n.* 立法者)；legislature(*n.* 立法机关)

legislative [ˈledʒɪslətɪv]

a. 立法的，有立法权的；根据法规执行的；立法机关的 *n.* 立法机关

搭 a legislative assembly 立法议会；legislative powers 立法权；legislative changes 立法变革

例 The United Nations has taken new ***legislative*** measures to stem the flow of weapons into the developing countries. 联合国已采取新的法律措施来阻止武器流入发展中国家。

legitimacy [lɪˈdʒɪtɪməsi]

n. 合法性；正统性

例 The young man was accused because the victim's families were serious doubts about the ***legitimacy*** of his so-called self-defense action. 这个年轻人遭到指控，因为受害人家属严重质疑他所谓的正当防卫的合法性。

legitimate

[lɪˈdʒɪtɪmət] *a.* 合法的，法定的；正当的，合情合理的

[lɪˈdʒɪtɪmeɪt] *vt.* 使合法

记 词根记忆：leg(法律) + itim + ate → 合法的，法定的

例 The majority of scientists believe it is ***legitimate*** to use monkeys in medical research. 大多数科学家认为使用猴子进行医学研究是合法的。

派 legitimately(*ad.* 合情合理地)

同 legal(*a.* 法定的，合法的)；lawful(*a.* 合法的，法定的)

legitimize [lɪˈdʒɪtəmaɪz]

vt. 使合法；赋予合法权利

记 词根记忆：leg(法律) + itim + ize(使…) → 使被法律认可 → 使合法；赋予合法权利

例 Some parents are concerned that a lot of violent films will be ***legitimized***, which will pose a threat to their children's mental health. 一些家长担心，大量的暴力电影被合法化会对孩子的心理健康构成威胁。

leisure* [ˈleʒə(r)]

n. 空闲时间；悠闲

例 Some people believe that children's ***leisure*** activities must be educational, otherwise they are a complete waste of time. 一些人认为，孩子们的休闲活动必须具有教育意义，否则纯粹是浪费时间。

lenient [ˈliːniənt]

a. (执法时)宽大的，宽容的；厚道的，仁慈的

记 词根记忆：len(软) + ient → 心肠软的 → 仁慈的

例 According to the recent survey, most of the job applicants prefer to work at companies whose rules and regulations are ***lenient***. 最新调查显示，大多数求职者喜欢在规章制度宽松的公司工作。

派 leniency(*n.* 宽大；仁慈)

lens* [lenz]

n. 透镜；镜片；镜头

记 联想记忆：借(lend)你透镜(lens)用用

例 ***Lenses*** can be used to concentrate the sun's rays. 透镜可用来聚集太阳光。

□ legislation □ legislative □ legitimacy □ legitimate □ legitimize □ leisure
□ lenient □ lens

leopard * [ˈlepəd]	*n.* 豹，美洲豹 记 联想记忆：leo(狮子) + pard(豹) → 像狮子一样凶猛的豹 → 美洲豹 例 One such weapon was the "basket of fire" or, as directly translated from Chinese, the "arrows like flying *leopards*". 这种武器就是"火篮"，直接从中文翻译过来就是"如飞豹般快速的箭"。
less than *	小于，少于 例 Each page takes *less than* a minute to produce. 每页的制作时间不到一分钟。
lethal * [ˈliːθl]	*a.* 致命的，破坏性的，毁灭性的；有害的 记 词根记忆：leth(死，僵) + al → 致死的 → 致命的 例 Bugs and weeds become resistant to poisons, so next year's poisons must be more *lethal*. 臭虫和野草对农药产生了抗药性，所以来年农药的杀伤力就需要再强一些。
leukaemia * [luːˈkiːmiə]	*n.* 白血病 例 Latency periods for *leukaemia* average about five years. 白血病的潜伏期平均约为五年。
level * [ˈlevl]	*n.* 水平面，水平线；高度，水平；等级 *a.* 平的，水平的；同高度的，同等程度的；平稳的；冷静的 *v.* (使)变平坦 搭 at the level of 在…水平上 例 The noise *levels* at the site can reach 45 decibels. 在这种场所，噪声值可达 45 分贝。
lever [ˈliːvə(r)]	*vt.* (用杠杆)撬动 *n.* 杠杆；施压手段 记 词根记忆：lev(举起) + er → 给我一根杠杆，我能撬动地球 → 撬动；杠杆 例 He *levered* a box open to reveal an antique vase. 他撬开箱子，里面露出一个古董花瓶。 同 tool (*n.* 工具，手段)；means (*n.* 方法，手段，工具) 
lexicographer * [ˌleksɪˈkɒgrəfə(r)]	*n.* 词典编纂者 记 词根记忆：lexico(词) + graph(书写) + er(表人) → 写词典的人 → 词典编纂者 例 The reform has transformed the way *lexicographers* work. 这种改革改变了词典编纂者的工作方式。 派 lexicographical(*a.* 词典编纂的)
liaise * [liˈeɪz]	*vi.* 做联络人；联络，联系 例 He had the right to *liaise* directly with the police while writing the report. 他在写报告的过程中，有权直接与警方联系。
libel [ˈlaɪbl]	*n.* (文字)诽谤，中伤；诽谤性文字 *vt.* 诽谤，中伤，诬蔑 记 词根记忆：lib(文字) + el → 以文字损害名誉 → (文字)诽谤 例 Recently, more and more movie stars are determined to sue the mass media for their *libels*, while they chose to keep silent in the past. 最近，越来越多的电影明星决定指控大众媒体损害其名誉，而在过去他们选择保持沉默。

28

□ leopard □ less than □ lethal □ leukaemia □ level □ lever
□ lexicographer □ liaise □ libel

liberty*
[ˈlɪbəti]

n. 自由，自由权；许可，准许；[常 *pl.*] 过于随便，放肆

搭 take liberties with sth.（尤指对书）任意改动；at liberty to do sth. 有权做…

例 You have ***liberty*** to use all the library facilities. 你们可以使用图书馆里的所有设施。

---

license
[ˈlaɪsns]

n. 许可（证），执照 *vt.* 批准，准许

搭 a driving license 驾驶执照；grant a license 批准许可证

例 They all have gone through a very tough training period to get a special taxi driving ***license***. 他们都经历了一段非常严格的训练才获得了专门的出租车驾驶执照。

---

likelihood
[ˈlaɪklihʊd]

n. 可能；可能性

记 联想记忆：likeli（看作 likely，很可能）+ hood（表性质，名词后缀）→ 可能性

例 The ***likelihood*** that animals living in forests will become extinct is increased when the forests are cut down. 砍伐森林会增加生活在森林中的动物灭绝的可能性。

---

limb
[lɪm]

n. 肢，臂；树枝

记 联想记忆：多喝点维 C 饮料，手臂（limb）有力就能爬（climb）上高山了

例 The body is pretty good at self-repair. A strain to a ***limb***, though painful at the time, generally resolves itself. 身体的自我修复功能很好。扭伤手臂当时虽然有些疼，但一般都能自我消退。

---

lime*
[laɪm]

n. 石灰

记 联想记忆：石灰（lime）需要时间（time）来锤炼

例 Countries use ***lime*** filtering to reduce the amount of chemical pollutant released into the atmosphere. 一些国家用石灰过滤法来减少排放到大气中的化学污染物。

---

limestone*
[ˈlaɪmstəʊn]

n. 石灰石，石灰岩

记 组合词：lime（石灰）+ stone（石头）→ 石灰石，石灰岩

例 The ***limestone*** has to be dug out of the mine and transported to the power station. 石灰石必须从矿山挖出，然后被运往发电站。

---

limitation*
[ˌlɪmɪˈteɪʃn]

n. 限制；局限

记 联想记忆：limit（限制）+ ation → 限制；局限

例 There is no ***limitation*** in the game, and you can use anything you want. 比赛没有什么限制，你可以使用任何你想用的东西。

---

limited*
[ˈlɪmɪtɪd]

a. 有限的

例 Some banks open for a ***limited*** time on Saturdays. 一些银行在周六限时开放。

□ liberty □ license □ likelihood □ limb □ lime □ limestone
□ limitation □ limited

limp *
[lɪmp]

a. 软的；无力的

记 联想记忆：和 limb(*n.* 肢；翼)一起记

例 Some of you may come from cultures that accept *limp* handshakes as normal. 你们有些人的文化习俗可能认为无力的握手很正常。

linen
[ˈlɪnɪn]

n. 亚麻织品；亚麻布

记 联想记忆：line(绳) + n → 亚麻编的绳 → 亚麻织品

例 All bed *linens* and towels are clearly embossed with the name of the manufacturer. 所有的床上用品和毛巾上都清楚地压印了生产商的名字。

linger *
[ˈlɪŋɡə(r)]

vi. 继续逗留；缓慢消失

例 The children *lingered* at the zoo until closing time. 动物园关门时孩子们才恋恋不舍地离去。

linguistic *
[lɪŋˈɡwɪstɪk]

a. 语言的；语言学的

记 词根记忆：lingu(语言) + istic → 语言的

搭 linguistic features 语言特征

例 Industrial training schemes have promoted an increase in *linguistic* and cultural awareness. 工业培训计划促进了语言和文化认知的进步。

link *
[lɪŋk]

n. 环节；联系，纽带 *v.* 连接，联系

记 联想记忆：网络上的"链接"就叫 link → 连接，联系

搭 link A with B 把 A 与 B 联系起来；link between air pollution and heart disease 空气污染与心脏病之间的联系

例 Benefits and hours spent on the job are not necessarily *linked*. 工作所得与所付出的时间不是必然相关的。

liquor
[ˈlɪkə(r)]

n. 烈性酒；含酒精饮料

记 词根记忆：liqu(液体) + or → 烈性酒

例 David got hooked on hard *liquor*. 戴维喝烈酒成瘾。

28

literacy *
[ˈlɪtərəsi]

n. 有文化；有教养；读写能力

记 词根记忆：liter(文字) + acy → 有文化

例 There is a great concern in many nations about declining standards of *literacy* in schools. 学校文化教育标准的降低令许多国家十分担心。

派 illiteracy(*n.* 文盲)

literacy

literal
[ˈlɪtərəl]

a. 照字面的；逐字的

记 词根记忆：liter(文字) + al → 照字面的；逐字的

例 The *literal* meaning of the phrase "say what you like" is "feel free to say anything you want". "say what you like"这个短语的字面意思是"说你想说的，不用拘束"。

派 literally(*ad.* 逐字地；实际上)

同 verbatim(*a.* 逐字的，照字面的)

literate
[ˈlɪtərət]

a. 有读写能力的；有文化的；博学的

记 词根记忆：liter(文字) + ate → 有读写能力的；有文化的

例 Though nearly twenty, Sara was barely *literate*. 尽管快 20 岁了，萨拉却几乎一点读写能力都没有。

□ limp □ linen □ linger □ linguistic □ link □ liquor
□ literacy □ literal □ literate

literature
[ˈlɪtrətʃə(r)]

n. 文学(作品)；文献

记 词根记忆：liter(文字) + ature → 文学(作品)；文献

例 Jane taught English *literature* at my old high school. 简在我的中学母校教英国文学。

litter
[ˈlɪtə(r)]

v. 使乱七八糟；乱扔 *n.* 废弃物，垃圾；一窝幼崽

记 联想记忆：把 little 的“l”乱丢，错拿成“r” → 乱扔

例 Cow pats would *litter* pastures, making grass inedible to cattle and depriving the soil of sunlight. 牛粪会弄脏牧草，使草变得不适合牛群食用，也使土壤得不到阳光的照射。

同 trash(*n.* 垃圾，废物)；rubbish(*n.* 垃圾，废物)

livelihood*
[ˈlaɪvlihʊd]

n. 生活，生计

例 We understand a port as a centre of land-sea exchange, and as a major source of *livelihood* and a major force for cultural mixing. 我们把港口理解为一个海陆交流的中心，人们赖以生存的重要资源，文化融合的主要推动力量。

liver
[ˈlɪvə(r)]

n. 生活者，居住者；肝脏

记 联想记忆：没有肝脏(liver)，人类便无法生存(live)

搭 liver cells 肝细胞

例 Some scientists think that the condition of your *liver* determines how the perfume will smell on you. 一些科学家认为，人体肝脏的健康状况决定香水在人身上的味道。

livestock
[ˈlaɪvstɒk]

n.〈总称〉家畜，牲畜

记 组合词：live(活) + stock(东西) → 活物 → 家畜，牲畜

例 The country banned the import of all ruminant *livestock* from Europe. 该国禁止从欧洲进口任何反刍类家畜。

load
[ləʊd]

v. 装载；装(胶卷、弹药等) *n.* 负荷；装载

例 Our camera could be *loaded* in daylight. 我们的相机可以在日光下装胶卷。

loan*
[ləʊn]

n./vt. 贷款，借

记 发音记忆：“漏” → 账本有漏洞，因为把钱借出去了 → 贷款，借

例 Does this mean I'm not eligible for a student *loan*? 这是不是意味着我不符合学生贷款的条件？

loath
[ləʊθ]

a. 不情愿的，勉强的

搭 nothing loath 很愿意，很高兴

例 We've had a tradition of doctors being fairly powerful and I guess they are pretty *loath* to allow any pretenders to their position to come into it. 我们的固有观念是医生一定非常强势，我想他们一定非常不愿意让任何觊觎者达到他们的地位。

□ literature □ litter □ livelihood □ liver □ livestock □ load
□ loan □ loath

lobby [ˈlɒbi]

v. 游说 *n.* 大厅；游说团

例 They were *lobbying* for stronger environmental protection. 他们在为加强环境保护而进行游说。

locality [ləʊˈkæləti]

n. 位置；地区

记 来自 local(*a.* 地方的)

例 A species may have more chances to survive if the individuals do not gather in a single *locality*. 如果某一物种的个体不集中在某单独地区，那么该物种就有了更多的生存机会。

locate* [ləʊˈkeɪt]

vt. 找到；位于；使坐落于；把…设置在

记 词根记忆：loc(地点) + ate(动词后缀) → 发现地点 → 找到；位于

搭 factory located far away 坐落在远处的工厂

例 The college is *located* at London Road. 这所大学位于伦敦路上。

location [ləʊˈkeɪʃn]

n. 位置，场所；(电影的)外景拍摄地

搭 a good location 好地段；the best/golden location 黄金地段

例 Which picture shows the correct *location* of the administration office? 哪一幅图显示的是管理处的正确位置？

log [lɒg]

n. 原木；航海或飞行日志 *vt.* 记录

例 The earliest peoples probably stored fire by keeping slow burning *logs* alight. 早期的人类很可能是通过让原木保持缓慢燃烧的状态来保存火种的。

logic [ˈlɒdʒɪk]

n. 逻辑；逻辑学

记 词根记忆：log(言语) + ic → 言语正确的 → 逻辑；逻辑学

例 Miranda holds the belief that science and *logic* will unlock the mysteries of the plague. 米兰达坚信科学和逻辑学会解开这一瘟疫的不解之谜。

28

longitude [ˈlɒndʒɪtjuːd]

n. 经度，经线

记 词根记忆：long(长) + itude → 连接南北两极的长线叫经线 → 经度

例 *Longitude* means the distance of an imaginary line from the top to the bottom of the Earth. 经线是人们想象出来的从地球顶部到其底部的距离。

longitudinal* [ˌlɒndʒɪˈtjuːdɪnl]

a. 经度的，经线的；纵的；长度的

记 联想记忆：和 latitudinal(*a.* 纬度的)一起记

例 A *longitudinal* study of nurses working in two Canadian hospitals examined the reasons why nurses took absence from work. 在对两家加拿大医院的护士进行了纵向调查后，他们发现了护士旷工的原因。

long-term* [ˈlɒŋtɜːm]

a. 长期的

例 The smoke may be doing you quite serious *long-term* damage. 吸烟可能会对你的身体造成长期严重的损害。

loop* [luːp]

n. 圈环；环状物；环路；循环 *v.* (使)成环，(使)成圈；成环形运动

例 These tunnels must *loop* around and connect. 这些隧道一定是成环状的而且是相通的。

□ lobby □ locality □ locate □ location □ log □ logic
□ longitude □ longitudinal □ long-term □ loop

loose
[luːs]

a. 松的；散漫的；不精确的

记 联想记忆：这样散漫（loose）下去，时间都丢（lose）了

例 The soil in which coffee is grown must be rich, moist and sufficiently *loose* to allow rapid drainage. 种植咖啡的土壤必须肥沃、潮湿且土质十分疏松以便迅速排水。

派 loosen（*v.* 解开，放松）

lounge*
[laʊndʒ]

vi. 懒洋洋地站（或坐、躺）*n.* 等候室；休息室

例 Some students were used to *lounging* in the dormitory to surf on the Internet at the weekends. 一些学生习惯于周末待在宿舍，懒洋洋地坐着，在网上冲浪。

lower*
[ˈləʊə(r)]

a. 较低的；下面的 *v.* 降低，减少

例 The *lower* end of the valley has become one huge camp site. 这条河谷下游的出口处已经变成了一个巨大的营地。

loyalty*
[ˈlɔɪəlti]

n. 忠诚，忠心

搭 national loyalty 对国家的忠诚

例 In the remote area, family and *loyalties* are still very important. 在偏远地区，家庭和忠诚仍然很重要。

luggage*
[ˈlʌɡɪdʒ]

n. 行李

例 The guys are here to take you and your *luggage* to the cabins. 这些人会带你们去房间，并帮你们把行李搬过去。

lull
[lʌl]

n. 间歇，暂停；平静期

例 In April a slight *lull* ensued, but the volcanologists remained pessimistic about this volcano. 四月接着出现了短暂的平静期，但是火山学家对此并不乐观。

lunar
[ˈluːnə(r)]

a. 月的；月亮的

搭 a lunar eclipse 月蚀

例 The Human Genome Project will take longer to accomplish than the *lunar* missions. 完成人类基因组工程的耗时将比人类成功登月花费的时间还要长。

luxuriant
[lʌɡˈʒʊəriənt]

a. 繁茂的；肥沃的；丰富的

记 词根记忆：lux（光）+ uri + ant(表性质，形容词后缀）→ 光线充足的 → 丰富的

例 WWF predicated early this year that the *luxuriant* Amazon Forest could become a grassy savannah by the end of this century. 世界野生动物基金会今年年初预测，茂盛的亚马孙森林将可能在本世纪末变为大草原。

□ loose □ lounge □ lower □ loyalty □ luggage □ lull
□ lunar □ luxuriant

Word List 29

音频

词根、词缀预习表

lux	光	luxury *a.* 奢华的	**magn**	大	magnify *vt.* 放大
main	手	maintain *vt.* 维修	**maj**	大	major *a.* 主要的
vol	意念	malevolent *a.* 有恶意的	**mand**	命令	mandarin *n.* 官僚
mani	手	manifest *a.* 明显的	**manu**	手	manual *a.* 手工的
mari	海	maritime *a.* 海的	**max**	大，高	maximize *vt.* 最佳化

luxury* [ˈlʌkʃəri]

n. 豪华(品)；奢侈(品) *a.* 奢华的

记 词根记忆：lux(光) + ury → 光彩的 → 奢侈(品)；奢华的

搭 live in luxury/lead a life of luxury 过奢侈的生活

例 He saved some money for *luxuries* such as fine paintings. 他积攒了一些钱，想买一些精品油画之类的奢侈品。

派 luxuriant(*a.* 繁茂的；肥沃的)

machinery* [məˈʃiːnəri]

n. 〈总称〉机械；机构

记 词根记忆：machin(机械) + ery → 机械

搭 industrial machinery 工业机械

例 The new mayor reformed the *machinery* of the government. 新市长对市政府机构进行了改革。

magic [ˈmædʒɪk]

n. 魔法，法术；魅力，魔力 *a.* 有魔力的，神奇的

记 联想记忆：mag(看作 magnet，磁铁) + ic → 像磁铁一样吸引人 → 魅力

例 There's no real *magic* in the world. 这世界上没有真正的魔法。

magma [ˈmæɡmə]

n. 岩浆

例 By collecting elements in rocks, Norman created artificial *magma* in his lab. 为收集岩石中的元素，诺曼在他的实验室里制造出了人工岩浆。

magnet [ˈmæɡnət]

n. 磁铁，磁石；磁体；有吸引力的人或物

例 Paris has always played a role of a *magnet* to attract people to seek romance and true love. 巴黎一直扮演着一个磁铁一样的角色，不断吸引着想要寻找浪漫和真爱的人们。

□ luxury □ machinery □ magic □ magma □ magnet

magnetic
[mæg'netɪk]

a. 磁的，有磁性的；有吸引力的

搭 magnetic fields 磁场；a magnetic needle 磁针

例 The electric and ***magnetic*** fields are formed due to a passing wave oscillating at a regular frequency. 电场和磁场是由振波以固定频率振荡而形成的。

magnificent**
[mæg'nɪfɪsnt]

a. 壮丽的，宏伟的，华丽的；高尚的

记 词根记忆：magn(大) + if(使…) + ic + ent(形容词后缀) → 宏伟的，壮丽的

搭 magnificent performance 出色表演

例 The garage around the corner contains the ***magnificent*** old Rolls-Royce which used to belong to George. 街角的车库里停着一辆漂亮的老式劳斯莱斯，它曾经是乔治的。

派 magnificently(*ad.* 壮观地；宏伟地)；magnificence(*n.* 壮丽，宏伟；华丽，富丽堂皇)

magnify
['mægnɪfaɪ]

vt. 放大，扩大

记 词根记忆：magn(大) + ify(使…) → 使…大 → 放大，扩大

例 This microscope can ***magnify*** an object 100, 000 times. 这个显微镜可将物体放大 10 万倍。

magnitude
['mægnɪtjuːd]

n. 广大，巨大；重要，重要性；星体的亮度

记 词根记忆：magn(大) + itude(表状态，名词后缀) → 广大，巨大

例 Stargazers were struck by the uncommon ***magnitude*** of the newly discovered comet. 这颗新发现的彗星尤其亮，令天文学家们非常吃惊。

mainly**
['meɪnli]

ad. 大体上，主要地

例 The weather is ***mainly*** cold and wet in England. 英格兰的天气以阴冷为主。

mainstream**
['meɪnstriːm]

n. 主要倾向，主要趋势，主流；主流派爵士乐(介乎传统与现代之间者)

a. 主流的

记 组合词：main(主要的) + stream(溪，流) → 主流，主要趋势，主要倾向

例 His radical views place him outside the ***mainstream*** of American politics. 他的激进观点使他脱离了美国政治的主流。

maintain**
[meɪn'teɪn]

vt. 维持，保持；维修，保养；坚持，主张；赡养，负担

记 词根记忆：main(手) + tain(拿住) → 用手牢牢握住 → 维持，保持

搭 maintain world peace 维护世界和平；maintain one's health 保持健康

例 Health promotion programs and policies would help people ***maintain*** healthy behaviors and lifestyles. 健康促进计划和方针能够帮助人们保持健康的生活习惯和生活方式。

maintenance**
['meɪntənəns]

n. 维持；保养；抚养费

搭 the maintenance of an automobile 汽车的保养

例 The school pays for heating and the ***maintenance*** of the buildings. 学校负担这些大楼的取暖和维修费用。

□ magnetic □ magnificent □ magnify □ magnitude □ mainly □ mainstream
□ maintain □ maintenance

major* ['meɪdʒə(r)]

a. 主要的 *n.* 专业(学生) *vi.* 主修，专攻

记 词根记忆：maj(大) + or → 较大的 → 主要的

例 In Mexico city, vehicle pollution is a *major* health hazard. 在墨西哥城，交通污染是人们健康的一个主要威胁。

majority* [mə'dʒɒrətɪ]

n. 多数，大多数

例 This treatment is not available in the vast *majority* of hospitals. 绝大部分医院都不提供这种治疗。

malevolent [mə'levələnt]

a. 有恶意的；恶毒的

记 词根记忆：male(恶) + vol(意念) + ent → 有恶意的；恶毒的

例 Stricken by a series of failures, he was *malevolent* toward those who were successful. 经过一连串失败的打击，他对那些成功人士充满了敌意。

mall [mɔːl]

n. 购物中心

例 Underground shopping *malls* are already common in China. 地下购物中心在中国已经极为普遍。

malleable ['mæliəbl]

a. 可塑的；易改变的

记 词根记忆：malle(锤子) + able → 可锤打的 → 易改变的

例 When dropped on the floor, *malleable* glass would bend rather than shatter into bits. 韧性玻璃掉在地上后，只会折弯而不会打碎。

malt [mɔːlt]

n. 麦芽；麦芽酒 *v.* 把…制成麦芽；(谷物)变成麦芽

例 A bottle of 15-year-old *malt* whisky is taken out by the hostess to entertain her guests. 女主人拿出一瓶 15 年陈酿的麦芽威士忌招待客人。

maltreat [ˌmæl'triːt]

vt. 虐待

记 词根记忆：mal(坏) + treat(=tract 拉) → 往坏处拉 → 虐待

例 It is necessary for the government to make relevant laws to punish people who *maltreat* domestic animals. 政府有必要制定相关法律来惩罚虐待家养动物的人。

29

mammal* ['mæml]

n. 哺乳动物

记 联想记忆：mamma(妈妈) + l → 靠吃妈妈的奶长大 → 哺乳动物

搭 marine mammals 海洋哺乳动物

例 The insect lives on small *mammals* and birds. 这种小虫子寄生在小型哺乳动物和鸟类身上。

派 mammalian(*a.* 哺乳动物的，哺乳纲的)

management* ['mænɪdʒmənt]

n. 管理(部门、人员)；处理

记 联想记忆：man(人) + age(年纪) + ment → 到了一定年龄，富有经验的人适合做管理人员 → 管理(部门、人员)

例 Why do you think that some changes have come about in the national revenue *management*? 你为什么会认为国家税收管理发生了改变呢？

managerial [ˌmænə'dʒɪəriəl]

a. 经理的；管理的，经营的

搭 managerial talent 管理人才

例 Such systems emphasize the *managerial* communications function and can be operated easily. 这些系统强调管理通信功能，便于操作。

□ major □ majority □ malevolent □ mall □ malleable □ malt
□ maltreat □ mammal □ management □ managerial

mandarin* [ˈmændərɪn]

n. 橘子；达官贵人，官僚；[M-] 普通话

记 词根记忆：mand(命令) + arin → 命令全国都要讲的 → 普通话

例 Which language would you like to learn? We offer French, Italian, *Mandarin*, Spanish and Portuguese. 您想学习哪种语言？我们提供法语、意大利语、普通话、西班牙语和葡萄牙语的学习。

manifest* [ˈmænɪfest]

a. 明显的 *vt.* 表明，显示 *n.* 货物清单

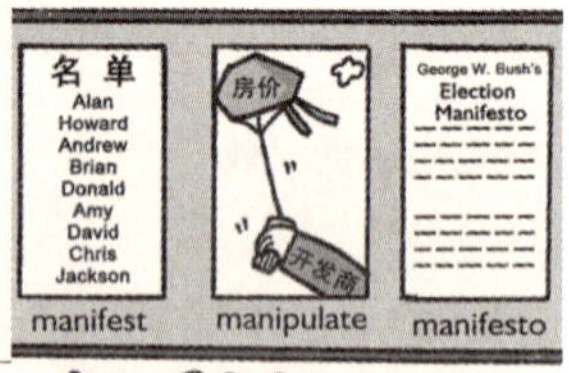

记 词根记忆：mani(手) + fest(打) → 用手打人，怒意很明显 → 明显的

例 The symptoms of the disease *manifested* themselves ten days later. 这种疾病的症状十天后表现了出来。

manipulate [məˈnɪpjuleɪt]

vt. 应付，处理；操纵，控制；影响

记 词根记忆：mani (手) + pul (拉) + ate → 用手拉 → 处理；操纵

例 Computers are very efficient at *manipulating* information. 计算机在处理信息方面效率极高。

同 handle(*v.* 操作，操纵)；manoeuvre(*v.* 操纵)

manipulative [məˈnɪpjələtɪv]

a. 操纵别人的；老于世故的

例 To handle with negative experiences, a child learns *manipulative* techniques that are hard to refrain later in life or even become set patterns. 为了应对这些负面体验，儿童学会了控制自己和他人，这种操纵技巧在日后的生活中很难被戒除，甚至会变成既定的行为模式。

manoeuvre [məˈnuːvə(r)]

n. 移动；策略，手段 *v.* 移动，转动；操纵，控制

例 We will be asked to perform some standard *manoeuvres* during the driving test. 驾照考试会要求我们做一些标准的操作。

manor [ˈmænə(r)]

n. 领地，庄园

记 联想记忆：man(人) + or(表物) → 人靠自己的力量建立起来的 → 领地

例 Within the grounds are a Georgian mansion, an Elizabethan dairy and the tower of a medieval *manor*. 在这片地区，有一所乔治时期的住宅，一个伊丽莎白时期的牛奶场，以及一座中世纪庄园的塔楼。

mansion [ˈmænʃn]

n. 大厦；(豪华的)宅邸

记 联想记忆：man(人) + sion → 有钱人住的地方 → 宅邸

例 Mary and her family lived in a *mansion*. 玛丽一家住在一座大房子里。

mantle [ˈmæntl]

n. 披风，斗篷；覆盖物；(煤气灯)纱罩；【解】外层；包膜；外表；(水库的)槽；【地】地幔 *vt.* 用斗篷盖；覆盖

例 Magma surged into the volcano from the Earth's *mantle*. 岩浆从地球的地幔涌入火山。

manual* [ˈmænjuəl]

n. 手册，指南 *a.* 手的，手工的，体力的

记 词根记忆：manu(手) + al(形容词后缀) → 手工的

搭 manual workers 手工劳动者；manual labour 体力劳动

例 You should read the *manual* instruction carefully before fixing the air-conditioner. 安装空调前你应该仔细阅读指导手册。

派 manually(*ad.* 用手地，手工地)

□ mandarin □ manifest □ manipulate □ manipulative □ manoeuvre □ manor
□ mansion □ mantle □ manual

manufacture [ˌmænjuˈfæktʃə(r)]	*vt.* 大量制造，成批生产 *n.* 大量制造；工业品 记 词根记忆：manu(手) + fact(制作，做) + ure → 用手制作 → 大量制造 例 Many automobile makers no longer *manufacture* cheap models. 很多汽车制造商不再生产低价位车型。
manufacturer [ˌmænjuˈfæktʃərə(r)]	*n.* 制造商，制造厂，生产者 记 词根记忆：manu(手) + fact(制作，做) + ure(表动作) + er(表人) → 用手做事的人 → 生产者 例 *Manufacturers* must sell these cleaner cars. 制造商必须卖掉这些清洁车。
marble [ˈmɑːbl]	*n.* 大理石；弹子；[*pl.*] 弹子游戏 记 联想记忆：mar(看作 March，三月) + ble → 大理三月好风光哎 → 大理石 例 In this game, you can insert a *marble* into a small hole to open the door. 在这个游戏中，你可以往一个小洞里塞入一颗弹子来把门打开。
margin* [ˈmɑːdʒɪn]	*n.* 差额，差距；页边空白；边缘；余地；幅度 *v.* 加旁注于；加边于 记 词根记忆：mar(是 mark 的变体，记号、符号) + in → 记号常标于书页空白处 → 页边空白 搭 by a small margin 以极小优势 例 I've made some suggestions in the *margins*. 我在页边空白处写了一些建议。
marginally* [ˈmɑːdʒɪnəli]	*ad.* 稍微，些微 例 Mother thought the products were *marginally* more expensive that she will not afford it this time. 妈妈认为这些商品稍有点贵，因此她决定这次不买。
maritime [ˈmærɪtaɪm]	*a.* 海的，海事的；海运的 记 联想记忆：mari(海) + time(时间) → 海上的时间 → 海的，海事的 搭 a maritime museum 海洋博物馆 例 You can call or send a message to someone aboard a ship by using our *Maritime* Services. 你可以通过我们的海运服务给船上的人打电话或发信息。
marker [ˈmɑːkə(r)]	*n.* 标记，标志 例 Travel is a *marker* of status in modern societies. 旅行是现代社会中一种身份标志。
marketplace* [ˈmɑːkɪtpleɪs]	*n.* 市场，集市 记 组合词：market(市场) + place(地点，场所) → 市场 例 Japan is the world's biggest *marketplace* for perfume. 日本是世界上最大的香水市场。
marsh [mɑːʃ]	*n.* 沼泽；湿地 记 联想记忆：mars(火星) + h → 火星上可能会有沼泽 → 沼泽 例 When they tried to cross the *marsh*, their cannons sank into the soft ground. 当他们试图穿过湿地时，他们的大炮陷进了松软的地面。

□ manufacture □ manufacturer □ marble □ margin □ marginally □ maritime
□ marker □ marketplace □ marsh

marsupial *
[mɑːˈsuːpiəl]

n./a. 有袋动物(的)

记 发音记忆："马修皮" → 马多修了一张皮，动物多了一张皮做口袋 → 有袋动物(的)

搭 marsupial animals 有袋动物

例 Arboreal *marsupials* may not recover to pre-logging densities. 树袋动物的密度可能无法恢复到伐木以前了。

marvellous *
[ˈmɑːvələs]

n. 令人惊奇的；奇特的，非凡的；奇迹般的，不可思议的；绝妙的

记 发音记忆："马虎了事" → 凡事只是马虎了事就不可能取得非凡的成就 → 非凡的

例 We'll come to a picture gallery where we've got a *marvellous* collection of paintings all by Australian artists. 接下来我们会来到一个画廊，这里有绝好的画作收藏，全都出自澳大利亚画家之手。

mass
[mæs]

a. 大量的 *n.* 团，众多；【物】质量；[*pl.*] 群众，民众 *v.* 聚集

记 联想记忆：和 less(*a.* 少的)一起记

搭 mass production 大规模生产

例 *Mass* use of motor vehicles has killed or injured millions of people. 机动车的大量使用已造成数百万人伤亡。

massive
[ˈmæsɪv]

a. 大而重的，厚实的，粗大的；大量的，大规模的

例 In Tokyo builders are planning a *massive* underground city to be begun in the next decade. 在东京，建筑者正计划在接下来的十年里建造一个大型地下城。

MasterCard *
[ˈmɑːstə(r)kɑːd]

n. 万事达信用卡

例 Have you got a Visa card or a *MasterCard*? 你有维萨卡或者万事达信用卡吗?

mastery *
[ˈmɑːstəri]

n. 精通，熟练；控制

记 联想记忆：master(精通) + y → 精通，熟练

例 A frequent change of roles is the training requisite for a *mastery* of the actor's art. 频繁地转换角色是掌握表演技能的必要训练。

match *
[mætʃ]

n. 火柴；比赛，竞赛；对手，敌手 *v.* 匹配，相称

搭 a football match 足球赛；man of the match 比赛中最优秀选手；home match 主场比赛；away match 客场比赛；match against/with 与…比赛

例 Why do people spend their money on a football *match*? 为什么人们会花钱看足球赛呢?

派 matchless(*a.* 无比的，无敌的)

mate *
[meɪt]

v. 交配，配种 *n.* 配偶；伙伴；(商船上的)大副

记 联想记忆：配偶(mate)相互为对方铺垫子(mat)

例 The scientist observed the rabbits as they *mated*. 科学家观察兔子交配。

material *
[məˈtɪəriəl]

n. 材料；素材 *a.* 物质的；重要的

例 Glass is the great building *material* of the future. 在未来，玻璃是主要的建筑材料。

□ marsupial □ marvellous □ mass □ massive □ MasterCard □ mastery
□ match □ mate □ material

materialistic* [məˌtɪəriəˈlɪstɪk]	*a.* 唯物主义的；物质享乐主义的，贪图享乐的 记 来自 material（*a.* 物质的） 例 Modern society is often called *materialistic*. 现代社会通常被称为是物质享乐主义的。
maternal [məˈtɜːnl]	*a.* 母亲的；母系的 记 词根记忆：mater（母亲）+ nal → 母亲的；母系的 搭 maternal instinct 母性本能 例 Susan's *maternal* grandmother is still alive. 苏珊的外祖母还健在。
mattress* [ˈmætrəs]	*n.* 床垫 例 A good *mattress* is a wise investment for people who want to avoid headaches. 对那些想避免头疼的人来说，买一张好床垫不失为一项聪明的投资。
mature [məˈtʃʊə(r)]	*a.* 成熟的；深思熟虑的 *v.* (使)成熟 记 联想记忆：自然（nature）中的 n 更换成 m 就是成熟的（mature） 搭 mature students 成年学生；on mature consideration/reflection 经过审慎考虑，经过深思熟虑 例 Jane is very *mature* for her age. 简年龄不大，却很成熟。
maturity* [məˈtʃʊərəti]	*n.* 成熟；完善，完备，准备就绪；到期(应付款) 搭 at maturity 成熟；full maturity 完全成熟 例 Almost all the fertilized eggs will hatch out into chicks which will in turn reach *maturity*. 几乎所有受精蛋都会孵出幼鸟，然后幼鸟就会慢慢成熟。
maximise* [ˈmæksɪmaɪz]	*vt.* 使增加到最大限度，最佳化；充分利用 记 词根记忆：max（大，高）+ im + ise（使…）→ 使增至最大限度 → 最佳化 例 Some airlines have cancelled less popular routes in an effort to *maximise* profits. 为实现利润最大化，一些航空公司取消了不太火爆的路线。
maximum* [ˈmæksɪməm]	*n.* 最大量，极限 *a.* 最大的，最高的 记 词根记忆：max（大，高）+ imum → 最大的，最高的 例 Students on a visitor visa or work permit may study for a *maximum* of 3 months. 持旅行签证或工作许可证的学生最多可有三个月的学习时间。
meadow [ˈmedəʊ]	*n.* 草地 记 联想记忆：mea（看作 meal，美餐）+ dow（看作 cow，母牛）→ 母牛在草地上吃草，享受美餐 → 草地 例 In order to protect the ecosystem, the country determined to convert 11 percent of its cropped land to *meadow* or forest. 为了保护生态系统，该国决定将 11%的农耕地变为草地或森林。
meagre [ˈmiːgə(r)]	*a.* 少量的，粗劣的 例 His *meagre* salary couldn't afford the basic consumption in the time of inflation. 通货膨胀期间，他那点可怜巴巴的工资不足以维持最基本的开销。
meaningful* [ˈmiːnɪŋfl]	*a.* 有目的的；有意义的 记 联想记忆：meaning（含义，意义）+ ful → 有目的的，有意义的 搭 a meaningful experience 一次有意义的经历

29

□ materialistic □ maternal □ mattress □ mature □ maturity □ maximise
□ maximum □ meadow □ meagre □ meaningful

meantime [ˈmiːntaim]	*n.* 其时 *ad.* 同时，当时 搭 in the meantime 与此同时 例 The country was urgently calling for peace while in the *meantime* secretly doing nuclear tests. 该国急切呼吁和平，同时却又秘密进行核试验。
meanwhile [ˈmiːnwaɪl]	*ad.* 与此同时 记 组合词：mean(意味) + while(当…时) → 就在那个时候 → 与此同时 例 Tina's due to arrive on Sunday. *Meanwhile*, what do we do? 蒂娜定于星期天到，这期间我们做什么呢?
mechanic [məˈkænɪk]	*n.* 机修工；[-s] 力学，机械学 记 词根记忆：mechan(机械) + ic → 机修工 例 The article gave the readers a summary of the life of a *mechanic*. 这篇文章向读者简略介绍了一个机修工的生活。
mechanical* [məˈkænɪkl]	*a.* 机械的，机械制造的；呆板的；习惯性的；体力的 搭 mechanical labour 体力劳动 例 Practise that and stop until it becomes *mechanical*. 坚持练习，直到习惯成自然。
mechanism [ˈmekənɪzəm]	*n.* 机械装置；机制，机理；办法 例 Tom replaced the button *mechanism* in the machine. 汤姆换掉了机器上的按钮装置。
medical* [ˈmedɪkl]	*a.* 医学的，医疗的；内科的 搭 medical centre 医疗中心；medical science 医学；medical service 医疗服务；family medical history 家族病史 例 The injured students required emergent *medical* attention. 那些受伤的学生急需医疗护理。
medication* [ˌmedɪˈkeɪʃn]	*n.* 药；药物 记 词根记忆：med(医疗，治疗) + ication → 药；药物 搭 be on medication for sth. 因…而吃药 例 The doctor writes what *medication* you need on the prescription. 医生在处方上写了你需要吃的药。
medieval [ˌmediˈiːvl]	*a.* 中世纪的；中古(时代)的 记 词根记忆：medi(中间) + ev(时代) + al → 中世纪的 搭 medieval Italy 中世纪的意大利 例 The tourists were shut in the tower of a *medieval* manor by the kidnappers. 游客被绑架者关在一座中世纪庄园的塔楼里。
mediocre* [ˌmiːdiˈəʊkə(r)]	*a.* 平庸的，平凡的 记 词根记忆：medi(中间) + ocre → 中间状态 → 平庸的，平凡的 搭 a mediocre writer 平庸的作家 例 I thought the play was only *mediocre*. 我认为这部戏剧只是平庸之作。
Mediterranean* [ˌmedɪtəˈreɪniən]	*a.* 地中海(式)的 *n.* 地中海 记 词根记忆：medi(中间) + terr(地球，土地) + anean → 在地球中间的 → 地中海；地中海(式)的 例 We enjoyed such *Mediterranean* climate very much. 这种地中海式气候让我们很享受。

□ meantime □ meanwhile □ mechanic □ mechanical □ mechanism □ medical
□ medication □ medieval □ mediocre □ Mediterranean

medium [ˈmiːdiəm]	*n.* 媒质，媒介；工具，手段；(细菌等的)生存环境 *a.* 中等的；平均的 记 词根记忆：medi(中间) + um → 中间的 → 中等的；媒介 搭 medium sized 中等尺寸的 例 Mary uses the ***medium*** of poetry to make her ideas known. 玛丽使用诗歌来表达思想。// Tom got a job in a ***medium***-sized firm. 汤姆在一家中等规模的公司里找到了一份工作。
megacity [ˈmegəsɪti]	*n.* (人口超过 100 万的)大城市 例 For any ***megacity*** wishing to remain a sustainable social and economic development, healthy environment is a must. 对于任何一个想保持社会和经济可持续发展状态的大城市来说，良好的城市环境都是必不可少的。
melatonin* [ˌmeləˈtəʊnɪn]	*n.* 褪黑激素 例 Some scientists think that ***melatonin*** plays an important part in the seasonal behaviour of certain animals. 一些科学家认为褪黑激素对某些动物的季节性行为有着重要作用。
melt [melt]	*v.* (使)融化；(使)消散 例 Salt helps ***melt*** ice. 盐可以使冰融化。 派 melting(*a.* 熔化的；融化的)
membership [ˈmembəʃɪp]	*n.* 会员身份；全体会员 例 You can pay the ***membership*** fee by cheque. 你可以用支票交会员费。

Growth and change are the law of all life. Yesterday's answers are inadequate for today's problems—just as the solutions of today will not fill the needs of tomorrow.

生长与变化是一切生命的法则。昨日的答案不适用于今日的问题——正如今天的方法不能解决明天的需求。

——美国总统 罗斯福 .F. (Franklin Roosevelt, American President)

Word List 30

音 频

词根、词缀预习表

memor	记忆	memorable *a.* 容易记住的	**ment**	思想，心智	mental *a.* 心理的，精神的
merg	沉没	merge *v.* 结合	**phor**	带来	metaphor *n.* 隐喻
meteor	陨石；天气	meteorology *n.* 气象学	**micro-**	微小的	microcosm *n.* 微观世界
scop	看，视野	microscope *n.* 显微镜	**migr**	迁移	migrant *n.* 移居者
milit	打架	militant *a.* 好战的	**mim**	模仿	mime *v.* 模拟，模仿

memorable* [ˈmemərəbl]

a. 容易记住的；难忘的

记 词根记忆：memor(记忆) + able(可…的) → 可记忆的 → 容易记住的

搭 a memorable experience 一次难忘的经历

例 The trip to that village was *memorable* for us. 去那个村庄旅游是我们难忘的一次经历。

memorandum [ˌmeməˈrændəm]

n. 备忘录，摘要

记 词根记忆：memor(记忆) + and + um → 辅助记忆的东西 → 备忘录

memorise [ˈmeməraɪz]

vt. 记住，熟记

例 Before sailing to the sea, prudent navigators will study the sailing directions, and *memorise* lighthouse locations to prepare themselves for any conditions they might encounter. 出海前，细心的航海员会研究航海说明并记住灯塔的位置，为他们可能会遇到的任何情况作准备。

menace* [ˈmenəs]

n. 威胁；危险的人(或物) *vt.* 威胁到，危及

记 联想记忆：men(人) + ace(看作 race，赛跑) → 和你赛跑的人对你构成了威胁 → 威胁

搭 a menace to sb./sth. 对…的威胁

例 Let's look at some of the reasons why back pain is developing into such a unique *menace*. 让我们来看一看为什么背疼会演变成一种顽疾。

同 threat(*n.* 威胁，恐吓)；threaten(*v.* 威胁，恐吓)

mental* [ˈmentl]

a. 心理的，精神的；智力的

记 词根记忆：ment(思想，心智) + al → 心理的，精神的

例 Health is a complete state of physical, *mental* and social well-being. 健康是生理、心理以及交际情况的一种整体良好状态。

mention* [ˈmenʃn]

n./v. 提及，说起

搭 not to mention 更不用说；更不必说

例 He *mentioned* in his letter that he might be moving abroad. 他在信中提到他可能要移居国外。

mentor [ˈmentɔː(r)]	*n.* 导师；顾问，指导者 记 词根记忆：ment(思想，心智) + or(表人) → 在精神上影响他人的人 → 导师；顾问 例 Every great leader who has created great achievement has a *mentor*, who can advise, help and point him to success. 每一个创造了巨大成就的伟大领袖都有一个能够给他建议、帮助他并指引他走向成功的导师。
merchandising* [ˈmɜːtʃəndaɪzɪŋ]	*n.* 销售规划 例 Their activities of *merchandising* did not provide sufficient funds for them. 他们的销售活动并没有给他们带来足够的资金。
mercury [ˈmɜːkjəri]	*n.* 水银 例 The *mercury* in the thermometer rose to 35°C yesterday. 昨天温度计的水银柱升到了 35 摄氏度。
mere [mɪə(r)]	*a.* 仅仅的；纯粹的 记 联想记忆：仅仅(mere)在这儿(here)徘徊是不行的 例 *Mere* denunciation will not solve this great problem. 仅仅靠谴责是解决不了这个大问题的。
merely* [ˈmɪəli]	*ad.* 仅仅，只不过 例 You don't have to be present. *Merely* send a letter of explanation. 你不一定非出席不可，只要寄封信去说明一下就可以了。// I meant it *merely* as a joke. 我只不过是开个玩笑。
merge [mɜːdʒ]	*v.* (使)结合 记 词根记忆：merg(沉没) + e → 沉没其中 → 结合 例 Fact and fiction *merge* together in his latest thriller. 在他最新的惊险小说中，真实和虚构相互交织。
mess [mes]	*n.* 凌乱 *v.* 弄糟，搞乱 搭 make a mess 弄乱，搞砸 例 The celebration locale is in a *mess*. 欢庆场地一片狼藉。// The wind *messed* up our hair. 风弄乱了我们的头发。
metaphor* [ˈmetəfə(r)]	*n.* 隐喻，暗喻 记 词根记忆：meta(变化) + phor(带来) → 以意义有变化的方式表达 → 隐喻 例 In literature the dove is often a *metaphor* for peace. 在文学作品中鸽子通常是和平的象征。
metaphorical [ˌmetəˈfɒrɪkl]	*a.* 隐喻的 例 The word has a literal as well as a *metaphorical* meaning. 这个单词有字面意思，也有隐喻义。
meteorology* [ˌmiːtiəˈrɒlədʒi]	*n.* 气象学 记 词根记忆：meteor（陨石；天气）+ ology（…学）→ 研究天气的学科 → 气象学 例 The diagram shows how the Australian Bureau of *Meteorology* collects up-to-the-minute information on the weather. 该图表显示了澳大利亚气象局如何收集最新天气信息。
methane* [ˈmiːθeɪn]	*n.* 甲烷，沼气

30

□ mentor □ merchandising □ mercury □ mere □ merely □ merge
□ mess □ metaphor □ metaphorical □ meteorology □ methane

metro* [ˈmetrəʊ]	*n.* 地下铁路 例 The cinema is in the main square, just two minutes' walk from the *Metro*. 电影院位于主广场，离地铁仅仅两分钟的步行路程。
microbiology* [ˌmaɪkrəʊbaɪˈɒlədʒi]	*n.* 微生物学 记 组合词：micro(微小的) + biology(生物学) → 微生物学 例 The *microbiology* lecture goes for one hour, and then it's followed immediately by a lab. 微生物课持续一个小时，然后学生们直接进实验室做实验。
microcosm* [ˈmaɪkrəʊkɒzəm]	*n.* 微观世界；缩影 记 词根记忆：micro(微小的) + cosm(宇宙，世界) → 微观世界 例 Malaysia's universities have always been a *microcosm* of Malaysian society. 马来西亚的大学往往是整个马来西亚社会的缩影。
microprocessor* [ˌmaɪkrəʊˈprəʊsesə(r)]	*n.* 微处理器 记 组合词：micro(微小的) + processor(处理器) → 微处理器 例 Now not even the humblest household object is made without a *microprocessor*. 现在即便是最简陋的家居用品在制造时也离不开微处理器。
microscope [ˈmaɪkrəskəʊp]	*n.* 显微镜 记 词根记忆：micro(微小的) + scop(看，视野) + e → 用来看很小的东西 → 显微镜 例 A *microscope* can magnify these germs. 显微镜可以将这些细菌放大。
midst [mɪdst]	*n.* 中间 记 词根记忆：mid(中间的) + st → 中间 例 In the *midst* of the glade were several huts. 森林空地的中间有几间小木屋。
migrant [ˈmaɪgrənt]	*n.* 移居者，移民；迁移动物，候鸟 记 词根记忆：migr(迁移) + ant(表人或物) → 移居者；迁移动物 例 The *migrants* fly to the south before winter. 候鸟在冬天来临之前飞往南方。
migrate* [maɪˈgreɪt]	*v.* (候鸟等)迁徙；移居 记 词根记忆：migr(迁移) + ate → 迁徙；移居 例 About half the nation's 2,000 beekeepers *migrate* north to find more flowers for their bees. 在这个国家的 2000 个养蜂人中，约半数人为给蜜蜂找到更多的花而北迁。 同 emigrate(*v.* 移居国外)；immigrate(*v.* 移居入境)
migration* [maɪˈgreɪʃn]	*n.* 迁徙，移居，移民 记 来自 migrate(*v.* 迁移) 搭 language migration 语言迁徙 例 The *migration* patterns of animals are related to the number of the kind of animal. 动物的迁徙方式与其数量相关。

□ metro □ microbiology □ microcosm □ microprocessor □ microscope □ midst
□ migrant □ migrate □ migration

migratory* [ˈmaɪgrətri]	*a.* 迁徙的，移居的；流动的，游牧的 记 词根记忆：migr(迁移) + at + ory → 迁徙的；流动的 搭 migratory birds 候鸟 例 There are lots of birds in this national forest park, both resident and *migratory*. 这个国家森林公园里有很多鸟，有留鸟也有候鸟。
mild* [maɪld]	*a.* 温柔的；温和的；轻微的 记 联想记忆：温柔的(mild)mm 有时也野蛮(wild) 例 She is the *mildest* woman you could wish to meet. 她是你想见到的最温柔的女人。// The thief just got a *mild* punishment. 小偷只受到了轻微的惩罚。
milestone [ˈmaɪlstəʊn]	*n.* 里程碑；转折点 记 组合词：mile(英里) + stone(石头) → 标记英里数的石头 → 里程碑 例 This theory represents one of the great *milestones* in the history of scientific thought. 这一理论是科学思想史上一座伟大的里程碑。
militant* [ˈmɪlɪtənt]	*a.* 好战的，好斗的；激进的 *n.* 好斗的人，激进分子 记 词根记忆：milit(打架) + ant → 好战的 例 One *militant* group warned the government to take notice. 一个激进的团体警告政府要注意。 同 combative(*a.* 好斗的)；agitator(*n.* 鼓动者，煽动者)；firebrand(*n.* 引起(社会或政治)动乱的人) 反 dove(*n.* 主和派人物)；pacifist(*n.* 和平主义者，反战主义者)
military [ˈmɪlətri]	*a.* 军事的 *n.* [the ~] 军队 记 词根记忆：milit(打架) + ary → 军事的 例 The gizmo is called the Army Flashlight because it was developed initially for *military* use. 这种小发明被称为"军队闪光灯"，因为它最初是为军事目的研制的。
millennium [mɪˈleniəm]	*n.* 一千年，千禧年；(未来的)太平盛世 记 词根记忆：mill(千) + enn(年) + ium → 一千年 例 *Millennium* Bug was really bothering the scientists in 1990s, when the electron technology hadn't been developed as fast as today. 20 世纪 90 年代，电子技术的发展没有现在这样迅速，"千年虫"问题在当时确实困扰着科学家们。
mime* [maɪm]	*v.* 模拟，模仿 *n.* 哑剧表演；哑剧演员 记 词根记忆：mim(模仿) + e → 模拟，模仿 例 The naughty boy *mimed* his old grandfather. 这个淘气的孩子模仿他的老爷爷。// Several French *mime* artists will give some lectures this afternoon. 几位法国哑剧表演艺术家将在今天下午做几场讲座。
mineral [ˈmɪnərəl]	*n.* 矿物，矿石 记 联想记忆：mine(矿) + ral → 矿物，矿石 例 Topaz is a hard and transparent *mineral*. 黄玉是一种坚硬透明的矿石。

30

□ migratory □ mild □ milestone □ militant □ military □ millennium
□ mime □ mineral

mingle [ˈmɪŋgl]

v. (使)混合,(使)联结;相往来;混杂其中

记 联想记忆:和 single(*a.* 单一的)一起记

例 The waters of the two streams *mingled* to form one river. 两股溪水汇成了一条河流。

minimal [ˈmɪnɪməl]

a. 最小的,最低限度的

记 词根记忆:min(小) + imal → 最小的

例 The new couple stayed with their parents, so their expenses were *minimal*. 这对新婚夫妇和父母住在一起,所以他们的花费最少。

反 maximum(*a.* 最大的,最大限度的)

minimise [ˈmɪnɪmaɪz]

vt. 使减到最低限度;最小化

记 词根记忆:min(小) + im + ise(使…) → 使变成最小 → 最小化

例 The adoption of clean energy will help *minimise* air pollution. 采用清洁能源有助于将空气污染降到最低程度。

minimum [ˈmɪnɪməm]

n. 最小值,最低限度 *a.* 最低的,最小的

记 词根记忆:min(小) + imum → 最小的

例 The *minimum* speed on the freeway is 45 kms per hour. 这条高速公路上的最低时速为 45 公里。

minister* [ˈmɪnɪstə(r)]

n. 部长;外交使节;牧师

例 The Prime *Minister* has promised to help the drought-stricken farmers in the northern part of the country. 首相已经承诺援助本国北部地区遭受旱灾袭击的农民。

ministry [ˈmɪnɪstri]

n. (政府的)部

例 People can call the *Ministry* of Justice for free legal advice. 人们可以打电话到司法部进行免费的法律咨询。

minority* [maɪˈnɒrəti]

n. 少数;少数民族

记 词根记忆:min(小) + or + ity(名词后缀) → 少数

例 Human resources are in the *minority* as much of the work is done by automated machines controlled by computers. 许多工作被电脑控制的自动化机器完成,人力就占少数了。

miracle [ˈmɪrəkl]

n. 奇迹;奇事

记 词根记忆:mir(惊奇) + acle(表物) → 奇迹;奇事

例 The doctor said that Mary's recovery was a *miracle*. 医生说玛丽能够康复是个奇迹。

miscellaneous [ˌmɪsəˈleɪniəs]

a. 各种各样的;混杂的

记 联想记忆:miscellane(a)(杂记,杂录) + ous → 各种各样的;混杂的

搭 miscellaneous costs 杂费

例 A little child's pockets are likely to contain a *miscellaneous* collection of objects. 小孩子的口袋里往往装有各种各样的东西。

misconception [ˌmɪskənˈsepʃn]

n. 误解,错误想法

例 Some people often have a *misconception* that keeping in good shape need to be on a diet or even not to eat anything; in fact this idea is wrong. 有些人经常有种错误的想法,认为好身材需要节食甚至靠不吃东西来保持,事实上这个想法是错误的。

□ mingle □ minimal □ minimise □ minimum □ minister □ ministry
□ minority □ miracle □ miscellaneous □ misconception

miserable [ˈmɪzrəbl]

a. 悲惨的，痛苦的；令人难受的

记 词根记忆：miser(同情)+able(能…的)→令人同情的→悲惨的

搭 as miserable as sin 非常悲惨；a miserable failure 可悲的失败

例 Many female patients have completely given up exercise because the pain makes them so *miserable*. 很多女病人已经完全放弃了锻炼，因为疼痛让她们极其痛苦。

mishandle* [ˌmɪsˈhændl]

vt. 粗暴地对待；错误地处理，胡乱操作

搭 mishandled baggage 错运行李

例 In our experience some types of exercise are easily *mishandled* and can lead to more harm than good. 根据我们的经验，一些锻炼很容易操作不当，进而弊大于利。

misjudge* [ˌmɪsˈdʒʌdʒ]

vt. 判断错误

记 联想记忆：mis(错)+judge(判断)→判断错误

例 Politicians have *misjudged* the public mood. 政客们对公众的情绪判断失误。

missile* [ˈmɪsaɪl]

n. 发射物；导弹，飞弹

记 词根记忆：miss(发送)+ile(表物体)→发送出去的东西→发射物；导弹

例 A *missile* struck a closed shopping mall in Kuwait City. 一枚导弹击中了科威特城一家关闭的购物中心。

mission [ˈmɪʃn]

n. 使命，任务；代表团，使团；传教，布道

记 电影《碟中谍》*Mission Impossible*，可直译为《不可能完成的任务》

例 The forces were sent to complete a secret *mission* in an uncharted place. 这些军队被派遣到一个地图上未标明的地方去执行一项秘密任务。

mite* [maɪt]

n. 极小量；螨虫

记 联想记忆：天上的风筝(kite)像小虫(mite)；mite 原指"螨虫"

例 The hives will be replaced because of *mites* or an ageing or dead queen. 蜂箱会因为螨虫或者蜂后的衰老或死亡等情况而被更换。

mixture [ˈmɪkstʃə(r)]

n. 混合(物)

记 词根记忆：mix(混合)+t+ure(表状态，名词后缀)→混合

例 Today, scientists continue to experiment with new glass *mixtures*. 如今，科学家们继续对新型的玻璃混合物进行试验。

mock* [mɒk]

a. 假的；模拟的 *n.* 嘲弄；模仿，仿制品 *v.* 嘲笑，嘲弄

记 联想记忆：和尚(monk)没头发常被人嘲笑(mock)

例 There's a *mock* camp site where you can see inside an Antarctic tent and imagine yourself sleeping there. 这里有一个模拟的露营地，你可以看到里面有一个南极帐篷，想象一下自己睡在里面的情景。

modem* [ˈməʊdem]

n. 调制解调器

例 This *modem* is on-line with the computer. 这个调制解调器与计算机相连接。

□ miserable □ mishandle □ misjudge □ missile □ mission □ mite
□ mixture □ mock □ modem

moderate [ˈmɒdərət] *a.* 温和的；适度的 [ˈmɒdəreɪt] *v.* (使)减轻，缓和；使适中

记 词根记忆：mod(适合) + er + ate → 使适合的 → 适度的；缓和

例 The people can bear *moderate* price increases in the market. 人们能够忍受市场上适度的涨价。// The wind has *moderated*. We can sail now. 风小了，我们现在可以起航了。

派 moderately(*ad.* 适度地，不过分地，有节制地)

moderation* [ˌmɒdəˈreɪʃn]

n. 温和，中庸；适度，合理

记 词根记忆：mod(适合) + er + ation(名词后缀) → 适度

搭 in moderation 节制

例 In the middle of Health Diet Pyramid we find the things that we can eat in *moderation*. 我们可以适量吃处于健康饮食金字塔中部的食物。

modernism* [ˈmɒdənɪzəm]

n. 现代主义

例 Many architects contributed to the development of *modernism* in the first half of last century. 上世纪上半叶许多建筑师都为现代主义的发展作出了贡献。

派 modernist(*n.* 现代主义者，现代人)

modification [ˌmɒdɪfɪˈkeɪʃn]

n. 修改，改正

记 联想记忆：modifi(看作 modify，修改) + cation → 修改

例 Knowledge of the ill effects of tobacco can lead to a *modification* in smoking behaviour. 了解吸烟对健康的损害能够改变人们吸烟的行为。

modify [ˈmɒdɪfaɪ]

vt. 更改，修改；(语法上)修饰

记 词根记忆：mod(尺度) + ify(使…) → 使…调整尺度 → 更改，修改

例 The construction of the houses has to be somewhat *modified* from houses in most areas. 这些房屋的结构应该根据大多数地区房屋的样式稍作修改。

modish [ˈməʊdɪʃ]

a. 流行的，时髦的

记 词根记忆：mod(样式) + ish → 最新样式的 → 流行的，时髦的

例 Nowadays, there is an interesting phenomenon that some bygone fashions, such as mini-skirt, become *modish* again. 如今，一个有趣的现象是一些过去的时尚再度流行开来，如迷你裙。

module [ˈmɒdjuːl]

n. 模块；模式；(航空器中的)舱；组件；单元

记 联想记忆：和 model(*n.* 模型)一起记

例 The school offers you 10-week *modules* of English courses. 该学校为你提供为期 10 周的英语课程单元。

moist [mɔɪst]

a. 湿润的，潮湿的

记 联想记忆：薄雾(mist)中湿润的(moist)城市很美

例 The earthworm lives in *moist* and warm soil. 蚯蚓生活在潮湿温暖的土壤里。

派 moisture(*n.* 潮湿，湿气)

molecule* [ˈmɒlɪkjuːl]

n. 分子

记 联想记忆：mol(摩尔) + ecule → 分子

例 Watson demonstrated the structure of the DNA *molecule*. 沃森展示了 DNA 的分子结构。

□ moderate □ moderation □ modernism □ modification □ modify □ modish
□ module □ moist □ molecule

molten [ˈməʊltən]

a. 熔化的

搭 molten lava 熔岩

例 With the increasing activities of the inner earth, the earth was shaking, the sea was roaring, and the volcano was pouring out *molten* rock. 由于地球内部活动的不断加剧，地面在晃动，海水在咆哮，火山在不断地向外喷射熔岩。

momentum [məˈmentəm]

n. 动力，冲力，势头；动量

记 联想记忆：moment（瞬间）+ um → 冲力在瞬间迸发 → 冲力

例 She worked day and night with the *momentum* of going abroad for further education. 出国深造是她夜以继日辛勤工作的动力。

同 impetus（*n.* 促进；推动力）

monitor [ˈmɒnɪtə(r)]

n. 班长；监视器 *vt.* 监视；监测

记 词根记忆：mon（忠告）+ itor → 给你忠告的人 → 班长

例 Some worry that governments and industry will be tempted to use the technology to *monitor* individual behaviour. 有人担心政府和企业会企图利用这项技术来监控个人行为。

monopoly [məˈnɒpəli]

n. 垄断，专卖；垄断商品，专卖商品

记 词根记忆：mono（单个）+ poly（多）→ 独占某商品绝大多数的市场份额 → 垄断，专卖

搭 capital monopoly 资本垄断

例 In some countries, stamps are a government *monopoly*. 在一些国家，邮票为政府垄断品。

monotonous [məˈnɒtənəs]

a. 单调的，无聊的

记 词根记忆：mono（单个）+ ton（声音）+ ous → 一个声音的 → 单调的

搭 a monotonous diet 乏味的食物

例 The play became *monotonous* after a while. 过了一会儿，这部剧就变得单调乏味了。

monster [ˈmɒnstə(r)]

n. 怪物；巨人，庞然大物

记 发音记忆："蒙死他" → 怪物把他给吓蒙了 → 怪物

例 The moving van is a *monster* of a truck. 这辆搬家车是辆巨型卡车。

monumental [ˌmɒnjuˈmentl]

a. 纪念碑的，纪念物的；不朽的，有重大意义的

记 联想记忆：monument（纪念碑）+ al（形容词后缀）→ 纪念碑的；不朽的

例 Unprecedented construction of tens of thousands of *monumental* engineering projects have been done to control floods in the country. 该国史无前例地建造了成千上万的重要工程来控制水患。

mood* [muːd]

n. 心情，情绪

记 联想记忆：心情（mood）不好也不能暴饮暴食（food）

例 Longer exposure to sunshine puts people in a better *mood*. 多晒太阳会使人心情变好。

30

□ molten □ momentum □ monitor □ monopoly □ monotonous □ monster
□ monumental □ mood

moral
[ˈmɒrəl]

a. 道德的，伦理的 *n.* [*pl.*] 品行，道德；寓意，教训

记 词根记忆：mor(风俗，习惯) + al(形容词后缀) → 全社会约定俗成的 → 道德的，伦理的

搭 public morals 社会公德

例 Altering our genetic inheritance is a ***moral*** problem. 改变我们的遗传基因是一个伦理问题。

morality*
[məˈræləti]

n. 道德，美德

记 联想记忆：moral(道德的) + ity → 道德，美德

搭 public morality 公共道德

例 Mankind has undergone great improvement in intelligence or ***morality***. 人类无论在智力方面还是在道德方面都经历了巨大的进步。

moribund
[ˈmɒrɪbʌnd]

a. 垂死的，即将灭亡的；即将结束的

记 词根记忆：mori(死亡) + bund(接近的) → 垂死的，即将灭亡的

例 There is a big problem at present that how the world economy can be revived from its present ***moribund*** state. 眼下的一个大难题是世界经济如何从行将就木的状态中走向复苏。

mortality
[mɔːˈtæləti]

n. 死亡率

记 词根记忆：mort(死亡) + ality(表性质，名词后缀) → 死亡率

搭 infant mortality 婴儿死亡率

例 Although infant ***mortality*** varies by ethnicity, deaths among infants with birth defects are similar in all groups. 尽管婴儿的死亡率因种族而不同，但是因出生缺陷而导致的儿童死亡在各个群体中却是类似的。

mosquito
[məˈskiːtəʊ]

n. 蚊子

例 ***Mosquitoes*** will suck human's blood. What's even worse, they will transmit many diseases. 蚊子会吸人类的血。更糟的是，它们会传播多种疾病。

Only the educated are free.

只有受过教育的人才是自由的。

——古希腊哲学家 爱比克泰德（Epictetus, Ancient Greek philosopher）

Word List 31

音频

mot	移动	motion *n.* 运动	**mund**	世界	mundane *a.* 世界的；世俗的
mut	变	mutual *a.* 相互的；共同的	**nav**	船	navigable *a.* 可通航的
neg	否定	negative *a.* 否定的，反面的	**not**	知道	notable *a.* 值得注意的
nutri	营养	nutrient *n.* 滋养物	**ject**	扔	object *n.* 目标；对象
lig	捆绑	obligation *n.* 义务	**serv**	维持	observe *v.* 遵守

moss [mɒs]

n. 苔藓

例 Due to the moist weather without sunlight, the rocks near the river were easily covered with *moss*. 由于天气潮湿、没有光照，河边的石头很容易长青苔。

motion [ˈməʊʃn]

n. 运动；手势 *v.* (向…)打手势

记 词根记忆：mot(移动) + ion → 运动

搭 set/put sth. in motion 让…动起来，开动…

例 For years Newton had been curious about the cause of the orbital *motion* of the moon and planets. 多年来，牛顿一直对月球和行星轨道运动的成因好奇。

motivate [ˈməʊtɪveɪt]

vt. 使有动机；激励，激发

搭 motivate sb. to do sth. 激励某人做某事

例 Pictures are used to help *motivate* children to read because they are beautiful and eye-catching. 图片因其美丽和引人注目而被用来激发孩子们的阅读兴趣。

motivational [ˌməʊtɪˈveɪʃnl]

a. 动机的，有关动机的

例 The science-and-engineering students have *motivational*, cognitive and emotional barriers in English learning, according to a survey released by the Ministry of Education. 据教育部公布的一项调查结果显示，理工科学生在英语学习中存在着动机、认知和情感方面的障碍。

motive [ˈməʊtɪv]

n. 动机，目的

记 词根记忆：mot(移动) + ive → 移动的目的 → 动机，目的

例 The police couldn't find a *motive* for the murder. 警方未能找出这起谋杀的动机。

□ moss □ motion □ motivate □ motivational □ motive

mould* [məʊld]

n. 霉，霉菌；模型，铸模；(人的)性格，气质 *v.* 用模子制作，浇铸；使形成，把…塑造成

搭 break the mould (of sth.) 打破…模式，改变…模式；mould one's character 塑造性格

例 A *mould* might prove to be a successful antibody to bacterial infection. 某种霉可能会被证明是细菌感染的有效抗体。

mount [maʊnt]

n. 山，山峰；支架，底座 *v.* 登上；骑上；发起；镶嵌

记 本身为词根，意为"登上"

搭 mount up(尺寸和数量上的)增加，上升

例 The eruption in May 1980 of *Mount* St. Helens astounded the world with its violence. 1980 年 5 月，圣海伦斯山火山爆发，其威力震惊了世界。

mountainous* [ˈmaʊntənəs]

a. 多山的

记 联想记忆：mountain(山) + ous → 多山的

例 This is the most *mountainous* part of Astoria. 这里是阿斯托里亚最多山的地区。

muddle* [ˈmʌdl]

n. 一团糟，凌乱，混乱；(头脑)糊涂，困惑

vt. 将…弄成一团糟；使困惑，使糊涂；混淆

记 联想记忆：mud(泥) + dle → 把泥弄得到处都是 → 混乱

搭 in a muddle 混乱；muddle along 混日子，得过且过；muddle through 胡乱应付过去

例 I'm in such a *muddle* that I completely forget to do my homework. 我真糊涂，竟把家庭作业完全抛到了脑后。

multinational* [ˌmʌltiˈnæʃnəl]

a. 多国的，多民族的；跨国公司的 *n.* 跨国公司

例 When you think of any organization, a family business or a *multinational* company, they are all fundamentally a group of people working together. 当你想到任何组织、家族企业或跨国公司时，从根本上来说它们都是一群在一起工作的人。

multiple [ˈmʌltɪpl]

a. 多重的；多样的 *n.* 倍数

记 词根记忆：multi(多的) + ple(折叠) → 多重的；多样的

搭 multiple choice 多项选择；in multiple(s) 成倍地

例 Those devices have *multiple* purposes. 那些装置具备多重功能。

multiply [ˈmʌltɪplaɪ]

v. (使)增加，(使)繁殖；乘

例 Hot weather *multiplies* bacteria rapidly. 炎热的天气导致细菌迅速繁殖。

mundane [mʌnˈdeɪn]

a. 世界的；世俗的，现世的；平淡的

记 词根记忆：mund(世界) + ane → 世界的；世俗的

例 Susan busied herself with the *mundane* task of cleaning the house. 苏珊用打扫房间这样平常的工作让自己忙起来。

□ mould □ mount □ mountainous □ muddle □ multinational □ multiple
□ multiply □ mundane

municipal
[mjuːˈnɪsɪpl]

a. 市的，市政的；地区的；内政的

记 词根记忆：muni(服务) + cip(拿) + al(形容词后缀) → 提供城市公共服务的 → 市政的

搭 a municipal council 市政委员会；the municipal government 市政府；a municipal university 市立大学；municipal affairs 市政事务

例 In many Western cities, plans to erect mosques often stir more passion than any other local or *municipal* affairs which will make politicians to leap into the fray. 在西方的许多城市，比起其他地方性事务和市政事务，修建清真寺的计划通常会激起更多的不满，并引发政治家们的激烈争辩。

murder
[ˈmɜːdə(r)]

n./v. 谋杀，凶杀

搭 get away with murder 逍遥法外；commit (a) murder 犯谋杀罪

例 The *murder* seemed planned. 这场谋杀显然是蓄意策划的。

派 murderer(*n.* 杀人犯，杀人凶手)

murky
[ˈmɜːki]

a. 浑浊的；黑暗的；朦胧的；隐晦的

例 In early medieval Britain, every castle had a cold *murky* dungeon for prisoners. 在中世纪早期的英国，每个城堡都有一个冰冷阴暗的地牢，用于关押囚犯。

muscle
[ˈmʌsl]

n. 肌肉；体力；力量，实力

记 发音记忆："马瘦"→ 瘦马没有肌肉 → 肌肉

搭 movement of muscles 肌肉运动；leg muscles 腿部肌肉；stomach muscles 腹部肌肉

例 If your bed doesn't give enough support, back *muscles* and ligaments will work all night trying to correct spinal alignment. 如果你的床不能提供足够的支撑，那么背部肌肉和韧带就会整晚工作来校直脊椎骨。

mushroom
[ˈmʌʃrʊm]

vi. 迅速成长(或发展) *n.* 蘑菇

例 The profit of this company is expected to *mushroom* to $50 million by 2012. 这家公司的利润到 2012 年有望猛增到五千万美金。

31

mutual
[ˈmjuːtʃuəl]

a. 相互的；共同的

记 词根记忆：mut(变) + ual(形容词后缀) → 穷则思变，共同发展 → 相互的；共同的

搭 mutual understanding 相互理解；the principle of equality and mutual benefit 平等互惠的原则

例 They soon discovered a *mutual* interest in music. 很快，他们发现他们对音乐有着共同的兴趣。

mysterious*
[mɪˈstɪəriəs]

a. 神秘的，诡秘的

记 联想记忆：myster(=mystery 神秘) + i + ous → 神秘的

例 Writers transport their heroes to *mysterious* realms beyond the Earth. 作家们将其笔下的英雄带到地球之外的神秘地域。

同 strange(*a.* 神秘的)；mystical(*a.* 奥秘的)

□ municipal □ murder □ murky □ muscle □ mushroom □ mutual
□ mysterious

naive
[naɪ'iːv]

a. 幼稚的，天真的，不成熟的

记 联想记忆：native(原始的，土著的)去掉 t → 比土著人还要少一点阅历 → 天真的，幼稚的，不成熟的

搭 naive attitude 天真的态度

例 The second flaw in the document is the *naive* faith it places in its 1,000 core zoos. 这一文献的第二个瑕疵就是，它天真地信任了所谓的 1000 家核心动物园。

同 childish(*a.* 幼稚的，不成熟的)；puerile(*a.* 幼稚的，孩子气的)

naked
['neɪkɪd]

a. 裸体的，无遮蔽的

例 The luminaries that can be seen by our *naked* eyes are quite a small part of the universe. 我们肉眼所能看到的天体仅仅是宇宙中很小的一部分。

narrator*
[nə'reɪtə(r)]

n. 讲述者，叙述者

例 Peter worked as a *narrator* in the company. 彼得在该公司做解说员。

nasty*
['nɑːsti]

a. 令人讨厌的；不友好的，恶意的，下流的；恶劣的

记 联想记忆：做事总是草率的(hasty)，真是令人讨厌的(nasty)

搭 a nasty person 下流的人；nasty weather 恶劣的天气

例 Many people feel that it's dangerous to ride the subway—there have been some *nasty* attacks. 很多人认为乘坐地铁很危险，因为地铁上发生过一些可怕的袭击。

同 disgusting(*a.* 令人厌恶的，使人反感的)；offensive(*a.* 使人不快的，讨厌的)

nationality
[ˌnæʃə'næləti]

n. 国籍；民族

记 联想记忆：nation(国家)+ality(表状态，名词后缀)→ 属于哪个国家 → 国籍

例 Can you show any proof of your *nationality*? 你能出示可以证明你国籍的证件吗？

native*
['neɪtɪv]

a. 当地(人)的 *n.* 本地人，本国人

例 All teachers in this school have specialist qualifications in teaching English to foreign students, and are all *native* speakers. 这所学校所有的老师都具备教外籍学生英语的专业资格，且均为英语国家人士。

natural*
['nætʃrəl]

a. 正常的，普通的，自然的；自然界的，天然的；天赋的，固有的

搭 natural disaster 自然灾害；natural scenery 自然景观

例 It's *natural* for an old man of his age to be so quiet. 处于他这般年纪的老人如此安静是很自然的。

naturally*
['nætʃrəli]

ad. 当然，自然；天生地

例 Is extinction a *naturally* occurring phenomenon? 物种灭绝是一种自然发生的现象吗？

□ naive □ naked □ narrator □ nasty □ nationality □ native
□ natural □ naturallly

navigable* [ˈnævɪɡəbl]

a. 可通航的；适于航行的

记 词根记忆：nav（船）+ ig（开动）+ able（能…的）→ 船可以开动的 → 可通航的

例 The depth of the *navigable* channel of this river is 40 feet. 这条河可航行河段的水深为 40 英尺。

navigation [ˌnævɪˈɡeɪʃn]

n. 航空，航海，航行；导航，领航

记 词根记忆：nav（船）+ ig（开，驱动）+ ation → 开动船只 → 航海，航行

例 All the world now knows that bats, or rather natural selection working on bats, had perfected the system tens of millions of years earlier, and their radar achieves feats of detection and *navigation* that would strike an engineer dumb with admiration. 现在人们意识到，确切地说因为自然选择的作用，蝙蝠早在几千万年前就已经完善了它们的雷达系统，其在探测与导航方面的成功让工程师们赞叹不已。

派 navigator（*n.* 导航者，领航员；早期的航海探险者）

necessarily* [ˈnesəsərəli; ˌnesəˈserəli]

ad. 必要地；必然地

例 As an international student you'll not *necessarily* be eligible for all the facilities offered to resident students. 作为国际学生，你将没有资格享受当地学生享有的所有便利。

necessity [nəˈsesəti]

n. 必然，必要；必需品；必要性

记 来自 necessary（*a.* 必需的；必要的）

例 Out of *necessity* or out of interest, people return to school for the common goal of self-improvement. 不管是出于需要还是兴趣，人们重返学校都是为了一个共同的目标——提高自己。

派 necessitous（*a.* 贫困的；急需的）

negative* [ˈneɡətɪv]

a. 否定的，反面的；消极的；负的，阴性的 *n.* 负数；（照相的）底片

记 词根记忆：neg（否定）+ ative → 否定的

搭 a negative reply 否定的答复；a negative number 负数；the negative terminal of a battery 电池的阴极

例 This policy had a *negative* effect on their business. 这一政策给他们的生意带了消极影响。

反 positive（*a.* 正面的，积极的）

neglect [nɪˈɡlekt]

n./vt. 忽视；疏忽；遗漏

记 词根记忆：neg（不）+ lect（选择）→ 不去选择 → 忽视；疏忽

搭 neglect one's duty 玩忽职守

例 After years of *neglect*, single speed cycles still manage to function, though not always too efficiently. 在被忽视多年之后，单速自行车尽管往往效率不高，但依然发挥着作用。// Don't *neglect* writing to your mother. 别忘了给你母亲写信。

同 ignore（*vt.* 不理，忽视）；overlook（*vt.* 忽略，未注意到）

31

negotiate
[nɪˈɡəʊʃieɪt]

v. 洽谈，协商；商定，达成；顺利通过

例 By no means does everyone in the world know English well enough to *negotiate* in it. 要让世界上每个人的英语都好得可以用它来进行谈判是不可能的。// Tom *negotiated* the fence with ease. 汤姆轻易就跳过了篱笆。

neoclassical
[ˌniːəʊˈklæsɪkl]

a. 新古典主义的

例 Besides grandeur of scale and simplicity of geometric forms, the use of columns is also the representative feature of *neoclassical* architecture. 除了规模的宏伟和几何形状的简洁性外，使用圆柱也是新古典建筑的标志性特征。

nerve
[nɜːv]

n. 神经；勇敢

记 词根记忆：nerv(体力；神经；勇气) + e → 神经；勇敢

例 The animal's optic *nerves* are highly regenerative. 这种动物的视觉神经有非常强的再生能力。// Rock-climbing is a test of *nerve* and skill. 攀岩是对勇敢和技巧的考验。

neutral
[ˈnjuːtrəl]

a. 中立的；无明显特性的

例 The feminist took *neutral* ground during the first interview. 这名女权主义者在第一次采访中采取了中立的态度。

nevertheless
[ˌnevəðəˈles]

ad. 仍然；然而 *conj.* 然而，不过

例 He was tired, *nevertheless* he kept on working. 他累了，但仍然继续工作。

newsletter*
[ˈnjuːzletə(r)]

n. 时事通讯，业务通讯

记 组合词：news(消息，新闻) + letter(文字) → 时事通讯

例 There's David West who has volunteered to be the club secretary, and one of the many jobs he will have is to sent out *newsletters* to you regularly. 那位就是戴维·韦斯特，他自愿做俱乐部秘书，他的众多工作之一就是定期给你们分发时事通讯。

nickel
[ˈnɪkl]

n. 镍；(美国和加拿大的)五分镍币

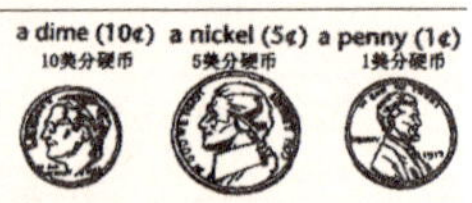

记 发音记忆："你抠" → 连五分钱都舍不得给 → 五分镍币

例 *Nickel* can be used to make batteries. 镍可以用来制造电池。

niggle*
[ˈnɪɡl]

v. 拘泥小节；挑剔，吹毛求疵；为小事操心；不断地烦扰

例 Tina wears a frown these days that there must be something *niggled* her. 蒂娜这些天眉头紧锁，一定是有什么事困扰着她。

nightmare
[ˈnaɪtmeə(r)]

n. 噩梦；可怕的事物

例 Traveling on those bad mountain roads is a *nightmare*. 在那些崎岖的山路上旅行真是件可怕的事。

□ negotiate □ neoclassical □ nerve □ neutral □ nevertheless □ newsletter
□ nickel □ niggle □ nightmare

nocturnal
[nɒkˈtɜːnl]

a. 夜晚的；夜晚发生的；夜晚活动的

记 词根记忆：noct(夜) + urnal → 夜晚的

搭 nocturnal vision 夜视能力；nocturnal animals 夜间活动的动物

例 It is probable that the ***nocturnal*** trades go way back in the ancestry of all mammals. 夜间进行活动可能是所有哺乳动物自祖先时起就有的行为。

nominal*
[ˈnɒmɪnl]

a. 名义上的；(金额、租金等)微不足道的

记 词根记忆：nomin(名字，名目) + al → 名义上的

搭 nominal head 名义上的领导；nominal assets 名义资产；nominal fee 很少的费用

例 The bonus to employees is merely a ***nominal*** sum. 雇员们只得到了一笔象征性的奖金。

派 nominally(*ad.* 有名无实地，名义上地)

同 titular(*a.* 有名无实的，名义上的)；minor(*a.* 较小的，较少的)

反 actual(*a.* 实际的，真实的)；genuine(*a.* 真正的)

Nordic
[ˈnɔːdɪk]

a. 北欧人的；北欧国家的

记 联想记忆：nor(看作 north，北) + dic → 北欧人的

例 Since the Winter Games began, 55 out of 56 gold medals in the men's ***Nordic*** skiing events have been won by competitors from Scandinavia or the former Soviet Union. 从首届冬季奥林匹克运动会开始，男子北欧式滑雪比赛所产生的 56 块金牌有 55 块被斯堪的纳维亚或前苏联的选手收入囊中。

normal*
[ˈnɔːml]

a. 正常的，平常的；标准的，规范的，正规的

记 联想记忆：norm(标准，规范) + al → 标准的，规范的

搭 normal education 师范教育；正规教育；normal state 标准状态，常态

例 The ***normal*** noise threshold for private housing is 55 decibels. 私人住宅区标准的噪音音量上限为 55 分贝。

派 normally(*ad.* 正常地，通常地)

notable*
[ˈnəʊtəbl]

a. 值得注意的；显著的，杰出的，显赫的 *n.* 名人，要人

记 词根记忆：not(知道) + able(可…的) → 可知道的 → 值得注意的

搭 a notable person 重要人物

例 The most ***notable*** of these activities was the Woman's Exhibition. 在这些活动中，最引人注目的是妇女(作品)展。

派 notably(*ad.* 显著地，特别地)

同 eminent (*a.* 杰出的，显赫的)；noteworthy (*a.* 显著的，值得注目的)；remarkable(*a.* 显著的，值得注意的)

notice board*

布告牌，公告牌

例 We go to the ***notice board*** to find out about lectures. 我们去公告牌那儿看看课程情况。

noticeable*
[ˈnəʊtɪsəbl]

a. 显而易见的；明显的

例 There has been a ***noticeable*** improvement in Tim's learning. 蒂姆的学业有了明显的提高。

31

□ nocturnal □ nominal □ Nordic □ normal □ notable □ notice board
□ noticeable

notify [ˈnəʊtɪfaɪ]	*vt.* 通知，报告 记 词根记忆：not(知道) + ify(使…) → 使人知道 → 通知，报告 例 If the library is not *notified* and you are 15 minutes late, your time can be given to someone else. 如果你没有通知图书馆，那么在你迟到 15 分钟后，你的时间就会给其他人。
notion [ˈnəʊʃn]	*n.* 概念，观念；想法 记 词根记忆：not(知道) + ion(名词后缀) → 知道的东西 → 观念；想法 例 The emergence of a new style of architecture reflects more idealistic *notions* for the future. 一种新建筑风格的出现反映了关于未来的更理想主义的观念。
notoriety [ˌnəʊtəˈraɪəti]	*n.* 声名狼藉，臭名昭著 记 词根记忆：not(知道) + oriety(多) → 坏事人所共知 → 臭名昭著 例 Even though you quit, that kind of *notoriety* will still follow you from one workplace to another. 即使你辞职了，这样的恶名还是一样跟着你，从一个岗位到另一个岗位。
notorious [nəʊˈtɔːriəs]	*a.* 著名的，众所周知的；声名狼藉的 例 Tom was a *notorious* liar. 汤姆是一个声名狼藉的骗子。 派 notoriously(*ad.* 出名地，声名狼藉地) 同 infamous(*a.* 声名狼藉的，臭名昭著的)；disreputable(*a.* 声名狼藉的)
nourish [ˈnʌrɪʃ]	*vt.* 养育，滋养；培养（情绪、观点等） 例 All the children were well *nourished* and in good physical condition. 所有这些孩子都营养良好，身体健康。 派 nourishing(*a.* 有营养的) 同 nurture(*vt.* 抚育，教养)；foster(*v.* 培养，培育)
novice [ˈnɒvis]	*n.* 生手，新手；初学者；新信徒，初学修士(或修女) 记 词根记忆：nov(新) + ice → 新手 例 In 2001, China, a *novice* in WTO, had many different opportunities and challenges to face. 2001 年，作为 WTO 的新成员，中国面临着许多不同的机遇和挑战。
nuclear* [ˈnjuːklɪə(r)]	*a.* 核能的，原子能的 记 联想记忆：nu + clear(清除) → 清除核危机 → 核能的 例 France derives three quarters of its electricity from *nuclear* power. 法国四分之三的电来自核能。
numerous [ˈnjuːmərəs]	*a.* 众多的 记 词根记忆：numer(数) + ous(多…的) → 数目众多的 → 众多的 例 *Numerous* overseas visitors have come to see how the program works. 众多海外游客到这里来观看这个项目是如何运作的。
nursery* [ˈnɜːsəri]	*a.* 幼儿教育的 *n.* 托儿所；苗圃 记 来自 nurse(*v.* 看护) 例 a nursery teacher 幼儿教师 例 Whether the state should provide free *nursery* education or not is being discussed on the table. 国家是否应该提供免费的幼儿教育这一问题正在讨论之中。

□ notify □ notion □ notoriety □ notorious □ nourish □ novice
□ nuclear □ numerous □ nursery

nurture [ˈnɜːtʃə (r)]	*vt.* 培养；滋养 *n.* 营养品 记 联想记忆：大自然(nature)滋养(nurture)着人类 例 We need to grow and *nurture* new talents. 我们需要增加和培养新人才。 同 nourish(*vt.* 养育，喂养)；cultivate(*vt.* 教养，培养)；foster(*v.* 养育，培养)
nutrient [ˈnjuːtriənt]	*n.* 滋养物，营养品 记 词根记忆：nutri(营养) + ent(名词后缀) → 滋养物，营养品 例 Embryos absorb mineral and other *nutrients* from their mothers. 胎儿从母体中吸收矿物质和其他营养物质。
nutrition* [njuˈtrɪʃn]	*n.* 营养；营养学 记 词根记忆：nutri(营养) + tion → 营养；营养学 搭 food nutrition 食品营养；good nutrition 营养丰富；nutrition science 营养学 例 Female are more conscious of food *nutrition*. 女性更关注食品营养。 派 nutritionist(*n.* 营养学家)；malnutrition(*n.* 营养不良) 同 nourishment(*n.* 营养品)；sustenance(*n.* 食物，营养物)
nutritional [njuˈtrɪʃənl]	*a.* 营养的，滋养的；营养物的，食物的 例 This book provides *nutritional* information on over 3,000 different food. 这本书介绍了 3000 多种食物的营养知识。
nutritious [njuˈtrɪʃəs]	*a.* 有营养的，营养丰富的 记 词根记忆：nutri(营养) + ti + ous(形容词后缀) → 有营养的，营养丰富的 例 In additional to a *nutritious* diet, a healthy body also depends on an appropriate exercise. 除了营养的饮食之外，健康的身体还需要适当的运动。
oak [əʊk]	*n.* 橡树，橡木 记 联想记忆：ok 中间有个 a → 一棵好橡树 → 橡树
object* 	[ˈɒbdʒɪkt] *n.* 物体；对象；目标；宾语 [əbˈdʒekt] *v.* 反对，不赞成 记 词根记忆：ob(向) + ject(扔) → 向某一方向扔去 → 目标；对象 例 The importance of these acquisitions extends beyond the *objects* themselves. 这些收获物的重要性超过了事物本身。
objectify [əbˈdʒektɪfaɪ]	*vt.* 使客观化；使具体化；物化 例 In the old time, many companies *objectify* their employees, ignoring sometimes they are also more sensible and need to be treated subjectively. 在过去，很多公司把员工当作物品，忽略了他们有时候也是比较感性的，需要得到主观对待。
objection [əbˈdʒekʃn]	*n.* 反对；反对的理由 例 If no one has any *objection* against the decision, I'll declare the meeting is closed. 如果没人反对这个决议，那么我将宣布会议结束。
objective* [əbˈdʒektɪv]	*n.* 目标，目的 *a.* 客观的 搭 strategic objective 战略目标；achieve the objective 达到目的；be objective about sth. 客观看待某事；objective reality 客观事实 例 The *objective* of the Human Genome Project is simple to state. 人类基因工程的目标很容易说明。

31

□ nurture □ nutrient □ nutrition □ nutritional □ nutritious □ oak
□ object □ objectify □ objection □ objective

obligation [ˌɒblɪˈgeɪʃn]

n. 义务，职责，责任

记 词根记忆：ob(表加强) + lig(捆绑) + ation → 用力捆绑 → 义务，职责

搭 under no obligation to do sth. 没有做某事的义务

例 Every government has the right and ***obligation*** to run its own internal affairs well. 每一任政府都有管理好国家内政的权利和职责。

obscene [əbˈsiːn]

a. 淫秽的，猥亵的，下流的；可憎的，可恶的；(数量)大得惊人的，骇人听闻的

搭 an obscene bird 乌鸦

例 Many parents think the government should take effective measures to prevent ***obscene*** videotapes from spreading among the youngsters. 许多家长认为政府应该采取有效措施阻止淫秽录像带在青少年间传播。

派 obscenely(*ad.* 猥亵地，污秽地)；obscenity(*n.* 淫秽的语言；下流的行为)

obscurity [əbˈskjʊərəti]

n. 模糊；费解；不出名

记 来自 obscure(*a.* 朦胧的，模糊的)

例 This opening chapter tells us how to avoid ambiguity and ***obscurity*** of expression. 开篇第一章告诉我们如何避免模糊和晦涩的语言表达。

observation* [ˌɒbzəˈveɪʃn]

n. 观察，观测；监视；评述，评论

记 词根记忆：ob(表加强) + serv(维持) + ation → 观测；监视

例 Can we mail out a questionnaire, or do face-to-face interviews, or maybe even ***observation***? 我们是邮寄调查表，还是面对面采访，亦或是进行观察？

observe [əbˈzɜːv]

v. 察觉；观察；遵守

记 词根记忆：ob(表加强) + serv(维持) + e → 遵守

例 She has ***observed*** that if a left-handed person is brain-damaged in the left hemisphere, the recovery of speech is quite often better than that of a right-handed person. 她观察到，如果一个左撇子的大脑左半球受损，他的语言恢复能力会比右撇子好很多。

obsession [əbˈseʃn]

n. 牵挂，惦念；迷住，困扰；萦绕于心的事物或人；固执的念头

记 词根记忆：ob(逆) + sess(=sit 坐) + ion → 坐立不安 → 困扰

例 It is said that General Charles De Gaulle had an ***obsession*** with *Mona Lisa* which is one of the masterpieces of the Renaissance. 据说戴高乐将军对《蒙娜丽莎》这幅文艺复兴时期的名作非常着迷。

派 obsessional (*a.* 痴迷的，迷恋的；耿耿于怀的)；obsessive (*a.* 迷恋的 *n.* 强迫症患者)

Word List 32

音频

词根、词缀预习表

struct	建造	obstruct *v.* 妨碍，阻止	tain	拿住	obtain *v.* 获得，得到
cur	跑	occur *vi.* 发生；存在	fens	打	offensive *a.* 冒犯的
opa	不透明	opaque *a.* 不透明的	opt	眼睛	optical *a.* 视力的
optim	最好	optimism *n.* 乐观	orb	轨道	orbit *n.* 轨道
ori	产生	origin *n.* 起源	orn	装饰	ornament *n.* 装饰；装饰物

obstacle
[ˈɒbstəkl]

n. 障碍，妨碍物，干扰

记 词根记忆：ob(反) + st(=stand 站) + acle(表小东西) → 反着站的小物体 → 障碍，妨碍物

搭 obstacle course 障碍赛跑赛场；重重困难；natural obstacles 天然障碍

例 Payment has been an *obstacle* to the development of e-commerce in China, because a large number of Chinese people don't get accustomed to credit cards or cheques. 付费方式一直是中国电子商务发展的障碍，因为很多中国人不习惯使用信用卡和支票。

obstruct
[əbˈstrʌkt]

v. 妨碍，阻止；阻塞；截断

记 词根记忆：ob(反) + struct(建造) → 反着建造 → 妨碍，阻止

搭 obstruct the investigation 阻碍调查；obstruct the highway 阻塞高速公路

例 Fish and dolphins that live in extremely muddy water cannot see because, although there is light, it is *obstructed* and scattered by the dirt in the water. 生活在极其浑浊的水域里的鱼和海豚是看不见东西的，因为尽管有光，但水里的泥土阻塞、分散了光线。

obtain
[əbˈteɪn]

v. 获得，得到；通用，流行

记 词根记忆：ob + tain(拿住) → 拿到 → 获得，得到

搭 obtain a degree 获得学位

例 Today fibre optics are used to *obtain* a clearer image of smaller objects. 现在，纤维光学被用于获取较小物体的更清晰图像。

occasion*
[əˈkeɪʒn]

n. 时刻，时候；场合；重大(或特殊)活动，盛会；时机，机会；起因，理由

vt. 引起，惹起

记 词根记忆：oc(近，往) + cas(掉落) + ion → 掉落到某物上 → 发生的时机 → 时机

例 It should have been an *occasion* for rejoicing, but she could not feel any real joy. 原本应该是高兴的时刻，她却丝毫未感到真正的快乐。

□ obstacle □ obstruct □ obtain □ occasion

occasional
[ə'keɪʒənl]

a. 偶尔的，间或发生的

例 There will be *occasional* congruity between prophecy and fact. 预言与事实偶尔会一致。

派 occasionally(*ad.* 有时候，偶尔)

occupation
[ˌɒkju'peɪʃn]

n. 占领；职业；消遣

搭 a regular occupation 固定职业

例 Please state your name, age and *occupation* on the form. 请在表格里填写姓名、年龄和职业。

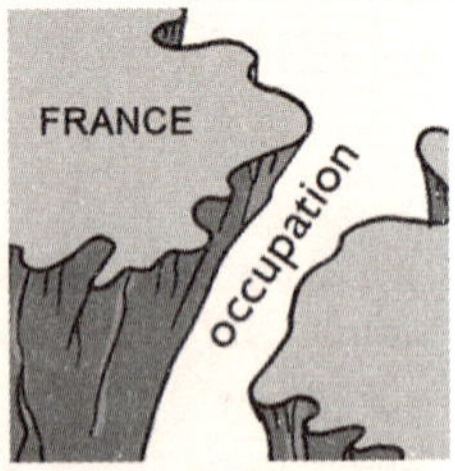

occupy
['ɒkjupaɪ]

vt. 占用，占领；(使)忙碌于；(使)从事

记 联想记忆：发生（occur）了大事，敌人占领(occupy)了该市

例 Any individual in any situation *occupies* a role in relation to other people. 任何个体，无论处于何种环境下，都扮演着与他人相关联的某种角色。

occur
[ə'kɜː(r)]

vi. 发生；存在

记 词根记忆：oc(向) + cur(跑) → 跑向 → 发生

搭 occur to 被想到；(主意)浮现于脑中

例 Generally, molt *occurs* at the time of least stress on the birds. 通常，换毛发生在小鸟压力最小的时候。

派 occurrence(*n.* 事故；发生的事件)

odd
[ɒd]

a. 奇特的；临时的；奇数的

记 联想记忆：奇奇(odd)相加(add)为偶

例 We are attracted by the *odd* behavior of the boy. 男孩古怪的行为吸引了我们。

派 oddly(*ad.* 奇特地)

odour
['əʊdə(r)]

n. 气味

例 Some people are known as *odour*-blind. 一些人闻不到气味。

offend
[ə'fend]

v. 冒犯；使厌恶；违犯

记 联想记忆：off(离开) + end(最后) → 冒犯了她，最后离开了 → 冒犯

例 You should remind yourself not to *offend* against the customs when you are in the minority region. 当你在少数民族地区的时候，要提醒自己不要冒犯他们的风俗。

派 offense(*n.* 犯规；冒犯)

offensive
[ə'fensɪv]

a. 冒犯的；使人不快的；无礼的；攻击性的，进攻性的 *n.* 进攻，攻击；攻势

记 词根记忆：of + fens(打) + ive → 打击别人 → 冒犯的；使人不快的

例 Every year, BBC receives plenty of complaints from the public about their *offensive* remarks during the interviews. BBC 每年都会收到公众对采访中出现的冒犯性话语的大量投诉。

派 offensively(*ad.* 冒犯地)；offensiveness(*n.* 冒犯；无礼)

反 inoffensive(*a.* 无害的)

□ occasional □ occupation □ occupy □ occur □ odd □ odour
□ offend □ offensive

offset
[ˈɒfset]

vt. 抵消，补偿，弥补

记 来自词组 set off（抵消）

例 Prices have risen in order to *offset* the increased cost of materials. 为弥补原料成本的增加而提高了价格。

offspring
[ˈɒfsprɪŋ]

n. 子女，后代；产物

记 联想记忆：off（出来）+ spring（春天）→ 春天出生的 → 子女，后代

例 With one right- and one left-handed parent, 15 to 20 percent of the *offspring* will be left-handed. 如果父母中有一个是左撇子，另一个惯用右手，那么他们的后代是左撇子的概率是 15%到 20%。

on the horizon

即将发生的

例 *On the horizon* are optical computers. 即将诞生的是光学计算机。

ongoing*
[ˈɒngəʊɪŋ]

a. 进行中的 *n.* 前进，发展

记 组合词：on（在…中）+ going（进行，进展）→ 进行中的

例 Manufacturers usually consider quality control to be an *ongoing* process. 制造商们通常认为质量管理是一个不断发展的过程。

onslaught
[ˈɒnslɔːt]

n. 猛攻，猛袭

记 联想记忆：on + slaught(er)（打击）→ 猛攻，猛袭

例 The *onslaught* of media attention has brought unnecessary distraction to the boxer who should focus exclusively on his competition. 媒体过分的关注使这个拳击手很分心，他本应该只专注于比赛的。

onwards*
[ˈɒnwədz]

ad. 向前地，前进地

搭 from...onwards 从（某时）起一直

例 The Romans left from the country in 410, at the beginning of the fifth century, and from then *onwards* the country suffered a series of invasions. 罗马人在公元 410 年，也就是五世纪初撤离该国，之后，这个国家遭受了一系列的侵略。

opaque
[əʊˈpeɪk]

a. 不透明的；晦涩的，难懂的

记 词根记忆：opa（不透明）+ que → 不透明的

例 His paper, with *opaque* cases, made the tutor dizzy. 他论文中晦涩难懂的案例让导师感到头晕目眩。

派 opaquely（*ad.* 不透明地，无光泽地）；opaqueness（*n.* 含糊）

同 obscure（*a.* 模糊的；费解的）；vague（*a.* 含糊的，不明确的）

反 transparent（*a.* 透明的）

operate
[ˈɒpəreɪt]

v. 运转；动手术；起作用；操作；经营

搭 operate a tutorial system 开设一个辅导系统；operating cost 运转费用

例 The lift didn't *operate*. 电梯坏了。// The doctor decided to *operate* on Tom immediately. 医生决定马上给汤姆动手术。// His father *operates* three big companies. 他父亲经营着三家大公司。

operational
[ˌɒpəˈreɪʃənl]

a. 运转的；操作的；运营的，业务的

记 来自 operate（*v.* 操作；运转）

例 We need some advanced *operational* staff. 我们需要一些高级操作人员。

opponent*
[əˈpəʊnənt]

n. 敌手，对手；反对者 *a.* 对立的，对抗的

记 词根记忆：op（反）+ pon（放）+ ent → 处于对立面的 → 对手，敌手；对立的，对抗的

例 The American Medical Association represents about half of all US doctors and is a strong *opponent* of smoking. 美国医学协会代表着全美一半左右的医生，这一机构强烈反对吸烟。

opportunity
[ˌɒpəˈtjuːnəti]

n. 机会，时机

记 联想记忆：opportun(e)（合适的，适当的）+ ity → 合适的时机 → 机会，时机

搭 take the opportunity to do sth./of doing sth. 趁机做…，借机做…

例 The film gave them an *opportunity* to let their imaginations run wild. 电影给了他们一个放任想象力纵情驰骋的机会。

oppose
[əˈpəʊz]

v. 反对，反抗

记 词根记忆：op（反）+ pos（放）+ e → 反着放 → 反对，反抗

搭 be opposed to 反对…；oppose oneself to 反对

例 Some environmentalists have *opposed* economic development of any kind. 一些环保主义者反对任何形式的经济发展。

opposite*
[ˈɒpəzɪt]

prep. 在…对面 *a.* 对面的，对立的；相反的，相对的 *n.* 对立面，对立物

例 The classroom is near the main entrance, just *opposite* the reception desk. 教室位于主入口附近，正对着接待处。

派 opposition（*n.* 反对）

optic*
[ˈɒptɪk]

a. 眼的，视觉的；光学的 *n.* 光学仪器

记 词根记忆：opt（眼睛）+ ic → 眼的，视觉的

搭 fiber optic cable 光缆；an optic examine 视力检查

例 The wound hurt his *optic* nerve that he could no longer see things. 伤口触及他的视觉神经，他再也看不到东西了。

optical*
[ˈɒptɪkl]

a. 视力的；光学的

记 词根记忆：opt（眼睛）+ ical → 视力的

搭 optical aids 助视器

例 We'll discuss *optical* fibres and how they could be used in the future to improve *optical* instruments. 我们将讨论光纤以及将来如何把它们用于改善光学仪器等问题。

optimism
[ˈɒptɪmɪzəm]

n. 乐观，乐观主义

记 词根记忆：optim（最好）+ ism（抽象名词后缀）→ 认为自己是最好的 → 乐观，乐观主义

例 The document does seem to be based on an unrealistic *optimism*. 这一文献似乎是建立在一种不现实的乐观主义的基础之上。

反 pessimism（*n.* 悲观，悲观主义）

□ operational □ opponent □ opportunity □ oppose □ opposite □ optic
□ optical □ optimism

optimistic*
[ˌɒptɪˈmɪstɪk]

a. 乐观的，乐观主义的

记 词根记忆：optim(最好) + istic → 什么都往最好处想的 → 乐观的

例 Psychologists have conducted studies showing that people become more *optimistic* when the weather is sunny. 心理学家已进行的研究表明，人们在阳光灿烂的日子里会更加乐观。

optimistic

optimum
[ˈɒptɪməm]

a. 最好的；最有利的

记 词根记忆：optim(最好) + um → 最好的

例 The *optimum* time for playing would depend on when it was most advantageous for the young of a particular species to do so. 玩耍的最佳时间取决于何时玩耍对某一特定物种的幼崽最为有利。

同 optimal(*a.* 最佳的，最理想的)；ideal(*a.* 理想的，完美的)

option
[ˈɒpʃn]

n. 选择(权)；(供)选择的物(或人)；选课

记 联想记忆：opt(选择) + ion → 选择

例 To increase the output of crops per acre, a farmer's easiest *option* is to use fertilisers and pesticides. 为增加每英亩农作物的产量，农民最简单的选择是使用肥料和杀虫剂。

optional*
[ˈɒpʃənl]

a. 可选择的，非强制的，随意的

记 联想记忆：option(选择) + al → 可选择的

搭 an optional course 选修课

例 Is geography an *optional* course, or does everyone have to learn it? 地理是选修课吗，还是每个人都必须学习？

optometrist
[ɒpˈtɒmətrɪst]

n. 验光师，视力测定者

记 词根记忆：opto(眼睛) + metr(测量) + ist(表人) → 验光师，视力测定者

例 Students will have a chance to ask *optometrists* any questions at the end of the lecture. 讲座结束时，学生们将有机会向验光师提问。 32

opulence
[ˈɒpjələns]

n. 财富，富裕；丰富，富饶

例 The lecture hall was decorated with stagy *opulence*. 演讲大厅装点着丰富的舞台装饰。

opulent*
[ˈɒpjələnt]

a. 豪华的，华丽的，富裕的；丰富的，丰饶的

记 词根记忆：op(财富) + ul + ent(形容词后缀) → 富裕的

例 The research suggests that even the most *opulent*, luxurious hotels seem to have underestimated the most basic needs of their customers. 调查显示，即使是最华丽、最奢侈的酒店似乎也低估了顾客最根本的需求。

orbit
[ˈɔːbɪt]

n. 轨道；影响范围，势力范围 *v.* 沿轨道运行；围绕…运动

记 词根记忆：orb(轨道) + it → 轨道

例 There have been hundreds of satellites put into *orbit* round the earth this year. 今年数以百计的人造卫星被送入环绕地球的轨道。

□ optimistic □ optimum □ option □ optional □ optometrist □ opulence
□ opulent □ orbit

orchestra [ˈɔːkɪstrə]	*n.* 管弦乐队 记 联想记忆：or + chest（胸腔）+ ra → 管弦乐队的成员大都需借助胸腔的力气吹奏乐器 → 管弦乐队 例 Which *orchestra* do you think is the finest in our country? 你觉得我国最棒的管弦乐队是哪一支？
organ* [ˈɔːgən]	*n.* 器官；(官方的)机构 例 The main *organs* of communication for the WSPU were its two newspapers. 妇女社会与政治联盟的主要联络机构是其创办的两家报纸。
organic* [ɔːˈgænɪk]	*a.* 器官的；有机的；有机体的；组织的 搭 organic being 有机体；organic food 有机食品；organic fiber 有机纤维 例 Many synthetic polymers are *organic* compounds. 很多合成聚合物都是有机化合物。
organism [ˈɔːgənɪzəm]	*n.* 生物；有机体 例 This insect is on a list of *organisms* known to be harmful. 这种昆虫属于有害物种。
organize [ˈɔːgənaɪz]	*v.* 组织，使有条理；成立 搭 organize an activity 组织活动；organized crime 团伙犯罪 例 Classes are *organized* according to ability level. 根据能力水平进行分班。
orientate* [ˈɔːrienteɪt]	*vt.* 使适应，使熟悉情况(或环境等)；给…定位，给…定向；使朝向；转至特定方向；适应（=orient） 例 The course at this university has a vocational focus on preparing its graduates for work, so students are *orientated* at employment. 这所大学的课程以职业为中心，注重毕业生工作之前的准备工作，因此将学生朝着就业方向培养。
orientation* [ˌɔːrienˈteɪʃn]	*n.* 定位；方向，方位；情况介绍；培训，训练 记 来自 orient(*vt.* 给…定向) 搭 an orientation meeting 介绍会；an orientation course 上岗培训课 例 Now that everyone knows what team they're in, we'll get on with the *orientation* programme. 既然每个人都明确了自己所在的小组，我们接着就开始进行培训项目。
orientation meeting	新生报到会 例 This information is all in the handout which you should have received at the *orientation meeting.* 这些信息在你从新生报到会上领到的手册上都有。
origin* [ˈɒrɪdʒɪn]	*n.* 起源；[常 *pl.*] 出身 记 词根记忆：ori(产生) + gin → 开始，本源 → 起源 搭 have origins in 源于 例 The *origins* of what is now generally known as modern architecture can be traced back to the social and technological changes of the 18th and 19th centuries. 通常意义上的现代建筑学的起源可以追溯到 18、19 世纪的社会和科技变革。

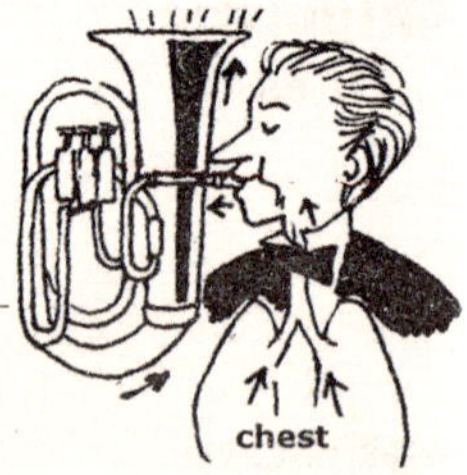

□ orchestra □ organ □ organic □ organism □ organize □ orientate
□ orientation □ orientation meeting □ origin

original* [əˈrɪdʒənl]

a. 最初的，原始的；新颖的，有独创性的 *n.* 原物，原作

搭 original handwriting 真迹；an original viewpoint 全新观点；an original play 原创剧

例 Their *original* house was converted into a residential college. 他们最初的房子被改建成了一所寄宿学校。// How important do you think it is for a film-maker to remain true to the *original* story? 你认为电影制片人忠于原著有多重要?

originate* [əˈrɪdʒɪneɪt]

v. 起源，发生；首创，创造

记 联想记忆：origin(起源) + ate(动词后缀) → 起源，发生

搭 originate in/from 起源于，由…引起/产生

例 According to my research, this type of banana actually *originated* in China. 根据我的研究，事实上，这种香蕉起源于中国。

派 origination(*n.* 起源); originator(*n.* 发起者，发明人); originative(*a.* 有创作力的)

ornament* [ˈɔːnəmənt]

n. 装饰；装饰物 *vt.* 装饰，修饰，美化

记 词根记忆：orn(装饰) + ament → 装饰；装饰物

搭 for ornament 以作装饰；be ornamented with sth. 用…装饰

例 The exhibition wall is covered with paintings and *ornaments*. 这面展示墙上满是油画和装饰物。

派 ornamenter(*n.* 装饰者)

ornamental* [ˌɔːnəˈmentl]

a. 装饰性的，装饰的

例 If you look out here to the south, you can see a circular *ornamental* pond. 如果你从这里往外向南看，可以看到一个环形的装饰性水池。

orthodox [ˈɔːθədɒks]

a. 正统的，传统的

记 词根记忆：ortho(正) + dox(观点) → 正统观点的 → 正统的

搭 orthodox views 传统观念

例 In many other industralised countries, *orthodox* and alternative medicine have worked "hand in glove" for years. 在其他的工业化国家里，传统医学与替代医学已经紧密结合多年了。

派 orthodoxy(*n.* 正统观念)

同 conventional(*a.* 传统的); customary(*a.* 习惯的，惯例的)

otherwise* [ˈʌðəwaɪz]

ad. 另样，用别的方法；在其他方面 *conj.* 要不然，否则

例 It's a ten-minute taxi ride from the station and will cost you £5, *otherwise*, you can take the bus which runs every half and an hour from the station. 从车站打车(到这)要十分钟，车费是五英镑。另外，你还可以乘从车站出发的公共汽车，一个半小时一班。

ounce [aʊns]

n. 盎司

例 This can weighs about 0.48 *ounces*. 这个罐子约重 0.48 盎司。

outcome [ˈaʊtkʌm]

n. 结果，成果；后果；结局；出口，输出量

记 来自词组 come out(出来)

例 Some environmentalists worry about this *outcome*. 一些环境保护主义者对这个结果表示担心。

32

□ original □ originate □ ornament □ ornamental □ orthodox □ otherwise
□ ounce □ outcome

outdo* [ˌaʊtˈduː]

vt. 超越，胜过

记 组合词：out(超过) + do(做) → 超越，胜过

例 The two universities are always trying to *outdo* each other academically. 这两所大学总是试图在学术上超过对方。

outlaw [ˈaʊtlɔː]

n. 亡命之徒，逃犯，被剥夺法律权益者 *vt.* 宣布…为非法，使…成为非法

记 组合词：out(超过) + law(法律) → 超出法律范围 → 宣布…为非法，使…成为非法

例 So far, the government's attempt to *outlaw* drunken driving has proved to be unsuccessful. 到目前为止，事实证明该政府试图使酒后驾车成为非法行为的努力失败了。

outline [ˈaʊtlaɪn]

n. 提纲；梗概；轮廓；草图 *vt.* 概述；列提纲

记 组合词：out(外部的) + line(线条) → 外部线条 → 轮廓；草图

搭 an outline of a speech 讲话提纲

例 The guide gave us a brief *outline* of the museum's history. 导游向我们大致介绍了这座博物馆的历史。 // He *outlined* his proposals to us. 他向我们概述了他的提案。

outlook [ˈaʊtlʊk]

n. 观点，见解；展望，前景

记 组合词：out(外面) + look(看) → 向外看 → 展望

例 The highly respected old man has a fairly positive *outlook* on life. 这位德高望重的老人对待生活非常乐观。

outpost [ˈaʊtpəʊst]

n. 前哨(站)；偏远村落

记 组合词：out(外面的) + post(柱；岗位) → 靠外的岗位 → 前哨(站)

例 There is a remote *outpost* in the most north part of the town. 小镇的最北端有一处偏僻的哨站。

output* [ˈaʊtpʊt]

n. 产量；输出量；输出功率 *vt.* 输出

记 组合词：out(外面) + put(放) → 输出

搭 farm output 农业生产量；the annual output of steel 钢的年产量

例 In the rich countries，subsidies for growing crops and price supports for farm *output* drive up the price of land. 在富裕的国家，农作物种植补助金以及针对农业产量的政府津贴抬高了地价。

outsell* [ˌaʊtˈsel]

vt. 卖得比…多

例 This kind of digital camera *outsells* all others on the market. 这款数码相机在市场上较其他型号畅销。

outward [ˈaʊtwəd]

a. 外面的；外表的，表面的

例 The scientist warned the local population against being deceived by the volcano's *outward* calm. 科学家警告当地居民不要被这座火山表面的平静所欺骗。

□ outdo □ outlaw □ outline □ outlook □ outpost □ output
□ outsell □ outward

outweigh* [ˌaʊt ˈweɪ]

vt. 比…重；(在重要性、影响上)比…更重要；胜过，强于

记 组合词：out(超过) + weigh(称重) → 比…更重要

例 The risks are vastly *outweighed* by the potential benefits. 潜在的利益要远远高于所要承担的风险。

overall* [ˌəʊvər ˈɔːl]

a. 全面的；全部的

记 组合词：over(从头到尾) + all(所有的) → 全面的；全部的

搭 overall checkup 全面检查

例 The *overall* absence rate of the company was 3.6 percent in the first year. 公司第一年度的总缺勤率为3.6%。

overcome* [ˌəʊvə ˈkʌm]

vt. 战胜，克服；(感情等)压倒

记 来自词组 come over(战胜；支配)

例 I don't believe limited resources and ecological constraints are *overcome* by personal skills. 我相信个人技术不能克服资源有限和生态限制的困难。

overdraft* [ˈəʊvədrɑːft]

n. 透支；透支额

例 Some workers have a huge *overdraft* to pay off every month. 一些工人每个月都要偿还巨额透支款。

overdue* [ˌəʊvə ˈdjuː]

a. 过期未付的；逾期的；过度的，过火的；迟到的，延误的

记 组合词：over(超过) + due(预期的) → 超过期限的 → 逾期的

例 The landlord is not very pleased because the rent is *overdue*. 因为房租过期未付，房东不是很高兴。

overestimate* [ˌəʊvər ˈestɪmeɪt] *vt.* 对…估计过高 [ˌəʊvər ˈestɪmət] *n.* 过高的估计 32

例 The company *overestimated* his ability when they employed him. 这家公司在雇用他时高估了他的能力。

overexploit [ˌəʊvərɪk ˈsplɔɪt]

vt. 过度开采

例 Many valuable natural resources, like coal and oil, are in the verge of exhaustion because people are *overexploiting* them. 由于人们过度开采，像煤和石油之类宝贵的自然资源正濒临枯竭。

overfill* [ˈəʊvəˌfɪl]

v. 装得太多，装到满溢

记 组合词：over(过度) + fill(装满) → 装得太多，装到满溢

例 It's dangerous to *overfill* liquid storage tanks. 贮罐过量充装液体是危险的。

overgraze [ˈəʊvəgreɪz]

v. 过度放牧

记 组合词：over(过度) + graze(放牧) → 过度放牧

例 Once the grass land is *overgrazed*, the vegetation will be damaged and the ground will become liable to erosion. 一旦草地遭到过度放牧，就会导致植被受损，土壤易于流失。

□ outweigh □ overall □ overcome □ overdraft □ overdue □ overestimate
□ overexploit □ overfill □ overgraze

overhead* [ˈəʊvəhed] *a.* 在头顶上的；高架的 *n.* 天花板；企业管理费用

[ˌəʊvəˈhed] *ad.* 在空中，在头顶上，在高处

记 组合词：over(在…之上) + head(头) → 在头顶上，在高处

搭 overhead projector 高射投影仪

例 The *overhead* cable will be harmful to the transport security. 高架电缆会危及交通安全。

overlap [ˌəʊvəˈlæp]

v. (使)部分重叠，交叠

记 联想记忆：over(在…之上) + lap(大腿) → 把一条腿放在另一条腿上 → (使)部分重叠

例 Our jobs *overlap* slightly, which causes difficulties. 我们的工作略有重叠，所以有时引起一些困难。

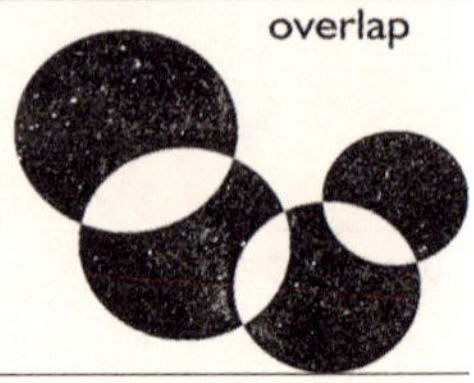

overlapping* [ˌəʊvəˈlæpɪŋ]

a. 重叠的；共通的

例 The two girls of *overlapping* interests went shopping together. 两个兴趣相同的女孩一起去购物了。

overlie [ˌəʊvəˈlaɪ]

v. 躺在…上面；置于…上面

记 组合词：over(在…之上) + lie(躺；放) → 躺在…上面；置于…上面

例 It is recognized by the public that *overlying* on the beach is very comfortable. 大家公认躺在海滩上很舒服。

The brotherly spirit of science, which unites into one family all its votaries of whatever grade, and however widely dispersed throughout the different quarters of the globe.

科学的博爱精神把分散在世界各地，各种热心科学的人联结成一个大家庭。

——美国总统 罗斯福 .F.（Franklin Roosevelt, American President）

Word List 33

音频

词根、词缀预习表

ox	氧气	oxide *n.* 氧化物	**par**	并列	parallel *a.* 类似的，相对应的
path	病痛	pathology *n.* 病理学	**ped**	脚	pedal *n.* 踏板
pen	惩罚	penalize *vt.* 惩罚，处罚	**pens**	悬挂	pension *n.* 养老金
meter	测量	perimeter *n.* 周长；周边	**pher**	带来	peripheral *a.* 外围的
man	流动	permanent *a.* 永久的，持久的	**mea**	流过	permeate *v.* 扩散，弥漫

overrate* [ˌəʊvəˈreɪt]

vt. 对…评价过高，高估

记 组合词：over(过度) + rate(估价) → 对…评价过高

例 Do you think the good team player is *overrated*? 你认为那个优秀的队员被高估了吗？

overseas* [ˌəʊvəˈsiːz]

a. 在海外的 *ad.* 在海外

记 组合词：over(越过) + seas(海) → 漂洋过海 → 在海外(的)

例 *Overseas* students may enrol for a course at the college from their home country. 留学生可以在本国报名学习大学的课程。

oversee* [ˌəʊvəˈsiː]

vt. 监督，监视(某人或某物)；俯瞰，眺望

记 组合词：over(在…之上) + see(看) → 监督

搭 oversee the project 监督这个项目

例 You must appoint someone to *oversee* the project. 你得指派个人监督这个项目。

overshadow [ˌəʊvəˈʃædəʊ]

vt. 给…蒙上阴影；使扫兴；使黯然失色

记 联想记忆：over(在…之上) + shadow(阴影) → 使黯然失色

例 News of the severe accident *overshadowed* the whole day's events. 那场严重的交通事故使得一整天的新闻都显得无足轻重了。

overview* [ˈəʊvəvjuː]

n. 综览，概述

例 Susan usually gives us a brief *overview* of what this class will involve. 苏珊通常在上课之前会就这节课的内容做一个概述。

overweight* [ˌəʊvəˈweɪt]

a. 超重的，过重的 *n.* 超重，过重 *vt.* 使负担过重

搭 overweight baggage 超重行李

例 Being *overweight* is a reason why back pain becomes worse. 超重负荷是导致背部疼痛恶化的一个原因。

□ overrate □ overseas □ oversee □ overshadow □ overview □ overweight

overwhelm [ˌəʊvəˈwelm]	*vt.* 征服；淹没 记 组合词：over(在…之上) + whelm(淹没，压倒) → 征服 例 The village was ***overwhelmed*** by the flood. 那个村庄被洪水淹没了。 派 overwhelming(*a.* 势不可挡的，压倒性的；巨大的)
overwork [ˌəʊvəˈwɜːk]	*v.* 使劳累过分；对…使用过度；滥用(词等) *n.* 过重的工作；工作过度 例 He has been ***overworking*** for two months, at last he fell ill in the workplace. 他已经连续劳累工作两个月之久，最后病倒在了工作岗位上。
owe* [əʊ]	*vt.* 欠；把…归功于 例 I ***owed*** the bank rather a lot of money a few years ago. 几年前，我欠了银行一大笔钱。
owl [aʊl]	*n.* 猫头鹰 例 The ***owl*** sleeps in the day and comes out to catch mice in the night. 猫头鹰白天睡觉，晚上出来抓老鼠。
oxide [ˈɒksaɪd]	*n.* 氧化物 记 词根记忆：ox(=oxy 氧) + ide → 氧化物 例 The greenhouse effect is a natural phenomenon due to the presence of greenhouse gases—water vapour, carbon dioxide and nitrous ***oxide***—in the atmosphere. 温室效应是一种由大气中的水蒸气、二氧化碳和一氧化二氮这些温室气体形成的自然现象。 派 oxidant(*n.* 氧化剂)
oxygen* [ˈɒksɪdʒən]	*n.* 氧，氧气 记 词根记忆：oxy(酸) + gen(产生) → 产生酸的 → 氧，氧气 例 ***Oxygen*** masks are used by the scientists for a shortage of oxygen at the top of the mountain. 由于山顶缺氧，科学家需要戴氧气罩。
ozone [ˈəʊzəʊn]	*n.* 臭氧 搭 ozone hole 臭氧洞 例 Carbon dioxide, nitrogen dioxide, ***ozone*** were among the pollutants monitored by the WHO. 二氧化碳、二氧化氮和臭氧都属于世界卫生组织监控的污染物。
ozone layer	臭氧层 例 Among green consumers, animal testing is the top issue—followed by concerns regarding the ***ozone layer***, river and sea pollution, and forest destruction. 绿色消费者最关注的是动物试验的问题，其次是臭氧层、河流和海洋的污染以及森林破坏的问题。
pack* [pæk]	*v.* (把…)打包，收拾(行李)；包装，包裹；塞满 *n.* 包 搭 pack up 收拾行装，打点行李；停止，放弃，辞掉 例 The canteen was absolutely ***packed***. 餐厅挤满了人。
pad [pæd]	*n.* 软垫；便笺本 *v.* (用软材料)填塞；蹑手蹑脚地走 例 Secretary always puts a ***pad*** by the telephone for taking notes. 秘书总是在电话机旁放一个便笺本以便做记录。

□ overwhelm □ overwork □ owe □ owl □ oxide □ oxygen
□ ozone □ ozone layer □ pack □ pad

painstaking
[ˈpeɪnzteɪkɪŋ]

a. 需细心的，辛苦的，煞费苦心的；勤勉的；刻苦的 *n.* 辛苦；勤勉；刻苦

记 组合词：pains(痛苦) + taking(花费…的) → 煞费苦心的

搭 work with painstaking 尽心地工作

例 It is a *painstaking* task of interpretation, so that we come to understand what these things mean for the human story. 诠释工作需要非常细心，这样我们才能了解这些事情对人类历史意味着什么。

pamper*
[ˈpæmpə(r)]

vt. 纵容，娇惯；精心护理

例 There is something very powerful in our need to be *pampered* and looked after; it's almost as if we return to being a baby, when everything was done for us and we felt safe and secure. 我们需要被纵容和照顾的情绪很强烈，当所有事情都为我们做好，我们感到安全无忧的时候，几乎就像回到了婴儿状态。

pamphlet
[ˈpæmflət]

n. 小册子

例 The *pamphlet* was regarded as a masterpiece of wit. 这本小册子被看成智慧的杰作。

panic*
[ˈpænɪk]

a. 恐慌的 *n.* 恐慌，惊惶 *v.* (使)惊慌失措

例 In fact I'm starting to *panic* as the project deadline is in two weeks and I don't seem to be making any progress at all. 事实上，当距工程的最后期限还剩两个星期时我开始惊慌失措起来，那时我还是一点进展也没有。

parallel
[ˈpærəlel]

n. 可相比拟的事物(或人)，相似处；纬线 *a.* 平行的；类似的，相对应的；并行的 *vt.* 与…相似；比得上

记 词根记忆：par(并列) + all(其他的) + el → 把不同的东西并列放置 → 类似的，相对应的

搭 parallel to 与…平行；parallel lines 平行线；parallel bars 双杠

例 The expressway is *parallel* to the railway. 这条高速公路与铁路平行。// Tom's experiences *parallel* mine in many instances. 在很多方面，汤姆的经历都与我的相似。

paralysis
[pəˈræləsɪs]

n. 瘫痪，麻痹，中风

记 词根记忆：para(半) + lys(分开) + is → 身体裂成两半 → 瘫痪，麻痹

例 The doctor injects the patient to *paralysis* before the medical operation, to lower the pain. 在做手术之前，医生通常会给病人注射麻醉剂，来减轻疼痛。

paramount
[ˈpærəmaʊnt]

a. 最重要的，决定性的 *n.* 最高统治者

记 联想记忆：par + amount(数量) → 在量上超过别的 → 最重要的，决定性的

例 We believed that it is of *paramount* importance to disseminate knowledge, so that patient care will continue to improve across the Europe and beyond. 我们相信传播知识是最重要的，以使欧洲及其他地方的患者护理得到持续改善。

parcel [ˈpɑːsl]	*n.* 包裹 例 She sent a ***parcel*** of books to her younger sister. 她寄给妹妹一包书。
pardon* [ˈpɑːdn]	*excl.* (用于请求别人重复某事)什么，请再说一遍 *n./vt.* 原谅，宽恕；赦免 例 A: Hurry up, Lucy! B: ***Pardon***? A: I said hurry up! A: 露西，快点！ B: 什么？ A: 我说快点！
parental [pəˈrentl]	*a.* 父的；母的；父母(般)的 例 The government repeatedly stressed its support for ***parental*** choice in the selection of a child's school. 政府一再重申其支持家长对孩子教育的选择权。
parliament [ˈpɑːləmənt]	*n.* 议会，国会 记 联想记忆：parlia(看作 parle，谈判) + ment → 谈判的地方 → 议会 例 The exhibition met with great opposition from ***Parliament***. 这次展览遭到了国会的强烈反对。
partial [ˈpɑːʃl]	*a.* 部分的，不完全的；偏爱的，癖好的；偏向一方的，偏心的 搭 partial imitation 部分模仿 例 Parents should not be ***partial*** to any one of their children. 父母不该对某个孩子偏心。 派 partially(*ad.* 部分地)
participant* [pɑːˈtɪsɪpənt]	*n.* 参加者，参与者 记 联想记忆：parti(看作 party，聚会) + cip + ant → 参加聚会的人 → 参与者 例 Group tours encourage ***participants*** to look at new objects and places. 团体旅游鼓励游客多去看新景点。
participate* [pɑːˈtɪsɪpeɪt]	*vi.* 参加，参与 记 词根记忆：part(部分) + i + cip(拿，取) + ate → 拿住部分 → 参加 搭 participate in 参加 例 More and more women are ***participating*** in politics. 越来越多的女性投身政治。
participation* [pɑːˌtɪsɪˈpeɪʃn]	*n.* 分享；参与 记 来自 participate(*vi.* 参与) 例 The students below 20 years old are not given the ***participation*** in the ball. 20 岁以下的学生不允许参加舞会。
particle [ˈpɑːtɪkl]	*n.* 极少量；微粒 记 联想记忆：part(部分) + icle(看作 article，物品) → 物品的一部分 → 极少量 例 This type of smoke contains more, smaller ***particles*** and is therefore more likely to be deposited deep in the lungs. 这种烟含有更多更小的颗粒，因此更可能沉淀到肺部深处。

□ parcel □ pardon □ parental □ parliament □ partial □ participant
□ participate □ participation □ particle

particular* [pəˈtɪkjələ(r)]	*a.* 特殊的，特别的；特定的，个别的；详细的 *n.* 详情，细目，细节 记 词根记忆：part(部分) + icular(属于…的) → 只属于部分的 → 特别的 搭 in particular 特别，尤其 例 Does the course has anything in *particular*? 这个课程有什么特殊之处吗? 派 particularity(*n.* 特性；特殊性)
particularly* [pəˈtɪkjələli]	*ad.* 特别，尤其 记 联想记忆：particular(特别的) + ly → 特别，尤其 例 Mary was *particularly* fond of bananas. 玛丽特别爱吃香蕉。
particulate [pəˈtɪkjəleɪt]	*a.* 粒子状的，微粒的，颗粒的 *n.* 粒子，微粒状物质 搭 particulate matter 颗粒物质 例 *Particulate* matter in soils and aquatic systems reacts with and influences the biological activity of pesticides. 土壤和水系统中的颗粒物质都与农药的生物活动起反应，并影响后者。
passionate [ˈpæʃənət]	*a.* 充满激情的，热切的，狂热的 记 联想记忆：passion(激情) + ate → 充满激情的 例 People in the primitive tribe have a *passionate* nature. 原始部落里的人富有激情。
passport* [ˈpɑːspɔːt]	*n.* 护照；途径，路子，手段 记 联想记忆：pass(通过) + port(港口) → 通过港口所需的文件 → 护照 例 This country is working to stop the illegal sale of its *passports* to suspected terrorists. 这一国家正在阻止向有恐怖分子嫌疑的人非法出售该国护照。
pasture [ˈpɑːstʃə(r)]	*n.* 牧场，草原 *vt.* 放牧 记 联想记忆：pas(看作 pass，通过) + ture → 牛羊通过的地方 → 牧场，草原 例 More than 1,000 acre fields were planted with crops several years ago, but now are returned to *pasture* for the cattle. 数年前，这里是 1000 多英亩的农田，如今退耕还牧，成为牧场。 派 pasturage(*n.* 放牧) 同 meadow(*n.* 草地，牧场)；grassland(*n.* 牧草地，草原)
patent	[ˈpætnt；ˈpeɪtnt] *vt.* 取得专利权 *n.* 专利(权) [ˈpeɪtnt] *a.* 显而易见的；有专利的，受专利保护的 搭 patent device 专利设备；apply for a patent 申请专利 例 Walker never *patented* his invention. 沃克从未为自己的发明申请专利。
pathology* [pəˈθɒlədʒi]	*n.* 病理学；病变 记 词根记忆：path(病痛) + ology(…学) → 病理学 例 My first class in this term is plant *pathology*. 这学期我的第一节课是植物病理学。
pathway* [ˈpɑːθweɪ]	*n.* 路径，途径 记 组合词：path(小路) + way(道路) → 路径，途径 例 There are new pedestrian *pathways* being built alongside the road. 这条路周围要修建新的步行路。

33

□ particular □ particularly □ particulate □ passionate □ passport □ pasture
□ patent □ pathology □ pathway

patriotic
[ˌpætriˈɒtɪk; ˌpeɪtriˈɒtɪk]

a. 爱国的，有爱国心的；显示出爱国精神的

搭 patriotic emotion 爱国感情

例 Teenagers felt it's *patriotic* to serve in the army to maintain world peace. 年轻人认为，为维护世界和平而服兵役是爱国的表现。

派 patriotism（*n.* 爱国主义，爱国精神）；patriot（*n.* 爱国者）

patriotic

patronage
[ˈpætrənɪdʒ]

n. 赞助；支持；光顾；任免权

记 联想记忆：patron（赞助人）+ age → 赞助；支持

例 "That gave those party bosses handy powers of *patronage*, but it was deadly for democracy," he said angrily. 他愤怒地指出："那等于给了党派领袖们便利的任免大权，却给民主判了死刑。"

pattern
[ˈpætn]

n. 样式；模式 *vt.* 构成图案；使形成，促成

例 How do you think the Internet will affect buying *patterns* in the future? 你认为互联网会如何影响未来的购买模式？

pavement
[ˈpeɪvmənt]

n. 人行道；地面，路面

例 According to the report, 30% of graduates will spend about four months pounding the *pavement* in search of a job. 据报道，30%的毕业生要花大约四个月的时间四处奔波寻找一份工作。

payable
[ˈpeɪəbl]

a. 可支付的；应支付的

记 联想记忆：pay（支付，给予）+ able（能…的）→ 可支付的；应支付的

例 Our company was asked a 10% deposit *payable* in advance. 我们公司需要预付 10%的定金。

payment*
[ˈpeɪmənt]

n. 支付；支付的款项

例 You may spread your *payments* over a longer period. 你可以将你的支付期顺延得更长。

pearl
[pɜːl]

n. 珍珠

例 The young lady was wearing a *pearl* necklace. 那个年轻的女士戴着一根珍珠项链。

pedal
[ˈpedl]

v. 骑车；踩踏板 *n.* 踏板

记 词根记忆：ped（脚）+ al → 脚踏的东西 → 踏板

例 The riders *pedaled* fast along the rocky road. 车手们在崎岖的路上飞快地骑着脚踏车。

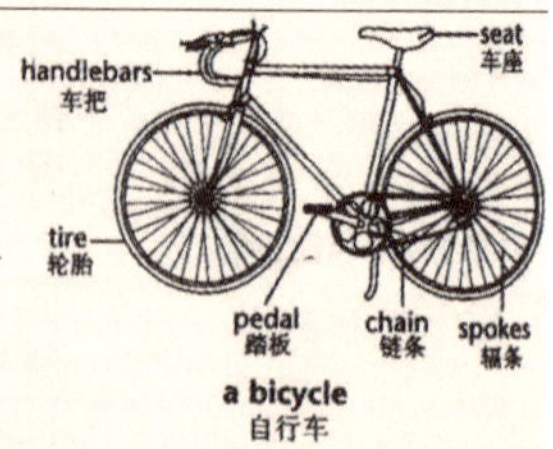

pedestrian*
[pəˈdestriən]

n. 行人 *a.* 徒步的；缺乏想象力的

记 词根记忆：ped（脚）+ estrian → 用脚走的人 → 行人

例 Two *pedestrians* were injured when a car skidded round them. 一辆汽车失控滑向两名路人并将其撞伤。

pedigree
[ˈpedɪgriː]

n. 家谱；门第；血统

例 He was adopted as a child, so he had no opportunity of learning his own *pedigree*. 他从小被人收养，没有机会了解自己的身世。

□ patriotic □ patronage □ pattern □ pavement □ payable □ payment
□ pearl □ pedal □ pedestrian □ pedigree

penalize [ˈpiːnəlaɪz]

vt. 惩罚，处罚；判罚；使处于不利地位

记 词根记忆：pen(惩罚) + al + ize(使…) → 惩罚，处罚

例 It's unfair that the whole medical staff should be *penalized* just because a nurse made a mistake. 仅仅因为一个护士犯错误，就惩罚所有的医务人员，这是不公平的。

penalty [ˈpenəlti]

n. 惩罚；罚金

记 词根记忆：pen(刑事的) + al + ty(名词后缀) → 惩罚；罚金

搭 death penalty 死刑

例 People who work reduced hours pay a huge *penalty* in career terms. 缩短工作时间的人事业上会遭到严重损失。

penetration [ˌpenɪˈtreɪʃn]

n. 进入，穿过；洞察力，领悟力

例 The company's successful *penetration* into E-business environment survived the depression. 这个公司成功地进军电子商务领域，终于挺过了大萧条时期。

pension [ˈpenʃn]

n. 养老金，抚恤金；年金

记 词根记忆：pens(悬挂，引申为“付钱”) + ion → 养老金

搭 live on a pension 靠退休金/抚恤金生活；receive a retirement pension 领退休金；a state pension 国家抚恤金

例 Even hourly employees receive benefits—such as *pension* contributions and medical insurance—that are not tied to the number of hours they work. 即使小时工也享受养老金和医疗保险等福利，但这些福利与他们工作的时间没有关系。

pepper [ˈpepə(r)]

n. 胡椒(粉) *vt.* 在…上撒(胡椒粉等)

例 Only a dash of *pepper* is enough for the dish. 这道菜只需放一点儿胡椒粉就可以了。

perceive [pəˈsiːv]

vt. 感知，察觉；认识到，理解

记 词根记忆：per(全部) + ceiv(拿住) + e → 全部拿住 → 感知，察觉

例 While I was examining the small stars, I *perceived* one that appeared visibly larger than the rest. 我观察那些小星星时，发现有一颗明显比其他的大。// Tom *perceived* Mary's comment as a challenge. 汤姆认为玛丽的批评是对他的一种激励。

同 detect(*vt.* 察觉，发觉)；comprehend(*v.* 领会，理解)

percentage* [pəˈsentɪdʒ]

n. 百分比，百分率

记 联想记忆：percent(百分比) + age(集体名词后缀) → 百分比，百分率

例 What *percentage* of the workforce was employed in agriculture in this country in the mid 1900s? 在 20 世纪中期，这个国家从事农业的劳动力在总劳动力中占多大比例?

□ penalize □ penalty □ penetration □ pension □ pepper □ perceive □ percentage

perception [pə'sepʃn]

n. 看法；感觉；洞察力

记 来自 perceive（*vt.* 感知，察觉）

例 Your *perception* and mine are different from the *perception* of someone who speaks French, for instance. 例如，你的想法与我的想法跟那些说法语的人的想法是不一样的。

派 perceptible（*a.* 可以感觉到的，看得出来的）；perceptive（*a.* 感知的；有理解力的，有识别力的）

perform* [pə'fɔːm]

v. 履行，执行，完成；表演，演出；（机器）运作

记 联想记忆：per（每）+ form（形式）→ 表演是各种艺术形式的综合 → 表演，演出

搭 perform on 演奏

例 Why did the divers *perform* worse in colder conditions? 为什么在较冷的条件下潜水者会表现得差些呢？// We are going to *perform Sleep Beauty* tonight. 我们今晚将表演《睡美人》。

performance* [pə'fɔːməns]

n. 演出，表演；履行，执行；功能，性能表现

搭 live performances 现场表演

例 Profits continue to grow, with strong *performance* in Asia and South America. 利润持续增长，这一点在亚洲及南美市场表现尤为明显。

perimeter [pə'rɪmɪtə(r)]

n. 周长；周边

记 词根记忆：peri（周围）+ meter（测量）→ 周长

例 A river runs along one side of the field's *perimeter*. 小河沿着这块地的一边延伸。

periodical* [ˌpɪəri'ɒdɪkl]

n. 期刊，杂志 *a.* 周期的，定期的

记 来自 period（*n.* 时期，周期）

例 The professor's paper has been issued in the latest *periodical*. 教授的论文已经发表在最近的一期期刊上。

派 periodically（*ad.* 周期地；定期地，按时地）

同 journal（*n.* 定期刊物，杂志）；magazine（*n.* 杂志，期刊）

peripheral [pə'rɪfərəl]

a. 外围的；次要的，附带的 *n.* 外围设备

记 词根记忆：peri（周围）+ pher（带来）+ al → 外围的

搭 peripheral information 辅助信息

例 If we think of a book we studied months or years ago, we will find it easier to recall *peripheral* details. 当我们回想几个月或几年前读过的一本书时，我们更容易记起一些细枝末节。

periphery [pə'rɪfəri]

n. 不重要的部分；外围

记 词根记忆：peri（周围）+ pher（带来）+ y → 带到周围 → 不重要的部分；外围

例 Ideas on this matter are also expressed by some scholars on the *periphery* of education area. 教育领域之外的一些学者也对此发表了看法。

□ perception □ perform □ performance □ perimeter □ periodical □ peripheral □ periphery

permanent *
[ˈpɜːmənənt]

a. 永久的，持久的

记 词根记忆：per(贯穿) + man(流动) + ent(形容词后缀) → 川流不息的 → 永久的，持久的

搭 an permanent address 永久住址

例 Instead of moving from place to place the family needed *permanent* dwellings. 这家人需要一个长期的居住地，而不是不断地搬家。

派 permanency(*n.* 永存)；permanently(*ad.* 永久地)

permeate
[ˈpɜːmieɪt]

v. 扩散，弥漫；渗透，渗入

记 词根记忆：per(全部) + mea(经过，流过) + te → 全部经过 → 扩散，弥漫；渗透

例 As a kind of research study, this method is *permeated* in all the courses as well as all activities of students. 作为一种研究性学习，这种方法渗透于学生的所有学科和所有活动中。

派 permeation(*n.* 渗入，透过)；permeant(*a.* 浸透的)

同 penetrate(*v.* 穿透，渗透)；saturate(*vt.* 浸透，使充满)

permission *
[pəˈmɪʃn]

n. 允许，准许

记 词根记忆：per(贯穿，自始至终) + miss(送) + ion → 始终送出 → 允许，准许

搭 without permission 未经许可；special permission 特许；planning permission 规划许可

例 Students living in the hall do not need *permission* to park their cars. 住宿生(在宿舍停车场)停车无须得到许可。

perpetrate
[ˈpɜːpətreɪt]

vt. 做(坏事)，犯(罪)

例 Nowadays, there is a common phenomenon in society that more and more criminals make use of new scientific technologies to *perpetrate* crimes. 如今，社会上出现一个普遍的现象，越来越多的犯罪分子利用新的科学技术从事犯罪活动。

perpetual
[pəˈpetʃuəl]

a. 连续不断的；长期的；永久的

记 词根记忆：per(自始至终) + pet(追求) + ual → 自始至终追求的 → 长期的；永久的

例 Life itself was a *perpetual* and punishing search for food. 生活本身就是一个不断辛苦找寻食物的过程。

同 eternal(*a.* 永恒的，永远的)；permanent(*a.* 永久的，持久的)；continuous(*a.* 连续的，持续的)

反 temporary(*a.* 暂时的，临时的)

perpetuate
[pəˈpetʃueɪt]

vt. 使永存；使持续

记 词根记忆：per(自始至终) + pet(追求) + uate → 永远追求 → 使持续

例 The pressure from the pain, when used correctly, can dispel fear and *perpetuate* motive power. 源自痛苦的压力，如果运用得当，能驱散恐惧并使动力持久。

33

perplex* [pə'pleks]

vt. 使困惑；使复杂化

记 词根记忆：per(完全) + plex(重叠) → 完全重叠在一起 → 使困惑；使复杂化

例 The leukaemia has continued to ***perplex*** doctors on how to heal. 白血病如何治愈的问题始终困扰着医生。

派 perplexity(*n.* 困惑)；perplexing(*a.* 复杂的)

同 baffle(*vt.* 使困惑)；mystify(*vt.* 使迷惑)；puzzle〔*v.* (使)迷惑〕

perquisite ['pɜːkwɪzɪt]

n. 利益；特权

记 词根记忆：per + quisit(要求) + e →要求(得到全部利益) → 利益

例 Fringe benefits, ***perquisites*** and perks are various non-wage compensations provided to employees in addition to their normal wages or salaries. 额外福利、补贴和津贴是除了正常工资之外，提供给雇员的几种非工资补偿形式。

persist [pə'sɪst]

vi. 坚持；维持，保持，持续

记 词根记忆：per(自始至终) + sist(坐) → 始终坐着 → 坚持；持续

例 If you ***persist*** in indifference, do not make me your confidante. 如果你坚持这么冷漠，就别让我做你的好朋友。

派 persistent(*a.* 持久稳固的)；persistence(*n.* 坚持，持续)

personal* ['pɜːsənl]

a. 个人的，私人的；亲自的，本人的；身体的，人身的

搭 personal loan 个人贷款；personal item 个人物品；personal information 个人信息

例 The woman who lost her briefcase gave the policeman some ***personal*** details. 丢失公文包的那个妇女向警察提供了一些个人信息。

派 personally(*ad.* 个人地)

Every person has two education, one which he receives from others, and one, more important, which he gives himself.

每个人都受两种教育，一种来自别人，另一种更重要的是来自自己。

——英国历史学家 吉朋 .E.（Edward Gibbon, British historian）

Word List 34

音 频

词根、词缀预习表

spect	看	perspective *n.* 角度，方法	**vas**	走	pervasive *a.* 遍布的
plagi	斜的	plagiarism *n.* 剽窃，抄袭	**plaus**	鼓掌	plausible *a.* 似有道理的
pli	弯，折	pliable *a.* 柔韧的	**pol**	磨	polish *v.* 磨光
pos	放	positive *a.* 积极的	**tent**	伸展	potential *a.* 潜在的
ced	前进	precedent *n.* 先例；惯例	**pred**	掠夺	predator *n.* 食肉动物

personality*
[ˌpɜːsəˈnæləti]

n. 人格；个性；名人，人物

搭 personality cult 个人迷信，个人崇拜

例 If you are in a role for long, it eventually becomes part of you, part of your ***personality***. 如果你长久地处于一个角色中，最终它将成为你的一部分，成为你个性的一部分。

personalize
[ˈpɜːsənəlaɪz]

vt. 使成为私人的；在(物品)上标出主人姓名(或记号)；个人化

例 All the towels and cups were ***personalized*** with the initial names of the owners. 所有的毛巾和杯子上都标注了物主姓名的首字母。// Netizens hoped Google search could soon evolve to the point where it is able to answer direct questions and ***personalize*** results. 网民希望谷歌搜索能很快发展到新水平，那时它能直接回答问题并将搜索结果个性化。

personnel
[ˌpɜːsəˈnel]

n. 全体人员，员工

记 联想记忆：员工(personnel)应该有个人(personal)时间

例 All ***personnel*** were asked to participate in the meeting. 此次会议要求全体员工参加。

perspective
[pəˈspektɪv]

n. (判断事物的)角度，方法；透视法

记 词根记忆：per(贯穿) + spect(看) + ive → 贯穿看 → 角度，方法；透视法

例 We were encouraged to see the issue from a different ***perspective*** of view. 我们受到鼓励从不同的视角来看待事物。

persuade*
[pəˈsweɪd]

v. 说服，劝说；使相信

搭 persuade sb. to do sth. 劝说某人做…；persuade sb. into/out of sth. 劝说某人做/不做…

例 I had tried my best to ***persuade*** Bob to join the club. 我竭尽全力说服鲍勃加入俱乐部。

□ personality　□ personalize　□ personnel　□ perspective　□ persuade

pervasive
[pəˈveɪsɪv]

a. 遍布的，弥漫的

记 词根记忆：per(完全) + vas(走) + ive(形容词后缀) → 走遍的 → 遍布的，弥漫的

例 Ageism is *pervasive* and entrenched in our society. 年龄歧视在我们的社会中非常普遍，而且根深蒂固。

pest*
[pest]

n. 害虫

搭 plant pests 作物害虫

例 Some varieties of food plants are especially vulnerable to *pests* or diseases. 一些粮食作物尤其容易受害虫和疾病的危害。

pesticide*
[ˈpestɪsaɪd]

n. 杀虫剂，农药

记 词根记忆：pest(瘟疫) + i + cide(杀) → 杀害虫的东西 → 杀虫剂

例 The main factors that could be contributing to the decline of the species include acid rain and the spread of the *pesticide* residues. 导致这个物种灭绝的主要因素包括酸雨和农药残留物的扩散。

petrol
[ˈpetrəl]

n. 汽油

记 发音记忆："派车" → 汽车有油才能往外派 → 汽油

例 In several countries they have become interested in the possibility of using fuel produced from crop residues as a replacement for *petrol*. 可以将农作物残渣制成燃料并替代汽油，一些国家已经对这种可能性产生兴趣。

petroleum
[pəˈtrəʊliəm]

n. 石油

记 词根记忆：petr(岩石) + ole(油) + um → 石油

例 This newly discovered substance can burn like *petroleum*. 这种新发现的物质可以像石油一样燃烧。

phenomenon*
[fəˈnɒmɪnən]

n. 现象，迹象；非凡的人(或事物)

记 词根记忆：phen(出现) + omen(预兆) + on → 出现预兆的 → 迹象

例 The greenhouse effect is a natural *phenomenon*. 温室效应是一种自然现象。

philosophy
[fəˈlɒsəfɪ]

n. 哲学；哲理

记 词根记忆：philo（爱）+ soph（聪明，智慧）+ y（名词后缀）→ 爱智慧的学问 → 哲学；哲理

例 Try your best to succeed—that's my *philosophy*. 竭尽全力，取得成功——这就是我的人生哲学。

派 philosopher(*n.* 哲学家，哲人)

photocopy*
[ˈfəʊtəʊkɒpi]

v. 影印，复印 *n.* 影印本，复印件

记 组合词：photo(照片，图片) + copy(复制) → 复制照片、图片 → 影印，复印

例 Let's go and *photocopy* the article. 我们去把这篇文章复印一份吧。

□ pervasive □ pest □ pesticide □ petrol □ petroleum □ phenomenon
□ philosophy □ photocopy

photography [fəˈtɒɡrəfi]

n. 摄影术，摄影

记 词根记忆：photo(照片) + graph(书写) + y → 摄影术，摄影

例 He is looking for ways of simplifying *photography*. 他正在寻找简化摄影的方法。

派 photographer(*n.* 摄影师)；photographic(*a.* 摄影的)

physical* [ˈfɪzɪkl]

a. 身体的，肉体的；物理的，物理学的；物质的，有形的 *n.* 体检

搭 physical examination 体检；physical endurance 身体的忍耐力；physical exercise 体育锻炼

例 The *Physical* Fitness Instructor's course is offered as a six-month course. 健身教练培训课程为期六个月。

physician [fɪˈzɪʃn]

n. 内科医生，医师

记 词根记忆：physic(医学) + ian(表人) → 医师

例 The *physician* said smoking was harmful to my health. 医生说吸烟对我的健康有害。

picturesque [ˌpɪktʃəˈresk]

a. 美丽如画的；(语言)生动的

搭 a picturesque village 风景如画的村庄

例 In addition to enjoying the *picturesque* scenery, travelers can visit quaint gift shops, country stores and other local attractions. 除了欣赏如画的美景，游客也可造访雅致的礼品店、乡村店铺和当地其他名胜。

pilot* [ˈpaɪlət]

n. 飞行员，引航员 *vt.* 驾驶，为…引航

记 发音记忆："派了他" → 派他去开飞机 → 飞行员

例 They owed their lives to the skill of the *pilots*. 是飞行员的技术挽救了他们的生命。

pine [paɪn]

v. 难过，悲伤 *n.* 松树，松木

记 联想记忆：松树(pine)的叶子像根针(pin)

搭 pine away(因思念等)憔悴，虚弱；pine for 怀念，思念；渴望

例 The old generation had been *pining* for home since the separation with families nearly half a century ago. 在与家人分离的近半个世纪中，老一辈一直怀念着自己的家。

34

pirate [ˈpaɪərət]

n. 侵犯版权者；海盗 *vt.* 盗用，盗版

记 联想记忆：和 private(*a.* 私人的；秘密的)一起记

例 Anybody can *pirate* our music and software without proper laws. 如果没有适当的法规出台，任何人都可以盗用我们的音乐和软件。

派 piracy(*n.* 海上抢劫；盗版行为)

□ photography □ physical □ physician □ picturesque □ pilot □ pine
□ pirate

pitch*
[pɪtʃ]

v. 投掷；颠簸；为…定音高 *n.* 沥青；场地；程度；最高点；音高

搭 a football/rugby pitch 足球/橄榄球场地；on the pitch 在场上比赛；off the pitch 在场下

例 The little device can give off a high *pitched* noise when you whistle. 当你吹口哨时，这个小装置就会发出尖锐刺耳的声音。

派 pitcher(*n.* 投球手；大水壶)

---

plagiarise
[ˈpleɪdʒəraɪz]

v. 剽窃，抄袭

记 词根记忆：plagi(斜的) + ar + ise → 做歪事 → 剽窃，抄袭

例 If you compare the two essays side by side, it is obvious that the author of the first has *plagiarised*. 如果你对比这两篇文章，就会发现很明显第一篇文章的作者抄袭了第二篇。

---

plagiarism*
[ˈpleɪdʒərɪzəm]

n. (文章、学说等的)剽窃，抄袭；剽窃物

记 词根记忆：plagi(斜的) + ar + ism(抽象名词后缀) → 做歪事 → 剽窃，抄袭

例 I'd like to mention the question of *plagiarism* in particular. 我想特别提一下剽窃问题。

---

plaster
[ˈplɑːstə(r)]

n. 灰泥，石膏；膏药

例 Two layers of *plaster* board will be needed for the interior bedroom walls. 卧室的内墙需要用双层石膏板。

---

plastic*
[ˈplæstɪk]

a. 塑料(制)的

例 The growers put *plastic* bags around the bunches to protect bananas. 种植者用塑料袋把香蕉束罩起来予以保护。

---

plateau
[ˈplætəʊ]

n. 高原；(上升后的)稳定时期(或状态)

记 联想记忆：plat(平的) + eau → 高出平地的地 → 高原

例 In the Deccan *Plateau* in Western India, there are more than two million cubic kilometers of lava. 在印度西部的德干高原，有超过 200 万立方公里的熔岩。

---

platform
[ˈplætfɔːm]

n. 平台，站台；纲领

记 联想记忆：plat(平的) + form(形态) → 形状是平的 → 平台

例 This 520-hectare island serves as the *platform* for the new military airport. 这个 520 公顷的小岛是新的军用机场起落台。

---

plausible
[ˈplɔːzəbl]

a. 似有道理的，貌似真实的；嘴巧的

记 词根记忆：plaus(鼓掌) + ible(可…的) → 可给予鼓掌的 → 似有道理的

例 The little boy could not find *plausible* explanation for the breaking of the beautiful vase. 小男孩找不到任何说得过去的理由来解释漂亮的花瓶怎么碎了。

派 plausibility(*n.* 似乎有理；善辩)；implausible(*a.* 难以置信的，不像真实的)；plausibly(*ad.* 似真地)

同 colorable(*a.* 似是而非的)

反 actual(*a.* 真实的)

pledge* [pledʒ]	*v.* 正式承诺；发誓，保证；抵押，典当 *n.* 誓约，保证；抵押 记 联想记忆：pled(看作 plead，恳求) + ge(音似：哥) → 哥哥发誓要改邪归正，恳求大家的饶恕 → 发誓 搭 fulfill one's pledge 履行诺言；make/give a pledge to do sth. 保证做某事 例 The prime minister has *pledged* today that he will make 250 million dollars available to help the drought-stricken farmers. 总理今天承诺将拨25亿美元帮助受旱灾影响的农民。
pliable* [ˈplaɪəbl]	*a.* (指人或思想)容易受影响的；顺从的；易弯的，柔韧的 记 词根记忆：pli(=ply 弯，折) + able(能…的) → 能弯曲的 → 柔韧的 例 This pair of shoes are made of *pliable* leather. 这双鞋是用软皮做的。
plot [plɔt]	*n.* 情节；阴谋；小块土地 例 The *plot* of this film was too complicated for me. 这部电影的情节对我来讲太复杂了。// Some families grew manioc and other starchy crops in small garden *plots*. 一些家庭在花园的小块地里种植树薯和其他淀粉类作物。
plough [plaʊ]	*n.* 犁 *v.* 耕地；开(路)；破(浪) 搭 plough around 试探 例 The farmer abandoned his *plough* and waited by the tree stump, hoping to get another hare. 那个农民荒废了耕作，在树桩旁等着，希望能再得到一只兔子。
plus [plʌs]	*prep.* 加上；和，以及 *n.* 加号；正号 *a.* 比所示数量多的 记 联想记忆：pl(看作 play，玩) + us(我们) → 加上我们，大家一起玩儿 → 加上 例 The psychologist found a word without a picture was superior to a word *plus* a picture for children. 心理学家发现，没有附上图片的词对孩子们而言比加了图片的词更好一些。
plush* [plʌʃ]	*a.* 豪华的，舒适的 *n.* 长毛绒 例 They investigated the so-called boutique hotels in the heart of downtown business districts, stately mansions located in the depths of beautiful countryside, and *plush* hotels built at the edge of tropical beaches surrounded by palm trees and idyllic blue ocean. 他们调查了位于城市中心商业区的所谓的精品酒店、坐落在美丽乡村深处的庄严的官邸，以及建在被棕榈树和田园般蓝色海洋环绕的热带沙滩边缘的豪华酒店。
point* [pɔɪnt]	*n.* 尖，尖端；点，小数点；条款，细目；分数，得分；要点，论点，观点 *v.* 指，指向；表明；瞄准 搭 come to the point 说到要点，扼要地说；on the point of 即将…的时候；point out 指出 例 A: I'd like to give a lecture. How do you think? B: Well, short and to the *point*. A: 我想做个演讲。你认为如何? B: 唔，注意要简短且紧扣主题。 派 pointed(*a.* 有尖的；犀利的)；pointer(*n.* 指针)

□ pledge □ pliable □ plot □ plough □ plus □ plush
□ point

poison*

[ˈpɔɪzn]

n. 毒，毒药 *vt.* 毒害

记 联想记忆：毒害(poison)百姓，被送进监狱(prison)

例 White phosphorus is a deadly *poison*. 白磷是一种致命的毒药。

poisonous*

[ˈpɔɪzənəs]

a. 有毒的，有害的；恶毒的，邪恶的

记 联想记忆：poison(毒) + ous(形容词后缀) → 有毒的

例 They ate a species of *poisonous* mushroom. 他们吃了一种有毒的蘑菇。

polish*

[ˈpɒlɪʃ]

v. 磨光，擦亮；使优美，润饰 *n.* 擦光剂，上光蜡

记 词根记忆：pol(磨) + ish(使…) → 磨光，擦亮

搭 polish one's English 补习英语；polish furniture 抛光家具

例 After the axe had been chipped into shape, the workers needed water and sand for grinding and *polishing*. 在斧子被削成形之后，工人们需要用水和沙子来打磨和抛光。// The stone should be cut and *polished*. 这块石头应该被切开并打磨。

派 polished(*a.* 磨光的，擦亮的)

poll*

[pəʊl]

n. 民意测验；政治选举，大选 *v.* 对…进行民意测验；获得…选票

记 联想记忆：大选(poll)费用(toll)上涨幅度惊人

搭 public opinion poll 民意调查；conduct a poll on 对…进行调查

例 The team is conducting a *poll* among freshmen. 这个小组正在新生中进行一次民意调查。

派 polling(*n.* 投票)

pollinate

[ˈpɒləneɪt]

vt.【植】给…授粉

记 联想记忆：pollin(看作 pollen，花粉) + ate → 给…授粉

例 A well-known scientist recently reported that air pollution may prevent bees from finding flowers to *pollinate*. 一位著名科学家最近报道，空气污染可能会妨碍蜜蜂找到花进行授粉。

pollutant

[pəˈluːtənt]

n. 污染物质(尤指排入水中和空气中的有害化学物质)，有害物质

记 来自 pollute(*vt.* 污染)

例 There is a tax on all industrial *pollutant* emissions, not just those over state-prescribed standards. 所有工业污染排放物都要征税，而不仅仅是超出国家规定标准范围的污染物。

pollution*

[pəˈluːʃn]

n. 污染，污染物；玷污

例 Air *pollution* is increasingly becoming the focus of government and citizen concern around the globe. 大气污染正逐渐成为全球范围内政府和市民关注的焦点。

populace

[ˈpɒpjələs]

n. (一个国家或地区的)人口，全体居民；平民，大众

记 词根记忆：popul(人民) + ace → 平民，大众

例 Workers in the nuclear industry are more likely than the general *populace* to have cancer in accordance with some authoritative inquiry. 根据一些权威调查，从事核能行业的劳动者比普通民众更可能患癌症。

popularity
[ˌpɒpjuˈlærəti]

n. 普及，流行

记 联想记忆：popular（流行）+ ity → 流行

例 There is an increasing *popularity* of organic food these days. 现在有机食品越来越流行了。

popularize
[ˈpɒpjələraɪz]

vt. 宣扬，宣传，推广；使普及，使通俗化

记 词根记忆：popul（人民）+ ar + ize（使…）→ 使广为人民所知 → 宣扬，宣传，推广；使普及

例 Internet has an important role to play in *popularizing* new scientific knowledge and spreading new information. 因特网在普及新的科学知识以及传播新信息方面起着重要的作用。

派 popularization（*n.* 普及）

populate*
[ˈpɒpjuleɪt]

vt.（大批地）居住于，生活于

记 词根记忆：popul（人）+ ate（使…）→ 使人在某处 →（大批地）居住于

例 The dinosaurs used to *populate* the earth. 恐龙曾经生活在地球上。

population*
[ˌpɒpjuˈleɪʃn]

n. 人口

搭 population explosion 人口爆炸；population control 人口控制

例 There is still a large portion of the world *population* living in poverty. 世界上还有一大部分人生活在贫困之中。// By the year 2021, the world *population* will increase by 24%. 到 2021 年，世界人口将增加 24%。

pore over

仔细阅读

例 They love to *pore over* weighty tomes. 他们喜欢钻研大部头的书。

portable
[ˈpɔːtəbl]

a. 便于携带的；手提式的

记 词根记忆：port（拿，运）+ able（可…的）→ 可以拿的 → 便于携带的；手提式的

搭 portable computer 手提电脑，笔记本；portable telephone 移动电话

例 A quiver is a *portable* case for holding arrows. 箭囊是可以随身携带的用来装箭的盒子。

portion
[ˈpɔːʃn]

n. 部分；一份 *vt.* 划分，分配

记 联想记忆：port（看作 part，部分）+ ion → 部分

例 The energy system uses the visible *portion* of the solar spectrum to light buildings. 该能源系统利用太阳光谱中的可见光来为建筑照明。

position*
[pəˈzɪʃn]

n. 位置，方位；职位，职务；姿势，姿态；见解，立场 *vt.* 安放，安置

搭 be in a position to do sth. 能够做…，有做…的机会；leave sth./sb. in the position of 使…处于…

例 The *position* of women in society has changed markedly in the last twenty years. 在过去的 20 年间，妇女的社会地位有了显著的改变。

positive*
[ˈpɒzətɪv]

a. 明确的；肯定的；积极的

记 词根记忆：pos（放）+ it + ive（形容词后缀）→ 放正心态的 → 积极的

搭 positive role 积极的作用；a positive example 积极的榜样；a positive number 正数

例 Customer comments, both *positive* and negative, are recorded by staff. 对于顾客的意见，无论是肯定的还是否定的，都由职员予以记录。

□ popularity □ popularize □ populate □ population □ pore over □ portable
□ portion □ position □ positive

possess
[pə'zes]

vt. 具有；拥有

记 联想记忆：poss(看作 boss，老板) + ess → 老板占有很多财产 → 具有；拥有

搭 possess an interest in 对…感兴趣

例 My professor *possessed* a surrealistic canvas by Dali. 我的教授拥有一幅达利的超现实主义油画。

possession*
[pə'zeʃn]

n. 持有，拥有；所有权；所有物，财产，财富；领土

搭 in sb.'s possession 被某人占有；in possession of sth. 占有某物

例 It would be a good idea to get some insurance for the furniture and other personal *possessions*. 给家具和其他一些个人财产上保险是一个不错的主意。

postcode*
['pəʊstkəʊd]

n. 邮政编码

例 A: Do you know your *postcode*?

B: Yes. It's GU8 9EW.

A: 你知道邮编吗？

B: 知道，是 GU8 9EW。

postgraduate
[ˌpəʊst'grædʒuət]

n. 研究生

搭 a postgraduate student 研究生

例 I've got a place in a *Postgraduate* Certificate in Education course starting in September. 我已经参加了 9 月份开学的教育学研究生文凭课程。

post-mortem
[ˌpəʊst'mɔːtəm]

a. 事后的 *n.* 检尸，尸体解剖；事后反思(或剖析)

搭 do/conduct/carry out a post-mortem on sb. 进行剖尸验证

例 When businesses fail, the *post-mortem* analysis is traditionally undertaken by accountants and market strategists. 生意失败后，通常是由会计师和市场战略家来进行事后分析。

postpone
[pə'spəʊn]

v. 延迟，延期

记 词根记忆：post(在…后面) + pon(放) + e → 放到后面 → 延迟，延期

例 The sports meet was finally *postponed* because of the bad weather. 由于天气恶劣，运动会最终被推迟了。

posture
['pɒstʃə(r)]

n. 姿势；心情；态度

posture

记 词根记忆：post(放) + ure → 姿势

搭 a comfortable/relaxed posture 舒适的/轻松的姿势；adopt an aggressive posture on... 对…采取强硬的态度

例 Back pains can be the result of a bad *posture*. 背部疼痛可能是不良姿势造成的。

potential*
[pə'tenʃl]

a. 潜在的；可能的 *n.* 潜力，潜能

记 词根记忆：po + tent(伸展) + ial → 无限伸展的 → 潜在的；可能的；潜能

搭 a potential customer/client 潜在顾客/客户；potential threat 潜在威胁；potential abilities 潜能

例 After the final interview, *potential* recruits were divided into three categories. 经过最后一轮面试，有可能被录用的人被分成三类。

□ possess □ possession □ postcode □ postgraduate □ post-mortem □ postpone
□ posture □ potential

poultry* [ˈpəʊltri]

n. 家禽；禽肉

记 词根记忆：poul(小鸡) + try → 家禽；禽肉

例 The *poultry* farmers keep ducks as well as chickens. 这些家禽养殖户既饲养鸭子也养鸡。

pour* [pɔː(r)]

v. 灌，倒；倾泻，涌流；喷发；不断涌现

记 联想记忆：穷(poor)困潦倒(pour)

例 Old customers *pour* out of the shopping centres cheering wildly at the weekends. 周末，老顾客欢欣雀跃地从购物中心蜂拥而出。

poverty [ˈpɒvəti]

n. 贫穷

搭 live in poverty 在贫困中成长；combat poverty 和贫困作斗争；poverty line 贫困线

例 In this country people were experiencing *poverty*, unemployment and famine. 在这个国家，人们正在经受贫困、失业和饥饿的煎熬。

practical* [ˈpræktɪkl]

a. 实际的，实用的；实践的，应用的

记 来自 practice(*v./n.* 实践)

搭 practical experience 实践经验；practical value 实用价值；practical material 实用材料

例 The new invention was very *practical*. 这项新发明很实用。

practically [ˈpræktɪkli]

ad. 几乎，简直；实际上

例 There is evidence that the reaction principle was applied *practically* well before the rocket was invented. 有证据证明，反作用原理在火箭发明前就得到了很好的实际应用。

pragmatic [præɡˈmætɪk]

a. 务实的；实事求是的；实用主义观点的

记 词根记忆：prag(做) + matic → 切实去做 → 务实的

例 The company hired this young man because of his *pragmatic* attitude towards the problems of work. 公司雇用这个年轻人是因为他能务实地对待工作中的问题。

precarious [prɪˈkeəriəs]

a. 不安全的，充满危险的；不牢靠的，不稳固的

记 联想记忆：pre(在…前面) + car(汽车) + ious → 坐在汽车前面 → 不安全的

例 The peninsula's peace and the fate of the Korean nation will face a *precarious* situation if the negotiation breaks down. 如果谈判破裂，半岛的和平和朝鲜民族的命运将面临岌岌可危的局面。

precede [prɪˈsiːd]

v. 领先，先于

记 词根记忆：pre(在…前面) + ced(走) + e → 走在前面 → 先于

例 If people were to *precede* the comprehensive notion of environmental protection, species would not face the situation of becoming extinct any more. 如果人类早些对环境保护有一个全面的概念，就不会有更多物种面临灭绝的危险了。

派 precedable(*a.* 可能被超前的，可能先发生的)

□ poultry □ pour □ poverty □ practical □ practically □ pragmatic
□ precarious □ precede

precedent [ˈpresɪdənt]

n. 先例，范例；惯例

记 词根记忆：pre(在…前面) + ced(走，前进) + ent → 走在前面的 → 先例；惯例

搭 set a precedent for 为…提供先例

例 The October Revolution was without *precedent* in recent history, which made a significant influence in Russia. 十月革命在近代历史上是没有先例的，对俄国产生了深远的影响。

同 tradition(*n.* 常例，常规)

反 following(*n.* 下列各项；部下)

派 precedence(*n.* 优先；优先权)

precipitation [prɪˌsɪpɪˈteɪʃn]

n. 降雨(量)，降水(量)；仓促，急躁；【化】沉淀作用

搭 an increase in annual precipitation 年降水量的增加

例 According to the statistic released by the Office of State Flood Control and Drought Relief Headquarters, *precipitation* in many parts of central China has been 50 to 80 percent below normal. 国家防汛抗旱总指挥部办公室公布的数据显示，华中很多地区的降水量比同期正常降雨量低了50%~80%。

precise [prɪˈsaɪs]

a. 精确的，准确的；严谨的

搭 to be precise 准确地说；precise measurements 精确的尺寸；a very precise man 非常严谨的人

例 The company serves its clients with professional and *precise* attitudes. 该公司本着专业和严谨的态度为客户服务。

派 precisely(*ad.* 精确地；正好)

precise

precision* [prɪˈsɪʒn]

n. 准确，精确；精确度

搭 precision instruments 精密仪器

例 The manufacturers exercise much attention and *precision* in producing their products. 在产品的生产过程中，制造商们倾注了大量心血，非常注重产品的精密性。

predator [ˈpredətə(r)]

n. 捕食性动物；食肉动物；奴役他人者(尤指在财务或性关系上面)；剥削者，掠夺者

记 词根记忆：pred(掠夺) + at + or(表人或物) → 掠夺肉食 → 食肉动物

例 To avoid being taken over by their counterpart *predator*, the company has made great effort and got fully preparation. 为了免遭强敌的接管，公司已经做了充分的准备工作。

predatory [ˈpredətri]

a. 食肉的；掠夺的

记 词根记忆：pred(掠夺) + atory → 掠夺的

搭 predatory pricing 掠夺性定价

例 The owl is a kind of cruel *predatory* bird which kills its prey with its claws. 鹰是一种残忍的食肉鸟类，它用锋利的爪子捕杀猎物。

predict* [prɪˈdɪkt]

v. 预言；预告

记 词根记忆：pre(在…之前)+dict(说)→预言

例 The United Nations *predicts* that the global population may stabilise between 8 and 14 billion in the twenty-first century. 联合国预言，在21世纪全球人口将稳定在80亿到140亿之间。

predictable [prɪˈdɪktəbl]

a. 可预言的，可预报的；按老一套办事的，墨守成规的

搭 a predictable result 可预见的结果

例 But volcanoes are not very *predictable*. 但是火山爆发很难预测。

Education is a progressive discovery of our ignorance.

教育是一个逐步发现自己无知的过程。

——美国历史学家 杜兰特(Durant, American historian)

Word List 35

音频

词根、词缀预习表

gn	出生	pregnant *a.* 怀孕的	**mis**	放	premise *n.* 前提
par	安排	prepare *v.* 准备，预备	**scrib**	写	prescribe *v.* 规定
val	力量	prevalent *a.* 流行的	**vi**	路	previous *a.* 以前的
prim	第一	primary *a.* 最初的	**priv**	私有	private *a.* 私人的
prob	检查	probation *n.* 试用期	**claim**	大声呼喊	proclaim *v.* 宣告

prediction [prɪˈdɪkʃn]

n. 预言，预料，预报

例 A growing interest in cultural identity may prevent the direst *predictions* from coming true. 日益增长的对文化认同的兴趣可能会阻止最可怕的预言成真。

predispose* [ˌpriːdɪˈspəʊz]

v. 事先(在某方面)影响某人；偏爱；(使)易受感染(或患病)

记 联想记忆：pre(预先) + dispose(处理) → 预先处理，不然容易感染 → 易受感染

例 Exposure to too much noise may *predispose* you to a headache. 听了太多的噪音会让你头疼。

派 predisposition(*n.* 倾向，癖好)

predominant* [prɪˈdɒmɪnənt]

a. 卓越的，突出的；支配的，主要的；盛行的

记 联想记忆：pre(在…前面) + dominant(统治的) → 在前面统治的 → 支配的

例 Singers have a *predominant* role in this performance. 歌手在这场表演中担任主要角色。

派 predominantly(*ad.* 主要地；重要地；显著地)

predominate [prɪˈdɒmɪneɪt]

vi. 统治，支配；(数量、力量上)占优势

记 联想记忆：pre + dominate(统治) → 处于统治地位 → 占优势

例 Red colour *predominates* in clothes of this brand. 这个品牌的衣服，红色占据了主流。

prefabricate [ˌpriːˈfæbrɪkeɪt]

vt. 预制构件(用以组装建筑物、船舶等)

例 If implanting subcutaneous blood vessel to superficial fascia, thin transferable axial pattern skin flaps can be *prefabricated*. 如果将皮下组织血管移位至浅筋膜，可预制可转换的薄轴型皮瓣。

preface
[ˈprefəs]

n. 序言，引言 *vt.* 为…写序言；以…为开端

记 联想记忆：pre(在…前面) + face(面) → 写在正文前面的话 → 序言

例 I will not delay you by a long *preface*. 我的开场白不会很长，免得耽误你们的时间。

preferable
[ˈprefrəbl]

a. 更可取的，更好的，更合意的

记 联想记忆：prefer(更喜欢) + able(能…的) → 更喜欢就觉得更好 → 更可取的，更好的，更合意的

例 I'm not sure the cure is *preferable* to the disease. 我不能肯定这种疗法是否更适用于医治这种疾病。

preference
[ˈprefrəns]

n. 喜爱；偏爱的事物(或人)；优先

记 联想记忆：prefer(更喜欢) + ence(名词后缀) → 偏爱的事物

搭 a matter of personal preference 个人爱好问题

例 Many people expressed a strong *preference* for the original plan. 许多人强烈表示喜欢原先的计划。

pregnancy*
[ˈpregnənsi]

n. 怀孕；怀孕期

记 来自 pregnant(*a.* 怀孕的)

例 They are especially vulnerable because of *pregnancy* but also because of osteoporosis, which I personally believe to be the major cause of the problem for women. 她们特别容易受到（背部疼痛的）攻击，一方面是因为怀孕，一方面是因为骨质疏松，而后者，我个人认为是导致这一问题的主要原因。

pregnant
[ˈpregnənt]

a. 怀孕的，妊娠的；充满的

记 词根记忆：pre(在…之前) + gn(=gen 出生) + ant(形容词后缀) → 在出生之前的 → 怀孕的

搭 get pregnant 怀孕

例 The tablets are not given to children under 12 years of age or *pregnant* or breastfeeding women. 12 岁以下的儿童以及处于妊娠期或哺乳期的妇女禁用此药。

35

preliminary
[prɪˈlɪmɪnəri]

a. 开端的，预备的，初步的 *n.* [常 *pl.*] 初步做法，起始行为

记 词根记忆：pre(预先) + limin(门槛；起点) + ary → 预先开始的 → 预备的

搭 without preliminaries 直截了当地；a preliminary trial 初步审讯；preliminary remarks 开场白

例 Although *preliminary* experimental evidence suggests that their in-air vision is poor, the accuracy with which dolphins leap high to take small fish out of a trainer's hand provides evidence to the contrary. 尽管先前的试验证明海豚在空气中的视力很差，但它们可以一跃到空中获取训练者手中的鱼儿，这种准确度成为与之前的结论相反的证据。

premier
['premiə(r)]

n. 总理；首相 *a.* 首要的，第一位的；最著名的

例 The *premier* was injured in a bomb attack. 总理在一次炸弹袭击中受伤。// He is a scientist at the Australian Government's *premier* research organization. 他是一位来自澳大利亚政府最好的研究机构的科学家。

premise*
[pre'mɪs]

n. 前提，假设；[*pl.*]（企业、机构等使用的）房屋和地基，经营场址

记 词根记忆：pre（在…前面）+ mis（放）+ e → 放在前面的东西 → 前提

搭 the major premise 主要前提

例 His agreement of this investment is based on the *premise* that all people are equally share the risk. 基于所有人平均分担风险的前提，他同意了该项投资。

同 hypothesis（*n.* 假设）

premium*
['priːmiəm]

a. 高级的，优质的；售价高的 *n.*（投保人向保险公司支付的）保险金；额外费用，加付款；奖品，赠品；额外津贴

记 词根记忆：pre（预先）+ m（=em 拿取）+ ium → 为…提前拿取的东西 → 保险金

搭 at a premium 稀少

例 The coffee we're drinking is *premium*. 我们喝的是特级咖啡。

preparation
[ˌprepə'reɪʃn]

n. 准备（工作），预备；制剂

例 The team has been training hard in *preparation* for the big game. 为备战这场重要比赛，队伍一直在坚苦训练。

prepare*
[prɪ'peə(r)]

v. 准备，预备

记 词根记忆：pre（预先）+ par（安排）+ e → 提前安排 → 准备，预备

搭 be prepared for 为…做准备，准备好

例 We need two more weeks to *prepare* the assignment because we have had difficulty obtaining the reference books. 我们还需要两周时间准备作业，因为我们在收集参考书上遇到了困难。

prerequisite*
[ˌpriː'rekwəzɪt]

n. 先决条件，前提；必备条件 *a.* 必备的

例 A degree is an essential *prerequisite* for employment. 学位是就业必备的条件。

prescribe
[prɪ'skraɪb]

v. 开处方，开药；规定，指示

记 词根记忆：pre（预先）+ scrib（写）+ e → 预先写好 → 规定；指示

搭 prescribe sb. sth 为某人开…药

例 Doctors diagnose before they *prescribe* a drug. 医生在开药前要先对病人进行诊断。

prescription
[prɪ'skrɪpʃn]

n. 处方，药方；开处方，开药方

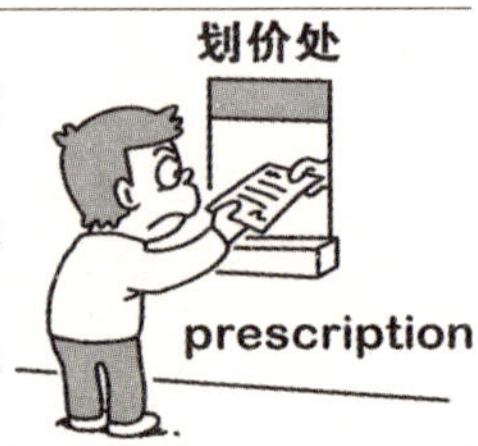

记 词根记忆：pre（预先）+ script（写）+ ion → 预先把要抓的药写在方子上 → 药方

搭 prescription drugs/medication 处方药；fill a prescription 按方配药；give a prescription 开药方

例 This medicine is not available without a *prescription*. 这种药只能凭处方购买。

□ premier □ premise □ premium □ preparation □ prepare □ prerequisite
□ prescribe □ prescription

presence* [ˈprezns]

n. 出席；存在；仪态

记 联想记忆：pre(在…前面) + senc(看作 send，送) + e → 送到前面 → 出席

例 Elliot discovered the ***presence*** of five rings encircling the equator of Uranus. 埃利奥特发现有五个光环围绕着天王星赤道。

presentation* [ˌprezn ˈteɪʃn]

n. 赠送；赠品，礼物；授予，提供；显示；引荐，介绍；报告；表演，上演

记 联想记忆：present(现在的) + ation(名词后缀) → 现在开始为我们做介绍吧 → 介绍

搭 make/give a presentation 做报告；on presentation of sth. 展示某物

例 We'd better fix the problem before the ***presentation***. 我们最好在做报告之前解决这个问题。

preserve [prɪ ˈzɜːv]

vt. 保护；维持；保存，保藏；腌渍

记 联想记忆：pre（在…前面）+ serve（服务）→ 在前面提供服务 → 保护；维持；保存

搭 preserve one's eyesight 保护视力

例 As a nurse, my profession is to ***preserve*** life, and to prevent disease. 身为一名护士，我的职责是保护生命以及预防疾病。

president* [ˈprezɪdənt]

n. 总统，校长，会长，(大会)主席

例 A lecture will be given by the ***president*** of the Union. 该协会主席将发表演讲。

派 presidential(*a.* 总统的)

pressure* [ˈpreʃə(r)]

n. 压力，压强；强制，压迫 *vt.* 对…施加压力（或影响）；迫使，说服

记 联想记忆：press(压) + ure → 压力，压强；强制；对…施加压力

搭 under pressure 处于压力之下；put pressure on 给…以压力；atmospheric pressure 大气压；take one's blood pressure 量血压

例 His father's blood ***pressure*** is a little high. 他父亲的血压有点高。// Mary was ***pressured*** into resigning. 玛丽被迫同意辞职。

35

presumably* [prɪ ˈzjuːməbli]

ad. 推测起来，大概

记 来自 presumable(*a.* 可能的)

例 ***Presumably*** consumers have bought such poisonous food. 大概消费者已经购买了这种有毒食品。

派 presume〔*v.* 假定(某事)是事实，(没有证据地)相信〕

presuppose [ˌpriːsə ˈpəuz]

vt. 预先假定…属实；认为，假设；以…为先决条件，以…为前提

记 联想记忆：pre(预先) + suppose(假定) → 预先假定…属实

例 The construction of this project ***presupposes*** that flexible money will be available during the following months. 该项目开工的前提是在接下来的几个月里要有活动资金。

□ presence □ presentation □ preserve □ president □ pressure □ presumably
□ presuppose

pretend [prɪˈtend]	*v.* 装作，假装 记 联想记忆：pre(预先)+tend(趋向)→预先就有了趋向→装作，假装 例 Many people ***pretend*** that they understand modern art. 很多人都假装自己懂得现代艺术。 派 pretence(*n.* 假象，伪装；标榜)
pretension* [prɪˈtenʃn]	*n.* 声称，自命；自负，自命不凡 记 词根记忆：pre(向前)+tens(伸展)+ion→无限地向前伸展→自负 例 The woman, having fewer ***pretensions***, is far more willing to learn. 这个女人并没有自命不凡，而是非常愿意学东西。
pretentious [prɪˈtenʃəs]	*a.* 自命不凡的，自负的；炫耀的；做作的 记 词根记忆：pre(向前)+tent(伸展)+ious→向前伸展的→自命不凡的，自负的 例 The writer took a book review in ***pretentious*** language to express his biased criticism. 该作者写了一篇书评，言语间满是自负，表达了相当偏执的评论意见。
prevail [prɪˈveɪl]	*vi.* 流行，盛行；占优势，战胜 搭 prevail on/upon 说服，劝说 例 The use of horses for ploughing still ***prevails*** in this area. 在这一地区用马耕地还很普遍。
prevalence [ˈprevələns]	*n.* 普及，流行，盛行 记 词根记忆：pre(领先)+val(力量)+ence→力量领先→普及，流行，盛行 例 The illness on neck, which used to bother the elderly, is of ***prevalence*** among young office workers nowadays. 过去常常烦扰老年人的颈椎病现在盛行于年轻的上班族之中。
prevalent [ˈprevələnt]	*a.* 流行的，普遍的 记 词根记忆：pre(在…前面)+val(力量)+ent→有走在前面的力量的→流行的 例 The use of child soldiers has been ***prevalent*** in these two countries. 使用儿童兵在这两个国家很普遍。 同 widespread(*a.* 分布广的，普遍的)；universal(*a.* 普遍的，全体的) 反 rare(*a.* 稀有的，罕见的)；uncommon(*a.* 不凡的，罕有的)
preventative [prɪˈventətɪv]	*a.* 预防性的 例 It is possible that the police were able to take ***preventative*** action and avoid a possible riot. 警察能够采取一些预防措施以避免可能发生的暴动，这是可能的。
previous* [ˈpriːviəs]	*a.* 以前的；在…之前的；早先的，稍前的 记 词根记忆：pre(在…前面)+vi(路)+ous→更早上路的→以前的 搭 previous to 在…之前 例 Coffee became cheaper than it had been for the ***previous*** years. 咖啡的价格比前些年低。

□ pretend □ pretension □ pretentious □ prevail □ prevalence □ prevalent
□ preventative □ previous

prey* [preɪ]

n. 猎物，捕获物；牺牲品，战利品 *vi.* 捕食；折磨，使烦恼；掠夺

记 联想记忆：兔子天天祈祷（pray）不要成为狼的猎物（prey）

搭 prey on insects 捕食昆虫为生

例 Most animals hunt their *prey* by means of their eyesight. 大多数动物靠视力进行捕猎。

同 quarry（*n.* 猎物）；victim（*n.* 受害者，牺牲品）；afflict（*vt.* 使苦恼，折磨）；bother（*v.* 打扰，麻烦）

---

primary [ˈpraɪməri]

a. 最初的，初级的；首要的，基本的

记 词根记忆：prim（第一）+ ary → 最初的；主要的

搭 the primary stage of civilization 文明的最初阶段；a primary school 小学；primary education 初等教育

例 The *primary* reason for advertising is to sell more goods. 做广告的首要目的是要售出更多的货物。// This event detracts them from their *primary* purpose. 这一事件让他们偏离了初衷。

派 primarily（*ad.* 首先；主要地，首要地）

---

prime* [praɪm]

a. 首要的；最好的

记 词根记忆：prim（第一）+ e → 首要的；最好的

例 He's a *prime* candidate to captain the team this season. 他是本赛季队长的最佳人选。

---

primitive [ˈprɪmətɪv]

a. 原始的，上古的；简单的，粗糙的 *n.* 原始人；原始事物

记 词根记忆：prim（第一）+ it + ive（具…性质的）→ 第一时间的 → 原始的

搭 primitive society 原始社会；a primitive measuring method 原始的测量方法

例 Studies of *primitive* societies suggest that the earliest method of making fire was through friction. 对原始社会的研究表明，人们最早是通过摩擦生火的。

---

principal [ˈprɪnsəpl]

a. 主要的 *n.* 校长；资本；主角

记 词根记忆：prin（第一）+ cip（拿，取）+ al → 最先拿取 → 主要的；校长

例 The Yellow River is one of the *principal* rivers of Asia. 黄河是亚洲的主要河流之一。// The *principal's* talk will last about fifteen minutes. 校长的讲话会持续大概 15 分钟。

---

principle [ˈprɪnsəpl]

n. 原则，原理；规范，准则；基本信念，信条

记 词根记忆：prin（第一）+ cip（拿，取）+ le → 须第一位选取的 → 原则，原理

搭 in principle 原则上，理论上；大体上，基本上

例 How does the reaction *principle* work? 反作用原理是如何起作用的呢？

□ prey □ primary □ prime □ primitive □ principal □ principle

prior
[ˈpraɪə(r)]

a. 在前的，优先的

记 词根记忆：pri(第一) + or → 排在第一的 → 在前的，优先的

搭 prior to 在…之前；a prior consideration 事先的考虑

例 This degree course needs no *prior* qualifications. 这种学位课程不需要先决条件。

priority
[praɪˈɒrəti]

n. 优先(权)，重点；优先考虑的事

搭 give priority to 给…优先权，优先考虑；time priority 时间先后顺序

例 The film stars went onto the stage according to *priority* of their appearance in the film. 影星们按照他们在影片中出现的先后顺序依次上台。// You should decide what your *priorities* are. 你应该分清事情的轻重缓急。

privacy
[ˈprɪvəsi]

n. 隐私，私事；隐私权

记 词根记忆：priv(私有) + acy → 隐私

例 Biometrics raise thorny questions about *privacy* and the potential for abuse. 生物测验学会引发一些有关隐私的棘手问题，同时它还很可能会被滥用。

同 secrecy(*n.* 秘密，保密)；seclusion(*n.* 归隐；私人的范围)

反 publicity(*n.* 公开)

private*
[ˈpraɪvət]

a. 私人的；私下的；私立的

记 词根记忆：priv(私有) + ate → 私人的

例 May I ask you a *private* question? 我能问你一个私人问题吗？

privilege
[ˈprɪvəlɪdʒ]

n. 特权，优惠，特许 *vt.* 给予特权，特别优待

记 词根记忆：priv(单个) + i + leg(法律) + e → 法律上的独享权利 → 特权

例 Education is not a *privilege* of some people but a right of all citizens. 受教育不是某些人的特权，而是所有公民的权利。

派 privileged(*a.* 有特权的)

probability*
[ˌprɒbəˈbɪləti]

n. 可能性；概率

记 来自 probable(*a.* 很可能的)

例 This is a tool for predicting the *probability* that a species will become extinct in a particular region over a specific period. 这是一种用来预测某一物种在某个特定时期、特定区域灭绝可能性的工具。

probable*
[ˈprɒbəbl]

a. 很可能的，大概的

例 It is *probable* that, some time in the tenth century, gun powder was first compounded from its basic ingredients of saltpetre, charcoal and sulphur. 火药很可能最早在十世纪的某个时间由硝石、木炭和硫磺等基本成分混合而成。

probation*
[prəˈbeɪʃn]

n. 缓刑(制)；(对人的)试用；试用期

记 词根记忆：prob(检查，试验) + ation → 察看 → 试用；试用期

例 I was just a servant who was on *probation*. 我只是一个处于试用期的仆人。

□ prior □ priority □ privacy □ private □ privilege □ probability
□ probable □ probation

probe [prəʊb]

v. 探索，查究；(用探针或探测器等)探查，探测 *n.* 探针；探测器，探测飞船；探索，调查

记 词根记忆：prob(检测) + e → 探测，查究

例 The space *probe* sent back useful information to us. 太空探测器给我们发回了有用的信息。

派 probing(*a.* 探查性的；逼视的)

同 investigate(*v.* 调查)；survey(*v.* 调查；检查)

procedure [prəˈsiːdʒə(r)]

n. 程序，手续；过程

记 联想记忆：proce(e)d(前进) + ure → 程序；过程

搭 regular procedure 正规手续；the registration procedure 登记手续；emergency procedure 紧急状况的处理程序；follow accepted procedure 遵循惯用的步骤

例 I hate the cumbersome administrative *procedures*. 我讨厌这些麻烦的行政手续。

proceed* [prəˈsiːd]

vi. 进行；前进；继续

记 词根记忆：pro(向前) + ceed(行走) → 进行；前进

例 Our work is *proceeding* slowly. 我们的工作进程缓慢。

process* [ˈprəʊses]

n. 过程；步骤，程序 *vt.* 加工；处理；办理

记 词根记忆：pro(向前) + cess(行走) → 向前走 → 过程

搭 a peaceful process 一个平静的过程；in the process of doing 在做某事的过程中

例 Reforming the educational system will be a difficult *process*. 教育制度的改革将是一个艰难的过程。// Your application will be *processed* promptly. 我们将迅速办理您的申请。

procession [prəˈseʃn]

n. 队伍，行列

记 联想记忆：队伍(procession)在行军的过程(process)中遭遇暴风雪

例 The soldiers lined the route of the *procession*. 士兵们沿行进的道路排成一列。

processor [ˈprəʊsesə(r)]

n. 加工机；加工工人；处理器

记 来自 process(*vt.* 处理)

例 A word *processor* is the basic part of a computer to produce printed documents. 文字处理器是电脑制作印刷文件的基本部分。

proclaim [prəˈkleɪm]

v. 宣告，宣布，声明；显示

记 词根记忆：pro(在…前面，向前) + claim(大声呼喊) → 在前面大叫 → 宣告，声明；显示

例 It was the famous speech delivered by the President in which he *proclaimed* that the country was independent. 在这次著名的演说中，总统宣布该国独立了。

派 proclamation(*n.* 公告，布告，声明)

同 declare(*v.* 正式宣布；宣称)；announce(*v.* 宣布，声称)

35

□ probe □ procedure □ proceed □ process □ procession □ processor □ proclaim

procrastinate
[prəʊˈkræstɪneɪt]

v. 耽搁，拖延

记 词根记忆：pro(向前) + crastin(明天) + ate → 拖到明天再干 → 耽搁，拖延

例 People were dying of starvation in the disaster area while governments *procrastinated*. 灾区的人们快要饿死了，而政府行动却拖拖拉拉。

productive
[prəˈdʌktɪv]

a. 生产性的；多产的；富有成效的

例 Without irrigation many *productive* areas of the country would not be able to be farmed. 如果没有灌溉，这个国家的很多多产地区将不能进行农业生产。

productivity
[ˌprɒdʌkˈtɪvəti]

n. 生产力；生产率

记 联想记忆：product(产品) + ivity → 生产力；生产率

例 This process enhanced our ability to improve *productivity* and quality. 这一方法增强了我们提高生产力和质量的能力。

同 output(*n.* 产量；输出量)；capacity(*n.* 容量；生产力)

profession
[prəˈfeʃn]

n. 行业，职业；宣称，表白

记 联想记忆：这位教授(professor)从事历史学专业(profession)

例 In this highly competitive world, if a man has no *profession*, there isn't much choice. 在这个竞争非常激烈的世界里，一个人如果没有专长就没有多少选择的机会。

professional*
[prəˈfeʃənl]

a. 职业的；专业的 *n.* 自由职业者；专业人员

搭 professional misconduct 失职；professional knowledge 专业知识

例 Sports psychologists spend time with *professional* athletes helping them approach competition with a positive mental attitude. 运动心理学家花时间帮助职业运动员以一种积极的心态去迎接挑战。

profile*
[ˈprəʊfaɪl]

n. 面部的侧影，侧面轮廓；传略，人物简介 *vt.* 扼要介绍；写传略(或简介)

记 词根记忆：pro(在…前面) + fil(线条) + e → 外部的线条 → 侧面轮廓

搭 an employee profile 雇员简介；keep a high/low profile 保持高/低姿态

例 The successful entrepreneur's career is *profiled* in this month's journal. 这期月刊概述了这位成功企业家的工作生涯。

profit*
[ˈprɒfɪt]

n. 利润；益处 *v.* 有利于；获益

搭 pursue maximum profit 追求最大利润；net profit 纯利润；profit from... 从…中受益

例 Some firms are even downsizing as their *profits* climb. 一些公司甚至在利润上升时还裁员。

派 profitless(*a.* 无利可图的，无益的)

profitable [ˈprɒfɪtəbl]

a. 有利可图的，赚钱的；有益的

记 联想记忆：profit(利益) + able(能…的) → 能获利的 → 有利可图的，赚钱的

搭 a highly profitable business 非常有利可图的生意

例 It is *profitable* for employers to work their existing employees hard. 雇主让他们的雇员努力工作是有利可图的。

同 beneficial(*a.* 有益的，有利的)；lucrative(*a.* 赚钱的；有利可图的)

反 unprofitable(*a.* 无利益的，不赚钱的)；worthless(*a.* 无价值的，无益的)

profound [prəˈfaʊnd]

a. 深切的，深远的；知识渊博的，见解深刻的，深奥的

记 联想记忆：pro(在…前面) + found(创立) → 有超前创见性 → 深远的；深奥的

搭 a profound sleep 酣睡；a profound idea 思想深刻

例 Globalization effects very *profound* changes in modern lifestyles. 全球化使现代人的生活方式发生了深刻的变化。

同 abstruse(*a.* 深奥的)；recondite(*a.* 深奥的，难以理解的)

反 shallow(*a.* 肤浅的，浅薄的)

prohibit* [prəˈhɪbɪt]

v. 禁止，阻止

记 词根记忆：pro(在…之前) + hibit(拿住) → 提前拿住 → 禁止，阻止

搭 prohibit sb. from doing sth. 阻止某人做某事

例 Smoking is *prohibited* on most occasions. 大多数场合都禁止吸烟。

派 prohibition(*n.* 禁令，禁止)

prohibitive [prəˈhɪbətɪv]

a. 禁止的，抑制的；令人望而却步的

记 词根记忆：pro(在…之前) + hibit(拿住) + ive → 提前拿住 → 抑制的

例 This doesn't require a *prohibitive* amount of energy. 这并不要求具有强大的能量。

project*

[ˈprɒdʒekt] *n.* 计划，方案；课题，项目；工程 [prəˈdʒekt] *v.* 放映；投射，发射；(使)突出，(使)伸出；设计，规划

记 词根记忆：pro(向前) + ject(投，掷) → 向前掷 → (使)突出，(使)伸出

搭 draw up a project 制订方案；carry out a project 执行方案

例 I think this *project* could be adapted to suit any age. 我觉得可以将该计划加以改动以适合所有年龄的人群。

prolonged [prəˈlɒŋd]

a. 持久的，长期的

记 词根记忆：pro(向前) + long(长) + ed → 向前拉长的 → 持久的，长期的

例 As the recent experiment shows, *prolonged* use of the new drug might have harmful side effects on patients. 最新的实验表明，长期使用这种新药物可能会对病人产生有害的副作用。

派 prolongable(*a.* 可延长的，可拖延的)；prolongation(*n.* 延长，延伸)

同 elongate(*v.* 伸长，拉长)；extend(*v.* 延展，延长)

反 shorten[*v.* (使)缩短，变短]

35

prominence
[ˈprɒmɪnəns]

n. 突出，显著；卓越；重要

记 词根记忆：pro(向前) + min(突出) + ence → 向前突出 → 突出，显著

例 Giving ***prominence*** to characteristic and increasing innovation is a pillar for enterprise's further development. 突出特色和勇于创新是企业进一步发展的支柱。

prominent
[ˈprɒmɪnənt]

a. 突出的；著名的；显著的

记 词根记忆：pro(向前) + min(突出) + ent(形容词后缀) → 突出的；显著的

例 Suzhou is one of the earlier ***prominent*** port cities. 苏州是较早的著名港口城市之一。

promise*
[ˈprɒmɪs]

n./ v. 允诺，保证；预兆，预示

例 The dark clouds ***promise*** rain. 乌云密布预示有雨。

promising
[ˈprɒmɪsɪŋ]

a. 有希望的；有前途的

记 联想记忆：promis(e)(承诺) + ing → 承诺了的 → 有希望的

例 Other members of the tribe scoured the country for ***promising*** fish holes. 这个部落的其他成员在全国范围内寻找能捕到鱼的场所。

同 hopeful〔*a.* (怀)有希望的〕；bright(*a.* 前景光明的，充满希望的)

反 hopeless(*a.* 没有希望的)

promote*
[prəˈməʊt]

vt. 促进；提升；促销

记 词根记忆：pro(向前) + mot(动) + e → 向前动 → 促进

搭 promote mutual understanding 促进相互理解；promote the sale of sth. 促销；promote cultural communication 增进文化交流

例 The band has gone on tour to ***promote*** their new album. 这个乐队已开始巡回宣传他们的新唱片。

Experience is a hard teacher because she gives the test first, the lesson afterwards.

经验是一位先行测试然后才授课严厉的教师。

——英国作家 弗农 .L.(Law Vernon, British writer)

Word List 36

音 频

词根、词缀预习表

pel	推	propel *vt.* 推进	**sper**	希望	prosper *vi.* 繁荣，兴旺
typ	模型	prototype *n.* 原型	**trud**	伸出	protrude *v.* (使)伸出
ven	来	provenance *n.* 出处，起源	**prox**	近	proximity *n.* 接近
punct	刺	punctual *a.* 守时的	**pur**	干净	purify *vt.* 使洁净
radi	光	radiate *v.* 发光；发热	**ceipt**	拿，取	receipt *n.* 收入

promotion* [prəˈməʊʃn]

n. 提升，晋级；促进，增进；发起，发扬；宣传，推销

例 Would you be willing to attend any of the special *promotions* for the new channel? 你愿意参加新频道的任何特别宣传活动吗？

pronounceable [prəˈnaʊnsəbl]

a. (指声音)发得出的；(指词)可发音的

记 联想记忆：pronounce(发音) + able(能…的)→ 可发音的

例 We wonder if there is a way to generate random but *pronounceable* passwords. 我们想知道是否有一种方法能够产生可读的随机密码。

proof* [pruːf]

n. 证据，证明；校样，样张 *a.* 能防…的，耐…的

记 联想记忆：屋顶(roof)有了p(棚)就能防雨 → 能防…的

搭 proof of purchase 购物证明

例 Can you provide any *proof* of identity? 你能提供任何身份证明吗？

propagate [ˈprɒpəgeɪt]

v. 繁殖，增殖；传播，宣传，使普及

记 词根记忆：pro(向前) + pag(扎牢，系牢) + ate → 向前系牢 → 繁殖；传播

例 Those false television advertising on medicine, with the famous as their spokesman, had *propagated* a false image in the public. 那些由名人代言的虚假医药广告在公众中宣传了一种虚假形象。

派 propagation(*n.* 繁殖；传播)

同 produce(*vt.* 生产；繁殖)；multiply(*v.* 增加；繁殖)

propel [prəˈpel]

vt. 推进，推动；驱使

记 词根记忆：pro(向前) + pel(推) → 推进

例 This does not mean that it was immediately used to *propel* rockets. 这并不意味着它立即就被用来推进火箭。

同 stimulate(*vt.* 刺激，激励)；impel(*vt.* 驱使；推进)

propellant
[prəˈpelənt]

n. 喷射剂；推进物，推进剂

A rocket motor's "bullets" are minute, high-speed particles produced by burning ***propellants***. 火箭发动机的"子弹"是微小的高速粒子，由推进剂的燃烧产生。

property
[ˈprɒpəti]

n. 财产，所有物；性质，特性；房产，地产

记 联想记忆：proper(固有的) + ty(表物) → 固有物 → 财产，所有物

搭 intellectual property 知识产权；assignment of property 产权转让；lost property 失物招领

例 Malleability is a physical ***property***. 延展性是(物质的)一个物理特性。

proportion
[prəˈpɔːʃn]

n. 比例；部分；相称

记 联想记忆：pro + portion(部分) → 比例；部分

搭 in proportion (to) (与…)成比例；out of proportion to sth. 与某物不成比例；proportion of …的比例；take a small proportion 占少量比例

例 The ***proportion*** of the population still speaking this language is very small. 只有少数人还在说这种语言。

proposal
[prəˈpəʊzl]

n. 提议，建议；求婚

记 来自 propose(*v.* 提议，建议)

例 The school master has accepted ***proposals*** to renovate the old schoolhouses. 校长已经接受了翻新旧校舍的提议。

propose*
[prəˈpəʊz]

v. 提议，建议；提名，推荐；打算；(向某人)求婚

记 词根记忆：pro(在…前面) + pos(放) + e → 在前面放出 → 行动之前指出 → 建议，提议

例 I understand that Bob is familiar with Manchester Park and ***propose*** let him show you around. 我知道鲍勃对曼彻斯特公园很熟，建议让他带你去逛逛。

prospective
[prəˈspektɪv]

a. 预期的；未来的；可能的

记 词根记忆：pro(向前) + spect(看) + ive(形容词后缀) → 向前看的 → 预期的；未来的

搭 prospective damage 预计损失

例 Department heads composed ***prospective*** teams using a combination of people from all three categories. 部门领导从现有所有三组人中选出一些人组成未来的团队。

同 imminent(*a.* 即将来临的)；anticipated(*a.* 预期的)

prospectus*
[prəˈspektəs]

n. 内容说明书，简章，简介

例 I picked up a really detailed ***prospectus*** for Tom. 我为汤姆挑选了一本内容相当详尽的说明书。

prosper
[ˈprɒspə(r)]

vi. 繁荣，兴旺；成功

记 词根记忆：pro(在前面) + sper(希望) → 希望在前，成功在后 → 繁荣，兴旺；成功

例 Over the next decades, our life will change a lot and our motherland will also ***prosper*** and be strong. 再过几十年，我们的生活会发生巨大变化，我们的祖国也会繁荣富强。

prosperous* [ˈprɒspərəs]

a. 繁荣的，兴旺的；成功的

搭 a prosperous city 繁华都市

例 My grandfather once was a *prosperous* Britain businessman. 我祖父曾是个成功的英国商人。

prototype [ˈprəʊtətaɪp]

n. 原型，蓝本

记 词根记忆：proto(首先) + typ(模型) + e → 首先的模型 → 原型

例 Toyota has invested hundreds of millions of dollars into R&D efforts, so as to take the market share in *prototype* hydrogen vehicles. 丰田汽车公司已经投入数亿美元的研发经费，以便在氢能源原型车市场占有一定的份额。

同 archetype(*n.* 原型)；original(*n.* 原物，原作)

protrude [prəˈtruːd]

v. (使)伸出；(使)突出

记 词根记忆：pro(向前) + trud(伸出) + e → 向前伸出 → (使)伸出；(使)突出

例 The climber tried to hang on to a piece of rock *protruding* from the cliff face. 攀岩者设法抓住悬崖外突出的岩石。

provenance [ˈprɒvənəns]

n. 出处，起源

记 词根记忆：pro(在…之前) + ven(来) + ance → 先于…来到的东西 → 出处，起源

例 According to the theory of Sigmund Freud, the author of this book searched for some doubtful *provenance* of jealousy. 根据西格蒙德•弗罗伊德的理论，本书作者寻找产生嫉妒的可能原因。

provided* [prəˈvaɪdɪd]

conj. 倘若，只要，假如

例 I'll buy the cup, *provided* that the price is right. 倘若价格合适，我就买这个杯子。

provision* [prəˈvɪʒn]

n. 供应，(一批)供应品；准备，预备；条款，规定；给养，口粮

记 来自 provide(*vt.* 供应，提供)

搭 make provision 做好准备，预先采取措施；under the provision of sth. 依据…条款

例 The country has enough *provisions* of grain for the future several years. 这个国家为未来几年备有足够的粮食储备。

同 preparation(*n.* 准备，预备)；clause(*n.* 条款)；food(*n.* 食物)

prowess [ˈpraʊəs]

n. 杰出的才能，高超的技艺，专长，造诣

记 联想记忆：prow(英勇的) + ess → 杰出的才能

例 He found that the way the cats played had no significant effect on their hunting *prowess* in later life. 他发现，猫咪的玩耍方式对它日后的捕猎生活没有重大的影响。

proximity* [prɒkˈsɪməti]

n. 接近，邻近；亲近

记 词根记忆：prox(近) + im + ity → 接近，邻近；亲近

搭 proximity to 邻近；亲近；in close proximity 非常接近

例 I chose the flat for its *proximity* to my company. 我选这个公寓是因为它离我们公司近。

同 vicinity(*n.* 邻近，附近)

反 distance(*n.* 远离，远隔)

□ prosperous □ prototype □ protrude □ provenance □ provided □ provision
□ prowess □ proximity

psychiatric* [ˌsaɪki ˈætrɪk]

a. 精神病的；治疗精神病的

例 Jim suffered from a ***psychiatric*** disorder. 吉姆精神紊乱。

publicity* [pʌb ˈlɪsətɪ]

n. 宣传，宣扬；公众的注意，名声

记 联想记忆：产品可凭借其独特性(peculiarity)，不用宣传(publicity)也能大为流行(popularity)

搭 seek publicity 想出风头

例 The company launched a ***publicity*** campaign on a large scale. 这家公司发起了一场大规模的宣传活动。

派 public(*a.* 公众的；公共的；公开的 *n.* 公众，民众)；publicly(*ad.* 公然地；舆论上地)；publicize〔*vt.* 宣传(尤指通过广告)〕

pudding [ˈpʊdɪŋ]

n. 布丁

记 发音记忆："布丁"

例 There's traditional plum ***pudding*** or apple pie for tonight's dessert. 今晚的甜点是传统的李子布丁或苹果派。

pull up stakes*

离开，搬家

例 About half the nation's 2,000 commercial beekeepers ***pull up stakes*** each spring. 全国 2000 名商业养蜂人中大约有一半每年春天都要搬家。

pulley [ˈpʊli]

n. 滑轮；滑车

记 联想记忆：pull(推) + ey → 滑轮；滑车

例 The lifting device is a rope and ***pulley*** system. 这种起重装置是由缆索和滑轮组成的。

pulverise [ˈpʌlvəraɪz]

vt. 碾磨成粉，粉碎

记 词根记忆：pulver(粉尘) + ise(动词后缀) → 粉碎

例 ***Pulverised*** rock will climb as a dust cloud into the atmosphere. 石粉会像尘雾一样上升到大气中。

pumice [ˈpʌmɪs]

n. 浮石，浮岩 *vt.* 用浮岩磨

例 Is the ***pumice*** light and full of the holes? 浮岩是既轻又密布坑洞的吗?

pump [pʌmp]

v. 用泵抽(水)；涌出，奔流 *n.* 泵，抽水机

搭 pump sth. into sb. 强行向某人灌输；pump sth. out 大量生产

例 The villagers were tired of getting water from thousand miles away, so they invented an machine for ***pumping*** groundwater. 村民们厌倦了到千里之外的地方打水，于是他们发明了一种可以抽地下水的机器。

punch* [pʌntʃ]

v. 穿孔，打孔；重击，猛击 *n.* 猛击；冲床，穿孔机；力量，效力

记 发音记忆："乓哧"(重击的声音) → 穿孔；重击

例 The robber ***punched*** the shopkeeper on his head and robbed the cash. 盗贼重击了店主的头部而后抢走了现金。

punctual [ˈpʌŋktʃuəl]

a. 守时的；准时的

记 词根记忆：punct(刺) + ual(形容词后缀)→ 像针刺那么准确 → 守时的；准时的

例 Being ***punctual*** shows your clients that you respect their schedule and that you can be counted on. 守时会让你的客户觉得，你尊重他们的安排，并且值得信赖。

派 punctually(*ad.* 准时地)；punctuality(*n.* 准时)

□ psychiatric □ publicity □ pudding □ pull up stakes □ pulley □ pulverise
□ pumice □ pump □ punch □ punctual

purchase* [ˈpɜːtʃəs]

vt. 买，购买 *n.* 购买的物品

记 联想记忆：pur + chase(追逐) → 为得到紧俏的商品而竞相追逐 → 购买

搭 purchase from 从…处购买

例 If you'd like to ***purchase*** any of George's books or other souvenirs, leave the house by the side entrance. 如果你想购买乔治的书或其他纪念品，请从房子的侧门离开。

派 purchaser(*n.* 购买者，采购人)

purify [ˈpjʊərɪfaɪ]

vt. 使洁净，使纯洁，净化；提纯，精炼

记 词根记忆：pur(干净的) + ify(使…) → 使洁净，净化；提纯

例 As is well-known, one of the main doctrines of this religion is that people should try to ***purify*** their mind. 众所周知，该宗教的一条主要教义是人们要净化自己的心灵。

派 purification(*n.* 净化，提纯)；purist(*n.* 纯粹主义者)

同 cleanse(*vt.* 清洗；净化)；refine(*vt.* 提纯，提炼；改善)

反 contaminate(*vt.* 污染，玷污)

purpose* [ˈpɜːpəs]

n. 目的，意图；用途，效果 *v.* 打算，企图，决心

搭 on purpose 故意，有意；with the purpose of 为了；statement of purpose 目的陈述

例 Bob was absent from school on ***purpose***. 鲍勃故意逃学。

pursuit [pəˈsjuːt]

n. 追求，寻求；[常 *pl.*] 花时间和精力等做的事；消遣，爱好

记 联想记忆：钱包(purse)被小偷偷去，赶忙追赶(pursuit)

搭 in pursuit of 追求

例 Archaeology is both a physical activity out in the field and an intellectual ***pursuit*** in the study or laboratory. 考古学既是一种野外的体力活动，也是研究室或实验室里的知性探索。

同 chase(*n.* 追逐)；hobby(*n.* 业余爱好)

qualification* [ˌkwɒlɪfɪˈkeɪʃn]

n. 资格，合格；技能；限定，条件；合格证

记 来自 qualify(*v.* 合格，具备资格)

搭 qualification test 资格考试；minimum qualification 最低资格

例 You can select someone—even a friend—who has the ***qualifications***, degrees and certificates. 你可以选有资格、学位和证书的人，甚至可以是朋友。

qualitative [ˈkwɒlɪtətɪv]

a. 性质的，质量的；定性的

记 联想记忆：qualit(y)(质量) + ative → 质量的；定性的

例 There is little ***qualitative*** improvement in their work. 他们的工作没有什么实质性的改进。

quantity [ˈkwɒntəti]

n. 数量，数目；量；众多，大宗

例 This medicine will reduce the ***quantity*** of blood flowing through the body. 这种药会减少体内的血流量。

quartz [kwɔːts]

n. 石英

记 联想记忆：quart(看作 quarter，一刻钟) + z → 钟表，石英钟 → 石英

例 The Eskimos produced a slow-burning spark by striking ***quartz*** against iron pyrites. 爱斯基摩人利用硫化铁矿石击打石英获得缓慢燃烧的火花。

36

□ purchase □ purify □ purpose □ pursuit □ qualification □ qualitative
□ quantity □ quartz

questionnaire* [ˌkwestʃəˈneə(r)]
n. 问卷，调查表
例 They did a lot of research using *questionnaires*. 他们借助问卷调查进行了大量研究。
同 questionary(*n.* 调查表，问卷)

quiver [ˈkwɪvə(r)]
v. 颤抖，抖动
例 The moth *quivered* its wings in front of the fire. 蛾子在火堆前抖动着翅膀。
同 quake(*vi.* 震动；颤抖)；shake[*v.* (使)颤抖，(使)震动]

quota [ˈkwəʊtə]
n. 定额，限额，配额
记 发音记忆："阔的"→出手阔绰，没有限额→限额
派 a quota system for …的限额制度
例 Your sales are always below *quota*. 你们的销售量总是低于限额。
同 allotment(*n.* 分配；份额)

quote* [kwəʊt]
n. 引文，引语；估价，报价；[*pl.*] 引号 *v.* 引用，引述，引证；提出，提供；报价
记 词根记忆：quot(数目)+e→引用，引述
搭 quote from 从…引用
例 The student *quotes* a paragraph from the Bible. 那名学生引用了《圣经》中的一段话。
派 quotation(*n.* 引文；报价)

racket [ˈrækɪt]
n. (网球、羽毛球等的)球拍
记 联想记忆：这副球拍(racket)被火箭(rocket)带入过太空
例 The player was fined for throwing his *racket* to the ground in anger. 那名球员一气之下将球拍摔到地上，因此遭到判罚。

radiate [ˈreɪdieɪt]
v. 发光；发热；辐射
记 词根记忆：radi(光线)+ate(使…)→发光；发热
例 The scientist said that the heat, light, and energy that were *radiated* from the sun filled the entire solar system. 那个科学家说太阳发出的热、光和能量遍布整个太阳系。
派 radiation(*n.* 发光；辐射)

radius* [ˈreɪdiəs]
n. 半径；周围，范围
记 词根记忆：rad(光线)+ius→半径就像是从同一点散发出的许多光线→半径
搭 with a twenty-meter radius 半径是20米
例 Some local carpenters could only accept jobs in a three-kilometer *radius*. 当地的一些木匠只能接受方圆三千米内的工作。
同 range(*n.* 幅度，范围)；parameter(*n.* [常 *pl.*] 界限，范围)

rampant [ˈræmpənt]
a. (犯罪、疾病等)猖獗的，肆虐的，泛滥的；(植物)蔓生的，疯长的
例 If one day inflation is *rampant*, it means that people's increased wage will be worth nothing soon. 如果有一天通货膨胀泛滥成灾，那就意味着人们增长的工资很快就会一文不值。

□ questionnaire □ quiver □ quota □ quote □ racket □ radiate
□ radius □ rampant

random [ˈrændəm]

a. 任意的，随机的，随意的 *n.* 随机，随意

记 联想记忆：ran(跑) + dom(领域) → 可以在各种领域跑的 → 任意的

搭 at random 随机地，任意地；random selection 随机的选择；random sampling 随机取样；random access 随机存取

例 The robots follow their own *random* paths around the plant busily getting on with their jobs. 机器人在工厂里沿着各自的随机路线忙碌地工作着。

同 irregular(*a.* 不规则的，无规律的)；arbitrary(*a.* 任意的)

反 designed(*a.* 有计划的)；arranged(*a.* 安排好的)

range* [reɪndʒ]

n. 范围，领域；系列；(山)脉；射程 *v.* (在一定范围内)变化，变动；排列

搭 a wide range of 一系列；range between... and... 范围在…与…之间不等；range from 延伸；(在一定程度或范围内)变动，变化

例 We'd like to produce the equipment with a *range* of sizes. 我们想生产大小规格不同的设备。

派 ranger(*n.* 护林员)

rank [ræŋk]

v. 排列；分等 *n.* 等级；军衔

记 联想记忆：银行(bank)拥有不同社会阶层(rank)的客户

例 How did Kant *rank* the senses? 康德如何对感觉进行分类?

rarity [ˈreərəti]

n. 稀有；稀有的事物

例 Nowadays, men who do the cooking are something of a *rarity*. 现在会做饭的男人十分稀少。

ratio [ˈreɪʃiəʊ]

n. 比，比率

记 词根记忆：rat(清点) + io → 比，比率

例 The male to female *ratio* of volunteers is 4 to 5. 志愿者中男女比例为4比5。

ration* [ˈræʃn]

n. 配给量，定量；给养，口粮 *vt.* 配给，定量供应

记 联想记忆：rat(老鼠) + ion → 老鼠正在开大会，讨论口粮问题 → 配给量，定量；口粮

搭 the weekly meat ration 每周的食肉量；be on ration 定量

例 Eggs are on *ration* during the war. 战争期间，鸡蛋都实行定量供应。

raw material

原材料

例 Firms have a standard *raw material* inspection procedure. 公司对原材料有一套标准的检验程序。

realistic* [ˌrɪəˈlɪstɪk; ˌriːəˈlɪstɪk]

a. 现实(主义)的，实际的；恰如其分的；逼真的

记 来自 real(*a.* 真的，真实的)

例 We must be more *realistic* towards the tough problem. 面对这个棘手的问题，我们应该更现实一点。

派 unrealistic(*a.* 不切实际的)；realistically(*ad.* 现实主义地；实事求是地)

□ random □ range □ rank □ rarity □ ratio □ ration
□ raw material □ realistic

realm
[relm]

n. 界，领域，范围；王国，国度

记 联想记忆：real(真正的)+ m → 真正的好东西(如音乐、艺术)无国界 → 领域；王国

搭 beyond/within the realms of possibility 超出/在可能范围；in the realm of literature 在文学领域内

例 It is strange that the rocket was generally ignored by writers of fiction to transport their heroes to mysterious ***realms*** beyond the Earth, even though it had been commonly used in fireworks displays in China since the thirteenth century. 尽管从 13 世纪起火箭就已经普遍应用在了中国的烟花表演中，奇怪的是，小说作者却很少会用火箭将他们的主人公带到地球以外的神秘地域。

rear*
[rɪə(r)]

a. 后方的，后部的；背后的 *n.* 后部，尾部 *v.* 饲养，抚养；种植

搭 at/in the rear of 在…的后面；rear sb. on sth.(用…)喂养；bring up the rear 站在队尾，落在后面

例 Mary's office is next to the ***rear*** entrance. 玛丽的办公室挨着后门。

reasonable*
[ˈriːznəbl]

a. 合理的，有道理的；通情达理的；适度的

记 联想记忆：reason(道理)+ able(能…的)→ 能讲理的 → 通情达理的

搭 at reasonable prices 以公道的价格

例 I think you'll find the methods very ***reasonable***. 我想你会觉得这些方法很合理。

派 unreasonable(*a.* 不合理的)

recalcitrant
[rɪˈkælsɪtrənt]

a. 顽抗的，反抗的

例 When someone is ***recalcitrant***, he might resist following orders, or going along, even too stubborn to deal with. 如果一个人很倔强，他可能拒绝服从命令或者与他人合作，甚至固执到无法应付的地步。

recapture
[ˌriːˈkæptʃə(r)]

vt. 重获，收复

例 Their attempt to ***recapture*** the city was failed by a traitor. 他们重新夺回这座城市的企图被一个叛徒毁掉了。

receipt
[rɪˈsiːt]

n. 收到，接到；发票，收据；[*pl.*] 收入，进款

记 词根记忆：re + ceipt(拿，取)→ 拿到的，取到的 → 收入，进款

搭 receipt invoice 收妥发票，钱货两讫发票；make out a receipt 写收据；net/gross receipts 净/总收入

例 It is a common rule that goods will be delivered on ***receipt*** of payment. 只有在支付货款后才可以交货，这是一条普遍的规则。

receiver
[rɪˈsiːvə(r)]

n. (电话)听筒；接收器

搭 pick up the receiver 拿起听筒

例 He put his hand over the ***receiver*** in order to get the signal better. 他将手放到接收器上以便收到更清晰的信号。

□ realm □ rear □ reasonable □ recalcitrant □ recapture □ receipt
□ receiver

reception * [rɪˈsepʃn]	*n.* 接收，接受；接待，招待会；接收效果 记 词根记忆：re(表加强) + cept(拿，取) + ion → 拿住 → 接受 搭 reception center/desk 接待处 例 The students' dormitory is to the right of the *reception* desk. 学生宿舍在接待处的右边。
receptionist * [rɪˈsepʃənɪst]	*n.* 接待员 例 The patient goes to a *receptionist* and ask her about his disease. 病人向接待员询问他的病情。
recession [rɪˈseʃn]	*n.* (经济的)衰退，衰退时期；撤回，退回 记 词根记忆：re(反) + cess(行走) + ion → 向后走 → 衰退；撤回 搭 economic recession 经济衰退期 例 During the economic *recession*, more and more countries begin to take trade protectionist measures, which is block to the global economic recovery. 经济衰退期间，越来越多的国家开始采取贸易保护措施，阻碍了全球经济的复苏。 派 recessionary(*a.* 引起经济衰退的)
recipe [ˈresəpi]	*n.* 食谱；方法，秘诀，秘方 记 词根记忆：re + cip(拿，取) + e → 抓住关键，才是诀窍 → 秘诀，秘方 搭 a recipe book 烹饪书 例 Errors in the genetic *recipe* for haemoglobin give rise to the most common single-gene disorder in the world. 血红蛋白中遗传密码出现问题会导致世界上最常见的单基因病变。 同 secret(*n.* 秘密；秘诀)；knack(*n.* 技巧，诀窍)
recipient [rɪˈsɪpiənt]	*n.* 接受者 记 词根记忆：re(反) + cip(拿，取) + ient → 不主动拿 → (被动的)接受者 例 This aritificial heart *recipient* will recover in three weeks. 人造心脏接受者将在三个星期后康复。 同 receiver(*n.* 接收器；接受者)
reciprocate [rɪˈsɪprəkeɪt]	*v.* 回报，回应；报答 例 Generally speaking, people will *reciprocate* the kindness that have been shown to them before. 一般而言，人们以前受过别人的恩惠，他们会进行报答。
reckon * [ˈrekən]	*v.* 认为，估计；测算，测量；料想，指望 记 词根记忆：reck(注意，留心) + on → 估计；测算 搭 reckon in 把…算在内；reckon without 未把…考虑在内；reckon on 指望，依赖；reckon with 重视，认真处理；把…考虑进去 例 Did you *reckon* in the cost of these raw materials? 你把买这些原材料的费用算进去了吗?

□ reception □ receptionist □ recession □ recipe □ recipient □ reciprocate
□ reckon

reclaim
[rɪˈkleɪm]

vt. 纠正；要求归还，收回；开垦(土地)

记 联想记忆：re(一再)+claim(大声叫喊)→一再叫喊，要求归还→要求归还

例 As he stopped the payment by installment, the finance company tried to *reclaim* his house. 在他停止分期付款后，该信贷公司试图收回他的房屋。

派 reclamation(*n.* 开垦；回收)

同 retrieve(*v.* 重新得到)；retake(*vt.* 取回，夺回)；recycle(*vt.* 使再循环，回收)

recognition*
[ˌrekəgˈnɪʃn]

n. 识别；认出；承认，确认，认可；赏识，表彰

记 来自 recognize(*vt.* 认出；承认)

例 The machine detected briefly towards her, but there was no sign of *recognition*. 机器对她进行了检测，但是没有一丝识别出来的迹象。

recognize
[ˈrekəgnaɪz]

vt. 认出；承认，认可

记 词根记忆：re(再，又)+co(=com 共同)+gn(知道)+ize→再次共同知道→认出；承认

搭 be recognized as sth. 被认为某物

例 Companies should *recognize* that their employees are a significant part of their financial assets. 公司应该认识到雇员是其金融资产的重要组成部分。

recommend
[ˌrekəˈmend]

vt. 推荐；劝告；使受欢迎

记 联想记忆：re(一再)+com(共同)+mend(修)→这本书是大家一再修改的成果，强力推荐→推荐

搭 recommend sb. sth. 向某人推荐某物；We recommend that... 我们建议…

例 As treatment for back pain the clinic mainly *recommends* relaxation therapy. 至于背部疼痛的治疗，诊所主要推荐采用放松疗法。

recommendation*
[ˌrekəmenˈdeɪʃn]

n. 推荐，推荐信；劝告，建议

搭 letter of recommendation 推荐信；on sb.'s recommendation 在某人的推荐下

例 The skills of making presentation are on the *recommendation* of a professor. 这些做报告的技巧是一位教授推荐的。

reconstruction*
[ˌriːkənˈstrʌkʃn]

n. 重建；再现

搭 economic reconstruction 经济重建；facial reconstruction 面貌复原

例 There will be a huge project for the post-war *reconstruction* for the tribe. 这个部落的战后重建将是非常巨大的工程。

Word List 37

音 频

词根、词缀预习表

cre	制造	recreation *n.* 娱乐，消遣	**fer**	带来	refer *v.* 参考，查阅
frain	笼头	refrain *v.* 抑制，克制	**reg**	统治	regent *n.* 摄政者
hab	拥有	rehabilitate *vt.* 使恢复原状	**lat**	搬运	relate *v.* 有关联
lax	松开	relax *v.* (使)放松	**lev**	举	relevance *n.* 相关性
loc	摆放	relocate *v.* 重新安置	**der**	给	render *vt.* 提供

recourse
[rɪˈkɔːs]

n. 依靠；求助，求援

例 A linguist's personal judgements are often uncertain, or disagree with the judgements of other linguists, at which point ***recourse*** is needed to more objective methods of enquiry, using non-linguists as informant. 语言学家的个人判断通常是不可靠的，或者与其他语言学家的判断不一致，这时就需要求助于更加客观的调查方法，选择非语言学家作为语料供应人。

recover*
[rɪˈkʌvə(r)]

v. 重新获得，重新得到；使复原，使康复；收回，换回

记 联想记忆：re(再，又) + cover(包括) → 重新获得

搭 recover oneself 使自己振作；recover from 恢复

例 After a few days of cough, my roommate began to ***recover***. 咳嗽了几天后，我的室友开始康复了。

派 recovery(*n.* 恢复)

recreate*
[ˌriːkriˈeɪt]

vt. 再现，再创造

例 Since very few people will ever experience the Antarctic first-hand, the visitor's centre aims to ***recreate*** the atmosphere of Antarctic. 由于很少有人能够亲自登上南极体验一把，因此游客中心旨在再现南极所特有的氛围。

recreation*
[ˌrekriˈeɪʃn]

n. 娱乐，消遣

recreation

记 词根记忆：re(再，又) + cre(制造) + ation(表结果，名词后缀) → 一遍遍地制造出来的 → 娱乐，消遣

搭 recreation area 娱乐休闲区；open-air/outdoor recreation 户外娱乐活动

例 As you can see, the building you are in now contains this main lounge, the dining room and the ***recreation*** room. 如你所见，你现在所在的这幢大楼包括主休息室、餐厅和娱乐室。

派 recreate〔*v.* (使)得到休养；(使)得到娱乐〕

□ recourse □ recover □ recreate □ recreation

recreational* [ˌrekriˈeɪʃənl]

a. 消遣的，娱乐的；游戏的

例 Sports facilities are set aside in the corner for the community's *recreational* use. 角落里设置了运动器材，以供社区人们娱乐之用。

recruit* [rɪˈkruːt]

v. 招募(新兵)，招收(新成员)；复原，恢复；补充

n. 新兵，新成员，新会员

记 词根记忆：re + cruit(=cres 成长)→ 使成长壮大 → 招募(新兵)，招收(新成员)

搭 recruit... to 招募，征募；recruit method 招聘方法

例 You are among the two hundred staff *recruited* to help look after the old. 你是被招聘来帮忙照顾老年人的 200 名员工之一。

派 recruitment(*n.* 招聘；吸收新成员)；recruiter(*n.* 征兵人员；为学校招生的人)

rectangle* [ˈrektæŋgl]

n. 长方形，矩形

记 词根记忆：rect(直的)+ angl(角)+ e → 长方形的每个角均为直角 → 长方形，矩形

例 Tom's room is in the shape of *rectangle*. 汤姆的房间是长方形的。

rectangular [rekˈtæŋgjələ(r)]

a. 长方形的，矩形的

记 词根记忆：rect(直的)+ angul(角)+ ar → 所有内角都为直角的平行四边形 → 长方形的

例 In front of the Empire State Building is a long *rectangular* wading pool. 帝国大厦前面是一个长方形的浅水池。

recycle* [ˌriːˈsaɪkl]

v. 回收利用

记 联想记忆：re(重新)+ cycle(循环)→ 循环利用 → 回收利用

例 The man collects the waste bins and deposits the waste into a shredder for *recycling*. 这个人把垃圾箱收集起来，把垃圾倒进搅碎机进行回收利用。

派 recyclable(*a.* 可回收利用的，可再循环的)

同 reclaim(*vt.* 回收)

redevelopment* [ˌriːdɪˈveləpmənt]

n. 重新规划；重新建设

搭 downtown redevelopment 市区重建；economic redevelopment 经济重建

例 Now, the theatre is reopening soon after its three-year *redevelopment*. 经过三年的重建，现在这家剧场很快就要重新开放了。

reduce* [rɪˈdjuːs]

v. 减少，缩小；简化

例 Catastrophes such as fire, flood, drought or epidemic may *reduce* population sizes to a small fraction of their average level. 火灾、洪水、干旱或流行病之类大灾难会降低人口数量，使其远远低于正常水平。

派 reduction(*n.* 减少，缩小；减价)

□ recreational □ recruit □ rectangle □ rectangular □ recycle □ redevelopment □ reduce

redundant* [rɪˈdʌndənt]	*a.* (因人员过剩而)被解雇的；多余的，过剩的；累赘的，冗长的 记 词根记忆：red(=re 一再) + und(波动) + ant(形容词后缀)→ 反复波动，反复出现 → 多余的，过剩的；累赘的 例 Jill was unlucky to be made ***redundant*** from her job. 吉尔不幸被解雇。 派 redundancy(*n.* 裁员；过多，过剩) 同 superfluous(*a.* 多余的，过剩的)；excessive(*a.* 过多的；过分的) 反 indispensable(*a.* 不可或缺的)；scanty(*a.* 不够的，贫乏的)
reel [riːl]	*n.* 卷轴，卷筒，卷盘，线轴 *v.* 摇摇晃晃地移动，蹒跚；眩晕，发昏；卷，绕 记 联想记忆：喝醉酒步履蹒跚(reel)，感觉(feel)墙走我不走 搭 reel off 一口气说出，滔滔不绝地讲(或重复) 例 There are another three new ***reels*** of film for use. 还有三卷胶卷可以使用。 同 roller(*n.* 滚筒；滚轴)；shamble(*vi.* 蹒跚)；stagger(*v.* 踉跄，蹒跚)；spool(*vt.* 把…缠绕在线轴上)
refectory* [rɪˈfektri]	*n.* (学院)餐厅，食堂 例 I agree with what you said earlier about fish and chips in the ***refectory***. 我同意你之前在食堂说的关于鱼和炸薯条的看法。
refer* [rɪˈfɜː(r)]	*v.* 参考，查阅，查询；提到，谈及；引用；提交，上呈 记 词根记忆：re(又) + fer(带来，拿来)→ 参考，查阅；提到，谈及 搭 refer to 参考，查阅；涉及，提到；refer to...as 把…称作，把…当作 例 In his speech, Martin ***referred*** to education reform several times. 马丁在演讲中几次提到教育改革的问题。 同 consult(*v.* 查阅，参考)
referee* [ˌrefəˈriː]	*v.* 裁判；仲裁，调停 *n.* 裁判(员)；仲裁人，调停人；证明人，介绍人 记 联想记忆：refer(查阅，咨询) + ee(表人) → 有问题时能够咨询的人 → 调停人；裁判 搭 to be the referee of a game 成为一项运动的裁判 例 Instead of spending much time ***refereeing*** between the two students, I went to the library. 我没有花太多时间调停这两名学生，而是去了图书馆。
reference* [ˈrefrəns]	*n.* 参考，参考书目；提及，涉及；证明书(或人)；介绍(人) 记 来自 refer(*v.* 参考；提到) 搭 with/in reference to 关于；reference source 参考源；reference letter 推荐信；reference book 参考书 例 The teachers will not give the range of ***reference*** books. 老师们不会给出参考书的范围。
refinement [rɪˈfaɪnmənt]	*n.* 精巧的附件，精制的改良品；精炼；文雅 搭 an atmosphere of refinement 优雅的气氛 例 The progress in ***refinement*** of machine tools has been substantial in recent years. 近年来，机床的改进取得了实质性的进展。

37

□ redundant □ reel □ refectory □ refer □ referee □ reference
□ refinement

refrain [rɪˈfreɪn]

v. 抑制，克制 *n.* 反复句，(诗歌的)叠句；副歌；经常重复的评价

记 词根记忆：re(回，向后) + frain(笼头) → 笼头往后 → 抑制，克制

搭 refrain from 克制

例 The survey finds that the majority of people can ***refrain*** from smoking in public places such as theater and museum. 调查发现，在剧院和博物馆这类公共场所大多数人能够克制住不抽烟。

同 restrain(*vt.* 抑制，控制)；abstain(*vi.* 戒除)

反 indulge(*v.* 纵容，放纵)

refresh [rɪˈfreʃ]

v. (使)复原，更新；(使)精神振作，(使)精力恢复

记 联想记忆：re(再，又) + fresh(新鲜的) → 使(复原)，更新

搭 refresh sb.' s memory 恢复某人的记忆

例 My job is to make sure that you all feel relaxed and ***refreshed***. 我的工作就是保证你们都感觉放松且精力充沛。

refresher* [rɪˈfreʃə(r)]

n. 提神物；帮助记忆的东西或人；补习课程

搭 refresher course 进修课程；refresher leave 进修假期

例 I'd like to enquire about the ***refresher*** courses that you run. 我想咨询一下您开办的进修课程的情况。

refreshment [rɪˈfreʃmənt]

n. (精力的)恢复；[*pl.*] 茶点，点心，饮料

记 联想记忆：refresh(使精神振作) + ment → (精力的)恢复

例 You can use the members' lounge for ***refreshment*** when you feel tired. 你感到疲倦时可以在会员休息室休息一下。

同 beverage(*n.* 饮料)

refrigerator* [rɪˈfrɪdʒəreɪtə(r)]

n. 冰箱；冷藏库

记 联想记忆：refrigerat(e)(冷藏) + or → 冰箱

例 I've left a meal in the ***refrigerator*** for you. 我在冰箱里给你留了饭。

refund

[ˈriːfʌnd] *n.* 退款 [rɪˈfʌnd] *vt.* 退还(钱款)，偿付

记 联想记忆：re(向后) + fund(资金) → 给回资金 → 偿付；退款

搭 full refund 全额偿还；give sb. a refund 给某人退款

例 You can't get a ***refund*** if you don't have any invoices. 如果你没有发票就不能获得退款。

refundable* [rɪˈfʌndəbl]

a. 可退还的，可归还的，可偿还的

例 The deposit on the house is ***refundable***. 这个房子的押金是可以退还的。

refusal [rɪˈfjuːzl]

n. 拒绝

记 来自 refuse(*v.* 拒绝)

例 The journalists received outright ***refusal*** of the foreign spokesman. 记者们遭到了外交发言人的断然拒绝。

regarding [rɪˈɡɑːdɪŋ]

prep. 关于

记 联想记忆：regard(关心) + ing → 关于

例 You are allowed to ask questions ***regarding*** the fees you are paying. 你们可以就自己的付费问题进行提问。

□ refrain □ refresh □ refresher □ refreshment □ refrigerator □ refund
□ refundable □ refusal □ regarding

regardless* [rɪ'ɡɑːdləs]	*ad.* 不顾后果地；无论如何 记 组合词：regard(关心)+less(少)→很少关心→不顾后果地 搭 regardless of 不管 例 *Regardless* of the theory or model that we choose, a reduction in population size decreases the genetic diversity of a population. 无论我们选择何种理论或研究样本，人口减少都会降低该种群的基因多样性。
regent ['riːdʒənt]	*n.* 摄政者(代国王统治者) 记 词根记忆：reg(统治)+ent(表人)→统治者→摄政者 例 George acted as a *regent* when the present king was a child. 当现任国王还是孩子时，乔治担任摄政王。
region* ['riːdʒən]	*n.* 地区；范围 记 词根记忆：reg(统治)+ion→统治的区域→地区；范围 例 Although the UK is a fairly small country, the geology and climate vary a good deal from *region* to *region*. 尽管英国的国土面积很小，但是不同地区间的地况和气候却大相径庭。
regional* ['riːdʒənl]	*a.* 局部范围的；地方(性)的，区域性的；全地区的，整个地区的 搭 regional accent 地方口音 例 Our group won the *regional* laurels. 我们小组赢得了地区冠军。
register ['redʒɪstə(r)]	*n.* 注册，登记；登记表 *v.* 注册，登记 记 词根记忆: re(回) + gist(=gest 带来) + er → 带回来 → 登记 搭 registered capital 注册资本；register a trademark 注册一个商标；register for 登记参加，报名参加；register with 向…登记，给…留下印象；registered mail 挂号信 例 You must remember to bring the ID card with you when you come to *register*. 你来登记的时候一定要记得带上身份证。
registration* [ˌredʒɪ'streɪʃn]	*n.* 登记，注册；(邮件等的)挂号；登记或注册的项目 例 There is a strict management in the *registration* of a child's birth. 对新生儿的登记进行严格管理。
regularity* [ˌregju'lærəti]	*n.* 规律性，规则性；整齐，匀称 记 来自 regular(*a.* 有规律的) 例 Climate change is disrupting the *regularity* of the seasons. 气候的变化打破季节的规律性。
regulate ['regjuleɪt]	*v.* 管制，控制；调节，校准；调整 记 词根记忆：reg(统治)+ul+ate(动词后缀)→统治并加以管理→管制 搭 regulate the traffic 管制交通；regulate one's spending 控制开支 例 More than 300 dams *regulate* river flows around the country. 有300多座大坝控制着全国的河水流量。 派 regulation(*n.* 规章；管理)
regurgitate [rɪ'ɡɜːdʒɪtet]	*vt.* 涌回，流回；【动】(使)反胃，将(咽下的食物)返回到口中，反刍 例 The cormorant *regurgitates* half-digested fish to feed its young. 鸬鹚将消化了一半的鱼回翻，喂给幼鸟。

37

□ regardless □ regent □ region □ regional □ register □ registration
□ regularity □ regulate □ regurgitate

rehabilitate
[ˌriːəˈbɪlɪteɪt]

vt. 改造(罪犯等)，使恢复正常生活；使恢复原状，修复；复职；恢复…的名誉

记 词根记忆：re + hab(拥有) + ilit + ate → 重新拥有 → 使恢复原状，修复

例 The prison service should try to *rehabilitate* prisoners rather than merely imprisonment. 监狱服务应该尽力改造罪犯而不是单纯地羁押。

reinforce
[ˌriːɪnˈfɔːs]

vt. 加强；增援

记 联想记忆：re(又，再) + in(向内) + force(力量) → 再次给予力量 → 加强

例 Concrete with steel bars in it is known as *reinforced* concrete. 水泥中加入钢条就成了我们所知的钢筋混凝土。

reinforcement
[ˌriːɪnˈfɔːsmənt]

n. 增援，加强，加固

例 The Red Cross blasted the authorities' response to the disaster, making an urgent plea for *reinforcements* and aid. 红十字会严厉抨击当局对灾难的反应，并紧急呼吁要求增援和救助。

reinvigorate
[ˌriːɪnˈvɪɡəreɪt]

vt. 使重新振作；使恢复活力

例 To *reinvigorate* the rural economy, the government proposes to exploit more highways to connect villages in the nationwide. 为促进农村经济振兴，政府计划在全国范围内建设更多的乡间公路。

reiterate
[riˈɪtəreɪt]

vt. 重复，反复；反复地说，重申

记 词根记忆：re(再，又) + it(走) + erate → 重复地去 → 反复地说，重申

例 As the United Nations report on access to water *reiterated* in November 2001, more than one billion people lack access to clean drinking water. 2001 年 11 月联合国关于获取水资源的报告重申了一个事实，即 10 亿多人口无法获取纯净的饮用水。

reject

[rɪˈdʒekt] *vt.* 拒绝 [ˈriːdʒekt] *n.* 被拒货品，不合格品

记 词根记忆：re(反) + ject(扔) → 被扔回来 → 拒绝

例 They are cheap because they are *rejects*. 它们是不合格品，所以便宜。

rekindle
[ˌriːˈkɪndl]

vt. 重新点燃；使复苏

记 联想记忆：re(重新) + kindle(点燃) → 重新点燃

例 In New Zealand, classes for children have slowed the erosion of Maori and *rekindled* interest in the language. 在新西兰，面向孩子们的课程减缓了毛利语的退化，重新引起了人们对这种语言的兴趣。

relate
[rɪˈleɪt]

v. 有关联；讲述，叙述

记 词根记忆：re + lat(搬运) + e → 有关联

例 That's the office that deals with all matters *related* to student welfare. 那间就是负责处理所有有关学生福利待遇问题的办公室。

relation*
[rɪˈleɪʃn]

n. 关系，联系；亲属，亲戚

搭 in/with relation to 关系到；have no relation to 与…没有关系；diplomatic relations 外交关系；international relations 国际关系

例 The *relation* between students and teachers is generally good in this university. 这所大学里师生间的关系总体来说很好。

relative* [ˈrelətɪv]

a. 相对的；比较的；有关的，相关的 *n.* 亲属，亲戚

搭 close/distant relatives 近/远亲

例 They now live in ***relative*** comfort. 他们现在过得比较舒适。

派 relatively(*ad.* 相当地；相对地)

relative

relax* [rɪˈlæks]

v. (使)放松

记 词根记忆：re（一再）+ lax（松开）→ 一再放开 →（使）放松

例 Watching TV can help me ***relax***. 看电视可以帮助我放松。

派 relaxation(*n.* 放松；休息)

relay

[ˈriːleɪ] *n.* 接力赛；中继设备 [ˈriːleɪ; riˈleɪ] *vt.* 传送；转播

记 联想记忆：re(重新) + lay(放置) → 重新放置 → 转播

例 The Olympic Games are ***relayed*** all round the world. 奥运会实况向全世界转播。

release* [rɪˈliːs]

vt. 释放，解放；发表，发行 *n.* 释放；发表，发布；排放，泄露

搭 release news 发布新闻

例 The thief was ***released*** on bail. 窃贼交了保释金后获释。

relentless [rɪˈlentləs]

a. 无情的，残酷的

记 联想记忆：relent(变温和) + less → 缺少温和 → 无情的，残酷的

例 Even a millionaire, he is still ***relentless*** in requiring his employees working day and night. 虽然身为百万富翁，他仍然冷酷无情地要求员工们没日没夜地为他工作。

relentless

relevance* [ˈreləvəns]

n. 中肯，适当；相关性

记 词根记忆：re(一再) + lev(举) + ance → 被一再举起 → 相关性

例 I'm left-handed myself and I actually didn't see any ***relevance*** to my own life when I happened to start reading an article by a sports psychologist called Peter Matthews. 我自己就是左撇子，当我碰巧开始读运动心理学家彼得·马修斯所写的一篇文章时，我实际上并未意识到这与自己的生活有何联系。

relevant* [ˈreləvənt]

a. 有关的，相应的；适当的，中肯的；有重大意义的

记 词根记忆：re(一再) + lev(举) + ant(形容词后缀) → 要不断举出相关的论据 → 有关的，相应的

搭 relevant to 与…相关的，有关的，相应的；relevant details 相关细节

例 You should support your arguments with examples and ***relevant*** evidence. 你应该用实例和相关证据来支持你的论点。

派 irrelevant(*a.* 不相关的；不切题的)

37

□ relative □ relax □ relay □ release □ relentless □ relevance
□ relevant

reliable*
[rɪˈlaɪəbl]

a. 可靠的，可信赖的

例 Three speed cycles are simple and ***reliable*** to ride around the town. 在城里还是骑三速自行车比较简便可靠。

reliance
[rɪˈlaɪəns]

n. 依靠，依赖

例 Long-term ***reliance*** on sleeping pills is dangerous. 长期依赖安眠药是危险的。

同 trust(*n.* 信任，信赖)；dependence(*n.* 信任，信赖)

反 distrust(*n.* 不信任)

relief*
[rɪˈliːf]

n. (痛苦等)减轻，解除；援救，救济；安慰；缓合剂

记 联想记忆：坚定的信念(belief)是痛苦的缓和剂(relief)

搭 to one's relief 令人感到放心的是；a sense of relief 解脱感；breathe a sigh of relief 如释重负地松了口气

例 The ***relief*** material was flown to the flood-hit districts. 救灾物资被空运至洪灾区。

relieve
[rɪˈliːv]

vt. 救济；缓解

例 These tablets are used to help ***relieve*** hay fever and symptoms due to allergies. 这些药片用于缓解花粉热及其他因过敏引发的症状。

religion
[rɪˈlɪdʒən]

n. 宗教；宗教信仰

记 词根记忆：re(一再) + lig(绑) + ion → 反复用某种信念约束→ 宗教；宗教信仰

例 The speaker explained the relevance of the ***religion*** to the local people. 演讲者说明了宗教对于当地人的重要意义。

派 religious(*a.* 宗教上的)

relocate
[ˌriːləʊˈkeɪt]

v. 重新安置，(使)搬迁，迁移

记 词根记忆：re(重新) + loc(摆放) + ate → 重新摆放 → 重新安置，(使)搬迁

例 The factory is to ***relocate*** its headquarters in the coastal area, which would create redundancy of 60 workers. 工厂将把总部迁往沿海地区，将导致60名员工失业。

reluctant*
[rɪˈlʌktənt]

a. 不情愿的，勉强的；难得到的，难处理的

记 发音记忆："驴拉坦克" → 不情愿的，勉强的

例 Although most trainers know how important handedness is, at present they are rather ***reluctant*** to make use of the insights scientists like Matthews can give. 尽管多数训练者知道用手习惯的重要性，但是目前他们仍然不愿采纳像马修斯这样的科学家的见解。

rely
[rɪˈlaɪ]

vi. 依靠；信赖

记 联想记忆：re（一再）+ ly（音似：lie“撒谎”）→ 一再撒谎的人完全不值得信赖 → 信赖

搭 rely on/upon 依靠

例 Most inland farmers ***rely*** on underground water for irrigation. 大部分内陆农民都依靠地下水灌溉土地。

remain*
[rɪˈmeɪn]

v. 保持；仍旧是；剩下 *n.* [*pl.*] 残余；遗迹；残骸，遗体

例 Though rockets have been used for several hundred years, they ***remained*** a relatively minor artefact of civilisation until the twentieth century. 尽管火箭的使用已有几百年的历史，但它们一直被看作是人类文明中相对次要的发明，直到 20 世纪才发生了变化。

remark*
[rɪˈmɑːk]

v. 评论，谈论；注意到，察觉 *n.* 评语，评论；注释

记 联想记忆：re（一再）+ mark（做标记）→ 一再做标记 → 评论

搭 remark about/on 评论；make a remark on 对…发表评论

例 Can you ***remark*** the differences between the two paintings? 你能说出这两幅画的不同之处吗?

remarkable*
[rɪˈmɑːkəbl]

a. 引人注目的，显著的，值得注意的；异常的，非凡的

搭 remarkable achievements 非凡的成就

例 More than 4,000 species of these ***remarkable*** creatures have evolved and adapted to the world's different climates. 这些极不平常的生物中已有 4000 多种进化并适应了地球上不同的气候。

remedy
[ˈremədi]

n. 药品；治疗法；补救 *vt.* 治疗；补救

记 词根记忆：re + med（治疗）+ y → 治疗

搭 remedy for 对…的治疗法或药物/补救

例 Without ***remedies***, the two men who ate poisonous mushroom died within days. 由于没有药物，那两个吃了毒蘑菇的人几天后就死了。

remind*
[rɪˈmaɪnd]

vt. 提醒，使想起；使发生联想

记 联想记忆：re（又，再）+ mind（注意）→ 使再次注意 → 提醒

搭 remind sb. of sth. 提醒，使想起

例 The notice ***reminds*** students that if they park a motor vehicle on university premises without a valid permit, they will be fined. 这个通知提醒学生们：未经允许就在校园里停放机动车会被罚款。

37

remote*
[rɪˈməʊt]

a. 远的，长久的；遥远的，偏僻的；远程的；关系疏远的，脱离的；绝少的，微乎其微的；孤高的，冷淡的

记 词根记忆：re（反）+ mot（移动）+ e → 向后移动 → 关系疏远的，脱离的

搭 remote control 遥控器；remote chance/possibility 机会很小；remote sensing technology 遥感技术；a remote village 偏僻的村庄

例 His ultimate goal was to discover an earth-like planet in ***remote*** galaxies. 他的最终目标是在遥远的星系中找到一颗类地行星。

同 distant（*a.* 遥远的）；isolated（*a.* 孤立的）

□ rely □ remain □ remark □ remarkable □ remedy □ remind
□ remote

removal [rɪˈmuːvl]

n. 除去；免职；搬迁

例 I saw a *removal* van outside your house yesterday afternoon. 昨天下午我看见你家屋外停着一辆搬家卡车。

remove* [rɪˈmuːv]

vt. 排除，消除；搬迁，移动；开除，解除 *n.* 距离，间距

记 联想记忆：re + move(移动) → 排除

搭 be far removed from sth. 和…差别很大

例 Water soluble vitamins are *removed* rapidly from the body. 水溶性维生素可以很快排出体外。

派 remover(*n.* 清除剂；搬家工人，搬家公司)

remuneration [rɪˌmjuːnəˈreɪʃn]

n. 报酬

例 To meet the requirements of public interest, the investment of the investors could be expropriated in comply with legal procedure with a due *remuneration*. 为了满足公共利益的需求，可以依照法律程序没收投资者的投资，并给予相应报酬。

renaissance [rɪˈneɪsns]

n. [the R-] (欧洲14至16世纪的)文艺复兴，文艺复兴时期；(文学、艺术等的)复兴，新生

记 词根记忆：re(重新) + naiss(=nasc 出生) + ance → 获得新生 → 复兴，新生

例 The significance of *Renaissance* lies in rediscovering the world and the human, and bringing the resurge of politics. 文艺复兴的意义在于重新发现了世界，也重新发现了人，并带来了政治学的复兴。

同 revival(*n.* 苏醒，复兴)；renewal(*n.* 复兴，恢复)

反 collapse(*n.* 倒塌；瓦解)；decline(*n.* 衰败，衰落)

render* [ˈrendə(r)]

vt. 使得，致使；给予，以…回报；提供；呈报，递交；表达；表演；翻译

记 词根记忆：ren(回，向后) + der(给) → 还给 → 以…回报；提供

例 Thousands of people were *rendered* homeless by the terrible earthquake. 可怕的地震过后，成千上万的人们流离失所。

派 rendering(*n.* 表演；翻译)

rendition [renˈdɪʃn]

n. 表演，扮演，演唱；翻译；视觉再现

例 The singer gave a moving *rendition* of Michael Jackson's "You Are Not Alone". 这位歌手深情演绎了迈克尔·杰克逊的《你不孤单》。

renew* [rɪˈnjuː]

v. 重新开始；恢复；更换，更新；续借

记 联想记忆：re(再，又) + new(新的) → 重新开始

例 The swift increase of population *renewed* the demand for building houses quickly and cheaply. 人口的迅速增长再次要求加快房屋的建造速度并降低建筑成本。

renewable [rɪˈnjuːəbl]

a. 可更新的，可再生的，可恢复的；可延长有效期的，可续期的

搭 renewable raw materials 可再生原材料；a renewable lease 可展期的租约

例 Scientists all over the world have made utmost efforts to develop *renewable* energy sources such as wind and tide power. 全世界的科学家都竭尽全力开发风能和潮汐能等可再生能源。

□ removal □ remove □ remuneration □ renaissance □ render □ rendition
□ renew □ renewable

renewal* [rɪˈnjuːəl]	*n.* 更新，恢复；重新开始；重建；复兴；续期；重申 搭 urban renewal 市区改造 例 There is a *renewal* of interest in traditional Chinese medicine therapy. 最近传统的中医疗法重新开始受到关注。// The lease comes up for *renewal* at the end of the month. 本租约到月底需要办理延期。

Tough-minded optimists approach problems with a can-do philosophy and emerge stronger from tragedies.

意志坚强的乐观主义者用“世上无难事”人生观来思考问题，越是遭受悲剧打击，越是表现得坚强。

——古罗马哲学家 西尼加 L. A.

（Lucius Annaeus Seneca, Ancient Roman philosopher）

Word List 38

音频

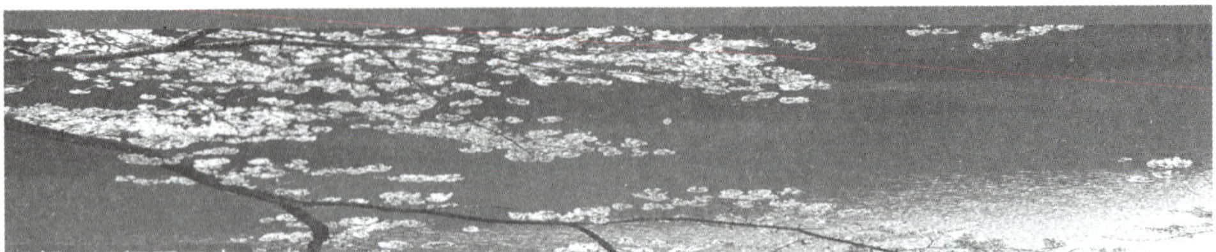

词根、词缀预习表

patr	祖国	repatriate *v.* 归国	**plen**	填满	replenish *vt.* 添加；补充
plic	重叠	replicate *vt.* 复制	**rept**	爬	reptile *n.* 爬行动物
put	想	reputation *n.* 名誉，名声	**quir**	追求	require *vt.* 需要；要求
sembl	一样	resemble *vt.* 像	**sent**	感觉	resent *v.* 愤恨
sist	站	resist *v.* 抵抗	**solv**	解开	resolve *v.* 解决，解答

rent*
[rent]

v. 租借；出租 *n.* 租金

搭 a high/low/fair rent 高的/低的/合理的租金

例 This house *rents* for RMB 5,000 a month. 这房子月租 5000 人民币。

rental
[ˈrentl]

n. 租金额；出租，租赁 *a.* 租用的；出租(业)的

搭 rental agreement 租约；car rental company 汽车租赁公司

例 Having one of these following cases, lessor shall terminate *rental* agreement in advance. 如有下列情形之一，出租人可以提前终止房屋租赁合同。

reorient*
[ˌriːˈɔːrient]

vt. 重新定方位；重新定位；使适应

记 联想记忆：re(重新) + orient(确定方向) → 重新定位

例 Our students are *reoriented* towards social development. 我们的学生要被培养成适应社会发展的类型。

repack
[rɪˈpæk]

vt. 重新包装；重新填塞；再装配；拆修

例 He had to *repack* his case after the customs officers opened it during the security inspection. 在海关人员打开包裹安检后，他必须重新打包他的行李。

派 repackage(*v.* 重新包装；改变…的形象)

repaint*
[rɪˈpeɪnt]

v. 重新油漆，重画

搭 repaint the wall 重新刷墙

例 The first thing people will see when they go in is that the foyer has been *repainted* gold. 人们走进来首先就会看到门廊被重新漆成了金色。

 □ rent □ rental □ reorient □ repack □ repaint

repatriate [ˌriːˈpætrieɪt]

v. 把(某人)遣返回国；归国

记 词根记忆：re(重新) + patr(父亲；祖国) + iate → 重新送回祖国 → 把(某人)遣返回国；归国

例 Some western nations were hit hard by global financial crisis since late 2008, and tried to ***repatriate*** migrant workers to their own countries. 一些西方国家在2008下半年受到全球金融危机的重创，因此想方设法将外籍劳工遣送回国。

repay [riˈpeɪ]

v. 归还(款项)；报答

例 You should ***repay*** principal and interest. 你应该偿还本金和利息。

repel [rɪˈpel]

vt. 击退，驱逐；抵制，拒绝；使反感，使厌恶

记 词根记忆：re(=back 向后) + pel(推) → 向后推 → 击退，驱逐

例 Ants store food, ***repel*** attackers and use chemical signals to contact one another in case of attack. 蚂蚁储存食物，击退进攻者，通过化学信号联系同伴以防御攻击。

派 repellent(*a.* 令人反感的)

同 disgust(*vt.* 使作呕)；repulse(*vt.* 击退，驱逐)

反 attract(*v.* 吸引)；allure(*v.* 吸引，诱惑)

repertoire [ˈrepətwɑː(r)]

n. (剧团等)常备剧目；(剧团、演员等的)全部节目

记 词根记忆：re(一再) + pert(带) + oire → 反复带着的剧目 → (剧团等)常备剧目

例 The Royal Shakespeare Company also have many modern plays in their ***repertoire***. 英国皇家莎士比亚剧团也演很多现代剧。

replace* [rɪˈpleɪs]

vt. 代替；更换；把…放回原处

记 联想记忆：re(重新) + place(位置) → 重新定位 → 代替；更换

例 The new fuel is as inefficient as the one they have ***replaced***. 这种新型燃料和被它们取代的燃料一样效率低下。

派 replacement(*n.* 代替；更换；归还)

replenish [rɪˈplenɪʃ]

vt. 再斟(或装)满；添加，补充

记 词根记忆：re(重新) + plen(填满) + ish → 添加；补充

例 The plunge of oil is crippling the Kremlin's ability to ***replenish*** its gold and foreign-currency reserves, just when it needs them most. 油价下跌正在削弱俄政府补给黄金和外汇储备的能力，而现在正是它最需要这些的时候。

replicate [ˈreplɪkɪt]

vt. 重复，复现或复制；再制造；再生

记 词根记忆：re(一再) + plic(重叠) + ate → 一再重叠 → 复制

例 A new computer virus was reportedly found in the new operating system by ***replicating*** themselves and passing along from user to user. 据报道，在新的操作系统中发现了一种新型电脑病毒，它通过自我复制在电脑用户间传播。

□ repatriate □ repay □ repel □ repertoire □ replace □ replenish
□ replicate

represent* [ˌreprɪˈzent]

vt. 代表；表示；表现

记 联想记忆：re + present(出席) → 代表出席 → 代表

例 The discovery of the reaction principle ***represents*** one of the great milestones in the history of scientific thought. 在科学思想史上，反应原理的发现是一座伟大的丰碑。

representative* [ˌreprɪˈzentətɪv]

n. 代表，代理人 *a.* 典型的，有代表性的

搭 sales representative 销售代表

例 Your examiner is a Student Union ***representative***. 你的主考官是学生会代表。

reproduce* [ˌriːprəˈdjuːs]

v. 繁殖，生育；复制，仿造，翻版；再现，使…在脑海中重现

记 联想记忆：re(一再) + produce(生产) → 不断生产 → 繁殖

例 Photographs, postcards and films enable memories to be endlessly ***reproduced***. 照片、明信片和电影让往事在脑海中不断重现。

派 reproduction(*n.* 复制品；繁殖)

reptile [ˈreptaɪl]

n. 爬行动物，爬虫类；卑鄙的人

记 词根记忆：rept(爬) + ile → 爬行动物

例 There were images of the ancient Mayas gods in the form of feathered serpents, crouching ***reptiles*** and dozens of human figures. 那里满是古代玛雅人的神明的图像：形似长着羽毛的大毒蛇、缩着的爬虫和大量的人形。

派 reptilian(*a.* 爬虫类的；卑鄙的)

reputable [ˈrepjətəbl]

a. 名声好的，高尚的；受尊敬的；值得信赖的

例 I insured my property and my health with a ***reputable*** insurance company. 我在一家著名的保险公司购买了财产及健康保险。

reputation* [ˌrepjuˈteɪʃn]

n. 名誉，名声

记 词根记忆：re(重新) + put(想) + ation(表状态) → 反复想想，名气只是过眼烟云 → 名誉，名声

搭 have a reputation for 因…而闻名；ruin reputation 损害名声；live up to its reputation 与其名气相符

例 The college has already established a national ***reputation*** for its excellence. 该校凭借着自己的卓越表现已经享誉全国。

request* [rɪˈkwest]

n./vt. 要求；请求

记 联想记忆：re(再，又) + quest(寻求) → 请求；要求

例 I'd like to make a ***request*** for leave. 我想请求离开一下。

require* [rɪˈkwaɪə(r)]

vt. 需要；命令；规定，要求

记 词根记忆：re(再，又) + quir(追求) + e → 不断地追求自己需要的 → 需要；要求

例 Every house built nearest to the airport ***requires*** the exterior walls to be double-brick to reduce noise. 所有建造在机场附近的住房都要求采用双层砖的外墙来降低噪音。

□ represent □ representative □ reproduce □ reptile □ reputable □ reputation
□ request □ require

requirement* [rɪˈkwaɪəmənt]

n. 需要，需求，要求；需要的东西；必要条件

记 来自 require(*v.* 需要，要求)

例 The Director of Studies will talk to you about the courses and different *requirements* for each. 教务主管将和你谈论课程问题以及每门课程的不同要求。

requisite [ˈrekwɪzɪt]

a. (情况)需要的；(成功)必要的 *n.* 必需品；要素

记 词根记忆：re(再，又) + quisit(要求) + e → 一再要求 → 需要的，必要的

例 The keyboard is a *requisite* hardware device of a computer, also a dialogue tool between a man and a computer. 键盘是计算机必要的硬件设备，也是人与计算机对话的工具。

requisition* [ˌrekwɪˈzɪʃn]

n./vt. 正式要求；征用

例 For the terrible civil war, there is a *requisition* for lots of guns by the government. 因为可怕的内战，该政府要求征用大量枪支。

rescue* [ˈreskjuː]

n./vt. 营救，救援

搭 rescue sb. from danger 营救某人脱险；rescue work 营救工作

例 Several school children were *rescued* from the burning building. 几名小学生被从燃烧的大楼里成功救出。

resemble [rɪˈzembl]

vt. 与…相似，像

记 词根记忆：re(又) + sembl(一样，相同) + e → 与…相似，像

例 When we tested four totally blind volunteers using the same list, we found that their choices closely *resembled* those made by the sighted subjects. 当使用同样的列单对四位盲人志愿者进行测试时，我们发现他们的选择与视力正常的实验对象的选择极其相似。

resent [rɪˈzent]

v. 愤恨；对…表示愤恨，感到气愤

记 词根记忆：re(再，又) + sent(感觉) → 再一次痛彻心扉的感觉 → 愤恨

例 The elder sisters in the family would *resent* all the attention that the coming baby was getting, especially when it was a little brother. 姐姐会对家庭里的新生儿，尤其是小弟弟，所得到的关注感到愤恨。

reservation* [ˌrezəˈveɪʃn]

n. 保留意见，存疑；预定，预订

记 来自 reserve(*vt.* 保留)

搭 an airline reservation 预订航班；make a reservation 预订；confirm a reservation 确认预订；cancel one's reservation 取消预订

例 I was advised to make a *reservation* in advance for the seats. 别人建议我提前预订座位。

38

reserve* [rɪˈzɜːv]

vt. 预订，预约；保留；储备 *n.* 储备(量)；自然保护区

记 词根记忆：re(再，又) + serv(保持) + e → 预订；保留

例 We *reserved* the room a week ago. 我们一星期前就预订了这个房间。

□ requirement □ requisite □ requisition □ rescue □ resemble □ resent
□ reservation □ reserve

reserved*
[rɪˈzɜːvd]

a. 说话不多的，内向的；有所保留的，预订的

搭 closed reserved 只读不借

例 Ellen was a shy, ***reserved*** girl and she rarely took part in the club activities. 埃伦是一位害羞内向的女孩，她很少参加社团活动。

residence
[ˈrezɪdəns]

n. 住宅，住处；居住

记 来自 resident(*a.* 居住的)

例 Without permission, students may not be allowed to keep motor vehicles at their ***residence*** in this university. 未经校方同意，学生不允许在校内的住宿区停放机动车辆。

resident
[ˈrezɪdənt]

n. 居民，住户 *a.* 常驻的，居住的

例 It's completely free as long as you're a ***resident*** here. 只要你是这里的住户，就可以完全免费(享受这项服务)。

residential
[ˌrezɪˈdenʃl]

a. 居住的，住宅的；寄宿的

搭 residential property 住宅地；residential school 寄宿学校；Asian residential area 亚洲人居住地；residential quarters 住宅小区

例 Smith House is one of the oldest ***residential*** colleges of the university. 史密斯学院是这所大学最古老的寄宿学院之一。

resign
[rɪˈzaɪn]

v. 辞职；辞去；放弃

记 联想记忆：re(回) + sign(签名) → 要回签名 → 辞职；放弃

例 The minister was forced to ***resign*** in 1989. 1989 年，该部长被迫辞职。

resilience
[rɪˈzɪliəns]

n. 弹性，弹力；复原力；适应性；(指人)乐观的性情

记 来自 resilient(*a.* 有弹性的；适应力强的)

例 Scientists can't explain the great ***resilience*** of Japanese pagodas in the earthquake. 科学家无法解释为什么日本宝塔在大地震中有强大的抗震力。

resist*
[rɪˈzɪst]

v. 抵抗；抗(病等)；耐(热等)

记 词根记忆：re(反) + sist(站) → 站在对立面 → 抵抗

例 Bugs and weeds will begin to ***resist*** poisons. 害虫和野草会开始产生抗药性。

resistance
[rɪˈzɪstəns]

n. 反抗，抵制；抵抗力，抵抗性；阻力；电阻

搭 resistance to chemicals 抵制化学药品

例 The defenders put up strong ***resistance*** to the demonstrators. 防卫者采取强硬的措施来阻止示威游行者。

resistant*
[rɪˈzɪstənt]

a. 抵抗的，有抵抗力的

搭 be resistant to 对…有抵抗力；acid resistant 抗酸的

例 A balanced diet helps us create a ***resistant*** body to disease. 均衡的饮食可以帮助我们对疾病产生抗体。

派 quake-resistant (*a.* 抗震的)；wind-resistant (*a.* 挡风的)

□ reserved □ residence □ resident □ residential □ resign □ resilience
□ resist □ resistance □ resistant

resit * [ˌriːˈsɪt]	*v./n.* 重修，补考 搭 resit the exam 参加补考 例 The four students *resat* the final examinations and passed this time. 这四名学生参加了期末考试补考，这次都通过了。
resolve * [rɪˈzɒlv]	*v.* 解决，解答；决定，决意；分解，分析 *n.* 决心，决意 记 词根记忆：re(完全) + solv(解开) + e → 解决，解答 搭 resolve to do sth. 决定做 例 Attempts are continued being made to *resolve* the problem of security in school. 人们不断尝试着解决学校的安全问题。
resort * [rɪˈzɔːt]	*n.* 求助；诉诸；胜地 *vi.* 求助；诉诸 记 联想记忆：报告(report)上级，紧急求助(resort) 例 The east coast *resorts* are only a short twenty-minute drive from here. 从这儿开车去东海岸的旅游胜地只需 20 分钟。
resource * [rɪˈsɔːs; rɪˈzɔːs]	*n.* [*pl.*] 资源，财力；应付办法，谋略；应变之才 记 联想记忆：re(再，又) + source(源泉) → 可再用的源泉 → 资源 搭 human resources 人力资源；productive resources 生产资料；teaching resources 教学资源；resource management 资源管理 例 How developing countries can advance their economies without destroying their natural *resources* is a burning question. 如何既发展经济又不破坏自然资源是发展中国家面临的一个迫在眉睫的问题。
respect * [rɪˈspekt]	*vt.* 尊敬 *n.* 尊敬；方面 记 词根记忆：re(一再) + spect(看) → 一再注视，以示尊敬 → 尊敬 例 I *respect* you for your honesty. 因为你为人诚实，所以我尊敬你。// We have the greatest *respect* for our teacher. 我们非常尊敬我们的老师。// It is said that the price will rise in *respect* of gas and water costs. 据说煤气费和水费要涨价。 派 respectable(*a.* 值得尊敬的)
respond * [rɪˈspɒnd]	*vi.* 回答，答复；响应；作出反应 搭 respond to 回答；对…作出反应；响应；respond by doing sth. 做…进行回应 例 Companies should *respond* to this kind of situation in an honest and open way. 公司应该采取诚实和公开的方式来应对这类情况。
respondent * [rɪˈspɒndənt]	*n.* 回答者，响应者；调查对象；被告 例 Our *respondents* are both men and women, but the women were just slightly in the majority. 我们的调查对象包括男性和女性，但女性在数量上略占上风。
response * [rɪˈspɒns]	*n.* 回答，答复；反应，响应 记 词根记忆：re(再，又) + spons(允诺，约定) + e → 回答；反应 搭 response for... 对…负责，是造成…的原因；in response to 答复，响应；适应 例 The news provoked an angry *response*. 这条消息引起了人们的愤怒。 派 responsive(*a.* 反应积极的)

38

□ resit □ resolve □ resort □ resource □ respect □ respond
□ respondent □ response

responsibility* [rɪˌspɒnsəˈbɪləti]

n. 责任，责任心；职责，任务

记 来自 responsible(*a.* 有责任感的；可靠的)

搭 perform one's responsibilities 履行或行使职责；assume the responsibility 承担责任

例 The company needs a sales manager with ***responsibility*** for North American market. 该公司需要一位负责北美市场的销售经理。

responsible* [rɪˈspɒnsəbl]

a. 有责任感的；可靠的

记 词根记忆：re（再，又）+ spons（承诺，约定）+ ible(能…的) → 能一再遵守承诺、约定的 → 有责任感的

搭 be responsible for 承担…的责任，有责任…

例 Smoking, as it is believed, is ***responsible*** for 30 percent of all deaths from cancer. 在因癌症导致的死亡中，有30%被认为是由吸烟引起的。

restore [rɪˈstɔː(r)]

vt. 恢复，使复位；修复，整修，重建；归还，交还

记 联想记忆：灾后重建(restore)，包括商店(store)

例 The government has been trying to ***restore*** public confidence in its management of the economy since the breakout of economic crisis. 自经济危机爆发以来，该政府就一直试图重建公众对其掌控经济能力的信心。

派 restoration(*n.* 恢复；修复)

restrain [rɪˈstreɪn]

vt. 阻止；抑制

记 词根记忆：re(回) + strain(拉紧) → 阻止；抑制

例 The doctors ***restrained*** the patient from hurting himself. 医生制止了病人的自残行为。

派 restraint(*n.* 抑制；约束措施)

restrict* [rɪˈstrɪkt]

vt. 限制，约束

记 联想记忆：re + strict(严格的) → 对人非常严格 → 限制，约束

例 A student loan is not ***restricted*** to those who receive a maintenance grant in this school. 在这所学校，学生贷款并不限于那些领生活补助金的学生。

restriction* [rɪˈstrɪkʃn]

n. 限制，约束

搭 speed restriction 速度限制；impose restriction on sth. 对…进行限制

例 There's an open ticket which doesn't have any ***restrictions*** on time. 有一种不定期客票，对时间没有任何限制。

resume [rɪˈzjuːm]

v. (中断后)重新开始，继续恢复

记 词根记忆：re(又，再) + sum(拿，取) + e → 重新拿起 → 重新开始

例 He ***resumed*** his reading after a nap. 小睡了一会儿后，他继续阅读。

retail* [ˈriːteɪl]

n. 零售 *v.* 零售，以…价格销售

记 词根记忆：re + tail(切割) → 切割成小块卖 → 零售

搭 retail price 零售价；retail trade 零售业；a retail shop 零售店

例 What sorts of shop do you like best, the department store or the small ***retails***? 你最喜欢哪种商店，百货商场还是小零售店？

□ responsibility □ responsible □ restore □ restrain □ restrict □ restriction
□ resume □ retail

retailer* [ˈriːteɪlə(r)]

n. 零售商人；复述者，传播者

例 Many *retailers* are facing their slowest business period during the financial crisis. 在金融危机中，许多零售商正处在最低迷时期。

retailing [ˈriːteɪlɪŋ]

n. 零售业

例 With the developing and popularizing of *retailing*, brand has changed into a symbol of products reputation for these manufacturers. 随着零售业的发展和普及，品牌变成制造商产品声誉的象征。

retain* [rɪˈteɪn]

vt. 保留；保持

记 词根记忆：re(再，又) + tain(拿住) → 一再拿住 → 保留；保持

例 The young lady *retained* her tennis title for the third year. 那个年轻女孩第三年仍保住了网球冠军的头衔。

retaliate [rɪˈtælieɪt]

vi. 报复，反击；复仇

搭 retaliate against his persecutor 报复迫害者；retaliate against an attack 对攻击展开报复

例 Since 911, American government has promised to take tough measures to *retaliate* against the terrorists. 自从 911 以来，美国政府承诺采取严厉的措施来反击恐怖分子。

retire* [rɪˈtaɪə(r)]

v. 退休；引退，退隐，撤退

记 联想记忆：re(再，又) + tire(劳累) → 不再劳累 → 退休

例 In this hospital, children under 16 don't need to pay, and the same thing goes for people who have *retired*. 在这家医院，16 岁以下的儿童免费就诊，退休人员也可享受同等待遇。

retrenchment [rɪˈtrentʃmənt]

n. 节省；削减

记 联想记忆：retrench(紧缩，节省) + ment → 节省；削减

例 Macro-control and *retrenchment* curbed sizable speculation venture capital in real estate, leading to the reduction of housing market demand. 宏观调控和费用削减，抑制了大量房地产风险投资，致使住房市场需求有所减少。

reunion* [riːˈjuːniən]

n. 重聚，团聚；(久别后的)聚会，联谊活动

记 联想记忆：re(再，又) + union(联合，结合) → 重聚，团聚

搭 annual reunion 年度聚会；family reunion 家庭聚会

例 All the members of the club gathered to have a *reunion* dinner last weekend. 上周末，这个俱乐部的所有成员进行了一次聚餐。

38

reunite* [ˌriːjuːˈnaɪt]

v. (使)结合；(使)重聚

例 The lost child was *reunited* with his parents in the police station. 那个走失的孩子和他的父母在警察局重聚。

reveal* [rɪˈviːl]

vt. 揭露；泄露；展现

记 联想记忆：re(相反) + veal(看作 veil，面纱) → 揭开面纱 → 揭露；展现

搭 reveal secret 泄露秘密

例 The Human Genome Project will *reveal* a new human anatomy—the complete genetic blueprint for a human being. 人类基因工程将开启人类解剖学的新篇章——描绘完整的人类基因蓝图。

□ retailer □ retailing □ retain □ retaliate □ retire □ retrenchment
□ reunion □ reunite □ reveal

revegetate
[riːˈvedʒəteɪt]

v. 再生长，再植

例 To *revegetate* is to replant and rebuild the soil of disturbed land. 再植是指重新种植、复原被破坏的土壤。

revelation
[ˌrevəˈleɪʃn]

n. 被揭示的真相，(惊人的)新发现；揭示，显示；泄露

记 联想记忆：revel(=reveal 揭露) + ation → 揭示，显示

例 The *revelation* of the commercial secrets would bring legal punishment to this multinational enterprise. 泄露商业机密将使这家跨国公司受到法律制裁。

同 disclosure(*n.* 揭发；败露)；exposure(*n.* 暴露；曝光)

反 concealment(*n.* 隐藏)

revenue*
[ˈrevənjuː]

n. (尤指大宗的)收入；税收

记 词根记忆：re(回) + ven(来) + ue → 回来的东西 → 收入

搭 anticipated revenue 预期收入；financial revenue 财政收入；tax revenue 税收

例 A new strategy for pricing known as "*revenue* management" is now being used by many large companies. 现在许多大公司都采用一项名为"收入管理"的新定价策略。

reverse*
[rɪˈvɜːs]

n. 相反，颠倒；背面，后面 *a.* 相反的；倒转的，颠倒的 *v.* 颠倒，(使)倒退

记 词根记忆：re(反) + vers(转动) + e → 反转 → 颠倒

搭 in reverse 顺序相反，反向；in reverse order 以颠倒的次序

例 Small rooms aren't quite cheap in *reverse*. 小房间反而不是很便宜。

派 reversal(*n.* 颠倒，倒转)；reversible(*a.* 可反转的，可逆的)

同 revoke(*vt.* 撤销，撤回)；invert(*vt.* 使颠倒；使转化)；converse(*n.* 相反的事物 *a.* 相反的，颠倒的)

review*
[rɪˈvjuː]

vt. 回顾；复习；评论 *n.* 回顾；评论

记 联想记忆：re(重新，再) + view(看) → 回顾；复习

例 Before going to bed, please *review* the day's classes. 睡觉前，请复习一下白天的课程内容。

派 reviewer(*n.* 评论家)

revise*
[rɪˈvaɪz]

v. 修订；复习

记 词根记忆：re(一再) + vis(看) + e → 反复看 → 修订；复习

例 Teaching methodology should be constantly *revised* to keep the pace with the time. 教师应该不断调整教学方法以跟上时代发展的步伐。

revival
[rɪˈvaɪvl]

n. (健康、力量或知觉的)恢复，复原；苏醒，复活；复兴；重新使用；重新流行

记 词根记忆：re(又) + viv(生命，生活) + al → 生命重现 → 复活；复兴

例 A written form is essential for this, so the mere possibility of *revival* has led many speakers of endangered languages to develop systems of writing where none existed before. 书写形式对这(语言的复兴)非常重要，这一线复兴的希望促使一些濒临灭绝的语言的使用者都开始开发之前没有的书写体系。

□ revegetate □ revelation □ revenue □ reverse □ review □ revise
□ revival

revive [rɪˈvaɪv]

v. (使)苏醒，复活；重新使用

记 词根记忆：re(重新) + viv(生命；生活) + e → 重新生活 → 复活；重新使用

例 In recent years, the government has encouraged folk artists to ***revive*** traditional skills by funding them. 近年来，政府已通过资金援助鼓励民间艺人复兴传统工艺。

同 restore(*vt.* 恢复；使复职)；revitalize(*vt.* 使恢复生机)

反 languish(*vi.* 憔悴，枯萎；变得衰弱)

revolution* [ˌrevəˈluːʃn]

n. 革命；巨变，大变革

记 词根记忆：re + volu(滚，卷) + tion → 不断向前席卷而来的 → 革命

例 Acid rain in fact started around the time of the industrial ***revolution*** of the 19th century. 酸雨实际上是在 19 世纪工业革命时期开始出现的。

派 revolutionary(*a.* 革命的；巨变的)

revolve [rɪˈvɒlv]

v. (使)旋转

记 词根记忆：re(再) + volv(卷，转) + e → 不断滚动 → (使)旋转

搭 revolve about/round 围绕…旋转

例 Fifteen satellites all ***revolve*** about the planet's equator. 15 颗卫星都绕着这颗行星的赤道旋转。

reward [rɪˈwɔːd]

n. 奖赏；报酬 *vt.* 酬谢；奖励

记 联想记忆：re + ward(看作 word，话语) → 领导再次发话，要给予他奖赏 → 奖赏

例 Those employees who never take sick leave think that they should be ***rewarded***. 那些从来不请病假的员工认为他们应该因此得到奖励。

派 rewarding(*a.* 值得做的，有益的；报酬高的)

ridiculous [rɪˈdɪkjələs]

a. 荒谬的；可笑的

记 词根记忆：rid(笑) + icul + ous(形容词后缀) → 可笑的

例 The fat old man looked ***ridiculous*** in his tight pink trousers. 那个胖老头穿着粉色的紧身裤，显得滑稽可笑。

rig [rɪg]

vt. 操纵，垄断 *n.* 船桅(或船帆等)的装置；成套器械

记 联想记忆：挖(dig)个洞把器械(rig)藏起来

例 The defeated candidate claimed that the election was ***rigged***. 落选的候选者称选举被人操纵了。

38

Word List 39

音频

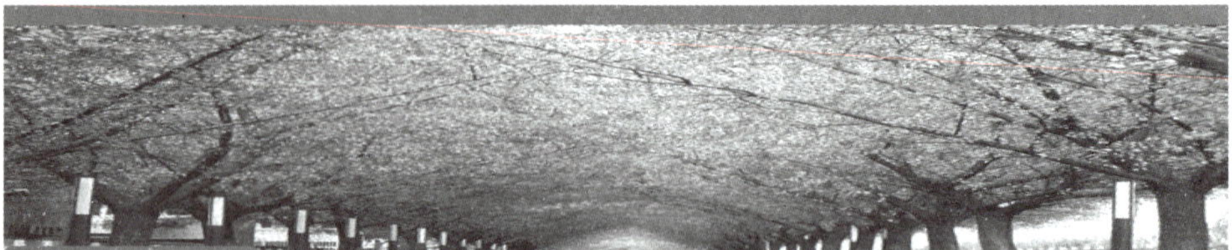

词根、词缀预习表

rig	直的	righteous *a.* 正直的	**rot**	旋转	rotate *v.*（使）旋转
rud	天然的	rude *a.* 粗糙的	**rur**	乡村	rural *a.* 乡村的
sacr	神圣的	sacrifice *n.* 牺牲	**sal**	盐	saline *a.* 含盐的
san	健康	sanitation *n.* 卫生	**sat**	充足	saturate *vt.* 使饱和
scen	设置	scenery *n.* 舞台布景	**sect**	切割	section *n.* 部分；部门

righteous [ˈraɪtʃəs]

a. 正义的，正直的；公正的；正当的

记 词根记忆：rig（直的；正确的）+ hte + ous（形容词后缀）→ 正直的；公正的

例 No matter how good and *righteous* one thinks his action is, he shouldn't break the law. 不管一个人认为他的行为多么友善多么正义，他都不应该犯法。

rigid [ˈrɪdʒɪd]

a. 严格的，死板的；刚硬的，僵硬的

例 Although glass is comparatively *rigid*, the atoms are arranged in a random disordered fashion. 虽然玻璃相对较硬，但是其分子结构排序杂乱无章。

rigorous [ˈrɪɡərəs]

a. 严密的；严格的，严厉的；严酷的

记 联想记忆：rig（看作 rog，要求）+ orous → 不断要求 → 严格的

例 Once you have arrived at your hypothesis, you then proceed through a strictly logical and *rigorous* process. 一旦你提出了假设，你就可以进行一个逻辑性极强的严密的求证过程。

派 rigorously（*ad.* 严格地；严密地）

同 meticulous（*a.* 谨小慎微的）；rigid（*a.* 严格的）

反 careless（*a.* 粗心的，疏忽的）

rim [rɪm]

n.（圆形物体的）边，缘

记 联想记忆：打靶（aim）不能打边（rim）

例 The pattern around the *rim* of the plate was very beautiful. 那个盘子边缘的图案非常漂亮。

ripe [raɪp]

a.（水果或庄稼）成熟的；时机成熟的

记 联想记忆：稻熟（ripe）米（rice）香

例 When one banana is *ripe*, it will give off a gas which then helps all the others to ripen. 当一根香蕉成熟了，它便会释放出一种气体催熟其他香蕉。

派 ripen（*v.* 使成熟；成熟）

ritual [ˈrɪtʃuəl]

n. 典礼，(宗教等的)仪式；例行公事，老规矩 *a.* 作为仪式一部分的，仪式的；例行的

记 联想记忆：rit(e)(典礼，仪式) + ual → 典礼，仪式

例 It is interesting to observe, for instance, some decline in the emphasis given to marriage ***rituals***. 我们发现很有意思的情况，例如，人们对结婚典礼的热衷程度在减弱。

同 ceremony(*n.* 仪式，典礼)；formality(*n.* 礼节；仪式)

rival [ˈraɪvl]

n. 竞争者，竞争对手；可与匹敌的人(或物) *a.* 竞争的，对抗的 *vt.* 与…竞争；与…匹敌，比得上；竞争，对抗

记 联想记忆：对手(rival)隔河(river)相望，分外眼红

搭 have no rivals 没有竞争对手，独领风骚

例 The *rival* team lost by 12 points in the first round. 第一轮比赛中，对手队以 12 分之差败北。

roam* [rəʊm]

v. 随便走，漫游；徜徉；漫谈某事 *n.* 漫步；徘徊

记 联想记忆：晚饭后，他在院子的狭小空间(room)里漫步(roam)

搭 roam over/around/about 闲逛，徘徊

例 If we go back ten thousand years ago we would find that there were lions ***roaming*** vast sections of the globe. 如果我们回到一万年前，就会发现地球上的大部分地方都有狮子出没。

roast [rəʊst]

a. 烤过的 *n.* 烤肉 *v.* 烤，炙

记 联想记忆：在海岸(coast)边烤(roast)肉

例 *Roast* dinner sounds ordinary but it is really tasty. 烧烤大餐听起来很普通，但味道的确很好。

robotic* [rəʊˈbɒtɪk]

a. 机器人的；像机器人的，呆板而机械的

例 Thanks to all of you for coming along today to hear about how the *robotic* float project is helping with ocean research. 感谢大家今天来听关于机器人浮筒工程是如何促进海洋研究的讲座。

robust [rəʊˈbʌst]

a. 健壮的，强壮的；坚定的

robust

记 "乐百氏"矿泉水用的就是 robust 这个单词

例 Some of the misconceptions are erroneous, more ***robust*** but also accessible to modification. 一些错误的想法是不正确的，尽管它可能会更加顽固但是仍然可以进行修改。

派 robustness(*n.* 健壮)；robustly(*ad.* 有活力地；强健地)

同 sturdy(*a.* 强健的)；healthy(*a.* 健壮的，健康的)

反 delicate(*a.* 脆弱的)

roll film

胶卷

例 At the end of 1889 Eastman launched a new *roll film* on a celluloid base. 1889 年底，伊斯门在赛璐珞胶片的基础上研制了一种新型胶卷。

39

□ ritual □ rival □ roam □ roast □ robotic □ robust
□ roll film

roller
[ˈrəʊlə(r)]

n. 滚筒；滚轴

记 来自 roll(*v.* 滚动)

例 The huge *roller* can press melted metal into thin sheet which is the raw material of knife. 大型滚筒可以将熔化的金属压成薄片，作为刀具的原材料。

romance
[rəʊˈmæns]

n. 恋爱；浪漫爱情；爱情小说，传奇故事

记 发音记忆："罗曼史"→ 浪漫爱情 → 恋爱；浪漫爱情

例 That was nothing but a spicy Hollywood *romance*. 那简直就是一部粗俗的好莱坞浪漫故事片。

rot
[rɒt]

n. 腐烂 *v.* (使)腐烂

例 Root *rot* is a serious problem in such a situation. 在这种情况下根部腐烂是一个很严重的问题。

rotate
[rəʊˈteɪt]

v. (使)旋转，转动；轮流，轮换

记 词根记忆：rot(旋转) + ate(使…) → (使)旋转，转动

例 European peasants in the ancient time would insert a wooden drill into a round hole in a stone and *rotate* it briskly to make fire. 古时，欧洲的农民将木钻插入石头的圆孔中，通过快速旋转木钻来取火。

route*
[ruːt;raʊt]

n. 路线；路程

搭 cycling route 骑自行车游览路线；shipping route 海运航线；air route 空运航线

例 This map will show the *route* across the mountains. 这张地图上有穿越群山的路线。

routine*
[ruːˈtiːn]

n. 例行公事；惯例 *a.* 例行的；常规的

例 Physical fitness instructors prepare *routines* of exercises to suit the individual client's age and level of fitness. 健身教练根据每位顾客的年龄及健康状况为他们量身打造锻炼计划。

rude
[ruːd]

a. 粗鲁的；粗糙的

记 词根记忆：rud(天然的) + e → 粗鲁的；粗糙的

例 Across the room stand three *rude* and high-backed chairs. 房间的那头放着三把做工粗糙的高背椅。

rudimentary
[ˌruːdɪˈmentri]

a. 基本的，初步的；未充分发展的，发育不成熟的；退化的

记 词根记忆：rud(天然的；粗鲁的) + iment + ary(形容词后缀) → 天然的状态 → 初步的；未充分发展的

例 New staffs were given only *rudimentary* training at the beginning of their work. 新员工在工作之初只接受了最基本的训练。

rumour
[ˈruːmə(r)]

n. 谣传，谣言

记 发音记忆："辱骂"→ 谣言往往比辱骂更伤人 → 谣言

搭 start/spread a rumour 制造/散布谣言

例 The *rumour* soon gained currency. 谣言很快流传开了。

□ roller □ romance □ rot □ rotate □ route □ routine
□ rude □ rudimentary □ rumour

rural*
[ˈrʊərəl]
a. 农村的，乡村的
记 词根记忆：rur(乡村) + al→ 农村的，乡村的
搭 rural areas 农村地区
例 Technological advance will bring about the decline of ***rural*** industries and an increase in urban populations at the same time. 科技进步将会导致农村产业的衰退，同时会带来城市人口的增长。

ruthless
[ˈruːθləs]
a. 无情的，冷酷的，残忍的
记 联想记忆：ruth(怜悯) + less(无) → 没有怜悯的 → 无情的，冷酷的，残忍的
例 Most of the surveyed citizens argued that the government had shown a ***ruthless*** disregard for their basic human rights. 大部分接受调查的公民争论道，政府残忍地无视他们的基本人权。
派 ruthlessly(*ad.* 残忍地)
同 cruel(*a.* 残酷的)

sack*
[sæk]
n. 麻袋，粗布袋；解雇；劫掠 *vt.* 解雇；劫掠
记 联想记忆：因为缺少(lack)竞争力，公司解雇(sack)员工
搭 get the sack 被解雇，被开除；give sb. the sack 开除 / 解雇某人
例 The corn was stored in large ***sacks*** in the barn. 谷物用大麻袋装着储存在粮仓里面。

sacrifice
[ˈsækrɪfaɪs]
n. 牺牲，牺牲品；献祭，供奉；祭品，供物 *v.* 牺牲，献祭
记 词根记忆：sacr(神圣的) + i + fic(做) + e → 为了神圣的事情而去做 → 牺牲，献祭
搭 make the final sacrifice 牺牲生命
例 Linda's parents made ***sacrifices*** so that she could have a good education abroad. 为了让琳达能在国外接受良好的教育，琳达的父母作出了牺牲。
派 sacrificial(*a.* 供奉的，献祭的，牺牲品的)

saline
[ˈseɪlaɪn]
a. 含盐的，咸的 *n.*【医】盐水
记 词根记忆：sal(盐) + ine → 含盐的，咸的
搭 saline solution 盐溶液
例 In medicine, ***saline*** is mainly used to kill bacteria. It is also widely used in cell biology experiments. 在医学中，盐水主要用于杀菌，还广泛应用于细胞生物学实验。

39

salinity*
[səˈlɪnəti]
n. 盐分，盐度
例 As the float rises to the surface it collects all sorts of data, most importantly variations in ***salinity***. 当浮筒上升到表面，就会收集各种数据，最重要的是盐度的变化。

□ rural □ ruthless □ sack □ sacrifice □ saline □ salinity

sample*

['sɑːmpl]

n. 样品，样本 *vt.* 从…抽样，采样；品尝

记 联想记忆：简单的(simple)的样品(sample)

搭 blood sample 血液样本；size of sample 样本的大小

例 The World Health Organization predicts that all of the ***samples*** of twenty megacities would have more than eighteen million inhabitants in the year 2020. 世界卫生组织预计，到 2020 年，全部 20 个抽样大城市的人口都将超过 1800 万。

sanction

['sæŋkʃn]

v. 批准，认可 *n.* 批准，认可；约束因素，约束力；[常 *pl.*] 国际制裁

记 词根记忆：sanct(神圣的) + ion → 神圣之物，原指教会的法令，引申为“批准，赞许” → 批准，认可

例 The economic ***sanctions*** have long been imposed on the nation due to refusing to sign multilateral agreement. 由于拒绝签署多边协议，长久以来，这个国家一直遭受着经济制裁。

派 sanctionist(*n.* 制裁国)

sanctuary*

['sæŋktʃuəri]

n. 圣堂，圣殿，圣坛；圣地；庇护所，避难所；禁猎区，动物保护区

sanctuary

记 词根记忆：sanct(神圣) + u + ary(表场所、地方，名词后缀) → 圣堂；避难所(圣堂经常成为避难所，因此有避难所之意)

搭 bird sanctuary 鸟类保护区；wildlife sanctuary 野生动植物保护区；seek sanctuary 寻找避难所

例 Despite living in a ***sanctuary***, which makes them safe from hunters, the animals still face a number of problems that threaten their survival. 尽管生活在保护区，得以远离猎人，这些动物仍然面临很多威胁它们生存的问题。

sanitary*

['sænətri]

a. 清洁的；保健的，卫生的 *n.* (有卫生设备的)公共厕所

记 词根记忆：san(健康) + it + ary → 健康的 → 清洁的；保健的

搭 sanitary facilities 卫生设施；sanitary conditions 卫生条件

例 People living in the district suffered from appalling ***sanitary*** conditions. 住在这一区域的人们卫生条件差得出奇。

sanitation

[ˌsæniˈteiʃn]

n. (公共)卫生，卫生设施

记 词根记忆：san(健康) + it + ation → 要想健康，得讲卫生 → 卫生

例 Production enterprises of aquatic products without ***sanitation*** registration are forbidden to produce, process or store any exit aquatic products. 未获得卫生注册登记的水产品生产企业禁止生产、加工或储存任何出境水产品。

saturate

['sætʃəreit]

vt. 使湿透，浸透；使充满，使饱和

记 词根记忆：sat(充足) + ur + ate(使…) → 使充足 → 使饱和

搭 saturate with 以…使饱和

例 Since some Asian countries' investment markets have now been ***saturated***, western countries are looking for a bigger market. 由于一些亚洲国家投资市场现在已经饱和，西方国家正在寻求一个更大的市场。

同 drench(*vt.* 使湿透，使浸透)；soak(*v.* 浸透，湿透)

sausage [ˈsɒsɪdʒ]

n. 香肠

例 These beetles make *sausage*-shaped brood chambers along the tunnels. 这些甲虫顺着地道建造香肠形状的育卵室。

savour [ˈseɪvə(r)]

vt. 品尝，品味；欣赏；体会，体味 *n.* 味道，风味；情趣，吸引力

记 词根记忆：sav(=sap 品尝) + our → 品尝，品味；味道，风味

例 Every day, people should afford a short moment to *savour* the gain and loss of the whole day before going to bed. 每天，人们都应该在睡觉前抽出片刻来品味一天的得与失。

scale [skeɪl]

n. 规模，大小；[*pl.*] 天平，磅秤；刻度，标度；(鱼等的)鳞；(音乐)音阶；等级，级别；比例(尺) *vt.* 攀登，爬越

搭 on a large scale 大规模地；in scale 成比例，相称；out of scale 不成比例，不相称；scale sth. down 缩小，减少

例 In a recent research, the tropical forest has been depicted as ecologically unfit for large-*scale* human occupation. 最近的一项调查显示，从生态学角度来看，人们认为热带森林不适合大规模人群居住。

scamper [ˈskæmpə(r)]

vi. 奔跑，快跑

scamper

记 联想记忆：s(音似：嘶) + camper(露营者) → 露营者嘶喊着快跑 → 快跑

例 I shouted for help and the dog *scampered* off. 我大声喊救命，狗便跑开了。

scan* [skæn]

v. 扫描；浏览 *n.* 扫描

记 发音记忆："四看" → 眼睛像扫描仪一样四处看 → 扫描；浏览

例 Customers at some Japanese banks will have to present their faces for *scanning* before they can enter the building. 在日本，某些银行需要客户经过面部扫描才可以进入。

派 scanner(*n.* 扫描仪)

scandal* [ˈskændl]

n. 丑事，丑闻；恶意诽谤；流言飞语；反感，愤慨

记 联想记忆：scan(扫描) + dal → 扫描时事，揭露丑闻 → 丑事，丑闻

搭 financial scandal 财政丑闻

例 The *scandal* destroyed the government's image completely. 这件丑闻完全毁了政府的形象。

派 scandalize [*vt.* 使(某人)愤慨或震惊]；scandalous(*a.* 出丑的，可耻的；诽谤的)

scarce [skeəs]

a. 缺乏的，不足的；稀少的，罕见的

记 联想记忆：scar(伤疤) + ce → 有伤疤 → 美中不足 → 不足的

搭 scarce metals 稀有金属

例 Many natural materials are becoming *scarce*. 许多天然原料濒临枯竭。

scare [skeə(r)]

n. 惊恐，恐慌 *v.* 吓，使害怕；受惊吓，感到害怕

例 The decoy camera can be fixed to the wall to *scare* off burglars. 可以在墙上安装假摄像头来吓走盗贼。

□ sausage □ savour □ scale □ scamper □ scan □ scandal
□ scarce □ scare

scatter
[ˈskætə(r)]

v. (使人或动物)散开，驱散；撒；撒播

記 联想记忆：s + cat(猫) + ter → 老鼠一见到猫就四处逃散 → 散开

搭 scatter... over... 把…撒在…；scatter strength 分散精力

例 The farmer ***scattered*** the seeds on the field. 农民在地里播种。

scenery*
[ˈsiːnəri]

n. 舞台布景；风景，景色

記 词根记忆：scen(设置) + ery(表场所，名词后缀) → 设置景色的场所 → 舞台布景；景色

搭 natural scenery 自然风景；magnificent scenery 壮丽的风景；impressive scenery 令人难忘的风景

例 The ***scenery*** is as beautiful as a painting. 这里风景美丽如画。

scent
[sent]

n. 香味；气味 *vt.* 嗅到；察觉

記 联想记忆：开放的花朵送出(sent)沁人心脾的香气(scent)

例 Doctors mix light, sounds, breezes and ***scents*** to stimulate the patients. 医生同时采用光、声音、微风和香味来刺激病人。

sceptical*
[ˈskeptɪkl]

a. 怀疑的，猜疑的

例 People become less ***sceptical*** and more optimistic when the weather is sunny. 人们在晴朗的日子里会变得少猜忌并且更乐观。

schedule*
[ˈʃedjuːəl]

vt. 安排；列入，收进(清单等) *n.* 时刻表；清单

記 发音记忆："筛斗" → 古代拿筛漏计时 → 时刻表

搭 ahead of schedule 提前；a train/flight schedule 火车/航班时刻表；on schedule 按约定时间，按时，准时；behind schedule 落后于计划进度，晚于规定时间，晚点；be scheduled for 定在某时(进行)

例 The lectures are ***scheduled*** for Tuesday and Thursday. 讲座安排在星期二和星期四。

scheme
[skiːm]

n. 计划，方案；体系，体制；阴谋 *v.* 计划，策划；密谋

記 联想记忆：根据图解(schema)来计划(scheme)行程

例 The government has been funding a loans ***scheme*** for students in higher education since September 1990. 自 1990 年 9 月起，政府就开始为大学生贷款计划提供资金。

scholar*
[ˈskɒlə(r)]

n. 学者；奖学金获得者

記 联想记忆：schol(看作 school，学校) + ar(表人) → 学者

例 The database is collected not merely for ***scholars***, but for people involved in a whole range of educational and artistic purposes. 收集这些数据库不仅仅是为了给学者提供资料，也为所有从事教育和艺术工作的人们提供资料。

scholarship*
[ˈskɒləʃɪp]

n. 奖学金；学问，学识

例 Susan won a ***scholarship*** to study at Harvard. 苏珊获得了在哈佛大学学习的奖学金。

□ scatter □ scenery □ scent □ sceptical □ schedule □ scheme
□ scholar □ scholarship

scope* [skəʊp]

n. 眼界，见识；(活动、影响等的)范围；(发挥能力等的)余地，机会

记 联想记忆：s + cope(对付，处理) → 人处理的事情多了，眼界自然就会开阔 → 眼界

例 The *scope* of the environmental problem facing the world's cities is immense. 世界上的许多城市面临着大范围的环境问题。

scorching [ˈskɔːtʃɪŋ]

a. 酷热的；激烈的

记 联想记忆：scorch(烧焦) + ing → 能烧焦的 → 酷热的

例 The *scorching* summer left people enervated and listless. 炎热的夏天让人虚弱无力，情绪低落。

score* [skɔː(r)]

v. 得分，记分；给(试卷等)打分，给…评分；刻痕于，画线于；获胜，成功

n. 得分，分数；乐谱；抓痕，划痕；二十

记 联想记忆：分，分(score)，考试的核心(core)

搭 a low score 低分

例 The composition was *scored* with corrections in red ink. 这篇作文用红笔批改过。

scour [ˈskaʊə(r)]

vt. 四处搜寻，细查；擦洗，擦亮；冲刷出，冲刷成

记 发音记忆："四 call" → 一连四个电话(call) → 四处搜寻

例 The rainstorm raced down the slope and *scoured* out the bed of a stream. 暴雨顺着斜坡倾泻而下，冲刷着河床。

派 scourer(*n.* 刷锅等用的尼龙丝或金属丝；去污粉)

scout [skaʊt]

n. 侦察员(或机、舰)；童子军 *v.* 侦察；寻找；搜索

记 联想记忆：sc + out(外面) → 在外面巡逻的人 → 侦察员

例 Both my brothers were *scouts* and I really want to join the *scout* troop. 我的两个哥哥都曾是童子军成员，我也很想加入童子军。

scrap* [skræp]

n. 碎屑 *vt.* 废弃；抛弃

记 联想记忆：刮(scrape)下许多碎屑(scrap)

例 *Scrapping* farm-price support and protection for coal-mining offers a two-fold bonus: a cleaner environment and a more efficient economy. 废除农产品价格补贴和对采煤业的保护有双重好处，可以获得更清洁的环境和更高效的经济。

同 debris(*n.* 碎片，残骸)；abandon(*vt.* 放弃，遗弃)

scrape [skreɪp]

v./n. 刮，擦

记 联想记忆：scrap(碎屑) + e → 碎屑是被刮下来的 → 刮

例 He *scraped* the mud off his shoes with the knife. 他用小刀刮去鞋上的泥土。

scratch* [skrætʃ]

n. 划伤，抓痕 *v.* 抓，搔；划破，划损

搭 from scratch 从头做起，从零开始；up to scratch 达到应有的水平

例 There is a small *scratch* on my bag. 我的包上有一道不长的划痕。

□ scope □ scorching □ score □ scour □ scout □ scrap
□ scrape □ scratch

scream* [skriːm]

v. 尖叫 *n.* 尖叫声

记 联想记忆：孩子们见到冰淇淋(ice-cream)，立刻尖叫(scream)起来

例 The students *scream* in excitement. 学生们激动得尖叫起来。

screen* [skriːn]

n. 屏幕，银幕；遮蔽；屏风，帘；筛子

vt. 掩蔽，遮蔽；包庇；筛选；放映（电影），播放(电视节目)

例 Everything on the *screen* interests those children. 那些孩子觉得屏幕上的一切都很有趣。

screw [skruː]

v. 用螺钉固定 *n.* 螺丝(钉)

记 联想记忆：s + crew(一群人) → 一群工人在流水线上生产螺丝钉 → 螺丝(钉)

例 He *screwed* the painting onto the wall. 他用螺丝钉把画固定在墙上。

scrub [skrʌb]

v. 用力擦洗，把…擦净；取消(计划等) *n.* 矮树丛，灌木丛

记 联想记忆：sc + rub(摩擦) → 用力擦洗

例 When the cleaner *scrubbed* the building interior, it has a brand-new look. 当清洁工把建筑内部擦洗干净后，整个建筑焕然一新。

同 scour(*v.* 冲洗，擦亮)；thicket(*n.* 灌木丛)

scrupulous [ˈskruːpjələs]

a. 多顾虑的，谨慎的(尤指道德方面)；一丝不苟的，严谨的

记 来自 scruple(*n./vi.* 顾忌，顾虑)

搭 be scrupulous in (doing) sth. 小心谨慎对待(做)某事

例 For larger studies, *scrupulous* attention has been paid to the sampling theory employed, and in all cases, decisions have to be made about the best investigative techniques to use. 对于更大的课题研究，就需要特别注意抽样理论的应用，在所有情况下，要注意选择使用最佳的调查方法。

scrutiny [ˈskruːtəni]

n. 详细检查，细看；监视

记 联想记忆：scru(音似：四顾) + tiny(微小的) → 连微小的都要顾到 → 详细检查，细看

例 The world of the ant has come in for considerable *scrutiny* lately, and the idea that ants demonstrate sparks of cognition has not been rejected by those involved in these investigations. 近期有大量针对蚂蚁王国的研究，参与研究的人员并未否定那种认为蚂蚁能表现出认知迹象的想法。

同 inquiry(*n.* 调查，审查)；inspection(*n.* 检查，审查)

反 neglect(*n.* 疏忽，忽视)

scuffle [ˈskʌfl]

n./vi. 扭打，混战

例 After a *scuffle* in the stands, the security guards soon subsided the crowd, and the football match returned to normal. 看台上一阵混战之后，保安人员快速疏散了人群，球赛得以正常进行。

□ scream □ screen □ screw □ scrub □ scrupulous □ scrutiny □ scuffle

sculpture [ˈskʌlptʃə(r)]	*n.* 雕塑品 记 联想记忆：sculpt(雕塑，雕刻) + ure → 雕塑品 例 Tom now has a new commission—making a glass ***sculpture*** for the headquarters of a pizza company. 现在汤姆有了新任务：为一家比萨公司总部的建筑制作一个玻璃雕像。
seal* [siːl]	*vt.* 封，密封 *n.* 封铅，封条；印，图章；海豹 记 联想记忆：sea(海洋) + l(看作 love，爱) → 海水也不会冲走爱的印迹 → 印，图章 例 Please ***seal*** the envelope and stick an eight-cent stamp on it. 请封好信封并贴上一张 8 分邮票。
seam [siːm]	*n.* 缝，接缝；煤层 例 The sailors couldn't find anything to caulk the ***seams*** in the boat. 水手们找不到任何东西来填塞船上的裂缝。
seasonal [ˈsiːzənl]	*a.* 季节性的，随季节而变化的；节令性的 例 ***Seasonal*** weather fluctuations depend on factors such as proximity to oceans or other large bodies of water, currents in those oceans, and prevailing winds. 周期性的气候变化取决于与海洋或者其他大型水体的临近程度、洋流及季风等因素。
seclude [sɪˈkluːd]	*vt.* 使隔离，使孤立 记 词根记忆：se(分离) + clud(关闭) + e → 脱离，过着封闭的生活 → 使隔离，使孤立 例 The monks ***secluded*** themselves from the rest of society. 僧侣们将自己与世隔绝。
secondary [ˈsekəndri]	*a.* 次要的，二级的；(教育、学校等)中等的；辅助的，从属的 记 联想记忆：来自 second(*num.* 第二) 搭 be secondary to 仅次于…；secondary school 中学 例 It took us three hours to decide the primary and ***secondary*** targets of this term. 我们花了三个小时才确定了这个学期的主要目标和次要目标。 派 secondarily(*ad.* 在第二，其次，在第二位)
section* [ˈsekʃn]	*n.* 部分；部门；截面 记 词根记忆：sect(切割) + ion → 从整体切割出来的 → 部分；部门 例 Here is the non-smoking ***section***. 这里是禁烟区。
sector [ˈsektə(r)]	*n.* 部分，部门；防御地段，防区；扇形 例 Nowadays more women are being employed in the business ***sector***. 现在，就职于商业部门的女性越来越多。
secure* [sɪˈkjʊə(r)]	*v.* 得到某物，获得；防护，保卫 *a.* 安全的；可靠的，放心的 记 联想记忆：se(看作 see，看) + cure(治愈) → 亲眼看到治愈，确定其是安全的 → 安全的；可靠的 搭 be secure from interruption 不受打扰 例 The person won his eighth Olympic gold medal, and ***secured*** his place in history. 那个人赢得了他的第八块奥运会金牌，巩固了其历史地位。 派 securely(*ad.* 安全地；安心地)；securable(*a.* 可得到的)

□ sculpture □ seal □ seam □ seasonal □ seclude □ secondary
□ section □ sector □ secure

security*
[sɪˈkjʊərəti]

n. 安全，保障；抵押品；[*pl.*] 证券

记 来自 secure(*v.* 保卫，防护；获得)

搭 security checks 安全检查；job securities 工作保障

例 such insurance plan can offer your families financial ***security*** in the event of the loss of properties. 这种保险计划可以在你失去财产的情况下向你的家人提供经济保障。

sedentary
[ˈsedntri]

a. (工作、活动等)需要久坐的；(人)惯于久坐不动的；(人或动物)定居的，不迁徙的；沉积的

记 词根记忆：sed(坐) + ent + ary(有关的) → 与坐着的状态相关联的 → 需要久坐的

搭 a sedentary lifestyle 长期伏案的生活方式

例 People doing ***sedentary*** jobs usually eat less than those who are in more active occupations. 从事久坐工作的人通常需要比那些从事活动量非常大的人吃得少。

sediment
[ˈsedɪmənt]

n. 沉淀物；沉积物(如沙、砾、石、泥等)

记 词根记忆：sedi(坐) + ment(名词后缀) → 坐下去的东西 → 沉淀物

例 There was heavy brown ***sediment*** in the bottom of the bottle. 水壶的底部有厚厚的棕色沉淀物。

派 sedimentation(*n.* 沉淀，沉降)；sedimentary(*a.* 沉积的，沉积形成的)

Rejoicing in hope, patient in tribulation.
从希望中得到欢乐，在苦难中保持坚韧。
——美国总统 肯尼迪 .J.(John Kennedy, American President)

Word List 40

音频

词根、词缀预习表

duc	引导	seduce *vt.* 勾引，引诱	**lect**	选择	select *v.* 选择
sem	符号，意义	semantic a. 语义的	**semi**	半	seminar *n.* 研讨会
sen	老的	senior *a.* 年长的	**sens**	感觉	sensible *a.* 合情理的
sequ	继续	sequence *n.* 顺序，次序	**sign**	标记	signature *n.* 签名
simul	相同	simulate *vt.* 模仿	**sinist**	左手	sinister *a.* 不吉祥的

seduce [sɪˈdjuːs]

vt. 勾引，引诱；诱使，唆使

记 词根记忆：se(分开)+duc(引导)+e → 引开 → 勾引，引诱

例 Customers were ***seduced*** into buying such household appliances as the washing machine and fridge by the offer of a free delivery. 顾客受商家免费送货的利诱而买诸如洗衣机和冰箱之类的家电。

派 seduction(*n.* 诱奸；诱惑力，魅力，吸引力)；seductive(*a.* 迷人的，有吸引力的)

seek [siːk]

v. 寻找；探索；追求

搭 seek one's fortune 寻找发财机会，外出闯荡

例 They ***sought*** in vain for somewhere to shelter. 他们怎么也找不到一个藏身之处。

seep [siːp]

vi. 漏出，渗漏

记 联想记忆：深(deep)层渗漏(seep)

例 Some parts of Australia are dry because rainwater ***seeps*** quickly through sandy soils and into the rock below. 澳大利亚的一些地区非常干燥，因为雨水很快渗过砂土，进入下面的岩石层。// Gradually the pain ***seeped*** away. 疼痛慢慢消失了。

派 seepage(*n.* 渗，渗透)

segment* [ˈsegmənt]

n. 片段；部分；节；线段；(橘子等的)瓣

记 词根记忆：seg(=sec 切割)+ment → 片段；部分

例 He claimed that the essence of reasoning lied in putting together two "behaviour ***segments***" in some novel way. 他称推理的本质就是将两个"行为片段"以新的方式整合在一起。

□ seduce □ seek □ seep □ segment

segregate
['segrɪgeɪt]

vt. 隔离，(使)分开

记 词根记忆：se(分离)+greg(人群)+ate→使脱离人群→隔离，(使)分开

搭 segregate from 与…隔离

例 It is necessary to ***segregate*** two groups of fans in the stadium, in case of unnecessary fight after the game. 为了避免赛后不必要的争斗，将体育场的两部分球迷隔开是非常必要的。

派 segregated(*a.* 隔离的)；segregation(*n.* 隔离)

同 isolate(*vt.* 使隔离，使孤立)；separate(*v.* 分开，隔离)

反 unite(*v.* 联合)

---

select
[sɪ'lekt]

v. 选择，挑选 *a.* 精选的，优等的

记 词根记忆：se+lect(选择)→选择，挑选

搭 selected poem of sb. 诗选

例 More and more employers are making use of what are called "personality questionnaires" to help them ***select*** new staff. 越来越多的雇主正在利用所谓的"性格调查问卷"来帮助自己挑选新员工。

派 selective(*a.* 选择的；选择性的)；selection(*n.* 选择)

---

self-esteem
[ˌselfɪ'stiːm]

n. 自尊；自负

例 Sam suffers from low ***self-esteem*** and it prevents him from pursuing his goals. 萨姆的自信心不足，这阻碍了他追求自己的目标。

---

semantic
[sɪ'mæntɪk]

a. 语义的

记 词根记忆：sem(符号，意义)+ant+ic→有关符号的→语义的

例 It is well-known that the professor is expert in language teaching and ***semantic*** analysis. 众所周知，该教授擅长语言教学和语义分析。

---

semester*
[sɪ'mestə(r)]

n. 学期

记 联想记忆：seme(看作semi，半)+s+ter(看作term，学期)→半学期也是学期→学期

例 In the first ***semester***, you'll be taking four subjects. 你在第一学期要选四门课。

---

seminar*
['semɪnɑː(r)]

n. (大学的)研究班，研讨会

记 词根记忆：semi(半)+nar→研讨会每半年举行一次→研讨会

例 You should prepare before you attend this ***seminar***. 参加这次研讨会之前你应该准备一下。

---

senior
['siːniə(r)]

a. 资格较老的；年长的 *n.* 较年长者；(中学或大学的)毕业班学生

记 词根记忆：sen(老的，年长的)+ior→年长的；较年长者

搭 senior citizens 老年人；senior students 大四学生

例 Women who apply for jobs in the middle or ***senior*** management have a higher success rate than men, according to an employment survey. 一项就业情况调查显示，申请从事中级或高级管理工作的女性比申请同等职位的男性就业成功率高。

□ segregate □ select □ self-esteem □ semantic □ semester □ seminar □ senior

sensation
[sen'seɪʃn]

n. (感官的)感觉能力；感觉，知觉；轰动，引起轰动的事件(或人物)

记 词根记忆：sens(感觉) + ation → 感觉，知觉

搭 cause a great sensation 引起很大轰动；heat sensation 热觉

例 This discovery would cause not much more *sensation* than Herschel's discovery of Uranus, in 1781. 这一发现的影响不会比赫舍尔于 1781 年首次发现天王星时更轰动。

sensational*
[sen'seɪʃənl]

a. 轰动性的，引起哗然的；耸人听闻的；极好的；绝妙的

搭 sensational discovery 轰动性的发现；sensational headlines 耸人听闻的头条新闻

例 The performance given by the newcomers is a *sensational* success. 新来者的表演相当成功。

sensible*
['sensəbl]

a. 明智的；合情理的；能觉察到的

记 词根记忆：sens(感觉) + ible(可…的) → 可感觉到的 → 合情理的

搭 a sensible idea 合乎情理的想法

例 This week's lecture is on *sensible* eating. 本周的讲座是关于合理饮食的。

sensitive*
['sensətɪv]

a. 敏感的，灵敏的；神经过敏的，容易生气的；易受伤害的

记 词根记忆：sens(感觉) + itive → 敏感的

例 The "environmentally *sensitive*" landscape was threatened by some buildings. 这处易受"环境影响的"风景受到了一些建筑物的威胁。

派 sensitivity(*n.* 敏感，灵敏性)

sensory*
['sensəri]

a. 感觉的，感官的

记 联想记忆：sens(e)(感觉) + ory → 感觉的

搭 a sensory organ 感觉器官

例 Mr. Roger is a scientist working in the field of *sensory* perception. 罗杰先生是感官知觉领域的一名科学家。

sentient
['senʃnt; 'sentiənt]

a. 有感觉能力的，有知觉力的；知悉的

记 词根记忆：sent(感觉) + ient → 有感觉能力的，有知觉力的；知悉的

例 Because animals are living and *sentient* beings, they deserve special protection and respect. 动物是活生生、有知觉的生物，它们应该受到特殊的保护和尊重。

separate

['sepəreɪt] *v.* 使分离，使分开；划分，区分；分离，分开；分居

['seprət] *a.* 分离的，分开的；不同的，特别的

搭 separate bedrooms 单独的卧室

例 The solution is not to *separate* teaching and research, but to recognize that the combination is difficult. 这种解决方案不是要将教学与研究分离开，而是承认它们的结合是困难的。

40

□ sensation □ sensational □ sensible □ sensitive □ sensory □ sentient
□ separate

sequence* [ˈsiːkwəns]

n. 一系列，一连串；顺序，次序

记 词根记忆：sequ(后续，继续) + ence → 顺序，次序

例 Scientists were able to analyse the ***sequence*** of events. 科学家能够分析事件发生的先后顺序。

serial [ˈsɪəriəl]

n. 连续剧 *a.* 连续的；顺序排列的

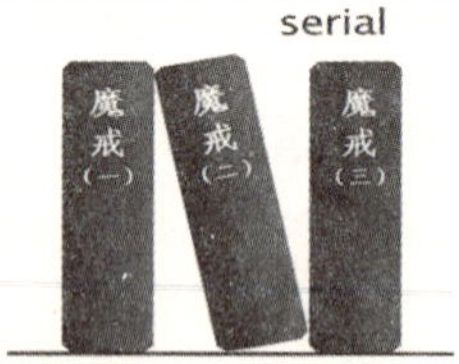

记 联想记忆：连续剧(serial)就是以某个主题为系列(series)的电视剧

例 A lot of people complained that American police ***serials*** were particularly violent. 许多人抱怨美国的警匪片太暴力了。

series* [ˈsɪəriːz]

n. 一系列，连续；丛书

记 联想记忆：电视连续剧可用 TV serial 和 TV series 表示

搭 a series of 一系列，一连串

例 This ***series*** of lectures is organized by the Students' Union. 这一系列演讲由学生会组织。

service* [ˈsɜːvɪs]

n. 服务，帮助；公共设施，公用事业；维修，保养；行政部门，服务机构 *vt.* 维修，保养

搭 airline coach service 航空公司汽车服务处；Student Service 学生服务中心；door-to-door service 门到门服务；service charge 服务费用；interlibrary service 图书馆馆际服务

例 The airline companies want to improve the ***service***. 航空公司想提升服务质量。

session [ˈseʃn]

n. 一场，一节；会议；集会

记 联想记忆：ses(看作 see，看见) + sion → 看见彼此 → 会面 → 会议

搭 special session 特别会议；in session 正在开会；training session 培训期；reading session 阅读课

例 This course is made up of 15 ***sessions***. 这门课共上 15 节。

setting* [ˈsetɪŋ]

n. 环境；背景；安置

记 联想记忆：set(布置) + t + ing → 布置(新居) → 环境；安置

例 The Waikato river, the longest river in New Zealand, flows through the center of the city of Hamilton, providing a picturesque and park-like ***setting*** of riverside walks and gardens. 怀卡托河是新西兰最长的河流，流经汉密尔顿市中心，两岸的人行道和花园为人们提供了公园般美丽如画的环境。

settle* [ˈsetl]

v. 定居，安家；解决，调停；安排，安放；支付，结算；安置于；(鸟等)飞落，停留，栖息

记 联想记忆：set(放置) + tle → 放置在一个地方就好像定居了下来 → 定居，安家

搭 settle down 定居，过安定的生活

例 They are offspring of the first Europeans who ***settled*** in China. 他们是最早在中国定居的欧洲人的后裔。

派 settler(*n.* 移民，殖民者)；settlement(*n.* 解决；协议；定居点)

□ sequence □ serial □ series □ service □ session □ setting
□ settle

severe* [sɪˈvɪə(r)]	*a.* 严重的；严厉的；剧烈的 搭 a severe consequence 严重后果；a severe storm 剧烈的暴风雨 例 The research completed in 1982 found that in the United States soil erosion was almost as ***severe*** as in India and China. 1982 年完成的调查显示，美国土壤侵蚀的状况和印度及中国的一样严重。 派 severely (*ad.* 严重地；严格地；激烈地)
shade [ʃeɪd]	*n.* 阴凉处；(灯)罩；暗部；色度；细微差别 *vt.* 遮蔽，遮光；把…涂暗 例 Dark colours give an aura of authority while lighter pastel ***shades*** suggest approachability. 深色调给人一种权威的感觉，而清淡柔和的色调使人感到亲切。
shaft* [ʃɑːft]	*n.* 轴，柄，杆；矛柄，把柄；(光的)束，光线；竖井，(电梯的)升降井 记 联想记忆：变速杆(shaft)用来改变(shift)速度 例 A small iron was attached to the 1.5m bamboo ***shaft*** as a weapon. 小铁块被固定在 1.5 米长的竹竿上作为一件武器。 同 spindle(*n.* 轴，杆)；beam〔*n.* (光线的)束〕
shallow [ˈʃæləʊ]	*a.* 浅的；肤浅的，浅薄的 记 联想记忆：顾影(shadow)自怜，浅薄(shallow)也 例 To the elephant, the stream is quite ***shallow*** so it is able to walk across it. But to the rabbit, it can be a murderer. 对大象来说，河流很浅，能够跨过去；但对兔子来说，就很危险，可能会被淹死。
shareholder [ˈʃeəhəʊldə(r)]	*n.* 股票持有人；股东 记 组合词：share(分享；股票) + holder(持有者) → 股票持有人
shark [ʃɑːk]	*n.* 鲨鱼；诈骗者 例 ***Sharks*** infest the waters. 这片海域有大批鲨鱼出没。
sharpen* [ˈʃɑːpən]	*v.* 削尖，磨快；使敏锐，使敏捷 记 联想记忆：sharp(锋利的) + en(使…) → 使锋利的 → 削尖；使敏锐 搭 sharpen pencils 削铅笔 例 The course can help the students ***sharpen*** their oral skills. 这门课程可以帮助学生们练就流利的口语表达能力。
shatter [ˈʃætə(r)]	*v.* (使)破碎，碎裂；给予极大打击 记 发音记忆："筛它"→(使)破碎 例 This event ***shattered*** all his previous ideas. 这件事粉碎了他以前所有的想法。// The vase ***shattered*** as it hit the floor. 花瓶掉在地上，碎了。
shave [ʃeɪv]	*n./v.* 修面 记 联想记忆：不要在阴暗处(shade)修面(shave) 例 How do you ***shave*** your beard so clean? 你是怎样把胡须刮得那么干净的?
sheer* [ʃɪə(r)]	*a.* 十足的；纯粹的；陡峭的 记 联想记忆：she(她) + er(表人) → 她是个十足的女人 → 十足的 例 Mary won the skating competition by ***sheer*** luck. 玛丽能在这次滑冰比赛中获胜纯属运气好。

□ severe □ shade □ shaft □ shallow □ shareholder □ shark
□ sharpen □ shatter □ shave □ sheer

shell [ʃel]	*n.* 壳；炮弹 *v.* 给…去壳；炮击 例 Anne removed the oyster from its ***shell*** and began to eat. 安妮从壳里挖出牡蛎，吃了起来。
shelter* [ˈʃeltə(r)]	*n.* 掩蔽(处)，隐蔽(处)；住所；保护 *v.* 掩蔽；躲避 记 联想记忆：shel(看作 shell，壳) + ter → 像壳一样的地方 → 掩蔽；住所 例 Harbour is a physical concept, a ***shelter*** for ships, while port is an economic concept, a centre of land-sea exchange. Harbour 是物质概念，即船的"家"；而 port 是经济概念，即海陆货物交换的中心。
shift* [ʃɪft]	*v.* 移动，转移；改变，转变 *n.* 转换，转变；轮(或换)班 记 联想记忆：电脑键盘上的切换键即 Shift 键 例 Fishermen protested, and the port was ***shifted*** a further five kilometres to the south. 由于渔民的反对，港口又向南移了五公里。
shilling* [ˈʃɪlɪŋ]	*n.* 先令 例 Those matches cost a ***shilling*** a box. 那些火柴一先令一盒。
shin [ʃɪn]	*n.* 胫，胫部，胫骨 *v.* (手脚并用沿某物)爬 搭 shin up/down sth. 爬上/下 例 You should punch him in the nose and kick him in the ***shins*** without fear when a stranger tries to sexually harass you. 当有陌生人试图对你性骚扰的时候，应该毫无畏惧地打他的鼻子踢他的小腿。
shipment [ˈʃɪpmənt]	*n.* 装运，运输；装载(或运输)的货物，装货量 记 联想记忆：ship(船运) + ment → 装运 例 Finally the honey is poured into barrels for ***shipment***. 最终蜂蜜被倒进桶里运走。 同 cargo(*n.* 货物)；freight(*n.* 货物；重载)
shore [ʃɔː(r)]	*n.* 滨，岸，海滩 例 The passengers spared no effort to swim for the ***shore*** when their aeroplane landed in the sea. 飞机在海上迫降后，乘客奋力朝海滩游去。
shortage* [ˈʃɔːtɪdʒ]	*n.* 不足，缺少 记 联想记忆：short(缺乏) + age → 不足，缺少 搭 financial shortage 缺钱；shortage of spare time 缺少空闲时间 例 The development project was greeted because of Holland's chronic ***shortage*** of land. 由于荷兰土地长期短缺，这一开发项目在荷兰大受欢迎。 同 lack(*n.* 缺少)；deficiency(*n.* 不足)
shorthand [ˈʃɔːthænd]	*n.* 速记法；速记 记 联想记忆：short(短的) + hand(手) → 人手短缺时，也不影响记录的速度 → 速记 例 The book contained some strange ***shorthand*** symbols. 这本书上有一些奇怪的速记符号。
short-term* [ˈʃɔːttɜːm]	*a.* 短期的 记 组合词：short(短的) + term(期间) → 短期的 例 Such ***short-term*** increases in production are obtained only at a substantial and serious cost to the organisation. 产量的这种短期增长只能以公司的巨额成本为代价。

□ shell □ shelter □ shift □ shilling □ shin □ shipment
□ shore □ shortage □ shorthand □ short-term

shrewd
[ʃruːd]

a. 机灵的；精明的

记 发音记忆：“熟的” → 对某事很熟，因此反应灵敏 → 机灵的

搭 a shrewd businessman 精明的商人

例 This politician was compassionate and ***shrewd***. 这位政治家富有激情又不失精明。

同 smart(*a.* 聪明的)；keen(*a.* 敏锐的，聪明的)

反 dull(*a.* 迟钝的)

shrink *
[ʃrɪŋk]

v. (使)收缩；萎缩

记 联想记忆：童话故事里，人喝(drink)了巫婆的药水就能收缩(shrink)身体

例 Employees found their time on the job ***shrinking*** to 10 hours daily. 雇员们发现他们的工作时间已经减少到每天十小时。

派 shrinkage(*n.* 收缩；收缩程度)

shrub
[ʃrʌb]

n. 灌木

记 联想记忆：sh + rub(擦伤) → 灌木擦伤皮肤 → 灌木

搭 shrub layer 灌木层

例 The volunteers raked around ***shrubs*** and trees to look for the lost children. 志愿者在灌木丛和树林里四处寻找迷路的孩子。

同 bush(*n.* 矮树丛)；scrub(*n.* 灌木)

shrug
[ʃrʌg]

n./v. 耸肩

记 联想记忆：shru(像拼音 shu 舒) + g(音似：胳) → 耸肩

例 Joey and Monica looked at each other and ***shrugged***. 乔伊和莫妮卡互相对视，耸了耸肩。

shutter *
[ˈʃʌtə(r)]

n. 百叶窗；(照相机的)快门

记 来自 shut(*v.* 关闭)

例 In 1889 an improved model with a new ***shutter*** design was introduced, and it was called the No. 2 Kodak camera. 1889 年推出的“柯达二号”是一款装有新型快门的改良型相机。

shuttle
[ˈʃʌtl]

n. 航天飞机

记 联想记忆：shut(关闭) + tle → 封闭的空间 → 航天飞机

例 The ***shuttle*** can carry devices for scientific inquiry. 这架航天飞机能携带科学考察装置。

siesta *
[siˈestə]

n. 午睡，午休

例 These workers have no time for a ***siesta*** in summer. 这些工人在夏天都没有时间午睡。

sift *
[sɪft]

v. 细查；筛；过滤

记 联想记忆：坐(sit)下来慢慢筛(sift)面粉

例 We ***sift*** through the information carefully to find a clue that will help us. 我们仔细研究资料以便找出对我们有帮助的线索。

40

□ shrewd □ shrink □ shrub □ shrug □ shutter □ shuttle
□ siesta □ sift

signal [ˈsɪgnəl]	*n.* 信号；暗号；标志 *v.* (向…)发信号；标志着 记 联想记忆：sign(签名) + al → 用签名作为自己的标志 → 标志 例 Serotonin is a chemical substance involved in sending *signals* in the nervous system. 血清素是一种在神经系统中参与传递信号的化学物质。// Tom *signaled* to the waiter to bring the menu. 汤姆示意服务员把菜单拿来。
signature [ˈsɪgnətʃə(r)]	*n.* 签名，签字；签署 记 词根记忆：sign(标记) + at + ure(表行为、状态，名词后缀) → 在文件上做记号 → 签名 例 Corbett ran into the bedroom and scribbled his *signature* on the notebook. 科比特冲进卧室，在笔记本上潦草地签上了自己的名字。
significance* [sɪgˈnɪfɪkəns]	*n.* 重要性，意义 例 The real *significance* of the first Kodak camera was that it was backed up by a developing and printing service. 第一代柯达相机的真正意义在于它可以连接冲洗和打印设备。
significant* [sɪgˈnɪfɪkənt]	*a.* 有意义的；重大的，重要的 记 来自 signify(*v.* 有重要性)；sign(标记) + ify(使…) → 重点部分标上记号 → 有重要性 例 Modifications to houses come at a *significant* cost to the home buyers. 房屋装修对购房人来说是一笔不菲的开销。 派 insignificant(*a.* 不重要的)；significantly(*ad.* 重大地；明显地)
signpost* [ˈsaɪnpəʊst]	*vt.* 在…设置路标 *n.* 路标 记 组合词：sign(标记) + post(放置) → 在…设置路标 例 The Education Centre is *signposted* at every crossing in the college. 该大学的每个十字路口处都设有通往教育中心的路标。
silicon [ˈsɪlɪkən]	*n.* 硅 例 The *silicon* chip is one of the most significant inventions in the past 50 years. 硅片是过去 50 年中最重要的发明之一。
silt* [sɪlt]	*n.* 淤泥 *v.* (用淤泥)阻塞 记 联想记忆：坐(sit)于淤泥(silt)而不染 例 Volcanic ash *silted* up the Columbia River 35 miles away. 哥伦比亚河中的火山灰淤积长达 35 英里。
silver* [ˈsɪlvə(r)]	*n.* 银；银器 例 A German alchemist tried to transmute *silver* into gold. 一位德国的炼金术士试图将白银炼成黄金。
similarly [ˈsɪmələlɪ]	*ad.* 同样地，类似地 例 All students in this school wear *similarly* unconventionally-cut suits. 这所学校的所有学生都穿着剪裁新颖、款式相同的服装。
simplicity [sɪmˈplɪsəti]	*n.* 简单(性)，简易；朴素；直率，单纯 记 联想记忆：simpl(e)(简单的；直率的) + icity → 简单，直率 例 For the sake of *simplicity*, the teacher might recommend the student to use this reference book. 为简便起见，老师可向学生推荐使用这本参考书。

□ signal □ signature □ significance □ significant □ signpost □ silicon
□ silt □ silver □ similarly □ simplicity

simplify
[ˈsɪmplɪfaɪ]

vt. 使简化

例 These self-help books are designed for people who want to ***simplify*** their lives. 这些自助书籍是为那些想简化生活的人设计的。

simplistic
[sɪmˈplɪstɪk]

a. 过分单纯化的，过分简单化的

例 But a closer inspection reveals this interpretation as too ***simplistic***. 进一步的调查显示，这种解释过于简单化了。

simulate
[ˈsɪmjuleɪt]

vt. 模仿，模拟；假装，伪装；扮演

记 词根记忆：simul（相同）+ ate（使…）→ 使相同 → 模仿

例 The experiment ***simulated*** a natural environment. 这个试验模拟了一种自然环境。

同 imitate（*vt.* 模仿，效仿）；ape（*vt.* 模仿）；affect（*v.* 假装）

simulate

simulation
[ˌsɪmjuˈleɪʃn]

n. 假装；模拟

例 The manager was beforehand with a computer ***simulation*** of likely sales performance in advance of the Christmas festival. 经理在圣诞来临前就事先用计算机模拟出了可能的销售业绩。

simultaneous
[ˌsɪmlˈteɪniəs]

a. 同时的，同时发生的，同时存在的；同步的

记 词根记忆：simul（相同）+ taneous → 相同时间的 → 同时发生的

例 Any ceasefire would be ***simultaneous*** with the withdrawal of troops. 任何一次的停火都是与撤军同时发生的。

派 simultaneously（*ad.* 同时地）

同 coinstantaneous（*a.* 同时发生的，同时的）

sincere
[sɪnˈsɪə(r)]

a. 真挚的，诚挚的，真诚的，诚恳的

记 联想记忆：sin（罪）+ cere → 把罪过一一坦白，态度真诚 → 真诚的

例 My respect to you is very ***sincere***. 我对您的尊敬是非常诚挚的。

sinew*
[ˈsɪnjuː]

n. 肌腱；力量的来源

例 The athletes were so nervous that we could see all their ***sinews*** tense. 运动员非常紧张，以致我们能看到他们紧绷的肌肉。

sinister*
[ˈsɪnɪstə(r)]

a. 不吉祥的，凶兆的；险恶的，邪恶的

记 词根记忆：sinist（左手）+ er → 古罗马时人们认为左边代表着"不祥、邪恶" → 不吉祥的；邪恶的

例 In your remarks you allude to certain ***sinister*** developments. 你的话语中暗示了一些不祥的势头。

40

sip
[sɪp]

v. 小口地喝；吸吮

例 As you ***sip*** the wine, you'll find something special in it. 当你小口啜饮这种酒时，你会发现它的独特之处。

situated*
[ˈsɪtʃueɪtɪd]

a. 位于…的；处于…境地的

例 The Newton Park site is ***situated*** four miles west of Bath. 牛顿公园位于巴思以西 4 英里的地方。

sizeable
[ˈsaɪzəbl]

a. 相当大的

例 Income from tourism accounts for a ***sizeable*** proportion of the total government revenue. 旅游收入占政府全部税收相当大的一部分。

□ simplify □ simplistic □ simulate □ simulation □ simultaneous □ sincere
□ sinew □ sinister □ sip □ situated □ sizeable

Word List 41

音频

词根、词缀预习表

sland	障碍物	slander *n.* 诋毁，中伤	**log**	说	slogan *n.* 标语，口号
soci	结交	sociable *a.* 友善的，友好的	**sol**	太阳	solar 太阳的；太阳能的
sol	单独	sole *a.* 唯一的，独有的	**solid**	坚实的	solidarity *n.* 团结，一致
solu	溶解	soluble *a.* 可溶的，可解决的	**sou**	在某地	souvenir *n.* 纪念品，纪念物
spec	看	spectator *n.* 观众，旁观者	**spher**	球	sphere *n.* 范围，领域

sketch [sketʃ]

v. 画素描；概述 *n.* 素描；速写

例 Tom's not willing to ***sketch*** Mary. 汤姆不愿为给玛丽画素描。

skew* [skjuː]

vt. 使偏；曲解 *a.* 歪斜的

例 She says the U.S. market for goods has become ***skewed*** by the assumption. 她说美国商品市场已被这种假设扭曲了。// The painting was a little ***skew***. 这幅画有点歪。

skim [skɪm]

v. 撇去；掠过，擦过；浏览，略读

记 联想记忆：一眼掠过(skim)，只见皮(skin)毛

例 My reading approach is to ***skim*** the book first to see what's important and what isn't. It saves hours. 我的阅读方法是先浏览全书，看看什么是重点，什么不是，这样会节省很多时间。

skip [skɪp]

v. 跳，蹦；漏过；逃学

例 She ***skips*** the difficult words when she reads English novels. 看英文小说时她经常跳过难词。

同 leap(*v.* 跳，跳跃；跳过)；overlook(*vt.* 忽视，略过)

skull [skʌl]

n. 颅骨；脑袋

记 联想记忆：据说大脑袋(skull)的人掌握技能(skill)比较快

例 The anthropologist unearthed the ***skull*** of an ancient human at the site. 人类学家在该遗址挖掘出一个古人类的头骨。

skyscraper* [ˈskaɪskreɪpə(r)]

n. 摩天楼

记 组合词：sky(天) + scrape(摩擦) + er(表人或物) → 楼高得可以擦到天 → 摩天楼

例 As construction techniques improved, the ***skyscraper*** became a reality. 随着建筑技术的进步，建造摩天大楼成为现实。

slacken [ˈslækən]	*v.* (使)松弛，放松；放慢；萧条 例 The pace of export and import *slackened* during the last quarter due to trade barrier between the two countries. 由于两国间的贸易壁垒，进出口步伐在上一季度有所放缓。
slander [ˈslɑːndə(r)]	*n.* 诋毁，中伤，诽谤(罪) *vt.* 诋毁，诽谤 记 词根记忆：sland(=scandal 障碍物，绊脚石) + er → 设置障碍物，使人绊倒 → 诋毁，诽谤 例 Nowadays, it is not rare that stars sue the news agency for their *slanders* on their good reputation in the entertainment circle. 如今，在娱乐圈明星指控新闻机构诋毁他们的名誉已屡见不鲜。 派 slanderous(*a.* 诽谤性的)
slash [slæʃ]	*n.* 砍痕，伤痕；斜线号 *v.* 砍；大幅度削减 记 联想记忆：一条斜线(slash)在他脑海里闪闪发光(flash) 搭 slash costs/prices 大幅度降低成本/价格 例 Their habits of hunting, fishing, and *slash*-and-burn cultivation have been often harmful to the habitat. 他们渔猎和刀耕火种的习性通常会破坏他们的生存环境。
slat [slæt]	*n.* 板条，狭板 *vt.* 用板条制作 记 联想记忆：和 slate(*n.* 板岩，石板)一起记 例 Try out an orthopaedic mattress or a spring *slatted* bed which can be beneficial for certain types of back pain. 你可以尝试使用矫形床垫或是板条弹簧床，这有助于缓解某些背痛。
sledge* [sledʒ]	*n.* 雪橇 *vi.* 乘雪橇 例 Supplies were brought to us on large *sledges* from a ship fifteen kilometers away. 供给品是从 15 公里外的船上用大雪橇拉来的。
sleek* [sliːk]	*a.* (毛发等)光滑而有光泽的；时髦的；豪华的 *vt.* 使(毛发等)光滑发亮 例 Not only sleeping and living accommodation, but also a *sleek* modern kitchen allows guests to cook and entertain if they wish at no additional cost. 如果客人愿意，不仅可以免费住宿，还可以免费在豪华厨房中做饭和招待客人。
slender* [ˈslendə(r)]	*a.* 修长的，细长的，苗条的；微小的，微薄的 记 联想记忆：并非所有女孩子都得温柔(tender)纤细(slender)才好看 例 Many families are still living on *slender* earnings. 许多家庭仍然靠微薄的收入度日。 派 slenderness(*n.* 苗条，纤细)
slice [slaɪs]	*v.* 把…切成片，削 *n.* 薄片，切片；份，部分 记 联想记忆：sl + ice(冰) → 把冰块切碎 → 切片 搭 a slice of 一片；一部分；a slice of bread 一块面包 例 I brought you a *slice* of pizza. 我给你带了一块比萨。

41

□ slacken □ slander □ slash □ slat □ sledge □ sleek
□ slender □ slice

slide* [slaɪd]

v. 滑动，下滑；(使)悄悄地移动 *n.* 滑动，下滑；滑坡，滑道，滑面；幻灯片；(土、泥等的)突然崩落

记 联想记忆：s + lid(盖子) + e → 盖子太滑，从桌子上滑了下去 → 滑动，下滑

搭 slide into 不知不觉地陷入；slide projector 幻灯片放映机；slide ruler 计算尺

例 For frequent usage, the drawers ***slide*** in and out easily. 由于频繁使用，抽屉很容易拉出、推进。

派 sliding(*a.* 滑行的)

slight* [slaɪt]

a. 轻微的，不足道的；纤细的，瘦弱的 *vt./n.* 轻视，藐视，轻蔑

记 联想记忆：s + light(轻的) → 轻微的

搭 a slight girl 一个苗条的女孩

例 I had a ***slight*** headache this morning. 今天早上我有点头疼。

派 slightly(*ad.* 些微)

slim [slɪm]

a. 苗条的；薄的 *vi.* 变苗条

记 联想记忆：sim 卡通常很薄(slim)

例 Tom likes her ***slim*** and pretty hands so much. 汤姆非常喜欢她那双纤细美丽的手。

slip* [slɪp]

v. 滑倒，失足；减退；摆脱，闪开；塞入 *n.* 差错，疏漏；滑倒；纸片

例 Tom ***slipped*** on the ice and broke his leg. 汤姆在冰上摔了一跤，摔断了腿。// Payments can be made at any branch of the Federal Bank by completing the deposit ***slip*** attached to your account notice. 你只需填写账目通知单上附带的存款单，便可以在联邦银行的任何支行付款。

slippery [ˈslɪpəri]

a. 滑的，滑溜的；油滑的，狡猾的；棘手的

记 联想记忆：slipp(=slip 滑) + ery → 滑的

例 How damp and ***slippery*** the ground is! 地面又湿又滑！

slogan [ˈsləʊɡən]

n. 标语，口号

记 词根记忆：s + log(说) + an → 标语，口号

例 Their ***slogan*** is "Deeds not words". 他们的口号是"要行动不要空话"。

slope [sləʊp]

n. 斜坡；倾斜 *vi.* 倾斜

记 联想记忆：slo（看作 slow，慢的）+ pe → 慢慢地走下斜坡 → 斜坡

例 Steps were taken to evacuate the population. Most campers, hikers and timbercutters left the ***slopes*** of the mountain. 已经采取措施疏散人群。大多数露营者、徒步旅行者和伐木工人都离开了山坡。// This tower ***slopes*** to the north. 这座塔向北倾斜。

slothful [ˈsləʊθfl]

a. 怠惰的，懒惰的；迟钝的

例 The white-collar workers in big cities tend to suffer from fatigue easily which makes them ***slothful*** in the office. 大城市的白领阶层往往容易患上疲劳症，使他们在工作中反应迟钝。

□ slide □ slight □ slim □ slip □ slippery □ slogan
□ slope □ slothful

slouch [slaʊtʃ]

v. 懒散地站(或坐、走)；低头垂肩地站(或坐、走)

记 发音记忆："似老去"→懒散地站；低头垂肩地站

例 Studies have shown that just one hour sitting in a *slouched* position can strain ligaments in the back. 研究表明，保持懒散的坐姿一小时就会导致背部韧带受损。

slum* [slʌm]

n. 贫民窟，贫民区

例 Such rapid and uncontrolled growth helped to turn parts of cities into *slums*. 这种快速而无节制的增长使城市的某些地区变成了贫民窟。

slumber [ˈslʌmbə(r)]

v. 睡眠(尤指睡得安稳而舒服)，安睡 *n.* [常 *pl.*] 睡眠，安睡

记 联想记忆：s + lumber(木材)→睡得很沉，像根木头→安睡

例 To enjoy the beauty of cherry blossom, many foreigners visit the Mount Fuji which has *slumbered* for years. 为了一睹樱花盛放之美，很多国外游客前往休眠多年的富士山游览。

slump* [slʌmp]

vi. 大幅度下降，暴跌；突然倒下，猛然落下 *n.* 萧条期；低潮状态

记 联想记忆：sl + ump(看作 jump，跳下)→突然跳下→暴跌

搭 a slump in profits 利润锐减

例 Sales of clothing have *slumped* sharply this year. 今年衣服的销量大幅下降。

slurry* [ˈslʌri]

n. 泥浆

例 How effective is the use of limestone *slurry*? 使用石灰浆的效果怎么样?

sluttish [ˈslʌtɪʃ]

a. 懒惰的，邋遢的；放荡的

记 来自 slut(*n.* 邋遢女人，懒婆娘)

搭 sluttish behaviour 放荡的行为

smart* [smɑːt]

a. 漂亮的，时髦的；高明的

例 Most computer criminals are *smart* enough to cover their crimes. 大多数计算机犯罪分子都很聪明，能掩盖自己的罪行。

smear [smɪə(r)]

v. 胡乱涂抹；弄脏，弄污；诽谤，诋毁；变得模糊不清，把(图画等)弄得模糊不清 *n.* 污迹，污渍；(显微镜的)涂片；诽谤，诋毁

记 联想记忆：遭到诽谤(smear)，发誓(swear)报复

例 Tony explained to the police that, the blood which was *smeared* on the front of his car belonged to a wild cat. 托尼向警方解释说，他车头蹭到的血迹是一只野猫的。

smell* [smel]

v. 散发(或有)…的气味；闻到，嗅到

例 Flowers *smell* stronger in the late evening. 花香在深夜更加浓烈。

□ slouch □ slum □ slumber □ slump □ slurry □ sluttish
□ smart □ smear □ smell

smooth*
[smuːð]

a. 顺利的；流畅的；协调的

搭 a smooth transfer of political power 政权的顺利交接

例 The new bill had a *smooth* passage through Parliament. 新法案在议会得以顺利通过。// Good health has been connected to the *smooth* mechanical operation of the body. 良好的健康状况与身体机能协调工作密不可分。

---

smother*
[ˈsmʌðə(r)]

v. 厚厚地覆盖；(使)窒息；把(火)闷熄

记 联想记忆：s(看作 she，她) + mother(母亲) → 母亲的溺爱快让她窒息了 → (使)窒息

例 All the towns and settlements in the area were *smothered* in a coating of ash. 这一地区的所有城镇和居民区都被火山灰覆盖了。

---

snack
[snæk]

n. 快餐，小吃；点心

搭 snack bar 小吃店，快餐店

例 The sandwich shop for quick *snacks* is nearby. 出售快餐的三明治店离这很近。

---

snap*
[snæp]

v. 咔嚓折断，啪地绷断；(啪的一声)打开(或关上)；咬；厉声说话，怒声责斥 *n.* 咔嚓声 *a.* 突然的，匆忙的

记 联想记忆：s + nap(小睡) → 上课小睡时被老师抓住了，遭到了训斥 → 怒声责斥

搭 snap out 厉声说出；snap up 迅速抓住；抢购

例 The heavy snow storm *snapped* tree branches and power lines. 暴风雪折断了树枝和电线。

---

snap up

抢购

例 Products in those shelves are *snapped up*, so manufacturers pay a lot for those areas. 那些货架上的产品的销路很好，因此生产商租用那块区域的费用也很高。

---

snobbish
[ˈsnɒbɪʃ]

a. 势利的，谄上欺下的；自命不凡的

记 来自 snob(*n.* 势利小人，谄上欺下者；自命不凡的人)

例 In current society, some people are very *snobbish*, who'd like to make friends only with people of wealth and of high social status. 在当今社会，有些人非常势利，他们只愿意与有钱和社会地位高的人交朋友。

---

soak
[səʊk]

v. 浸泡

记 联想记忆：在肥皂(soap)水中浸泡(soak)

例 We'll get you up to your room and *soak* your feet; you'll be okay. 我们带你到房间里泡泡脚，这样你会感觉舒服些。

---

sociable*
[ˈsəʊʃəbl]

a. 友善的，友好的；好交际的，合群的

记 词根记忆：soci(同伴，结交) + able → 好交际的

搭 a sociable child 合群的孩子

例 The girl is such a *sociable* child that she likes talking to everyone here. 这个女孩非常友善，她喜欢跟这里的每个人聊天。

---

socialise
[ˈsəʊʃəlaɪz]

v. (同他人)来往，交往，交际；使(某人)适应社会生活

搭 socialised medicine 公费医疗制度；socialise with 与…来往

例 I enjoy *socialising* with the others. 我喜欢与人交际。

□ smooth □ smother □ snack □ snap □ snap up □ snobbish
□ soak □ sociable □ socialise

sociology* [ˌsəʊsiˈɒlədʒi]	*n.* 社会学 记 词根记忆：soci(同伴，结交) + ology(…学) → 社会学 例 In the first semester you'll be taking four subjects: psychology, ***sociology***, history and economics. 第一学期你将学习四门课：心理学、社会学、历史和经济学。
solar [ˈsəʊlə(r)]	*a.* 太阳的；(利用)太阳能的 记 词根记忆：sol(太阳) + ar → 太阳的 例 Of all the planets in our own ***solar*** system, the Earth is the only one on which life can survive. 在太阳系所有行星中，地球是唯一一颗生命可以存活的行星。
solar-powered [ˈsəʊləˌpaʊəd]	*a.* 由太阳能驱动的 例 ***Solar-powered*** battery can transform the energy of sunlight into electric energy. 太阳能电池能把光能转化为电能。
sole [səʊl]	*a.* 唯一的，独有的 *n.* 鞋底，袜底；脚底 记 词根记忆：sol(单独) + e → 唯一的 搭 sole parent 单亲 例 His ***sole*** motive was to make her happy. 他唯一的动机就是让她高兴。 派 solely(*ad.* 唯一地；独自地)
solemn [ˈsɒləm]	*a.* 庄严的，隆重的；严肃的，认真的 记 词根记忆：sol(太阳) + emn → 古时把太阳看作是神圣庄严的 → 庄严的 搭 a solemn cathedral 庄严肃穆的大教堂 例 Kit made a ***solemn*** vow that he would always stand beside me. 基特郑重起誓，说他将永远支持我。
solicitor [səˈlɪsɪtə(r)]	*n.* (城镇的)法务官；初级律师，事务律师 例 ***Solicitors*** in Australia are very popular. 律师在澳大利亚很受欢迎。 同 lawyer(*n.* 律师)；attorney(*n.* 律师)
solidarity [ˌsɒlɪˈdærəti]	*n.* 团结，一致 记 词根记忆：solid(坚实的) + arity → 坚实的状态 → 团结 例 Downtrodden people will never be able to make any effective protest until they achieve ***solidarity***. 被压迫的人们只有团结一致才能做出有效的抗议。 同 unity(*n.* 团结；一致)；concord(*n.* 一致；和谐) 反 split(*n.* 分裂)
solidify [səˈlɪdɪfaɪ]	*v.* 巩固，确保；凝固，(使)固化；团结 例 In either case, make it a habit of ***solidifying*** your thoughts in a pattern before you put it into practice. 在任何情况下，都要养成一个习惯：先使想法固化成一种模式，再着手实践。
soluble [ˈsɒljəbl]	*a.* 可溶的；可解决的 记 词根记忆：solu(溶解；解开) + ble(可…的) → 可溶的；可解决的 搭 soluble material 可溶性物质 例 Fat ***soluble*** vitamins can be stored for quite some time in the body. 能溶于脂肪的维生素可在体内储存很久。 同 resoluble(*a.* 可解决的；可分解的) 反 unsolvable(*a.* 不能溶解的；无法解决的)

41

□ sociology □ solar □ solar-powered □ sole □ solemn □ solicitor
□ solidarity □ solidify □ soluble

solution* [səˈluːʃn]	*n.* 解答，解决办法；溶解，溶液 例 It took time to find ***solution*** to the problem. 找到解决该问题的方法需要时间。
solve* [sɒlv]	*vt.* 解答；解决 例 Technology alone cannot ***solve*** the problem of vehicle pollution. 仅仅靠技术不可能解决机动车辆带来的污染问题。
sophisticate* [səˈfɪstɪkeɪt]	*n.* 久经世故的人；精通者 例 Susan isn't the ***sophisticate*** that her classmates imagine her to be. 苏珊并不像她的同学们想的那样是个久经世故的人。
sophisticated [səˈfɪstɪkeɪtɪd]	*a.* 老于世故的，老练的；精密的，尖端的，先进的；复杂的；高雅的，有教养的 搭 a sophisticated columnist 老练的专栏作家 例 Space management is now a highly ***sophisticated*** method of manipulating the way we shop to ensure maximum profit. 空间管理现在已成为一种非常尖端的技术，它通过控制我们的购物方式来实现利润最大化。 派 sophistication(*n.* 精致；复杂) 同 experienced(*a.* 经验丰富的)；proficient(*a.* 精通的，熟练的，娴熟的)；complicated(*a.* 复杂的) 反 unsophisticated(*a.* 不懂世故的；单纯的)
sore [sɔː(r)]	*a.* 痛的；恼火的；剧烈的 *n.* 疮 例 He's had so many colds and ***sore*** throats recently. 他最近常常感冒，嗓子也经常痛。
sorrow [ˈsɒrəʊ]	*n.* 悲哀；伤心事 搭 sorrow at/over sth. 为…感到悲伤 例 Carolyn's eyes filled with ***sorrow*** at thinking of how she had treated Kevin and lost him forever. 想到自己那样对待凯文并永远地失去了他，卡罗琳的眼中充满了悲伤。
source [sɔːs]	*n.* 来源，出处；(河的)源头，发源地；根源，起源 记 联想记忆：这些资源(resource)的来源(source)是哪里? 例 We understand a port as a centre of land-sea exchange, and as a major ***source*** of livelihood and a major force for cultural mixing. 我们把港口看作海陆交换的中心、生计的主要来源以及推动文化融合的重要力量。
souvenir [ˌsuːvəˈnɪə(r)]	*n.* 纪念品，纪念物 记 词根记忆：sou(=sub 在某地) + ven(来) + ir → 在某地游玩带回来的东西 → 纪念品，纪念物 搭 a souvenir shop 纪念品商店 例 We've gathered together a wonderful collection of ***souvenirs***. 我们已经收集了一大批精美的纪念物。
spacecraft [ˈspeɪskrɑːft]	*n.* 航天器，宇宙飞船 记 组合词：space(太空) + craft(技术) → 太空技术 → 航天器，宇宙飞船 例 We've done a lot on the study of ***spacecraft*** returning technique. 我们已在航天器返回技术上做了很多研究工作。

□ solution □ solve □ sophisticate □ sophisticated □ sore □ sorrow
□ source □ souvenir □ spacecraft

spacious* [ˈspeɪʃəs]
a. 宽广的，宽敞的
记 联想记忆：spac（看作 space，空间）+ ious（多…的）→ 空间很多的 → 宽广的，宽敞的
例 I haven't thought that the hotel rooms are so *spacious* and comfortable. 我从来没有想到这家宾馆的房间是如此宽敞而且舒服。

spade [speɪd]
n. 铁锹
例 We need a *spade* if we're going to dig a pit. 如果我们要挖个深坑，就需要一把铁锹。

span [spæn]
n. 跨距；一段时间 *v.* 横跨；持续
例 The workers completed the building within the *span* of three months. 工人们在三个月的时间内建成了这栋大楼。

spare* [speə(r)]
a. 闲置的；备用的，外加的；空闲的 *v.* 省出，抽出(时间等)；饶恕，赦免；免去；不吝惜(时间、金钱等) *n.* 备用品；[*pl.*] 配件
搭 spare part 备件，配件；spare time 闲暇时光；spare a thought for sb. 为某人着想；to spare 多余
例 Thank you very much for *sparing* so much of your time to talk with me. 非常感谢您抽出这么长的时间与我谈话。

spark [spɑːk]
n. 火花
记 联想记忆：s + park（公园）→ 公园经常是燃起爱情火花的地方 → 火花
例 In the Stone Age, tool-makers discovered that chipping flints produced *sparks*. 在石器时代，工匠们发现敲凿燧石能产生火花。

spasm [ˈspæzəm]
n. 痉挛；抽搐；(活动、情感等的)突发，阵发
记 联想记忆：掉入深坑（chasm）突发痉挛（spasm）
搭 facial spasm 面部痉挛；muscle spasm 肌肉痉挛
例 The patient shudders with a sudden *spasm*. 病人突然抽搐，全身发抖。

spasmodic [spæzˈmɒdɪk]
a. 痉挛的；间歇性的
记 联想记忆：spasm（痉挛，阵发）+ odic → 痉挛的
例 Since the arrival of Europeans, the region experienced a period of *spasmodic* activity, between 1831 and 1857. 自从欧洲人来到这个地区，在 1831 到 1857 年间它经历了一个间歇性的活跃时期。

specialise* [ˈspeʃəlaɪz]
v. 专门研究，专攻；专用于，使适应特殊目的
记 来自 special（*a.* 特殊的，专门的）
搭 specialised equipment 专用设备
例 Two years later, we will *specialise* and take courses in one or two subjects. 两年后，我们将专攻一两门学科并学习这些学科的课程。// As the brain evolved, one side became *specialised* for fine control of movement. 随着大脑的进化，大脑的一边开始专门负责对运动进行精密控制。
派 specialisation（*n.* 专门化，特殊化）

41

□ spacious □ spade □ span □ spare □ spark □ spasm
□ spasmodic □ specialise

specialist * [ˈspeʃəlɪst]	*n.* 专家；专科医生 记 联想记忆：special(专门的) + ist(从事某职业的人) → 专家 搭 specialist knowledge 专业知识 例 The professor is one of the world's leading ***specialists*** in the field. 这位教授是该领域内的顶级专家。 派 special(*a.* 特别的；专门的；附加的，额外的)
specialty [ˈspeʃəltɪ]	*n.* 特产；特长 记 来自 special(*a.* 专门的) 例 Cross-country skiing events are a ***specialty*** of cold-weather countries. 越野滑雪赛事是气候寒冷的国家中一道独特的风景线。
species * [ˈspiːʃiːz]	*n.* 种，物种 记 联想记忆：科学家从一些生物物种（species）中选取好的制成标本(specimen) 例 Between 1968 and 1982, the country imported about 50 different ***species*** of dung beetle, from Asia, Europe and Africa. 在 1968 年到 1982 年间，该国从亚洲、欧洲和非洲进口了大约 50 种不同种类的蜣螂。
specific [spəˈsɪfɪk]	*a.* 特定的；明确的 例 Do you have any ***specific*** studying goals for this year? 今年你有具体的学习目标吗? 派 specifically(*ad.* 特定地；明确地)
specification [ˌspesɪfɪˈkeɪʃn]	*n.* [常 *pl.*] 规格，规范；明确说明；(产品等的)说明书 记 联想记忆：specific(明确的) + ation → 明确说明 → 说明书 搭 the specification of a microwave oven 微波炉说明书 例 The house has been built exactly to our ***specifications***. 房子完全是按照我们的工程设计书建造的。 同 clause(*n.* 条款)；instruction(*n.* 指示；用法说明)
specify [ˈspesɪfaɪ]	*v.* 指定；详细说明 记 词根记忆：spec(看) + ify(使…) → 让人看清楚 → 详细说明 例 It is not necessary to ***specify*** quantity when ordering beer. 预定啤酒时无需指定数量。
specimen [ˈspesɪmən]	*n.* 范例，样品；样本，标本 例 Anton is observing the ***specimen*** with a magnifying glass. 安东正在用放大镜观察这个标本。
spectacular [spekˈtækjələ(r)]	*a.* 壮观的；令人惊叹的 *n.* 壮观的场面；精彩的表演 搭 a spectacular success 巨大的成功；make a spectacular of oneself (因行为、穿着)出丑，出洋相 例 Tyler and Jack are seated near floor-to-ceiling windows affording a ***spectacular*** view of the city. 泰勒和杰克坐在落地窗边，壮观市景尽收眼底。
spectator [spekˈteɪtə(r)]	*n.* 观众；旁观者 记 词根记忆：spect(看) + ator → 观众；旁观者 搭 spectator sport 吸引很多观众的体育项目 例 The ***spectators***, as well as the participants, of the ancient Olympics were all male. 古代奥林匹克运动会的观众和运动员全都是男性。

□ specialist □ specialty □ species □ specific □ specification □ specify
□ specimen □ spectacular □ spectator

Word List 42

音频

词根、词缀预习表

splend	明亮	splendid *a.* 壮观的，壮丽的	**stagn**	池塘	stagnate *v.* 停滞；不发展
stan	站立	stance *n.* 姿势；观点	**stat**	坐	static *a.* 静止的，静态的
sti	刺	stimulus *n.* 刺激，促进(因素)	**stat**	声明	statue *n.* 塑像
-less	没有	stainless *a.* 不锈的；无污点的	**stereo**	三维的	stereo *a.* 立体声的
urb	城市	suburb *n.* 郊区	**cess**	走	succession *n.* 连续；接替

spectrum
[ˈspektrəm]

n. 谱，光谱，频谱；范围，幅度

记 词根记忆：spect(看) + rum → 能看到光的颜色 → 光谱

搭 electromagnetic spectrum 电磁光谱

例 Sufferers can fight back by spending a few hours each day under special, full-*spectrum* lamps. 患者可以通过每天在特殊的全光谱灯下照射几小时来缓解(身体的不适)。

同 range(*n.* 范围，幅度)

speculate
[ˈspekjuleɪt]

v. 推测；投机

例 I began to *speculate* about how she was spending her time. 我开始猜测她是如何打发时光的。

speculation
[ˌspekjuˈleɪʃn]

n. 推测，思索；投机活动，投机买卖

例 Rumours that the two singers are about to marry have been dismissed as pure *speculation*. 关于两位歌手要结婚的谣言被证实仅仅是猜测，无人再理会。

sphere*
[sfɪə(r)]

n. 球(体)；范围，领域

记 词根记忆：spher(球) + e → 球(体)

例 Mary's *sphere* of interests is very limited. 玛丽兴趣不广。

spice
[spaɪs]

n. 香料，调味品 *vt.* 使增添趣味；往…加香料

记 联想记忆：曾经风靡一时的英国乐队 Spice Girls (辣妹组合)

例 Variety is the *spice* of life. 多彩的生活才有趣。

spill*
[spɪl]

v. (使)溢出；涌出

记 联想记忆：s + pill(药丸) → 药丸太满了，洒了一地 → 溢出

例 The beer *spilled* from the glass. 啤酒从玻璃杯里溢出来了。

spill

□ spectrum □ speculate □ speculation □ sphere □ spice □ spill

spin* [spɪn]
v. (使)旋转 n. 旋转
例 This action *spins* a series of gears. 这个操作使一连串的齿轮旋转起来。

spine [spaɪn]
n. 脊椎，脊柱；(动植物的)刺，刺毛；书脊；〈喻〉中心
记 联想记忆：s + pine(松树) → 像松树一样挺拔 → 脊柱
例 Twisting movements can place unusual force on your *spine*. 扭转动作会给脊椎带来不寻常的压力。
派 spinal(a. 脊椎的)
同 backbone(n. 脊椎)

spiral [ˈspaɪərəl]
a. 螺旋形的，盘旋的 v. 盘旋上升(或下降)；(物价等)急剧增长 n. 螺旋形；逐渐加速上升(或下降)
记 联想记忆：spir(看作 spire，螺旋) + al → 螺旋形的
搭 spiral staircase 螺旋形楼梯
例 A *spiral* of smoke rose from the chimney. 烟囱里的烟袅袅升起。
派 spire(n. 螺旋)
同 loop(n. 环；线圈)；twist(n. 扭曲；螺旋状)；coil(v. 盘绕，卷)

spiritual [ˈspɪrɪtʃuəl]
a. 精神的；心灵的；宗教的
记 联想记忆：spirit(精神) + ual(形容词后缀) → 精神的
搭 spiritual damage 精神伤害
例 Human *spiritual* needs should match material affluence. 人类的精神需求应该与物质富足相匹配。

spit [spɪt]
v. 吐唾沫(或痰)；喷出 n. 唾液，唾沫
记 联想记忆：s + pit(坑) → 往坑里吐痰 → 吐唾沫
搭 spit out 吐出
例 Don't *spit* at random. 不要随地吐痰。

spite [spaɪt]
n. 恶意，怨恨
搭 in spite of 不管，尽管
例 He put the house up for sale out of *spite* at his family. 他将房子出售是出于对家人的怨恨。

splash [splæʃ]
v. 溅；泼
搭 splash out (on sth.) 花大笔的钱(买某物等)
例 I refreshed myself by *splashing* cold water on my face. 我往脸上扑冷水让自己精神起来。
同 splatter(v. 飞溅)；sprinkle(v. 喷洒)

splendid [ˈsplendɪd]
a. 壮观的，壮丽的，极好的；堂皇的，豪华的；灿烂的，辉煌的
记 词根记忆：splend(明亮) + id → 让人眼前一亮的 → 壮观的
搭 a splendid scene 壮观的场面
例 They marry rich men merely because they are rich and have *splendid* houses. 她们嫁给富人，仅仅是因为富人有钱和豪华的房子。// We've all had a *splendid* time. 我们大家都玩得很开心。

□ spin □ spine □ spiral □ spiritual □ spit □ spite
□ splash □ splendid

splint* [splɪnt]

n. 细木梗；【医】(用于固定受伤肢体的)夹板 *vt.* 用夹板夹

记 联想记忆：sp + lint（棉绒）→ 用棉绒和夹板把病人受伤的腿包扎好 → 夹板

例 These kinds of matches were *splints* coated with sulphur and tipped with potassium chlorate. 这种火柴是由涂上了硫磺、头部黏有氯酸钾的细木梗制成的。

split [splɪt]

v. (使)分裂，分离；(被)撕裂，裂开；劈开；分担，分享 *n.* 裂口；分化，分裂

记 发音记忆："死劈了它" → 劈开 → 分裂

搭 split into... 分成，分开；split from/with sb. 与某人断绝关系，离开某人；split second 瞬间，刹那

例 The party *split* up into several groups. 这个党派分裂成几个集团。

spoil* [spɔɪl]

v. 损坏，破坏，糟蹋；宠坏，溺爱；(食物)变质 *n.* [*pl.*] 战利品，掠夺物，赃物

记 联想记忆：破坏(spoil)土地(soil)，损人不利己

搭 the spoils of office 利用官职捞取的私利

例 He wasn't going to let a headache *spoil* his holidays. 他不想因为头疼而使假期泡汤。

spoilage* [ˈspɔɪlɪdʒ]

n. 变质；损坏

例 Bitterness, he says, alerts us of toxins in the food, while sourness warns us of *spoilage* and saltiness signals the presence of minerals. 他说，苦味提醒我们食物中有毒素，酸味提醒我们食品已变质，而咸味代表存在矿物质。

sponge [spʌndʒ]

n. 海绵 *v.* 用湿海绵(或布)擦，揩

记 发音记忆："死胖子" → 海绵吸饱水像个死胖子 → 海绵

例 He squeezed out water from a *sponge*. 他拧出海绵里的水。

同 rinse(*vt.* 清洗)

sponsor* [ˈspɒnsə(r)]

n. 发起者，赞助人，主办者；主顾 *vt.* 发起，主办；赞助，资助；惠顾

记 联想记忆：spons(看作 spoon，勺子) + or(表人) → 揭勺而起者 → 发起者

例 He is the main *sponsor* of the conference. 他是这次会议的主要发起者。

派 sponsorship(*n.* 资助；赞助款)

sporadically* [spəˈrædɪkli]

ad. 偶发地；零星地

例 Rockets had been used *sporadically* for several hundred years. 在过去的几百年间，火箭被人们偶尔使用。

spot [spɒt]

vt. 认出，发现；看见，注意到 *n.* 地点，处所；斑点，污点；少量

搭 on the spot 当场，在现场；put sb. on the spot 使某人为难；hot spot 热点；a scenic spot 景点

例 You'll *spot* the cinema right next to the underground station. 你会在地铁站旁边看到这家电影院。

spot on

恰好的(地)，准确的(地)

例 I think your idea is *spot on*. 我认为你的主意不错。

□ splint □ split □ spoil □ spoilage □ sponge □ sponsor
□ sporadically □ spot □ spot on

spouse* [spaʊs]	*n.* 配偶 记 联想记忆：sp(看作 spend，度过) + ouse(看作 house，房子) → 在同一间房子里共度人生的人 → 配偶 例 How your child adapts to your divorce is largely dependent on how you and your ***spouse*** act. 你的孩子如何适应你的离婚主要取决于你和你配偶的行为举止。 同 mate(*n.* 配偶)
sprawl* [sprɔːl]	*n.* 四肢伸开的姿势或动作；(城市的)无计划发展 *v.* 伸开四肢坐、卧或倒下；杂乱无序地延伸 记 联想记忆：伸展手脚趴在地上(sprawl)潦草地写(scrawl) 例 Urban ***sprawl*** means that life without a car is next to impossible. 城市的无计划扩张意味着生活中如果没有车几乎寸步难行。
spray* [spreɪ]	*n.* 浪花；喷雾；飞沫 *v.* 喷射，(使)溅洒 记 联想记忆：sp(音似：四泼) + ray(光线) → 光线向四面射去 → 喷射 例 Farmers are ***spraying*** the crops with pesticide. 农民们正在给庄稼喷洒杀虫剂。
spring* [sprɪŋ]	*n.* 春天，春季；弹簧，发条；弹性，弹力；(源)泉；跳跃 *v.* 跳跃；涌现，突然出现；突然提出(或说出) 记 联想记忆：sp + ring(铃声) → 泉水叮咚似铃声 → 泉 搭 spring up 跳起来 例 He was born in the ***spring*** of 1985. 他出生于 1985 年春天。
spur [spɜː(r)]	*n.* 刺激(物)；激励；靴刺，马刺 *vt.* 刺激，激励，鞭策；(用马刺)策马加速 记 联想记忆：NBA 的马刺队就是 Spur 例 Whenever the official holidays approach, many supermarkets ***spur*** the sales by means of promotion. 每当法定假日临近，许多超市就通过促销活动来刺激销售。
squash [skwɒʃ]	*n.* 软式墙网球，壁球 *v.* 压碎，挤压；挤进，塞入；镇住，镇压；制止 记 联想记忆：squ(看作 squeeze，挤) + ash(灰) → 挤成灰 → 挤压 例 The new gym has got an ice rink and a sports hall for ***squash***, badminton, volleyball and several other indoor sports. 新体育馆设有溜冰场和一个可以打壁球、羽毛球、排球和进行其他室内运动的运动大厅。
squeeze [skwiːz]	*v.* 压榨，榨取；捏，挤压；挤入，挤过；向…勒索 *n.* 挤压，捏；紧缺，拮据，经济困难；减少，削减 记 联想记忆：s + quee(看作 queen，女王) + ze → 想与女王握手的人很多 → 挤入，挤过 搭 squeeze toothpaste 挤牙膏；squeeze sth. out 把…挤出来；squeeze your eyes shut 紧紧闭上你的眼睛 例 I made the toast and ***squeezed*** orange juice every morning. 我每天早上都烤面包、榨橙汁。
stab [stæb]	*v.* 刺，戳 例 A lot of people get shot, ***stabbed,*** and decapitated in the fight. 在这场争斗中，有很多人被枪杀、刺死，被斩首。

□ spouse □ sprawl □ spray □ spring □ spur □ squash
□ squeeze □ stab

stabilise [ˈsteɪbəlaɪz]

v. (使)稳定，(使)稳固

记 来自 stable(*a.* 稳定的)

例 The patient's condition has now ***stabilised***. 现在病人的情况已经稳定下来了。

派 stability[*n.* 稳定(性)；稳固(性)]

stable* [ˈsteɪbl]

a. 稳定的，稳固的，安定的；沉稳的，持重的 *n.* 马厩

记 联想记忆：那张破桌子(table)居然很稳(stable)

例 The society will remain ***stable*** over the long term. 社会将保持长期稳定。

stack [stæk]

n. 整齐的一叠(或一堆) *v.* 把…叠成堆，堆放于；堆积，堆起

记 联想记忆：库存(stock)就是一堆(stack)商品

搭 reference stacks 书库；stack-pile wood 堆贮木材；stack up 把…堆起；a stack of hay 一堆草

例 Dishes are ***stacked*** up in a drying rack. 盘子被堆放在一个烘干架上。

staff [stɑːf]

n. 全体职工，工作人员；棒；(军队的)全体参谋人员 *vt.* 为…配备人员；任职于

记 联想记忆：与 stuff(*n.* 材料)一起记

搭 office staff 办公室文员；teaching staff 教职员工

例 Managers estimate ***staff*** productivity in terms of their working hours. 经理通过职员的工作时间来评估他们的生产效率。

stage* [steɪdʒ]

n. 舞台；戏剧；阶段

搭 on/off stage 在台上/台下；stage fright 怯场；at this stage of life 处于这个人生阶段

例 The next ***stage*** of the project was the design phase. 该项目的下一个阶段是设计阶段。

stagnate* [stægˈneɪt]

v. (使)停滞；不发展

记 词根记忆：stagn(=pool 池塘)+ate → 池塘的水不流动 → (使)停滞

例 Real wages have ***stagnated*** since that year. 实际工资从那一年开始就没再涨过。

stain [steɪn]

vt. 染污；给…着色 *n.* 污点

记 联想记忆：一下雨(rain)，到处都是污点(stain)

例 The ink ***stained*** his shirt blue. 墨水给他的衬衫染上了蓝色。

stainless [ˈsteɪnlis]

a. 不锈的；无污点的，无瑕疵的

记 联想记忆：stain(污点)+less(没有) → 无污点的；不锈的

搭 stainless steel 不锈钢

例 It's made of ***stainless*** steel which is guaranteed for 50 years. 它由不锈钢制成，确保可以使用 50 年。

staircase [ˈsteəkeɪs]

n. 楼梯

记 组合词：stair(楼梯)+case(箱，盒) → 楼梯

例 On hearing the fire alarm, all people in the building should evacuate via the ***staircase***. 听到火警后，楼里的所有人都应该通过楼梯撤出大楼。

42

□ stabilise □ stable □ stack □ staff □ stage □ stagnate
□ stain □ stainless □ staircase

stake* [steɪk]	*n.* 桩；火刑柱；利害关系；股份；赌金 *vt.* 以…打赌；拿…冒险 记 联想记忆：s + take(带来) → 带来赌金 → 赌金 搭 at stake 在危险中，处于成败关头 例 They burned this man at the ***stake*** as a heretic. 他们将这个人当作异教徒，对其处以火刑。
stale [steɪl]	*a.* 不新鲜的；陈腐的 记 联想记忆：s + tale(传说) → 传说说多，陈词滥调 → 陈腐的 例 There was a smell of ***stale*** vegetables in the air. 空气中有一股不新鲜的蔬菜的味儿。 同 obsolete(*a.* 陈旧的，废弃的)
stall [stɔːl]	*n.* 货摊；小隔间 记 联想记忆：sta(看作 stand，立) + ll(像两根柱子) → 两根柱子撑起的狭小空间 → 货摊；小隔间 例 Remember to visit the souvenir ***stalls*** in the car park in front of the main entrance to the stadium. 记得到体育馆正门前停车场内的纪念品小店看看。
stammer* [ˈstæmə(r)]	*n.* 结巴，口吃 *v.* 口吃 记 联想记忆：stamm(看作 stamp，邮票) + er → 嘴被贴上了邮票 → 口吃 例 Left-handed children, forced to use their right hand, often develop a ***stammer***. 本来惯用左手的小孩在被迫改用右手后，通常会患口吃。
stamp [stæmp]	*v.* 跺(脚)，重踏；在…上盖(字样或图案等)；重步走 *n.* 邮票，印花；印，图章；标志，印记；跺脚，顿足 搭 stamp tax 印花税；stamp collecting 集邮；commemorative stamp 纪念邮票；visa stamps 签证章 例 You'll have to get this card ***stamped*** and then you come back here with it and pay your union fee. 你先拿这张卡去盖章，然后拿回来交会费。
stance* [stæns]	*n.* 姿势；观点，立场 记 词根记忆：stan(=stand 站立) + ce → 站姿 → 姿势 例 Can you feel how much more comfortable a relaxed ***stance*** is? 以这样一种放松的姿势，你能感觉舒适多了吗?
standard* [ˈstændəd]	*n.* 标准 *a.* 标准的 搭 standard of education 教育标准；better standard of living 更高的生活水平；up to standard 合格 例 Chains of KFC's and McDonald's are setting a new ***standard*** of customer service. 肯德基和麦当劳的连锁店正在制定一套新的顾客服务标准。// Those firms have a ***standard*** raw material inspection procedure. 那些工厂有一套标准的原料检查流程。
standpoint [ˈstændpɔɪnt]	*n.* 立场；观点 记 组合词：stand(站立) + point(观点) → 立场；观点 例 From a completely economical ***standpoint***, the ad is actually more important than the film itself. 单以经济学观点看，这则广告实际上比电影本身更重要。

□ stake □ stale □ stall □ stammer □ stamp □ stance
□ standard □ standpoint

starchy* [ˈstɑːtʃi]

a. 含淀粉的

记 联想记忆：starch(淀粉) + y → 含淀粉的

例 You eat too much ***starchy*** food. 你吃含淀粉类食物太多了。

stare [steə(r)]

n./vi. 盯

记 联想记忆：凝视(stare)星(star)空

例 He ***stared*** at the word trying to remember what it meant. 他盯着这个单词，努力想记起它的意思。

stark* [stɑːk]

a. 光秃秃的，赤裸的；荒凉的；完全的

记 联想记忆：star(星球) + k → 许多星球没有大气，没有生命 → 荒凉的

例 The language barrier presents itself in ***stark*** form to firms who wish to market their products in other countries. 对于那些想把自己的产品销售到其他国家的企业来说，语言成了他们明显的障碍。// Mary was in a ***stark*** madness. 玛丽彻底疯了。

starve* [stɑːv]

v. (使)挨饿；(使)饿死

记 联想记忆：star(明星) + ve → 和明星养尊处优的生活正相反 → 挨饿

例 Thousands of people ***starved*** during the war. 战争中，成千上万的人饿死。

stash* [stæʃ]

vt. 藏匿；贮藏

记 联想记忆：st(看作 stay，在) + ash(灰) → 放在灰里 → 藏匿

例 The bees ***stash*** honey to eat later. 蜜蜂将蜂蜜贮藏起来供以后食用。

statement* [ˈsteɪtmənt]

n. 陈述；声明；报表

记 来自 state(*vt.* 声明)

例 The ***statement*** contradicts the views of the writer. 这些陈述与作者的观点相反。

static [ˈstætɪk]

n. 静电；[-s] 静力学 *a.* 静止的，静态的；呆板的

记 词根记忆：stat(坐) + ic → 坐着的 → 静止的

搭 static electricity 静电，静位觉

例 Some people get ***static*** in their hair. 有些人的头发会产生静电。

stationary [ˈsteɪʃənrɪ]

a. 静止的，不动的，固定的；稳定的

记 联想记忆：station(位置) + ary → 总在同一位置的 → 静止的

搭 a stationary target 固定的目标

例 It seemed to me that there were almost as many serious problems when cars were ***stationary*** as when they were travelling at 90 miles an hour. 对我来讲，车停止不动和以每小时 90 英里的速度行驶出现的严重问题几乎一样多。

同 motionless(*a.* 不动的，静止的)；fixed(*a.* 固定的)

反 mobile(*a.* 移动的)

42

stationery [ˈsteɪʃənri]

n. 文具

例 They manage the Student Union paper shop, selling magazines and newspapers as well as ***stationery*** and sweets. 他们负责管理学生会的报刊亭，销售杂志、报纸，还有文具和糖果。

statistic [stə'tɪstɪk]

n. 统计数值；统计学

记 联想记忆：stat（看作 state，国家）+ istic → 常听到新闻说：据国家统计数据表明 → 统计数值

例 The writer pointed out that the employment ***statistic*** was deceptive. 作者指出这个就业统计数据不可信。

statistically* [stə'tɪstɪkli]

ad. 统计上地

例 If that information is ***statistically*** valid, we can find out what the majority of students prefer. 如果统计数据可靠的话，我们就可以找出大多数学生所喜欢的（课程）。

statistics* [stə'tɪstɪks]

n. 统计数字，统计资料；统计学

例 I'm quite interested in ***statistics*** about the schools in the different zones. 我对不同区域的学校的统计资料很感兴趣。

statue ['stætʃuː]

n. 塑像

记 词根记忆：stat（站）+ ue → 总是站立的东西 → 塑像

搭 the Statue of Liberty 自由女神像

例 The ***statue*** would be perfect but for a few small flaws in its base. 如果不是底座有一些小瑕疵，这尊雕像堪称完美。

派 statuesque（*a.* 雕塑般的）

status ['steɪtəs]

n. 地位；身份；状况

记 联想记忆：stat（看作 state，声明）+ us（我们）→ 声明我们是谁 → 身份

搭 marital status 婚姻状况

例 The chart shows the amount of leisure time enjoyed by men and women of different employment ***status***. 这张图表显示了不同职业身份的男性和女性所享有的闲暇时间量。

steady ['stedi]

a. 稳步的；稳定的 *v.* （使）稳定，（使）平稳；（使）镇定

记 联想记忆：st + eady（看作 ready，准备好的）→ 事先有准备，心里就有底 → 稳的；稳定的

例 The van is making ***steady*** progress through the dark night. 货车在黑夜中平稳行驶。

派 steadily（*ad.* 平稳地）

steam* [stiːm]

n. （蒸）汽，汽雾 *v.* 发出蒸汽；（火车、轮船）行驶；用蒸汽开动

搭 steam engine 蒸汽机

例 The old train is powered by ***steam*** engine. 老式火车由蒸汽机驱动。

steep* [stiːp]

a. 陡峭的；（价格等）过高的；急剧的

记 联想记忆：step（阶梯）中又加一个 e → 更高了 → 陡峭的

例 It's very ***steep*** here and the surface is a little slippery. 这儿很陡，地面还有点滑。

steer [stɪə(r)]

v. 引导；驾驶

记 联想记忆：当你驾驶（steer）的时候，眼睛一定要盯住（stare）前方

例 He ***steered*** his car very carefully along the narrow mountain roads. 他非常小心地驾车行驶在狭窄的山路上。

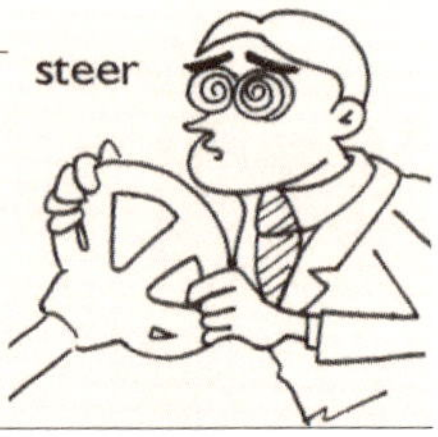

□ statistic □ statistically □ statistics □ statue □ status □ steady
□ steam □ steep □ steer

stem* [stem]

n. 茎；(树)干；词干 *vt.* 止住，抑止，堵住，阻止

搭 stem from 源于

例 As the axe cut through the *stem*, the tree fell. 斧子砍断树干时，树倒了下来。

stereo [ˈsteriəʊ]

a. 立体声的 *n.* 立体声(装置)

记 本身为词根，意为"三维的，立体的"

搭 personal stereos 随身听

例 I've got a fridge and a *stereo* system which I've just bought from a friend. 我刚从一个朋友那里买了一台冰箱和一套立体声音响。

stereoscopic [ˌsteriəˈskɒpɪk]

a. 有立体视觉的；有立体效果的

例 The position of the eyes so restricts the field of vision in baleen whales that they probably do not have *stereoscopic* vision. 由于须鲸眼睛的位置限制了视野，它们可能没有立体视觉。

stick* [stɪk]

v. 刺，戳；黏贴，黏住；卡住，陷住

搭 be stuck on 被…迷住，特别喜欢；get stuck 被迷住

例 The pictures on the wall were simply *stuck* on and so could easily become detached. 墙上的画只是被简单地固定住，所以很容易摘下来。

sticky [ˈstɪki]

a. 黏性的；(天气)湿热的

记 联想记忆：stick(黏贴) + y → 黏性的

例 My fingers are *sticky* from that candy bar. 糖块把我的手指弄得黏糊糊的。

stiff* [stɪf]

a. 硬的，僵硬的 *ad.* 极其，非常

记 联想记忆：可与 still(*a.* 静止的)一起记

例 We felt *stiff* after a long walk. 走了很长一段路后，我们感觉腿脚发僵。// This movie bored me *stiff*. 这部电影让我烦透了。

stimulate [ˈstɪmjuleɪt]

vt. 刺激；使兴奋；激发，激励

例 Why don't we try massaging the feet to *stimulate* blood flow? 我们为什么不试试按摩双足来促进血液循环呢？// The overload principle refers to an athlete *stimulating* a muscle beyond its current capacity. 超负荷法则是指运动员对肌肉施以超过目前承受力的刺激。

stimulus [ˈstɪmjələs]

n. 刺激(物)，促进(因素)

记 词根记忆：sti(刺) + mul + us → 刺激(物)，促进(因素)

例 The bright light is a *stimulus* to the eyes. 强光会刺激眼睛。

stint [stɪnt]

n. 定量；限额

记 联想记忆：定量(stint)支取染发剂(tint)

42

□ stem □ stereo □ stereoscopic □ stick □ sticky □ stiff
□ stimulate □ stimulus □ stint

Word List 43

音频

词根、词缀预习表

stip	一起按压	stipulate *v.* 规定，明确要求	**string**	捆绑	stringent *a.* 严格的，苛刻的
struct	建造	structure *n.* 结构，构造	**sub**	在下面	subordinate *a.* 下级的，次要的
mit	放	submit *v.* 屈从；提交	**merg**	浸没	submerge *v.* 浸没；潜入水中
st	站	substance *n.* 物质；实质	**sid**	坐	subsidy *n.* 津贴，补助金
sequ	跟随	subsequent *a.* 随后的	**scrib**	写	subscribe *v.* 订阅，订购

stipulate
[ˈstɪpjuleɪt]

v. 规定，明确要求；(作为条件)讲定，约定

记 词根记忆：stip(一起按压) + ul + ate(使…) → 使一起按压 → 规定，明确要求

例 The new regulation *stipulates* that every procedure has to comply to the relevant safety production standards. 新制度规定每一个步骤都要遵守相关的安全生产标准。

stir
[stɜː(r)]

v./n. 搅动；摇动；激动

记 本身是词根，意为“刺激”

例 You'd better give the coffee a *stir* before you drink it. 喝咖啡之前最好先搅拌一下。

stitch*
[stɪtʃ]

vt. 缝，缝合 *n.* 一针，针脚

记 联想记忆：stit(看作 sit，坐) + ch → 坐在那里做针线活 → 缝；针脚

搭 drop a stitch (织毛衣时)掉针了；cross stitch 十字绣；back stitch 回针，返针；stitch sth. up 把某物缝合

例 Susan is *stitching* her old clothes. 苏珊正在缝旧衣服。

stock
[stɒk]

n. 储备品；股票；〈总称〉家畜 *v.* 储备 *a.* 常备的

例 Fish *stocks* here began to decline in the 1950s in South Scotland. 在苏格兰南部，鱼类储量从 20 世纪 50 年代开始减少。

stockpile*
[ˈstɒkpaɪl]

n. 囤聚的物资 *vt.* 大量贮备

记 组合词：stock(储备) + pile(堆) → 成堆地储备 → 大量贮备

例 The owner of the factory intended to build up his *stockpile* of raw materials. 该厂主打算增大原料库存。

storey
[ˈstɔːri]

n. 楼层

记 联想记忆：可与 store(*n.* 商店)一起记

例 To the west of where I'm standing, we can see the construction of a seventeen-*storey* building. 从我站的地方往西，可以看到一座 17 层的建筑。

storyline [ˈstɔːrilaɪn]

n. 故事情节

记 组合词：story（故事）+ line（线条）→ 故事情节

例 The pure, innocent love of a young couple became the main *storyline* of this film. 一对年轻夫妻纯真无瑕的爱情是这部电影的主要故事情节。

stout * [staʊt]

a. 发胖的，肥胖的，强壮的；结实的，牢固的；顽强的，坚毅的

记 联想记忆：st（=stand 站）+ out（出来）→ 歹徒行凶，壮小伙站出来 → 强壮的

搭 stout wind 暴风；a stout ship 牢固的船

例 This machine was completely encased in a *stout*, iron cylinder. 这台机器完全置于一个结实的铁筒内。

stove [stəʊv]

n. 炉

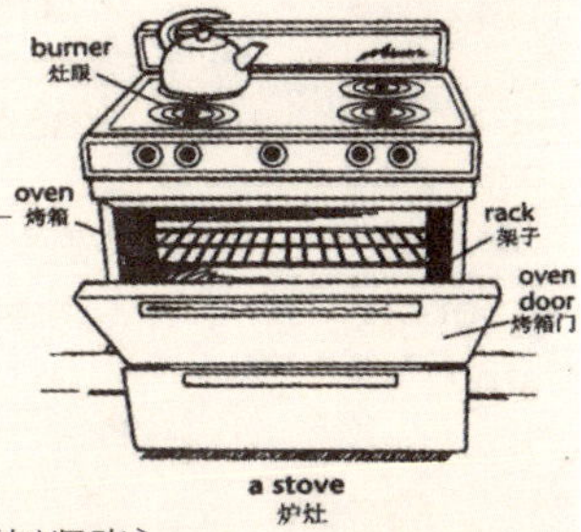

例 This dorm got a television, a fridge, a washing machine, and a new *stove*. 这个宿舍有电视、冰箱、洗衣机和一个新炉子。

strain [streɪn]

v./n. 拉紧，绷紧；扭伤，拉伤；（使）过劳，（使）极度紧张

记 本身为词根，意为"拉紧"

例 Tom *strained* his muscle in the match. 汤姆在比赛中拉伤了肌肉。

同 stretch（*v./n.* 拉伸，伸展）；tense〔*v./n.*（使）紧张〕

strand [strænd]

n. 股，缕；部分，方面

例 There are three distinct *strands* to Sports Studies and you would need to choose fairly early on just which direction you wanted to follow. 运动研究有三个不同的分支，你需要尽早确定研究方向。

同 string（*n.* 线，细绳）；thread（*n.* 线，细丝）

strap * [stræp]

n. 带子 *vt.* 捆扎；（用绷带）包扎

记 联想记忆：和 strip（*n.* 条，带）一起记

例 This *strap* on my briefcase is broken. 我公文包的这根带子断了。

派 strapless（*a.* 无吊带的，无肩带的）；strapped（*a.* 缺钱的，手头紧的）

strategist [ˈstrætədʒɪst]

n. 战略家

记 联想记忆：strateg(y)（战略）+ ist（表人）→ 战略家

例 The Japanese *strategist* talked about the impact of globalization on nations. 那位日本战略家谈到了全球化给各国带来的影响。

strategy [ˈstrætədʒi]

n. 战略，策略

记 联想记忆：str（看作 strange，奇怪的）+ ate（吃）+ gy → 用奇怪的方法吃掉对手 → 战略，策略

搭 marketing strategies 营销策略；reading strategy 阅读策略；research strategy 研究策略

例 The Ottawa Charter presents fundamental *strategies* and approaches in achieving health for all. 《渥太华宪章》提出了实现全民健康的基本策略和方法。

□ storyline □ stout □ stove □ strain □ strand □ strap
□ strategist □ strategy

straw* [strɔː]

n. 稻草；吸管

例 Agnes has a wheelbarrow full of *straw* and manure. 阿格尼丝推着满满一推车的稻草和肥料。

stream* [striːm]

n. 溪流；一股 *v.* 流出

记 联想记忆：s + tream(看作 dream，梦想) → 梦想的河流 → 溪流

例 The leaves were washed by rain into *streams* and rivers. 树叶被雨水冲进小溪与河流。// The wound *streamed* blood. 伤口流血了。

strengthen [ˈstreŋθn]

vt. 加强，巩固

记 联想记忆：strength(力量) + en(使…) → (使)有力量 → 加强，巩固

例 The conference will *strengthen* linkages between the two countries. 本次会议将加强两国的联系。

stress* [stres]

n. 压力；重音；强调，重点，着重 *vt.* 强调；重读

记 联想记忆：s + tress(看作 dress，穿衣) → 穿衣强调个人风格 → 强调

搭 stress management 压力管理

例 Bookstores now abound with manuals describing how to manage time and cope with *stress*. 现在书店里有很多关于如何安排时间、缓解压力的手册。

stretch [stretʃ]

v. 伸展；延伸，延续，拉长；使倾注全力，使紧张 *n.* 一段(时间、路程)；伸展，延伸，延续

搭 at a stretch 一口气地，连续；at full stretch 非常紧张，尽力而为；stretch out 伸展，伸手

例 His feet are *stretched* out to an electric heater. 他的脚伸到了电暖气上。// Mary has not been sufficiently *stretched* at school this term. 玛丽这个学期学习不是太紧张。

strike [straɪk]

v. 打；折磨 *n.* 罢工

例 A small stone *struck* me on the head. 一颗小石块击中了我的头部。// The *strike* quickly spread to other states. 罢工很快波及其他州。

striking [ˈstraɪkɪŋ]

a. 显著的，惹人注目的

例 The most *striking* quality of satiric literature is its freshness. 讽刺文学最显著的特征是它的新颖。

string [strɪŋ]

n. 线；弦；细绳；一串 *vt.* (用绳等)缚；扎；挂；(用线)串起；使排成一列

记 联想记忆：st + ring(铃) → 一串清脆的铃声 → 一串

搭 a piece of string 一根带子；shoe string 鞋带

例 When the motor runs, the *string* will wind up around the shaft. 当发动机开始运转，细绳就会绕着把柄卷起来。

stringent [ˈstrɪndʒənt]

a. (法律、规则等)严格的，苛刻的；(财政状况)紧缩的，短缺的，银根紧的；迫切的

记 词根记忆：string(捆绑) + ent(形容词后缀) → 捆绑起来的 → 银根紧的；苛刻的

例 A *stringent* regulation on security has guaranteed the success of Olympic Games. 严格的安保制度确保了奥运会的成功举办。

□ straw □ stream □ strengthen □ stress □ stretch □ strike
□ striking □ string □ stringent

strip [strɪp]

v. 剥夺；夺去，使空无一物；拆卸，拆开 *n.* 带状物；条纹；狭长地带，带状水域

记 联想记忆：s(音似：死) + trip(旅行) → 死亡剥夺了人的尘世之旅 → 剥夺

例 Topsoils are ***stripped*** and stockpiled prior to mining for subsequent dispersal over rehabilitated areas. 在采矿前先将地表土层挖去并贮存起来用于之后铺在矿区需要恢复的地区。

stripe* [straɪp]

n. 条纹

记 联想记忆：和 strip(*n.* 条纹)一起记

例 This skirt has a red ***stripe*** around the edge. 这条裙子的边上有一圈红色条纹。

stroke [strəʊk]

n. 击，打；(病)突然发作，中风；(体育中的)击球；笔触，一笔；(游泳或划船的)划，划法；一击；报时的钟声；抚摸 *vt.* 抚摸

记 联想记忆：与 strike(*v.* 打击)一起记

例 People who suffer ***strokes*** on the left side of the brain usually lose their power of speech. 左脑中风的人常常会丧失语言能力。

structure* [ˈstrʌktʃə(r)]

n. 结构；构造；建筑物 *vt.* 系统安排；精心组织

记 词根记忆：struct(建造) + ure → 建筑物

搭 management structure 管理结构；economic structure 经济结构

例 The biologist is giving a lecture on cellular ***structures***. 那位生物学家正在做一个有关细胞结构的讲座。

studio [ˈstjuːdiəʊ]

n. 工作室；摄影室；练习室

例 On the other side of the reception area is the dance ***studio***. 接待区的另一边是舞蹈室。

studious [ˈstjuːdiəs]

a. 好学的，学习勤勉的；专心的；谨慎的，认真的，仔细的

记 来自 study(*n./v.* 学习)

例 A belief of "Learning to the ***Studious***" drives him to enter China's most famous university. "学会勤学苦练"这个信仰一直鞭策着他，直到进入中国最好的大学。

同 diligent(*a.* 勤勉的，用功的)

stuff [stʌf]

n. 原料，材料 *vt.* 填进；让…吃饱

搭 stuff... with 填满，塞满；have a stuffed nose 鼻子不通气；the stuff of sth. …的材料

例 The premium coffee like the ***stuff*** we're drinking now is from a type of bean called Arabica. 特级咖啡，就像我们现在喝的，是由一种叫阿拉比卡的咖啡豆制成的。// I am ***stuffed***. 我吃饱了。

stuffy* [ˈstʌfi]

a. 不透气的，(空气)不新鲜的，不通风的；乏味的

记 联想记忆：stuff(填进) + y → 填得满满当当的，很闷 → 不透气的

例 We've installed air conditioning, so it won't get so hot and ***stuffy***. 我们安装了空调，因此不会太闷热。

stylish* [ˈstaɪlɪʃ]

a. 时髦的；漂亮的

搭 stylish hairstyle 时髦的发型

例 Their uniforms are ***stylish***. 他们的制服很时髦。

43

□ strip □ stripe □ stroke □ structure □ studio □ studious
□ stuff □ stuffy □ stylish

subject*

[ˈsʌbdʒɪkt] *n.* 题目；学科；主语 [ˈsʌbdʒekt] *a.* 受…支配的，取决于…的；易遭受…的

搭 be subject to 经受…

例 I'm giving some thoughts to a new book on a different *subject*. 我在构思一本不同题材的新书。

subjective [səbˈdʒektɪv]

a. 主观(上)的

例 Taste and smell were *subjective* senses. 味觉和嗅觉都是主观感觉。

派 subjectivism(*n.* 主观主义，主观论)

同 personal(*a.* 个人的)；intuitive(*a.* 直觉的)

反 objective(*a.* 客观的)

subliminal [ˌsʌbˈlɪmɪnl]

a. 下意识的，潜意识的

记 联想记忆：sub(在…下面) + limin(=limen 最小限度的神经刺激) + al (形容词后缀) → 下意识的，潜意识的

例 How we look sends all sorts of *subliminal* messages to other people. 我们的外表向其他人传达了各种潜在的信息。

派 subliminally(*ad.* 下意识地，潜意识地)

submarine [ˌsʌbməˈriːn; ˈsʌbməriːn]

n. 潜水艇 *a.* 水底的，海底的

submarine

记 联想记忆：sub(在…下面) + marine(海洋的；船舶的) → 在海底航行的 → 潜水艇

搭 submarine cable 海底电缆

例 Residual heat in the *submarine* would disappear very quickly in these Arctic waters. 在北极水域，潜水艇里的余热会迅速消失。

同 underwater(*a.* 水面下的)；submerged(*a.* 在水下的)

submerge [səbˈmɜːdʒ]

v. 浸没；潜入水中

记 词根记忆：sub(在…下面) + merg(浸没) + e → 浸没；潜入水中

例 The city was *submerged* by the flood. 这座城市被洪水淹没了。

submit* [səbˈmɪt]

v. 屈从；提交

记 词根记忆：sub(在…下面) + mit(放) → 放在下面 → 屈从；提交

搭 submit to 递交；屈服

例 After many failures, I *submitted* to fate. 多次失败后，我向命运屈服了。

subordinate

[səˈbɔːdɪnət] *n.* 下属 *a.* 下级的；次要的

[səˈbɔːdɪneɪt] *vt.* 使处于次要地位，把…列在下级；使服从

记 词根记忆：sub(在…下面) + ordin(顺序) + ate → 顺序在下 → 次要的

例 He was always friendly to his *subordinates*. 他一向对下属和蔼可亲。

同 inferior(*a.* 下等的，下级的)；secondary(*a.* 次要的，二级的)

反 superior(*a.* 上级的)

□ subject □ subjective □ subliminal □ submarine □ submerge □ submit □ subordinate

subscribe* [səbˈskraɪb]

v. 订阅，订购；申请，预订

记 词根记忆：sub(在…下面) + scrib(写) + e → 在下面写上名字 → 订阅，订购

例 Which magazines did your father ***subscribe*** to? 你父亲订阅了哪些杂志？

派 subscriber(*n.* 订阅者；用户)

subscription* [səbˈskrɪpʃn]

n. 订阅，订购；订阅费，订购款；捐赠，捐助；签字，签署

例 A statue in his memory was erected by public ***subscription***. 由公众捐资建起一座纪念他的雕像。

subsequent* [ˈsʌbsɪkwənt]

a. 继…之后的，随后的

记 词根记忆：sub(在…下面) + sequ(跟随) + ent → 继…之后的，随后的

搭 subsequent on 作为…的结果发生；subsequent events 后来发生的事

例 This incident was of great importance in the ***subsequent*** development of events. 这一事件对后续事态的发展影响重大。

派 subsequently(*ad.* 随后；接着)

subsidiary [səbˈsɪdiəri]

n. 子公司；附属机构；支流 *a.* 次要的；辅助的，附设的

记 词根记忆：sub（在…下面）+ sid（坐）+ iary → 坐在下面的 → 次要的；辅助的

搭 subsidiary unit 从属单位；a subsidiary company 分公司

例 Ports attract many ***subsidiaries*** and independent industries. 港口城市吸引了很多附属公司和独立产业。

同 subordinate(*a.* 次要的；下级的)；affiliate(*n.* 分支机构)；branch(*n.* 分支，分部)

subsidise* [ˈsʌbsɪdaɪz]

vt. 津贴，资助

记 来自 subsidy(*n.* 津贴，补助金)

例 They actually ***subsidise*** the exploitation and consumption of natural resources. 他们实际上为自然资源的开发和利用提供资助。// Farmers are ***subsidised*** in this country. 该国对农民发放津贴。

subsidy [ˈsʌbsədi]

n. 津贴，补助金

记 词根记忆：sub(在…下面) + sid(坐) + y → 在台下就坐领津贴 → 津贴，补助金

搭 housing subsidies 住房补贴

例 In the rich countries, the annual value of farm ***subsidies*** is immense — about $250 billion. 在经济发达国家，每年的农业津贴都高达约 2500 亿美元。

subsoil* [ˈsʌbsɔɪl]

n. 底土，下层土

记 联想记忆：sub(在…下面) + soil(土壤) → 下面的土壤 → 底土

例 They are analysed to assess the ability of the soil or ***subsoil*** material to support vegetation. 通过分析它们来测定土壤或底土滋养植被的能力。 43

substance* [ˈsʌbstəns]

n. 物质；实质

记 词根记忆：sub(在…下面) + st(站) + ance → 站立的根本 → 实质

例 Tobacco contains 43 cancer-causing ***substances***. 烟草中含有 43 种致癌物质。

□ subscribe □ subscription □ subsequent □ subsidiary □ subsidise □ subsidy
□ subsoil □ substance

substantial* [səb'stænʃl]

a. 可观的，大量的；坚固的，结实的；实质的；大体上的

记 词根记忆：sub(在…下面)+stant(站立)+ial(形容词后缀)→站在下面的→实质的

例 The smoke experienced daily by many people is enough to produce *substantial* adverse effects on the heart and lungs. 很多人日常所吸入的(香烟)烟雾就足以对他们的心脏和肺造成巨大的危害。

派 substantially(*ad.* 充分地；可观地；实质上)

substitute ['sʌbstɪtjuːt]

v. 代替，替换 *n.* 代替者，代替物，代用品

搭 substitute for 代替

例 It is better for a company to employ more workers because people are available to *substitute* for absent staff. 对公司来说，多雇用一些员工大有好处，因为有足够的人手去替代缺勤人员。

substitution [ˌsʌbstɪ'tjuːʃn]

n. 代替，置换；代入法

例 It seems that the director is going to make a *substitution* for the old program. 看起来导演准备替换掉老节目。

subtle ['sʌtl]

a. 细微的，微妙的，难以捉摸的；隐约的；精巧的，巧妙的；诡秘的，狡诈的

记 词根记忆：sub(在…下面)+tle→暗藏于下面的→微妙的；隐约的

例 Many characteristics result from *subtle* interactions between genes and the environment. 许多特征都是通过基因和环境之间微妙的相互作用形成的。

同 delicate(*a.* 微妙的)；intricate(*a.* 难以理解的)；cunning(*a.* 狡猾的)

subtract [səb'trækt]

vt. 减去；去掉

记 词根记忆：sub(在…下面)+tract(拉)→拉下来→减去；去掉

例 That event *subtracts* nothing from his merit. 那件事丝毫没有减损他的美德。

subtropical* [ˌsʌb'trɒpɪkl]

a. 亚热带的

搭 a subtropical climate 亚热带气候

例 The storm is now retrograding to the southeast, into *subtropical* latitudes. 暴风雨正在向东南方退去，进入亚热带地区。

suburb ['sʌbɜːb]

n. 郊区

记 词根记忆：sub(在…下面)+urb(城市)→郊区

例 The hotel in Sydney's southern *suburbs* is the closest to Sydney Airport. 位于悉尼南郊的这家酒店是距悉尼机场最近的酒店。

succeed [sək'siːd]

v. 成功；接着发生

记 词根记忆：suc(在…下面)+ceed(走)→从下面走到上面→成功

搭 succeed in (doing) sth. 在…中取得成功

例 One Winter Olympics has *succeeded* another every four years since 1924, with a break only for the Second World War. 从1924年开始冬奥会每四年举办一次，只在二战期间中断过一次。

succession [sək'seʃn]

n. 连续；接替，继承

记 词根记忆：suc(=sub 在…下面)+cess(走)+ion→在下面走→连续

例 She has won the award for the third year in *succession*. 这是她连续第三年获得此奖项。

□ substantial □ substitute □ substitution □ subtle □ subtract □ subtropical
□ suburb □ succeed □ succession

successive [sək'sesɪv]	*a.* 连续的 例 China's industrial exports went up for five *successive* years. 中国的工业出口额连续五年呈上升趋势。
succumb* [sə'kʌm]	*vi.* 屈服，屈从；(因…)死亡 记 词根记忆：suc(在…下面)+cumb(躺)→躺下不再起来→死亡 例 Since white phosphorus is a deadly poison, match-makers exposed to its fumes often *succumbed* to necrosis. 因为白磷是一种剧毒物质，暴露在其粉尘中的火柴制作工人常常死于坏疽。
sucker ['sʌkə(r)]	*n.* 吸盘；吸根，根出条 记 联想记忆：suck(吸吮)+er→吸盘 例 Bananas are normally grown from *suckers* which spring up around the parent plant. 香蕉树通常由长于母树附近的根出条培育而形成。
suffer* ['sʌfə(r)]	*v.* 遭受，忍受；忍耐；容许；患病；受损失 记 词根记忆：suf(在…下面)+fer(拿来，带来)→带到下面去→遭受，忍受 例 They all *suffer* from chronic back pain. 他们都患有慢性背部疼痛。
suffice [sə'faɪs]	*v.* (使)满足，(使)满意；足够 记 词根记忆：suf(表加强)+fic(做)+e→拼命地工作→(使)满意；足够 搭 suffice (it) to say 只要说…就够了 例 No more boring lectures, painful seminars or tiring presentations. A few sentences will *suffice.* 没有枯燥的说教、痛苦的研讨会或令人厌倦的演讲，几句话就够了。 派 sufficiency(*n.* 充足，足量) 反 lack(*vt.* 缺乏)
sufficient* [sə'fɪʃnt]	*a.* 足够的，充分的 搭 be sufficient for 对…来说足够的，充分的 例 It takes only 10 to 20 minutes of exposure to sunlight a day to ensure *sufficient* vitamin D production. 一天只需接受阳光照射 10 到 20 分钟便可使身体产生足够的维生素 D。 派 self-sufficient (*a.* 自给自足的) 反 insufficient(*a.* 不足的)
suggest* [sə'dʒest]	*v.* 建议，提出；暗示 例 The research *suggests* that women avoid dealing effectively with their economic situation because of a lack of confidence. 研究表明女性由于缺乏信心而不能有效地处理自己的经济状况。 派 suggestive(*a.* 引起联想的)
suicidal* [suːɪ'saɪdl]	*a.* 自杀(性)的；有自杀倾向的 记 词根记忆：sui(自己)+cid(杀)+al(形容词后缀)→自杀(性)的 例 A telephone counseling service in this country gets more calls from people with *suicidal* feelings when it rains. 在这个国家，电话咨询服务在雨天会接到更多有自杀情绪的人打来的电话。

□ successive □ succumb □ sucker □ suffer □ suffice □ sufficient
□ suggest □ suicidal

suitable [ˈsuːtəbl]

a. 适当的，相配的；合适的，适宜的

记 组合词：suit(合适) + able(能…的) → 合适的 → 适当的

搭 suitable for 适宜；suitable time to do sth. 做…的适当时间；a suitable candidate 合适的人选

例 This medicine is not ***suitable*** for children under age 5. 这种药不适合五岁以下儿童服用。

派 suitability(*n.* 合适；适宜性)；suitably(*ad.* 合适地，适宜地，相称地)

suitcase [ˈsuːtkeɪs]

n. 手提箱；衣箱

记 组合词：suit(一套衣服) + case(箱子) → 衣箱

例 Tom travelled by plane last week and his ***suitcase*** was lost. 汤姆上周坐飞机去旅行，把手提箱弄丢了。

sulphuric acid

硫酸

例 He broke a bottle filled with ***sulphuric acid***. 他打碎了一个装有硫酸的瓶子。

summarise [ˈsʌməraɪz]

v. 总结，概括

记 来自 summary(*n.* 摘要，概要)

例 The speaker ***summarised*** the important points of her lecture. 演讲者概括了她演讲中的重点。

派 summarisation(*n.* 摘要，概要)

summary* [ˈsʌməri]

n. 摘要，概要 *a.* 概括的，简略的

记 词根记忆：summ(=sum 总的) + ary → 摘要，概要

搭 in summary 总括

例 Tina gave a ***summary*** of the activity last night. 蒂娜昨晚给出了活动的概要。

summit [ˈsʌmɪt]

n. (山等的)最高点，峰顶

例 A gigantic explosion tore much of the volcano's ***summit*** to fragments. 巨大的爆炸几乎将火山山顶全部炸成碎片。

sundial [ˈsʌndaɪəl]

n. (通过太阳知道时间的)日规；日晷(仪)

例 Moonlight was frosting the dew, and an old ***sundial*** threw a long shadow. 月光把露水照得雪白，一座旧日晷投出一道长长的影子。

superb [suːˈpɜːb]

a. 极好的；高质量的

搭 superb advertisements 精彩的广告

例 The mountains of the central island provide ***superb*** ski facilities in winter. 岛中部的山脉为冬天滑雪提供了绝佳的场地。

superficial [ˌsuːpəˈfɪʃl]

a. 表面的；肤浅的

记 词根记忆：super(在…上面) + fic(做) + ial → 做表面文章 → 表面的

搭 a superficial resemblance 表面上的相似

例 Those who tend to show off in front of other people are so ***superficial*** indeed. 那些喜欢在别人面前炫耀的人实际上相当肤浅。

同 shallow(*a.* 浅的；浅薄的)

□ suitable □ suitcase □ sulphuric acid □ summarise □ summary □ summit
□ sundial □ superb □ superficial

superior
[suːˈpɪərɪə(r)]

a. 上级的，(在职位、地位等方面) 较高的；优越的，优于…的，较…多的；优良的，卓越的；有优越感的，高傲的 *n.* 上级，长官

记 联想记忆：super(在…上面) + ior → 上级的

搭 superior to 比…好的，超过…的

例 Researchers found that a word without a picture is ***superior*** to a word plus a picture in terms of reading efficiency. 研究人员发现，就阅读效率而言，不配图画的文字比配有图画的文字的阅读效率更高。

派 superiority(*n.* 优越性，优势；优越感)

It is not enough to do good; one must do it the right way.

人不仅要做好事，更要以正确的方式做好事。

——英国政治家 莫利 .J.（John Morley, British statesman）

Word List 44

音频

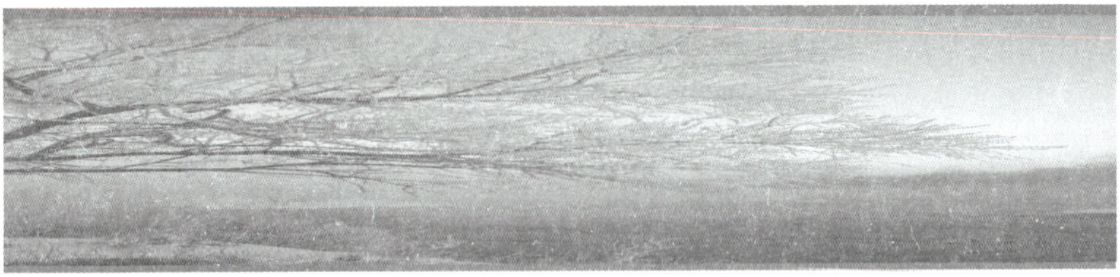

sed	坐	supersede *vt.* 代替，取代	**stit**	站立	superstitious *a.* 迷信的；根据迷信的
vis	看见	supervise *vt.* 监督；管理	**ple**	填满	supplementary *a.* 增补的；补充的
pos	放置	suppose *v.* 假想，假定	**fac**	脸	surface *n.* 表面；外表
cept	捕捉	susceptible *a.* 易受影响的	**vey**	看	survey *n.* 调查，勘察
tain	支持	sustain *v.* 支撑，撑住	**spend**	悬挂	suspend *vt.* 吊，悬挂

supersede [ˌsuːpəˈsiːd]

vt. 代替，取代

记 词根记忆：super(在…之上)+sed(坐)+e→坐在别人的位置上→代替；取代

例 The old theory has been ***superseded*** by more recent research. 旧的理论已经被较新的研究取代了。

superstitious [ˌsuːpəˈstɪʃəs]

a. 迷信的；根据迷信的，由迷信引起的；受迷信思想支配的

记 词根记忆：super(在…之上)+stit(站立)+ious→站立在他物之上的→迷信的；受迷信思想支配的

例 The majority of people don't believe in the old ***superstitious*** saying that the number 13 is unlucky. 大多数人都不相信"数字13不吉利"这一古老的迷信说法。

supervise [ˈsuːpəvaɪz]

vt. 监督，管理；指导

记 词根记忆：super(超过)+vis(看见)+e→在超出别人高度的地方看→监督，管理；指导

例 Mary ***supervises*** the work of the department. 玛丽指导该部门的工作。

派 supervisory(*a.* 管理的，监督的)

同 administer(*vt.* 管理)；superintend(*vt.* 管理，监督)

supervision [ˌsuːpəˈvɪʒn]

n. 监督，管理；指导

例 Students are prohibited from handling these chemicals unless they are under the ***supervision*** of a tutor. 学生们禁止接触这些化学药品，除非在老师的指导之下。

supervisor* [ˈsuːpəvaɪzə(r)]

n. 监督人，管理人，指导者；主管

例 We have to put ourselves into the role of the manager or ***supervisor***. 我们必须要融入经理或主管的角色。

supplement

[ˈsʌplɪment] *vt.* 补充，增补 [ˈsʌplɪmənt] *n.* 增补(物)，补充(物)；补遗；增刊；附录

记 联想记忆：supple(看作 supply，补给) + ment → 增补，补充

搭 supplement to 对…的补充；vitamin supplements 维生素补充剂

例 A student loan is intended to ***supplement*** living costs of students. 学生贷款旨在补贴学生的生活费用。

supplementary
[ˌsʌplɪˈmentri]

a. 增补的，补充的

记 词根记忆：sup(在下面) + ple(填满) + ment + ary → 在下面填满的 → 增补的，补充的

例 The man can clearly tell you the need for ***supplementary*** measures if one wants to assist the rural poor. 那个人可以清楚地告诉你扶助农村贫民过程中配套措施的必要性。

派 supplementation(*n.* 增补，补充)

同 additional(*a.* 另外的，附加的)；extra(*a.* 额外的)

supply*
[səˈplaɪ]

n. 供给，供应(量)；[常 *pl.*] 存货，必需品 *vt.* 供给，供应；满足(需要)，弥补(不足)

搭 supply sth. to sb. 为某人提供…

例 Underground water sources in Australia ***supply*** about 18% of the total water consumption. 澳大利亚用水供给的 18%来自地下水。

supportive*
[səˈpɔːtɪv]

a. 支持的，支援的；赞助的；鼓励的；同情的

记 来自 support(*vt.* 支持，拥护；赞助)

例 Children can often do better at school for they have ***supportive*** parents. 有父母的支持，孩子们在学校常常会表现得更好。

suppose*
[səˈpəʊz]

v. 假想，假定，猜想，推测；[用于祈使句]假定，让；[常用于被动语态] 期望做（某事），认为应该做（某事）

记 词根记忆：sup(在下面) + pos(放置) + e → 私下将某种猜测放在心中 → 假想，猜想

搭 be supposed to do sth. 应该做…

例 I ***suppose*** you're going to tell me the whole history of banana growing now, aren't you? 我猜你是打算现在给我讲解香蕉种植的整个历史，对吗？

suppress
[səˈpres]

vt. 压制，镇压；禁止发表，查禁；抑制(感情等)，忍住；阻止…的生长(或发展)

记 联想记忆：sup(向下) + press(压) → 压下去 → 压制，镇压

例 I know life is hard to you, so don't ***suppress*** the tears, as tears on the face is better than hurt to heart. 我知道你的生活很艰难，所以不要强忍泪水，脸上流泪总好过内心受伤！

派 suppressant(*n.* 抑制剂)

同 squash(*v.* 镇压，压制)；restrain(*vt.* 抑制，压制)

suppression* [səˈpreʃn]	*n.* 镇压，压制，抑制；扑灭 记 来自 suppress(*vt.* 镇压；抑制) 搭 fire suppression system 灭火系统
surf [sɜːf]	*v.* 冲浪 记 发音记忆："舒服"→冲浪很舒服→冲浪 例 The rugged west coast beaches were famous for ***surfing***. 蜿蜒曲折的西海滩因适合冲浪而闻名。
surface* [ˈsɜːfɪs]	*n.* 表面；外表，外观 *v.* 浮出水面；浮现，显露；在…上加表面 记 词根记忆：sur(在…之上)+fac(脸)+e→脸的上面→表面；外表 搭 on the surface 表面上，从外表看，乍一看 例 It seems like a difficult problem on the ***surface***, but in fact it is easy to solve. 这个问题表面上看起来很难，但实际上很容易解决。
surge* [sɜːdʒ]	*v.* (人群等)蜂拥而出；波动，涌动 *n.* (感情等的)洋溢；猛增 记 联想记忆：s+urge(急迫的)→水流湍急→波动，涌动；洋溢 例 Magma had ***surged*** into the volcano from the Earth's mantle. 岩浆从地幔流出，涌入火山。 同 throng(*v.* 大群地移动，拥塞)；gush(*v.* 涌出)；rise(*n./v.* 上升，增加)
surgeon* [ˈsɜːdʒən]	*n.* 外科医生 记 联想记忆：surge(波动)+on→做外科医生，情绪不能太波动→外科医生 搭 a dental surgeon 牙医 例 The ***surgeon*** sewed up the wound. 外科医生缝合了伤口。
surgery [ˈsɜːdʒəri]	*n.* 外科学；外科手术；手术室，诊疗室 搭 heart bypass surgery 心脏搭桥手术 例 They perform ***surgery*** between 9:00 and 11:30 every weekday. 他们在每个工作日的9:00到11:30做手术。
surpass* [səˈpɑːs]	*v.* 超过，超越，优于，胜过；超过…的界限，非…所能办到(或理解) 记 联想记忆：sur+pass(通过)→在上面通过→超过 例 His success has ***surpassed*** all expectations. 他所取得的成功远远超过了预期。 同 exceed(*vt.* 超越，胜过)；surmount(*vt.* 超越，战胜)
surround [səˈraʊnd]	*vt.* 围绕；包围 记 联想记忆：sur+round(圆)→在圆的外边→围绕；包围 搭 be surrounded by sth. 被…围绕；surround yourself with sth. 用…把自己包围住 例 We have ***surrounded*** this city. 我们已经包围了这座城市。
surroundings* [səˈraʊndɪŋz]	*n.* 周围的事物，环境 搭 working surroundings 工作环境 例 Those who could afford to live in more pleasant ***surroundings*** moved out. 那些支付得起更舒适的环境的人都搬了出去。

□ suppression □ surf □ surface □ surge □ surgeon □ surgery
□ surpass □ surround □ surroundings

surveillance
[sɜːˈveɪləns]

n. 监视，盯梢

记 联想记忆：survei(看作 survey，调查) + llance → 通过观看来调查 → 监视，盯梢

搭 surveillance equipment 监视设备

例 The diplomat was placed under police ***surveillance***. 这名外交官被置于警察的监视之下。

survey*

[ˈsɜːveɪ] *n.* 调查，勘察；测量，勘测；审视

[sɜˈveɪ] *vt.* 调查，检视(建筑物等)；测量，勘测；俯瞰，眺望

记 词根记忆：sur(在…之上) + vey(看)→ 从上往下看 → 调查

搭 sample survey 抽样调查；land survey 土地测量；survey of reading habits 阅读习惯调查；a geological survey 地质勘测

例 A recent ***survey*** of staff found that 90 percent welcomed having clothing which reflected the corporate identity. 最近的一项员工调查发现，90%的员工表示欢迎能够反映企业形象的工装。

survive*
[səˈvaɪv]

v. 活下来；幸免于；比…活得长，比…长命

记 词根记忆：sur(在…之上，越过) + viv(生活，度过) + e → 活得更长久→ 比…活得长

例 For most animal species, individuals are less likely to ***survive*** and reproduce. 对于大多数动物物种来说，个体似乎更难存活以及繁衍后代。

派 survival(*n.* 生存；幸存)

susceptible
[səˈseptəbl]

a. 易受影响的，易受伤害的；易受感染的；(人)敏感的，易动感情的；能经受…的，容许…的

记 词根记忆：sus(表加强) + cept(捕捉) + ible(能…的) → 容易被捕捉的 → 易受影响的，易受伤害的

搭 be susceptible to 易受…影响，对…过敏；be susceptible of 容许…的，可能…的

例 A large number of TV advertisement are aimed at ***susceptible*** young women who always buy goods they actually don't need. 大量的电视广告瞄准易受影响的年轻女性，她们总是购买一些实际上并不需要的东西。

派 susceptibility(*n.* 易感性)

同 allergic(*a.* 过敏的)；vulnerable(*a.* 易受攻击的；易受影响的)

反 immune(*a.* 免疫的，不受影响的)

suspect*
[səˈspekt]

v. 猜想，怀疑

记 词根记忆：su(s)(在…下面) + spect(看) → 在下面看一看 → 怀疑

搭 suspect of sth./doing sth. 怀疑…

例 Scientists ***suspected*** it to be a comet. 科学家怀疑它是一颗彗星。

派 suspicious(*a.* 疑心的；可疑的)

44

suspend* [sə'spend]

vt. 吊，悬挂；推迟；暂停，中止

记 词根记忆：sus(在…下面) + pend(悬挂) → 悬挂于之下 → 暂停

搭 suspend a driving license 吊销驾照；suspend payment 暂停付款

例 The party representative ***suspended*** the talk with the government. 该党代表暂停了和政府的对话。

派 suspended(*a.* 暂停的；缓期的)；suspender(*n.* [常 *pl.*]吊裤带)

sustain* [sə'steɪn]

v. 支撑，撑住，承受住；维持，保持；经受，遭受，忍耐

记 词根记忆：sus(在…下面) + tain(支持) → 维持，保持

搭 sustain hardships 忍受艰苦；sustain a person's spirit 使某人振作；sustain growth 维持增长

例 Thousands of lakes are so polluted that they can no longer ***sustain*** fish life. 数千个湖泊受到非常严重的污染，已无法再维持鱼类的生存。

sustainable [sə'steɪnəbl]

a. 可以忍受的；足以支撑的；养得起的

记 来自 sustain(*v.* 维持)

搭 sustainable development 可持续发展

例 As a win-win technology between human and nature, green science and technology is the essential way to ***sustainable*** development. 作为一种人与自然双赢的科学技术，绿色科技是通向可持续发展的必由之路。

swallow ['swɒləʊ]

v. 吞咽；忍受 *n.* 燕子

例 One should never ***swallow*** his words. 人们应坚守诺言。

swamp [swɒmp]

vt. 淹没；使应接不暇 *n.* 沼泽

例 The tsunami ***swamped*** the port city. 海啸吞没了这座港口城市。

同 overwhelm(*vt.* 淹没；压倒)；marsh(*n.* 湿地，沼泽)

swap* [swɒp]

v./n. 交换

例 Don't ***swap*** horses when crossing a stream. 过河勿换马/危难之时不宜作大变动。

同 exchange(*vt./n.* 交换)；trade(*v.* 交换)

swear [sweə(r)]

v. 宣(誓)；诅咒

例 Before giving evidence, you must ***swear*** what you're going to say is true. 作证前，你必须宣誓保证所说一切皆属实。

swell [swel]

v. 膨胀；增长，增强

记 联想记忆：那种气味(smell)在增长(swell)，越来越难闻

例 It was the pressure inside the mountain that made it ***swell***. 山体内部的压力使它膨胀。

swift [swɪft]

a. 快的；敏捷的，迅速的

例 Hong Kong has cheap, ***swift*** and effective public transport. 香港的公共交通便宜、快捷且高效。

swing* [swɪŋ]

v. 摇摆；(使)突然转向 *n.* 摇摆；秋千

记 联想记忆：s + wing(翅膀) → 摇摆翅膀，在风中盘旋 → 摇摆

例 The bus ***swung*** sharply to the left. 公共汽车猛地拐向左边。

□ suspend □ sustain □ sustainable □ swallow □ swamp □ swap
□ swear □ swell □ swift □ swing

switch* [swɪtʃ]

n. 开关；转换 *v.* (使)改变，转变；转换；对调

例 A *switch* was flipped and the machine began to whirl at 300 revolutions per minute. 按下开关，机器开始以每分钟 300 转的速度旋转。

swivel [ˈswɪvl]

v. 旋转 *n.* 转环，转节

例 The old man sat down on a squeaky *swivel* chair and dozed fitfully. 老人坐在嘎吱作响的转椅里，断断续续打着瞌睡。

symbol* [ˈsɪmbl]

n. 象征；符号

例 The sounds of boat whistles or the moving tides are *symbols* of a port city. 汽笛声和海浪声是港口城市的象征。

派 symbolic(*a.* 象征的；符号的)

symbolism [ˈsɪmbəlɪzəm]

n. 符号的使用；(尤指文艺中的)象征主义，象征手法

例 I have been exploring how well blind people understand the *symbolism* behind shapes such as hearts that do not directly represent their meaning. 我一直在探索盲人对形状(如心形)背后的象征意义的理解程度，这些形状并不直接代表它们自身的意义。

sympathetic [ˌsɪmpəˈθetɪk]

a. 同情的，体谅的；赞同的，支持的；和谐的

记 词根记忆：sym(共同) + path(感觉) + et + ic(形容词后缀) → 有着共同感觉的 → 同情的

例 Lena just needed someone who would lend a *sympathetic* ear to her. 丽娜只需要有人能听她诉诉苦。

sympathise [ˈsɪmpəθaɪz]

vi. 同情；赞同

例 Although he pretended to *sympathise*, I knew he was laughing up his sleeve. 虽然他装作同情，但我知道他正暗自偷笑。

sympathy [ˈsɪmpəθi]

n. 同情；赞同，支持

记 词根记忆：sym(共同) + path(感觉) + y → 怀有相同的感觉 → 同情

例 This seeming *sympathy* didn't soothe her distress. 这种表面上的同情并不能减轻她的悲痛。

symphony [ˈsɪmfəni]

n. 交响乐

记 词根记忆：sym(共同) + phon(声音) + y → 奏出共同的声音 → 交响乐

例 The audience were all enchanted by the engrossing *symphony*. 交响乐美妙绝伦，听众全都陶醉其中。

同 concord(*n.* 和谐，一致)；harmony(*n.* 协调，和谐)

反 discord(*n.* 不一致，不和谐)

symptom [ˈsɪmptəm]

n. 症状；征候，征兆

记 词根记忆：sym(一起) + pto(掉下) + m → 一起掉下来的 → 症状；征候

搭 symptom for …的症状；late symptoms 迟发症状；clinical symptoms 临床症状；deficiency symptoms 营养缺乏症状；the symptoms of cancer 癌症症状

例 This disease has some *symptoms* similar to a cold. 这种病的某些症状与感冒的相似。

synchronise*
[ˈsɪŋkrənaɪz]

v. (使)同步发生，同速进行

搭 synchronised swimming 花样游泳

例 There's an indoor arena for gymnastics, a stadium for track and field and a swimming pool for races and ***synchronised*** swimming and also diving. 这里有个室内体操馆、一个田径运动场，和一个用于游泳比赛、花样游泳和跳水的泳池。

synthesis
[ˈsɪnθəsɪs]

n. 综合，合成；综合体

记 联想记忆：syn(共同) + thesis(论题) → 将相同的论题综合起来 → 综合

搭 the synthesis of art 综合艺术

例 You need to make a ***synthesis*** of all the ideas I heard in the lecture. 你需要把我在演讲中听到的全部意见综合一下。

synthetic
[sɪnˈθetɪk]

a. 人造的；合成的，综合的 *n.* 合成物；合成纤维(织物)

记 词根记忆：syn(一起) + thet(放) + ic(形容词后缀) → 放到一起的 → 合成的，综合的

搭 synthetic material 合成材料；synthetic dye 合成染料

例 Some clothes in the market including natural fibre silk and ***synthetic*** ones could not be crushed easily. 市面上一些含天然纤维真丝和合成纤维的衣服不易起皱。

派 synthetically(*ad.* 综合地，合成地)

systematic*
[ˌsɪstəˈmætɪk]

a. 系统的，体系的

记 来自 system(*n.* 系统)

例 Experts in chemical are trying to find ***systematic*** attempt to destroy the organization. 化学方面的专家正致力于找出系统的方法去摧毁该组织。

tab
[tæb]

n. 标签

例 The girl wrote her name on the ***tabs*** of all her books. 那个女孩儿在自己所有书的标签上都写上了自己的名字。

tablet
[ˈtæblət]

n. 药片

例 Do not take Borodine ***tablets*** before consulting your doctor. 在咨询医生前请不要服用鲍罗丁药片。

tackle
[ˈtækl]

v. 对付，处理；向某人提起(问题或困难情况)；(足球等比赛中)抢截，抢球
n. 用具，器具；滑轮(组)，滑车；(足球等比赛中)抢截

记 联想记忆：tack(钉) + le → 除去眼中钉 → 对付，处理

搭 block and tackle 滑轮，滑车设备；fishing tackle 钓具；tackle sb. about sth. 与某人就其事进行交涉

例 The disappointing results of many conventional road transport projects in Africa led some experts to rethink the strategy by which rural transport problems were to be ***tackled*** at the beginning of 1980s. 因为非洲许多传统公路运输项目的结果令人失望，一些专家重新思考战略，希望农村交通问题能在20世纪80年代初得到解决。

派 tackler(*n.* (足球等的)拦截队员)

□ synchronise □ synthesis □ synthetic □ systematic □ tab □ tablet
□ tackle

tag
[tæg]

n. 标签；附加语 *v.* 跟随；给…加标签；添加

记 联想记忆：在包（bag）上贴标签（tag）

例 If you are going to see the film, would you mind if I *tag* along? 你要是去看电影，我也跟着去行吗？

tan
[tæn]

n. 棕褐色；晒黑 *v.*（使）晒成棕褐色，晒黑；硝（皮）

例 These shoes are *tan*, not dark brown. 这些鞋是棕褐色的，不是深褐色的。

同 sunburn（*n./v.* 晒黑）

tangibly*
[ˈtændʒəbli]

ad. 可触摸地；可感知地；有形地

记 词根记忆：tang（=touch 触摸）+ ibl（=ible 能…的）+ y → 可触摸地

例 This improvement, while not *tangibly* measurable, has increased the ability of management. 这一进步，虽然没法具体衡量，但是提高了管理能力。

tanker
[ˈtæŋkə(r)]

n. 油轮；油罐车；加油飞机

记 词根记忆：tank（大容器；油箱）+ er → 装油的大容器 → 油轮；油罐车

搭 an oil tanker 油轮；运油车

例 She looked around for any kind of vehicle and then found an abandoned fuel *tanker*. 她四处寻找车辆，随后发现了一辆废弃的油罐车。

tap
[tæp]

v. 轻拍；利用，开发

例 Water from these subterranean lakes can be pumped to the surface and *tapped*. 可以将这些地下湖泊中的水抽出地面加以利用。

target*
[ˈtɑːɡɪt]

n. 目标；对象，靶子 *vt.* 对准，面向

记 联想记忆：tar（音似：她）+ get（得到）→ 我的目标是得到她 → 目标

搭 target sth. at/on sb./sth. 把…作为…的目标

例 Everyone should have a *target* in mind for the first year of college life. 每个人在大学生活的第一年都应该有个目标。

tariff
[ˈtærɪf]

n. 关税，税率；（旅馆、饭店等的）价目表

例 Taxi companies are using revenue management to set their *tariffs*. 汽车租赁公司用收入管理来制定他们的收费标准。

taunt
[tɔːnt]

vt. 嘲笑，讥笑 *n.*［常 *pl.*］嘲弄的言语，讥讽

例 People used to tease and *taunt* him with his cowardice. 过去人们常嘲讽他的胆小怕事。

teamwork*
[ˈtiːmwɜːk]

n. 协力合作，团队合作；配合

例 An important part of *teamwork* is having trust in your colleagues' ability. 团队协作重要的一点就是要相信同事的能力。

tease
[tiːz]

v. 逗乐，奚落，戏弄；强求 *n.* 揶揄，戏弄，取笑；逗弄者，取笑者

记 联想记忆：tea（茶）+ se → 以茶代酒，戏弄别人 → 揶揄，戏弄

搭 tease sth. out 探讨，深入研究

例 I used to get *teased* about my name until I changed it last year. 在去年我改了名字之前，别人总笑话我的名字。

同 kid（*v.* 开玩笑，取笑）；toy（*vi.* 玩弄）

□ tag □ tan □ tangibly □ tanker □ tap □ target
□ tariff □ taunt □ teamwork □ tease

technical ['teknɪkl]

a. 技术的，工艺的

记 词根记忆：techn(技艺) + ical → 技术的

搭 technical suport 技术支持；a technical education 技术教育；technical college 工学院；technical hitch 技术故障，机件故障

例 This job requires someone with specialized *technical* knowledge. 该工作要求具备专门的技术知识。

technician [tek'nɪʃn]

n. 技术员，技师

记 词根记忆：techn(技艺) + ician(表人) → 技术员，技师

例 This looseness in molecular structure of glass allows *technicians* to tailor it to whatever they need. 玻璃松散的分子结构使技术人员可以按照自己的需求对其进行加工。

technique [tek'niːk]

n. 技巧，技艺；技术，技能

记 词根记忆：techn(技艺) + ique(看作 ic，…术) → 技术

搭 marketing techniques 营销技巧

例 A new style of architecture was made possible by new materials and construction *techniques*. 新的建筑材料和建筑技术使新的建筑风格得以实现。

tedious ['tiːdiəs]

a. 冗长乏味的，单调的

搭 a tedious story 乏味冗长的故事

例 The audience became sleepy by the speaker's *tedious* story. 演讲者冗长乏味的故事使得听众昏昏欲睡。

同 boring(*a.* 无聊的，乏味的)

teem

teem* [tiːm]

vi. 倾泻；充满，遍布

记 联想记忆：和 team(*n.* 群，队)一起记

例 To create new colonies, a healthy hive, *teeming* with bees, can be separated into two boxes. 为了培育新的蜂群，可以将一个装满蜜蜂的健康蜂箱分成两个。

telegraph ['telɪgrɑːf]

n. 电报机；电报 *v.* 打电报，发电报；(无意中)泄露，流露

记 词根记忆：tele(远的) + graph(写) → 以书写的方式带来远处的东西 → 电报机；电报

例 With development of technology, *telegraph* as a means of communication has been gradually replaced by mobile phone, Internet and other media means. 随着技术的进步，电报这种交流方式已经逐渐被手机、互联网和其他媒介所取代。

telescope* ['telɪskəʊp]

n. 望远镜

记 词根记忆：tele(远) + scop(看) + e → 往远处看时所借助的工具 → 望远镜

例 Through a *telescope* the planet appears as a small bluish-green disc. 这颗行星在望远镜里看起来就像是一张很小的蓝绿色光盘。

□ technical □ technician □ technique □ tedious □ teem □ telegraph □ telescope

temper *

['tempə(r)]

n. 情绪 *vt.* 使缓和

记 联想记忆：情绪（temper）会影响体温（temperature）

例 It is generally believed that *tempers* grow shorter in hot, muggy weather. 人们普遍认为在闷热的天气里更容易发脾气。

temporary

['temprəri]

a. 临时的，暂时的

搭 temporary employment/work 临时工作

例 Coal mining makes only *temporary* use of the land and produces no toxic chemical wastes. 采煤业只是暂时使用煤矿所在的土地，不会产生任何有毒的化学废弃物。

派 temporarily(*ad.* 临时地)

tempt *

[tempt]

vt. 引诱；吸引

记 本身为词根，意为"尝试"→受到诱惑而尝试→吸引；引诱

例 Some worry that governments and industries will be *tempted* to use the technology to monitor individual behaviours. 一些人担心，政府和企业有意使用这一技术来监控个人行为。

同 appeal(*vi.* 有吸引力)；entice(*vt.* 诱惑，怂恿)

tenable *

['tenəbl]

a. 站得住脚的；可防守的

记 词根记忆：ten(维持，保持)+able→能够维持的→站得住脚的

例 Tom thought his approach was *tenable*. 汤姆认为他的方法是站得住脚的。

tenant *

['tenənt]

n. 承租人；房客；佃户

记 联想记忆：ten(十)+ant(蚂蚁)→十只蚂蚁来住店，虽小也是客→房客

搭 a sitting tenant 老房客

例 The furniture was left by the former *tenant*. 这些家具是上个房客留下来的。

同 lodger(*n.* 投宿者)；leaseholder(*n.* 承租人)

tend *

[tend]

v. 倾向于，趋于；照料；招待

例 Women *tend* to research thoroughly before applying for positions or attending interviews. 在申请职位或是参加面试前，女性往往会(对应聘公司及职位)进行全面彻底的了解。

tendency *

['tendənsi]

n. 倾向，趋向

记 词根记忆：tend(伸展)+ency→倾向，趋向

搭 tendency to do sth. 做…的趋势；tendency towards sth. …的趋向/趋势

例 The effort to clean up cars may do little to cut pollution if nothing is done about the *tendency* to drive them more. 驾驶汽车的人越来越多，如果不采取措施遏制这一趋势，那么即使下力气对汽车进行清理整顿，这对减少污染也不会起到什么作用。

44

□ temper □ temporary □ tempt □ tenable □ tenant □ tend
□ tendency

Word List 45

音 频

词根、词缀预习表

log	说	terminology *n.* 专门用语，术语	terr	地	terrace *n.* 一层梯田；阳台
termin	边界	terminal *n.* 终点，终端	the	看，考虑	theory *n.* 理论，原理
text	编织	texture *n.* 质地，纹理	therm	热	thermal *a.* 热的，热量的
tim	害怕	timid *a.* 胆小的；羞怯的	tox	毒	toxin *n.* 毒素，毒质
tor	转动	torrent *n.* 洪流；爆发	tor	扭曲	torment *n.* 痛苦，折磨

tender
[ˈtendə(r)]

a. 嫩的；脆弱的；温柔的

记 联想记忆：婴儿太脆弱(tender)，需悉心照料(tend)

例 Chicken is *tender* and delicious. 鸡肉肉嫩味美。

tense
[tens]

a. 拉紧的 *v.* (使)拉紧

记 发音记忆："弹死"→没有弹性→拉紧的

例 When pain strikes, we attempt to keep the back as immobile as possible, which makes the muscles *tense* up. 当疼痛来袭时，我们尽最大努力保持背部不动，这样会使肌肉紧绷。

派 tension(*n.* 紧张)

tensile
[ˈtensaɪl]

a. 拉力的，张力的；可延展的，可伸长的

搭 tensile force 张力

例 The cables, made of high *tensile* steel, are the bridge's main support. 这种具有高抗拉强度的钢索是这座大桥的主要支撑。

terminal
[ˈtɜːmɪnl]

n. 终点，终端；终点站，航站楼 *a.* 末端的

记 词根记忆：termin(边界) + al → 末端的

例 There is an ink jet printer attached to each *terminal*. 每一个终端都连接有一台喷墨打印机。

terminology*
[ˌtɜːmɪˈnɒlədʒi]

n. (某学科的)专门用语，术语

记 词根记忆：termin(界限) + o + log(说) + y → 仅限于一部分人使用的语言 → 术语

例 I don't understand scientific *terminologies*. 我不懂科学术语。

terrace
[ˈterəs]

n. 一层梯田；一排并列的房子；阳台

记 词根记忆：terr(地) + ace → 一层梯田；一排并列的房子

例 A *terrace* of five homes is under way beside my house. 我的房子旁边正在建造一幢能够居住五户的连排房。

terrain [tə'reɪn]

n. 地形，地势

记 词根记忆：terr(地) + ain → 地形，地势

例 Five speed bicycles are best suited to riding over long distances or hilly *terrain*. 五档位变速自行车最适用于长途旅行或者崎岖多山的地形。

同 landform(*n.* 地形)

terrestrial [tə'restriəl]

a. 陆地的，陆生的，陆栖的；地球的

记 词根记忆：terr(地) + estr + ial → 陆地的，陆生的

搭 terrestrial life 地球生物

terrify* ['terɪfaɪ]

vt. 使恐怖，使惊吓

例 Uniforms for the military were originally intended to impress and even *terrify* the enemy. 穿着军装的最初目的是为了给敌人留下深刻印象甚至是将他们吓退。

territory* ['terətri]

n. 领土，版图；领域，范围

记 词根记忆：terr(地) + it + ory(表地点，名词后缀) → 领土；领域

例 We must realize that Antarctic *territory* belongs to everyone. 我们必须意识到南极的领土属于大家。

派 territorial(*a.* 领土的)

textile* ['tekstaɪl]

n. 纺织品

记 联想记忆：text(编织) + ile → 纺织品

例 From the seventeenth century, the company began to export *textiles* to North America. 从 17 世纪起，这家公司就开始向北美出口纺织品。

texture ['tekstʃə(r)]

n. 质地，纹理；口感

记 词根记忆：text(编织) + ure → 质地，纹理

例 This kind of meat has a similar taste and *texture* to beef. 这种肉的味道和口感与牛肉类似。

theoretical* [ˌθɪə'retɪkl]

a. 理论(上)的

搭 theoretical background 理论背景

例 In the first year students learn *theoretical* courses. 第一年学生学习理论课。

派 theoretically(*ad.* 理论上)

theory* ['θɪəri]

n. 理论，原理；学说；意见，看法

记 词根记忆：the(看，考虑) + ory → 做事时要考虑、参看的东西 → 理论，原理

例 Tom once put forward an attractive though unlikely *theory*. 汤姆曾经提出一个具有吸引力但不太可能的理论。

派 theoretical(*a.* 理论的)

therapy ['θerəpi]

n. 治疗，疗法

搭 radiation therapy 放射治疗；interferon therapy 干扰素治疗法；recreation therapy 娱乐疗法；be in therapy 接受治疗

例 We are beginning to realise the unique benefits of relaxation *therapy* in curing back pain. 我们正开始认识到放松疗法对背痛具有独特的疗效。

□ terrain □ terrestrial □ terrify □ territory □ textile □ texture
□ theoretical □ theory □ therapy

thereby* [ˌðeəˈbaɪ]

ad. 因此，从而

例 Mary became an American citizen, *thereby* gaining the right to vote. 玛丽成了美国公民，因此得到了投票权。

therefore* [ˈðeəfɔː(r)]

ad. 因此，所以

例 The earth is unique, *therefore*, we have to attain a sustainable balance between population, economic growth and the environment. 我们只有一个地球，因此必须保持人口数量、经济发展与环境之间的长久平衡。

thermal [ˈθɜːml]

a. 热的，热量的 *n.* 热气流

记 词根记忆：therm(=thermo 热) + al → 热的

搭 thermal energy 热能

例 A heat pump puts out more *thermal* energy than it consumes. 热泵产生的热能要高于它所消耗的热能。

同 warm(*a.* 暖和的，温暖的)；hot(*a.* 热的)

thesis* [ˈθiːsɪs]

n. 论文

例 The students could consult reference books when writing their graduate *theses*. 学生们在写毕业论文时可以查阅一些参考书。

thigh [θaɪ]

n. 大腿

记 联想记忆：跑完步感觉大腿(thigh)肌肉紧绷(tight)

例 The football player pulled his *thigh* muscle in the match. 那名足球运动员在比赛中拉伤了大腿肌肉。

thirsty [ˈθɜːsti]

a. 口渴的；饥渴的

例 The moisture is absorbed by *thirsty* plants. 饥渴的植物吸收了水汽。

thorny [ˈθɔːni]

a. 多刺的；痛苦的，棘手的

记 联想记忆：t + horn(角) + y → 有角的刺 → 多刺的

例 This *thorny* problem on environmental protection floored the new mayor. 这个关于环境保护的棘手问题把新市长难住了。

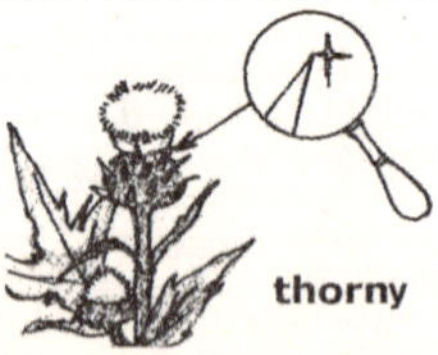

thoughtful [ˈθɔːtfl]

a. 沉思的；体贴的

例 It's so *thoughtful* of you to offer to drop me off at the train station. 你主动提出开车送我去火车站，真是太体贴了。

threaten [ˈθretn]

v. 威胁，恐吓；预示(危险)快要来临，是…的征兆，可能发生

搭 be threatened with sth. 被某物吓到

例 Soil erosion *threatens* the productivity of land in both rich and poor countries. 无论是富国还是穷国，土壤侵蚀都会危及土地的生产力。

派 threatening(*a.* 恐吓的；乌云密布的)

threshold [ˈθreʃhəʊld]	*n.* 入门，门槛；界限；开端，起点 记 联想记忆：thres(看作 thread，细线) + hold(拿着) → 手里拿根细线站在门口 → 入门，门槛 搭 be on the threshold of sth. 在…的开端 例 The normal noise *threshold* for people is 80 decibels. 80 分贝是人类所能忍受的最高的正常噪音。 同 doorway(*n.* 门口)；outset(*n.* 开端，开始)
thrifty [ˈθrɪfti]	*a.* 节俭的，节约的 记 来自 thrift(*n.* 节约，节俭) 例 In ancient time, Chinese people were usually brought up to be *thrifty* and hard-working. 在古代，中国人在成长过程中常常受到勤俭节约的教育。
thrill [θrɪl]	*v.* (使)非常激动；(使)发抖 搭 be thrilled to bits 非常愉快 例 The traveller *thrilled* us with his stories of adventure. 这位旅行者的冒险经历令我们激动不已。 同 excite(*vt.* 使激动，使兴奋)；delight[*v.* (使)高兴，(使)欣喜]
thrive* [θraɪv]	*vi.* 兴旺，繁荣 记 联想记忆：th + rive(r)(河) → 古时有河的地方大都是文明的发源地 → 兴旺，繁荣 例 Those societies *thrived* there for more than 1,000 years before the arrival of Europeans. 在欧洲人到来之前，那些社会已经繁荣了一千多年。
throughout* [θruːˈaʊt]	*prep./ad.* 各处；遍及；在整个…期间 例 There will be bus services to the university *throughout* the weekend. 整个周末都有公交车去这所大学。
thunder [ˈθʌndə(r)]	*n.* 雷；雷声 *v.* 打雷；轰隆响 记 联想记忆：th + under(在…下) → 打雷时切忌躲在树下 → 雷 例 *Thunder* accompanies lightning. 雷电交加。 派 thunderstorm(*n.* 雷暴)；thundercloud(*n.* 雷雨云)
tick off	用记号勾出，给…打核对号 例 If they agree I will ask them some multiple choice questions and *tick off* their answers on my sheet. 如果他们同意，我会提问一些选择题，并在我的问卷上记录他们给出的答案。
tickle* [ˈtɪkl]	*v.* (使)发痒；使高兴，逗乐 *n.* 痒 记 联想记忆：买张电影票(ticket)逗她高兴(tickle) 例 I *tickled* my little brother's feet with a feather. 我用一根羽毛来挠弟弟的脚。
tighten [ˈtaɪtn]	*v.* (使)变紧；使更加严格，加强 记 联想记忆：tight(紧的) + en(使…) → (使)变紧 搭 tighten up 变得更加严格 例 During three bad harvests in China, everyone must *tighten* their belt as a result of national income and foreign trade stagnation. 中国三年自然灾害期间，由于国内收益和国外贸易的停滞，每个人都要勒紧腰带过日子。

45

□ threshold □ thrifty □ thrill □ thrive □ throughout □ thunder
□ tick off □ tickle □ tighten

tillable
[ˈtɪləbl]

a. 适宜耕种的，可耕种的

记 联想记忆：till（耕作，犁地）+ able（能…的）→ 适宜耕种的，可耕种的

例 Scientists have found that *tillable* lands have declined sharply in recent years due to global warming. 科学家发现，近年来由于全球变暖，可耕种土地骤减。

tilt
[tɪlt]

v. （使）倾斜，倾侧；（使）倾向于，偏向 *n.* 倾斜，倾侧

例 Government's fiscal policy will be *tilting* toward agricultural development. 政府的财政政策将倾向于农业发展。

timber
[ˈtɪmbə(r)]

n. 木材，木料；栋木，大梁

记 联想记忆：timb（看作 time，时间）+ er → 树苗变成木材需要时间 → 木材，木料

搭 timber industry 木材业

例 Forests are cut down for *timber*. 人们为了木材而砍伐森林。

timid
[ˈtɪmɪd]

a. 胆小的；羞怯的

记 词根记忆：tim（害怕）+ id → 胆小的；羞怯的

例 Generally speaking, animals in the zoo are *timid* and cautious in comparison with wild animals in the forest. 一般而言，动物园的动物比森林中的野生动物胆小谨慎。

派 timidity（*n.* 胆小，羞怯）；timidly（*ad.* 胆小地，羞怯地）

同 cowardly（*a.* 胆小的，怯懦的）；shy（*a.* 害羞的）

反 bold（*a.* 大胆的）

tolerate
[ˈtɒləreɪt]

vt. 容忍，宽容；容许，承认

例 Younger people tend to *tolerate* noise better than their elders. 年轻人比年长者更能承受噪音。

tome*
[təʊm]

n. 册，大部头书；（有学术价值的）巨著

记 联想记忆：大部头书（tome）都放在家里（home）

例 They love to pore over weighty *tomes*. 他们喜欢钻研巨著。

tome

topple
[ˈtɒpl]

v. 倒塌，倒下；打倒，推翻

记 联想记忆：top（顶）+ ple → 使顶向下 → 打倒，推翻

例 The old man *toppled* backwards into the river, but no one came up to give a helping hand. 老人后仰翻入河里，但没有人上前伸出援助之手。

topple

topsoil*
[ˈtɒpsɔɪl]

n. 表层土

记 组合词：top（顶部）+ soil（土壤）→ 表层土

例 The United States discovered in 1982 that about one-fifth of its farmland was losing *topsoil*. 美国于 1982 年发现其约有五分之一的耕地存在极为严重的表层土流失现象。

□ tillable □ tilt □ timber □ timid □ tolerate □ tome
□ topple □ topsoil

torment [ˈtɔːment] *n.* 痛苦，折磨；令人痛苦的东西 [tɔːˈment] *vt.* 折磨，使痛苦，烦扰；纠缠；戏弄，捉弄

记 词根记忆：tor(=tort 扭曲) + ment → 扭曲的状态 → 痛苦，折磨

搭 be in torment 在痛苦中

例 It is hard for the rich to understand that the poor from the remote rural areas are undergoing a ***torment***. 富人很难理解偏远农村地区的穷人正遭受的苦难。

torrent [ˈtɒrənt] *n.* 洪流；爆发；(话语等的)连发

记 词根记忆：tor(=torn 转动) + rent → 水流转动不停地前进 → 洪流

例 As ice and snow melted, they touched off devastating ***torrents*** of mud and debris. 冰雪融化引发了破坏力极大的泥石流。

tortoise [ˈtɔːtəs] *n.* 龟，陆龟；行动迟缓的人

例 People in that tribe used to think that the ***tortoises*** and turtles came from hell. 那个部落的人过去常认为陆龟和海龟来自地狱。

tough* [tʌf] *a.* 难对付的；健壮的；(肉等食物)老的

搭 a tough nut 难对付的人，与之打交道有危险的人

例 Kangaroo meat is darker in color and ***tougher*** than that of rabbit. 与兔肉相比，袋鼠肉较硬且颜色较深。

townscape* [ˈtaʊnskeɪp] *n.* 市镇风光

记 组合词：town(市镇) + scape(景色) → 市镇风光

toxic [ˈtɒksɪk] *a.* 有毒的；中毒的

记 发音记忆："逃(一)个是(一)个" → 酒里有毒，快逃 → 有毒的

例 ***Toxic*** chemicals were spilled from the factory into the river. 有毒的化学物从工厂被排放到河里。

派 toxicity(*n.* 毒性)

同 poisonous(*a.* 有毒的)；noxious(*a.* 有害的，有毒的)

toxin* [ˈtɒksɪn] *n.* 毒素，毒质

记 词根记忆：tox(毒) + in → 毒素，毒质

例 Intake of nicotine encourages activity of other ***toxins*** in the blood. 吸入的尼古丁会激活血液中的其他毒素。

trace [treɪs] *vt.* 追踪，追查；追溯；描摹，标出 *n.* 痕迹；微量

记 联想记忆：描绘(trace)车轮的痕迹(track)

搭 without (a) trace 无影无踪；trace element 痕量元素，微量元素

例 The origin of modern architecture can be ***traced*** back to the social and technological changes of the 18th and 19th centuries. 现代建筑的起源可追溯到18、19世纪出现的社会和科技变革。

派 traceable(*a.* 可追踪的)

track* [træk] *n.* 小路；跑道 *v.* 跟踪，追踪

例 The road system here evolved from the goat ***tracks*** followed by the early inhabitants. 这里的道路系统在早期居民所走的羊肠小道的基础上发展了起来。

45

□ torment □ torrent □ tortoise □ tough □ townscape □ toxic
□ toxin □ trace □ track

track and field* 田径

例 When it comes to baseball, both universities have a poor record, and the same goes for *track and field*. 说到棒球比赛，这两所大学的比赛成绩都不怎么好，田径比赛也是如此。

tradition* [trəˈdɪʃn] *n.* 传统；惯例

例 Individuals often find it hard to escape from the role that cultural *traditions* have defined for them. 人们经常发现难以摆脱文化传统给自己限定的角色。

traditional* [trəˈdɪʃənl] *a.* 传统的，惯例的；口传的，传说的

搭 traditional views 传统观点；traditional belief 传统信条；traditional industry 传统工业；traditional methods 传统方法

例 Rosewood is a pure example of a *traditional* country house of this part of England. 红木建筑是英格兰这个地区传统乡间住宅的典型代表。

派 traditionally(*ad.* 传统地；惯例地)

tragic [ˈtrædʒɪk] *a.* 悲惨的；悲剧(性)的

记 联想记忆：t + rag(破旧衣服) + ic → 穿破旧衣服的 → 悲惨的

例 His trip to America is a *tragic* story. 他的美国之行就是个悲剧。

tram* [træm] *n.* 有轨电车，电车轨道 *v.* 乘电车

搭 tram tour 有轨电车游览

例 I am watching for my *tram* because sometimes it comes early. 我正留意我要坐的那班有轨电车，因为它有时候会早到。

tramp* [træmp] *v.* 跋涉；踩踏 *n.* 长途跋涉

例 Those poor people *tramped* for miles and miles without finding anywhere to stay. 那些可怜的人走啊走，始终找不到栖身之处。

tranquility* [træŋˈkwɪləti] *n.* 宁静，安静

记 联想记忆：tranquil(宁静的) + ity(名词后缀) → 宁静

例 Tom and Mary lead a life in the village in search of *tranquility*. 汤姆和玛丽为追求宁静而在乡下生活。

transaction* [trænˈzækʃn] *n.* 办理；处理；交易，业务；[*pl.*]会报，学报

记 词根记忆：trans(穿过) + act(做) + ion → 在两者之间进行 → 交易

例 The teller told me that the computer system was temporarily down, so they couldn't do any *transactions*. 出纳员告诉我计算机系统临时出故障了，所以他们不能进行任何交易。

同 deal(*n.* 交易)；exchange(*n.* 交换；交易)

transcend [trænˈsend] *vt.* 超越，胜过，优于

记 词根记忆：trans(越过) + (s)cend(爬) → 超越，胜过

例 The forest policy must *transcend* national frontiers and generations of people, and it must allow for the inevitable changes that take place in the forests, in needs, and hence in policy. 森林政策必须超越国界和世代的界限，必须考虑到森林、需求以及相关政策所发生的不可避免的变化。

□ track and field □ tradition □ traditional □ tragic □ tram □ tramp
□ tranquility □ transaction □ transcend

transcribe* [træn'skraɪb]	*vt.* 抄写，誊写；打印；转录 记 词根记忆：tran + scrib(写) + e → 转写 → 抄写，誊写 例 She *transcribed* a letter on the typewriter. 她用打字机打印了一封信。
transcript* ['trænskrɪpt]	*n.* 抄本，副本；文字记录 例 The professor was reading the *transcript* of the interview. 教授正在看面试的文字记录。
transcription [træn'skrɪpʃn]	*n.* 抄写，誊写；抄本，誊本；书面标注的事物；(乐曲的)改编 例 *Transcriptions* always benefit from any additional commentary provided by an observer. 手抄本总是能从阅评者的附加评注中得到完善。
transfer*	[træs'fɜː(r)] *v.* 搬，转移；调动，转学；转让，过户；转车，换乘 ['træsfɜː(r)] *n.* 转移；调动；转车，换乘 记 词根记忆：trans(穿过，越过) + fer(带来) → 转移；调动 搭 transfer property to sb. 把财产转让给某人；transfer from...to... 从…转换成…；bank transfer 银行转账 例 Pollen can be *transferred* by birds that come into contact with flowers. 花粉可以通过与花接触过的鸟来传播。 派 transference(*n.* 转移；转让)；transferable(*a.* 可转移的)
transform* [træns'fɔːm]	*v.* 使改观，改革，改善；变换，把…转换成 记 词根记忆：trans(越过；交叉) + form(形状) → 使形状交叉 → 使改观 例 The new genetical anatomy will *transform* medicine and reduce human suffering in the twenty-first century. 在21世纪，新的基因解剖学将彻底改变药品形式并减轻人类的痛苦。
transient ['trænziənt]	*a.* 短暂的，转瞬即逝的 *n.* 在某地短暂停留或工作的人 记 词根记忆：trans(穿过) + ient → 时光穿梭 → 短暂的 例 In recent years, there is a large *transient* population flowing into big cities. 近些年来，大量流动人口涌入大城市。 同 temporary(*a.* 暂时的，临时的)；passing(*a.* 短暂的) 反 permanent(*a.* 永久的，持久的)
transit* ['trænzɪt]	*n.* 运输，运载 *v.* 通过，经过；中转 记 词根记忆：trans(越过，穿过) + it(走) → 从一地走到另一地 → 运输，运载；通过，经过 例 They wish to put mass *transit* systems into and around cities and promote small low emission cars for urban use. 他们希望将公共交通系统用于城市和城际交通而将排气量低的小汽车用于市区交通。 同 transportation(*n.* 运输，运载)；delivery(*n.* 传送，运送)
transition [træn'zɪʃn]	*n.* 过渡，过渡时期；转变，转换，变革 记 词根记忆：trans(穿过) + it(走) + ion → 穿过一地走到另一地 → 转变 搭 in transition 转变中 例 The *transition* from planned economy to market economy is not an easy one. 从计划经济向市场经济转变并非易事。 派 transitional(*a.* 变迁的，过渡期的) 同 transformation(*n.* 转化)；change(*n.* 转变，改变)

□ transcribe □ transcript □ transcription □ transfer □ transform □ transient
□ transit □ transition

translate* [ˈtrænsleɪt]

v. 翻译

例 The name of the weapon was directly ***translated*** from Chinese. 这种武器的名字是从汉语直接翻译过来的。

transmit* [træns ˈmɪt]

v. 传送；传染；发射

记 词根记忆：trans(越过) + mit(送) → 越过去输送 → 传送

例 All the documents have been ***transmitted*** electronically to the printing centre. 所有文件已经被电传至印刷中心。

派 transmitter(*n.* 传送者；发射机)

transmute* [trænz ˈmjuːt]

v. 改变；(使)变化，变形，变质

记 词根记忆：trans(表加强) + mut(变化) + e → 改变

例 The alchemist tried to ***transmute*** iron into gold. 炼金术士试图将铁变成黄金。

transparent [træns ˈpærənt]

a. 透明的，清澈的；明显的；易懂的

记 联想记忆：trans(穿过) + parent(双亲) → 父母之间没有什么可隐瞒的 → 透明的

例 Clear, tough, ***transparent*** and flexible, the new film not only made the rollfilm camera fully practical, but provided the raw material for the introduction of cinematography. 这种新胶卷清晰、强韧、透明，还有弹性，不仅使卷式胶卷相机特别实用，也为电影摄影艺术的出现提供了原料。

transplant

[træns ˈplaːnt] *vt.* 移栽，移种(植物等)；移植(器官等)；使迁移，使移居 [ˈtrænsplaːnt] *n.* (器官等的)移植

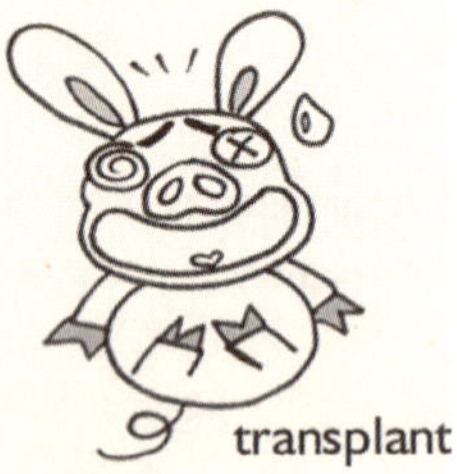

记 词根记忆：trans(改变) + plant(种植) → 改种到他处 → 移植

例 Every year, tens of thousands of patients are given organ ***transplants*** in developed countries. 发达国家每年有数以万计的病人接受器官移植。

派 transplantation(*n.* 移植；迁移)；transplantable(*a.* 可移植的)

同 graft(*v.* 移植；嫁接)；transfer(*v.* 转移，调动)

transport

[ˈtræspɔːt] *n.* 运输，运送；运输系统，运载工具

[træ ˈspɔːt] *vt.* 运输，运送，搬运

记 词根记忆：trans(穿过) + port(搬运) → 从一地搬到一地 → 运输，运送

搭 on/by public transport 乘坐公共交通工具；transport costs 运费；free transportation 免费交通

例 Better integration of ***transport*** systems is highly desirable and made more feasible by modern computers. 人们迫切要求运输系统进一步一体化，而现代计算机使这一要求更易实现。

transportation* [ˌtrænspɔː ˈteɪʃn]

n. 运输，运输系统，运输工具

搭 preservation and transportation of samples 样品的保存和运输

例 There is a need of huge promotion in public ***transportation***. 公共交通系统需要大幅度的提高和改善。

□ translate □ transmit □ transmute □ transparent □ transplant □ transport □ transportation

trap* [træp]

n. 陷阱，圈套，诡计 *vt.* 诱捕，诱骗，使中圈套；使陷入困境，使受限制

搭 fall into a trap 陷入圈套；the unemployment trap 失业的困境；debt trap 负债困境；avoid the trap of doing sth. 避免掉进陷阱

例 The parents were a bit concerned about the side bar of the baby chair, because they felt babies could ***trap*** their fingers in it. 父母有点担心这个婴儿座椅的侧板，因为他们觉得侧板会夹住婴儿的手指。

Morality is not really the doctrine of how to make ourselves happy but of how we are to be worthy of happiness.

道德确实不是指导人们如何使自己幸福的教条，而是指导人们如何配享有幸福的学说。

——德国哲学家 康德 .I.（Immanuel Kant, German philosopher）

45

Word List 46

音频

词根、词缀预习表

trem	害怕	tremendous *a.* 极大的，巨大的	**tres**	越过	trespass *vi.* 侵犯；擅闯
tri	三	triple *a.* 三部分的，三倍的	**tribut**	给予	tribute *n.* 贡品；颂词
trop	转	tropical *a.* 热带的；炎热的	**turb**	晃动	turbine *n.* 涡轮机；汽轮机
ultim	最后	ultimate *a.* 最后的；最终的	**ulter**	远	ulterior *a.* 较远的；不可告人的
anim	精神	unanimous *a.* 一致同意的	**uni**	一个	union *n.* 协会，工会

trapeze*
[trəˈpiːz]

n. 高空秋千；吊架

记 联想记忆：trap(陷阱) + eze(看作 eye，眼睛) → 乱吊秋千，陷阱无眼 → 高空秋千

例 The brothers' *trapeze* act is unique. 那对兄弟的高空秋千表演独一无二。

treadmill*
[ˈtredmɪl]

n. (人或畜力的)踏车；累人的活；单调的例行工作，乏味繁重的工作

记 联想记忆：tread(踩踏) + mill(磨坊) → 在磨坊里踩踏车 → 累人的活

例 I can't get off the office *treadmill*. 我无法摆脱单调的坐班工作。

treatise
[ˈtriːtɪz]

n. 论文；专著

例 "Your feedback helped me to improve this *treatise*, which ultimately helped everybody in the class," the teacher said. 老师说："你们的反馈帮我改进了这篇论文，这最终也帮了班里的每个人。"

treatment*
[ˈtriːtmənt]

n. 治疗；对待

记 来自 treat(*vt.* 对待；治疗)

搭 require hospital treatment 需要住院治疗

例 People were dissatisfied with the *treatment* of animals at the zoo. 动物园对待动物的方式令人不满。

trek*
[trek]

vi./n. 牛拉车；艰苦跋涉

例 We are organizing a ten-day holiday, from the sixteenth of November, with eight days actual walking, *trekking* in the Semira Mountains. 我们计划组织一个为期十天的假期旅行，从 11 月 16 日开始，其中包括在赛米拉山进行八天的实地步行和跋涉。

□ trapeze □ treadmill □ treatise □ treatment □ trek

tremendous
[trəˈmendəs]

a. 极大的，巨大的；非常的，惊人的

记 词根记忆：trem(害怕)+end+ous(多…的)→(多得、好得)让人害怕的→非常的，惊人的

例 This looseness in molecular structure gives the material *tremendous* "formability". 分子结构如此松散使这种材料极具"可塑性"。

同 enormous(*a.* 巨大的，庞大的)；marvelous(*a.* 非凡的，惊奇的)

反 tiny(*a.* 微小的)

trench
[trentʃ]

n. 沟，壕沟 *v.* 挖沟

记 联想记忆：t+rench(看作bench，长凳)→像长凳一样狭长的地区→沟，壕沟

搭 trench coat 军用防水短上衣；trench warfare 堑壕战

例 The next stage of the project involves *trench* excavation, cable laying, construction backfilling and reinstatement, and landscaping works. 该工程的下一阶段包括坑道挖掘、电缆铺设、建筑回填和修复以及景观美化工程。

同 channel(*n.* 水道)；ditch(*n.* 沟渠)

trend
[trend]

n. 倾向；趋势；流行，时尚 *vi.* 伸向；倾向

记 联想记忆：tend(倾向)加r还是倾向(trend)

搭 a downward trend 向下的趋势；an upward trend 向上的趋势；economic trend 经济趋势；recent trend 最近的趋势；sweeping trends 席卷一切的潮流

例 In your opinion, will this *trend* continue into the future? 依你看，这种趋势在未来还会继续吗？

trespass
[ˈtrespəs]

vi. 侵犯(某人的财产)；擅闯(某人的领地)；利用(某物)；冒犯，触犯

记 词根记忆：tres(=trans 越过)+pass(大步走)→越过去大步走→侵犯；冒犯，触犯

例 Farmers have barricaded their fields to stop wild elephants from *trespassing* on the land in the south of Asia. 在南亚地区，农民在田地里设置障碍物来阻止野象侵犯他们的土地。

trial*
[ˈtraɪəl]

n. 审讯；试验 *a.* 试验性的

搭 clinical trials 临床试验；trial period 试用期；time trial 计时游，计时比赛；on trial (指人)在试用期间；(指物)在试验中

例 The *trial* lasted for three days. 审讯持续了三天。// They fed themselves on the food as a sort of *trial* run. 他们自己吃这种食物，就算对这种食物的初步试验。

triangle
[ˈtraɪæŋgl]

n. 三角(形)

记 联想记忆：tri(三)+angle(角)→三角(形)

例 You can draw a *triangle* by connecting three points not in a straight line. 连接不在一条直线上的三个点就可以画出一个三角形。 46

tribal [ˈtraɪbl]

a. 部落的，部族的；集团意识强的

记 来自 tribe(*n.* 部落)

例 At the first sight of ***tribal*** arts and dress on the island, tourists will certainly be attracted. 当游客第一眼看到岛上的部落艺术和服饰时，就一定会被其吸引。

tribute* [ˈtrɪbjuːt]

n. 贡品；颂词，称赞；(表示敬意的)礼物

记 词根记忆：tribut(给予) + e → 给予(皇室)的东西 → 贡品

例 In ancient times, people had to pay ***tribute*** to the king. 在古代，人们必须向国王进贡。

同 compliment(*n.* 称赞，恭维)；praise(*n.* 赞扬)

trick* [trɪk]

n. 诡计，花招 *vt.* 欺诈，哄骗

记 联想记忆：西方国家的小孩子在万圣节喜欢玩 treat or trick 的游戏

例 They used a decoy camera to ***trick*** burglars. 他们用一台伪装相机来哄骗窃贼。

派 tricky(*a.* 不易处理的，需要技巧的)

trigger* [ˈtrɪgə(r)]

vt. 引发，导致 *n.* 扳机

记 联想记忆：扣动扳机(trigger)射杀了一只老虎(tiger)

搭 trigger a war 引发战争

例 The earthquake ***triggered*** an avalanche. 地震引发了一场雪崩。

同 stimulus(*n.* 刺激物)；initiate(*vt.* 发起，开始)；cause(*vt.* 引起，导致)

trim [trɪm]

vt./n. 修剪；整理 *a.* 苗条的，修长的；整齐的，整洁的

记 联想记忆：tri(看作 try，试) + m(end)(修理) → 试着去修理 → 修剪

搭 trim one's nails 修剪指甲；trim sth. off/away 把某物去除掉；trim off 修剪；trim with 用…装饰；trim with brass 用铜器装饰；trim lawns 齐整的草坪

例 The top of the can is ***trimmed*** and then bent over to secure the lid. 罐子的顶部经过修整后微微向上隆起以便固定好盖子。

trimester* [traɪˈmestə(r)]

n. 三月期；学期

例 The academic year is divided into three ***trimesters***. 一学年分为三学期。

trinket* [ˈtrɪŋkɪt]

n. 小装饰品；不值钱的珠宝

例 The lady had some ***trinkets*** on her dress. 这位女士在衣服上挂了一些饰品。

triple [ˈtrɪpl]

a. 三部分的；三倍的 *v.* (使)增至三倍

记 词根记忆：tri(三) + ple → 三部分的，三倍的

例 As a whole, European countries see forests as performing a ***triple*** function: biological, economic and recreational. 整体来看，欧洲国家认为森林在以下三方面起到了作用：生物、经济以及休闲娱乐。

triumphant
[traɪˈʌmfənt]

a. 得胜的；得意洋洋的；狂欢的

记 联想记忆：triumph（胜利）+ ant → 得胜的；得意洋洋的

例 The newborn infant is ***triumphant*** and joyful at each development taken by each consciousness, and he revels and marks great joy in the slightest creative act of each of his issues. 新生婴儿对自己有意识地取得的每一个进展感到得意和高兴，并为他所做出的每一个最轻微的创造性行为而陶醉、喜悦。

trivial *
[ˈtrɪviəl]

a. 无价值的，琐屑的；平庸的，普通的

记 词根记忆：tri（三）+ vi（路）+ al（形容词后缀）→ 三岔路的 → 琐屑的

例 They think that tourism is a ***trivial*** subject. 他们认为旅行是一个无价值的主题。

同 trifling（*a.* 不重要的）；petty（*a.* 小的，不重要的）

反 important（*a.* 重要的，重大的）；main（*a.* 主要的，重要的）

trivialize
[ˈtrɪviəlaɪz]

vt. 使显得不重要，轻视，淡化

例 There's a serious social problem today that too many films are ***trivializing*** the seriousness of violent and sex scenes. 当今有一个严重的社会问题，那就是过多影片都在淡化暴力以及情色场面的严重性。

tropical *
[ˈtrɒpɪkl]

a. 热带的；炎热的

记 词根记忆：trop（转）+ ical → 热得令人晕头转向 → 热带的；炎热的

搭 tropical condition 热带环境；tropical disease 热带病；tropical rainforests 热带雨林；tropical marine climate 热带海洋气候

tropospheric *
[ˌtrɒpəˈsferɪk]

a. 对流层的

搭 tropospheric ozone 对流层臭氧

troupe *
[truːp]

n. （演出的）班子，团，队；（尤指）马戏团，芭蕾舞团

记 联想记忆：部队（troop）里的一群（group）人组建了一个剧团（troupe）

例 A ***troupe*** of dancers from Italy is one of the leading attractions in the festival. 一支来自意大利的舞蹈队在节日里最引人注目。

truant *
[ˈtruːənt]

vi. 逃避责任；旷课 *n.* 逃学者；逃避者

例 Jason has been ***truanting*** three days this week. 贾森本周逃了三天课。

truce
[truːs]

n. 休战（协定）

记 联想记忆：休战协定（truce）确认了战败属实（true）

例 A sacred ***truce*** was declared to allow men to travel to the games in safety. 宣布了神圣的休战协定以使人们安全地去参加比赛。

trunk
[trʌŋk]

n. 树干，躯干；大箱子；象鼻

记 联想记忆：卡车（truck）撞向树干（trunk）

例 White poplar, as the symbol of a real man, is always eulogized by writers for its tall and straight ***trunk***. 作为伟丈夫象征的白杨树，总因其高大笔直的枝干备受作家们的赞美。

trustworthy
[ˈtrʌstwɜːði]

a. 值得信赖的，可靠的

例 Yang is an experienced and ***trustworthy*** guide. 杨是一位经验丰富且值得信赖的向导。

46

□ triumphant □ trivial □ trivialize □ tropical □ tropospheric □ troupe
□ truant □ truce □ trunk □ trustworthy

tube*

[tjuːb]

n. 管道，试管；〈英〉地铁

记 联想记忆：立方形(cube)的管道(tube)

例 When the *tube* was broken, air rushed in, causing the phosphorus to combust spontaneously. 当试管破裂后，空气涌进造成磷自燃。

tug

[tʌg]

v. 用力拖(或拉)

记 发音记忆："探戈"→跳探戈时脚步拖拉要有力→用力拖(或拉)

例 The fisherman *tugged* the small boat out of the water. 渔民用力把小船拖到岸上。

tune

[tjuːn]

vt. 调音；调节，调整 *n.* 调子；和谐

记 联想记忆：转动(turn)旋钮调音(tune)

例 Engines of old cars were *tuned* to reduce the exhausts they emitted. 调整老式汽车的发动机以减少废气排放量。

tunnel*

[ˈtʌnl]

n. 隧道；地道 *v.* 挖(地道)，开(隧道)

记 联想记忆：海峡(channel)像条长长的地道(tunnel)

例 The prisoner had escaped by *tunnelling*. 犯人挖地道逃跑了。

turbid

[ˈtɜːbɪd]

a. 混浊的；紊乱的

例 Vision is obviously more useful to species inhabiting clear open waters than to those living in *turbid* rivers and flooded plains. 显而易见，与生活在浑浊的小河里或者河漫滩里的物种相比，视力对生活在干净清澈水域里的物种更加重要。

turbine*

[ˈtɜːbaɪn]

n. 涡轮机，汽轮机

记 词根记忆：turb(晃动)＋ine→涡轮机

例 Ultraclean coal can be used in advanced power systems such as coal-fired gas *turbines*. 超纯煤可以用在诸如燃煤的燃气涡轮机之类的先进动力系统中。

turnover

[ˈtɜːnəʊvə(r)]

n. 营业额；人事变动率；货物周转率

记 来自词组 turn over(营业额达到；翻转；交换)

例 The company tried its best to decrease the *turnover*. 公司竭尽全力降低人事变动率。

同 shift(*n.* 移动，移位；轮班)

turret

[ˈtʌrət]

n. 塔楼，角楼

例 From the castle *turret*, people could oversee this beautiful river. 从城堡的塔楼上，人们可以俯瞰这条美丽的河流。

tutor*

[ˈtjuːtə(r)]

v. (给…)当家庭教师 *n.* 导师；家庭教师

例 Jane *tutored* this little girl in English. 简给这个小女孩当英文家教。

tutorial*

[tjuːˈtɔːriəl]

n. 大学导师的辅导课；指南 *a.* 家庭教师的，辅导教师的，大学导师的；辅导的，指导的

例 I think you should be ready for today's *tutorial* on "how to find a good job". 我认为你已经为今天的辅导课"如何找到好工作"做好了准备。

□ tube □ tug □ tune □ tunnel □ turbid □ turbine
□ turnover □ turret □ tutor □ tutorial

twist* [twɪst]

v. 缠绕；捻；扭曲，弯曲 *n.* 弯曲

记 联想记忆：tw(看作 two，两个) + ist(表人) → 两个人扭打在一起 → 缠绕

例 Research shows that spasms can cause *twisting* of the spine. 研究显示，痉挛会导致脊椎扭曲。

twofold* [ˈtuːfəʊld]

a. 两倍的，双重的；两部分的 *ad.* 两倍地，双重地

例 There has been a *twofold* increase in the number of rare birds in the past decade. 在过去的十年，珍稀鸟类的数量增加了两倍。

typhoon* [taɪˈfuːn]

n. 台风

记 发音记忆："台风"

例 The brunt of a *typhoon* will be deflected by the neighbouring islands. 来袭的台风会因为邻近的岛屿而偏离方向。

typical* [ˈtɪpɪkl]

a. 典型的

记 联想记忆：typ(e)(典型) + ical → 典型的

例 The *typical* farm in the North is a small, family-run concern, producing mainly wool and timber for the market. 北部的典型农场规模小且由家庭经营，主要生产市场上所需的羊毛及木材。

派 typically(*ad.* 典型地)

ulterior [ʌlˈtɪəriə(r)]

a. 较远的；不可告人的，隐秘的，秘密的

记 词根记忆：ulter(远) + ior → 较远的；不可告人的，隐秘的

例 In current society, when one actively supports someone who needs help, he may be suspected of having an *ulterior* motive by some people. 在当今社会，当一个人积极帮助需要帮助的人时，有些人可能怀疑他别有用心。

ultimate* [ˈʌltɪmət]

a. 最后的，最终的；根本的 *n.* 最好(或先进、伟大等)的事物，极品，精华

记 词根记忆：ultim(最后) + ate → 最后的，最终的

搭 the ultimate authority 最高当局；the ultimate principle 基本原理；in ultimate 到最后，结果

例 For early explorers, it was the *ultimate* survival contest. 对于早期探险家来说，这是终极生存竞赛。

派 ultimately(*ad.* 最后，终于)

ultraclean* [ˌʌltrəˈkliːn]

a. 超净的，特净的

例 They decided to put superclean coal and *ultraclean* coal into the production. 他们决定在生产中使用超净煤和特净煤。

unanimous* [juˈnænɪməs]

a. 一致同意的；一致通过的

记 词根记忆：un(=uni 一个) + anim(精神) + ous → 大家都秉持一种精神 → 一致同意的

例 *Unanimous* agreement should be reached for this plan to go ahead. 这项计划需要全体人员一致通过才能进行。

派 unanimously(*ad.* 全体一致地，一致同意地)

unanimous

46

□ twist □ twofold □ typhoon □ typical □ ulterior □ ultimate
□ ultraclean □ unanimous

unaware* [ˌʌnəˈweə(r)]

a. 未意识到的

记 联想记忆：un(不，没有) + aware(意识到的) → 未意识到的

例 He was *unaware* of my entry into the room. 他没意识到我已经走进了房间。

unbeatable [ʌnˈbiːtəbl]

a. 无敌的，不可战胜的

例 The emerging market, with great curious about new things, has *unbeatable* advantage to grasp the investor's eyes. 新兴市场更容易接受新事物，在吸引投资方面拥有绝对优势。

unbeatable

unbiased* [ʌnˈbaɪəst]

a. 公正的，没有偏见的

记 联想记忆：un(无) + biased(有偏见的) → 公正的，没有偏见的

搭 unbiased opinions 没有偏见的想法

例 I wanted to get her *unbiased* comments on my article. 我想要的是她对我的文章给出不偏不倚的评论。

unblemished [ʌnˈblemɪʃt]

a. 无瑕疵的，完好的

例 Some states indicated that, it would be legal to get a remission if a prisoner in jail keeps an *unblemished* record in 3 years. 一些州政府表示，如果服刑期的囚犯三年内没有任何不良记录，就可以合法获得减刑。

uncertainty* [ʌnˈsɜːtnti]

n. 犹豫，迟疑；不确定；无把握

例 These fluctuations of environment add another degree of *uncertainty* to the survival of many species. 这些环境变化给很多物种的生存带来了另一种不确定性。

unconcerned* [ˌʌnkənˈsɜːnd]

a. 漠不关心的；不烦恼的

例 Only 22 percent say they are *unconcerned* about this issue. 只有 22% 的人称他们不关心此事。

unconquerable* [ˌʌnˈkɒŋkərəbl]

a. 不可征服的

例 This place in their hearts was *unconquerable*. 这个地方在他们心目中是不可征服的。

underestimate* [ˌʌndərˈestɪmeɪt] *vt.* 低估 [ˌʌndərˈestɪmət] *n.* 低估

记 组合词：under(不足) + estimate(估计) → 估计不足 → 低估

例 The statistics show that the number of people affected by the H1N1 has been seriously *underestimated*. 这项数据显示之前严重低估了甲流患者的数量。

undergraduate* [ˌʌndəˈgrædʒuət]

n. 大学本科生，大学生，大学肄业生

记 组合词：under(不足) + graduate(毕业生) → 还不是毕业生 → 大学本科生

例 The Universities of Oxford and Cambridge recently held joint conferences to discuss the noticeably rapid decline in literacy among *undergraduates*. 牛津和剑桥这两所大学近期召开了几次联合会议，讨论本科生文化水平显著下降的问题。

□ unaware □ unbeatable □ unbiased □ unblemished □ uncertainty □ unconcerned
□ unconquerable □ underestimate □ undergraduate

underground* [ˈʌndəgraʊnd] *a.* 地下的 *n.* 地铁 [ˌʌndəˈgraʊnd] *ad.* 在地(面)下

记 组合词：under(在…下) + ground(地面，土地) → 地下的；在地(面)下

搭 underground railway 地铁

例 Water from the ***underground*** rivers bubbles to the surface as springs. 地下河的水以泉水的形式冒出地表。

underline* [ˌʌndəˈlaɪn] *vt.* 画线于…之下；强调

记 组合词：under(在…下) + line(画线) → 在…下面画线 → 画线于…之下；强调

例 You can ***underline*** new words encountered in your reading. 你可以在阅读中遇到的新单词下面画线做标记。

underling* [ˈʌndəlɪŋ] *n.* 职位低的人，下属

记 联想记忆：under(在…管辖下) + ling → 职位低的人

例 Many corporate managers find it difficult to measure the contribution of ***underlings*** to a firm's well-being. 许多公司的经理发现很难衡量下属对公司正常运作所作的贡献。

underlying* [ˌʌndəˈlaɪɪŋ] *a.* 表面下的，下层的，在下面的；根本的；潜在的，隐含的

记 组合词：under(在…下) + lying(躺着的) → 在下面躺着的 → 在下面的

例 Our understanding of the ***underlying*** causes of El Nino events is being confirmed by float data. 浮筒采集到的数据证实了我们对厄尔尼诺现象的潜在原因的了解。

undermine* [ˌʌndəˈmaɪn] *vt.* 削弱；破坏

记 组合词：under(在…下) + mine(挖) → 在下面挖 → 削弱；破坏

搭 undermine one's position 削弱某人的地位；undermine one's credibility 破坏某人的信用

例 The constant failure was starting to ***undermine*** my confidence. 接连的失败开始削弱我的自信心。

派 underminer(*n.* 暗中破坏者)

同 weaken〔*v.* 削弱；(使)变弱〕

反 strengthen(*vt.* 加强，巩固)；intensify(*v.* 增强，加强)；reinforce(*vt.* 加强，加固)

underneath [ˌʌndəˈniːθ] *ad.* 在下面 *prep.* 在…下面 *n.* 下部

例 Each of the 900 pillars of this building can be individually jacked up, allowing wedges to be added ***underneath***. 这座建筑的 900 根柱子都可以分别被托起以便在下面放入楔子。

underpin [ˌʌndəˈpɪn] *vt.* 加固…的基础；加强，巩固

例 The Copenhagen Conference appeals to all developed countries to reduce emissions by at least 80% in the same period and ***underpin*** these efforts through robust and comparable mid-term reductions. 哥本哈根会议呼吁所有发达国家在同一时期内至少减排 80%，同时通过中期有力的类似减排措施来巩固这一成绩。

□ underground □ underline □ underling □ underlying □ undermine □ underneath □ underpin

understandable* [ˌʌndəˈstændəbl]

a. 可以理解的，能懂的；可同情的

例 Only I have got to put the trial into practice can it be *understandable* to everyone. 只有我将此试验实现大家才会理解。

understanding [ˌʌndəˈstændɪŋ]

n. 理解；谅解 *a.* 体谅的；宽容的

例 The Human Genome Project will open up new *understanding* of many ailments that afflict humanity. 人类基因工程将开启人们对于困扰人类的很多疾病的全新认识。

undertake [ˌʌndəˈteɪk]

v. 承担(某事物)，负起(某事物的)责任；同意或答应做某事

搭 undertake responsibility 承担责任

例 Mary *undertook* the organization of the whole scheme. 玛丽负责整个计划的组织工作。// The firm *undertook* to keep price increases to a minimum. 公司承诺价格涨幅保持最低标准。

undetected* [ˌʌndɪˈtektɪd]

a. 未被发现的

记 联想记忆：un(不) + detect(发现) + ed → 未被发现的

例 The family had managed to live *undetected* for six years outside the border town of Breda, Holland. 这一家人成功地在荷兰布雷达这个边镇外度过了六年不为人知的生活。

undisguised* [ˌʌndɪsˈgaɪzd]

a. 无伪装的；坦率的

记 联想记忆：un(不，无) + disguise(装饰；伪装) + d → 无伪装的

例 They looked upon the creature with a loathing *undisguised*. 他们看那动物时眼神中流露出明显的厌恶。

undoubtedly [ˌʌnˈdaʊtɪdli]

ad. 毋庸置疑地，确凿地

例 The shift of food-production from Europe to regions without farm subsidies will *undoubtedly* mean more pressure to convert natural habitat into farmland. 毫无疑问，粮食生产从欧洲转向没有农业补贴的地区意味着自然栖息地被转为农田的压力日益增大。

uneasy [ˌʌnˈiːzi]

a. 心神不安的；担心的

记 联想记忆：un(不) + easy(安心的) → 不安心的 → 心神不安的

例 He was *uneasy* about the results of the final exams. 他为期末考试成绩忧心忡忡。

unemployment [ˌʌnɪmˈplɔɪmənt]

n. 失业；失业人数

记 联想记忆：un(不) + employ(雇用) + ment → 不被雇用 → 失业

例 The graph shows the *unemployment* rates in the US and Japan between March 1993 and March 1999. 这张图表显示了从1993年3月至1999年3月六年间美国和日本的失业率。

派 employment(*n.* 雇用；使用；工作)

unexpected [ˌʌnɪkˈspektɪd]

a. 想不到的，意外的

例 Some *unexpected* difficulties have arisen in his life. 他的生活中出现了一些意想不到的困难。

□ understandable □ understanding □ undertake □ undetected □ undisguised □ undoubtedly
□ uneasy □ unemployment □ unexpected

unfortunately* [ʌnˈfɔːtʃənətli]	*ad.* 不幸地 例 *Unfortunately*, they cannot come to our party. 很遗憾，他们来不了我们的晚会了。
uniform* [ˈjuːnɪfɔːm]	*n.* 制服 *a.* 相同的，一致的 记 词根记忆：uni(单一) + form(形式) → 单一形式的 → 相同的，一致的 搭 in uniform 穿着制服的 例 Traditionally *uniforms* were manufactured to protect the workers. 传统上，生产制服的目的是保护工人。 派 uniformity(*n.* 同样，一致)
union* [ˈjuːniən]	*n.* 协会，工会，同盟；联合，合并 记 词根记忆：uni(一个) + on(表人、物) → 使人都朝着同一个方向走 → 协会，同盟；联合 搭 the European Union 欧洲联盟；labour union 工会 例 The speech contest is presided by the Student *Union*. 这个演讲比赛是由学生会主办的。

Although the world is full of suffering, it is full also of the overcoming of it.
虽然世界多苦难，但是苦难总是能战胜的。
——美国作家 海伦·凯勒（Hellen Keller, American writer）

Word List 47

音频

词根、词缀预习表

vers	转	universe *n.* 宇宙，天地万物	**ut**	用	utilise *vt.* 利用，运用
vac	空	vacant *a.* 未占用的，空的	**var**	改变，变化	variety *n.* 品种，种类
van	空	vanish *vi.* 突然消失；不复存在	**val**	价值	valid *a.* 有效的，具有法律效力的
vag	漫游	vague *a.* 模糊的；含糊的	**veloc**	快的	velocity *n.* 速度，效率
verb	言语	verbal *a.* 口头的；言辞的	**ver**	真实	verdict *n.* 裁定；定论

unique* [juˈniːk]

a. 唯一的，独一无二的；极不寻常的，极好的

记 词根记忆：uni(单一) + que(有…特点的) → 唯一的，独一无二的

搭 a unique style 独特的风格；unique copy 珍本，孤本；a unique talent 奇才；be unique to sb./sth. 独具，特有

例 Biometric security systems operate by storing a digitised record of some *unique* human features. 生物测定安全系统通过储存某些独特的人类特征的数字化记录来运行。

universe [ˈjuːnɪvɜːs]

n. 宇宙，天地万物；世界；领域

记 词根记忆：uni(单一) + vers(转) + e → 一个旋转着的整体空间 → 宇宙

例 Not only did the rocket solve a problem that had intrigued man for ages, but, more importantly, it literally opened the door to exploration of the *universe*. 火箭不仅解决了困扰几代人的一个问题，更重要的是，它开启了探索宇宙的大门。

派 universal(*a.* 普遍的；通用的)

unload* [ˌʌnˈləʊd]

v. 从…卸下货物；摆脱

记 联想记忆：un + load(负荷，重担) → 从…卸下货物

例 Loading and *unloading* costs can be minimised by refining raw materials or turning them into finished goods. 可以通过对原材料进行加工或将其制成成品来将它们的装卸成本降至最低。

unobtrusive [ˌʌnəbˈtruːsɪv]

a. 不显著的，不引人注目的；不张扬的

记 联想记忆：un(不) + obtrusive(突出的) → 不引人注目的

例 Listening to some quiet and *unobtrusive* music is one of the ways for me to find the inner tranquility after a long day. 漫长的一天过后，听一些轻柔平和的音乐是我寻求内心平静的方式之一。

 □ unique □ universe □ unload □ unobtrusive

unparalleled
[ʌn'pærəleld]

a. 无双的，无比的，空前的

记 联想记忆：un(无) + parallel(平行) + ed → 没有东西可以与之平行的 → 无双的，无比的

例 It was an *unparalleled* opportunity for Mary to develop her studies. 这对于玛丽发展学业来说是一个绝好的机会。

---

unprejudiced*
[ˌʌn'predʒədɪst]

a. 无偏见的；公正的

例 The formation of scientific theory starts with simple, *unprejudiced* observation. 科学理论的形成始于简单、无偏见的观察。

---

unquote*
[ˌʌn'kwəʊt]

v. 结束引语

例 The President *unquoted* his quotation with "have a nice day here". 总统先生通过"祝你们在这儿玩得愉快"来结束他的引语。

---

unrealistic*
[ˌʌnrɪə'lɪstɪk]

a. 不现实的，不切实际的

记 联想记忆：un(不) + realistic(现实的) → 不现实的，不切实际的

搭 unrealistic ideas 不切实际的想法

例 It is *unrealistic* to expect people to give up private cars in favour of mass transit. 期望人们放弃使用私家车转而支持公交系统是不切实际的。

---

unregistered*
[ʌn'redʒɪstəd]

a. 未注册的

例 It is *unregistered* for his car that he can not drive it in the street. 他的小汽车还没有进行注册，因此不可以在大街上行驶。

---

unsanitary
[ʌn'sænətri]

a. 不卫生的 (=insanitary)

例 According to a survey by WHO, millions of people from developing countries are living in *unsanitary* conditions. 世界卫生组织的一项调查显示，数百万发展中国家的人正生活在不卫生的环境中。

---

unsatisfactory*
[ˌʌnˌsætɪs'fæktəri]

a. 不能令人满意的

例 Reception of television programmes is *unsatisfactory* here. 这个地区电视节目的接收情况不能令人满意。

---

untrustworthy*
[ʌn'trʌstwɜːði]

a. 不值得信任的，靠不住的

记 组合词：un(不) + trust(信任) + worthy(值得的) → 不值得信任的

例 They think left-handed people are *untrustworthy*. 他们认为惯用左手的人不可靠。

---

unveil
[ˌʌn'veɪl]

v. 揭去面纱或覆盖物；揭幕；首次公开、揭露或展示(某事物)

记 联想记忆：un(解开) + veil(面纱) → 揭去面纱

例 The municipality decided to *unveil* its 2010 budget plan finally after several rounds of seminars with lawmakers and economic experts. 经过立法者和经济学家数回合的研究讨论，市政当局终于决定公布2010年的预算方案。

---

unwrap
[ˌʌn'ræp]

vt. 打开，解开；除去包装

例 Christmas activities incorporate winter activities like sipping hot cocoa, decorating Christmas trees and *unwrapping* Christmas gifts. 圣诞活动并入各种冬季活动，如喝热可可饮料，装扮圣诞树和拆圣诞礼物。

47

unyielding* [ʌnˈjiːldɪŋ]
a. 顽强的；坚硬的；不能弯曲的，坚固的
记 联想记忆：un（不）+ yielding（屈从的，易弯曲的）→ 顽强的；坚固的
例 Mary was *unyielding* in her opposition to the plan. 玛丽坚决反对这一计划。// The mattress was hard and *unyielding*. 床垫很硬，不能弯曲。

upgrade [ˌʌpˈɡreɪd]
n. 向上的斜坡；增加，改善 *vt.* 使(机器等)升级，提高，改进；提拔，提升；改善
记 组合词：up(向上) + grade(等级) → 使升级，提高；提拔，提升；改善
例 With the increase in terrorism attacks, more and more international airports plan to *upgrade* the safety check systems. 随着恐怖主义袭击的增加，越来越多的国际机场计划升级安检系统。
同 improve(*v.* 改善，改进)

uphill [ˌʌpˈhɪl]
ad. 向上，往上；上坡；艰难地
例 We cycled *uphill* for over an hour. 我们骑自行车爬了一个多小时的山坡。

upper* [ˈʌpə(r)]
a. 上面的；地位较高的
例 Helen lived on the *upper* floor. 海伦住在楼上。

upset
[ʌpˈset] *vt.* 使苦恼；搅乱；推翻，颠倒 [ˌʌpˈset] *a.* 心烦的；(肠胃等)不适的
记 联想记忆：up(向上) + set(放置) → 底朝天放着 → 颠倒
例 The coming final exam *upsets* the students a lot. 期末考试即将来临，学生们心烦意乱。

up-to-date [ˌʌptəˈdeɪt]
a. 直到最近的；现代的
例 The data gave lexicographers access to an *up-to-date* daily language. 这些资料为词典编纂者提供了最新的日常用语。

urban [ˈɜːbən]
a. 都市的；住在都市的
记 发音记忆："饿奔"→ 初到大都市闯荡，饿得狂奔 → 都市的
搭 urban areas 城市地区；urban residents 城市居民
例 The concentration of vehicles makes air quality in *urban* areas unpleasant. 汽车大量集中在市区使得这里的空气污浊不堪。

urbanization [ˌɜːbənaɪˈzeɪʃn]
n. 城市化，都市化
例 The intervention of government plays an important role in solving the problems in the process of *urbanization*. 政府干预对解决城市化过程中出现的问题起着重要作用。

urge [ɜːdʒ]
v. 敦促，力劝；鼓励；竭力主张
例 My boss *urged* me to unfold my market strategy. 老板鼓励我详细阐述我的市场策略。

urgent [ˈɜːdʒənt]
a. 紧急的，紧迫的；催促的，急切的
例 His car is in *urgent* need of repair. 他的汽车急需修理。
派 urgently(*ad.* 紧急地)

□ unyielding □ upgrade □ uphill □ upper □ upset □ up-to-date
□ urban □ urbanization □ urge □ urgent

utilise* [ˈjuːtəlaɪz]

vt. 利用，运用

记 词根记忆：ut(用) + ilise → 利用

例 I guess the two main things to remember are to identify individual talent and then to *utilise* it. 我想需要记住的两个主要内容是确认个人天赋，然后再加以利用。// The engineer has a knowledge of natural science acquired by study and practice which is applied to develop ways to *utilise* the materials and forces of nature for the benefit of mankind. 工程师从学习和实践中得来的自然科学知识可以用来研究利用自然界的材料和力量的途径，从而为人类造福。

utility* [juːˈtɪləti]

n. 功用，效用；[常 *pl.*] 公用事业

记 词根记忆：ut(用) + ility → 使用的效果如何 →功用，效用

例 One of many reforms came in the area of public *utilities*. 众多改革措施中有一条涉及公用事业的变革。

派 utilitarian(*a.* 实用的，功利的)

utilisation [ˌjuːtəlaɪˈzeɪʃn]

n. 利用

例 This research provides the scientific foundation for rational *utilisation* of land. 这项调查为合理使用土地提供了科学依据。

utterance [ˈʌtərəns]

n. 用言语表达，讲话；话语，言语，言论

例 Linguists ask their informants for *utterances* that describe certain actions, objects or behaviours. 语言学家让他们的语料供应人描述某些动作、物体或行为。

vacancy [ˈveɪkənsi]

n. 空位，空房间；(职位的)空缺，空职；无主意，空虚，茫然若失

记 来自 vacant(*a.* 空的，未被占用的)

例 We have *vacancies* for salesmen. 我们销售人员的职位有空缺。

vacant* [ˈveɪkənt]

a. 未占用的，空的

记 词根记忆：vac(空) + ant(形容词后缀) → 未占用的

搭 a vacant position 空缺职位；a vacant seat 空位；a vacant expression 茫然的表情

例 A *vacant* room is very difficult to find in this district after nine o'clock. 九点之后，很难在这个区找到空房间。

派 vacate〔*vt.* 腾出，空出；离(职)，退(位)〕

vacation [vəˈkeɪʃn]

n. 假期；休假

记 词根记忆：vac(空的) + ation → 有空的 → 假期；休假

例 She's going to Florida for *vacation*. 她要去佛罗里达度假。

vacuum [ˈvækjuəm]

n. 真空；[*pl.*] 真空吸尘器 *v.* 用吸尘器清扫

记 词根记忆：vac(空的) + uum → 真空

搭 vacuum desiccator 真空干燥器

例 The *vacuum* flask can keep drinks hot. 保温瓶可以保持饮料的温度。

□ utilise □ utility □ utilisation □ utterance □ vacancy □ vacant
□ vacation □ vacuum

vague [veɪɡ]	*a.* 模糊的；含糊的 记 词根记忆：vag(漫游) + ue → 思路四处游走 → 模糊的；含糊的 例 He gave a ***vague*** answer and we couldn't understand what he meant. 他的回答太含糊了，我们不明白他的意思。
valid [ˈvælɪd]	*a.* 有效的，具有法律效力的；正当的；有根据的，有理的 记 词根记忆：val(价值) + id → 价值大的 → 有效的，具有法律效力的 例 The suggestion will be implemented within 48 hours, if a ***valid*** reason is not given for nonimplementation. 如果不能提出正当的反对理由，该建议将在 48 小时内被执行。
valuable* [ˈvæljuəbl]	*a.* 贵重的，有价值的 *n.* 贵重物品，财宝 搭 valuable belongings 贵重的财产 例 The province is abundant in ***valuable*** minerals. 该省富含贵重的矿物质。
van [væn]	*n.* 运货车 记 联想记忆：运货车(van)能(can)载多少货物 例 We hired a ***van*** to move the furniture to our new house. 我们雇了辆运货车将家具搬往新家。
vanish* [ˈvænɪʃ]	*vi.* 突然消失；不复存在，消逝 记 词根记忆：van(空) + ish → 空无一物 → 不复存在 例 Topsoil in India and China is ***vanishing*** faster and faster. 在印度和中国，地表土流失的速度越来越快。
variability* [ˌveəriəˈbɪləti]	*n.* 可变性，易变性 记 联想记忆：variab(=variable 可变的) + ility → 可变性，易变性 例 Without genetic ***variability*** the species will lose the capacity to evolve. 如果没有基因变异，物种就会失去进化能力。
variant [ˈveəriənt]	*a.* 不同的 *n.* 变量；变体 例 In its most recent ***variant*** (1980), the book consists of the reading of vocabulary and text while the class is listening to music. 在这本书的最新版(1980 年版)中，学生可以边听音乐边阅读词汇与篇章。
variation* [ˌveəriˈeɪʃn]	*n.* 变化，变动；变种，变异；变更；变奏 记 词根记忆：vari(改变，变化) + ation(表状态，名词后缀) → 变化，变动；变异 例 ***Variations*** and combinations of these two hat shapes formed the basis of the pupil's final designs. 这两种帽子外形的改变和相互融合形成了小学生最终设计的基础。
variety* [vəˈraɪəti]	*n.* 品种，种类；变化，多样化 记 词根记忆：var (改变，变化) + iety → 有很多变化 → 品种；变化 搭 a variety of 许多 例 The places we will visit offer a ***variety*** of shopping. 我们将参观的地方可提供各种购物活动。 
various* [ˈveəriəs]	*a.* 各种各样的；不同的；多方面的 例 The professor has studied the languages of ***various*** countries. 这位教授研究过多个国家的语言。

□ vague □ valid □ valuable □ van □ vanish □ variability
□ variant □ variation □ variety □ various

vary
[ˈveərɪ]

v. 改变；(使)多样化；变化；不同

例 The price of a bed in different hotels always ***varies*** so much. 不同旅馆的床位价格总是大不相同。

搭 variable(*a.* 易变的 *n.* 变量)

vast *
[vɑːst]

a. 巨大的；大量的

记 联想记忆：古老的东方(east)地大物博，人口众多(vast)

例 Cutting down forests on a large scale has continued apace over ***vast*** areas. 在很多地区大规模砍伐森林仍在快速进行。

派 vastly(*ad.* 巨大地；大量地)

vegetarian
[ˌvedʒəˈteəriən]

n. 素食者 *a.* 素食者的

搭 a vegetarian restaurant 素食饭馆

例 The restaurant offers special meals for ***vegetarians***. 这家饭店为素食者准备了特别的食物。

vegetation
[ˌvedʒəteɪʃn]

n. 植物，草木

例 There are more and more ***vegetation*** disappearing every year and we couldn't find them forever. 每年都有越来越多的植物灭绝，我们永远也找不到它们了。

同 plant(*n.* 植物)

veil *
[veɪl]

n. 面纱；遮蔽物 *vt.* 蒙着面纱；掩饰

记 联想记忆：邪恶的(evil)人总是试图掩饰(veil)自己

例 They lifted the ***veil*** of this ancient tomb. 他们揭开了这座古代陵墓的神秘面纱。

velocity
[vəˈlɒsəti]

n. 速度，速率；迅速，快速

记 词根记忆：veloc(快的) + ity → 速度，速率；迅速，快速

搭 gain/lose velocity 加/减速

例 The parameters involved in this essay includes mass ratio, initial relative impact ***velocity***, absolute mass and relative acceleration. 这篇论文涉及的参数有：质量比、初始相对碰撞速度、绝对质量和相对加速度。

同 speed(*n.* 迅速；速度，速率)；rapidity(*n.* 迅速)

venomous
[ˈvenəməs]

a. 有毒的；分泌毒液的；恶意的，狠毒的

记 联想记忆：venom(毒液) + ous → 有毒的；分泌毒液的

搭 venomous snake 毒蛇

例 There are some ***venomous*** snakes to beware of in the forest. 森林中有一些需要提防的毒蛇。

ventilation
[ˌventɪˈleɪʃn]

n. 空气流通；通风设备，通风方法

记 来自 ventilate(*vt.* 使通风)

搭 rooms with good ventilation 通风良好的房间；ventilation system 通风系统

例 In the noisiest areas mechanical ***ventilation*** will have to be installed in the exterior walls. 在噪音最大的区域，必须在外墙安装机械通风设备。

□ vary □ vast □ vegetarian □ vegetation □ veil □ velocity
□ venomous □ ventilation

venture
[ˈventʃə(r)]

v. 敢于去；拿…冒险，冒…的险 *n.* 风险投资，(商业等的)风险项目

记 发音记忆："玩车"→玩车一族追求的就是冒险→冒…的险

搭 venture into the unknown 闯入未知的领域；venture into/on sth. 冒险做…

例 Allan, a doctoral student in anthropology, ***ventured*** deep into the jungle to search for the primitive natives. 艾伦是一名人类学博士生，他冒险深入丛林腹地寻找原始土著。

venue
[ˈvenjuː]

n. (聚集、审判、比赛等的)地点

记 联想记忆：ven(来)+ue→大家都来的地方→(聚集、审判、比赛等的)地点

搭 sport venue 运动场馆；outdoor venue 户外场所

例 This team will play here or at other ***venues*** all over the country. 这支队伍将会在这或者国内的其他赛场比赛。

verbal
[ˈvɜːbl]

a. 口头的；言辞的，文字的，词语的；动词的

记 词根记忆：verb(言语)+al(形容词后缀)→口头的；言辞的，文字的

例 The engineer was too excited to give a ***verbal*** description of what the success of moon landing means. 工程师太兴奋了，以至于无法用言语表达登月成功意味着什么。

verdict*
[ˈvɜːdɪkt]

n. 裁定；定论；判断；意见

记 词根记忆：ver(真实的)+dict(说)→说出事实→裁定；判断

搭 reach a verdict 作出裁定

例 The judge will announce court ***verdict*** tomorrow. 法官明天将宣布法院的裁定。

同 opinion(*n.* 主张，判断)；judgment(*n.* 判断；看法)

verification
[ˌverɪfɪˈkeɪʃn]

n. 确认

例 The customs will make a ***verification*** whether there is record filing before the goods release. 在货物放行之前，海关会先确认一下该批货物是否有备案。

verify*
[ˈverɪfaɪ]

vt. 证明；证实

记 词根记忆：ver(真实的)+ify(使…)→使…真实→证明；证实

例 In some California housing estates, a key alone is insufficient to get someone in the door; his or her voiceprint must also be ***verified***. 在加州的一些住宅区，进入房间仅靠一把钥匙是不够的，还需要确认声波纹。

派 verification(*n.* 确认)

vernacular*
[vəˈnækjələ(r)]

n. 本国话；方言；土语；(建筑的)民间风格 *a.* 本国语的

记 发音记忆："我奶哭了"→离乡多年，我奶奶一听到熟悉的乡音就激动地哭了→方言

搭 vernacular dwellings 民居；an incomprehensible vernacular 无法理解的方言

例 This ***vernacular*** language has never really been studied before. 这种方言从未被真正研究过。

□ venture □ venue □ verbal □ verdict □ verification □ verify □ vernacular

versatile
[ˈvɜːsətaɪl]

a. 多才多艺的，多面手的；多用途的，通用的

记 词根记忆：vers（转）+ at + ile → 可以向各个方向转的 → 多才多艺的，多面手的；多用途的，通用的

搭 a portable and versatile inspection tool 便携式多功能检测工具

例 Because honey is *versatile* and not expensive, it is widely used in every aspect of our daily life. 蜂蜜具有多种功能，价格不贵，被广泛应用于日常生活的各个方面。

派 versatility（*n.* 多才多艺；多功能性）；versatilely（*ad.* 多才多艺地；多功能地）

同 all-round（*a.* 多方面的，多才多艺的）

---

version*
[ˈvɜːʃn]

n. 样式；型号；种类；说法；版本；译本

记 词根记忆：vers（转）+ ion → 从原文转化而来 → 译本

例 The British rocket differed from the Indian *version*. 英国火箭和印度火箭不同。

---

versus*
[ˈvɜːsəs]

prep. 与…相对，对抗

记 词根记忆：vers（转）+ us → 转向我们 → 与…相对

例 The performance tomorrow is Rocket *versus* Cavaliers. 明天的表演将是火箭队对骑士队。

同 against（*prep.* 与…相反；对）

versus

宿命的对决

---

vertebrate*
[ˈvɜːtɪbrət]

n. 脊椎动物 *a.* 有脊椎的

记 来自 vertebra（*n.* 脊椎骨）

搭 vertebrate animals 脊椎动物

例 Even without further expansion they could save around 2,000 species of endangered land *vertebrates*. 即使没有更大规模的扩展，他们仍能拯救大约 2000 种濒危陆生脊椎动物。

---

vertical
[ˈvɜːtɪkl]

a. 垂直的；竖式的 *n.* 垂直线

搭 a vertical line 垂直线

例 The climber managed to find a support on the *vertical* cliff. 登山者成功地在陡直的峭壁上找到了一个支撑点。

---

vessel*
[ˈvesl]

n.〈总称〉船只；容器；血管

例 Sea ports have been transformed by the advent of powered *vessels*. 机动船只的出现改变了海港的外观。

vessel

---

vested*
[ˈvestɪd]

a. 法律规定的；既定的

记 联想记忆：到了法律规定的（vested）年龄，就被授予（vest）选举的权利

例 The politicians didn't have the courage to confront the *vested* interest that subsidies create. 政治家们没有勇气去对抗补贴带来的既得利益。

□ versatile □ version □ versus □ vertebrate □ vertical □ vessel
□ vested

vet* [vet]

vt. 审查，仔细检查 *n.* 兽医

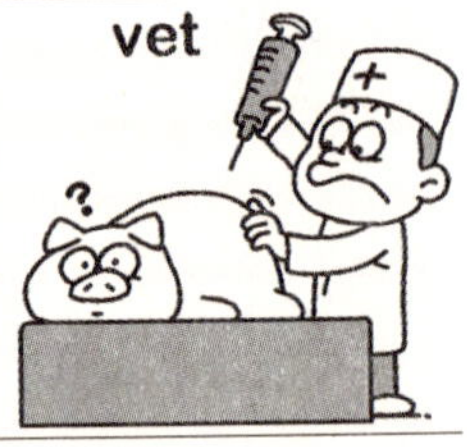

例 Students who want loans are not "means tested" or "credit *vetted*". 想要贷款的学生不用接受家庭经济状况调查，也不用接受信用审查。// I have to take the cat to the *vet's* tomorrow. 明天我得把猫带到兽医诊所去诊治。

同 screen(*vt./n.* 审查，检查)

---

veterinarian* [ˌvetərɪˈneəriən]

n. 兽医

例 The woman wanted to be a *veterinarian* when she was a little girl, but she became a singer when she grew up. 这个女人小时候想成为一名兽医，而长大后成了一名歌手。

---

veterinary* [ˈvetnri]

a. 兽医的

搭 veterinary medicine 兽药

例 This zoo was closed down following a report by a *veterinary* inspector. 这家动物园因为兽医检查员的一份报告而被关闭。

---

viable* [ˈvaɪəbl]

a. 可行的，可实施的；【生】能自行生长发育的

记 词根记忆：vi(道路) + able(能…的) → 有路可走 → 可行的，可实施的

例 In order to develop an economically *viable* hotel organisation model, they decided to implement some new policies. 为了能够开发一种在经济上切实可行的酒店管理模式，他们决定采用一些新政策。

派 viability(*n.* 可行性)

---

vibrant [ˈvaɪbrənt]

a. 振动的；活泼的，充满生气的；兴奋的

例 As we honor this past, we also recognize that the future of the world will benefit from a strong and *vibrant* Russia. 在铭记这一历史的同时，我们也认识到世界的未来将得益于一个强大、富有生机的俄罗斯。

---

vibrate [vaɪˈbreɪt]

v. (使)颤动

例 The rattlesnake would swiftly shake and *vibrate* its tail when it felt threat. 响尾蛇在感到威胁时会急速地摇晃并抖动尾巴。

派 vibration(*n.* 颤动，振动)

---

vice versa*

反之亦然

例 Acids neutralize alkalis and *vice versa*. 酸能中和碱，反之亦然。

---

vicious [ˈvɪʃəs]

a. 罪恶的，邪恶的；残酷的，残忍的；凶猛的；恶性的

记 来自 vice(*n.* 罪行；堕落，邪恶)

搭 vicious circle 恶性循环；a vicious criminal 残忍的罪犯

例 A group of tourists suffered a *vicious* attack by a gang of local people. 一群旅游者遭到一帮当地流氓的恶意攻击。

派 viciously(*ad.* 恶毒地；剧烈地)；viciousness(*n.* 恶毒；严重)

同 savage(*a.* 野蛮的；凶猛的；残忍的)；malicious(*a.* 怀恶意的，恶毒的)；spiteful(*a.* 怀恨的，恶意的)

□ vet □ veterinarian □ veterinary □ viable □ vibrant □ vibrate
□ vice versa □ vicious

victim*
[ˈvɪktɪm]

n. 牺牲者；受害者

记 联想记忆：胜利者（victor）的荣耀是牺牲者（victim）的鲜血换来的。

搭 fall victim to 成为…的牺牲品；成为…的受害者

例 The majority of the *victims* in this earthquake were children. 这次地震中的主要受害者是儿童。

victimise
[ˈvɪktɪmaɪz]

v. （使）受害，迫害

记 联想记忆：victim（受害者）+ ise（使…）→（使）成为受害者 →（使）受害

例 The World Health Organization reported that environmentally related diseases *victimise* the most of Africa continent, followed by parts of Southeast Asia. 世界卫生组织称，与环境相关的疾病危害着非洲大陆的绝大部分地区，其次是东南亚的部分地区。

viewpoint
[ˈvjuːpɔɪnt]

n. 观点，看法

记 组合词：view（见解）+ point（点）→ 观点

例 They held obstinately to the purely military *viewpoint*. 他们顽固地坚持纯粹的军事观点。

vigorous
[ˈvɪgərəs]

a. 朝气蓬勃的；有力的

记 联想记忆：vigor（活力）+ ous → 有活力的 → 朝气蓬勃的

搭 vigorous students 朝气蓬勃的学生

例 The small group of the survivors was to become a *vigorous*, self-sustaining island population. 那一小队幸存者成了精力充沛、自力更生的岛上居民。

The purpose of education is to replace an empty mind with an open one.
教育的目的是用能接受新思想的头脑去取代一个空虚的灵魂。
——美国教育家 福布斯 .M.（Malcolm Forbes, American educator）

Word List 48

音 频

词根、词缀预习表

vil	无耻的	vile *a.* 可恶的；卑鄙的	**vit**	生命	vital *a.* 极其重要的；有生命力的
vis	看	visual *a.* 视觉的；用于视觉的	**volunt**	意愿	voluntary *a.* 自愿的，志愿的
vuln	受伤	vulnerable *a.* 易受攻击的	**voy**	路	voyage *n.* 旅行；航行
vulg	人们，大众	vulgar *a.* 大众的	**ten**	维持	tenable *a.* 站得住脚的；可防守的
scop	看	telescope *n.* 望远镜	**graph**	写	telegraph *n.* 电报机；电报

vile [vaɪl]

a. 糟糕透顶的，可恶的；恶劣的，卑鄙的

记 词根记忆：vil(无耻的) + e → 恶劣的，卑鄙的

例 Study shows that children who live in violent surroundings may use more *vile* languages than ordinary children. 研究表明，与普通孩子相比，生活在暴力环境中的孩子可能会使用更多肮脏的语言。

派 vileness(*n.* 讨厌；卑劣)

violate [ˈvaɪəleɪt]

vt. 违反，违犯，违背；亵渎；侵犯，干扰

例 The legislative should take measures to prevent the mass media from *violating* the public's privacy. 立法机构应该采取措施制止大众媒体侵犯人们的隐私。

派 violation(*n.* 违反)

violence [ˈvaɪələns]

n. 暴力行为；激烈，猛烈

记 发音记忆："为尔冷死" → 多么激烈的爱啊！ → 激烈

例 Capital punishment is essential to control *violence* in society. 死刑对控制社会上的暴力事件具有重要意义。

violent* [ˈvaɪələnt]

a. 暴力的；带有强烈感情的；猛烈的

例 Although news broadcasts are *violent*, people felt they shouldn't be banned. 虽然新闻广播言辞激烈，但人们还是觉得不应该将其取消。

virtually [ˈvɜːtʃuəli]

ad. 几乎，差不多；实际上，事实上

例 There is *virtually* no evidence to support his argument. 事实上没有任何证据可以支持他的论点。

virtue* [ˈvɜːtʃuː]

n. 美德；优点

搭 by/in virtue of 凭借，依靠

例 The *virtue* of job descriptions is that they lessen role ambiguity. 工作描述的优点是能减少角色模糊性。

 □ vile □ violate □ violence □ violent □ virtually □ virtue

virtuous [ˈvɜːtʃuəs]

a. 有道德的，品性好的，品德高的；自命清高的；贞洁的

记 来自 virtue(*n.* 德行；美德)

例 Compared with intelligent people, ***virtuous*** and hard-working people will be more welcomed in the office. 与聪明的人相比，品德高尚、刻苦工作的员工在办公室更受欢迎。

virus [ˈvaɪərəs]

n. 病毒

例 It was a deadly ***virus*** spread by field mice. 这是一种通过田鼠传播的致命病毒。

visa* [ˈviːzə]

n. 签证

记 联想记忆："维萨卡"就是 visa card

搭 exit visa 出境签证；entry visa 入境签证；transit visa 过境签证；work visa 工作签证；study visa 学习签证

例 If you want to re-enter the island, you must get a multi-entry ***visa***. 如果你想要重新进入这个岛屿，就必须持有多次入境签证。

viscous [ˈvɪskəs]

a. 黏滞的，黏性的

例 Numerous tiny worms were floating in a ***viscous*** liquid. 黏稠的液体里飘浮着无数的小蠕虫。

visible* [ˈvɪzəbl]

a. 可见的，看得见的；有形的；明显的，显而易见的

记 词根记忆：vis(看) + ible(可…的) → 可见的，看得见的

例 Comets are only normally ***visible*** in the immediate vicinity of the sun. 彗星只有在最接近太阳时才可见。

派 invisible(*a.* 看不见的，无形的)

vision* [ˈvɪʒn]

n. 想象力；视力，视觉；梦幻，幻觉

例 This type of tablet may cause problems with your ***vision***. 这类药品可能会给你带来视力问题。

visual [ˈvɪʒuəl]

a. 视觉的，用于视觉的

记 词根记忆：vis(看) + ual(形容词后缀) → 视觉的

搭 visual acuity 视敏度；visual aid 直观教具；visual arts 视觉艺术；visual cell 视觉细胞；visual fatigue 视觉疲劳

例 The exhibition of London Museum is largely ***visual***, with a huge number of items on show. 伦敦博物馆的展览会展出了大量物品，让人大开眼界。

vital* [ˈvaɪtl]

a. 生死攸关的；极其重要的；有生命力的

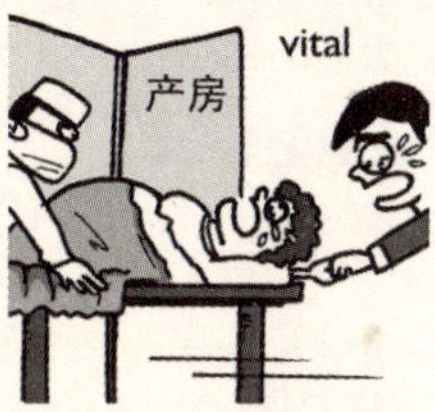

记 词根记忆：vit(生命) + al → 事关生命的 → 生死攸关的

搭 vital to/for sth. 对…极重要的，对…必不可少的；at the vital moment 在关键时刻；a vital error 致命的错误；a vital decision 重要决定

例 The Department has a ***vital*** role to play in providing information to visitors and scholars. 该部门在为来访者及学者提供信息方面发挥着极其重要的作用。

48

□ virtuous □ virus □ visa □ viscous □ visible □ vision
□ visual □ vital

vitality* [vaɪˈtæləti]

n. 生命力，活力

记 词根记忆：vit (生活，生命) + al + ity(名词后缀) → 生命力，活力

搭 be full of vitality 充满活力；exceptional vitality 精力旺盛

例 When you see the Asiatic lion in India, what you sense is enormous *vitality*. 当你在印度看到亚洲狮时，你能感觉到的就是它们旺盛的生命力。

vivid* [ˈvɪvɪd]

a. 鲜艳的；生动的

记 词根记忆：viv(生命) + id → 有生命力的 → 生动的

例 The photos depicted *vivid* scenes of a suffragette's life. 这些照片生动地表现了一名妇女参政论者的生活。

vocational* [vəʊˈkeɪʃənl]

a. 职业的，业务的

记 来自 vocation(*n.* 职业)

例 This is a *vocational* training institute. 这是一个职业培训机构。

volcano* [vɒlˈkeɪnəʊ]

n. 火山

记 联想记忆：vol(=will 意志力) + can(会) + (n)o → 火山爆发不以人的意志为转移 → 火山

例 The majority of the world's *volcanoes* encircle the Pacific Ocean. 世界上的大多数火山都位于环太平洋地区。

volcano

volt [vəʊlt]

n. 伏特

例 He removed a medium sized, 20 *volt* battery from the machine. 他从机器中拿掉了一节 20 伏特的中号电池。

voltage [ˈvəʊltɪdʒ]

n. 电压

例 The *voltage* made her hair shoot straight out. 电压使得她的头发立了起来。

volume* [ˈvɒljuːm]

n. 卷，册；体积；音量

记 联想记忆：和 volute(*a.* 向上卷的)一起记

例 This liquid was 10 litres in *volume*. 这一液体的体积为十升。// Would you turn down the *volume*, please? 你能将音量开小点吗？

voluntary* [ˈvɒləntrɪ]

a. 自愿的，志愿的

记 词根记忆：volunt(意愿) + ary → 出于自身意愿的 → 自愿的

例 I decided to join a *voluntary* organization and was sent to Ecuador to carry out land surveys. 我决定加入一个志愿者组织，并且被派往厄瓜多尔执行土地测量任务。

派 voluntarily (*ad.* 自愿地，自动地，主动地)

volunteer* [ˌvɒlənˈtɪə(r)]

v. 自愿做，无偿做 *a.* 志愿的，义务的，无偿的 *n.* 志愿者

搭 volunteers for Olympic Games 奥运会志愿者

例 Mary *volunteered* to work as a teacher in West Africa. 玛丽自愿去西非做一名教师。

vomit [ˈvɒmɪt]

n. 呕吐，呕吐物；催吐剂 *v.* 呕吐，恶心；喷出

记 联想记忆：v + o(形似嘴) + mit(词根 mit 指"发送") → 张嘴发送 → 呕吐

搭 vomit up 呕吐

例 The strange smell made her want to *vomit*. 这种奇怪的味道让她很恶心。

□ vitality □ vivid □ vocational □ volcano □ volt □ voltage
□ volume □ voluntary □ volunteer □ vomit

voyage [ˈvɔɪɪdʒ]

n./v. 旅行，航行，飞行

记 词根记忆：voy(路) + age → 旅行，航行

搭 maiden voyage 首航；voyage of discovery 发现之旅；first voyage 第一航程

例 They made a *voyage* across the Atlantic. 他们作了一次横越大西洋的航行。

vulgar [ˈvʌlgə(r)]

a. 庸俗的，粗俗的，下流的，缺乏教养的；大众的，通俗的

记 词根记忆：vulg(人们，大众) + ar → 大众的，通俗的

搭 vulgar tastes 低级趣味；vulgar jokes 粗俗的笑话

例 It seems pretty *vulgar* to give a woman your business card in public asking for a date or dinner. 当众给女性名片要求约会或共进晚餐似乎非常粗俗。

派 vulgarity(*n.* 庸俗，粗俗)；vulgarly(*ad.* 粗野地；庸俗地)

同 coarse(*a.* 粗鄙的)

反 exquisite(*a.* 优美的，高雅的，精致的)；elegant(*a.* 雅致的，高雅的)

vulnerable* [ˈvʌlnərəbl]

a. 易受攻击的，易受伤的

记 词根记忆：vuln(受伤) + er + able(易…的) → 易受伤的

搭 be vulnerable to 易受…伤害；vulnerable group 弱势群体

例 Women are especially *vulnerable* to back pain because of pregnancy. 由于怀孕，女性尤其容易背痛。

派 vulnerability(*n.* 易受攻击；弱点)；vulnerably(*ad.* 易受伤害地；易受攻击地)

同 assailable(*a.* 可攻击的，易攻击的)

反 strong(*a.* 强壮的，强大的；坚固的)；tough(*a.* 强硬的；坚韧的)

wage [weɪdʒ]

n. 工资；[常 *pl.*] 报酬

例 In this company, *wages* are paid at the end of every month. 这家公司每到月末发工资。

wagon* [ˈwægən]

n. 四轮马车；大篷车

记 联想记忆：大众汽车 Volkswagon → 客货两用车 → 大篷车

例 The horses were harnessed and hooked to the *wagon*. 这些马被装上挽具，套到马车上。

waist* [weɪst]

n. 腰，腰部

搭 strip to the waist 光着上半身

例 Tom tied a walkman recorder to his *waist*. 汤姆在腰上别了一台随身听。

wander [ˈwɒndə(r)]

v. 徘徊，闲逛，漫步；偏离正道；走神，(神情)恍惚

记 联想记忆：在十字路口徘徊（wander），想知道(wonder)下一步该怎么走

搭 wander from/off 偏离…，游离…；wander from the subject/point 离题；wander about/over the world 漫游世界

例 They enjoyed *wandering* in this old town. 他们喜欢在这个古镇上闲逛。// The teacher realized the students' attention was beginning to *wander*. 老师发现学生的精神开始不集中了。

□ voyage □ vulgar □ vulnerable □ wage □ wagon □ waist
□ wander

warrant * [ˈwɒrənt]	*v.* 保证；证明…正当 *n.* 授权；许可证 例 The situation scarcely ***warrants*** them being dismissed. 这种情况很难证明解雇他们是正当的。
wastage * [ˈweɪstɪdʒ]	*n.* 消耗量；损耗；（雇员的）减员 记 联想记忆：waste（浪费，消耗）+ age（集体名词后缀）→ 消耗量；损耗 例 Quality control cuts ***wastage*** and saves time. 质量管理既降低损耗又节省时间。
water-borne [ˈwɔːtəbɔːn]	*a.* 水运的，水传播的，饮水传染的 记 组合词：water（水）+ borne（bear 的过去分词，携带）→ 由水带来的 → 水运的，水传播的 例 Cholera, a ***water-borne*** disease, could cause severe diarrhea, vomiting and often death. 霍乱是一种由水传播的疾病，能引起严重的腹泻和呕吐，往往还导致死亡。
waterfront * [ˈwɔːtəfrʌnt]	*n.* 滨水路，滨水区，码头区 记 组合词：water（水）+ front（面向，朝向）→ 滨水路，滨水区，码头区 例 Those countries still maintain their business centres near the port ***waterfront***. 那些国家的商业中心仍然靠近码头。
waterproof [ˈwɔːtəpruːf]	*a.* 不透水的；防水的 记 组合词：water（水）+ proof（防…的）→ 防水的 搭 waterproof fabric 防水布，防雨布 例 The ***waterproof*** match can still work after eight hours in water. 防水火柴放在水里八小时后仍能使用。
wax [wæks]	*n.* 蜡；蜂蜡 *v.* 给…上蜡，给…打蜡；（月亮）渐圆，渐满 搭 candle wax 蜡烛 例 In the extracting room, rotating blades shaved away the ***wax*** that covered each cell. 在提取室里，旋转的刀片刮掉覆盖每间蜂房的蜂蜡。
weaken * [ˈwiːkən]	*v.* （使）变弱，（使）减弱 例 He ***weakened*** as the illness grew worse. 他病情加重，身体日益衰弱。
weakness * [ˈwiːknəs]	*n.* 虚弱；缺点；偏好，嗜好 例 Iridology can help doctors discover any constitutional ***weakness*** long before its clinical outbreak. 虹膜学能够帮助医生早在体质虚弱症出现临床症状前就发现它。
wealthy * [ˈwelθi]	*a.* 富的，富裕的；充裕的 例 Some people hold the view that ***wealthy*** nations should share their wealth with poorer nations by providing such things as food and education. 有些人认为富国应以提供食品和教育等方式让穷国分享它们的财富。
wean * [wiːn]	*vt.* （使）断奶，（使）戒掉 例 It is hard to ***wean*** children off picture books when pictures have played a major part throughout their reading experiences. 当图画在孩子们的阅读中扮演着主要角色时，很难让他们去阅读不带图画的书籍。

□ warrant □ wastage □ water-borne □ waterfront □ waterproof □ wax
□ weaken □ weakness □ wealthy □ wean

weapon [ˈwepən]	*n.* 武器，兵器 例 They were interested in the possibilities of using the rocket itself as a *weapon* of war. 他们对将火箭自身用作战争武器的可能性非常感兴趣。
wedge* [wedʒ]	*n.* 楔子，楔形 *vt.* 楔入 记 联想记忆：楔子(wedge)的边缘(edge)很尖锐 例 The window doesn't stay closed unless you *wedge* it. 这扇窗关不严，除非用楔子楔上。
weed [wiːd]	*n.* 杂草 例 Bugs and *weeds* become resistant to poisons, so next year's poisons must be more lethal. 害虫和杂草会产生抗药性，所以来年的农药必须更加致命。
weigh [weɪ]	*v.* 称重；认真考虑，权衡 搭 weigh advantages and disadvantages 权衡利弊；weigh sb. down 使…烦恼，使…忧心忡忡；weigh out 称出 例 These boxes are heavy with honey and may *weigh* up to 90 pounds each. 装满蜂蜜后的这些盒子非常重，每个都可能重达 90 磅。 派 weight(*n.* 重量，分量)
welfare [ˈwelfeə(r)]	*n.* 福利 记 联想记忆：wel(看作 well，好的) + fare(费用) → 让人过上好生活的费用 → 福利 搭 welfare work 福利事业；welfare state 福利制度；福利国家；welfare benefits 福利待遇 例 The office deals with all matters related to student *welfare*. 该办公室专门处理与学生福利相关的各种事务。
well-being [ˌwelˈbiːɪŋ]	*n.* 安宁；福利 记 组合词：well(好，健康) + being(存在) → 安宁；福利 例 They stated, "health is a complete state of physical, mental and social *well-being* and is not merely the absence of disease." 他们声称，"健康是集生理、精神和社会安宁为一体的完整状态，而不仅仅是不生病。"
whaling* [ˈweɪlɪŋ]	*n.* 捕鲸 记 来自 whale(*n.* 鲸) 例 The town was first established as a *whaling* base although there isn't any *whaling* today. 这个城镇建立之初是一个捕鲸基地，但如今这里已经不再捕鲸了。
wheelchair [ˈwiːltʃeə(r)]	*n.* (病人等用的)轮椅 记 组合词：wheel(车轮) + chair(椅子) → 带轮子的椅子 → 轮椅 例 Many public places have *wheelchair* access for the handicapped. 许多公共场所都为残疾人设有轮椅通道。
whereas [ˌweərˈæz]	*conj.* 然而，但是 例 Some of the studies show positive results, *whereas* others do not. 一些研究结果令人满意，其他则不然。

□ weapon □ wedge □ weed □ weigh □ welfare □ well-being
□ whaling □ wheelchair □ whereas

whisper
[ˈwɪspə(r)]

n./v. 低语

记 联想记忆：whi(看作 who) + sper(看作speaker) → 谁在小声说话 → 低语

例 I saw Peter *whisper* something to Michael. 我看见彼得跟迈克尔小声说了些什么。

whistle
[ˈwɪsl]

v. 吹口哨 *n.* 口哨；呼啸而过

记 联想记忆：w + hist(嘘) + le → 嘘的一声 → 吹口哨；口哨

例 This is where you *whistle* so the key holder will open the door for you. 你就在这里吹口哨，看门人就会给你开门。

widespread
[ˈwaɪdspred]

a. 分布广的；普遍的

记 组合词：wide(宽广的) + spread(传播，分布) → 分布广的

搭 widespread vegetables 广泛种植的蔬菜

例 The use of friction to make fire was also *widespread* in Europe. 摩擦生火的办法在欧洲也广为流传。

wildlife
[ˈwaɪldlaɪf]

n. 野生生物

记 组合词：wild(野生的) + life(生命) → 野生生物

例 Most of the *wildlife* in the rainforest are gentle and harmless. 雨林中的大多数野生动植物都是温和无害的。

willing
[ˈwɪlɪŋ]

a. 愿意的，乐意的

例 Would you be *willing* to attend any of our promotions? 你愿意参加我们的宣传活动吗，无论哪个都成？

派 willingness(*n.* 自发；愿意)

windscreen
[ˈwɪndskriːn]

n. 挡风玻璃，风挡

记 组合词：wind(风) + screen(屏，遮蔽物) → 挡风玻璃

例 You must attach it to the front *windscreen* of your car. 你必须把它贴在汽车前面的挡风玻璃上。

wire*
[ˈwaɪə(r)]

n. 金属丝；电线

例 The pulses would travel over glass fibres, not copper *wire*. 这些脉冲将通过玻璃纤维而不是铜丝传输。

withdraw
[wɪðˈdrɔː]

v. 收回；撤退；缩回，退出；提取(钱)

搭 withdraw one's promise 收回诺言；a withdrawn letter 撤回的信函；withdraw money from a bank 从银行取钱

例 ATMs are extremely useful as they enable you to *withdraw* cash from your account whenever you want. 自动取款机非常有用，因为它可以使你随时从账户内取款。

□ whisper □ whistle □ widespread □ wildlife □ willing □ windscreen
□ wire □ withdraw

withstand [wɪð'stænd]

vt. 抵挡；经受住

记 联想记忆：with(与…在一起)+stand(站)→武警官兵手拉手站在一起抵挡洪流→抵挡

例 A desert animal can *withstand* high body temperatures. 生活在沙漠中的动物可以忍受较高的体温。

witness ['wɪtnəs]

n. 证据；目击者 *v.* 目击；为…作证

例 Tom *witnessed* the accident. 汤姆目睹了那起意外事故。

womb* [wuːm]

n. 子宫；发源地

记 联想记忆：生命的过程就是从子宫(womb)到坟墓(tomb)

例 Foetuses can be tested while in the *womb*. 胎儿在子宫的时候可以进行检查。

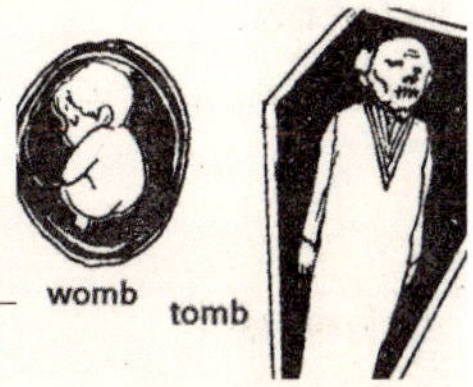

wonder* ['wʌndə(r)]

v. 诧异，奇怪；纳闷，想知道 *n.* 惊奇，惊异；奇迹，奇事

搭 no wonder 难怪，怪不得

例 Excuse me, I'm *wondering* if you'd mind answering a few questions? 打扰了，我想知道你是否介意回答几个问题?

workaholic* [ˌwɜːkə'hɒlɪk]

n. 工作狂

记 联想记忆：work(工作)+aholic(着迷于…的，上瘾的)→工作狂

例 Many people criticised this *workaholic* economy. 很多人批评这种工作狂经济。

workforce ['wɜːkfɔːs]

n. 受雇的或现有的工作人员总数；劳动人口

记 组合词：work(工作)+force(队伍)→劳动人口

例 The rise in the female *workforce* in the European Community is a positive trend. 欧共体中女性劳动人口的增加是一个积极的趋势。

world-wide ['wɜːldwaɪd]

a./ad. 遍及全球的/地

例 The use of artificial fertilizers *world-wide* increased by 40 percent per unit of farmed land between the mid 1970s and late 1980s. 从20世纪70年代中期到80年代末，在全世界范围内每单位耕地的人造化肥使用量增长了40%。

worm [wɜːm]

n. 虫，蠕虫；蜗杆，螺纹

例 There are two *worm* gears, one vertical and one horizontal. 有两种涡轮，一种是垂直的，另一种是水平的。

worthwhile [ˌwɜːθ'waɪl]

a. 值得花费时间(或金钱)的，值得做的

记 组合词：worth(值得)+while(一段时间)→值得花费时间的

搭 be worthwhile to do sth./doing sth. 值得做…

例 I'm sure you've done *worthwhile* things in the last ten years. 我确信在过去的十年里，你做了很多有意义的事。

worthy ['wɜːði]

a. 有价值的；值得的

例 I would praise him, but he is not *worthy*. 我想表扬他，但他自己不争气。

反 unworthy(*a.* 没有价值的；不值得的)

□ withstand □ witness □ womb □ wonder □ workaholic □ workforce
□ world-wide □ worm □ worthwhile □ worthy

wrap [ræp]	*v.* 裹；包；缠绕 记 联想记忆：w + rap(使着迷) → 被缠绕着 → 缠绕 例 I will *wrap* all of your Christmas gifts. 我会把你所有的圣诞礼物都包起来。
wrestle [ˈresl]	*v.* 摔跤；全力对付；用力移动 搭 wrestle with 与…摔跤；与…斗争 例 The police officer tackled the man and *wrestled* him to the ground. 警方制服了那个男人并将他摔倒在地。
wretch* [retʃ]	*n.* 不幸的人 记 联想记忆：wre(看作 wreck，遇难) + t(看作 to，去) + ch(看作 China) → 保罗开车去中国，撞了！ → 不幸的人 例 He is really a poor *wretch* that he lost his mother when he was five years old. 他五岁的时候就失去了母亲，真是一个不幸的人。
wrinkle [ˈrɪŋkl]	*n.* 皱纹 *v.* (使)起皱纹 记 联想记忆：眨眼(twinkle)容易起皱纹(wrinkle) 例 Those ladies wanted to make their looks free of *wrinkles*. 那些贵妇们希望自己的脸上没有皱纹。 
yield [jiːld]	*n.* 产量 *v.* 出产；放弃 搭 yield up 放纵；yield to 向…屈服；boost crop yield 提高作物产量 例 Higher *yields* have been achieved by increased irrigation and better crop breeding. 通过增加灌溉和提高育种质量实现了产量的增长。 派 yielding(*a.* 出产的；柔顺的，顺从的)
zone [zəʊn]	*n.* 地区，地带；区域 记 联想记忆：爱尔兰组合 Boy Zone(男孩地带) 例 There are many different climatic *zones* in Australia. 澳大利亚有很多不同的气候带。
zoological* [ˌzəʊəˈlɒdʒɪkl; ˌzuːəˈlɒdʒɪkl]	*a.* 动物学的 记 来自 zoology(*n.* 动物学) 例 I believe that 10,000 is a serious underestimate of the total number of *zoological* establishments in this world. 我认为全球动物学机构的总量远不止一万个。

□ wrap □ wrestle □ wretch □ wrinkle □ yield □ zone
□ zoological

附录一　2000个最常用词汇

A

a *art.* 一(个、张、块 …)
ability *n.* 能力
about *prep.* 关于
above *prep.* 在…上面 *ad.* 在上面 *a.* 上面的
abroad *ad.* 在国外，到国外
absence *n.* 缺席
absent *a.* 缺席的
accept *v.* 接受
acceptable *a.* 可接受的
accident *n.* 事故
accordance *n.* 符合，一致
according *a.* 符合的
according to 根据
account *n.* 账目
ache *v.* 痛
acid *a.* 酸的
across *prep.* 穿过
act *v.* 表演
action *n.* 动作，表演
active *a.* 积极的
activity *n.* 活动
actor *n.* 男演员
actress *n.* 女演员
actual *a.* 真的
add *v.* 增加
addition *n.* 添加
address *n.* 地址
adjective *n.* 形容词
admiration *n.* 仰慕
admire *v.* 崇敬
admit *v.* 承认
adult *n.* 成年人
advance *n.* 前进 *v.* 推进，促进
advantage *n.* 优势
adventure *n.* 冒险
adverb *n.* 副词
advertise *v.* 做广告
advertisement *n.* 广告
advice *n.* 建议
advise *v.* 建议
affair *n.* 事情
afford *v.* 承担
afraid *a.* 害怕的
after *prep.* 在…以后 *conj.* 在…以后
afternoon *n.* 下午
afterwards *ad.* 之后
again *ad.* 再一次
against *prep.* 与…相对
age *n.* 年龄
ago *ad.* 之前
agree *v.* 同意
agreement *n.* 同意
ahead *ad.* 在前
aim *n.* 目标
air *n.* 空气
aircraft *n.* 飞机
airforce *n.* 空军
airport *n.* 机场
alcohol *n.* 酒精
alike *ad.* 相像
alive *a.* 活的
all *a.* 全部的 *pron.* 全体
allow *v.* 允许
almost *ad.* 几乎
alone *a.* 单独的
along *ad.* 沿着
aloud *ad.* 大声地
alphabet *n.* 字母表
already *ad.* 已经
also *ad.* 也
although *conj.* 虽然
altogether *ad.* 总共
always *ad.* 总是
among *prep.* 在…之中
amount *n.* 数量
amuse *v.* 使愉快
amusement *n.* 娱乐
amusing *a.* 有趣的
an *art.* 一(个、张、块 …)
ancient *a.* 古老的
and *conj.* 和
anger *n.* 生气
angle *n.* 角度
angry *a.* 生气的
animal *n.* 动物

ankle *n.* 脚踝
annoy *v.* 惹恼
annoyance *n.* 恼怒
another *a.* 另一的
answer *n.* 答案 *v.* 回答
ant *n.* 蚂蚁
anxiety *n.* 焦虑
anxious *a.* 焦虑的
any *a.* 任何
anyhow *ad.* 无论如何
anyone *pron.* 任何人
anything *pron.* 任何事
anywhere *pron.* 任何地方
apart *ad.* 分开
apparatus *n.* 器械
appear *v.* 出现
appearance *n.* 模样
apple *n.* 苹果
appoint *v.* 指定
approval *n.* 同意
approve *v.* 同意
arch *n.* 拱形
area *n.* 地域
argue *v.* 争论
argument *n.* 争论
arm *n.* 胳膊
armor *n.* 盔甲
arms *n.* 武器
army *n.* 军队
around *prep.* 在…周围
arrange *v.* 安排
arrangement *n.* 安排
arrival *n.* 到达
arrive *v.* 到达
art *n.* 艺术
article *n.* 文章
as *ad.* 就像
conj. 因为，当…时
ash *n.* 灰尘
ashamed *a.* 羞愧的
aside *ad.* 在旁边
ask *v.* 问
asleep *ad.* 睡着地
association *n.* 联合
at *prep.* 在
atom *n.* 原子
attack *v.* 攻击
attempt *v.* 试图
attend *v.* 参加
attendance *n.* 参加
attention *n.* 注意
attract *v.* 吸引
attractive *a.* 有吸引力的
aunt *n.* 阿姨
autumn *n.* 秋季
average *a.* 平均的 *n.* 平均
avoid *v.* 避免
awake *a.* 醒着的
away *ad.* 离开
awkward *a.* 尴尬的

B

baby *n.* 婴儿
back *a.* 后面的 *ad.* 在后面
n. 后背
background *n.* 背景
backward *ad.* 向后
backwards *ad.* 向后
bacterial *a.* 细菌的
bad *a.* 坏的
bag *n.* 书包
bake *v.* 烘烤
balance *n.* 平衡
ball *n.* 球
banana *n.* 香蕉
band *n.* 品牌
bank *n.* 银行；河岸
bar *n.* 木棒 *v.* 拴住
bare *a.* 秃的
barrel *n.* 桶
base *n.* 基础 *v.* 以…为基础
basket *n.* 篮子
bath *n.* 洗澡
bathe *v.* 洗澡
battle *n.* 战役
be *v.* 是
beak *n.* 喙
beam *n.* 梁
bean *n.* 豆子
bear *v.* 忍受
beard *n.* 胡子
beat *n.* 敲打 *v.* 敲打
beautiful *a.* 美丽的
beauty *n.* 美人
because *conj.* 因为
become *v.* 成为
bed *n.* 床
bee *n.* 蜜蜂
beer *n.* 啤酒
before *prep.* 在…之前
beg *v.* 乞求
begin *v.* 开始
beginning *n.* 开始
behave *v.* 表现

behavior *n.* 行为
behind *ad.* 在后面较远处
prep. 在…后面
belief *n.* 信仰
believe *v.* 相信
bell *n.* 铃声
belong *v.* 属于
below *ad.* 在下面 *prep.* 在…下面
belt *n.* 带子
bend *v.* 弯折
beneath *prep.* 在…下面
berry *n.* 浆果
beside *prep.* 在…旁边
besides *conj.* 另外
best *a.* 最好的
better *a.* 较好的
between *prep.* 在…之间
beyond *ad.* 在更远处
bicycle *n.* 自行车
big *a.* 大的
bill *n.* 账单
bind *v.* 捆绑
bird *n.* 鸟
birth *n.* 出生
birthday *n.* 生日
bit *n.* 一点儿
bite *v.* 咬
bitter *a.* 苦的
black *a.* 黑的 *n.* 黑色
blade *n.* 刀片
blame *v.* 责怪
bleed *v.* 流血
bless *v.* 祝福
blind *a.* 盲的
block *v.* 阻塞
blood *n.* 血
blow *v.* 吹
blue *a.* 蓝色的
board *n.* 木板
boat *n.* 船
body *n.* 身体
boil *v.* 煮
bomb *n.* 炸弹
bone *n.* 骨头
book *n.* 书
boot *n.* 靴子
border *n.* 边境
born *a.* 出生的
borrow *v.* 借
both *pron.* 两者
bottle *n.* 瓶子
bottom *n.* 底部
bowel *n.* 肠子
bowl *n.* 碗
box *n.* 盒子
boy *n.* 男孩
brain *n.* 脑子
branch *n.* 分支
brass *n.* 铜
brave *a.* 勇敢的
bread *n.* 面包
breadth *n.* 宽度
break *v.* 打破
breakfast *n.* 早餐
breast *n.* 胸
breath *n.* 呼吸
breathe *v.* 呼吸
breed *v.* 教养
brick *n.* 砖
bridge *n.* 桥
bright *a.* 明亮的
bring *v.* 带来
broad *a.* 宽的
broadcast *v.* 广播
brother *n.* 兄弟
brown *a.* 棕色的 *n.* 棕色
brush *n.* 刷子
bucket *n.* 木桶
build *v.* 建筑
building *n.* 建筑物
bullet *n.* 子弹
bunch *n.* 许多
burial *n.* 埋葬
burn *v.* 燃烧
burst *v.* 爆发
bury *v.* 埋葬
bus *n.* 公共汽车
bush *n.* 灌木丛
business *n.* 生意
busy *a.* 忙的
but *conj.* 但是
butter *n.* 黄油
button *n.* 按钮
buy *v.* 买
by *prep.* 通过

C

cage *n.* 笼子
cake *n.* 蛋糕
calculate *v.* 计算
calculator *n.* 计算器
call *v.* 叫

calm *a.* 冷静的
camera *n.* 摄像机
camp *n.* 营地 *v.* 扎营
can *n.* 容器 *v.* 能，会
candle *n.* 蜡烛
cap *n.* 帽子
capital *n.* 资金；首都
captain *n.* 船长
car *n.* 汽车
card *n.* 卡片
cardboard *n.* 纸板
care *v.* 关心
careful *a.* 细心的
careless *a.* 粗心的
carriage *n.* 车辆
carry *v.* 携带
cart *n.* 大车
case *n.* 案子
castle *n.* 城堡
cat *n.* 猫
catch *v.* 抓住
cattle *n.* 牛
cause *n.* 原因
cell *n.* 细胞
cement *n.* 水泥
cent *n.* 分
center *n.* 中心
centimeter *n.* 厘米
central *a.* 中心的
century *n.* 世纪
ceremony *n.* 庆祝
certain *a.* 确定的
chain *n.* 链子
chair *n.* 椅子
chairperson *n.* 主席
chalk *n.* 粉笔
chance *n.* 机会
change *v.* 改变
character *n.* 性格
charge *v.* 索取
charm *n.* 魅力
chase *v.* 追逐
cheap *a.* 便宜的
cheat *v.* 欺骗
check/cheque *n.* 支票
cheek *n.* 面颊
cheer *v.* 欢呼
cheerful *a.* 高兴的
cheese *n.* 奶酪
chemical *a.* 化学的
chemistry *n.* 化学
chest *n.* 胸
chicken *n.* 鸡
chief *a.* 主要的
child *n.* 孩子
childhood *n.* 童年
children *n.* 孩子
chimney *n.* 烟囱
chin *n.* 下巴
chocolate *n.* 巧克力
choice *n.* 选择
choose *v.* 选择
church *n.* 教堂
cigarette *n.* 香烟
cinema *n.* 影院
circle *n.* 圆圈
circular *a.* 圆的
citizen *n.* 市民
city *n.* 城市
civilization *n.* 文明
claim *n.* 声明
class *n.* 班级
clay *n.* 泥土
clean *a.* 清洁的 *v.* 清洁
clear *a.* 清楚地 *v.* 弄清楚
clerk *n.* 书记员
clever *a.* 聪明的
cliff *n.* 悬崖
climb *v.* 爬
clock *n.* 钟
close *a.* 紧密的，关着的 *ad.* 紧密地 *v.* 关闭
cloth *n.* 布
clothes *n.* 衣服
clothing *n.* 服装
cloud *n.* 云
club *n.* 俱乐部
coal *n.* 煤
coast *n.* 海岸
coat *n.* 外套
coffee *n.* 咖啡
coin *n.* 硬币
cold *a.* 寒冷的
collar *n.* 衣领
collect *v.* 收集
college *n.* 大学
color *n.* 颜色
comb *n.* 梳子
combination *n.* 结合
combine *v.* 结合
come *v.* 来
comfort *v.* 安慰
comfortable *a.* 舒服的
command *v.* 要求
committee *n.* 委员会

common *a.* 平常的
companion *n.* 同伴
company *n.* 公司
compare *v.* 比较
comparison *n.* 比较
compete *v.* 竞争
competition *n.* 竞争
competitor *n.* 竞争者
complain *v.* 抱怨
complaint *n.* 抱怨
complete *a.* 完全的
computer *n.* 计算机
concern *v.* 关于
concerning *prep.* 关于
concert *n.* 音乐会
condition *n.* 条件
confidence *n.* 信心
confident *a.* 有信心的
confuse *v.* 使糊涂
connect *v.* 连接
conscience *n.* 良心
conscious *a.* 有意识的
consider *v.* 考虑
consist *v.* 组成
contain *v.* 包括
content *n.* 内容
continue *v.* 继续
contract *n.* 合同
control *v.* 控制
convenient *a.* 方便的
conversation *n.* 谈话
cook *v.* 烹饪
cool *a.* 凉快的
copper *n.* 紫铜
copy *v.* 复制

cord *n.* 绳索
corn *n.* 玉米
corner *n.* 拐角
correct *a.* 正确的
cost *n.* 成本
cotton *n.* 棉花
cough *v.* 咳嗽
could *v.* 能，会
council *n.* 委员会
count *v.* 计算
country *n.* 国家
courage *n.* 勇气
course *n.* 课程
court *n.* 法院
cover *v.* 覆盖
cow *n.* 奶牛
coward *n.* 胆小鬼
cowardly *a.* 胆小的
crash *n.* 碰撞 *v.* 碰撞
cream *n.* 奶油
creature *n.* 生物
creep *v.* 爬行
cricket *n.* 蟋蟀
crime *n.* 罪行 *v.* 犯罪
criminal *a.* 有罪的
crop *n.* 庄稼
cross *n.* 十字架 *v.* 穿过
crowd *n.* 人群
cruel *a.* 残忍的
cruelty *n.* 残忍
crush *v.* 压碎
cry *v.* 哭
cup *n.* 杯子
cupboard *n.* 橱柜
cure *v.* 治愈

curl *n.* 卷发
current *a.* 最近的
curse *v.* 诅咒
curtain *n.* 窗帘
curve *v.* 雕刻
custom *n.* 风俗
customer *n.* 顾客
cut *v.* 切割
cycle *v.* 循环

D

daily *a.* 每天的 *ad.* 每天
damage *v.* 破坏
dance *v.* 跳舞 *n.* 舞蹈
danger *n.* 危险
dangerous *a.* 有危险的
dare *v.* 敢
daring *a.* 大胆的
dark *a.* 黑的
date *n.* 日期
daughter *n.* 女儿
day *n.* 白天
dead *a.* 死的
deal *n.* 事情
dear *a.* 亲爱的
death *n.* 死亡
debt *n.* 债务
decay *v.* 腐朽
deceit *n.* 欺骗
deceive *v.* 欺骗
decide *v.* 决定
decimal *n.* 小数
decision *n.* 决定
declaration *n.* 声明

declare *v.* 声明
decorate *v.* 装饰
decoration *n.* 装饰
decrease *v.* 减少
deep *a.* 深的
deer *n.* 鹿
defeat *v.* 打败
defend *v.* 防御
defense *n.* 防御
degree *n.* 程度
delay *v.* 推迟
delicate *a.* 精细的
delight *n.* 高兴
deliver *v.* 传送
demand *v.* 要求
department *n.* 部门
depend *v.* 取决于
dependent *a.* 依赖的
depth *n.* 深度
descend *v.* 下降
describe *v.* 描写
description *n.* 描写
desert *n.* 沙漠
deserve *v.* 应得
desirable *a.* 想要的
desire *v.* 想要
desk *n.* 书桌
destroy *v.* 破坏
destruction *n.* 破坏
detail *n.* 细节
determination *n.* 决定
determined *a.* 决定的
develop *v.* 发展
devil *n.* 魔鬼
diamond *n.* 钻石
dictionary *n.* 字典
die *v.* 死
difference *n.* 不同
different *a.* 不同的
difficult *a.* 困难的
difficulty *n.* 困难
dig *v.* 挖掘
dinner *n.* 正餐
dip *v.* 舀，汲取
direct *a.* 直接的 *v.* 指导
direction *n.* 方向
dirt *n.* 灰尘
dirty *a.* 脏的
disappoint *v.* 使失望
discourage *v.* 使气馁
discouragement *n.* 气馁
discover *v.* 发现
discovery *n.* 发现
dish *n.* 菜肴
dismiss *v.* 解除
distance *n.* 距离
distant *a.* 遥远的
ditch *n.* 沟
divide *v.* 分开
division *n.* 分开
do *v.* 做
draw *v.* 拖，拉
drawer *n.* 抽屉
dream *v.* 做梦 *n.* 梦想
dress *n.* 衣服 *v.* 穿衣
drink *v.* 喝
drive *v.* 驾驶
drop *v.* 掉落
drown *v.* 溺死
drug *n.* 药物；毒品
drum *n.* 鼓
drunk *a.* 喝醉的
dry *a.* 干燥的
duck *n.* 鸭子
dull *a.* 阴暗的
during *prep.* 在…期间
dust *n.* 灰尘
duty *n.* 责任

E

each *a.* 每一个的 *pron.* 每个
eager *a.* 热切的
ear *n.* 耳朵
early *a.* 早的
earn *v.* 赢得
earth *n.* 地球
east *n.* 东方
eastern *a.* 东方的
easy *a.* 容易的
eat *v.* 吃
edge *n.* 边缘
educate *v.* 教育
education *n.* 教育
effect *n.* 影响
effective *a.* 有效的
effort *n.* 努力
egg *n.* 蛋
eight *num.* 八
eighth *num.* 第八
either *pron.* (两者)任一个
elbow *n.* 肘
elect *v.* 选举
election *n.* 选举
electric *a.* 电的

electricity *n.* 电
elephant *n.* 大象
else *a.* 另外的
employ *v.* 雇用
employer *n.* 雇主
employment *n.* 雇用
empty *a.* 空的 *v.* 清空
enclose *v.* 包围
enclosure *n.* 包围
encourage *v.* 鼓励
encouragement *n.* 鼓励
end *n.* 结局
enemy *n.* 敌人
engine *n.* 发动机
engineer *n.* 工程师
English *n.* 英语
enjoy *v.* 享受
enjoyment *n.* 享受
enough *a.* 足够的
enter *v.* 进入
entertain *v.* 给…娱乐
entertainment *n.* 娱乐
entrance *n.* 入口
envelope *n.* 信封
equal *a.* 平等的 *n.* 同等的人 *v.* 使平等
equality *n.* 平等
escape *v.* 逃跑
especially *ad.* 特别地
establish *v.* 建立
establishment *n.* 建立
even *a.* 平坦的 *ad.* 即使
evening *n.* 晚上
event *n.* 事件
ever *ad.* 永远
every *a.* 每一个的
everyone *pron.* 每个人
everything *pron.* 每件事
everywhere *pron.* 每个地方
evil *a.* 邪恶的
exact *a.* 准确的
examination *n.* 考试
examine *v.* 考察
example *n.* 例子
excellent *a.* 优秀的
except *conj.* 除了
exchange *v.* 交换
excite *v.* 使兴奋
excited *a.* 兴奋的
exciting *a.* 使人兴奋的
excuse *v.* 原谅
exercise *v.* 练习
exist *v.* 存在
existence *n.* 存在
expect *v.* 期望
expensive *a.* 昂贵的
experience *n.* 经历
explain *v.* 解释
explanation *n.* 解释
explode *v.* 爆炸
explosion *n.* 爆炸
explosive *a.* 爆炸的
express *v.* 表达
expression *n.* 表达
extreme *a.* 极其的
eye *n.* 眼睛
eyelid *n.* 眼睑

F

face *n.* 脸
fact *n.* 事实
factory *n.* 工厂
fail *v.* 失败
failure *n.* 失败
faint *a.* 晕的 *v.* 晕倒
fair *a.* 公平的
fairy *n.* 仙女
faith *n.* 信仰
faithful *a.* 忠实的；虔诚的
fall *v.* 掉落
false *a.* 错误的
fame *n.* 声誉
familiar *a.* 熟悉的
family *n.* 家庭
famous *a.* 著名的
fancy *n.* 想像力
far *a.* 遥远的
farm *n.* 农场
farmer *n.* 农民
fashion *n.* 时髦
fashionable *a.* 时髦的
fast *a.* 快的 *ad.* 快地
fasten *v.* 加快
fat *a.* 肥胖的
fate *n.* 命运
father *n.* 父亲
fault *n.* 错误
favor *n.* 喜爱
favorable *a.* 喜爱的
favorite *a.* 最爱的
fear *v.* 害怕

feather *n.* 羽毛
feed *v.* 喂养
feel *v.* 感觉
feeling *n.* 感受
fellow *n.* 伙伴
female *n.* 女性
fence *n.* 栅栏
fever *n.* 发烧
few *a.* 很少的
field *n.* 土地
fierce *a.* 凶猛的
fifth *num.* 第五
fight *v.* 战斗
figure *n.* 数字
fill *v.* 填补
film *n.* 电影
find *v.* 找到
fine *a.* 好的
finger *n.* 手指
finish *v.* 结束
fire *n.* 火
fireplace *n.* 壁炉
firm *a.* 坚定的 *n.* 公司
first *num.* 第一
fish *n.* 鱼
fisherman *n.* 渔夫
fit *a.* 合适的 *v.* 使适合
five *num.* 五，五个
fix *v.* 安装
flag *n.* 旗帜
flame *n.* 火焰
flash *n.* 闪光 *v.* 闪光
flat *a.* 平的，平坦的
flesh *n.* 肉
flight *n.* 飞
float *v.* 漂流
flood *n.* 洪水
floor *n.* 地板
flour *n.* 面粉
flow *v.* 流动
flower *n.* 花
fly *n.* 苍蝇 *v.* 飞
fold *v.* 折叠
follow *v.* 跟随
fond *a.* 喜爱的
food *n.* 食物
fool *n.* 傻瓜
foolish *a.* 愚蠢的
foot *n.* 脚
football *n.* 足球
footpath *n.* 小路
footstep *n.* 脚步
for *prep.* 为了
forbid *v.* 禁止
force *n.* 力量
forehead *n.* 额头
foreign *a.* 外国的
foreigner *n.* 外国人
forest *n.* 森林
forget *v.* 忘记
forgive *v.* 原谅
fork *n.* 叉子
form *v.* 形成
formal *a.* 正式的
former *a.* 以前的
formerly *ad.* 以前
fort *n.* 堡垒
fortunate *a.* 幸运的
fortune *n.* 财富
forward *ad.* 向前
forwards *ad.* 向前
four *num.* 四
fourth *num.* 第四
fox *n.* 狐狸
frame *n.* 框架
free *a.* 自由的；免费的
freedom *n.* 自由
freeze *v.* 冰冻
frequent *a.* 频繁的
fresh *a.* 新鲜的
friend *n.* 朋友
friendly *a.* 友好的
frighten *v.* 使惊吓
frightening *a.* 吓人的
from *prep.* 从
front *a.* 前面的 *n.* 前面
fruit *n.* 水果
fulfill *v.* 履行
full *a.* 满的
fun *n.* 乐趣
funeral *n.* 葬礼
funny *a.* 有趣的
fur *n.* 皮毛
furnish *v.* 装饰
furniture *n.* 家具
further *a.* 更远的 *ad.* 更远地
future *n.* 未来

G

gain *v.* 得到
game *n.* 游戏
garage *n.* 车库
garden *n.* 花园
garment *n.* 衣服

gas *n.* 气体
gasoline/petrol *n.* 汽油
gate *n.* 大门
gather *v.* 收集
general *a.* 一般的
generous *a.* 慷慨的
gentle *a.* 温柔的
gentleman *n.* 绅士
get *v.* 得到
gift *n.* 礼物
girl *n.* 女孩
give *v.* 给
glad *a.* 高兴的
glass *n.* 玻璃
glory *n.* 荣誉
glue *n.* 胶水
go *v.* 去
goat *n.* 山羊
god *n.* 神
God *n.* 上帝
gold *n.* 金子
golden *a.* 金的
good *a.* 好的
good-bye *n.* 再见
goods *n.* 货物
govern *v.* 统治，管理
government *n.* 政府
grace *n.* 优雅
graceful *a.* 优雅的
gradual *a.* 逐渐的
grain *n.* 谷物
gram *n.* 电报
grammar *n.* 语法
grand *a.* 宏伟的
grandfather *n.* 祖父
grandmother *n.* 祖母
grass *n.* 草
grateful *a.* 感激的
grave *n.* 坟墓
gray *a.* 灰色的 *n.* 灰色
great *a.* 伟大的
green *a.* 绿色的 *n.* 绿色
greet *v.* 问候
greeting *n.* 问候
grief *n.* 痛苦
grieve *v.* 感到悲痛，伤心
ground *n.* 土地
group *n.* 小组
grow *v.* 生长
growth *n.* 生长
guard *v.* 保卫
guess *v.* 猜想
guest *n.* 客人
guidance *n.* 指导
guide *v.* 指导
guilt *n.* 罪行
gun *n.* 枪

H

habit *n.* 习惯
hair *n.* 头发
hairy *a.* 毛的，多毛的
half *n.* 一半
hall *n.* 大厅
hammer *n.* 鼓槌；铁锤
hand *n.* 手
handkerchief *n.* 手绢
handle *v.* 处理，解决
hang *v.* 悬挂
happen *v.* 发生
happy *a.* 高兴的
hard *a.* 坚硬的
harden *v.* 变硬
hardly *ad.* 几乎不
hardship *n.* 辛苦
harm *n.* 害处
harmful *a.* 有害的
harmless *a.* 无害的
hasty *a.* 匆忙的
hat *n.* 帽子
hate *v.* 憎恨
hatred *n.* 憎恨
have *v.* 有
he *pron.* 他
head *a.* 头部的 *n.* 头
health *n.* 健康
healthy *a.* 健康的
hear *v.* 听
heart *n.* 心
heat *n.* 热量
heaven *n.* 天堂
heavy *a.* 重的
heel *n.* 脚后跟
height *n.* 高度
help *v.* 帮助
helpful *a.* 有益的
hen *n.* 母鸡
her *pron.* 她
here *ad.* 这里，在这里
hers *pron.* 她的
herself *pron.* 她自己
hide *v.* 躲藏
high *a.* 高的 *ad.* 高
hill *n.* 小山

him *pron.* 他
himself *pron.* 他自己
hire *v.* 雇用
his *pron.* 他的
historical *a.* 历史的
history *n.* 历史
hit *v.* 打击
hold *v.* 抓住，持有
holiday *n.* 假期
hollow *a.* 空的
holy *a.* 神圣的
home *ad.* 在家 *n.* 家
honest *a.* 诚实的
honesty *n.* 诚实
honor *n.* 荣誉
honorable *a.* 光荣的
hook *n.* 钩子
hope *v.* 希望 *n.* 希望
hopeful *a.* 有希望的
hopeless *a.* 没希望的
horizon *n.* 地平(线)
horn *n.* 角
horse *n.* 马
hospital *n.* 医院
host *n.* 主人
hot *a.* 热的
hotel *n.* 旅店
hour *n.* 小时
hourly *a.* 小时的
house *n.* 房子
how *ad.* 怎样
human *n.* 人类
humor *n.* 幽默
humorous *a.* 幽默的
hundred *num.* 百
hundredth *num.* 第一百
hunger *n.* 饥饿
hungry *a.* 饥饿的
hunt *v.* 打猎
hurry *v.* 匆忙
hurt *v.* 伤害
husband *n.* 丈夫
hut *n.* 小屋

I

I *pron.* 我
ice *n.* 冰
icy *a.* 冰的
idea *n.* 主意
if *conj.* 如果
ill *a.* 生病的
image *n.* 形象
imaginary *a.* 想象的
imagination *n.* 想象
imagine *v.* 想象
importance *n.* 重要性
important *a.* 重要的
improve *v.* 提高
improvement *n.* 提高
in *ad.* 进入 *prep.* 在里面
include *v.* 包括
income *n.* 收入
increase *v.* 增加
indoor *a.* 室内的
indoors *ad.* 室内
industrial *a.* 工业的
industry *n.* 工业
infect *v.* 传染
infection *n.* 传染
influence *v.* 影响
inform *v.* 通知
information *n.* 信息
ink *n.* 墨水
inner *a.* 内部的
inquire *v.* 询问
inquiry *n.* 询问
insect *n.* 昆虫
inside *n.* 里面
instead *ad.* 作为替代
instruct *v.* 说明
instruction *n.* 说明
instrument *n.* 器具
insurance *n.* 保险
insure *v.* 保险
intend *v.* 想要
intention *n.* 目的，意图
interest *n.* 兴趣
interesting *a.* 有趣的
international *a.* 国际的
interrupt *v.* 打扰
interruption *n.* 打扰
into *prep.* 到里面
introduce *v.* 介绍
introduction *n.* 介绍
invent *v.* 发明
invention *n.* 发明
invitation *n.* 邀请
invite *v.* 邀请
inwards *ad.* 向内
iron *a.* 铁的 *n.* 铁
island *n.* 岛
it *pron.* 它
its *pron.* 它的
itself *pron.* 它自己

J

jaw *n.* 下巴
jealous *a.* 妒忌的
jealousy *n.* 妒忌
jelly *n.* 果冻
jewel *n.* 珠宝
jewelry *n.* [总称]珠宝
job *n.* 工作
join *v.* 加入
joint *n.* 关节
joke *n.* 笑话
journey *n.* 旅行
joy *n.* 高兴
judge *v.* 判断
judgment *n.* 判断
juice *n.* 果汁
jump *v.* 跳跃
just *a.* 公平的
justice *n.* 公平

K

keen *a.* 热切的
keep *v.* 保持
key *n.* 答案
kick *v.* 踢
kill *v.* 杀
kilo *n.* 千
kilogram *n.* 千克
kilometer *n.* 千米
kind *n.* 种类
king *n.* 国王
kingdom *n.* 王国
kiss *v.* 吻
kitchen *n.* 厨房
knee *n.* 膝盖
kneel *v.* 跪下
knife *n.* 刀子
knock *v.* 敲
knot *n.* 结
know *v.* 知道
knowledge *n.* 知识

L

labor *n.* 劳动力
lack *v.* 缺少
ladder *n.* 梯子
lady *n.* 女士
lake *n.* 湖
lamb *n.* 羔羊
lamp *n.* 灯
land *n.* 土地
language *n.* 语言
large *a.* 大的
last *ad.* 最后 *a.* 最后的 *v.* 持续
late *a.* 晚的
lately *ad.* 最近
laugh *v.* 笑
laughter *n.* 笑，笑声
law *n.* 法律
lawyer *n.* 律师
lay *v.* 放
lazy *a.* 懒惰的
lead *n.* 领导；榜样 *v.* 领导
leaf *n.* 树叶
lean *v.* 倾斜
learn *v.* 学习
least *a.* 最少的
leather *n.* 皮子
leave *v.* 离开
left *a.* 左边的 *n.* 左边
leg *n.* 腿
legal *a.* 合法的
lend *v.* 出借
length *n.* 长度
less *ad.* 更少 *a.* 更少的
lesson *n.* 课程；教训
let *v.* 让
letter *n.* 信；字母
level *a.* 水平的 *ad.* 水平地 *n.* 水平
library *n.* 图书馆
lid *n.* 盖子
lie *v.* 放；躺下
life *n.* 生活
lift *v.* 举起
light *n.* 灯光 *a.* 轻的 *v.* 点亮
lightning *n.* 闪电
like *prep.* 像 *v.* 喜欢
likely *a.* 可能的
limb *n.* 四肢
limit *v.* 限制 *n.* 限制
line *n.* 线
lion *n.* 狮子
lip *n.* 嘴唇
liquid *n.* 液体
list *n.* 名单
listen *v.* 听
liter *n.* 升
literature *n.* 文学
little *a.* 很少的

live *v.* 居住
load *n.* 担子
loaf *n.* 面包
local *a.* 当地的
lock *v.* 锁住
lodging *n.* 寄宿
log *n.* 原木
lonely *a.* 孤独的
long *a.* 长的 *ad.* 长期地
look *v.* 看
loose *a.* 松散的
lord *n.* 地主
lose *v.* 失去
loss *n.* 损失
lot *n.* 一批
loud *a.* 大声的
love *v.* 爱 *n.* 爱
low *a.* 低的
lower *v.* 降低
loyal *a.* 忠诚的
loyalty *n.* 忠诚
luck *n.* 运气
lump *n.* 大量，多数
lung *n.* 肺

M

machine *n.* 机器
machinery *n.* [总称]机器
mad *a.* 疯的
magazine *n.* 杂志
magic *a.* 神奇的
magician *n.* 魔术师
mail *v.* 邮寄 *n.* 信件
main *a.* 主要的
make *v.* 做
male *n.* 男性
man *n.* 人；男人
manage *v.* 管理
manager *n.* 经理
manner *n.* 礼貌
many *a.* 许多的
map *n.* 地图
march *v.* 前进
mark *n.* 记号
market *n.* 市场
marriage *n.* 婚姻
marry *v.* 结婚
mass *n.* 大量
master *n.* 主人；硕士
mat *n.* 席子
match *n.* 比赛
material *n.* 物质，材料
matter *n.* 事情
may *v.* 可以
me *pron.* 我
meal *n.* 一顿饭
mean *v.* 意思是
meaning *n.* 意思
means *n.* 方法
measure *n.* 措施，方法
meat *n.* 肉
medical *a.* 药物的；医学的
medicine *n.* 药物
meet *v.* 会面
meeting *n.* 会议
melt *v.* 融化
member *n.* 成员
memory *n.* 记忆
mend *v.* 修理
mention *v.* 提到
merry *a.* 快乐的
message *n.* 信息
messenger *n.* 信使
metal *n.* 金属
meter *n.* 米
method *n.* 方法
metric *a.* 公制的
microscope *n.* 显微镜
middle *a.* 中间的 *n.* 中间
might *v.* 可能
mile *n.* 英里
military *a.* 军队的
milk *n.* 牛奶
million *num.* 百万
millionth *num.* 第一百万
mind *n.* 思想 *v.* 介意
mine *n.* 矿山 *pron.* 我的
mineral *a.* 矿物的
minister *n.* 部长
minute *n.* 分钟
mirror *n.* 镜子
miss *v.* 错过，想念
mist *n.* 薄雾
mistake *n.* 错误
mix *v.* 混合
mixture *n.* 混合物
model *n.* 模特
modern *a.* 现代的
moment *n.* 时刻
money *n.* 钱
monkey *n.* 猴子
month *n.* 月
monthly *a.* 每月的 *ad.* 每月
moon *n.* 月亮

moral *a.* 道德的
morals *n.* 道德
more *a.* 更多的
morning *n.* 早晨
most *a.* 最多的
mother *n.* 母亲
motor *v.* 驾驶汽车 *n.* 汽车
mountain *n.* 山
mouse *n.* 老鼠
mouth *n.* 嘴
move *v.* 运动
much *a.* 很多的
mud *n.* 泥土
multiply *v.* 增加
murder *v.* 谋杀
muscle *n.* 肌肉
music *n.* 音乐
musician *n.* 音乐家
must *v.* 必须
my *pron.* 我的
myself *pron.* 我自己
mysterious *a.* 神秘的
mystery *n.* 神秘性；谜

N

nail *n.* 指甲
name *n.* 名字
narrow *a.* 狭窄的
nasty *a.* 肮脏的
nation *n.* 国家；民族
national *a.* 国家的；民族的
nature *n.* 自然
naval *a.* 海军的
navy *n.* 海军
near *a.* 近的；亲近的
ad. 近 *prep.* 在附近
nearly *ad.* 几乎
neat *a.* 整洁的
necessary *a.* 必须的
neck *n.* 脖子
need *v.* 需要
needle *n.* 针
neighbor *n.* 邻居
neighborhood *n.* 邻里
neither *a.* 两者都不的
nerve *n.* 神经
nervous *a.* 紧张的
nest *n.* 巢
net *n.* 网
network *n.* 网络
never *ad.* 从来不
new *a.* 新的
news *n.* 新闻
newspaper *n.* 报纸
next *a.* 下一个的 *ad.* 下一个
nice *a.* 美好的，漂亮的
night *ad.* 夜晚
nine *num.* 九
ninth *num.* 第九
no *ad.* 不
no one 没有人
noble *a.* 贵族的 *n.* 贵族
nobleman *n.* 贵族
noise *n.* 噪音
none *pron.* 没有人
nonsense *n.* 废话
nor *conj.* 也不
north *n.* 北方
northern *a.* 北方的
nose *n.* 鼻子
not *ad.* 不
nothing *pron.* 没有任何事
notice *n.* 通知 *v.* 注意
noun *n.* 名词
now *ad.* 现在
nowhere *ad.* 没有任何地方
number *n.* 数字
nurse *n.* 护士
nut *n.* 坚果
nylon *n.* 尼龙

O

o'clock *ad.* …点钟
obedience *n.* 顺从
obedient *a.* 顺从的
obey *v.* 遵从
object *n.* 物体
obtain *v.* 获得
occasion *n.* 场合
ocean *n.* 海洋
odd *a.* 奇数的
of *prep.* …的
off *ad.* 离开 *prep.* 从…离开
offend *v.* 冒犯
offense *n.* 冒犯
offensive *a.* 冒犯的
offer *v.* 提供
office *n.* 办公室
officer *n.* 官员
official *a.* 官方的
often *ad.* 经常
oil *n.* 油
old *a.* 老的

old-fashioned *a.* 过时的
on *ad.* 在上面 *prep.* 在…上面
once *ad.* 曾经
one *num.* 一个
oneself *pron.* 某人自己
onion *n.* 洋葱
only *ad.* 只有
open *a.* 开着的 *v.* 打开
operate *v.* 经营；做手术
operation *n.* 经营；手术
opinion *n.* 主意
opponent *n.* 对手
oppose *v.* 反对
opposite *a.* 相反的
opposition *n.* 反面
or *conj.* 或者
orange *n.* 柑橘；橙汁
order *v.* 命令 *n.* 秩序
ordinary *a.* 普通的
organ *n.* 器官
organization *n.* 组织
origin *n.* 来源
other *a.* 其他的
otherwise *ad.* 否则
ought *v.* 应该
our *pron.* 我们的
ours *pron.* 我们的
ourselves *pron.* 我们自己
out *a.* 外面的 *ad.* 外面
outdoor *a.* 户外的
outdoors *ad.* 户外
outer *a.* 外部的
outside *ad.* 外面
over *ad.* 在上面；超过
    prep. 在…上面
owe *v.* 亏欠
owing to 由于
own *a.* 自己的 *v.* 拥有
oxygen *n.* 氧气

P

pack *v.* 包裹
packet *n.* 包裹
page *n.* 页
pain *n.* 疼痛
painful *a.* 疼痛的
paint *v.* 绘画
painting *n.* 绘画
pair *n.* 一对
palace *n.* 宫殿
pale *a.* 苍白的
pan *n.* 平底锅
paper *n.* 纸张
parcel *n.* 包裹
parent *n.* 父(母)亲
park *n.* 公园
parliament *n.* 议会
part *n.* 部分
participle *n.* 分词
particular *a.* 特别的
partner *n.* 搭档
party *n.* 党；聚会
pass *v.* 路过
passage *n.* 段落
passenger *n.* 过路人
past *a.* 过去的
pastry *n.* 糕点
path *n.* 道路
patience *n.* 耐心
patient *a.* 耐心的
pattern *n.* 形式
pause *v.* 暂停
pay *v.* 支付
payment *n.* 支付
peace *n.* 和平
peaceful *a.* 和平的
pen *n.* 钢笔
pence *n.* 分
pencil *n.* 铅笔
people *n.* 人
pepper *n.* 辣椒
per *prep.* 每，每一
perfect *a.* 完美的
perform *v.* 表演；表现
perhaps *ad.* 可能
period *n.* 时期，阶段
permission *n.* 允许
permit *v.* 允许
person *n.* 人
personal *a.* 私人的
persuade *v.* 劝说
pet *n.* 宠物
photograph *n.* 照片
photography *n.* 摄影
phrase *n.* 词组，短语
physical *a.* 物质的
piano *n.* 钢琴
pick *v.* 采摘；拾起
picture *n.* 照片
piece *n.* 片断
pig *n.* 猪
pile *n.* 一堆
pilot *n.* 飞行员
pin *n.* 别针

pink *a.* 粉红色的 *n.* 粉红色
pipe *n.* 管子
pity *n.* 可惜
place *n.* 地方
plain *a.* 平坦的；朴素的；简单的 *n.* 平原
plan *n.* 计划 *v.* 计划
plane *n.* 飞机
plant *v.* 种植 *n.* 植物
plastic *n.* 塑料 *a.* 塑料的
plate *n.* 盘子
play *v.* 演奏；玩
pleasant *a.* 愉快的
please *v.* 使高兴 *ad.* 请
pleased *a.* 高兴的
pleasure *n.* 愉快
plenty *a.* 许多的
plural *a.* 复数的
pocket *n.* 口袋
poem *n.* 诗
poet *n.* 诗人
poetry *n.* 诗
point *n.* 点 *v.* 指出
pointed *a.* 显著的，突出的
poison *n.* 毒药
poisonous *a.* 有毒的
pole *n.* 竿
police *n.* 警察
polish *v.* 擦亮
polite *a.* 有礼貌的
political *a.* 政治的
politician *n.* 政治家
politics *n.* 政治
pool *n.* 水池
poor *a.* 贫穷的
popular *a.* 受欢迎的
popularity *n.* 受欢迎度
population *n.* 人口
port *n.* 港口
position *n.* 位置
possess *v.* 拥有
possession *n.* 财产，所有物
possibility *n.* 可能性
possible *a.* 可能的
possibly *ad.* 可能地
post *n.* 邮政
pot *n.* 锅；罐；壶
potato *n.* 土豆，马铃薯
pound *n.* 英镑
pour *v.* 倾泻，倒
powder *n.* 粉末
power *n.* 力量
powerful *a.* 强大的
practical *a.* 实际的
practice *n.* 练习
praise *v.* 夸奖
pray *v.* 祈祷
prayer *n.* 祈祷者
precious *a.* 宝贵的
preparation *n.* 准备
prepare *v.* 准备
presence *n.* 存在
present *a.* 当前的 *n.* 礼物
preserve *v.* 维护，保留
president *n.* 主席，总统
press *v.* 按，压
pressure *n.* 压力
pretend *v.* 假装
pretty *a.* 漂亮的
prevent *v.* 防止
price *n.* 价格
prickly *a.* 多刺的
pride *n.* 骄傲
priest *n.* 牧师
prince *n.* 王子
principle *n.* 原则，准则
print *v.* 印刷
prison *n.* 监狱
prisoner *n.* 囚犯
private *a.* 私人的
prize *n.* 奖励
probability *n.* 可能性
probable *a.* 可能的
problem *n.* 问题
process *n.* 过程
procession *n.* 列队
produce *v.* 生产
product *n.* 产品
production *n.* 生产
profession *n.* 专业
profit *n.* 利润
promise *v.* 承诺 *n.* 承诺
pronounce *v.* 发音
pronunciation *n.* 发音
proof *n.* 证明
proper *a.* 适当的
property *n.* 财产
protect *v.* 保护
protection *n.* 保护
protective *a.* 保护的
proud *a.* 骄傲的
prove *v.* 证明
provide *v.* 提供
public *a.* 公共的
pull *v.* 拉

pump *v.* 用泵汲水
punish *v.* 惩罚
punishment *n.* 惩罚
pupil *n.* 小学生
pure *a.* 纯正的
purple *n.* 紫色
purpose *n.* 目的
push *v.* 推
put *v.* 放

Q

quality *n.* 质量
quantity *n.* 数量
quarrel *v.* 吵架
quarter *n.* 四分之一
queen *n.* 王后
question *n.* 问题
quick *a.* 迅速的
quiet *a.* 安静的 *n.* 安静
quite *ad.* 非常

R

rabbit *n.* 兔子
race *n.* 竞赛
radio *n.* 收音机
railway *n.* 铁路
rain *n.* 雨
raise *v.* 举起
range *n.* 范围
rank *n.* 阶级
rapid *a.* 迅速的
rare *a.* 稀少的
rat *n.* 老鼠
rate *n.* 比率
rather *ad.* 很，非常
raw *a.* 生的；未加工的
reach *v.* 到达
read *v.* 读书
ready *a.* 准备好的
real *a.* 正确的；真实的
really *ad.* 真正地
reason *n.* 原因
reasonable *a.* 合理的
receive *v.* 收到
recent *a.* 最近的
recently *ad.* 最近
recognition *n.* 确认，认识
recognize *v.* 确认，认识
record *n.* 纪录 *v.* 纪录
red *a.* 红的
reduce *v.* 减少
reduction *n.* 减少
refusal *n.* 拒绝
refuse *v.* 拒绝
regard *v.* 认为
regular *a.* 有规律的
related *a.* 有关的
relation *n.* 关系
relative *a.* 相对的
religion *n.* 宗教
religious *a.* 宗教的
remain *v.* 留下
remark *n.* 评论
remember *v.* 记住
remind *v.* 提醒
remove *v.* 移动
rent *v.* 租住
repair *v.* 修理
repeat *v.* 重复
reply *v.* 回答
report *v.* 报告
represent *v.* 代表
representative *a.* 代表的
republic *a.* 共和的
request *v.* 要求
respect *v.* 尊重
respectful *a.* 尊重的
responsible *a.* 负责的
rest *n.* 休息
restaurant *n.* 饭店
result *n.* 结果
return *n.* 收益 *v.* 回来
reward *n.* 奖励
rice *n.* 大米
rich *a.* 富有的
rid *v.* 摆脱
ride *v.* 骑
right *a.* 正确的，对的 *n.* 正确 *ad.* 向右
ring *n.* 铃声；戒指
ripe *a.* 成熟的
rise *v.* 升起
risk *n.* 风险
river *n.* 小河
road *n.* 道路
rob *v.* 抢劫
rock *n.* 岩石
rod *n.* 竿；棒
roll *v.* 滚动
roof *n.* 屋顶
room *n.* 房间
root *n.* 根源

rope *n.* 绳子
rose *n.* 玫瑰
rough *a.* 粗糙的
round *a.* 圆的 *ad.* 在周围
  prep. 在…周围
row *n.* 排 *v.* 使排成排
royal *a.* 皇室的
rub *v.* 摩擦
rubber *n.* 橡胶
rude *a.* 粗鲁的
ruin *v.* 毁灭
rule *n.* 规则 *v.* 统治
ruler *n.* 统治者
run *v.* 跑
rush *v.* 冲

S

sad *a.* 伤心的
safe *a.* 平安的，安全的
safety *n.* 平安，安全
sail *v.* 航海
sale *n.* 出售
salt *a.* 咸的 *n.* 盐
same *a.* 同样的
sand *n.* 沙子
satisfaction *n.* 满意
satisfactory *a.* 令人满意的
satisfy *v.* 使人满意
save *v.* 储蓄
say *v.* 说
scale *n.* 规模
scatter *v.* 散布
scene *n.* 风景
scenery *n.* 景色
school *n.* 学校
science *n.* 科学
scientific *a.* 科学的
scientist *n.* 科学家
scissors *n.* 剪刀
screw *n.* 螺钉
sea *n.* 海洋
search *v.* 搜寻
season *n.* 季节
seat *n.* 座位
second *num.* 第二 *n.* 秒
secrecy *n.* 秘密
secret *a.* 秘密的
secretary *n.* 秘书
see *v.* 看
seed *n.* 种子
seem *v.* 好像
seize *v.* 抓住
sell *v.* 出售
send *v.* 发送
sensation *n.* 感觉
sense *n.* 感觉
senseless *a.* 没有感觉的
sensible *a.* 合理的
sensitive *a.* 敏感的
sentence *n.* 句子
separate *a.* 分开的，独立的
  v. 分开
serious *a.* 严重的
servant *n.* 仆人
serve *v.* 服务
service *n.* 服务
set *n.* 套，副，批 *v.* 设置
settle *v.* 安排；解决
seven *num.* 七
seventh *num.* 第七
several *a.* 几个的
severe *a.* 严重的
sew *v.* 缝
sex *n.* 性
sexual *a.* 性的
shade *n.* 阴凉处
shadow *n.* 影子
shake *v.* 震撼，摇动
shall *v.* 应该
shame *n.* 羞耻
shape *n.* 形状
share *v.* 分享
sharp *a.* 尖锐的
she *pron.* 她
sheep *n.* 羊
sheet *n.* 纸张
shelf *n.* 架子
shell *n.* 壳
shelter *v.* 遮蔽，防护
shield *n.* 保护物
shine *v.* 闪光
ship *n.* 船
shirt *n.* 衬衫
shock *n.* 震撼 *v.* 震撼
shoe *n.* 鞋
shoot *v.* 射击
shop *n.* 商店
shopkeeper *n.* 店主
shore *n.* 海岸
short *a.* 短的；矮的
shot *n.* 射击
should *v.* 应该
shoulder *n.* 肩膀
shout *v.* 叫喊

show *n.* 展览 *v.* 展示，指出
shut *v.* 关闭
sick *a.* 生病的
side *a.* 旁边的 *n.* 旁边
sideways *n.* 旁边
sight *n.* 视力
sign *n.* 符号
signal *v.* 指示
signature *n.* 签名
silence *n.* 安静
silent *a.* 安静的
silk *n.* 丝
silly *a.* 傻的
silver *n.* 银子
similar *a.* 相似的
similarity *n.* 相似性
simple *a.* 简单的
since *conj.* 从…以来
sincere *a.* 真诚的
sing *v.* 唱
single *a.* 单身的
singular *a.* 单一的
sink *v.* 下沉
sister *n.* 姐妹
sit *v.* 坐
situation *n.* 形势
six *num.* 六
sixth *num.* 第六
size *n.* 尺寸
skill *n.* 技术
skillful *a.* 熟练的
skin *n.* 皮肤
skirt *n.* 短裙
sky *n.* 天空
slave *n.* 奴隶
sleep *v.* 睡觉
slide *v.* 滑行
slight *a.* 轻微的
slip *v.* 滑行
slippery *a.* 滑的
slope *n.* 斜坡
slow *a.* 缓慢的
small *a.* 小的
smell *v.* 闻，嗅
smile *v.* 笑
smoke *n.* 烟
smooth *a.* 平滑的
snake *n.* 蛇
snow *n.* 雪
so *conj.* 所以
soap *n.* 肥皂
social *a.* 社会的
society *n.* 社会
sock *n.* 短袜
soft *a.* 柔软的
soil *n.* 泥土
soldier *n.* 士兵
solemn *a.* 庄严的，肃穆的
solid *n.* 固体
some *a.* 有些的 *pron.* 一些
somehow *ad.* 以某种方法
someone *pron.* 有的人
something *pron.* 有的事
sometimes *ad.* 有时
somewhere *pron.* 有的地方
son *n.* 儿子
song *n.* 歌曲
soon *ad.* 很快
sore *a.* 痛的
sorrow *n.* 悲伤
sorry *a.* 抱歉的
sort *n.* 种类
soul *n.* 灵魂
sound *n.* 声音 *v.* 听起来
soup *n.* 汤
sour *a.* 酸的
south *n.* 南方
southern *a.* 南方的
space *n.* 空间
spacecraft *n.* 宇宙飞船
spade *n.* 铲，锹
speak *v.* 说
spear *n.* 矛，枪
special *a.* 特别的
specialist *n.* 专家
speech *n.* 演讲
speed *n.* 速度
spell *v.* 拼写
spend *v.* 花费
spin *v.* 纺纱，纺线
spirit *n.* 精神
spite *n.* 怨恨
splendid *a.* 美好的
split *v.* 劈开
spoil *v.* 损坏，溺爱
spoon *n.* 汤匙
sport *n.* 体育
spot *n.* 斑点
spread *v.* 传播
spring *n.* 春季
square *a.* 平方的，四方的 *n.* 平方；广场
stage *n.* 舞台
stair *n.* 楼梯
stamp *n.* 邮票

stand *v.* 站立
standard *n.* 标准
star *n.* 星星
start *v.* 开始
state *n.* 国家
station *n.* 车站
stay *v.* 停留
steady *a.* 稳定的
steal *v.* 偷窃
steam *n.* 蒸汽
steel *n.* 钢铁
steep *a.* 陡峭的
stem *n.* 树干
step *n.* 台阶
stick *v.* 粘贴
sticky *a.* 粘性的
stiff *a.* 硬的
still *a.* 静止的 *ad.* 仍然
sting *v.* 刺
stitch *v.* 缝
stomach *n.* 胃
stone *n.* 石头
stop *v.* 停止
store *n.* 商店
storm *n.* 暴风雨
story *n.* 故事
straight *a.* 直的，直接的 *ad.* 直地，直接地
strange *a.* 奇怪的，陌生的
stranger *n.* 陌生人
stream *n.* 小溪
street *n.* 街道
strength *n.* 优势
stretch *v.* 伸展
strike *v.* 打击
string *n.* 细绳
stroke *n.* 打，击
strong *a.* 强壮的
structure *n.* 结构
struggle *v.* 挣扎
student *n.* 学生
study *v.* 学习
stupid *a.* 愚笨的
style *n.* 形式
subject *n.* 学科
substance *n.* 物质
subtract *v.* 减去
succeed *v.* 成功
success *n.* 成功
successful *a.* 成功的
such *ad.* 这样地 *pron.* 这样的人 *a.* 这样的
suck *v.* 吮吸
sudden *a.* 突然的
suffer *v.* 遭受
sugar *n.* 糖
suggest *v.* 建议
suit *n.* 衣服
suitable *a.* 合适的
sum *n.* 数量
summer *n.* 夏季
sun *n.* 太阳
supper *n.* 晚饭
supply *n.* 供给 *v.* 供给
support *v.* 支持
suppose *v.* 猜想
sure *a.* 肯定的
surface *n.* 表面
surprise *v.* 使吃惊
surround *v.* 包围
swallow *v.* 吞咽
swear *v.* 发誓
sweep *v.* 打扫
sweet *a.* 甜的 *n.* 糖果
swell *v.* 膨胀
swim *v.* 游泳
swing *v.* 摇摆
sword *n.* 剑
sympathetic *a.* 有同情心的
sympathy *n.* 同情
system *n.* 体系

T

table *n.* 桌子
tail *n.* 尾巴
take *v.* 带走，拿去
talk *v.* 讲话
tall *a.* 高的
taste *v.* 品尝
tax *n.* 税收
taxi *n.* 出租车
tea *n.* 茶
teach *v.* 教
team *n.* 小组
tear *v.* 撕毁
telephone *n.* 电话
television *n.* 电视
tell *v.* 告诉
temper *n.* 性情，脾气
temperature *n.* 温度
temple *n.* 塔
tend *v.* 照料
tendency *n.* 趋势，倾向
tender *a.* 纤弱的

tennis *n.* 网球
tense *n.* 时态
tent *n.* 帐篷
terrible *a.* 可怕的
terror *n.* 恐惧
test *n.* 测验
than *conj.* 比
thank *v.* 感谢
that *conj.* 因为，由于
pron. 那个
the *art.* 这
theater *n.* 戏院
their *pron.* 他们的
theirs *pron.* 他们的
them *pron.* 他们
themselves *pron.* 他们自己
then *ad.* 那时
there *ad.* 那里
therefore *conj.* 所以
these *pron.* 这些
they *pron.* 他们
thick *a.* 厚的
thief *n.* 小偷
thin *a.* 瘦的
thing *n.* 事情
think *v.* 想，思考
third *num.* 第三
thirst *n.* 渴
thirsty *a.* 口渴的
this *a.* 这 *pron.* 这个
thorough *a.* 彻底的
those *pron.* 那些
though *conj.* 虽然
thought *n.* 思想
thousand *num.* 千
thread *n.* 线
threat *n.* 威胁
threaten *v.* 威胁
three *num.* 三
throat *n.* 咽喉
through *ad.* 通过 *prep.* 通过
throw *v.* 扔
thumb *n.* 大拇指
thunder *n.* 雷
thus *conj.* 所以
ticket *n.* 票
tidy *a.* 整洁的 *v.* 打扫
tie *n.* 领带 *v.* 绑，系，拴
tiger *n.* 老虎
tight *a.* 紧的
time *n.* 时间
timetable *n.* 时刻表
tin *n.* 罐头
tire/tyre *n.* 轮胎
tire *v.* 感到劳累
title *n.* 称呼
to *prep.* 到
tobacco *n.* 烟草
today *ad.* 在今天 *n.* 今天
toe *n.* 脚趾
together *ad.* 一起
tomorrow *n.* 明天
tongue *n.* 舌头
tonight *ad.* 今晚
too *ad.* 也
tool *n.* 工具
tooth *n.* 牙齿
top *a.* 一流的 *n.* 顶部
total *a.* 总共的 *n.* 总共
touch *v.* 触摸
tour *v.* 旅游 *n.* 旅游
tourist *n.* 旅行者
towards *prep.* 向着
tower *n.* 塔
town *n.* 城镇
toy *n.* 玩具
track *n.* 轨迹
trade *n.* 贸易
traffic *n.* 交通
train *n.* 火车
translate *v.* 翻译
transparent *a.* 透明的
trap *n.* 陷阱
travel *v.* 旅行
treat *v.* 对待；治疗
treatment *n.* 治疗
tree *n.* 树木
tremble *v.* 颤抖
tribe *n.* 部落
trick *n.* 诡计，恶作剧 *v.* 欺骗，
哄骗
trip *n.* 旅行
tropical *a.* 热带的
trouble *n.* 麻烦
trousers *n.* 裤子
true *a.* 真实的
trunk *n.* 树干
trust *v.* 信任
truth *n.* 事实
try *v.* 试图，努力
tube *n.* 试管
tune *n.* 语调
turn *v.* 转动
twice *ad.* 两倍
twist *v.* 扭转

type *n.* 类型
typical *a.* 典型的

U

ugly *a.* 丑陋的
uncle *n.* 叔叔
under *prep.* 在…下面
understand *v.* 明白
undo *v.* 消除
uniform *n.* 制服
union *n.* 联合
unit *n.* 单位
unite *v.* 团结，联合
universal *a.* 普遍的
universe *n.* 宇宙
university *n.* 大学
until *ad.* 直到
up *a.* 向上的 *ad.* 在上面
  prep. 在…上面
upper *a.* 上面的
upright *a.* 垂直的 *ad.* 直立地
upset *v.* 颠覆
upside down 颠覆
upstairs *a.* 楼上的 *ad.* 到楼上
urge *v.* 敦促
urgent *a.* 紧急的
us *pron.* 我们
use *v.* 使用
useful *a.* 有用的
useless *a.* 无用的
usual *a.* 通常的

V

valley *n.* 山谷
valuable *a.* 有价值的
value *n.* 价值
variety *n.* 多样性
various *a.* 多样的
vary *v.* 改变
vegetable *n.* 蔬菜
vehicle *n.* 车辆
verb *n.* 动词
very *ad.* 非常
victory *n.* 胜利
view *n.* 观点
village *n.* 村庄
violence *n.* 暴力
violent *a.* 暴力的
visit *v.* 参观，拜访
voice *n.* 嗓音
vote *v.* 选举
vowel *n.* 元音
voyage *n.* 航海

W

wage *n.* 薪水
waist *n.* 腰
wait *v.* 等候
waiter *n.* 服务员
wake *v.* 叫醒
walk *v.* 步行
wall *n.* 墙
wander *v.* 漫游
want *v.* 想要
war *n.* 战争
warm *a.* 暖和的 *v.* 温暖
warmth *n.* 温暖
warn *v.* 警告
wash *v.* 洗
waste *v.* 浪费
watch *v.* 观看
water *n.* 水
wave *n.* 波浪
way *n.* 道路
we *pron.* 我们
weak *a.* 弱的
wealth *n.* 财富
weapon *n.* 武器
wear *v.* 穿着
weather *n.* 天气
weave *v.* 编织
wedding *n.* 婚礼
week *n.* 星期
weekly *a.* 每周的 *ad.* 每周
weigh *v.* 重
weight *n.* 重量
welcome *v.* 欢迎
well *ad.* 好的 *n.* 井
west *n.* 西方
western *a.* 西方的
wet *a.* 湿的
what *pron.* 什么
whatever *ad.* 无论什么
wheat *n.* 小麦
wheel *n.* 车轮
when *ad.* 何时 *conj.* 在…时
whenever *ad.* 无论何时
where *ad.* 哪里
whether *conj.* 是否
which *pron.* 哪个

whichever *ad.* 无论哪个
while *conj.* 当
whip *n.* 鞭子
whisper *v.* 小声说话
whistle *n.* 口哨
white *a.* 白的
who *pron.* 谁
whoever *pron.* 无论是谁
whole *a.* 整体的
why *ad.* 为什么
wicked *a.* 坏的
wide *a.* 宽广的 *ad.* 广大地
widespread *a.* 广泛传播的
width *n.* 宽度
wife *n.* 妻子
wild *a.* 野的
will *v.* 将要
willing *n.* 意愿
win *v.* 赢得
wind *v.* 蜿蜒
wind *n.* 风
window *n.* 窗子
wine *n.* 酒
wing *n.* 翅膀
winter *n.* 冬季
wire *n.* 电线
wisdom *n.* 智慧
wise *a.* 明智的
wish *n.* 愿望
with *prep.* 与…一起
within *prep.* 在…之内
without *prep.* 没有…
witness *n.* 证人
woman *n.* 女人
wonder *n.* 奇迹 *v.* 想知道
wood *n.* 木头
wooden *a.* 木质的
wool *n.* 羊毛
woolen *a.* 羊毛的
word *n.* 单词
work *n.* 工作
world *n.* 世界
worm *n.* 虫子
worry *v.* 担心
worse *a.* 更坏的
worship *n.* 尊敬
worst *a.* 最坏的
worth *prep.* 值…钱
worthy *a.* 值得的
worthy of 值得
would *v.* 愿意
wound *v.* 受伤
wrap *v.* 缠绕
wreck *v.* 失事
wrist *n.* 手腕
write *v.* 写
wrong *a.* 错的，错误的 *ad.* 错误地 *n.* 错误
wrongdoing *n.* 坏事

Y

yard *n.* 场院
year *n.* 年
yearly *a.* 每年的
yellow *a.* 黄色的 *n.* 黄色
yes *ad.* 是
yesterday *n.* 昨天
yet *conj.* 然而
you *pron.* 你
young *a.* 年轻的
your *pron.* 你的
yours *pron.* 你的
yourself *pron.* 你自己
youth *n.* 青年

Z

zero *n.* 零

附录二　雅思阅读主题词汇

环境类

accumulation *n.* 堆积物
alluvial *a.* 冲积的
avalanche *n.* 雪崩
boulder *n.* 大石头，漂石
carbon *n.* 碳
cascade *n.* 喷流
catastrophe *n.* 大灾难
Celsius *a.* (温度)摄氏的
circulation *n.* 流通，循环
climatic *a.* 气候上的
combustion *n.* 燃烧
conservation *n.* 保护，保存
contaminate *v.* 弄脏；污染
counterbalance *v.* 使平衡
crater *n.* 火山口
cropland *n.* 农田
debris *n.* 残骸
decompression *n.* 泻压
deforestation *n.* 采伐森林
delta *n.* 三角洲
demographic *a.* 人口统计学的
demolish *v.* 毁坏
deteriorate *v.* (使)恶化
deterioration *n.* 恶化
disaster *n.* 灾难
disintegrate *v.* (使)碎裂
disrupt *v.* 破坏
drought *n.* 干旱
dump *v.* 倾倒，倾销
ecological *a.* 生态学的
ecosystem *n.* 生态系统
embankment *n.* 筑堤
eruption *v.* 爆发
evacuate *v.* 排泄
extinction *n.* 灭绝
Fahrenheit *n.* 华氏温度计
gas emission 气体排放
glacier *n.* 冰川
granite *n.* 花岗岩
greenhouse *n.* 温室
habitat *n.* 居住地，栖息地
humid *a.* 湿润的
irreversible *a.* 不可撤销的
log *n.* 原木
luxuriant *a.* 肥沃的
magma *n.* 岩浆
mechanism *n.* 机理，机制
meteorology *n.* 气象学
ozone *n.* 臭氧
petroleum *n.* 石油
phenomenon *n.* 现象
prioritize *v.* 优先考虑
pulverised rock 碎石
radiation *n.* 辐射
reclaim *v.* 开垦，改造
recurrent *a.* 反复发生的
recycle *v.* 回收利用
resource depletion 能源耗尽
sediment *n.* 沉积(物)
slope *n.* 斜坡

solar *a.* 太阳的
sulphuric acid 硫酸
the Earth's mantle 地幔
thrive *v.* 兴旺，繁荣
timber *n.* 木材
tropical *a.* 热带的
ultraviolet light 紫外光
vegetation *n.* 植被
viability *n.* 生存能力
viscous lava 粘性熔岩
volcano *n.* 火山
volcanologist *n.* 火山学家
water consumption 水资源消耗

科技类

aperture *n.* 光圈
box camera 箱式照相机
cartridge *n.* 胶卷
cinecamera *n.* 电影摄影机
diaphragm *n.* 光圈
eyepiece *n.* 目镜
film *n.* 胶片
filter *n.* 滤光镜
flash / flashlight *n.* 闪光灯
folding camera 风箱式照相机
gelatine *n.* 白明胶
guide number 闪光指数
holder *n.* 固定器，支架
latitude *n.* 宽容度
lens *n.* 镜头
magazine *n.* 软片盒
mask *n.* 遮光黑纸
photoelectric cell 光电管
photometer *n.* 曝光表
plate *n.* 感光片
plateholder *n.* 胶片夹
sensitivity *n.* 灵敏度
shutter release 快门线
shutter *n.* 快门
spool *n.* 片轴
spotlight / floodlight *n.* 聚光灯
still camera 照相机
strain *n.* 压力
sunshade *n.* 遮光罩
telemeter *n.* 测距器
tripod *n.* 三角架
viewfinder *n.* 取景器
wide-angle lens 广角镜头
zoom lens 变焦镜头
versatile *a.* 通用的
alchemy *n.* 炼金术
metallurgy *n.* 冶金
alloy *n.* 合金
electrode *n.* 电极
distill *v.* 蒸馏
quartz *n.* 石英
phosphorus *n.* 磷
inflammable *a.* 易燃的
ceramic *a.* 陶瓷的
insulate *v.* 隔离，绝缘
fiber *n.* 纤维
optics *n.* 光学
retina *n.* 视网膜
iris *n.* 虹膜
opaque *a.* 不透明的
microprocessor *n.* 微处理器
binary *a.* 二进制的
buffer *n.* 缓冲区
browser *n.* 浏览器
hypertext *n.* 超文本

reticular *a.* 网状的
Ethernet *n.* 以太网
domain *n.* 域
patent *n.* 专利
artificial *a.* 人造的
dome *n.* 圆顶
sewage *n.* 污水；下水道
hydraulic *a.* 水力的
landfill *n.* 垃圾掩埋(地)
ventilation *n.* 通风
polytechnic *a.* 各种工艺的
geometric *a.* 几何(学)的
asymmetry *n.* 不对称
bilateral *a.* 双边的

医学类

pediatrician *n.* 儿科医师
gynecologist *n.* 妇科医师
neurologist *n.* 神经专家
psychiatrist *n.* 精神病学专家
dentist *n.* 牙医师
surgeon *n.* 外科医师
anesthetist *n.* 麻醉师
clinic *n.* 诊所
sanatorium *n.* 疗养院
wholesome *a.* 有益于健康的
vaccinate *n./v.* 接种
complaint *n.* 疾病
affection *n.* 疾病
ulcer *n.* 溃疡
lesion *n.* 损害
injury *n.* 损伤
eruption *n.* 疹
spot *n.* 斑
pimple *n.* 丘疹；小疮
blackhead *n.* 黑头粉刺
blister *n.* 水疱
boil *n.* 疖
scar *n.* 疤痕
wart *n.* 疣
corn *n.* 鸡眼
bruise *n.* 挫伤
bump *n.* 肿
swelling *n.* 肿胀
twist *n.* 扭伤
symptom *n.* 症状
diagnosis *n.* 诊断
case *n.* 病例
epidemic *n.* 流行病
attack *n./v.* 发作
sneeze *n.* 打喷嚏
faint *n.* 晕厥
dizziness *n.* 眩晕
lose consciousness 失去知觉
diet *n.* 饮食
treatment *n.* 治疗
cure *n./v.* 治愈
anemia *n.* 贫血
arthritis *n.* 关节炎
bronchitis *n.* 支气管炎
cancer *n.* 癌
indigestion *n.* 消化不良
influenza *n.* 流感
leukemia *n.* 白血病
measles *n.* 麻疹
paralysis *n.* 瘫痪；麻痹
pneumonia *n.* 肺炎
poliomyelitis *n.* 脊髓灰质炎
rabies *n.* 狂犬病
scarlet fever 猩红热

smallpox *n.* 天花
swamp fever 疟疾
tumour *n.* 瘤
surgery *n.* 外科
anesthesia *n.* 麻醉
blood transfusion 输血
transplant *n.*/*v.* 移植
stitch *v.* 缝线
operating theatre 手术室
instrument *n.* 手术器械
bandage *n.* 绷带
gauze *n.* 纱布
compress *n.* 敷布
sticking plaster 橡皮膏，胶布
plaster *n.* 石膏

职业类

labour exchange 职业介绍所
full employment 全职就业
piecework *n.* 计件工作
timework *n.* 计时工作
assembly line work 组装线工作
occupation *n.* 职务
vacancy *n.* 空缺
work permit 工作许可证
application *n.* 求职
engage *v.* 雇用
work contract 劳务合同
industrial accident 劳动事故
vocational guidance 职业指导
vocational training 职业训练
labour costs 劳力成本
permanent worker 长期工，固定工
staff *n.* 人员
skilled worker 技术工人
specialized worker 熟练工人
collaborator *n.* 合作者
foreman *n.* 工头
craftsman *n.* 工匠
specialist *n.* 专家
night shift *n.* 夜班
proletarian *n.* 无产者
trade union 工会
guild *n.* 行会
association *n.* 协会
emigration *n.* 移民；移居
representative *n.* 代表
works council 劳资联合委员会
labour law 劳工法
remuneration *n.* 报酬
wage index 工资指数
basic wage 基础工资
gross wages 全部收入
hourly wages 计时工资
bonus *n.* 奖励
payday *n.* 发工资日，付薪日
pay slip 工资单
payroll *n.* 薪水册
unemployment benefit 失业救济
old-age pension 养老金
retirement *n.* 退休
claim *n.*/*v.* 要求；索赔
go-slow *n.*/*v.* 怠工
strike pay 罢工津贴(由工会给的)
demonstration *n.* 示威
sanction *n.*/*v.* 制裁
unemployment *n.* 失业
discharge *n.*/*v.* 辞退
dismissal *n.* 开除，解雇
negotiation *n.* 谈判

生活类

accommodation *n.* (膳宿)供应
lodging *n.* 寄宿(处)
lease *n.* 出租
tenant *n.* 房客；佃户
landlord *n.* 房东
dormmate *n.* 室友
dormitory *n.* 寝室
real estate 房地产
vicinity *n.* 近邻
flat *n.* 公寓
deposit *n.* 押金
linen *a.* 亚麻的
stationery *n.* 文具
laundry *n.* 洗衣；洗衣店
cafeteria *n.* 自助餐厅
cater *v.* 满足(需要)
aerobics *n.* 有氧健身操
badminton *n.* 羽毛球(运动)
baseball *n.* 棒球
squash *n.* 壁球
amateur *n.* 业余爱好者
gathering *n.* 聚会
excursion *n.* 远足
illiterate *n.* 文盲
discipline *n.* 学科，纪律
terminology *n.* 术语学；〈总称〉术语
dean *n.* (大学)教务长
curriculum *n.* 课程
syllabus *n.* 课程提纲
calendar *n.* 日历；日程
compulsory *a.* 必修的
recruit *v.* 招生
prestige *n.* 声望，威信
esteem *n./v.* 尊敬
aptitude *n.* 智力
matriculation *n.* 录取入学
vocation *n.* 职业
transferable *a.* (学分等)可转换的
scholarship *n.* 奖学金
tutorial *n.* 辅导(课)
assignment *n.* 任务；(课外)作业
dissertation *n.* 论文
credential *n.* 证明；文凭

生物类

molecule *n.* 分子
amino acids 氨基酸
protein *n.* 蛋白质
enzyme *n.* 酶
botany *n.* 植物学
flora *n.* 植物群
fauna *n.* 动物群
bacteria *n.* [*pl.*] 细菌
fungi *n.* [*pl.*] 真菌
algae *n.* 海藻
fade *v.* 凋谢；褪色
organism *n.* 生物体，有机体
reptile *n.* 爬行动物
amphibian *n.* 两栖动物
mammal *n.* 哺乳动物
primate *n.* 灵长目动物
evolution *n.* 进化
gene *n.* 基因
genetics *n.* 遗传学
helix *n.* 螺旋，螺旋状物
mutation *n.* 突变
predator *n.* 捕食者
embryo *n.* 胚胎

grasshopper *n.* 蚱蜢
cricket *n.* 蟋蟀
pollen *n.* 花粉
hive *n.* 蜂房
larva *n.* 幼虫
pupation *n.* (化)蛹
hemisphere *n.* (脑)半球
somatic *a.* 躯体的
limb *n.* 肢
anatomy *n.* 解剖学
paralyze *v.* 使瘫痪
artery *n.* 动脉
gland *n.* 腺体
pancreas *n.* 胰
hormone *n.* 荷尔蒙，激素
cholesterol *n.* 胆固醇

学科类

Chinese *n.* 语文
English *n.* 英语
Japanese *n.* 日语
mathematics *n.* 数学
science *n.* 理科
gymnastics *n.* 体育
history *n.* 历史
algebra *n.* 代数
geometry *n.* 几何
geography *n.* 地理
biology *n.* 生物
chemistry *n.* 化学
physics *n.* 物理
physical geography 自然物理
literature *n.* 文学
sociology *n.* 社会学
psychology *n.* 心理学
philosophy *n.* 哲学
engineering *n.* 工程学
mechanical engineering 机械工程学
electronic engineering 电子工程学
medicine *n.* 医学
social science 社会科学
agriculture *n.* 农学
astronomy *n.* 天文学
economics *n.* 经济学
politics *n.* 政治学
commercial science 商学
biochemistry *n.* 生物化学
anthropology *n.* 人类学
linguistics *n.* 语言学
accounting *n.* 会计学
law / jurisprudence *n.* 法学
banking *n.* 银行学
metallurgy *n.* 冶金学
finance *n.* 财政学
mass-communication *n.* 大众传播学
journalism *n.* 新闻学
atomic energy 原子能学
civil engineering 土木工程
architecture *n.* 建筑学
chemical engineering 化学工程
accounting and statistics 会计统计
business administration 工商管理
library *n.* 图书馆学
diplomacy *n.* 外交
foreign language 外文
major *v.* 主修
minor *v.* 辅修

附录三　雅思口语、写作主题词汇

休闲、节日

Advent *n.* 基督降临节
aerobics dancing 健美操
aerobics *n.* 有氧运动
affectional film 爱情片
All Saints' Day 万圣节
altar *n.* 祭坛,圣坛
amber *n.* 琥珀
amethyst *n.* 紫水晶
ancient architectural complex 古建筑群
ancient tomb 古墓
aperture *n.* 光圈
bag-packer *n.* 背包自助旅行者
banquet hall 宴会厅
banquet *n.* 宴会
basin *n.* 盆地
blusher *n.* 腮红
book the ticket 订票
brook *n.* 小溪
buffet *n.* 自助餐
bushland *n.* 灌木丛
castle *n.* 城堡
cataract *n.* 大瀑布
causeway *n.* 堤道
cave *n.* 洞穴
chin-up *n.* 引体向上
coastland *n.* 沿海地区
comedy *n.* 喜剧片
concealer *n.* 遮瑕膏
continent *n.* 大陆
cooktail party 鸡尾酒会
coral island 珊瑚岛
corridor *n.* 走廊
cosmetic *n.* 化妆品
cruise *n./v.* 巡游
cycling *n.* 自行车运动
desert *n.* 沙漠
detective film 侦探片
diaphragm *n.* 光圈
dining room 餐厅
diving *n.* 潜水
Easter *n.* 复活节
ethical film 伦理片
eye gel 眼胶
eye mask 眼膜
eyepiece *n.* 目镜
facial mask 面膜
family reunion dinner 团圆饭
ferry *n.* 渡船
filmdom *n.* 电影界
filter *n.* 滤光器
flight number 航班号
flord *n.* 峡湾
foundation *n.* 粉底
fountain *n.* 泉水,喷泉
golf *n.* 高尔夫运动
Good Friday 耶稣受难节
greenbelt *n.* 绿化带
grotto *n.* 洞穴
hair conditioner 护发素
hand lotion 护手霜
hang gliding 悬挂式滑翔运动
hiking *n.* 徒步旅行
hilly areas 丘陵地带
hitch-hike *vi.* 搭便车旅行

hotspring *n.* 温泉
informal dinner 非正式晚餐
islet *n.* 小岛
jogging *n.* 慢跑
lens *n.* 镜头
lip gloss 润唇膏
liquid eye liner 眼线液
literary film 文艺片
lounge *n.* 休息室
lowland *n.* 低地
lunar calendar 农历
makeup remover 卸妆水
makeup removing lotion 卸妆乳
martial art 武术
mascara *n.* 睫毛膏
moisturizer *n.* 润肤露
monument *n.* 纪念碑
mousse *n.* 摩丝
musical *n.* 音乐剧
nail polish 指甲油
nursery *n.* 托儿所
paper-cut *n.* 剪纸
pavilion *n.* 亭子
peninsula *n.* 半岛
pressed powder 粉饼
propose a toast 敬酒
Ramadan *n.* 斋戒月
range *n.* 山脉
reef *n.* 礁石
refreshments *n.* 茶点
residential area 居民区
resort *n.* 度假胜地
ruby *n.* 红宝石
Sabbath *n.* 安息日
sapphire *n.* 蓝宝石
scuba diving 器械潜水
serial *n.* 连续剧
shampoo *n.* 洗发水
Shrove Tuesday 忏悔日
shutter release 快门键
shutter *n.* 快门
sit-up *n.* 仰卧起坐
skateboarding *n.* 滑板运动
skating *n.* 滑冰
skiing *n.* 滑雪运动
snack bar 小吃店
snack *n.* 小吃
sneaker *n.* 运动鞋
swordsmen film 武侠片
spotlight tour 经典游
stalactite *n.* 钟乳石
stalagmite *n.* 石笋
staying-up 守岁
stool *n.* 凳子
styling gel 发胶
summer resort 避暑胜地
surfing *n.* 冲浪
taboo *n.* 禁忌
tea party 茶会
telephoto lens 长焦镜头
terrace *n.* 阳台
terrain *n.* 地形
The Lantern Festival 元宵节
tourist guide 导游
tower *n.* 楼
track and field 田径运动
tragedy *n.* 悲剧片
trailer *n.* 预告片
travel agency 旅行社
tropical rain forest 热带雨林
ventilation *n.* 通风设备
viewfinder *n.* 取景器
water polo 水球
water skiing 滑水

waterfall *n.* 瀑布
wetland *n.* 沼泽地
wide-angle lens 广角镜头
yoga *n.* 瑜伽
zoom lens 变焦镜头

交　通

a chain collision 连环相撞
airport limousine 机场大巴
airport tax 机场税
airport terminal 航站楼
altitude *n.* 高度
artery traffic 交通干线
automatic traffic signal light 自动红绿灯
automobile industry 汽车工业
berth *n.* 卧铺
boarding card 登机牌
bumpy flight 不平稳的飞行
business class 商务仓
carbon dioxide 二氧化碳
careless driving 粗心驾驶
carriage-way *n.* 车行道
ceiling *n.* 上限
charge *v.* 充电
coach *n.* 长途汽车
connecting flight 换乘班机
crash *n./v.* 撞击
cross road 十字路口
cruising speed 巡航速度
curb *n./v.* 限制
curve road 弯路
dangerous driving 危险驾驶
dilemma *n.* 困境
direct flight 直飞
domestic *a.* 国内的
dual carriage-way 双程线
DUI 酒后驾车
duty-free shop 免税店
economy class 经济舱
energy-saving *a.* 节能的
fare *n.* 票价
first class 头等舱
flight connection centre 转机中心
flight *n.* 飞行
forced landing 迫降
freeway *n.* 高速公路
guide post 路标
head-on collision 迎面相撞
highway *n.* 公路
hit and run 肇事逃逸
landing *n.* 着陆
lane auxiliary 辅助车道
layover *n.* 短暂停留
light rail 轻轨
loop *n.* 回路
make a reservation 预定
night service 夜航
no through traffic 禁止通行
non-stop flight 连续飞行
one way only 单行道
overcrowded *a.* 过度拥挤的
pantomime *v.* 打手势
parking lot 停车场
parking permit 停车许可证
passing bay 让车道
pedestrian *n.* 行人
plane ticket 飞机票
private transport 私人交通
public transport 公共交通
pullman *n.* 卧铺车
reservation *n.* 预订
road junction 道路交叉点
road networks 公路网
round trip 往返旅程

safety island 安全岛
saver ticket 打折票
shuttle bus 班车
shuttle *n.* 短程穿梭的交通工具
single line 单行线
slight impact 轻微碰撞
speed limit 最高车速
steep hill 陡坡
gain height 爬升
toll *n.* 通行费
traffic congestion 交通拥挤
traffic control 流量管控
traffic police 交通警察
traffic regulation 交通规则
two-way traffic 双向交通
underground *n.* 地铁
vacant seat 空座
van *n.* 小货车
violator *n.* 违规者
winding road 弯路
zebra stripes 斑马线

饮 食

asparagus *n.* 芦笋
bean *n.* 菜豆
beer *n.* 啤酒
beet *n.* 甜菜
bitter *a.* 苦的
bland *a.* 清淡的
brandy *n.* 白兰地
broad bean *n.* 蚕豆
broccoli *n.* 花椰菜
cabbage *n.* 卷心菜
carrot *n.* 胡萝卜
cashew nut 腰果
cauliflower *n.* 花椰菜
celery *n.* 芹菜
champagne *n.* 香槟酒
chervil *n.* 山萝卜
chilli *n.* 红辣椒
chive *n.* 细香葱
cider *n.* 苹果酒
claret *n.* 红葡萄酒
cocktail *n.* 鸡尾酒
coconut *n.* 椰子
cod *n.* 鳕鱼
cognac *n.* 一种白兰地酒
cress *n.* 水芥
cucumber *n.* 黄瓜
cumin *n.* 小茴香
curried chicken 咖喱鸡
curry *n.* 咖喱
dried shrimps 虾米
eggplant *n.* 茄子
essence *n.* 香精
fennel *n.* 茴香
fragrant *a.* 芳香的
garlic *n.* 蒜
gherkin *n.* 小黄瓜
gin fizz 杜松子酒
gourmet powder 味精
greasy *a.* 油腻的
herring *n.* 青鱼
honey *n.* 蜂蜜
kale *n.* 甘蓝菜
kohlrabi *n.* 大头菜
lard *n.* 猪油
laurel *n.* 月桂
leek *n.* 韭菜
lemon juice 柠檬原汁
lemonade *n.* 柠檬水
lentil *n.* 小扁豆
lettuce *n.* 生菜;莴苣
light *a.* 清淡的

liqueur *n.* 白酒
margarine *n.* 人造奶油
marrow *n.* 西葫芦
melon *n.* 甜瓜
mineral water 矿泉水
mint *n.* 薄荷
mushroom *n.* 蘑菇
mustard *n.* 芥末
onion *n.* 洋葱
orange juice 橙汁
oyster sauce 蚝油
parsley *n.* 欧芹
peanut butter 花生酱
pepper *n.* 胡椒
pig bag 猪肚
pimiento *n.* 红色柿子椒
pumpkin *n.* 南瓜
radish *n.* 萝卜
red date 红枣
red wine 红葡萄酒
salty *a.* 咸的
seasoned *a.* 调过味的
seaweed soup 紫菜汤
sesame butter 芝麻油
shrimp sauce 虾酱
sliced noodles 刀削面
smoked bacon 熏肉
sour *a.* 酸的
soy sauce 酱油
soybean paste 豆瓣酱
spice *n.* 香料
squid *n.* 鱿鱼
stinky tofu 臭豆腐
sugar *n.* 糖
sweet *a.* 甜的
table salt 调味盐
tableware *n.* 餐具
tasteless *a.* 无味的
tasty *a.* 美味的
thyme *n.* [植] 百里香
tomato paste 西红柿酱
truffle *n.* 松露
turnip *n.* 萝卜
vinegar *n.* 醋
vodka *n.* 伏特加酒
watercress *n.* 豆瓣菜
whisky *n.* 威士忌酒
white wine 白葡萄酒
winkle *n.* 田螺

健　康

allergy *n.* 过敏症
antibiotic *n.* 抗生素
aspirin *n.* 阿司匹林
asthma *n.* 哮喘
bandage *n.* 绷带
capsule *n.* 胶囊
case history 病历
clinic *n.* 诊所
cold cure 感冒药
cough *n./v.* 咳嗽
cramp *n.* 痉挛
dentist *n.* 牙医
depression *n.* 沮丧
diabetic *n.* 糖尿病患者
diarrhea *n.* 腹泻
dizzy *a.* 头晕的
eyedrop *n.* 眼药水
febrifuge *n.* 退烧药
fever *n./v.* 发烧
flu *n.* 流感
gauze *n.* 纱布
have a runny nose 流鼻涕
hay fever 枯草热;花粉症

headache *n.* 头痛
injection *n.* 注射
medication *n.* 药物
mixture *n.* 合剂
oculist *n.* 眼科医生
ointment *n.* 药膏
penicillin *n.* 盘尼西林,青霉素
phlegm *n.* 痰
physician *n.* 内科医生
pill *n.* 药丸
preventive injection 预防针
stethoscope *n.* 听诊器
stomachache *n.* 胃痛
surgeon *n.* 外科医生
symptom *n.* 症状
syrup *n.* 糖浆
tablet *n.* 药片
toothache *n.* 牙痛
twisted *a.* 扭伤的
vet *n.* 兽医
vitamin *n.* 维他命
vomit *n./v.* 呕吐

校　园

academic record 学习成绩
academic year 学年
academy of fine arts 美术学院
accommodation *n.* 住宿
advanced *a.* 高级的
agricultural college 农学院
agricultural university 农业大学
Arabic *n.* 阿拉伯语
assessment *n.* 评估
assistant *n.* 助教
associate professor 副教授
attached middle school 附中
auditor *n.* 旁听生
basic course 基础课
boarder *n.* 住宿生
branch school 分校
cafeteria *n.* 自助餐厅
campus *n.* 校园
canteen *n.* 食堂
Cantonese *n.* 粤语
class discussion 课堂讨论
class for advanced studies 进修班
common room 公共休息室
comprehensive knowledge 广博的知识
compulsory course 必修课
compulsory education 义务教育
conservatory of music 音乐学院
content of courses 教学内容
correspondence school 函授学校
course *n.* 科目
credit *n.* 学分
curriculum *n.* 课程
deadline *n.* 最后期限
dining hall 食堂
diploma *n.* 毕业证书
elementary *a.* 基本的
engineering institute 工业学院
enlightening *a.* 富有启发的
enrollment *n.* 注册
exam-oriented education 应试教育
exchange experience 交流经验
extension *n.* 延期
extracurricular activity 课外活动
facility *n.* 设施
faculty *n.* 全体教员
fake diploma 假文凭
far-reaching *a.* 深远的
final test 期末考试
full-time teacher 专职教师
glossary *n.* 词汇表

grade *n.* 分数
graduate student 研究生
graduation announcement 毕业典礼请柬
graduation appraisal 毕业评估
graduation ceremony 毕业典礼
graduation field work 毕业实习
guest lecturer 客座教授
handout *n.* 文字资料
headmaster *n.* 校长
in-service training course 在职进修班
instruction after class 课外辅导
intermediate *a.* 中级的
Italian *n.* 意大利语
journal *n.* 学术期刊
key school 重点学校
lecturer *n.* 讲师
lecture *n.* 讲座
letter of reference 推荐信
literacy class 文字课
locker room 更衣室
mandarin *n.* 汉语普通话
medical university 医科大学
non-resident student 走读生
open class 公开课
optional course 选修课
outside reading 课外阅读
paper *n.* 论文
part-time teacher 兼职教师
people-oriented *a.* 以人为本的
period of schooling 学习年限
physical culture institute 体育学院
polytechnic university 工业大学
Portuguese *n.* 葡萄牙语
pre-service education 职前教育
professor *n.* 教授
quality education 素质教育
receive education 接受教育
reference *n.* 参考书
registration form 注册表
rote learning 机械学习
Russian *n.* 俄语
school report 成绩单
school timetable 课程表
scope of knowledge 知识面
self-taught examination 自学考试
semester *n.* 学期
seminar *n.* 讨论会
short-term training course 短训班
Spanish *n.* 西班牙语
special course 专修科
specialized course 专业课
staff room 教员办公室
structure *n.* 结构
students' union 学生会
summary *n.* 总结
syllabus *n.* 教学大纲
teaching and administrative staff 教职员工
teaching group 教学组
thesis *n.* 毕业论文
tuition *n.* 学费
tutorial *n.* 个别指导
vocational school 职业学校

职　场

accounting assistant 会计助理
achievement *n.* 工作成绩
active *a.* 主动的
adaptable *a.* 适应性强的
administer *v.* 管理
adroit *a.* 机敏的
advanced worker 先进工作者
aggressive *a.* 有进取心的
alert *a.* 机灵的
ambitious *a.* 有雄心的

amiable *a.* 和蔼可亲的
amicable *a.* 友好的
analytical *a.* 善于分析的
analyze *v.* 分析
apologetic *a.* 道歉的
appointed *a.* 被任命的
apprehensive *a.* 有理解力的
aspiring *a.* 有抱负的
assist *n./v.* 协助
audacious *a.* 无畏的
candid *a.* 坦白的
capable *a.* 有能力的
career *n.* 职业
cashier *n.* 出纳员
challenging *a.* 有挑战性的
charitable *a.* 仁慈的
citizenship *n.* 国籍
competent *a.* 有能力的
computer engineer 计算机工程师
confident *a.* 有信心的
conscientious *a.* 认真的
considerate *a.* 体贴的
constructive *a.* 建设性的
contemplative *a.* 沉思的
cooperative *a.* 有合作精神的
creative *a.* 富创造力的
dedicated *a.* 专注的
demonstrate *v.* 证明
dependable *a.* 可靠的
devoted *a.* 献身的
diplomatic *a.* 老练的
disciplined *a.* 守纪律的
discreet *a.* 谨慎的
dutiful *a.* 尽职的
duty *n.* 职责
dynamic *a.* 有活力的
earnest *a.* 认真的
efficient *a.* 有效率的
employment *n.* 就业
energetic *a.* 精力充沛的
enthusiastic *a.* 热情的
expressive *a.* 有表现力的
faithful *a.* 忠诚的
forceful *a.* 有说服力的
frank *a.* 直率的
frugal *a.* 朴素的
generous *a.* 大方的
genteel *a.* 有教养的
gentle *a.* 文雅的
hard-working *a.* 勤勉的
hearty *a.* 精神饱满的
honest *a.* 诚实的
hospitable *a.* 热情友好的
humble *a.* 谦虚的
humorous *a.* 幽默的
impartial *a.* 公正的
independent *a.* 有主见的
industrious *a.* 勤奋的
ingenious *a.* 有独创性的
initiative *n.* 首创精神
interpreter *n.* 口译员
knowledgeable *a.* 知识渊博的
legal adviser 法律顾问
marketing executive 销售主管
marketing representative 销售代表
motivated *a.* 积极的
nominated *a.* 被提名的
objective *a.* 客观的
position *n.* 职位
professional ethic 职业道德
sensitive *a.* 敏感的
well-educated *a.* 受过良好教育的

感　受

abominable *a.* 讨厌的
addicted *a.* 沉溺的
affectionately *ad.* 挚爱地
amazed *a.* 吃惊的
amused *a.* 被逗乐的
animated *a.* 活泼的
annoyed *a.* 烦闷的
apathetic *a.* 冷漠的
arrogant *a.* 傲慢的
astonished *a.* 吃惊的
astounded *a.* 被震惊的
awkward *a.* 笨拙的
bewildered *a.* 困惑的
bobbish *a.* 高兴的
bored *a.* 无聊的
charmed *a.* 着迷的
concerned *a.* 关心的
confident *a.* 自信十足的
confused *a.* 糊涂的
cynical *a.* 愤世嫉俗的
delighted *a.* 欣喜的
depressed *a.* 沮丧的
determined *a.* 坚决的
disappointed *a.* 失望的
disconsolately *ad.* 悲伤地
disgusted *a.* 厌烦的
dolorous *a.* 忧伤的
ecstatic *a.* 入迷的
elated *a.* 兴高采烈的
embarrassed *a.* 尴尬的
emotional *a.* 易激动的
energetic *a.* 精力充沛的
enthralled *a.* 被迷住的
exasperated *a.* 恼火的
fabulous *a.* 美妙的
flattered *a.* 感到荣幸的
flustered *a.* 慌乱的
forwearied *a.* 筋疲力尽的
frightened *a.* 害怕的
frustrated *a.* 沮丧的
gentle *a.* 温柔的
gratified *a.* 称心的
hopeful *a.* 有希望的
hopeless *a.* 绝望的
irritated *a.* 恼怒的
liberated *a.* 无拘束的
nervous *a.* 紧张不安的
overjoyed *a.* 狂喜的
overwhelmed *a.* 不堪重负的
perplexing *a.* 令人困惑的
pleased *a.* 高兴的
positive *a.* 积极的
proud *a.* 自豪的
puzzled *a.* 茫然的
rejuvenated *a.* 恢复活力的
relaxed *a.* 放松的
relieved *a.* 宽慰的
resolute *a.* 坚决的
sleepy *a.* 欲睡的
snuffy *a.* 闷闷不乐的
solitary *a.* 孤独的
teasingly *ad.* 烦恼地
terrified *a.* 感到恐惧的
thrilled *a.* 极为激动的
tired *a.* 疲惫的
touched *a.* 受感动的
unwearied *a.* 孜孜不倦的
upset *a.* 不安的
vigorous *a.* 精力充沛的
wonderful *a.* 极好的

语句衔接、转折

accordingly *ad.* 相应地
although *conj.* 尽管
believe it or not 信不信由你
by definition 明显地
consequently *ad.* 所以
considering that 考虑到
following this 在此之后
furthermore *ad.* 此外
given that 假定
henceforth *ad.* 今后
if necessary 必要时
if possible 如有可能
in any event 不论怎样
in brief 简言之
in case 万一
in order that 为了
in other words 换句话说
in particular 尤其
in reality 事实上
in summary 总之
in view of 考虑到
indeed *ad.* 真正地
inevitably *ad.* 不可避免地
meanwhile *ad.* 同时
naturally *ad.* 自然地
nevertheless *conj.* 不过
not to mention 更不必说
notwithstanding *conj.* 虽然
occasionally *ad.* 偶然地
on account of 因为
originally *ad.* 最初
owing to 由于
provided *conj.* 假如
seeing that 鉴于
similarly *ad.* 同样地
simultaneously *ad.* 同时地
still *ad.* 仍然
subsequently *ad.* 后来
therefore *ad.* 因此
thus *conj.* 因此
to be honest 诚实地说
to begin with 首先
to tell the truth 说实话
ultimate *a.* 最终的
undeniably *ad.* 不可否认地
while *conj.* 虽然
with a view to 考虑到
without reservation 毫无保留地
worse still 更糟的是

附录四　雅思听力常见同音异义词

同音异义词			
all together [ɔːl ˈtəːgeðə]	altogether [ɔːl ˈtəːgeðə]	bear[bɛə]	bare[bɛə]
band[bænd]	banned[bænd]	aloud[əˈlaud]	allowed[əˈlaud]
bread[bred]	bred[bred]	break[breik]	brake[breik]
check[tʃek]	cheque[tʃek]	compliment [ˈkɔmpliment]	complement [ˈkɔmpliment]
already[ɔːlˈredi]	all ready[ɔːlˈredi]	find[faind]	fined[faind]
flew[fluː]	flu[fluː]	floor[flɔː]	flaw[flɔː]
flower[ˈflauə]	flour[ˈflauə]	for[fɔː]	four[fɔː]
fourth[fɔːθ]	forth[fɔːθ]	hair[heə]	hare[heə]
wait[weit]	weight[weit]	waste[weist]	waist[weist]
heal[hiːl]	heel[hiːl]	here[hiə]	hear[hiə]
heroin[ˈherəuin]	heroine[ˈherəuin]	meet[miːt]	meat[miːt]
ours[ˈauəz]	hours[ˈauəz]	red[red]	read[red]
peace[piːs]	piece[piːs]	whether[ˈ(h)weðə]	weather[ˈ(h)weðə]
son[sʌn]	sun[sʌn]	rose[rouz]	rows[rouz]
story[ˈstɔːri]	storey[ˈstɔːri]	source[sɔːs]	sauce[sɔːs]
vain[vein]	vein[vein]	theirs[ðeəz]	there's[ðeəz]
alright[ɔːlˈrait]	all right[ɔːlˈrait]	whose[huːz]	who's[huːz]
altar[ˈɔːltə]	alter[ˈɔːltə]	always[ˈɔːlweiz]	all ways[ˈɔːlweiz]
anyone[ˈeniwʌn]	any one[ˈeniwʌn]	ware…wear	where[weə]
ascent[əˈsent]	assent[əˈsent]	vain[vein]	vein[vein]
berth[bəːθ]	birth[bəːθ]	tail[teil]	tale[teil]
boy[bɔi]	buoy[bɔi]	steel[stiːl]	steal[stiːl]

同音异义词			
buy…by	bye[bai]	stare[steə]	stair[steə]
cell[sel]	sell[sel]	sort[sɔːt]	sought[sɔːt]
cite	site[sait]…sight	some[sʌm]	sum[sʌm]
climb[klaim]	clime[klaim]	sail[seil]	sale[seil]
coarse[kɔːs]	course[kɔːs]	root[ruːt]	route[ruːt]
council['kaunsl]	counsel['kaunsl]	right…rite	write[rait]
crewed[kruːd]	crude[kruːd]	principal['prinsəpl]	principle['prinsəpl]
cycle['saikl]	psychal['saikl]	plain[plein]	plane[plein]
fair[feə]	fare[feə]	paw…pore	pour[pɔː]
formally['fɔːməli]	formerly['fɔːməli]	miner['mainə]	minor['mainə]
higher['haiə]	hire['haiə]	mail[meil]	male[meil]
in[in]	inn[in]	loan[ləun]	lone[ləun]
dear[diə]	deer[diə]	lessen['lesn]	lesson['lesn]
aunt[ɑːnt]	aren't[ɑːnt]	way[wei]	weigh[wei]

附录五　雅思听力单词英、美发音比较

单词	英音	美音	单词	英音	美音
aboard	[ə'bɔːd]	[ə'bɔːrd]	absolve	[əb'zɒlv]	[əb'zɑːlv]
accost	[ə'kɒst]	[ə'kɔːst]	across	[ə'krɒs]	[ə'krɔːs]
adieu	[ə'djuː]	[ə'duː]	aeration	[eə'reɪʃn]	[e'reɪʃn]
after	['ɑːftə(r)]	['æftə(r)]	arm	[ɑːm]	[ɑːrm]
assume	[ə'sjuːm]	[ə'suːm]	banana	[bə'nɑːnə]	[bə'nænə]
border	['bɔːdə(r)]	['bɔːrdə(r)]	borrow	['bɒrəʊ]	['bɑːroʊ]
brochure	['brəʊʃə(r)]	[broʊ'ʃʊr]	cadre	['kɑːdə(r)]	['kædri]
calf	[kɑːf]	[kæf]	carbon	['kɑːbən]	['kɑːrbən]
career	[kə'rɪə(r)]	[kə'rɪr]	cast	[kɑːst]	[kæst]
ceremony	['serəməni]	['serəmoʊni]	coarse	[kɔːs]	[kɔrs]
comet	['kɒmɪt]	['kɑːmət]	cord	[kɔːd]	[kɔrd]
costume	['kɒstjuːm]	['kɑːstuːm]	courage	['kʌrɪdʒ]	['kɜːrɪdʒ]
craft	[krɑːft]	[kræft]	curative	['kjʊərətɪv]	['kjʊrətɪv]
curious	['kjʊəriəs]	['kjʊriəs]	data	['deɪtə]	['dætə]
discard	[dɪs'kɑːd]	[dɪs'kɑːrd]	draft	[drɑːft]	[dræft]
electron	[ɪ'lektrɒn]	[ɪ'lektrɑːn]	elongate	['iːlɒŋgeɪt]	[ɪ'lɔːŋgeɪt]
enchant	[ɪn'tʃɑːnt]	[ɪn'tʃænt]	endure	[ɪn'djʊə(r)]	[ɪn'dʊr]
exotic	[ɪg'zɒtɪk]	[ɪg'zɑːtɪk]	expert	['ekspɜːt]	['ekspɜːrt]
explosive	[ɪk'spləʊsɪv]	[ɪk'splosɪv]	extraordinary	[ɪk'strɔːdnri]	[ɪk'strɔːrdəneri]
eyeglass	['aɪglɑːs]	['aɪglæs]	finale	[fɪ'nɑːli]	[fɪ'næli]
focus	['fəʊkəs]	['foʊkəs]	gasp	[gɑːsp]	[gæsp]
garage	['gærɑːʒ]	[gə'rɑːʒ]	geometry	[dʒi'ɒmətri]	[dʒi'ɑːmətri]
graft	[grɑːft]	[græft]	grant	[grɑːnt]	[grænt]
grassy	['grɑːsi]	['græsi]	hectare	['hektɑː(r)]	['hekter]
host	[həʊst]	[hoʊst]	intuit	[ɪn'tjuːɪt]	[ɪn'tuːɪt]
laboratory	[lə'bɒːrətri]	['læbrətɔːri]	laughing	['lɑːfɪŋ]	['læfɪŋ]
missile	['mɪsaɪl]	['mɪsl]	mysterious	[mɪ'stɪəriəs]	[mɪ'stɪriəs]
nerve	[nɜːv]	[nɜːrv]	necessary	['nesəsəri]	['nesəseri]
positive	['pɒzətɪv]	['pɑːzətɪv]	renewal	[rɪ'njuːəl]	[rɪ'nuːəl]
rural	['rʊərəl]	['rʊrəl]	sample	['sɑːmpl]	['sæmpl]
schedule	['ʃedjuːl]	['skedʒuːl]	secretary	['sekrətri]	['sekrəteri]
stationary	['steɪʃənri]	['steɪʃəneri]	turbine	['tɜːbaɪn]	['tɜːrbaɪn]

	雅思词汇词根+联想记忆法（加强版）	雅思词汇词根+联想记忆法（乱序版）	雅思词汇词根+联想记忆法
页数/开本	536/ 特16开（170*230）	528 / 特16开（170*230）	368 / 32开（145*210）
篇章结构	48个Word List 附录一　2000个最常用词汇 附录二　雅思阅读主题词汇 附录三　雅思口语、写作主题词汇 附录四　雅思听力常见同音异义词 附录五　雅思听力单词英、美发音比较	48个Word List 索引 附录一　雅思阅读词汇分类 附录二　雅思听力常见同音异义词 附录三　雅思听力单词英、美发音比较 附录四　雅思常考单词英美对照表	35个Word List 附录一　雅思阅读词汇分类 附录二　雅思听力常见同音异义词 附录三　雅思听力单词英、美发音比较 附录四　雅思常考单词英美对照表
配套MP3	录音时长400多分钟 内容包括：48个Word List 中的英文单词及其中文释义 音频下载：www.dogwood.com.cn/mp3/ysjq	录音时长400多分钟 内容包括：48个Word List中的英文单词及其中文释义 音频下载：www.dogwood.com.cn/mp3/yslx	录音时长200分钟 内容包括：35个Word List中的英文单词及其中文释义 音频下载：www.dogwood.com.cn/mp3/ysch
适用的学生层次	具有一定的词汇基础，有志于取得雅思高分的考生	具有一定的词汇基础，有志于取得雅思高分的考生	雅思词汇基础较为薄弱的考生
突出特色	1. 采用“词根+联想”记忆法，辅以谐音、组合词等多种记忆法，并配有幽默有趣的插图，更高效地记忆单词。 2. 精选大量真题例句，帮助考生熟悉考试难度。 3. 归纳常考词组和搭配，给出大量同、反义词和派生词，全面拓展考生的词汇量。 4. 用*标注听力、口语词汇，帮助考生备考听说。 5. 增设返记菜单，便于查找定位。	1. 采用“词根+联想”记忆法，辅以谐音、组合词等多种记忆法，并配有幽默有趣的插图，更高效地记忆单词。 2. 打破常规字母顺序，所有单词采用“乱序”编排，帮助考生自由灵活地记忆单词。 3. 精选大量真题例句，帮助考生熟悉考试难度。 4. 归纳常考词组和搭配，给出大量同、反义词和派生词，全面拓展考生的词汇量。 5. 用*标注听力、口语词汇，帮助考生备考听说。 6. 增设返记菜单和索引，便于查找定位。	1. 采用“词根+联想”记忆法，辅以谐音、分拆、形近等多种记忆法，并配有幽默有趣的插图，更高效地记忆单词。 2. 精选大量真题例句，帮助考生熟悉考试难度。 3. 归纳常考词组和搭配，给出大量派生词，使单词学习更全面。 4. 用*标注听力、口语词汇，帮助考生备考听说。
单词量	约4500个核心单词，1200个核心词组，补充大量同/反义词、派生词，共收录约8000个常用单词。	约4500个核心单词，1200个核心词组，补充大量同/反义词、派生词，共收录约8000个常用单词。	共收录约3500个核心单词。
相同点	1. 紧扣雅思考试，收录大量雅思核心词汇，精选单词释义。 2. 以“词根+联想”记忆法为主，辅以谐音、拆分、形近等多种记忆法，并配有幽默有趣的插图。 3. 大量真题例句，帮助考生熟悉考试难度。 4. 用 *标注听力、口语词汇，方便考生备考听说。 5. 专业播音人员朗读英文单词及其中文释义。 6. 附录中均收录了雅思阅读词汇分类，根据阅读常考主题进行分类，帮助考生高效记忆阅读词汇。		
不同点	1. 所有单词从A到Z按字母顺序编排。 2. 收录大量同、反义词。 3. 附录一收录了最常用的2000个词汇，考生可先学习本部分，掌握最基本的词汇。 4. 增设返记菜单，便于考生进行自测。	1. 所有单词“乱序”编排。 2. 收录大量同、反义词。 3. 增设返记菜单和索引，便于查找定位。	1. 所有单词从A到Z按字母顺序编排。 2. 收录的词汇相对简单，适用于词汇基础较为薄弱的考生。
学习建议	有的考生认为正序方便查阅，符合已有的背单词习惯，容易有成就感；有的考生认为乱序编排不容易形成上下单词的提示记忆，能保证背词的均匀性，效率更高。上述三本书采用不同的方式编排，在词汇量、例句难度上均有所不同。考生可先学习《雅思词汇词根+联想记忆法》打下基础，然后根据个人的学习方式和习惯选择“乱序版”或“加强版”，进一步学习雅思词汇，取得6.5分以上的分数。无论选择哪本词汇书，坚持到底就是胜利！		